Learning about Mental Health Practice

Edited by

D1285094

Theo Stickley
University of Nottingham, UK
and
Thurstine Basset
Thurstine Basset Consultancy Ltd, UK

John Wiley & Sons, Ltd

Other Wiley Editorial Offices

John Wiley & Sons Inc., 111 River Street, Hoboken, NJ 07030, USA

Jossey-Bass, 989 Market Street, San Francisco, CA 94103-1741, USA

Wiley-VCH Verlag GmbH, Boschstr. 12, D-69469 Weinheim, Germany

John Wiley & Sons Australia Ltd, 42 McDougall Street, Milton, Queensland 4064, Australia

John Wiley & Sons (Asia) Pte Ltd, 2 Clementi Loop #02-01, Jin Xing Distripark, Singapore 129809

John Wiley & Sons Canada Ltd, 6045 Freemont Blvd, Mississauga, Ontario, L5R 4J3, Canada

Wiley also publishes its books in a variety of electronic formats. Some content that appears in print may not be available in electronic books.

Library of Congress Cataloging-in-Publication Data

Learning about mental health practice / edited by Theo Stickley and
Thurstine Basset.
      p. cm.
   Includes bibliographical references and index.
   ISBN 978-0-470-51226-5 – ISBN 978-0-470-51227-2
   1.   Mental health services – Practice.   I.   Stickley, Theo.   II.   Basset,
Thurstine.
   RA790.75.L43 2008
   362.2 – dc22

                                           2007050286

British Library Cataloguing in Publication Data

A catalogue record for this book is available from the British Library

ISBN 978-0-470-51226-5 (H/B)   978-0-470-51227-2 (P/B)

Typeset in 10/13pt Scala and Scala Sans by Laserwords Private Limited, Chennai, India
Printed and bound in Great Britain by Antony Rowe Ltd, Chippenham, Wiltshire

In the time between contributing to one of the chapters in this book and its production, sadly one of the authors has died. This book is therefore dedicated to the memory of Magdalen Fiddler, a much loved and deeply missed friend who was an inspiration to all who met her.

Contents

**PART III: APPROACHES FOR MENTAL HEALTH
PRACTICE**   417

About the editors

Theo Stickley trained in counselling and mental health nursing, and practised in both professions for many years. He now teaches mental health at the University of Nottingham and has published widely in the nursing and mental health press. The focus of his research is mental health and the arts, and he has led on a number of research projects in collaboration with people who use mental health services. Theo is a keen gardener, motorcyclist and artist (but has not yet found a way to combine all three simultaneously).

Thurstine Basset trained as social worker and worked as a community worker and social work practitioner, mostly in the mental health field. He is now an independent training and development consultant and runs his own company, which is based in Brighton. He works for national voluntary agencies, such as Mind, Together and the Mental Health Foundation. With the Richmond Fellowship, he is the joint course leader for its Diploma in Community Mental Health, which is accredited by Middlesex University. He is a Visiting Fellow at the University of Brighton. He has written mental health learning materials, many of which are published by Pavilion Publishing, with which he works in an advisory role. He likes to walk and watch cricket.

Contributors

Peter Amsel
Composer, writer and health-care activist

Ian Baguley
Professor of Mental Health; Director, Centre for Clinical and Academic Workforce Innovation, University of Lincoln; and associate director, NIMHE National Workforce Programme

Thurstine Basset
Independent training and development consultant

Peter Bates
National Development Team

Anne Beales
Director of Service User Involvement, Together: Working for Wellbeing

Peter Bullimore
Survivor activist

Alison Cameron
Service user of mental health services in London

Peter Campbell
Mental health system survivor and freelance trainer

Anne Cooke
Clinical Psychologist and Third Year Director on the doctoral programme in clinical psychology at Salomons, Canterbury Christ Church University

Anthony Cotton
Community Support Worker with Bradford District Care Trust

Julie Cullen
Service improvement lead (Day Service Modernisation), Care Services Improvement Partnership, National Institute Mental Health, England

Sharon Lee Cuthbert
Independent training and development consultant

Pam Enderby
Professor of Rehabilitation and Dean of the Faculty of Medicine at the University of Sheffield

Anne Felton
Lecturer in mental health and social care, School of Nursing, University of Nottingham

Magdalen Fiddler
Postgraduate researcher, Manchester University

Daniel B. Fisher
Executive director, National Empowerment Center, Lawrence, Massachusetts

Dawn Freshwater
Professor of Healthcare and head of the School of Healthcare, University of Leeds

Bill (KWM) Fulford
Professor of philosophy and mental health, University of Warwick; Member of the Philosophy Faculty, University of Oxford; Co-Director, Institute for Philosophy, Diversity and Mental Health, Centre for Ethnicity and Health, University of Central Lancashire; and Special Adviser for Values-Based Practice, National Institute of Mental Health in England National Workforce Programme

Peter Gilbert
Professor of Social Work and Spirituality, Staffordshire University and NIMHE national Lead for Spirituality and Mental Health. Former national NIMHE/SCIE Fellow in Social Care (Policy and Practice)

Gordon Grant
Research professor in the Centre for Health and Social Care Research, University of Sheffield

Bob Grove
Director of the employment programme, The Sainsbury Centre for Mental Health, London

Paul Hammersley
Programme director for the COPE (Collaboration of Psychosocial Education) Initiative at the School of Nursing, Midwifery and Social Work at Manchester University

Roslyn Hope
Director, National Institute of Mental Health in England, National Workforce Programme

Laura Lea
Service user group coordinator, service user and mental health trainer

Sarah Lewis
Mental Health Team Secretary, Centre for Clinical and Academic Workforce Innovation, University of Lincoln

Tabitha Lewis
Senior lecturer in dual diagnosis at Middlesex University

Rufus May
Mental health activist and clinical psychologist with Bradford District Care Trust's assertive outreach team; and honorary research fellow with the centre for community citizenship and mental health at the University of Bradford.

Ian McGonagle
Workforce project manager, Centre for Clinical and Academic Workforce Innovation, University of Lincoln; and National Institute of Mental Health in England, National Workforce Programme

Joe Miller
Consultant clinical psychologist, Devon Partnership NHS Trust

Mike Nolan
Professor of gerontological nursing at the University of Sheffield

Madeline O'Carroll
Lecturer, City University, London

Steve Onyett
Senior development consultant with the Care Services Improvement Partnership South West; and visiting professor at the Faculty of Health and Social Care at the University of the West of England

Sara Owen
Professor of nursing, Centre for Clinical and Academic Workforce Innovation, University of Lincoln

David Pilgrim
Professor of mental health policy, University of Central Lancashire; and consultant clinical psychologist, Lancashire Care NHS Trust

Gary Platz
Service user leader, the Wellink Trust, Wellington, New Zealand

Lorraine Rayner
Lecturer, School of Nursing, University of Nottingham

John Read
Co-director of the doctorate of clinical psychology programme at the University of Auckland, New Zealand

Julie Repper
Associate professor/reader at the University of Nottingham

Liz Sayce
Director of policy and communications for the Disability Rights Commission

Joanne Seddon
National Development Team

Gemma Stacey
Lecturer in mental health and social care, School of Nursing, University of Nottingham

Theo Stickley
Associate professor in mental health at the University of Nottingham

Jerry Tew
Senior lecturer in social work at the University of Birmingham; Social Care Lead for the Heart of England Hub of the Mental Health Research Network; and executive member of the Social Perspectives Network

Premila Trivedi
Freelance mental health service user trainer and education and training adviser (service user involvement), South London & Maudsley NHS Foundation Trust

Jan Wallcraft
Service user consultant, researcher and activist

Lesley Warner
Registered mental nurse, formerly a senior researcher at the Sainsbury Centre for Mental Health, London

Jennie Williams
Director of Inequality Agenda Ltd.

Kim Woodbridge
Operational manager, Milton Keynes Council and Primary Care Trust

Norman Young
Consultant nurse for serious mental illness, complex needs, Cardiff and Vale NHS Trust

Preface

This book is written for students of mental health. It closely follows another book published by Wiley called *Teaching Mental Health*, which we have also edited. The first book is written as a kind of handbook of ideas for people involved in teaching and training students to prepare for mental health practice. What the two books have in common (as well as the editors) is that they have both been authored not just by academic 'experts' or policy writers, but also practitioners and people who are experts by their own experience of mental health problems and using mental health services. This is an important factor when you come to study sections of this book, because it is intended to be relevant and to incorporate service user perspectives as well as the views of researchers, professionals and academics.

This is not a book about medical diagnosis and treatment, neither is it a book just for nurses or social workers. What we have attempted is to present major issues and approaches that are relevant to mental health for practitioners from all professions in the 21st Century. This book is not intended to replace other medically oriented books, but it is intended to help students of mental health to think about much broader perspectives than the medical model offers. Modern problems require modern solutions and approaches; this book highlights what some of those solutions and approaches are. Although most of the contributors are from the UK, we are pleased to include contributions from people in Canada, the USA and New Zealand.

Acknowledgement

We would like to express our thanks to Peter Lindley, formerly of the Sainsbury Centre for Mental Health, who made a significant contribution to the ideas developed in this book.

Introduction

Theo Stickley and Thurstine Basset

This book is written for everyone who is learning about mental health practice. It is aimed at students from all the various disciplines involved in mental health work; this includes mental health workers who are not affiliated to a specific profession, as well as those from the established professions in mental health work. This is deliberate, in order to focus on what the different groups of worker have in common, rather than what separates them. One factor that is becoming more apparent in health and social care around the world is the need for the different professions to learn from each other. Contributors to this book therefore come from a range of professional backgrounds. Furthermore, some of the contributors either currently use or have used mental health services in the past. There have been many recent changes in mental health care provision and we feel that the two most important changes are the moves towards learning from each other, and learning from people who are experts on the care system through their experience of using the services. What can be learned about mental health practice is greatly increased if we are able to work across traditional barriers and learn from each other.

The main emphasis in this book is on mental health practice in relation to adults. The principles that underpin the practice can be applied to people of all ages, but the practical examples given throughout the book relate more specifically to the 16–65 age group of service users.

There have been many changes in mental health services in recent years. In the UK, when the National Health Service came into being after the Second World War it inherited many large mental hospitals. The majority of these institutions were built in the 19th Century. They were very full, overcrowded and barely meeting the needs of their inmates. Influenced in part by the work of Erving Goffman (Goffman, 1961) and other critics of these institutions, government policy to close these hospitals and move to community care began in the 1960s. The process of moving care from these large institutions into the community took decades rather than years. Policy has attempted to ensure that the shift from institutional care to community care has protected both the individuals involved and the public. When the 'Modernisation Agenda' arrived it was very welcome,

---

but it came rather late in the day and at a time when many were criticising what became known as 'care in the community'. It was not until the very last months of the last year of the 20th century that a new, modern and comprehensive plan for community care emerged in the UK with the publication of the National Service Framework for Mental Health (Department of Health, 1999).

While there has been progress since the 1960s, community care provides a huge challenge. Our mental health system is required to accommodate not only those who historically would have been considered 'mad', but also many people who struggle to cope with modern society and all of its inequalities. The gap between the rich and the poor has widened and many people who end up in the care of the mental health system have fallen prey to abuse, drugs, alcohol and the effects of poverty. In addition, many people with mental health problems who in the past might have been contained in large mental institutions are more likely these days to be inappropriately caught up in the justice system.

Mental health practitioners of the future, therefore, will need to understand the origins of contemporary mental health problems. That is why this book focuses on what has become known as 'the psycho-social'; in other words, the relationship between the psychological and the social. It is the argument of this book that the two are inseparable.

In the second half of the 20th Century, mental health learning, education, training and practice were mostly very institutional, with the large psychiatric hospitals holding sway at the centre of much of the training and education. The main professions in mental health work – nursing, occupational therapy, psychiatry, psychology and social work – tended to learn and train in isolation from each other. As the large hospitals closed, so many staff had to learn new skills in order to work in multidisciplinary teams in the community (Muijen, 1997). It was a difficult shift to make and there was always the chance that staff would merely transplant their institutional practices from the large hospitals to the community setting.

In 1997 in the UK, the Sainsbury Centre for Mental Health published a document called *Pulling Together* (SCMH, 1997), to help mental health workers to begin to make plans for their future roles and training needs. It was clear that the overlap of roles between professional staff was significant. Concentrating on the work that needed to be done rather than the profession of the worker, the Sainsbury Centre subsequently produced *The Capable Practitioner Framework* (SCMH, 2001), which explored the generic knowledge and skills needed for mental health work. Specialist work was then looked at in terms of both interventions and the service setting in which the intervention would take place. Subsequent work led to the development of the Ten Essential Shared Capabilities (Department of Health, 2004).

All the professional groups in mental health begun to look at new ways of working in the early 2000s. Mental health nurses form the second largest contingent in the mental health workforce (non-professionally affiliated workers being the largest group) and the review of mental health nursing *From Values to Action* (Chief Nursing Officer, 2006) calls for the adoption of a recovery-based holistic approach in mental health work. Other professions are calling for similar approaches, which take into account the physical, psychological, social and spiritual needs of service users. This book fully supports this initiative and seeks to put into context what this might mean in practice.

The Ten Essential Shared Capabilities form the basis for these new developments and for all learning about mental health practice, and they are the starting point for this book. This introductory chapter sets the context for the book and outlines the contents of the chapters, which are presented in three parts.

▶ Part I: Foundations for mental health practice – the ten essential shared capabilities

In Chapter 1, Roslyn Hope explores the background to the development of the Ten Essential Shared Capabilities. Roslyn is well placed to introduce the shared capabilities, as she is the director of the National Workforce Programme. In her chapter, she draws interesting parallels with the field of learning disability. She also gives some detail on each of the capabilities before discussing their implementation and future challenges. Ian McGonagle *et al.* (Chapter 2) build on the first chapter through exploring the underpinning philosophy and value base of the capabilities. They also illustrate their relevance to practice through some care studies.

Subsequent chapters (3 to 12) explore each of the Ten Essential Shared Capabilities in turn. In Chapter 3, Anne Beales and Gary Platz examine 'Working in Partnership', giving examples from an individual and organisational perspective from both the UK and New Zealand. Premila Trivedi, in Chapter 4, looks at 'Respecting Diversity' and presents her model of AVUDCI (Acknowledging, Valuing and Using Diversity and Challenging Inequality). In Chapter 5, Bill Fulford and Kim Woodbridge consider value-based practice and ethics in relation to 'Practicing Ethically'. David Pilgrim (Chapter 6) expands on the capability 'Challenging Inequality' through examining the link between socio-economic inequalities and the diagnosis and treatment of mental health problems. Inequality needs to be challenged by a broad political, national and local spectrum of actions, with progressive mental health workers allying themselves with the service user movement to challenge the status quo.

From the USA, Dan Fisher (Chapter 7) illustrates 'Promoting Recovery' through both personal experience and his involvement with the National Empowerment Center in Massachusetts. In Chapter 8, Lesley Warner considers 'Identifying People's Needs and Strengths' through an examination of assessment as part of the Care Programme Approach in the UK. In Chapter 9, Laura Lea draws on her experience as a service user trainer in exploring the aspiration of 'Providing Service User Centred Care'. She stresses the importance of goals being set by the service user and not by the service itself. Madeline O'Carroll *et al.* (Chapter 10) examine the use of psychosocial skills in practice as an example of the capability 'Making a Difference'. Anne Felton and Gemma Stacey (Chapter 11) explore 'Promoting Safety and Positive Risk Taking'. They argue that positive risk taking should form an integral part of mental health practice.

In the final chapter for this part of the book, Sharon Cuthbert and Thurstine Basset (Chapter 12) explore 'Personal Development and Learning' through developing portfolios, professional development planning, using supervision, and other supports such as mentoring and coaching.

▶ Part II: Issues for mental health practice

It is clear that in the emerging agenda for the 21st Century, mental health care needs to be very much broader in its approach than the traditional and narrow medical model of practice. People need to be seen in their social contexts. Chapter 13, written by Jerry Tew, emphasises social perspectives on mental distress. Chapter 14, by Peter Bates and Joanne Seddon, identifies practices that promote social inclusion. This is in an uphill struggle, however, when stigma and discrimination are entrenched in social attitudes. Chapter 15, by Liz Sayce, argues that equality and rights for people with mental health problems should be at the heart of strategies to overcome social exclusion and discrimination. Peter Campbell, who has been campaigning for many years for greater attention to the voice of people who use services, gives an informative overview in Chapter 16 of service user involvement from his perspective. Steve Onyett discusses how teams can work effectively in complex systems in Chapter 17.

There are many conceptual issues for mental health practice, not least of which is the contested nature of the concept of mental illness itself. In Chapter 18, Anne Cooke identifies the problems associated with the use of the concept of mental illness. In 21st Century society, growing attention is being given to the relationship between mental health problems and the use and misuse of substances. In Chapter 19, Tabitha Lewis and Alison Cameron give a useful overview of substances and the effects of their misuse, and offer a practical guide for practitioners. Chapter 20 by Jennie Williams and Joe Miller focuses on gender issues, especially issues of inequality and the mental health of both women and men. Chapter 21 by Paul Hammersley *et al*. introduces the trauma model of psychosis, which challenges the conventional wisdom of the causes of schizophrenia. Last but not least in this section, research into the needs of those who care for people with mental health problems is presented by Julie Repper *et al*. in Chapter 22.

▶ Part III: Approaches for mental health practice

This part of the book focuses on various approaches to mental health care. Theo Stickley and Dawn Freshwater argue in Chapter 23 that therapeutic relationships are fundamental to all mental health work. In Chapter 24, Rufus May *et al*. examine psychological approaches to mental health, not only theoretically but also experientially. Bob Grove (Chapter 25) looks practically at the employment needs of people who use mental health services and offers answers to what mental health workers should both know and do in this important area. The author of Chapter 26, Peter Amsel from Canada, is a composer and discusses the issue of how medication can dull creativity. He argues therefore that medication should be used minimally but wisely when practitioners are 'treating the creative mind'.

Students of mental health practice may struggle with maintaining a balance between psychosocial interventions and promoting social inclusion. In Chapter 27, Peter Bates and Julie Cullen clarify the issues and discuss the possible clashes and compromises inherent in working with the two approaches. In Chapter 28, the vast subject of spirituality and mental health is considered by Peter Gilbert, who wisely and sensitively offers a message for mental health students and practitioners today. While holism and complementary approaches have been generally accepted in the population, they stand little chance of becoming mainstream in mental health services. However, people want holistic and complementary approaches in care and Jan Wallcraft (Chapter 29) argues for greater acceptance of holism to meet people's needs and demands.

The editors conclude the book with a consideration of what the capable practitioner of the future will be like. How can we change with the times and what are the challenges for positive change for the future?

▶ References

Chief Nursing Officer (2006) *From Values to Action: The Chief Nursing Officer's Review of Mental Health Nursing.* London: Department of Health.

Department of Health (1999) *The National Service Framework for Mental Health.* London: Department of Health.

Department of Health (2004) *The Ten Essential Shared Capabilities – A Framework for the Whole of the Mental Health Workforce.* London: Department of Health/NHSU/Sainsbury Centre/NIMHE.

Goffman, E. (1961) *Asylums.* Anchor Books, New York.

Muijen, M. (1997) The future of training, *Journal of Mental Health*, 6(6): 535–538.

Sainsbury Centre for Mental Health (1997) *Pulling Together: The Future Roles and Training of Mental Health Staff.* London: The Sainsbury Centre for Mental Health.

Sainsbury Centre for Mental Health (2001) *The Capable Practitioner Framework: A Framework and List of the Practitioner Capabilities Required to Implement the National Service Framework for Mental Health.* London: Sainsbury Centre for Mental Health. Available to download from www.scmh.org.uk.

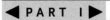

PART I

Foundations for mental health practice – the ten essential shared capabilities

The ten essential shared capabilities: their background, development and implementation

Roslyn Hope
National Institute of Mental Health in England

Services for people with mental health problems have undergone major structural changes. Although the plan to close long-stay institutions was first announced in 1962, the change did not fully begin to happen until 20 years later. Now, fortunately, practically all the old Victorian hospitals have gone.

Services for people with learning disabilities were similarly congregated into long-stay hospitals until the early 1980s. In this case, however, an important movement emerged that questioned the ways of thinking about and providing services to people with learning disabilities.

This movement or philosophy was described as 'normalisation' and was led by Wolf Wolfensberger. Normalisation was described as 'the use of culturally valued means in order to enable people to live culturally valued lives' (Wolfensberger, 1980). It stemmed from the hypothesis that a person can be considered 'deviant' or devalued when a significant characteristic (a 'difference') of theirs is negatively valued by the majority of society. While numerous differences do exist among individuals, these do not constitute 'deviancy' unless they are sufficiently negatively value charged in the mind of observers. Different cultures define different types of differences as deviant, but in all cultures they fall into one or more of three broad categories:

(a) Physical differences and bodily impairments that exist from birth, or that occur later because of disease, old age or other reasons.

Learning About Mental Health Practice.   Edited by Theo Stickley and Thurstine Basset
© 2008 John Wiley & Sons, Ltd

(b) Overt or covert behaviours (the latter including religious, political and other beliefs.

(c) Attributive identities of people, such as nationality, ethnicity, language spoken etc.

Wolfensberger (1980) argued that the consequences for people who were perceived as 'deviant' from social norms were, in turn, negative. He summarised these as follows:

(a) Devalued people will be badly treated. They will usually be accorded less esteem and status than that given to non-devalued citizens. They are apt to be rejected, even persecuted, and treated in ways that tend to diminish their dignity, adjustment, growth, competence, health, wealth, lifespan etc.

(b) The treatment accorded to devalued people will take forms that express the societal perception of the devalued person or group. For instance, people who may be perceived as risky or dangerous (perhaps for no realistic reason) may be provided in settings that are prison like.

(c) How a person is treated will, in turn, strongly influence how that person subsequently behaves. Negative expectations are more likely to lead to negative behaviour. 'On the other hand, the more social value is accorded to the person, the more s/he will usually be encouraged to assume roles and behaviours which are appropriate and desirable and the more will be expected of him/her, and the more she/he is apt to achieve.'

Normalisation, later to be called 'social role valorisation', had a great influence on services for people with learning disabilities. It was operationalised into service standards that could be used for evaluation and service design purposes (Wolfensberger & Truman, 1983). In England it was translated into 'An Ordinary Life', an approach to service design arguing that people with learning difficulties could live, like anyone else, in ordinary housing, rather than in hospitals or large hostels; that they were individual, with different strengths and needs; and that person-centred planning (called Individual Programme Planning at the time) was essential.

The term 'normalisation' was subsequently used indiscriminately, and often wrongly, and is no longer in current usage. The reader will recognise, however, that much of what is in current mental health policy can be traced back to the movement led by Wolfensberger and others. It was, perhaps, easier to apply the principles to people with learning difficulties, whose needs were primarily associated with social and educational challenges. It is interesting to reflect how far the approach was (not) taken up in mental health.

The author was struck, in moving from the field of learning disabilities at the end of the 1980s into the field of mental health, by how the formulation of needs by staff was focused through an illness lens. What 'patients' did or said was attributed to their presenting problem or diagnosis; there seemed little reflection on them as people, with the same hopes and aspirations as others. This in turn appeared to lead to low expectations from both staff and patients about what the future might hold. An old study carried out by Rosenhan (1973) still had resonance: it described how stooges who faked symptoms in order to be admitted to psychiatric hospital, but who resumed normal behaviour on admission, were not discharged quickly as what they did was perceived by staff to confirm their diagnosis. The researcher concluded that once a person had a label or diagnosis of mental illness, that diagnosis appeared to define them; they could not be listened to as an ordinary person and other aspects of their lives, such as physical illness, family and work issues, were not addressed appropriately.

Services for people with mental health problems in the early 1990s were still largely hospital based, with some small Community Mental Health Teams emerging as well as primary care links. A methodology known as 'SEARCH' conferences was developed to bring people with mental health problems, their families, practitioners and managers together to:

(a) explore what futures people wanted for themselves

(b) compare this with how things were at present

(c) identify what needed to happen to achieve those desirable futures

The outcomes of these conferences, replicated up and down the country, were largely the same. People wanted:

(a) access to services at all times (24 hours a day and at weekends)

(b) help focused at home or locally

(c) services that addressed key issues in their lives: home, work, education

(d) assistance in regaining their ability to manage their own lives, through psychological approaches

These messages, and other national and international studies, influenced the development of new models of care, which were finally formalised in the National Service Framework for Mental Health (Department of Health, 1999) and the NHS Plan (Department of Health, 2000), in which Assertive Outreach, Early Intervention and Crisis Resolution/Home Treatment Teams were made national targets or 'must dos'.

In many parts of England, a great deal of service redesign was underway. In Staffordshire, for instance, as part of the closure of St Matthews Hospital there was a radical programme of bed reduction and the establishment of locality teams specialising in primary care support, therapy and crisis response. All key stakeholders had influenced the service design and there was a high expectation of improved outcomes for service users and their families. Unfortunately, feedback from service users about the new services was that although the buildings and structures had changed, the expectations of them by staff and the way they felt they were treated had not.

Staff had moved into new roles; there had been very few retirements and redundancies. Training had been provided, largely orienting staff to their new teams, roles and settings. The training and development was only available for a few weeks during the period of transition. Some teams, with inspirational leaders and managers, began to operate them differently, with ongoing supervision and support; but the majority did not.

Over the same period, the Care Programme Approach (CPA), introduced in 1991, was hitting problems and was being carried out as a bureaucratic rather than a person-centred approach to assessment and care planning. Initiatives sprang up, however, such as the development of the Avon Mental Health Measure (see www.mind.org.uk) to enable service users to lead their own assessments and deliver meaningful objectives for their care plans. In the author's patch, a piece of work was commissioned to facilitate the engagement of service users and carers in the assessment and care planning process of CPA.

An important finding in the evaluation of this work was that service users were anxious about and therefore reluctant to articulate their aspirations, which may, for example, have been to get a job or to come off medication. They felt that this would not be taken seriously by staff and may even have been used as evidence of 'lack of insight'. This was echoed by the views of some staff. It clearly illustrated the importance of the need for an open dialogue between practitioners and service users; and for practitioners to re-evaluate their expectations of the views and contributions of the person on the other side of the desk.

It is ironic that what service users and carers describe as the gaps in staff skills are not generally perceived by staff themselves to be a problem. A training need analysis in Staffordshire, for example, of primary and secondary care staff of all professional backgrounds across health and social care, which also asked service users and carers what they most found wanting in staff, showed that staff felt the need for more skills in risk assessment and dealing with crises. Service users and carers described the need for more listening skills, being treated with respect and as a partner in the care process. This was still a common finding in 2007 across newly qualified as well as experienced practitioners in health and social care.

The report *Pulling Together: The Future Roles and Training of Mental Health Staff* (Sainsbury Centre for Mental Health, 1997) provided a timely position statement, highlighting the need for 'core' and 'distinctive' competences for all mental health staff. While identifying the importance of considering the needs of service users and carers, and highlighting concern about staff attitudes and values, particularly in inpatient care, these did not figure strongly in staff's proposed core competences.

Around this time, recovery was beginning to be talked about in mental health circles. Its origins were largely in North America and an early definition (Anthony, 1993), described how 'a person with mental illness can recover even though the illness is not "cured". (Recovery) is a way of living a satisfying, hopeful and contributing life even with the limitations caused by illness.' This movement was led and championed by service users, but met with early scepticism from the professions.

The National Service Framework for Mental Health implementation process at a national level included the establishment of a Workforce Action Team (WAT). The WAT commissioned work, including the Capable Practitioner Framework from the Sainsbury Centre for Mental Health in 2001, Mental Health National Occupational Standards from Skills for Health, and a national mapping of education and training. This showed significant gaps in pre- and post-qualification training of all staff. Significant omissions included user and carer involvement, mental health promotion, values- and evidence-based practice, working with families, multidisciplinary working and working with diversity. The WAT final report outlined all of the above and other aspects of workforce development and, significantly, recommended the need for the new role of 'Support Time and Recovery Worker' (STR). The purpose of the role was to do as it said on the tin, specifically addressing what service users said they wanted from staff: time to be listened to, support to try things out, and to achieve a life that had value and meaning for the person.

In 2002, the National Institute for Mental Health in England (NIMHE) was established. Its role was to help implement mental health policy at a local level. It took the form of a few national programmes: workforce, social inclusion, delivering race equality, acute inpatient care, and the establishment of eight Regional Development Centres to work with local stakeholders, including service users and carers.

The NIMHE National Workforce Programme started its work in 2003 and chunked its work into six key areas:

(a) workforce planning

(b) recruitment and retention

(c) new ways of working – for the existing workforce

(d) new roles – to bring new people into the workforce

(e) education, training and development – to create capable practitioners

(f) leadership – to facilitate organisational change and development

This was published in a Mental Health Workforce Strategy in 2004 (Department of Health, 2004a).

A key imperative for the education, training and development aspect of the programme was to prioritise the development of a 'core curriculum' or 'core skills' for the entire workforce based on the gaps from the Workforce Mapping Report. Furthermore, inquiry reports into untoward incidents had frequently criticised poor risk assessments or inappropriate management of violent behaviour, as well as poor communication and coordination between agencies. In considering how to approach these priorities, the NIMHE National Workforce Programme and the Sainsbury Centre for Mental Health (in a collaborative workforce support unit) reviewed the Capable Practitioner Framework and consulted service users and carers, practitioners, academics and managers specifically about the key gaps in core skills.

It came as no surprise that the frequently expressed concerns of service users and carers were reiterated once again, echoed to some extent by practitioners. Values underpinning skills, knowledge and behaviour were highlighted as the 'must do' aspect. This complemented the work being developed on values-based practice by Woodbridge and Fulford (2004). It was therefore agreed that service user and carer concerns should form the basis of our subsequent work at the National Workforce Programme: the Ten Essential Shared Capabilities.

▶ Development of the ten essential shared capabilities

In defining our work, we wanted to use language carefully. The term 'core', as linked with competences, has been used to mean 'shared across all' as well as 'specific to one profession'. We therefore decided to use the term 'shared' from the outset. We discussed whether we should use the word 'competences', but competences were much more detailed than we wanted and, in any case, Mental Health National Occupational Standards were already in development. We preferred broader descriptions of values-based practice, which would build on the well-received Capable Practitioner Framework, to enable the whole of the workforce to see the wood for the trees. So we opted for the word 'capabilities'. Finally, we wanted to emphasise the importance of the shared capabilities, so 'essential' was the final part of our description: Essential Shared Capabilities (ESC). We did not know at the outset that there would end up being 10!

The Ten Essential Shared Capabilities were developed into a framework for the whole of the mental health workforce, which was published in 2004 (Department of Health, 2004c). They are summarised as follows:

(a) 'Working in Partnership. Developing and maintaining constructive working relationships with service users, carers, families, colleagues, key people and wider community networks. Working positively with any tensions created by conflicts of interest of aspiration that may arise between the partners in care.'

People who use services need to be viewed as partners in care rather than passive recipients of services. Practitioners will need the ability:

■ to explain in an understandable way their professional role and any parameters they work within

■ to communicate with all stakeholders involved in an individual's care

■ to engage service users in a collaborative assessment process

■ to acknowledge the part that families and carers play in the service users' support network and be able to engage them as partners in care

■ to communicate across disciplines, professional and organisational boundaries

(b) 'Respecting Diversity. Working in partnership with service users, carers, families and colleagues to provide care and interventions that not only make a positive difference but also do so in ways that respect and value diversity including age, race, culture, disability, gender, spirituality and sexuality.'

Practitioners will need to:

- understand and acknowledge diversity
- understand the impact of discrimination and prejudice on mental health and mental health services
- demonstrate a commitment to equal opportunities for everyone
- respond to the needs of people sensitively
- promote people's rights and responsibilities and recognise the service users' rights to privacy, dignity, respect and confidentiality

(c) 'Practising Ethically. Recognising the rights and aspirations of service users and their families, acknowledging power differentials and minimising them wherever possible, providing treatment and care that is accountable to service users and carers within the boundaries prescribed by national (professional) legal and local codes of ethical practice.'
Practitioners will need to demonstrate:

- an understanding of and commitment to the legal and human rights of service users and carers
- an ability to respond to the needs of people in an ethical, honest and non-judgemental manner
- an ability to encourage active choices and participation in care and treatment

(d) 'Challenging Inequality. Addressing the causes and consequences of stigma, discrimination, social inequality and exclusion on service users, carers and mental health services. Creating, developing and maintaining valued social roles for people in the communities they come from.'

In order to challenge inequality, practitioners need to:

- understand the nature of stigma
- understand the effects of exclusion and discrimination and the role that mental health services play in this process
- demonstrate an ability to challenge discrimination and communicate concerns to others

This capability has further been developed in the light of what we know about social exclusion and what practitioners can do to promote social inclusion.

(e) 'Promoting Recovery. Working in partnership to provide care and treatment that enables service users and carers to tackle mental health problems with hope and optimism and to work towards a valued lifestyle within and beyond the limits of any mental health problem.'

Recovery is what people experience themselves as they become empowered to achieve a life that is meaningful in their own terms. Practitioners need to:

- understand that recovery is a process that is unique to each person
- understand the essential role of hope in the process
- accept that recovery is not about the elimination of symptoms or the notion of cure
- work in a way that is flexible and responds to the expressed needs of the person

(f) 'Identifying People's Needs and Strengths. Working in partnership to gather information to agree health and social care needs in the context of the preferred lifestyle and aspiration of service users, their families, carers and friends.'

The focus is to enable people to describe their experience in such a way as to identify their strengths and formulate their needs as a person. Practitioners need to:

- carry out (or contribute to) a systematic whole systems assessment, focusing on strengths and needs rather than on problems and symptoms

(g) 'Providing Service User Centred Care. Negotiating achievable and meaningful goals; primarily from the perspective of service users and their families. Influencing and seeking to achieve these goals and clarifying the responsibilities of the people who will provide any help that is needed, including systematically evaluating outcomes and achievements.'

Goals need to be, first and foremost, meaningful to the person for whom they are set; they need to have achievable and measurable steps so that success can be measured or so that the plan can be revised. Practitioners need:

- to work alongside service users to help them describe their goals as precisely and meaningfully as possible
- to help the service user identify and use their strengths to achieve their goals and aspirations

(h) 'Making a Difference. Facilitating access to and delivering the best quality, evidence-based, values-based health and social care interventions to meet the needs and aspirations of service users and their families and carers.'

Much of what is practised in mental health service has no evidence base. In some cases, service users describe those services as helpful, such as alternative therapies. What does have an evidence base (as defined by being included in National Institute for Health and Clinical Excellence guidance), on the other hand, is frequently not implemented. Both of these issues are a source of concern. Practitioners need to:

- be aware of and seek to implement evidence-based practice

■ gather information on a regular basis in order to develop evidence from practice

(i) 'Promoting Safety and Positive Risk Taking. Empowering the person to decide the level of risk that they are prepared to take with their health and safety. This includes working with the tension between promoting safety and positive risk taking, including assessing and dealing with possible risks for service users, carers, family members, and the wider public.'

Risk assessments and risk management are essential, but they can feed into defensive practice if they are not integrated into a person-centred assessment and care planning (CPA) process. Practitioners need to:

■ demonstrate the ability to form harmonious working relationships with service users and carers and involve them in risk management strategies

(j) 'Personal Development and Learning. Keeping up to date with changes in practice and participating in life long learning, personal and professional development for oneself and colleagues through supervision, appraisal and reflective practice.'

Practitioners need to be active participants in their own development and supported by their colleagues and employing organisation to do so. Staff are the most important resource and have the most impact on the experience of people using services. The vast majority come in to services to do the best they can for the people they are working with. The fact that they end up doing things that do not help people is due to a number of factors, including inadequate or outdated training, poor ongoing support and supervision to foster personal growth and self-questioning, and inadequate multidisciplinary working.

▶ Implementing the ten essential shared capabilities

It is one thing to produce a framework for the whole of the workforce; it is quite another to implement it! It was decided to develop learning materials as a first step towards implementation. The NHSU, at the time, agreed to fund the process and the first materials were printed and distributed for field testing in 46 sites across England in 2005. The materials were produced in both paper and CD-Rom versions.

A formal, external evaluation was completed and published (Brabban & Brooker, 2006). 579 learners and 75 facilitators took part in the evaluation and the overall results were highly positive. The key recommendations included:

(a) 'Experts by Experience' should be involved in the delivery of specific ESC (Essential Shared Capabilities) modules wherever possible.

(b) Group facilitation is the preferred mode of delivery rather than individual study alone, as it is important for values-based issues to be challenged by peers.

(c) The material needs to be made more relevant to non-clinical staff, by using different case study examples.

(d) 98% of participants used the paper version rather than the CD Rom, so revised materials need to be available in printable form.

(e) The hours of study are likely to be in excess of what was originally estimated (16 hours).

(f) There are opportunities for more in-depth learning through extensive references, to accommodate practitioners from a variety of backgrounds and with different levels of expertise.

In the light of the recommendations, the learning materials were modified and are now available on the website of the Centre for Clinical and Academic Workforce Innovation at the University of Lincoln (commissioned by NIMHE to undertake the work) www.lincoln.ac.uk/ccawi.

Discussions have been held with all of the key professions to ensure that the ESC are addressed within their pre-registration training programmes. They are now referred to explicitly in clinical psychology training, in the College of Occupational Therapists, and by the General Social Care Council for Social Work. They were included in the Chief Nursing Officer's review of mental health nursing in 2006, which emphasised a commitment to recovery. Active discussions have been held with the Royal College of Psychiatrists and the ESC have been addressed in some undergraduate medical training.

There is a danger, however, that the cross-referencing aspect of training can be a tick-box exercise rather than an in-depth scrutiny of the curricula. A separately funded project, Mental Health in Higher Education (see www.mhhe.heacademy.ac.uk) set up to facilitate interdisciplinary learning in mental health, is actively promoting the ESC with all its academic partners to engage them in a fundamental, root-and-branch review of their curricula.

All employing organisations have been encouraged to integrate the ESC into their training strategies and there are increasingly frequent examples of positive practice.

▶ Building on the ten essential shared capabilities

An induction module is being developed to enable the ESC to become integrated in the time-pressured induction programmes in health and social care organisations.

Additional, more in-depth materials have been developed or are in the process of development to expand on the ESC:

■ *Promoting Recovery*: A recovery module on a CD-Rom has been produced, which outlines a two-day programme with associated learning resources: 'Creating and Inspiring Hope' – Integrating recovery values and principles into everyday practice.

- *Respecting Diversity*: Race Equality and Cultural Capability (RECC) learning materials have been developed, field tested in four sites nationally and revised; they were published in 2007.

- *Challenging Inequality*: A framework called 'Capabilities for Inclusive Practice' has been developed, published in 2007.

- *Identifying People's Needs and Strengths; Providing Service User Centred Care; Promoting Safety and Positive Risk Taking*: Through the review of the Care Programme Approach (2007/2008), learning materials to cover the assessment, care planning and risk processes will be available in 2008.

▶ What are the continuing challenges?

Producing learning materials is only one step. They are now available as an 'off-the-shelf' resource for everyone. How they are delivered and facilitated will make the difference. This means that facilitators need to have undergone values-based training. Equally, it is increasingly recognised that service users and carers are a great source of trainers, not only in describing their experience but also as facilitators in their own right. Ways of involving service users and carers is described in a report by Tew, Gell and Foster (2004). This is one way of ensuring that training is values based and grounded in the experience of the person using them.

Training and development still tends to occur in an unsystematic manner, not related to the needs of service users and of the service as a whole. A 'Learning and Development Toolkit' for the whole of the mental health workforce (Department of Health, 2007a) has been produced to help local health and social care organisations identify their priorities and develop learning and development strategies.

What people learn and how they put what they have learned into practice is a key challenge for all students, practitioners, educators and employing organisations. It is unhappily all too common for people undertaking training, both at pre- and post-registration levels, to find that their new skills or attitudes do not sit well with existing models of service or with what the team or service has been doing traditionally. Training to provide psychosocial interventions is a case in point and, more recently, training for non-medical prescribing.

Person-centred values, which challenge the culture of many existing services, run the risk of being discouraged in new trainees and converts. This relates back to the earlier point that staff are often unaware that what they do is actually not focused on the needs and wishes of the service user and carer. The suggestion or impression that this is the case can lead to defensiveness and hostility. Indeed, feedback from employers suggests that the ESC are often seen as most appropriate for the non-professionally qualified workforce. While this is heartening on the one hand, it ignores the fact that mental health professionals also need to base their work on these capabilities. The experience of Support, Time and Recovery workers, for instance, shows that the greatest challenge to the successful implementation of their role is from experienced practitioners, who do not have a full understanding of, or commitment to, their recovery-oriented approach.

In seeking to ensure that we have capable practitioners in the future, therefore, we need to ensure that there are also capable teams and services in which they can work effectively.

▶ Conclusions and the way forward

The values that should underpin how services are designed and delivered have become clearer over the years. The Ten Essential Shard Capabilities have been specifically developed to articulate the primacy of person-centred values.

Making the ESC core to what practitioners do is not an easy task, as they challenge different professional perspectives. They overarch the medical, psychological and social models and their implications for formulating needs.

Help is at hand, however, in the approach of New Ways of Working (NWW). Work started on this in 2003 and since that time three key reports have been published: *New Ways of Working for Everyone* (Department of Health, 2007b) and its two preceding reports, *New Ways of Working for Psychiatrists: An Interim Report* (Department of Health, 2004b) and *New Ways of Working for Psychiatrists: Final Report – But Not the End of the Story* (Department of Health, 2005). NWW challenges custom and practice; it is about making jobs doable for staff, but it is also about delivering services more effectively to meet the needs of people with mental health problems and those of their carers. All three reports explicitly state that the ESC must underpin what all practitioners need in order to deliver effective New Ways of Working.

The Creating Capable Teams Approach (Department of Health, 2007c) provides a means for multidisciplinary teams to review what they are doing, based on service user and carer needs, to facilitate New Ways of Working and to develop more appropriate education and training for team members. The ESC are used to underpin the preparation of the team for the process.

The Ten Essential Shared Capabilities have considerable validity and present significant challenges to practitioners developing their practice. They make explicit the values that should underpin modern mental health services and what practitioners do to make their efforts more relevant to service users and carers. Who would argue with that?

▶ References

Anthony, W. (1993) Recovery from mental illness: The guiding vision of the mental health service system in the 1990s. *Psychosocial Rehabilitation Journal*, 16(4): 11–23.

Avon Mental Health Measure, www.mind.org.uk, under Information – Factsheets – User-centred Mental Health Assessments.

Brabban, A. & Brooker, C. (2006) *The Ten Essential Shared Capabilities Learning: An Evaluation of the Pilot Training Materials*. Sheffield: Sheffield University.

Department of Health (1999) *National Service Framework for Mental Health*. London: Department of Health.

Department of Health (2000) *The NHS Plan*. London: Department of Health.

Department of Health (2001) *Workforce Action Team (WAT) Report 2001*. London: Department of Health.

Department of Health (2004a) *National Mental Health Workforce Strategy*. London: Department of Health.

Department of Health (2004b) *New Ways of Working for Psychiatrists – Interim Report*. London: Department of Health.

Department of Health (2004c) *The Ten Essential Shared Capabilities: A Framework for the Whole of the Mental Health Workforce*. London: Department of Health.

Department of Health (2005) *New Ways of Working for Psychiatrists: Enhancing Effective, Person-centred Services through New Ways of Working in Multidisciplinary and Multi-agency Contexts. Final Report – But Not the End of the Story*. London: Department of Health.

Department of Health (2007a) *A Learning and Development Toolkit for the Whole of the Mental Health Workforce Across both Health and Social Care*. London: Department of Health.

Department of Health (2007b) *New Ways of Working for Everyone – Progress Report*. London: Department of Health.

Department of Health (2007c) *The Creating Capable Teams Approach*. London: Department of Health.

Rosenhan, D. L. (1973) On being sane in insane places. *Science*, **179**: 250–58.

Sainsbury Centre for Mental Health (1997) *Pulling Together: The Future Roles and Training of Mental Health Staff*. London: Sainsbury Centre for Mental Health.

Sainsbury Centre for Mental Health (2001) *The Capable Practitioner*. London: Sainsbury Centre for Mental Health.

Skills for Health (2003) *National Occupational Standards for Mental Health*. London: Skills for Health.

Tew, J., Gell, C. & Foster, S. (2004) *Learning form Experience: Involving Service Users and Carers in Mental Health Education and Training. A Good Practice Guide*. Birmingham: MHHE, NIMHE West Midlands & Trent WDC.

Wolfensberger, W. (1980) A brief overview of the principle of normalisation. In R. J. Flynn & K. E. Nitsch (eds), *Normalisation, Social Integration, and Community Services* (pp. 7–30). Baltimore, MD: University Park Press.

Wolfensberger, W. & Truman, S. (1983): *PASSING. Programme Analysis of Service System Implementation of Normalisation Goals*. Toronto: National Institute on Mental Retardation.

Woodbridge, K. & Fulford, K. W. M. (2004) *Whose Values? A Workbook for Values Based Practice in Mental Health Care*. London: Sainsbury Centre for Mental Health and Warwick Medical School.

Web sites

Centre for Clinical and Academic Workforce Innovation: www.lincoln.ac.uk/ccawi

New Ways of Working: www.newwaysofworking.org.uk

Skills for Health: www.skillsforhealth.org.uk

MHHE: www.mhhe.heacademy.ac.uk)

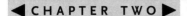
The ten essential shared capabilities in practice

Ian McGonagle, Ian Baguley, Sara Owen and Sarah Lewis
Centre for Clinical and Academic Workforce Innovation, University of Lincoln

This chapter examines the assumptions that underpin the Ten Essential Shared Capabilities and explores how the capabilities can be applied to mental health practice.

The authors have found that students and practitioners develop a greater understanding of the Ten Essential Shared Capabilities if they take the time to discuss them with their colleagues. This discussion and reflection also help people to consider how the ESC can then be transferred and translated into their daily practice with service users, carers and colleagues.

▶ Introduction

Mental health services are changing at a rapid rate. Old certainties about the roles, purpose and skill mix of mental health teams are under significant revision and review (CSIP/NIMHE, 2007). The current interest and activity around new ways of working in mental health have focused primarily on flexibility. For example, the workforce of the future will need to be flexible and adaptable in order to respond to the societal changes and workforce challenges that mental health and other services face. This flexibility refers not only to practitioners' roles, but also to the way practitioners think and behave. Underpinning all of this is the fundamental importance of the values that mental health practitioners bring to their work.

There is no doubt that the work of mental health practitioners has changed and is continuing to change. This has been greatly influenced by the rise of the consumerist movement, which has been reflected in much government policy since the late 1980s. This movement has supported and enabled the growth and

Learning About Mental Health Practice.   Edited by Theo Stickley and Thurstine Basset
© 2008 John Wiley & Sons, Ltd

23

influence of the voice of service users and carers at policy and service development level. From a purist consumer perspective, service users in receipt of poor services could 'take their business elsewhere'. In mental health services, however, clients often find this a difficult if not an impossible option. Instead, some service users and carers have sought to positively influence the types of services available and the way in which they are delivered. This reformist approach has filtered its way though many important policy initiatives both within mental health and in wider health and social care, such as *The National Service Framework (NSF) for Mental Health* (Department of Health, 1999) and *Our Health, Our Care, Our Say* (Department of Health, 2006). These policy documents incorporate the notion of citizenship, whereby all citizens have political, civil and social rights in determining the way health care and other services are planned, organised and delivered. The mental health service user movement has been at the forefront in demanding new or alternative mental health provision in addition to the improvement of the care provided within existing healthcare services.

The National Institute for Mental Health (England) (NIMHE) National Workforce Programme supports practitioners in mental health services to adopt flexible practices and to challenge long-held assumptions about the way care is organised and delivered. This challenge includes the need for practitioners to move beyond the rhetoric of user and carer involvement towards a greater emphasis on engagement and collaboration. Tools such as the Ten Essential Shared Capabilities (ESC) provide a practical and useful framework for practitioners to reflect on their practice with others, with the ultimate aim of promoting collaborative working with service users and carers, and flexibility and innovation in mental health practice.

Collaborative service user and carer involvement presents a number of challenges for mental health practitioners, particularly for those working in more traditionally organised services. For example, users and carers have employed what political leverage they have to criticise not only the services themselves but also the practice of professionals and other mental health workers. Service users and carers have repeatedly reported that services are not fit for purpose and that practitioners often seem unable to recognise, respond and respect their common and sometimes unique needs. This is supported by research that provides a consistent picture of requests from users and carers for warmth and humanity within a relationship of respect and understanding (see Godfrey & Wistow, 1997; Noble & Douglas, 2004; Rose, 2001). These issues are echoed in the review of services for Black and Minority Ethnic (BME) communities (Sainsbury Centre for Mental Health, 2002).

The service user and carer critique of contemporary mental health care in turn challenges the professional identity of practitioners, as professions are built on the use of expert knowledge and control over a discrete area of work. This can create a dissonance between the practice of care giving and the experience of mental health service users as partners in care. For practitioners wanting to address this dissonance and develop a more collaborative approach to their work, this can be hampered by the bureaucracy in large organisations, high caseloads and staff shortages.

Whatever the reasons for this dissonance, a positive response from practitioners is required so that mental health services truly meet the needs of those who use them. The NIMHE National Workforce Programme, together with colleagues from practice and education, is aiming to provide support and to produce a range of materials to guide practitioners in new ways of working. Much of this work is underpinned by an acknowledgement and understanding of professionalism and how this influences practice. For example, Ludmerer (1999) has considered professionalism in medical practice and argues that it is founded on three essential characteristics, namely:

- expert knowledge

- self-regulation

- a relationship based on trust where there is a responsibility to place the needs of the patient ahead of the physician's self-interest

It is this last element that has guided the development of the Ten Essential Shared Capabilities.

▶ The ten essential shared capabilities

The Ten Essential Shared Capabilities (ESC) were developed as an articulation of the core capabilities expected by service users and carers in their interactions with mental health practitioners. As noted in the previous chapter by Roslyn Hope (see Chapter 1), the Ten ESC statements arose out of a large-scale consultation exercise with service users and carers, mental health-care practitioners and colleagues in Higher Education; a process led by the Sainsbury Centre for Mental Health. The comprehensive material gathered from this consultation was refined into the ten core statements of shared capabilities applicable across the entire mental health practitioner workforce and at all levels of practice.

The Ten ESC are important because service users and carers strongly believe that they are essential components of a close, collaborative relationship built on mutual trust, respect and ethical practice. In essence, the Ten ESC are a set of values with associated behaviours that mental health practitioners should hold and display in all interactions. These values can and should underpin not only interactions with service users and carers, but also interactions with colleagues in mental health and other services.

The assumptions that underpin the ten essential shared capabilities

Acknowledgement of values

The first assumption that underpins the Ten ESC is the acknowledgement of values. Values are crucial because they are psychologically significant to individuals and have an effect on attitudes, social conduct and judgment of others (Rokeach, 1983). At one level values can be considered as fundamental truths; that is, the aspects of life that individuals really care about and think are important. These in turn influence the way individuals present themselves to the world and behave towards others.

Being aware of your own values is not enough, however. Individuals hold a number of values, and these may vary in importance. Personal values also provide a critical link to emotions and subsequent behaviour. For example, personal beliefs are frequently the catalyst for a specific course of action (Gollwitzer, 1996). Values therefore represent the criteria through which individuals evaluate actions, policies, people and events. Importantly for understanding the Ten ESC, values are seen as hierarchical (Schwartz, 1994). They are ordered in relative importance to one another and it is this that distinguishes values from attitudes. Values can be linked to moral statements about 'the way things should be', whereas attitudes refer to how individuals apply thinking to match those moral expectations. Values, attitudes (and associated behaviour) are therefore explicitly linked and are the cornerstones of how we act and who we are.

It is also important to note the dynamic nature of values. Pursuing a course of action that is consistent with one particular value may be inconsistent with another. For example, even if a practitioner subscribes to all of the Ten ESC, there may be times when two or more capabilities can be in direct conflict with each other. Mental health practitioners may wish to 'Work in Partnership (ESC 1), 'Provide Service User Centred Care' (ESC 7) and 'Promote Recovery' (ESC 5). These same practitioners may also be in the process of using mental health legislation to detain a person in hospital. In this scenario the values are inconsistent, as the overriding value in this case may be to 'Promote Safety' (ESC 9). Studying and reflecting on the Ten ESC provides a useful framework for understanding the dynamic nature of routine practice in mental health. Arguably, keeping personal and professional values in mind is the most effective way of articulating the rationale behind selected actions. Behaviour can be outside conscious thought, but keeping values accessible helps in maintaining behaviour that is consistent with our value base (Verplanken & Holland, 2002).

The Ten ESC provide a foundation for mental health practice that reflects the expectations of service users and carers. They also have a role in influencing agreed practice standards that can be used by all practitioners when making care-delivery decisions. The interest in how values held by practitioners can be used to aid understanding of practice is having resonance across the health and social care spectrum. In the care of older people, for example, the Department of Health and Social Care have developed the 'Dignity in Care' initiative, which is also founded on ten value statements that underpin the proposed dignity programme (see www.doh/dignityincare). This programme is consistent with the Ten ESC.

This interest in the core values that underpin practice almost certainly comes from the rise in the consumerist approach within health and social care. Taking a proactive stance and listening to the experiences of people who use services has provided the basis for understanding practice omission (what service users think is missing from services) and practice enhancement (what can be put in place to improve service delivery). The Ten ESC are focused on the individual care setting and on the interactions between practitioners, service users and their families. The flexibility of the framework allows individual practitioners to interpret and reframe each of the capabilities according to the demands of their day-to-day therapeutic interactions and behaviours.

Implementation on a cognitive and behavioural level

The second assumption underpinning the implementation of the Ten ESC is that it takes place on a cognitive and behavioural level (the expectation that practitioners behave in certain ways and that they can use the ESC as a framework through which they explain behaviours and actions). The Ten ESC and the associated national learning materials (download from www.lincoln.ac.uk/ccawi/ESC.htm) are available to assist practitioners to exert influence and control over their decision-making and action processes. This sense of control and responsibility links back to the earlier emphasis on professional identity and also to Bandura's construct of self-efficacy (Bandura, 1977, 1997). The theory of self-efficacy proposes that acting in a desired way with successful meaningful behaviours is based on the interplay between values (conviction) and desired behaviours (to achieve desired outcomes).

An individual's judgement on their ability to be effective in their behaviours (the effort given to a course of action) is based on four sources of information, namely:

- personal past performance at the task
- the performance of others deemed to be similar to oneself
- verbal persuasion that one is capable
- a person feels they want to act in this way

The desire to act and the subsequent action can be different. Bandura argues that we are contributors to our actions rather than the sole determiners (Bandura, 1997). This is because reciprocal interactions exist between our behaviour, cognitions, affect, biological processes and/or our environment. The dynamic nature of our values is a reflection of the feedback received from practitioners and those receiving mental health services. Service users, for example, reliably report degrees of dissatisfaction regarding basic customer care-type behaviours from mental health practitioners and services (i.e. interest, compassion, understanding and empathy). Mental health practitioners then begin to consider these values and associated behaviours as central to their practice and professional ethos. The Ten ESC can therefore be seen as an exercise in raising individual practitioners' awareness of their values and behaviours with a positive aim of encouraging and supporting the move towards values congruence (Verplanken, 2004).

Having a sense of self-efficacy also refers to the methods by which practitioners generate self-perceiving, self-reflecting and self-correcting activities (Bandura, 1997, p. 5). This is important in the Ten ESC, as they are descriptors of core practice behaviours for the entire mental health workforce. In a very real sense they support inter-professional learning and focus on the sharing of inter-professional uniqueness and similarities. The Ten ESC facilitate and support inter-professional education as a collaborative venture that supports positive service user-centred care from all disciplines (Barr, 1998).

Some authors have noted that inter-professional learning has been hampered by engrained stereotypes of practitioners with different models of mental health care, conflicting values and dichotomous approaches to care and treatment (Barnes, Carpenter & Dickinson, 2000). Opening a dialogue about values and practice is at the heart of all ESC activity.

While the ESC are self-evident as a description of core capabilities for mental health practice, what they mean in practice can raise different points of emphasis for different practitioners. Having different perspectives is not a bad thing; indeed, difference is a thing to be celebrated. No two people see the same football game or look at a painting in the same way. Having different views adds to the richness of our understanding of mental health. The key to learning and developing can be understanding differences in value and perspective with service users and colleagues. In sharing our points of view, negotiating and agreeing, a mutually beneficial way forward can be found.

We believe that the ESC help describe the complex interactions and negotiations with service users, carers and practitioners. This includes weighing up possible courses of action, understanding the consequences and the range of opinion, the agreement of care plans and the management of difference.

Therefore it is possible to differ widely on our perspective and understanding. Successful mental health care is, in part, being able to live with and manage difference and to negotiate agreement and positive ways of working with alternative views and actions. This is part of your emerging role as a mental health practitioner, both with service users, carers and colleagues.

▶ The positive impact of the ten ESC on practice

To illustrate the positive impact that the Ten ESC can have on practice, we present the following three care studies. As with many case vignettes, they can be seen as a composite of a number of experiences to illuminate key points for study. Care study 1 (Naomi) is written in the first person – because it really is Naomi's story. We consider that this reinforces the belief that practitioners were not able (for whatever reason) to keep their values at the forefront of their mind when they chose their actions in practice. It is also worth noting that what makes a difference for people can be so simple. Technical competence in counselling or any other intervention has limited worth without a set of values based on respect for the person with whom you are working.

Care study 2.1: Naomi (in her own words)

I'd been having some difficulties for a long period of time that I describe as depression and anxiety related. As an 18-year-old young woman I was really unsure what was happening to me and felt there was no one I could talk to or who could help me at home. I went to my GP and asked if I could see a counsellor, as I was sure I wanted someone who would listen to me and help me understand what was happening to me. When I met the counsellor I met someone who explained my symptoms in terms of an anxiety circle and said she was there to promote my self-help. Over a number of sessions she repeated again and again the anxiety circle but did not seem to be concerned with 'me'. I felt uncomfortable about doing breathing exercises, but the counsellor insisted we do them but I refused. She continued to insist and it got to the point where I had a panic attack in the session and I walked out.

At this time my boyfriend and I had to move away from home for his job. So leaving all family connections behind, we set off for another part of the country. I was going downhill fast and got to the point where I did not go out of our new house for a whole year. This was very hard for my boyfriend who was also away from home and with a partner who could not get out of the house. I continued to feel very depressed and anxious all the time.

We had to move again due to my partner's work and we began to plan our wedding. I visited my new GP, as I was unsure I would be able to walk down the aisle. He reviewed my notes and told me there was no prospect of me ever being able to manage my wedding day. The GP told me that based on his previous experience of people with my history he considered me incurable; in effect, he told me I was a hopeless case!

I was determined to do something so I registered with a new GP who then referred me to a community psychiatric nurse (CPN). On my first visit he instructed me that we would have four appointments only. After telling my story again he did nothing and I have to say he was useless. I don't know what he did; he was distant and uninvolved in what was happening to me. I carried on with the four appointments in the hope that something would happen, but even now I can't even remember what we talked about. I needed someone to help me, to encourage and support me, but I was not receiving it from people who were there (supposedly) to help me.

I was helping myself all the time, managing to go to the local library, reading books trying to work out a plan for myself to overcome my anxiety.

I went back to my GP and he suggested a referral to psychology and when I got the letter I was informed that there was to be a two-year wait before I could be seen!

I felt I had no options, I had not met anyone who seemed to care, I was worried sick, feeling anxious and increasingly depressed, but trying to find a way out by myself. So I waited the two years. My life was on hold while I waited and waited. I was still away from family and friends with just support from my now husband and even he was still unable to really comprehend how I felt.

After the two years I was seen by a psychologist who was still in training, but that didn't matter, because she seemed to care. Yes, she too explained to me the cycle of anxiety (I knew it pretty well by now), but she was kind and helped me set realistic goals and got me motivated. I was still frustrated though as she told me at our first meeting that there would only be five sessions. After a two-year wait, that's not the kind of thing you want to hear.

Due to my husband's work we had to move again, and so struggled on. In my new home, I was still feeling depressed and anxious and visited my new GP. He suggested a referral to another CPN who made another quick assessment of my difficulties. He asked if I would be interested in group therapy; as I was anxious to get as much help I agreed. He also suggested a referral to an assessment centre for a detailed assessment of my depression and anxiety. He promised to get back to me with information about my anxiety and depression and details of the group. I never heard from him again.

I did attend an assessment with yet another CPN and a student nurse. It lasted one hour and was quite a grilling; at the end of it they suggested a referral to a cognitive behaviour therapist. This was an improvement though as the waiting list would only be one year! It meant that I would have to wait yet again and so in the meantime, they also suggested an appointment with a graduate mental health worker for the 'books on prescription' scheme.

What can I say? This graduate worker was fantastic, a real breath of fresh air. Do you know what he did when we first met? He introduced himself and asked if I would like a cup of tea. Simple as that, he made me feel at ease, he made me feel like he wanted to help, to give me time and space to get through this time and he wanted us to work together on the problems. Of course he took me through the cycle of anxiety, but this time he asked what I knew and understood before he did so. I came away with a renewed sense of optimism. Life is still hard, I still have difficult times, but I have hope. He sets out the work for us; he is genuinely interested in me and what is happening to me. Telling your story is hard and you need people who care about you to help you through the story and through this experience.

I still have my frustrations with services (I'm still waiting to see a cognitive behaviour therapist); so much time is spent in offices talking. I still struggle going outside and I would benefit from working with people outside and not inside. But I am carrying on with my treatment programme with the graduate worker and am, at last, feeling the benefit.

Activity 2.1

Answer the following questions in relation to Naomi's story:

- *Working in Partnership (ESC 1)*: What are the factors in Naomi's experience that either do or do not demonstrate effective partnership working?

- *Identifying people's needs and strengths (ESC 6)*: Where in this experience did people demonstrate the ability to identify Naomi's needs...? ...and her strengths?

- *Making a difference (ESC 8)*: Where in this story did practitioners demonstrate the use of evidence-based care? What things do we need to understand about the delivery of evidence-based care?

- *Other ESC descriptors*: How could Naomi's care have been improved using any other of the ESC descriptors?

Care Study 2.2: Surinder

Surinder is a 23-year-old woman who left home eight months ago to complete a beautician's training course. She is now living in a shared flat with others who are on her course.

She is the middle child of three. Her younger brother has just started at university studying chemistry, while her older sister is married with one child. Surinder is from a Sikh family and describes her family life as more westernised than that of some of her school friends.

Surinder has always described her family life as happy, homely and stable, with good relations with her siblings. Her mother is reported to have had infrequent but recurring bouts of depression throughout her life, with the most significant experience following the birth of her son. However, Surinder can never recall any formal health services being called for in the care of her mother, other than a family GP.

Surinder was an average student at school, popular with her friends, but she did not excel in any subject other than art. She reports that most of the teachers liked her, but mainly because she did not 'cause anyone any bother'.

During one of her beautician classes, Surinder found herself feeling very tearful and had to leave hurriedly. One of her instructors suggested she visit her GP. The GP noted that Surinder was thin and easily tearful when questioned about her feelings. A referral was made to the local mental health services.

She was interviewed by a community psychiatric nurse (CPN), who stated that Surinder had failed to engage with the assessment, saying she 'felt homesick and that's all that is wrong with me'. Reporting that he was unable to suggest a treatment plan, Surinder was referred back to her GP.

Over the following weeks her friends and course instructors have noticed that Surinder has become increasingly withdrawn. She reports to friends that she is losing confidence and does not feel able to go out with the other girls on the course.

She withdraws to her bedroom in her flat. Staff and her colleagues become increasingly concerned for her welfare and her GP is called. Surinder does not respond to the GP, and following police intervention, Surinder is admitted to an acute psychiatric unit. While there, Surinder feels very uncomfortable, isolated and continually states she wants to go home.

On the ward the social worker is unhappy at her admission, stating that alternatives to hospital have not received sufficient attention, while the occupational therapist feels certain that Surinder needs the admission in order to treat her obvious depression.

During her admission, Surinder remains unresponsive to practitioners and withdrawn from the majority of other service users. Following a full multidisciplinary team meeting, the consultant psychiatrist felt that Surinder would be better off in her flat and she was discharged back to the original CPN. During her admission Surinder gives up on her beautician course, but also feels currently unable to return to the family home.

Activity 2.2

Use the ESC to review Surinder's care history.

- *Identifying People's Needs and Strengths (ESC 6)*: At what point do you think Surinder's needs and strengths were identified? Do you think the professionals worked collaboratively to aid Surinder and meet her needs and aspirations? What aspects of Surinder's life do you think are important to the maintenance of her mental and physical well-being?

- *Respecting Diversity (ESC 2)*: Do you think that Surinder's personal cultural needs were important and, if so, were they addressed in her care programme? What do you think these culturally important issues may have been?

■ *Providing Service User Centred Care (ESC 7)*: At what point do you think the people in services began to really consider the unique needs of Surinder? When did people in the service begin to think about working with Surinder to achieve some meaningful, achievable goals?

■ *Promoting Recovery (ESC 5)*: At what point do you think it is important to begin discussing Surinder's hopes and fears? How would you support and enable Surinder to have optimism for her future?

Care Study 2.3: John

John is a 44-year-old married man with three children, Brian (20), Lucinda (18) and Mike (15). John has had a diagnosis of schizophrenia for 25 years. Although his last admission to hospital was some 15 years ago, he continues to receive monthly medication by injection and is seen by the psychiatrist for review once a year. John is seen by a CPN every month when he has his medication.

Recently John reported that he thought he was becoming unwell again. Although he wasn't able to articulate exactly what this meant, he did describe some physical symptoms that could be associated with anxiety.

On review by the psychiatrist it was decided to increase John's medication as a preventive measure. Subsequently John described concerns that he had about his youngest son Mike, who had become a bit distant and solitary.

There were also tensions between John and his wife Mandy, and John hinted that there may be sexual difficulties.

Activity 2.3

Use the ESC to review John's care history.

■ *Working in Partnership (ESC 1)*: Who would be the partners in this care programme? How would you organise this partnership working?

■ *Personal Development and Learning (ESC 10)*: What are your personal development and learning needs to help you respond positively and meaningfully to John in his current situation? What approaches would you use to identify any learning needs in assisting John?

▶ Conclusion

The Essential Shared Capabilities form an important foundation for the work of the NIMHE National Workforce Programme. Importantly, this work has been and continues to be driven by service users and carers. The magnification of the importance of values and principles is a welcome addition to the range of evidence-based interventions available in mental health care. The ESC learning materials (download at www.lincoln.ac.uk/ccawi/ESC.htm) provide the opportunity for learners to use these foundation blocks when reflecting on any education subject or practice encounter. Basing practice reflection and action on robust and considered values as well as available research evidence is a surer method of providing the kind of partnership in mental health care that is consistent with the demands of service users and carers.

▶ Appendix: the ten essential shared capabilities, including 'lay descriptions'

1. Working in partnership

Developing and maintaining constructive working relationships with service users, carers, families, colleagues, lay people and wider community networks. Working positively with any tensions created by conflicts of interest or aspiration that may arise between the partners in care.

What this means

Getting on well with service users, carers, families, people you work with, people in the community and the general public. Coping with differences of opinion about what and how things should be done and goals that should be reached.

2. Respecting diversity

Working in partnership with service users, carers, families and colleagues to provide care and interventions that not only make a positive difference but also do so in ways that respect and value diversity, including age, race, culture, disability, gender, spirituality and sexuality.

What this means

Working with service users, carers, families and other workers to provide care and treatment that helps people, accepting each person for what they are and treating them well whatever their age, race, culture, disability, gender, spirituality or sexuality

3. Practising ethically

Recognising the rights and aspirations of service users and their families, acknowledging power differentials and minimising them whenever possible.

Providing treatment and care that is accountable to service users and carers within the boundaries prescribed by national (professional), legal and local codes of ethical practice.

What this means

Recognising the rights and hopes of service users and their families and treating people as equally as possible. Keeping to good-practice guidelines and working within the law.

4. Challenging inequality

Addressing the causes and consequences of stigma, discrimination, social inequality and exclusion on service users, carers and mental health services. Creating, developing or maintaining valued social roles for people in the communities they come from.

What this means

Hoping to overcome unfair treatment and unwelcoming attitudes that affect service users, carers and mental health services. Helping people to play an active part in their own community and to be accepted rather than shut out.

5. Promoting recovery

Working in partnership to provide care and treatment that enables service users and carers to tackle mental health problems with hope and optimism and to work towards a valued lifestyle within and beyond the limits of any mental health problem.

What this means

Helping service users and carers to deal with their mental health problems and to keep a sense of hope for the future. Helping them to find a way of life that is rewarding to them whether or not they continue to have mental health problems.

6. Identifying people's needs and strengths

Working in partnership to gather information to agree health and social care needs in the context of the preferred lifestyle and aspirations of service users, their families, carers and friends.

What this means

Working with others to agree someone's needs in all areas of their life, keeping in mind the way they like to live and things for which they, their family, carers and friends hope.

7. Providing service user centred care

Negotiating achievable and meaningful goals; primarily from the perspective of service users and their families. Influencing and seeking the means to achieve these goals and clarifying the responsibilities of the people who will provide any help that is needed, including systematically evaluating outcomes and achievements.

What this means

Agreeing on goals that fit with what the service user and their family/carers want and that can be reached. Helping to work out what needs to be done, who will do what and how progress and success will be measured

8. Making a difference

Facilitating access to and delivering the best-quality, evidence-based, values-based health and social care interventions to meet the needs and aspirations of service users and their families and carers.

What this means

Making sure that service users, their families and carers have access to a range of high-quality care and treatments that work well, are delivered appropriately, and meet their needs and hopes for the future.

9. Promoting safety and positive risk taking

Empowering the person to decide the level of risk they are prepared to take with their health and safety. This includes working with the tension between promoting safety and positive risk taking, including assessing and dealing with possible risks for service users, carers, family members, and the wider public.

What this means

Working with someone in a positive way to decide how much risk they are prepared to take with their health and safety. Making sure that their safety is be balanced against risk taking and that all decisions are based on improving the quality of life. This capability involves assessing and dealing with possible risks to service users, carers, family members and the general public.

10. Personal development and learning

Keeping up to date with changes in practice and participating in life-long learning, personal and professional development for oneself and colleagues through supervision, appraisal and reflective practice.

What this means

Keeping up to date with changes in the way services are delivered. Taking part in learning throughout the whole of your life. Making sure that you (and the people you work with) get advice and support through supervision, regular reviews of progress and opportunities to think about the ways things are done.

▶ **References**

Bandura, A. (1977) Self-efficacy: Toward a unifying theory of behaviour change. *Psychological Review*, **84**: 191–215.

Bandura, A. (1997) *Self-Efficacy: The Exercise of Control*. New York, Freeman.

Barnes, D., Carpenter, J. & Dickinson, C. (2000) Interprofessional education for community mental health: Attitudes to community care and professional stereotypes. *Social Work Education*, **19**: 565–83.

Barr, H. (1998) Competent to collaborate: Towards a competency–based model for inter-professional education. *Journal of Inter-professional Care*, **12**: 181–8

CSIP/NIMHE (2007) *Mental Health: New Ways of Working for Everyone*. London: Department of Health.

Department of Health (1999) *The National Service Framework for Mental Health*. London: Department of Health.

Department of Health (2006) *Our Health, Our Care, Our Say*. London: Department of Health.

Godfrey, M. & Wistow, G. (1997) The user perspective on managing for health outcomes: The case of mental health. *Health and Social Care in the Community*, **5**: 325–33.

Gollwitzer, P. M. (1996) The volitional benefits of planning. In P. M. Gollwitzer & J. A. Bargh, J.A. (eds) *The Psychology of Action*. London: Guildford Press.

Ludmerer, K. (1999) *Time to Heal*. Oxford: Oxford University Press.

Noble, L. M. & Douglas, B. C. (2004) What users and relatives want from mental health services. Services research and outcomes. *Current Opinion in Psychiatry*, **17**: 289–96.

Rokeach, M. (1983) *The Nature of Human Values*. New York: John Wiley & Sons Ltd.

Rose, D. (2001) *User's Voice: The Perspectives of Mental Health Services Users on Community and Hospital Care*. London: Sainsbury Centre for Mental Health.

Sainsbury Centre for Mental Health (2002) *Breaking the Cycles of Fear*. London: Sainsbury Centre for Mental Health.

Schwartz, S. H. (1994) Are there universal aspects in the content and structure of values? *Journal of Social Issues*, **50**: 19–45.

Verplanken, B. (2004) Value congruence and job satisfaction among nurses: A human relations perspective. *International Journal of Nursing Studies*, **41**: 599–605.

Verplanken, B. & Holland, R. W. (2002) Motivated decision making: Effects of activation and self-centrality of values on choices and behaviour. *Journal of Personality and Social Psychology*, **82**: 434–47.

Web sites

Department of Health and Social care Dignity in Care initiative: www.doh/dignityincare

The Ten Essential Shared Capabilities learning materials: www.lincoln.ac.uk/ccawi/ESC.htm

◀ **CHAPTER THREE** ▶

Working in partnership

Anne Beales
Together: Working for Wellbeing

Gary Platz
The Wellink Trust, Wellington, New Zealand

The first essential shared capability is Working in Partnership. The Department of Health (2004) describes this capability as:

> Developing and maintaining constructive working relationships with service users, carers, families, colleagues, lay people and wider community networks. Working positively with any tensions created by conflicts of interest or aspiration that may arise between the partners in care.

▶ Working in partnership with individuals (Gary Platz, New Zealand)

Thinking back over the years about experiencing partnerships, I would say there was an experience of being listened to that had quite a positive effect on me. Before this experience, I can't recall even thinking of partnership as a possibility.

I was at home and I was at a stage of distress a lot of service users will be familiar with: the stage of things starting to take off, but I was not at a level in which the crisis team would respond. However, I knew that within a period of time I would be at a level where they would have to. I rang the emergency response team and I told them who I was and that I wasn't too far gone yet, but I knew within myself that things would get worse. I wasn't expecting them to respond other than to say, 'Have a warm bath and a cup of tea and see how that goes.' What did happen was that they listened to me. They came to my house, listened to what I said I needed and worked for me. I went to a respite place, stayed three days, and went home without things getting out of hand. My past experiences of things getting out of hand had meant hospitalisation and months of working my way through it.

Learning About Mental Health Practice. Edited by Theo Stickley and Thurstine Basset
© 2008 John Wiley & Sons, Ltd

There were elements of that situation that are very necessary for true partnership.

The first element was that they actually knew me and were not just familiar with the name and file. I had been using services for a while and was known. That knowledge of me meant that they had developed a level of trust. In other words, they listened to me and they believed me (this can be an amazing experience when one is experiencing mental distress). In effect, they had an adult-to-adult relationship with me. They listened to me and I listened to them. We both valued what the other was communicating and responded appropriately.

Since that time in the early 1990s, I have been increasingly involved in campaigning and working as a service user in the mental health field. I have experienced counterfeit partnership, but I am also pleased to say that in recent times an increasing amount of true partnerships between service users, families, family organisations, charity providers and clinical services are being developed. These true partnerships contain strong elements of mutual trust and respect.

▶ Working in partnership with individuals (Anne Beales, UK)

I can recall a really supportive way of working in partnership with my General Practitioner. It would be fair to say he was a controversial doctor, and I remember how he included me when deciding to refer me to the local Community Mental Health Team (CMHT) for assessment and treatment. When the report was sent back to him from the CMHT (addressed to him even though it was about me!), he phoned me at home and I went to the surgery to read through the report with him. It felt empowering and gave me an insight not only about how others saw me, but also about what I wanted my next steps to be. The steps turned out to be with friends and with others who had similar experiences of distress, isolation, fears and hopes. No assessments were made, no negative judgements either, but there was so much support and shared learning about what helped me and what hindered my return to myself.

While working with others who had similar experiences to run a local service user group called CAPITAL (Clients And Professional In Training And Learning), members all worked in partnership with each other, though we all contributed in different ways as we had different skills. It felt liberating to be with people who just accepted me, appreciating I had something to offer. CAPITAL worked with professionals and staff at all levels in West Sussex, however this was often around an agenda set by the professionals. CAPITAL delivered through auditing the local assertive outreach team, conducting a best-value review of child and adolescent mental health services, delivering training on the Approved Social Worker courses at the local university among so much other activity. To do these things meant, most importantly, that we had to educate and support ourselves. We both supported developments within the NHS Trust and supported our own well-being, and in doing so we were able to inform and influence the wider mental health community. Partnerships can lead to success at every level.

Figure 3.1   Working in Partnership.

Activity 3.1

Consider, as a practitioner, how your work and intervention will act as a support in an empowering way. How prepared/able are you to wait to take action until mutual trust and respect for both your own and the service user's expertise has been established?

What would help you the most in achieving Working in Partnership?

(a) Supportive manager and team who can take positive risks.

(b) Familiarity with the person experiencing distress, their family, their circumstances etc.

(c) A robust knowledge of local resources, which would include self-help groups.

Would you act without having all of the above?

Consider how you would resist the pressure to act too quickly before a partnership is formed when facing a crisis situation.

▶ Partnership working at wellink (Gary Platz)

Wellink is a charitable trust that has provided community-based support services for mental health consumers in Wellington, New Zealand, since 1989. Its mission is to facilitate recovery support that meets the needs of people with experience of mental illness. And its philosophy is: 'Let understanding, acceptance, love and hope unite our community and lead us in the way we work.' You can find out more about Wellink at www.wellink.org.nz.

The following is an example of how The Wellink Trust was able to work in partnership with young people.

Headspace and the Youth Governance Group form an interesting case in point. In the Wellink Trust we were looking at how Wellink could be of most benefit to young people who experience severe mental distress (mental illness). My role in Wellink at the time was consumer adviser, and I was able to contact a service user who had been through youth early intervention services in the not too distant past in order that we could investigate and develop a proposal on how Wellink could be positioned to best meet the needs of local young people. The outcome was an additional service user position in the Wellink Trust: youth development worker. The primary task of this role was to establish a Youth Governance Group that was representative of the diversity of young people accessing mental health services and the diversity of their lived experience.

The Youth Governance Group was an integral part of a partnership set up between clinical hospital-based youth services, non-clinical Wellink charitable trust services, and direct youth service user input. Its input into to the partnership was in a shared leadership role. The area of expertise of young service users was in knowing the lived experience, knowing what it is like to receive services and knowing the issues. They were well positioned to create an environment that would be best suited for young people. Some of the areas in which the group took the lead were the interior decoration of the service, the name of the service and the reviewing and development of policies. An example was the development of a policy on self-harm, which reframed the whole perception of self-harm and reduced the shame and moral judgement that the very description of the act as self-harm conjures up. Young people also took the lead in training of staff on all issues as seen from a young service user perspective. There are two sides to every issue: the service provider's perspective and the service user's perspective. Both had to be considered to see the whole picture and to design and set up and run a successful service.

Another example in the Wellink Trust is a collaboration by peers (service users). Wellink Trust and the clinical hospital jointly run the services. This collaboration was once again led by service users, who set up what is called the 'Key We Way'. This service is a peer (service user) crisis recovery house, which sits in the community as an alternative to hospitalisation and is a part of the overall mental health system in the greater Wellington area of New Zealand. For this to be possible a lot of work was done in true collaboration, sharing with and working with philosophies and ideologies so as to have the 'Key We Way' as a seamless part of the overall system. Here, service users moved beyond inclusion and participation, which can sometimes be service users reacting to other people's agendas, towards the more proactive position of decision making, leading and implementing innovation.

▶ Partnership working at together (Anne Beales)

Together is a leading UK charity working for well-being. That means we support people with mental health needs to get what they want from life and to feel happier. We do this by:

- running a range of services
- campaigning and doing research
- educating local communities about their own mental health needs.

In everything we do we are inspired and guided by the hopes and wishes of the people we support. Find out more about us at www.together-uk.org.

In my current role as Director of Service User Involvement at Together, I'm able to work in partnership with senior managers within national bodies which influence the NHS at a policy-making level. I'm also serving as a management committee member in the recently formed National Survivor User Network, which aims to support service user-led shared learning, and signpost appropriate groups towards influence at a strategic level, getting their voice heard. The key factor in my work is working in partnership with people who access Together's services, and our intention is to ensure that our experiences lead to developments both within Together and outside. Service users' voices in the UK are becoming much more organised and proactive and are increasingly leading on the development of practice and on the internal and the external messages of organisations. One day a service user-led national charity that provides services will become a reality. In my view, good partnerships can lead to success at every level.

Together was involved in 2007 in responding to a consultation about the Care Programme Approach (CPA). Below is an extract from the response of people who access Together's services. It offers an insight into how service users would like to be involved in partnerships around CPA and demonstrates the emphasis people place on empowerment rather than the experience of having things done to or for them.

In Together's Service User Directorate's response to a review of the CPA in 2006–7, people who access Together's services stated:

> If the person going through the Care Programme Approach is to be at the centre, for example designing their own care plan, this would require a fundamental shift in thinking. We would cite that the dictionary definition of independence is self-governing, so we are not suggesting that people do everything for themselves, but play the governing role around everything to do with themselves.

- Service users need to be central to the CPA process. Rather than being involved in the process of care reviews, service users could arrange/negotiate their own CPA meetings in a manner/place and at a time of their choice, choose their Care Coordinator etc.

- Once the person who is working towards well-being is at the centre, care plans will then be sensitive to the person's culture, history, background, gender, status within the family etc. Indeed, this is the only guarantee that genuinely sensitive and supportive care plans can be designed and worked through. This would address many of the negative complaints service users have about care plans and access to them.

- If our suggested approach is adopted, it will facilitate an irreversible shift in everybody's thinking around attitudes to people experiencing distress. For example, training would be required for those who are designing their own care plan, whereas, at the moment, training resources are targeted towards staff.

Another example where people who require support have spoken about feeling empowered via partnerships is in the area of Direct Payments. Direct Payments place the emphasis correctly (in our view) with the person who is in receipt of the payments to enhance their well-being via buying what they consider helps. Below is a service user's comment about the Direct Payments scheme:

> It's a really good scheme. I think direct payments should be available to people who experience mental distress. Initially, I was put off trying to access it as I had to get in contact with social services and a social worker again. I don't know why we can't just refer ourselves, as we know what we need. I got direct payments and, although it was difficult at first having to set up a bank account, in the end it was OK because I just paid the personal assistant with cheques. I used my personal assistant for administrative help for me to keep up with the service-user movement activities. It took the pressure off me and she helped me with my written work. In the end I only had three hours per week but it made such a difference. I also have a friend who has used her direct payments to learn to drive, and it's altered her life for the better too. (Beales *et al.*, 2006)

One of the major successful components of self-help groups and service user-led groups is the solidarity that people experience. Practitioners therefore need to have an understanding of how this can be accessed by individuals they are working with and who may well experience their distress in terms of feeling alone and isolated, facing the stigma that is still attached to mental distress. The feeling of hope and the return of confidence cannot be given, but can be discovered by the person going through the experience. We can give people the maximum opportunity to make this discovery by referring individuals to groups. At Together, we provide locally based forums as well as a national forum for individuals to join, and believe that this offers an incredibly valuable opportunity for people to gain a route back towards having a purpose.

The following are people's views about taking part in Together's National Steering Group (Beales *et al.*, 2006):

- It feels like a very vibrant group.

- It is almost beyond belief how much work we do and everyone is included.

- It is special for everybody and this will be good stuff for the future – that's from my heart – I look forward to it as it gives me hope. I wish everyone has good health.

- It makes me feel important as my views are listened to.

- Change and hope for the future – I feel there is a good feeling of warmth around – its somewhere where it feels OK – it's nice.

▶ The future: wellink (Gary Platz)

Wellink sees itself as moving beyond partnership towards integration. The difference between partnership and integration could be looked at in this way.

Partnership means that both parties' points of view are heard and respected and acted on. Integration is combining parts to a whole. Instead of two parties and partnership, there would be a new culture that embraces all. This is the ideal that Wellink is aiming for. Integration is something that can grow out of strong partnership.

Wellink has had a partnership between the service user peer team and the rest of the organization; in other words, a service user/service provider partnership. This partnership has been functioning for eight years. Over that time, both parties in the partnership have developed the empathetic skills to see the culture and the issues of the partner with some success. Nevertheless, there are still difficulties at times and the peer workers, even in this environment, still experience role strain.

In 2004, we commissioned some specific work on the issue of sustainability for the peer workers in Wellink Trust. A company called TeamWorks (a coaching and training company) was selected to do the work. TeamWorks interviewed each member of the peer-workers team. TeamWorks collaborated with me (I was manager of the peer team at the time) in developing supervision and training sessions on maintaining well-being, while sustaining the role of a service user worker. TeamWorks facilitated the sessions. Six key issues were identified and the issues and session headings are listed below.

Issue 1

The peer team had a strong intrinsic motivation to give something back. What they wanted to give back was understanding! The majority of service user workers want the mental health system to understand the experience of mental illness, and what it is like to use mental health services. They wanted things to change. They wanted to help others who experience severe distress similar to their own experiences. They had experienced injustice, prejudice and displacement and wanted what caused it to change. Their passion was very strong, because their suffering had been great. While all these were good things, they also created problems. So the question was: How do I sustain myself and my role without being burnt out?

Training session 1: work/life balance

- What is it that nourishes me and sustains me?
- What is it that depletes me?
- How does this affect my work/life balance?

Issue 2

The team was made up of people who had a history of extreme experiences. How do they carry their experiences in their lives and their work?

Training session 2: today and yesterday

■ How much impact does the past have on me in the present?

■ What are my triggers, my responses?

■ How do I manage them?

■ The relationships I form with clients and peers – are they arising out of my neediness or out of fullness?

Issue 3

In a service user role, one is surrounded by mental illness. Is it healthy to be in such an environment? Does it hinder our recovery? Do we get stuck in the very same system for which we are advocating change? How do we balance the positive and negative?

Training session 3: lightness, play and observing self

■ How critical is my self-awareness?

■ Is it an instrument I use for moving forward in life or has it become a restrictive force?

■ Creating a positive vision of self.

Issue 4

Being seen as a role model. Having to prove that peer service user workers are up to the mark. Feeling we have to do twice as much as others to prove our worth. There is so much to be done, how do we not feel overly responsible for making a change happen?

Training session 4: personal power, self-determination and perfectionism

■ Exploring the fear of becoming unwell.

■ Giving myself permission to be unwell and to be who I am.

Issue 5

We are relatively new but operating in an established culture. Putting your heart and soul into doing a good job and not being taken seriously by some health professionals. When our personal experience of living with mental illness and using the mental health system is core to our roles as service user workers, it can impact on us personally when our role is not taken seriously by others.

Training session 5: the seers and feelers

■ A visible service user position: professionalism and credibility.

- What does 'being professional' mean to you, and to others?

- How do I manage the cultural prejudice – consumer and professional?

Issue 6

By the very nature of shared experience with people using mental health services, we have a different relationship with them compared to non-service user staff. This can create a blurriness in the area where we finish and the other person starts. Thus the issue is: How can we maintain sustainable peer relationships with people who use mental health services and still stay true to our role as service user workers? As a person who's lived with the experience of severe mental illness and has a passion for working in the field of mental health, it can be easy to spend most of our whole life in mental health issues. Do we want to stay working in mental health for ever, and what are our transferable skills?

Training session 6: fuzziness, blurriness

- Exploring the nature of boundaries.

- Community and belonging.

- Life and work at Wellink. Where to from here?

These sessions were a great help in supporting the peer workers and we would like to see more of this kind of tailored training and support sessions for service user workers in the future.

On a larger scale, an example in New Zealand of a collective perspective is New Zealand's Ministry of Health's second mental health plan (New Zealand Ministry of Health, 2005).

As part of the process of developing a plan, a forum was set up for a collective of service users from throughout the country. This was a group of about 35 people. They had one day to put together a service user's view of how the mental health plan should be. Interestingly enough, this was a fairly easy thing to do, as all the service users had very similar ideas. These ideas are outlined in *Our Lives in 2014: A Recovery Vision from People with the Experience of Mental Illness* (New Zealand Mental Health Commission, 2004).

The debate between collective view and representation is an interesting one. That group of service users who attended the forum were not truly mandated representatives of service users in New Zealand, though it was apparent through the acceptance of *Our Lives in 2014* that that group of service users held a collective view. The outcome of that forum influenced *Te Tāhuhu: Improving Mental Health* (New Zealand Ministry of Health, 2005). *Our Lives in 2014* is extensively used throughout the mental health system in New Zealand as the foundation document for planning recovery-focused mental health services.

One of the issues that has traditionally been a barrier to working in partnership in New Zealand and indeed in other countries has been the issue of pursuing personal and local agendas. In New Zealand, the service user movement has evolved away from that position. Even in the last three years there has been a tremendous change with all stakeholder groups. Though we still have our individual areas of concern, what has happened is that the environment has changed to one that is at least having the same conversation. That conversation is about recovery, and what it means for service users, for clinicians, for families, and, most importantly, there is also discussion about what a recovery-focused mental health system would actually look like. We have found that recovery is the key to this issue: a concentration on recovery moves everybody away from protecting their own patches. The mental health system has to have a philosophy around recovery and a focus towards mental well-being instead of mental illness. The focus on well-being is very important, and this brings people together. How? You may ask. Because of the simple reason that everybody needs the same sorts of things in place in their lives and thinking for some level of mental well-being. That very idea challenges the 'us and them' paradigm.

▶ The future – together (Anne Beales)

Figure 3.2 shows how Together involves people who access the services to work as a collective or as a group. Having been part of a group and undertaken training, people may wish to volunteer their time, regaining purpose to their days alongside re-acquainting themselves with their skills or learning new ones. The key is that this is a service user-led process, with trainers and coordinators having had experience of accessing services themselves. It is a virtual way of working and has become more explicit as the experience of working in this way has proved to be beneficial. People make their own decisions as to whether to attend the training and what voluntary work opportunities they want to pursue. Some people who attend may enjoy the lunchtime refreshments, while others use being part of the group to regain employment. It is self-directed and inclusive in every sense.

Together is aiming to use this model across its whole organisation to:

■ Increase awareness and understanding of well-being and how to support it from the service-user perspective, enabling self-management, self-directed support, and development of peer support and social inclusion.

■ Engage service users in involvement generally at all levels, ensuring that lived experience provides influence and insight into developments.

■ Act as a support for organisational change, which will make service user-led services more attractive to commissioners who are looking for innovation and new effective ways of providing services and support.

■ Be a practical impetus to make best use of current tools and expertise, for example care plans, leading to the development of new initiatives such as service-user portfolios mirroring staff portfolios for example, which will not only reduce inequality but support people to be mindful that the experience of distress is not wholly negative.

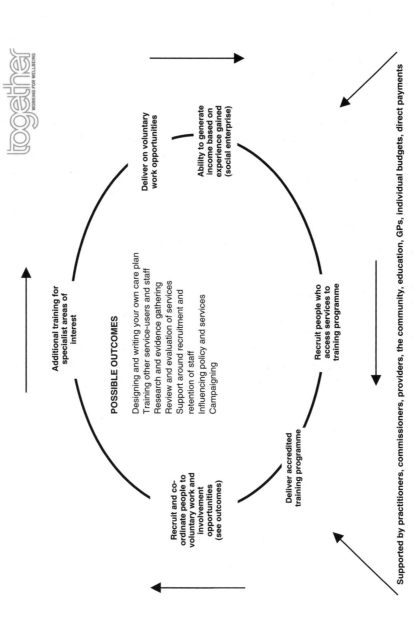

POSSIBLE OUTCOMES

Designing and writing your own care plan
Training other service-users and staff
Research and evidence gathering
Review and evaluation of services
Support around recruitment and
retention of staff
Influencing policy and services
Campaigning

Additional training for
specialist areas of
interest

Deliver on voluntary
work opportunities

Ability to generate
income based on
experience gained
(social enterprise)

Recruit people who
access services to
training programme

Deliver accredited
training programme

Recruit and co-
ordinate people to
voluntary work and
involvement
opportunities
(see outcomes)

Supported by practitioners, commissioners, providers, the community, education, GPs, individual budgets, direct payments

Figure 3.2 The work of Together.

■ Link to existing systems, for example current services and support to enhance what can be offered.

■ Promote employment and education opportunities, participating in training and research, support for peer-led review and evaluation of services, raising the profile of service user experience and the well-being agenda.

■ Enable support with people from marginalised and minority groups in a self-directed way.

In thinking about implementation, we have concluded that people can follow the process throughout, or opt in or out at various points. We hope that commissioners will buy time for individuals, or groups of individuals, or for a whole service to follow through the whole process or opt for parts of the approach. This approach can be delivered via geographical areas, small or large, specific services or community groups, and can be led and sensitively delivered by black and minority ethnic communities, gay, lesbian, bisexual and transgender groups, remaining culturally and gender sensitive, catering for people regardless of their current levels of distress. It can be used for people of any age, who currently access services, who have accessed services, who may need to access services or who refuse to access services. It can act as a conduit between services and agencies. It has the potential to attract income from previously untapped sources such as education or Department of Works and Pensions, alongside traditional sources such as primary care, local authorities and the health economy.

This would, by definition, become an integrated development within communities. It can become part of someone's care plan or, indeed, be the whole care plan. It can support people to access and maintain housing, rejoin and stay in employment, access education, remain in receipt of services or support or leave, in order to give support. It can be delivered in secure services and prisons. It is adaptable enough to enable current or new providers to deliver it, providing that service users lead on the implementation. It requires peer leadership, as it is the test of time and experience of using services that has led us to believe it is those with similar experiences who have the vision and ability to see our unique strengths at any point in our journey towards well-being.

▶ Concluding thoughts on partnership working

We would both argue that the approaches outlined in this chapter reflect the aspirations and experience of people who access services. Obviously, people would not attend and keep attending if it was of no use to them or did not meet their expectations of themselves and others. No compulsion has been necessary and having been through the process, many remain committed and highly motivated to changing services that have failed, and often badly, to meet their expectations. Collectively, people find their strength to use their voice to improve the experience of others who experience distress. Many describe giving back to their community as a fulfilling experience, something that has long escaped them during a period of distress. Obviously, we hope that people move on to resume what they consider an ordinary life, but for a time-limited period the harnessing of people's knowledge, skills and talents into a collective voice ensures that we can tap into a previously untapped resource that benefits the whole health community.

For there to be a real sense of partnership, service users need to be more than just 'involved'.

Goss and Miller (1995) presented a 'ladder of user and carer involvement', with no involvement at the bottom rung and user and carer control at the top rung. We would echo their point that partnership working requires both partners to have some element of control and self-determination. It will never happen if the worker has all the power and the service user has none.

Lea (2006) presents a continuum from her experiences as a service user trainer. She illustrates how important it is for service users to have their own education and training needs addressed if they are to progress from a starting point, which could be seen as tokenistic, towards a goal of real partnership.

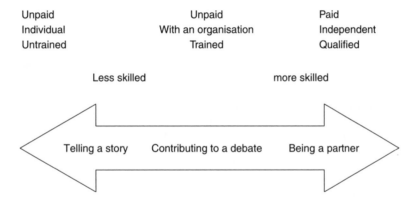

Motivation to train	Benefits in training	Changes
Giving something back	Personal learning	Being employed
Righting a wrong	Gaining confidence	Obtaining status
Informing ignorance	Finding meaning	Developing better
Seeking change	Professional learning	services
		Recovery
		Moving on

We hope that this chapter will support people's thinking around partnerships and that as a practitioner who may or may not have experienced mental distress, there is enough food for thought for you to focus on the abilities, talents and skills of those with whom you work in partnership.

Activity 3.2

Having read this chapter:

(1) Make a list of what you feel are the key components to working in partnership.

(2) What are the barriers to working in partnership?

(3) How can you overcome these barriers?

▶ Acknowledgement

Our thanks to Sarah Yiannoullou and Mandy Chainey for their help with this chapter.

▶ References

Beales, A., Beresford, P., Hitchon, G., Westra, A. & Basset, T. (2006) *Service-Users Together: A Guide for Involvement*. London: Together and Pavilion Publishing.

Department of Health (2004) *The Ten Essential Shared Capabilities: A framework for the whole of the mental health workforce*. London: Department of Health.

Goss, S. & Miller, C. (1995) *From Margin to Mainstream: Developing User and Carer Centred Community Care*. York: The Joseph Rowntree Foundation.

Lea, L. (2006) Acute solutions and beyond: Lessons on service user involvement. *Journal of Mental Health Workforce Development*, 1(2): 34–7.

New Zealand Ministry of Health (2005) *The Second New Zealand Mental Health and Addiction Plan – Te Tāhuhu: Improving Mental Health 2005–2015*. Wellington: New Zealand Ministry of Health.

New Zealand Mental Health Commission (2004) *Our Lives in 2014: A Recovery Vision from People with the Experience of Mental Illness*. Wellington: NZMHC.

◄ CHAPTER FOUR ►

Respecting diversity through acknowledging, valuing and using diversity and challenging inequalities (AVUDCI)

Premila Trivedi

South London & Maudsley NHS Foundation Trust

The second essential shared capability is Respecting Diversity. The Department of Health (2004) describes this capability as:

> Working in partnership with service users, carers, families and colleagues to provide care and interventions that not only make a positive difference but also do so in ways that respect and value diversity including age, race, culture, disability, gender, spirituality and sexuality.

'Excited', 'curious', 'apprehensive', 'valued', 'uncomfortable', 'ambivalent', 'challenged', 'politically correct', 'bullied'. These are just some of the replies that staff at a large NHS Trust gave when asked for their immediate response to seeing the word 'diversity' written in large letters on a flip chart. This wide range of (often impassioned) responses gives some clue as to the complexity of focusing on diversity.

In its simplest form, diversity can be defined as the very many ways in which people within one population differ from one another, in terms of personal dimensions (values, beliefs, personality), internal dimensions (race, age, gender, sexual orientation, class, physical ability, mental health, religion), external

Learning About Mental Health Practice. Edited by Theo Stickley and Thurstine Basset
© 2008 John Wiley & Sons, Ltd

dimensions (language, accent, education, work experience, socio-economic status, marital status, family structure, caring responsibilities) and organisational dimensions (role, status, team, union affiliation, work location etc.; Gardenswartz & Rowe, 2003). The advantages of such diversity are obvious, since a heterogeneous population will offer many more opportunities and options for active growth and development than a homogeneous one (Gardenswarz & Rowe, 2003). So why, then, does such a positive social construction as diversity evoke such mixed responses?

Clues probably lie in the fact that diversity has not always been viewed in such a positive light. In the 12th Century, the term was first used to mean 'difference, oddness, wickedness, perversity' and, in spite of much progress in our appreciation of difference, this negative view towards difference is still very prevalent today (Equalities Review, 2007). This is because when we interact with one another, we do not start from a neutral standpoint but bring with us power relations and ideologies of validity and status that determine how we see others within the context of existing structures and systems (Dalal, 2003). This results in certain groups being valued and privileged in terms of access to socially valued resources, such as money, status and power, while 'different' others are seen as being of lesser worth, with limited access to such resources and subjected to discrimination and subjugation in order to maintain societal power relations, hierarchies and ideologies (Dalal, 2003; Williams & Keating, 2005).

These facts are undisputed, and any focus on diversity has to include an understanding of the ways in which responses to diversity have resulted in social inequalities for whole sections of our society and adversely affected their lives (Equalities Review, 2007). Confronting this reality and becoming aware of our own (privileged or disadvantaged) position will inevitably be challenging, and may make us reluctant to engage in any detailed consideration of diversity and the ways in which we (as individuals, as groups and as a society) respond to the differences around us. But without facing these challenges, we can never hope to respect and value diversity and enable it to fulfil its true potential and create a more dynamic, creative, fair and just society. Learning about diversity is never going to be simple and needs to be both exciting and challenging, enlightening and baffling, personal and political and, perhaps most important of all, a lifelong process if we are really to embrace diversity as a positive social construct.

In this chapter an approach – AVUDCI – is explored in terms of diversity, particularly in relation to mental health settings. AVUDCI emphasizes the importance of:

- **A**cknowledging

- **V**aluing and

- **U**sing **D**iversity and

- **C**hallenging **I**nequalities (which arise because of difference)

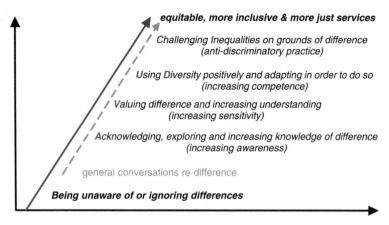

equitable, more inclusive & more just services

Challenging Inequalities on grounds of difference
(anti-discriminatory practice)

Using Diversity positively and adapting in order to do so
(increasing competence)

Valuing difference and increasing understanding
(increasing sensitivity)

Acknowledging, exploring and increasing knowledge of difference
(increasing awareness)

general conversations re difference

Being unaware of or ignoring differences

Figure 4.1 An AVUDCI approach to diversity – the importance of general conversations at every stage.

Within mental health, AVUDCI widens the scope of the essential shared capability 'Respecting Diversity' to encompass the importance of the essential shared capability 'Challenging Inequality', and also builds on Department of Health initiatives such as Positively Diverse and Delivering Race Equality (Department of Health, 2000, 2004, 2005). For some, AVUDCI will be seen as absolutely essential in our increasingly globalised world. For others, it may be seen as a rather meaningless buzzword bandied around by those who espouse political correctness.

This chapter aims to get beyond these polarised views by systematically exploring the notion of AVUDCI and its components, using a series of interactive activities. These are set in both personal and professional contexts, since how we react to diversity in one area of our life will inevitably influence our reaction in others (Johnson & Johnson, 2006). For example, mental health workers who aim to use AVUDCI with mental health service users may find it difficult to do so in a truly authentic way if they do not feel that they can (for whatever reason) openly use AVUDCI within their clinical teams. As a service user trainer I have too often found this situation, with staff often admitting that they are reluctant or unable actively to acknowledge, value and use diversity or challenge inequalities within their staff team, even though they do try to do this in terms of their clients/patients. Perhaps the answer to this mismatch is to go back to basics and make sure diversity becomes part of general, everyday conversations, which then become the starting point for becoming more aware, sensitive, competent and anti-discriminatory practitioners (Figure 4.1). The exercises in this chapter will hopefully generate such conversations – and more.

▶ Acknowledging diversity

Diversity is a fact of life, but one that is often difficult to acknowledge in societal contexts and between social groups. Our tendency is generally to focus on similarities, since these are what enable us to identify with others and feel part of an in-group (Landrine, 1992). Often there will be a reluctance to raise the topic of diversity unless we really have to, since people:

- May feel anxious in case talking about issues of difference may threaten relationships based on similarities.

- May lead to them being judged and marginalised if their beliefs, values and attitudes do not concur with the accepted 'norm' (e.g. being seen as 'politically correct').

- May feel they will cause offence or upset to others.

But not raising the subject of diversity because we are fearful that we will 'get it wrong' means that we inevitably close down any opportunities to 'get it right'. By avoiding the 'elephant in the room', we evade risks, miss out on different perspectives and controversies that enable us to be more creative in our thinking and decision making, and confine ourselves to static functioning rather than developing and moving on (Johnson & Johnson, 2006).

Activity 4.1: Identifying and acknowledging difference

Needs to be done in pairs:

- Find yourself a partner and discuss, identify and note down as many differences between yourself and your partner as you can.

Remember to note down the small differences as well as the more obvious ones. Only disclose what feels comfortable to you – feel OK to pass on certain differences if you wish. The temptation will be to get into a conversation about your differences, so try to avoid this as you need to list as many differences as possible.

Structured reflection

- How did it feel to focus specifically on difference? *This exercise may feel strange, uncomfortable or unreal initially as we usually tend to focus on similarities. But you may also have found the exercise interesting and*

---

stimulating, identifying differences automatically enabling you to identify similarities and this inevitably generating more meaningful and deeper communication.

■ Did some differences seem more difficult to talk about than others, or did you censor some out? *Often people will find themselves censoring out discussion of sensitive subjects, e.g. sexual orientation, or subjects that they feel very strongly about, e.g. religion or politics.*

■ Did you identify any differences that surprised you? *This can be very revealing, especially if you had made assumptions based on physical appearance or mannerisms etc.*

■ Look down your list of differences. Are there any that could affect the way people are treated in society? *Most differences, however small, could have either a negative or positive impact on the way in which people with that difference are treated, and most people will have had experience of this.*

■ What differences do we know have a *particular* impact on the way people are treated in society? *The impact of certain differences, e.g. race, class, age, gender, sexual orientation, disability, is very marked and leads to significant social inequalities.*

In its simplest form, diversity can be defined as the many ways in which people differ from one another, as identified in the previous activity. According to Gardenswartz and Rowe (2003), four layers of diversity form the filters through which each of us sees the world, with personality at the centre (the innately unique aspect that gives each of us our own particular style), internal dimensions over which we have little or no control (such as gender, age and race, sexual orientation) as the next layer, external dimensions (outside influences such as education, where you grew up or live now, marital status, political affiliation), with the final layer being work/organisational dimensions (what unit you work in, your status and position in the hierarchy and worksite in the organisation). Within many of these dimensions, there will be sub-dimensions that themselves may be further sub-divided into sub-sub-dimensions and so forth. For example, 'race' can be sub-divided into black and white; then black into African, Caribbean, Asian; then African into Nigerian, Ghanaian, Kenyan, Zimbabwean etc.; then Nigerian into Ibo, Hausa, Yoruba, Fulani etc. Other characteristics can be similarly sub-divided, each individual ending up being a complex and intricate mix of differences, which make them into the unique person they are but also with similarities to others.

Our complex inter-mix of differences contributes massively to our identity and where we see our place in the world. Acknowledging and feeling able to own our differences is crucial to our sense of self. For many people today, differences that were once masked or hidden are now claimed with pride and indicate solidarity and a refusal to be silenced, for example through the feminist, disability and mental health system survivors' movements and organisations such as Stonewall and Madpride. Openly to acknowledge and honour a person's individual attributes is to value and respect them, and by fostering a climate where equity and mutual respect are intrinsic, we can create a much more accepting, knowledgeable, fair and co-operative society. Within mental health services such acknowledgement is of particular importance, since our sense of self is so largely determined by how others respond to our differences (Landrine, 1992). For many mental health service users, this sense of self may be confused or fragile, at least in part, because of the often negative ways in which others have responded to aspects of our identity. In trying to make sense of such negativity, some of us may come to see it as justified, internalise it and live in a constant state of guilt for being who we are.

Low self-worth and self-esteem, poor confidence and self-hatred may manifest itself in self-harm or suicidal behaviour (Trivedi, 2002). If this is to be understood and meaningfully addressed, it is essential to acknowledge aspects of our identity that make us different from the mainstream, and also at the same time any consequences there may have been as a result of these differences and impacts on our mental health (Karlsen, 2007). By not raising these crucially important issues, service users may have no option but to assume that their differences or associated experiences are unacceptable, must not be acknowledged or explored, thereby increasing their internalised negativity and sense of hopelessness and unacceptability (Trivedi, 2002).

Activity 4.2: Acknowledging diversity

- Read the poem 'Internalization' (below) and identify two or three points in the writer's experience where diversity could have been usefully acknowledged by mental health services and how this could have been done with possible outcomes.

Point in poem where diversity could have been acknowledged	Practical ways in which this could have been done	Possible outcome

Your reflections on the value of acknowledging diversity:

Poem by Black MH service user
(shows consequences of not acknowledging diversity within clinical practice)

INTERNALIZATION

Sleepless nights, enveloping despair – guilt.
Guilt at being me – black, female, poor,
Part of a large family – part of an even larger society
Resounding with racism and rejection.

Valium, psychiatrists, falling more into the abyss
Of white man's medicine.
Hospital, enforced activity, constant cajoling
To fit their categorization of me,

All the time denying me my pain, my hurt, my confusion.
Reinforcing my 'badness' at feeling these things.
Isolating me – alone – with my problems,

Unexpressed anger, increasing guilt,
The silence growing louder.
Largactil, locked doors, ECT, eventually stillness.
Sinking deeper and deeper into the sanctuary of insanity:
Beautiful – silent – still – feelingless – internal death;
Pushing back the screaming agony, before I infect them with my poison –
The poison of my blackness, my culture, my very being;
All wrong, all contradicting the norms of their society,
All disrupting their ordered world.

And in the end I saw it their way, the guilt *was* mine.
So I tried – and battled – and pulled my self out of it –
And buried myself deeper, keeping me inside,
Smiling nicely, acting right, colluding with them,
Ensuring their equilibrium was maintained,
So I have the privilege of existing in their world –
Of experiencing their values, their beliefs,
Their prejudice, their power.
What does it matter that I died in the process?

What does it matter? One more black, crazy female,
One more drain on society, what does it matter?
To them nothing –
And ultimately to me it must mean nothing too,
Otherwise even existence becomes impossible
And internal death can only be mirrored in external reality.

Premila Trivedi (1992)

▶ Valuing diversity

With pluralism (a framework within which members of diverse groups maintain their cultures or special interests with respect and tolerance within a common shared culture and fruitfully co-exist without conflict or assimilation) and, in particular, with multiculturalism (a policy that endorses the principle of cultural diversity and supports the right of different cultural and ethnic groups to retain distinctive cultural identities), there are ample opportunities to value the diversity that surrounds us (Gardenswartz & Lowe, 2003). Most obviously, this is in terms of popular culture, music, food and so on, which enables individuals to try something new, value it and incorporate it into their lifestyle (in the process of acculturation) if that feels appropriate and beneficial. However, when it comes to more challenging aspects of diversity – such as aspects of faith, arranged marriages or social justice systems – valuing diversity and seeing the benefits may not be so straightforward and in some situations may be at serious odds with the norms and values we hold (Alibhai Brown, 2000). Trying to learn and understand these different behaviours, and the contexts in which they occur, and to work through our views and feelings about such contentious issues will inevitably be complex and challenging.

We need to be very mindful of where we stand personally, professionally and legally in terms of condoning such practices in the name of valuing 'diversity'. Cases like Victoria Climbie have highlighted the complexity of this, and for many people the answer seems to be to work on being very clear about one's own views on contentious issues of diversity (including being clear about the legal position), but not to let your view on one aspect of diversity in a group lead you to devalue all aspects of that group's diversity. When challenges arise (as they inevitably will when working with diversity), it is all too easy to let these mask the benefits. If we are really to value diversity, then it is important to keep these at the forefront of our mind.

Activity 4.3: Benefits and challenges of living and working in a diverse society

■ List some of the benefits and challenges of living and working in a diverse society.

Benefits

Challenges

Your reflections on the benefits and challenges of living in a diverse society:

Historically, social ideologies have, to a large extent, predicated against valuing difference (especially those differences that are seen as being somehow inferior to the 'norm', for instance in terms of class, gender, race etc.) and the benefits that diversity can confer, and still do so today (Equalities Review, 2007). In order to challenge such ideologies, it is essential to actively keep the benefits of diversity firmly in mind. For example, diversity can:

■ Create more interesting and exciting lives by providing a richness of experience, knowledge and understanding and inspiration for creativity.

■ Enable growth and development through increasing curiosity and a need to know those around us better.

■ Generate mutual respect and inter-dependence.

■ Produce more flexibility by considering other values, beliefs and norms, verifying our own values and considering whether there is a personal or societal need to adapt, for example by developing new practices.

■ Generate more open-mindedness by providing opportunities to confront our assumptions and challenge our stereotypes.

■ Reduce confrontation and decrease conflict by increasing our familiarity with, and tolerance of, understanding of difference.

■ Affirm our own difference as a social group and enable us to acknowledge the multiplicity of differences that exists within the group and how this could be better appreciated and utilised.

However, valuing the benefits of diversity is not as simple as making a list. It also involves recognising and confronting the, sometimes huge, challenges that diversity can bring. For example, diversity can:

■ Cause discomfort by taking us into areas of unfamiliarity and out of our comfort zone.

■ Bring about anxieties at having to acknowledge how fears of difference, stereotypes and prejudice may lead us to act in discriminatory (or sometimes patronising) ways.

■ Create confrontation and conflict because of misinterpretation, misunderstandings and misconceptions.

■ Raise fears and guilt because of having to consider power relations and associated issues of privilege, disadvantage and social inequalities.

- Produce practical difficulties in terms of time, resources, flexibility and the range of systems needed to enable equity and justice for all.

- Generate cynicism and derision, in terms of viewing diversity as just about political correctness, especially in terms of such things as language.

Being aware of these challenges, honestly being able to reflect on them and actively do something about them, will be the most effective ways of valuing diversity.

Perhaps one of the simplest ways to begin this process may be to look at the language we use in response to difference. This is particularly relevant within mental health services, where terminology is frequently used to devalue rather than value, and in many cases difference and beliefs and behaviours that are considered to deviate from the 'norm' become seen as a symptom of mental illness (Crawford *et al.*, 1999; Williams, Scott & Bressington, 2004). Being aware of this, working to understand the contexts and reasons behind behaviours and beliefs and using more appropriate, positive and inclusive language would form a simple, easily implemented and effective starting point to practically valuing diversity (Trivedi, 2004).

Activity 4.4: Valuing diversity through language

- Consider the terms given below, which are commonly used to describe people's behaviours in mental health services.

- Think about possible reasons behind these behaviours and then give alternative words or phrases, which could be used instead to show a better understanding of the ways in which people respond to and deal with consequences of diversity.

Terms commonly used in mental health services to describe behaviours	Alternative terms that show better understanding of difference and behaviour
Attention seeking *(as applied to a woman)*	
secretive *(as applied to a gay man)*	
obsessive *(as applied to a woman of faith)*	

Terms commonly used in mental health services to describe behaviours	Alternative terms that show better understanding of difference and behaviour
lacks insight (*as applied to a man from a less privileged class*)	
paranoid (*as applied to a young black man*)	
controlling (*as applied to an older adult*)	
non-compliant (*as applied to someone with a physical disability*)	

Your reflections on valuing diversity through language:

Exemplar for Activity 4.4: Valuing diversity through language

Language used in mental health services to describe behaviours	Alternative language that shows better understanding of difference and behaviour
attention seeking (*as applied to a woman*)	■ Distressed, frustrated and trying to get her needs met, knows from experience she's unlikely to achieve this simply by asking. ■ Relies on coping strategies she has developed in situations of oppression/abuse.
secretive (*as applied to a gay man*)	■ Cautious, protects his privacy – maybe in response to a previous negative experience. ■ Finds it difficult to be open with us, not at the point of trusting yet.

Language used in mental health services to describe behaviours	Alternative language that shows better understanding of difference and behaviour
obsessive *(as applied to a man of faith)*	■ Anxious and attempting to preserve sense of self through familiar rituals etc. ■ Seeking reassurance through placing trust in God when people have shown themselves not to be trustworthy.
lacks insight *(as applied to a man from a less privileged class and educational background)*	■ Views the situation differently to us and does not agree with our interpretations. ■ Has developed own understanding based on (often negative) experience. ■ Wants to share own interpretation with us.
paranoid *(as applied to a black man in a predominantly white society)*	■ Experiences the world and people around as hostile and threatening. ■ Letting us know how dangerous things feel.
controlling *(as applied to an older woman)*	■ Finds it hard to feel she has little control. ■ Not always wanting to do what staff want her to do. ■ Needs to be listened to and responded to better. ■ Has her own clear ideas of what she wants to do.
non-compliant *(as applied to a young woman with a physical disability)*	■ Knows that the way things are being done are not best suited to her needs. ■ Resents assumption that she will be grateful and good because she has an impairment.

▶ **Using diversity**

Using diversity involves working to create an environment that uses the unique skills and abilities of everyone within society, with the aim of creating an inter-dependent, more inclusive, respectful and equitable environment and community (Gardenswarz & Rowe, 2003; Department of Health, 2000; Royal College of Nursing, 2002). But diversity is not just about those who are perceived as being different. It is about everybody, and everybody working together and using diversity to make better lives for all. This may sound like idealistic rhetoric, but it is surprising how often we actually do this in our everyday lives in order to benefit ourselves and those around us.

Activity 4.5: Using diversity in everyday life

■ Consider two or three specific aspects of difference (e.g. gender, race, age, mental health etc.) and think of situations where you positively use the diversity around you in your everyday life. (NB This could be in terms of inter-dependent roles, learning more, experiencing other ways.)

Difference	How you use this practically	Benefit for you	Benefit for others around you

Your reflections on using diversity in everyday life:

While we may often use difference almost subconsciously in our everyday lives, doing this can be more challenging when the benefits are not so apparent or immediate, or using a particular difference goes against the prevailing ideology.

To really use all the differences around us, we therefore need to develop a set of conscious and active practices that

■ Move away from the idea of complete independence and focus more on an appreciation for interdependence.

■ Show mutual respect for values, qualities, behaviours and experiences that are different from our own and may not immediately be understandable, accessible or attractive.

■ Build alliances so that we can work together positively across differences.

Within the workplace, diversity should be a central part of an organisational strategy that provides opportunities (within a safe, positive and nurturing environment) for people to acknowledge, value and positively use values, qualities and behaviours that are different to their own, thereby moving beyond tolerance to actually embracing and utilising the diverse skills, talents and abilities of those around them (Department of Health 2000, 2004). At the same time, it is crucial that organisations and people within them look at their established values and standards to ensure that these are not discriminating (either deliberately or unwittingly) against people because of their differences (Department of Health, 2005). This is where the concept of equal opportunities comes in as a major feature of organisational policy. The assumption is often made that, because an organisation is very rigorous in terms of equal opportunities, it also acknowledges, values and uses the diversity and challenges inequalities (AVUDCI).

However, this is not necessarily so, and there are important differences between equal opportunities and AVUDCI. For example, many organizations may (University of Warwick, 2003):

■ Adopt equal opportunities policies in a reactive way because they have to due to external pressure (e.g. legislation) and see this as a cost. AVUDCI is more proactive and internally driven, reflects the core values of the organisation and is seen as an investment. Primarily, it works to create a more diverse workforce that better reflects the diversity of the community it serves and more positive working environments within which all individuals feel valued and diversity is used to benefit all.

■ Concern themselves rigorously with equal opportunity policies and procedures to meet their statutory obligations and 'neutralise' difference, but often do little more. AVUDCI is more strategic and is about respecting difference and actively using it to establish a more creative and positive working culture.

■ Consider equal opportunities to be about trying to 'right a wrong' for certain groups and create a level playing field. AVUDCI embraces different people as individuals and not simply as members of a disadvantaged group, and sees difference as potentially a resource, not a problem to be managed.

■ Concentrate on groups who, by law, must be seen to be treated equitably, for example ethnic minorities, older people and those with disabilities. AVUDCI does not specifically focus on certain groups, but rather works to develop all individuals and challenge discrimination in any form

■ Focus on developing equal opportunities within a single department (usually Human Resources/Personnel), with knowledge and expertise confined to a relatively small number of people with practice based on existing narrow and often very rigid models. AVUDCI is about a much greater plurality of human knowledge and experience, with creating and developing equity and justice being not the responsibility of just a few but of all.

Practically, organisations must use an equal opportunities approach, but should also consciously work to use an AVUDCI approach. This is particularly relevant in mental health settings where difference plays a key role in role and power relationships, and the interests of those who are perceived (or pathologised) as being different can all too easily be over-ridden by the interests of systems and organisational priorities (Royal College of Nursing, 2002). Identifying areas where difference can be proactively used in a positive way is a key starting point in implementing an AVUDCI approach.

Activity 4.6: Using difference proactively as part of an AVUDCI approach

■ Identify a situation in the workplace where difference can be positively used:

  o with service users

  o with teams

Opportunity	Practical steps you could take to use diversity	Benefits
With service users		
With team		

Your Reflections:

▶ Challenging inequality

Difference is an inevitable part of our lives and, while it certainly confers many benefits, it also brings significant challenges. This is because all human interactions inevitably have power structured into them. Such power relations sustain a version of reality in which certain identities and differences are made critical in the organisation of social and political relationships. In this way, different social groups are ascribed different status, with accompanying positions of privilege or disadvantage. Once this is established, then ideology does the work of sustaining these power relationships and consequent social inequalities by convincing everyone that this is the natural order of the world and must be maintained in order to preserve social stability and cohesion (Dalal, 2003). By utilising such a hegemonic approach (i.e. domination through consent rather than coercion), society maintains its status quo but perpetuates social inequalities, disadvantage and discrimination, which has serious impacts on whole sections of society (Equalities Review, 2007). For example, certain groups (e.g. women, older people, black people, gays and lesbians) come to be seen as of lesser worth and therefore afforded less access to socially valued resources, such as money, status and power (Williams & Keating, 2005).

Such social inequalities are obviously counter to the values and principles of equity and justice, and it is therefore essential to actively:

- Recognise that social inequalities result in personal, cultural and institutionalised discrimination, which creates and sustains privileges for some while creating and sustaining disadvantages for others.

- Recognise how power influences and determines social inequalities, but also how power can be used to counter social inequalities.

- Take responsibility for recognising, acknowledging and using our own power and use it positively to oppose discrimination in all its forms.

- Work together in social, political, professional and other groups to eradicate all forms of discrimination, which occur because of difference.

Activity 4.7: Challenging discrimination

■ Consider a situation in your life when you have (or wanted to) challenge stigma or discrimination either to yourself or someone else due to difference.

Situation	What you wanted to do	What you actually did	Outcome

Structured reflection

1. Would you do anything differently if the same thing happened again, and if so, why?

2. What would you do differently?

3. *What do you hope outcome will be?*

Other chapters in this book discuss social inequalities, discrimination and oppression in more detail, so here the topic is confined to specific examples of mental health service users. For many, discrimination and oppression on the grounds of difference can be a significant contributory factor to their mental health problems. Individual responses to such discrimination can vary according to the person's sense of self and self-esteem, personality, resilience, endurance and life experiences (Trivedi 2002, 2004). These responses can be most simply summarised as:

- *Counter response*, where individuals are very clear that their differences are an absolutely essential part of who they are and present themselves to mainstream society with these differences intact, certain that they have the right to do this. They deal with any negative consequences as they occur and many will, at the same time, work to raise awareness of the impact of discrimination and try to bring about some positive change.

- *Accepting response*, where individuals know that they need to maintain their differences in order to preserve their identity and sense of self, but may lack the confidence to present these to a mainstream society that essentially seeks to exclude them. They may therefore retreat into their group, where they can develop a kind of psychic envelope that strengthens their self-identity and sense of oneness to a belonging group.

- *Adaptation response*, where individuals adopt a more pragmatic approach and modify their differences in order to increase their chances of being socially included. They may therefore constantly juggle their identity, covering up or diminishing their 'unacceptable' differences while in mainstream society, but retain them within their own group in order constantly to reinforce and validate their true identity.

- *Assimilation response*, where individuals (perhaps with a weaker sense of self and/or poor family and community links) may consciously or unconsciously come to the conclusion that, since their differences are what cause them to be rejected by mainstream society, they should cover up or diminish them and assimilate them in order to increase their chances of being accepted and socially included. Perhaps of all the responses this is the most worrying, since it can, in some cases, lead to a dangerous loss of identity and sense of self and give rise to severe mental health problems such as:
  - feelings of guilt for being who they are
  - feelings of vulnerability, powerlessness and hopelessness
  - negative feelings about themselves, and about others like themselves
  - a loss of or denial of identity
  - depression, with physical and psychological symptoms, including 'psychosis'
  - self-destructive behaviour (e.g. self-harm, suicide)

All of these responses may lead to mental distress, initiating mental health problems or exacerbating those that already exist. If these individuals then find themselves in contact with systems or organisations that, rather than

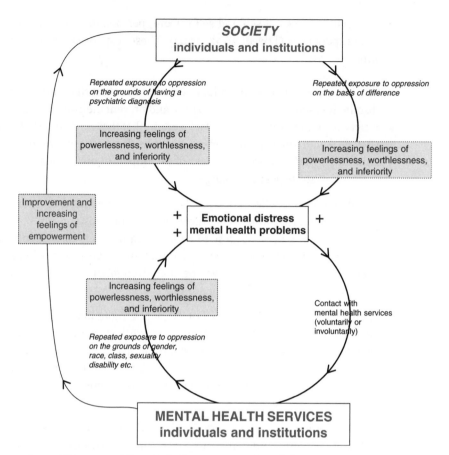

Figure 4.2 The spiral of oppression (adapted from Trivedi, 2002).

understanding and challenging oppression, reinforce that oppression with their own oppressive attitudes and practices, it may result in more distress, driving the person even further into 'madness' and the mental health system, and into a continuing spiral of oppression (see Figure 4.2).

The spiral of oppression in Figure 4.2 illustrates what oppressed groups in society experience once they come into contact with psychiatry and enter the mental health system. Discrimination, social inequalities and oppression in society on the grounds of difference can affect an individual's mental health by initiating emotional distress or compounding that which may already be present. Society's response to such distress is to treat it within an essentially medical context, in a system of mental and social health care that, rather than understanding and challenging oppression that gives rise to mental distress, reinforces it with its own oppressive attitudes and practices. This results in more distress, driving the person even further into the mental health system, and into a continuing spiral of oppression. For those individuals who do improve and leave mental health services and enter back into society, they now (in addition to the original oppression) also now become subject to the oppression of mentalism, since society has such a negative and pessimistic view of anyone who has a psychiatric diagnosis. Thus the spiral continues, leaving users of mental health services feeling trapped within a system that perpetuates oppression and discrimination.

Recognizing this spiral of oppression and how it perpetuates mental distress is crucial if the damaging effects of discrimination and oppression on mental health are to be worked with and addressed and resilience built to cope with (maybe inevitable) continuing discrimination. For individual mental health workers, a useful way of helping service users to fracture the spiral may be by using their power in a positive way to recognise, address and challenge inequalities that affect the individual (Tew, 2005).

Activity 4.8: Using power positively

■ Consider the situation below.

Situation

Ahmed complains to his primary nurse (Jon) that another patient, Billy, has been repeatedly taunting him by calling him racist names. Jon is a caring nurse, but unwittingly uses his power in a *negative* way to deal with this situation.

Action by Jon

Jon tells them both to stop winding each other up, and says they must keep out of each other's way. Jon also says the ward is very busy and they are not helping. Jon then tells Ahmed to go to his room and Billy to go to the smoking room. He makes sure they do and then goes back to office to finish the discussion he was having about another patient with the consultant.

Ahmed's reaction

Ahmed feels angry and resentful that his concerns and the effect on him have not been taken seriously by Jon. He also fears further abuse from Billy, and his sense of paranoia increases. The voices he hears start becoming more pervasive and threatening.

Billy's reaction

Billy feels that the confrontation was more to do with Ahmed and his illness than with him. He goes away feeling fine and not realising how unacceptable and damaging his racist language is. Billy continues to use

---

racist terms on the ward, to the distress of Ahmed and several other patients.

■ Now consider how Jon could have used his power in a more useful and positive way for both Ahmed and Billy (and indirectly other patients on the ward).

Jon's action (using his power in a positive way)

Ahmed's reaction

Billy's reaction

Exemplar for Activity 4.8: Using power positively

■ Now consider how Jon could have used his power in a more useful and positive way for both Ahmed and Billy (and indirectly other patients on the ward).

Jon's action (using his power in a positive way)

Jon acknowledges Ahmed's distress and says he just needs to tell the consultant where he is and then he'll come back to talk to Billy. He comes back in a couple of minutes and spends time talking to Ahmed about how he is feeling about Billy's comments. Jon states clearly that racist language is unacceptable on the ward, and he will talk to Billy about the situation and do everything he can to make sure the same thing doesn't happen in the future. Jon ensures that Ahmed feels reassured and is engaged in activity and then goes to talk to Billy. He tells Ahmed he will come back and tell him the outcome.

Jon tells Billy how upset Ahmed is, and reminds Billy how upset *he* was when some children were yelling abuse at him in the street last week. He ensures that he gives Billy an opportunity to explain why he uses such language or why he is trying to wind Ahmed up, but also reminds Billy that no matter what, racist language is completely forbidden in the hospital. He must therefore stop using such language and find a more useful way to express his emotions and address his issues. Jon offers to spend some time with Billy to do this, but makes it clear that racist language will not be tolerated on the ward, that illness is no excuse and that it is his (i.e. Jon's) responsibility to ensure that everyone on the ward feels safe.

Ahmed's reaction

Ahmed feels heard and respected. He has had a chance to express his distress and confirm that some action is going to be taken. He is now making some tea, and beginning to talk to another patient.

Billy's reaction

Billy initially feels angry at being confronted, but as Jon talks to him in a fairly relaxed way, he starts to engage. He expresses his anger and frustration at being locked up on the ward. Jon acknowledges Billy's feelings, but suggests that he should find more appropriate ways to express them. Jon makes some suggestions and offers to spend time with Billy to work this through some more. Billy feels acknowledged, but also realises that racist language will not be tolerated and if he uses it in the future, he will always be challenged.

▶ Conclusion

Difference is an inescapable and potentially invaluable part of our personal and working lives. However, incorporating difference into our lives so that it fulfils this potential is complex and requires societal, community and individual change at both political and social levels. Many initiatives in health have been put in place to develop such change (Department of Health, 2000, 2004, 2005) and there is certainly a huge push to address some of the issues around diversity. However, there is still some confusion (certainly at a heart if not a head level) about diversity and focusing on diversity, and in particular learning about it is not always as simple as it might seem.

In order to clarify the concept of diversity, this chapter has introduced the term AVUDCI explicitly to indicate the need to take a proactive approach to difference by acknowledging, valuing and using diversity and challenging inequalities, thereby creating fairer and more just institutions and organisations. Creating a new term in relation to diversity may be of questionable value when so many words already exist and often cause confusion by being used in misleading ways. But maybe this is the very reason to create a new term, AVUDCI, which very clearly spells out what the word means and can be easily distinguishable from the myriad of words associated with diversity already in use.

In addition, some of the activities and messages conveyed in this chapter may at first appear to be obvious and simplistic, but my experience as a service user trainer who has been delivering such messages and activities over a number of years suggests that there is often a great need to go 'back to basics' when considering diversity. Very often when service users talk about improving services and creating change in mental health services and clinical practice, it is about very seemingly simple things, like communication, positive relationship building and acceptance of patients as people with all the qualities (both positive and negative) that everyone in the world may have. By keeping it simple, using an AVUDCI approach and perhaps most importantly enabling diversity to become part of our everyday conversations without creating anxiety, fear and/or conflict, maybe one day diversity will reach its true potential.

For mental service users, this may in some ways be easier than for others. We become used to considering our differences and try to make sense of them. We are often placed in a position on wards or in the community with people with whom we may not have chosen to spend long times, and we often have amazing opportunities to see beyond the surface and really get to know a whole host of different people. Certainly my experience has been thus, and although it can really 'do your head in' at times, it also offers an amazing richness of experience. If you are part of a strong and positive service user group, an amazing and often new sense of belonging can also result (Trivedi & members of SIMBA, 2002). Hopefully, more mental health workers will be able to learn from the positive experiences of AVUDCI-ing that many of us service users have been privileged to have.

**Part of poem written for SIMBA (Share In Maudsley Black Action),
a black service user group**

Here I stand and see SIMBA
Diversity personified, marked differences
In skin colour, hair texture, facial features
Beauty in all its forms. Voices, dialects, accents
All differences openly acknowledged, accepted and respected
Each providing a new and distinctive facet to the whole
Forming a precious jewel, sparkling in all its glory
Proclaiming to the world the unique multiplicity of SIMBA's being.

© Premila Trivedi

Activity 4.9: Personal/professional action planning

■ Reflect on what you have discovered and/or learned from this chapter. Then think of one small, achievable action you can take to implement AVUDCI in your workplace/clinical practice.

Area of AVUDCI	Action to be taken	Resources needed	Outcome
Enable general conversation about diversity as an essential prerequisite to AVUDCI			
Acknowledge diversity			
Value diversity			
Use diversity			
Challenge **I**nequalities			

▶ **Acknowledgement**

Much of the information in this chapter comes from the experience of delivering training on diversity as part of the South London & Mausdsley NHS Foundation Trust corporate induction course for staff. The session was designed and developed in partnership with Esther Craddock, Education & Training Advisor (Diversity), Training Dept, South London & Maudsley NHS Foundation Trust.

▶ **References**

Alibhai Brown, Y. (2000) *After Multiculturalism*. London: Foreign Policy Centre.

Crawford, P., Johnson, A. J., Brown, B. J. & Nolan, P. (1999) The language of mental health nursing reports: Firing paper bullets? *Journal of Advanced Nursing*, **29**(2, February): 331–40.

Dalal, F. (2003) *Race, Colour and the Process of Racialization: New Perspectives from Group Analysis, Psychoanalysis and Sociology*. Hove: Brunner Routledge.

Department of Health (2000) *Positively Diverse*. London: Department of Health

Department of Health (2004) *The Ten Essential Shared Capabilities. A Framework for the Whole of the Mental Health Workforce*. London: Department of Health.

Department of Health (2005) *Delivering Race Equality in Mental Health Care: An Action Plan for Reform Inside and Outside Services and the Government's Response to the Independent Inquiry into the Death of David Bennett*. London: Department of Health.

Equalities Review (2007) *Fairness and Freedom: The Final Report of the Equalities Review*. Norwich: HMSO.

Gardenswartz, L. & Rowe, A. (2003) *Diverse Teams at Work: Capitalizing on the Power of Diversity*. Alexandra, VA: Society for Human Resource Management.

Johnson, D. W. & Johnson, F. P. (2006) Valuing diversity. In D. W. Johnson & F. P. Johnson (eds), *Joining Together: Group Theory and Group Skills*. London: Pearson International.

Karlsen, S. (2007) *Ethnic Inequalities in MH: The Impact of Racism*. London: Race Equality Foundation.

Landrine, H. (1992) Clinical implications of cultural differences: The referential versus the indexical self. *Clinical Psychology Review*, **12**: 401–15.

Royal College of Nursing (2002) *Diversity Appraisal Resource Guide*. London: RCN.

Tew, J. (2005) Power relations, social order and mental distress. In J. Tew (ed.), *Social Perspectives in Mental Health: Developing Social Models to Understand and Work with Mental Distress*. London, Jessica Kingsley.

Trivedi, P. (1992) In F. Bangay (ed.), *From Dark to Light*. London: Survivors' Poetry.

Trivedi, P. (2002) Racism, social exclusion and mental health – a Black user's perspective. In K. Bhui (ed.), *Racism and Mental Health*. London: Jessica Kingsley.

Trivedi, P. (2004) Are we who we say we are or who you think we are? *Asylum*, **14**(4): 4–5.

Trivedi, P. & members of SIMBA (2002) Let the tiger roar. *Mental Health Today*, August: 303–33.

University of Warwick Equal Opportunities Committee (2003) *Diversity*. http://www2. warwick.ac.uk/services/equalops/policies/.

Williams, J. & Keating, F. (2005) Social inequalities and mental health. In A. Bell & P. Lindley (eds), *Beyond the Water Towers: The Unfinished Revolution in Mental Health Services*. London: Sainsbury Centre for Metal Health.

Williams, J., Scott, S. & Bressington, C. (2004) Dangerous journeys: Pathways into and through secure MH services. In N. Jeffcote & T. Watson (eds), *Working Therapeutically with Women in Secure MH Settings*. London, Jessica Kingsley.

CHAPTER FIVE

Practising ethically: values-based practice and ethics – working together to support person-centred and multidisciplinary mental health care

Bill (KWM) Fulford
Universities of Oxford and Warwick

Kim Woodbridge
Milton Keynes Council and Primary Care Trust

The third essential shared capability is Practising Ethically. The Department of Health (2004) describes this capability as:

> Recognising the rights and aspirations of service users and their families, acknowledging power differentials and minimising them whenever possible. Providing treatment and care that is accountable to service users and carers within the boundaries prescribed by national (professional), legal and local codes of ethical practice.

Values-based practice is a clinical skills-based approach to working with complex and conflicting values in health care. This chapter introduces values-based practice and illustrates how, together with ethics, it offers a *process* for working more effectively with values in mental health and social care, particularly in

Learning About Mental Health Practice. Edited by Theo Stickley and Thurstine Basset
© 2008 John Wiley & Sons, Ltd

the context of the different perspectives represented by person-centred care and multidisciplinary teamwork.

Values-based practice is closely linked to evidence-based practice. Hence the chapter also:

- Describes the complementary relationship between values-based practice and evidence-based practice.

- Summarises the growing resources for values-based alongside evidence-based practice in mental health and social care from a range of policy, service development and training initiatives, in the UK and internationally.

The chapter concludes with a brief historical endnote locating values-based practice in the on-going development of mental health and social care as disciplines that are not only evidence based but also person centred.

▶ What are values? what is ethics?

'Values' and 'ethics' are both familiar terms, but in practice they generally mean very different things to different people. Table 5.1 shows the responses of one

Table 5.1   One group's responses to the differences between ethics and values

Values	Ethics
Personal	Rules
Emotive	Doing the right thing
Meaningful	Biomedical dilemmas
Taste	Something to rely on
Choice	Rules – certainty
Preferences	Absolutes
Wide range	Professional guidelines
Culture specific	Rules
Preferences	Respect for rights
Anything important	Right and wrong
Things	Values based
Places	Guide good decision making
People	
Subjective	Morals
Personal judgement	Integrity
Ideals	Conduct – taking a stand
Emotional judgement Worth	
Social conditioning	Prescriptions
Emotional judgement	Religion
Worth	Social coherence
Standards	Structured study of values
Principles	Code of conduct
Estimation	Institutional rules

group to an exercise in which we asked them to write down three words that they associate with 'ethics' and three words that they associate with 'values'.

As you can see, the responses from this group were very different. But on the whole, values are thought of as being wider than ethics and more individual. In particular, values associated with ethics often refer to moral values rather than the wider understanding of values within values-based practice, which includes personal preferences and aesthetic values. Values thus cover anything that matters to people and that motivates them, positively or negatively, whereas ethics tends to be more about rules and standards.

We need values-based practice and ethics because of the complexity and variety of values – personal, cultural and professional – that affect every decision we take in everyday mental health and social care. Case scenario 5.1 illustrates this complexity. Consider what answers you would give to the two questions. There are no right or wrong answers! But reflecting on this case scenario will help to bring out the diversity and complexity of the values influencing our practice, and hence why we need values-based practice as well as ethics.

Case Scenario 5.1: Dual diagnosis, values-based practice and ethics

A person has managed his severe mental health problems for all his adult life. His wife then dies of cancer and subsequently he begins to drink heavily and regularly. He is therefore identified as dual diagnosis (mental health problems and alcohol misuse). Coming up to the anniversary of his wife's death, his drinking increases and a concerned neighbour takes him to A&E. While in A&E, he makes the liaison mental health worker aware of his wish to die. The crisis team are then asked to complete a mental health assessment and risk assessment; however, he is too intoxicated to complete a useful assessment and they want to wait until he is more sober. A Mental Health Act Assessment is not considered to be appropriate as although at high risk, this is clearly a grief reaction. The substance misuse worker is concerned that he may experience delirium tremens if he abruptly stops his consumption of alcohol without support. The police are contacted when he absconds from A&E because of the perceived high risk of suicide. However, when he is found, he states he is on his way home to sleep off the alcohol and wants to be left alone.

Reflective questions

1. What values are reflected in this story?
Try writing a list – it will probably turn out to be a very long list, but it might include some of the following:

- Duty to care.

- Confidentiality (in relation to speaking to the neighbours).

- Autonomy.

- In primary mental health, the importance of mild to moderate depression, grief reactions and so on as against the history of severe mental health.

- Policy priorities around the issues of substance misuse.

- National government initiative on suicide prevention.

- Physical health.

2. Which of these values should have priority? And which should dominate decision making in practice?

Put this way, this is an impossible question to answer! Everything is important and everyone will balance these and other values in different ways. So even within our short list, we are presented with a whole series of direct conflicts of values. Often an issue that, at first glance, may seem obvious to one person may be given a very different answer by someone else; for example, the different priorities each of us might give to treat mild to moderate depression over severe mental health problems. Codes and guidelines can provide a supporting framework for decision making, but in themselves they cannot resolve all these conflicting values. This is why we need values-based practice as a *process* for balancing conflicting values.

As we shall see in this chapter, values-based practice and ethics both offer very practical tools to support decision making. We shall shortly look at how the two approaches fit together. To anticipate a little, we can summarise this briefly as follows: the tools of ethics tend to be outcome focused, providing rules and regulations that aim to prescribe 'right outcomes' for different situations; the tools of values-based practice, on the other hand, are process focused, supporting balanced decision making through the development of effective clinical skills for working with differences of values. Ethics tells us 'what to do'. Values-based practice tells us 'how to do it'.

▶ How values-based practice and ethics fit together

Just as there is a sense in which health care has always been evidence based (Sackett *et al.*, 2000), so there is a sense in which it has always been values based. The Hippocratic Oath, for example, was the first in a long line of ethical codes expressing key clinical values that are now the basis of modern ethical guidelines and related developments in health-care law.

Ethical codes and guidelines provide important frameworks for practice. However, the growing complexity of the values involved in health care is reflected in the fact that ethical codes themselves vary widely and there are often conflicts both within and between codes in the values they express. For example, respecting autonomy is often in conflict with acting in a patient's best interests, and maintaining confidentiality is often in conflict with the need to share information as the basis of good clinical care. In addition to conflicting values, furthermore, many widely adopted 'framework values' have complex interpretations. Acting in a patient's best interests, for example, means very different things in different contexts depending on the often very diverse values of the particular individuals concerned.

One response to such difficulties is to write ever more detailed codes, and indeed the size and variety of ethical codes and guidelines have increased enormously in recent years. Values-based practice (VBP) offers a very different, although complementary response. Values-based practice is based on the idea that, while codes do indeed provide a vital framework of shared values to guide practice, the processes of coming to balanced judgements where values conflict and of interpreting the applications of complex values, are matters, primarily, not for reference to a rule book, but for good clinical skills operating within an appropriate service framework (Fulford, 2004).

The complementary nature of the framework of values provided by ethical codes and guidelines and the skills-based approach of values-based practice is shown diagrammatically in Figure 5.1.

This is derived from work in jurisprudence by a former professor of philosophy and law: H. L. A. Hart (Hart, 1968). Lord Woolf, one of the UK's most senior lawyers and at the time the Lord Chief Justice, has recently applied a similar approach to Human Rights legislation. As Lord Woolf put it, the Human Rights Act is not about rights as conventionally understood by lawyers (and by implication by ethicists); it is, rather, a framework of values within which balanced judgements have to be made according to the particular circumstances of each individual situation (Lord Woolf, 2002).

The following brief case scenario illustrates the need for values-based practice to help us apply ethical codes in our day-to-day work. See what answers you would give to the reflective questions.

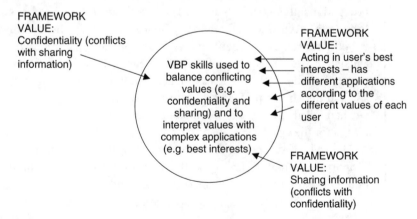

Figure 5.1 Shared framework values and values-based practice.

Case Scenario 5.2: Occupational therapy – Codes and clinical practice.

Scenario for reflection

The following extract is from an interview with an occupational therapist. Although a very brief extract, it describes vividly the conflicts that may arise between our own values and the values of others in our team or the values of management.

> I was sent to complete a functional assessment but when I got to his home the person I was assessing had lost his two dogs. I knew that this was really important to him so I helped him sort out what could be done and then helped him do it. But I also knew that, in relation to my colleagues, coming back without the assessment meant I had failed.

Reflective questions

1. Can you relate to this experience? Have you had similar experiences?
2. One way in which we may try to resolve these conflicting values is by referring to our own code of ethics. Think about a code that covers your own practice – in what ways would this help?

In this case, the College of Occupational Therapists' Code of Ethics and Professional Conduct (College of Occupational Therapists, 2005) sets out very clear guidance on practice under the following headings:

- Client Autonomy and Welfare
- Services to Clients
- Personal/Professional Integrity
- Professional Competence and Standards

This is a very useful starting point that helps to safeguard the values of an occupational therapist in practice. The first three of these headings appear to cover the occupational therapist in the scenario above: she was concerned with the welfare of the client and wanted to provide an appropriate service consistent with her own professional integrity. However, her colleagues, from what she says, might have taken a different view, suggesting that she had not shown professional competence (fourth bullet point) because she had failed to carry out the functional assessment that was the original reason for the visit.

The code of practice in this case does provide an explicit framework to support day-to-day clinical work. But when it comes to applying the code in the field situation, with all its complexity and unpredictability, we need values-based skills for balancing conflicting values as well.

▶ Pointers to good process in values-based practice

As a process-based approach, values-based practice covers four main areas, as shown in Figure 5.2. This is taken from a workbook for values-based practice, *Whose Values?*, developed jointly by the Sainsbury Centre for Mental Health and Warwick University Medical School (Woodbridge & Fulford, 2004). At the heart of the approach are four key areas of clinical skills (pointers 1–4). Also important, however, are two aspects of service delivery: that services should be user-centred and multidisciplinary (pointers 5 and 6). Equally important are close links between values-based practice and evidence-based practice (pointers 7–9), and a strong partnership in decision making between service users and service providers (pointer 10).

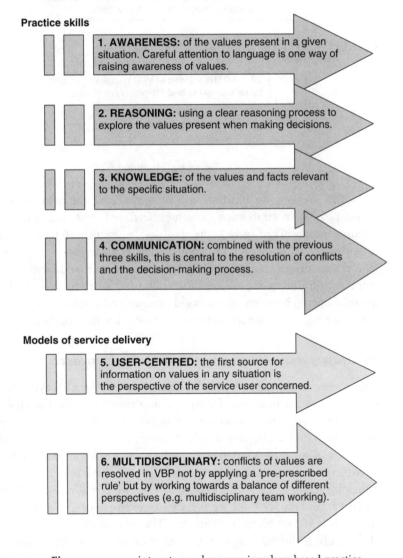

Practice skills

1. **AWARENESS:** of the values present in a given situation. Careful attention to language is one way of raising awareness of values.

2. **REASONING:** using a clear reasoning process to explore the values present when making decisions.

3. **KNOWLEDGE:** of the values and facts relevant to the specific situation.

4. **COMMUNICATION:** combined with the previous three skills, this is central to the resolution of conflicts and the decision-making process.

Models of service delivery

5. **USER-CENTRED:** the first source for information on values in any situation is the perspective of the service user concerned.

6. **MULTIDISCIPLINARY:** conflicts of values are resolved in VBP not by applying a 'pre-prescribed rule' but by working towards a balance of different perspectives (e.g. multidisciplinary team working).

Figure 5.2 10 pointers to good process in values-based practice.

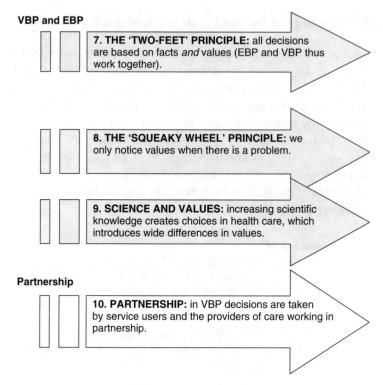

VBP and EBP

7. THE 'TWO-FEET' PRINCIPLE: all decisions are based on facts *and* values (EBP and VBP thus work together).

8. THE 'SQUEAKY WHEEL' PRINCIPLE: we only notice values when there is a problem.

9. SCIENCE AND VALUES: increasing scientific knowledge creates choices in health care, which introduces wide differences in values.

Partnership

10. PARTNERSHIP: in VBP decisions are taken by service users and the providers of care working in partnership.

Figure 5.2 *(continued).*

In this section, we illustrate the importance of the areas of clinical skill (pointers 1–4) in supporting person-centred and multidisciplinary teamwork within a framework of agreed ethical values. In practice, all four skills areas have to work together. But we will illustrate them by considering raising awareness and ethical reasoning as resources for person-centred care; and knowledge of values and communication as resources for multidisciplinary teamwork. We return to the relationship between values-based practice and evidence-based practice, and how these together support partnership in decision making, later in the chapter.

Awareness of values, ethical reasoning and person-centred care

Values are everywhere and, like the air we breathe, essential even though much of the time we are unaware of them. Raising awareness of values, therefore, and of the surprising extent to which our values differ, is the first and perhaps the most important training step in values-based practice. Table 5.1 at the start of this chapter, as a word-association exercise, illustrates one way of doing this.

A further approach to raising awareness of values is to reflect on our own values by standing back and looking at how we actually behave in practice as distinct from how we *think* we behave. An example of the effectiveness of this approach is shown given in Figure 5.3. This is taken from an exercise that one of the authors did with an assertive outreach team. The team was a very well-functioning multidisciplinary team with a strong ethos of service user-centred

1) Perspectives referred to in the meeting

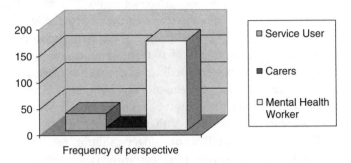

2) Subjects discussed in the meeting

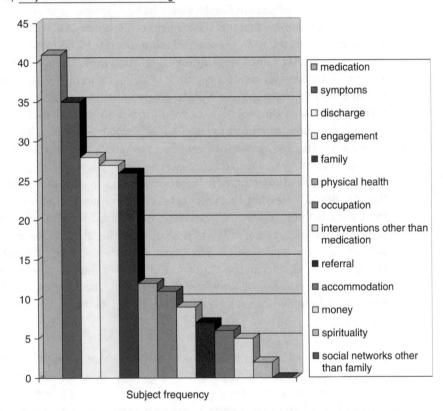

Figure 5.3 Values expressed in a Care Programme Approach review meeting.

care, and they had asked for training in values-based practice to support their approach. As a first step, the team agreed to monitor the values expressed in one of their Care Programme Approach review meetings.

These results were a surprise to the team! The first part of Figure 5.3 shows the frequencies with which the service user's, the carer's, and the mental health worker's perspectives were expressed in the meeting. As you will see, the perspectives of the mental health workers in the team dominated the meeting, with only occasional references to the perspectives of the service users concerned, and almost no references to the perspectives of carers. The second part of the figure shows the subjects actually discussed in the meeting. Again, the results for this strongly multidisciplinary team were a surprise. Far from a balanced approach, reflecting the perspectives of all team members, the first three most commonly discussed subjects were medication (frequency score 41), symptoms (frequency score 35) and discharge (frequency score 28). Engagement (frequency score 27) with family (frequency score 26) followed closely. But the four least frequently raised subjects were topics that have been widely recognised for some time (Faulkner and Layzell, 2000; Rogers, Pilgrim & Lacey, 1993) to be of particular importance to service users: accommodation (frequency score 6), money (frequency score 5), spirituality (frequency score of 2) and social networks (such as friends) other than family, which had a frequency score of zero.

Given their commitment to service user-centred care, the team were understandably very surprised by these results. But this raised their awareness of how strongly their own values were influencing their work, despite their commitment to a service user-centred approach. Raising awareness is, of course, only the first step in improving user-centred care, albeit an essential first step. As noted above, all of the 'pointers' to good process in values-based practice may be important here, but ethical reasoning, as pointer 2 of values-based practice, provides a particularly powerful example of how ethics and values-based practice are complementary in day-to-day decision making.

Ethics may be important, first, as providing a framework of shared values in the way described earlier in this chapter. Such frameworks, as we noted, are the basis of ethical codes and guidelines. But ethics may also be important in providing a whole series of different ways of reasoning about values derived from different areas of moral philosophy. Some key references for this are given at the end of this chapter in the Guide to Further Reading. In practice, there are three ways of reasoning about values that are particularly helpful for day-to-day decision making. We do not have space here to go into these in detail, but briefly they are:

- *Principles reasoning*: this is 'top-down' reasoning that relies on shared framework values of the kind illustrated in Figure 5.1. The most widely used form of principles reasoning focuses on the four principles of autonomy of service user choice, beneficence (service providers acting in service users' interests), avoiding harm, and fairness, in particular in the way resources are shared (see, for example, Beauchamp & Childress, 1989/1994).

- *Case-based reasoning*: this is the opposite of principles reasoning in that it is 'bottom up'; that is, thinking about an ethical problem by comparing different cases, and thinking about what would be right or wrong in different situations (see, for example, Jonsen & Toulmin, 1988).

- *Perspectives reasoning*: this way of reasoning about an ethical problem focuses on exploring the different perspectives of those concerned and is particularly

Table 5.2 Advantages and disadvantages of three different methods of ethical reasoning

Main approaches	Advantages	Disadvantages
Principles	Increases awareness Changes attitudes Points to relevant facts Improves thinking skills	Algorithmic approach Professional centred
Case based	Based on real-life links with case-based method Often leads to agreement in practice	Agreement can mean bias, prejudice, and hence abuse Professional centred
Perspectives	Patient centred Knowledge based	Relativism

closely related to communication skills (see, for example, Hope, Fulford & Yates, 1996).

Each of these ways of ethical reasoning has advantages and disadvantages, as summarised in Table 5.2. However, they all focus in different ways on the values of the service user concerned in a given situation. Principles reasoning emphasises autonomy of service user choice and the importance of service providers acting in the interests of service users. Case-based reasoning allows a more intuitive and personal way of understanding the values involved in a given situation, including those of the service user concerned. Perspectives reasoning is directly about understanding different perspectives and how a situation may look from different points of view, in particular that of the service user.

Case Scenario 3, Risk Assessment: Awareness of Values and Values-based Practice

Scenario for reflection

Neil was brought into the emergency out-of-hours mental health services by a neighbour because of fears that he would kill himself. Neil was in a very distressed and emotional state. Earlier that week Neil's wife had said she was definitely leaving permanently and taking their two children. They had been married for 17 years and Neil was described by the neighbour as being very dependent on his wife.

When interviewed by the mental health practitioner, John, Neil revealed he suspected that his wife was leaving him for his best friend who had been giving them both support during this bumpy time in their marriage. Neil also revealed that they had separated several times before because of Neil's violent temper, and there had been times that he had struck his wife and she had needed treatment as a result. Neil was very angry and tearful

---

during the interview and walked out several times, but would return and apologise for his behaviour.

Neil was adamant that although he had said some foolish things to the neighbour earlier, it was in temper and that he was fine now. What he really needed to do was to go home and start to deal with the situation. When asked by the mental health practitioner who was completing the assessment whether there was anyone who could be telephoned, Neil said he was a very proud and private person and that discussing this with anyone else would be humiliating. The only way to get his self-respect back was to deal with this himself.

The outcome from the assessment completed by the practitioner was that Neil did not present with any identifiable mental health problem; also he was not previously known to mental health services. Based on Neil's assurances that his earlier behaviour was just an initial outburst and that he had now calmed down and was seeing things more clearly and calmly, that he had no intentions of hurting himself or anyone else, and that he just wanted to get home to start picking up the pieces of his life, the practitioner concluded Neil was not currently a high-level risk.

However, the practitioner was very concerned that Neil would be leaving in an emotionally labile state and unsupported by friends or family, and that he was adamant that he wanted to resolve his distress alone.

Reflective question

1. When reading through the above account what would be your own response to the situation? How would you conclude the interview with Neil?

Note your ideas about this.

2. In deciding how to conclude the interview, whose values are relevant? Are there conflicting values in play?

Note your ideas. List the people involved and what you think their values – their concern, wishes, needs, expectations etc. – are in this situation. Then, note any conflicts of values. And think how these might be balanced in coming to a decision about what to do.

(We continue with this case scenario later in the chapter.)

Knowledge of values and communication as resources for multidisciplinary teamwork

Very important for effective teamwork is to become more aware of the different value perspectives of team members. Figures 5.4 and 5.5 show how awareness of differences of values between team members may be important, not only for good communication between team members, but also for service user-centred care. The figures look complicated, but they illustrate how research on values can support good decision making, and it is just the overall patterns that we will be concentrating on.

Figures 5.4 and 5.5 are taken from a study of the perspectives of different team members and of service users and carers, involved in the community care of people with a diagnosis of long-term schizophrenia (Colombo, 1997). Colombo explored these perspectives, not directly, by asking people what they thought about how people should be cared for, but indirectly, by getting them to respond to a case vignette. Using the case vignette, the respondents were asked to say what was important to them in a series of questions, covering diagnosis, behaviour, treatment and so on, as listed in the left-hand column of the figures. Their responses were then coded and allocated to different 'models' that reflected different service provider perspectives – medical, social, psychological and so on, as listed across the top of each figure. This produced a pattern for each group (called here a 'models grid'), reflecting the perspectives (the values and beliefs) of that group on the case vignette.

Looking at Figure 5.4, you will see that this compares the perspectives of psychiatrists (dark grey squares) with social workers (light grey squares) – and they are

ELEMENTS	PSYCHIATRISTS (P) AND SOCIAL WORKERS (S)					
	Medical (Organic)	Social Stress	Cognitive Behaviour	Psycho-therapeutic	Family (interaction)	Political
1 Diagnosis/description	P			S		
2 Interpretation of behaviour	P			S		
3 Labels	P			S		
4 Aetiology	P			S		
5 Treatment	P	S			S	
6 Function of the hospital	P S	P S				P S
7 Hospitality and community	P	S		S		
8 Prognosis	P			S		
9 Rights of the patient	P S	S				S
10 Rights of society	P S					
11 Duties of the patient	P		P S			
12 Duties of society	P	S				

Figure 5.4 Comparison of models grids for psychiatrists (dark grey) and social workers (light grey). Shared models cross-hatched (see text).

ELEMENTS	SERVICE USERS - Two Groups: 1, like psychiatrists (Up); 2, like social workers (Us)											
	Medical (Organic)		Social Stress		Cognitive Behaviour		Psycho-therapeutic		Family (interaction)		Political	
1 Diagnosis/ description	Up							Us				
2 Interpretation of behaviour					Up		Up	Us				
3 Labels	Up					Us		Us				
4 Aetiology	Up							Us				
5 Treatment	Up			Us				Us				
6 Function of the hospital	Up	Us	Up								Up	Us
7 Hospitality and community			Up	Us			Up	Us				
8 Prognosis	Up							Us				
9 Rights of the patient	Up	Us		Us							Up	Us
10 Rights of society			Up	Us								
11 Duties of the patient			Up	Us	Up	Us						
12 Duties of society	Up				Up	Us					Up	

Figure 5.5 Comparison of models grids for two groups of service users: Group 1 similar to psychiatrists (Up-dark grey), Group 2 similar to social workers (Us-light grey). Shared models cross-hatched (see text).

almost completely different! There are only six squares out of a possible 72 where their perspectives overlap (i.e. where the dark grey and light grey squares, representing psychiatrists and social workers respectively, come together). This was a particular surprise for both groups because they were working together in the same teams and yet had no idea just how different their perspectives (their values and beliefs) really were.

So this was an important awareness-raising exercise for the teams concerned. Better understanding of each other's perspectives, of their values and beliefs, and of how surprisingly different they were was the basis for improved communication and better-co-ordinated decision making. Even more important, though, for effective service user-centred care were the findings for the service user group. These are shown in Figure 5.5.

The models in Figure 5.5 for service users are shown in exactly the same way as those of the service providers in Figure 5.4. Again, the results were a surprise! As Figure 5.5 shows, the service users involved in the study turned out to have two different 'models', one group responding very like the psychiatrists in the study (shown dark grey in Figure 5.5; and compare with the dark grey squares in Figure 5.4), and a second group responding very like the social workers (shown light grey in Figure 5.5; and compare with the light grey squares in Figure 5.4).

The expected result from this part of the study was that the groups of service users would respond to the case vignette with a broadly political model; that is, with responses falling mainly in the right-hand column of Figure 5.5. Thus, the service users concerned were recruited not through clinical teams but as volunteers from local MIND; and they had all had a diagnosis of schizophrenia for some years. It was a reasonable expectation that their perspectives would reflect concerns about power imbalances, stigmatisation and other broadly 'political' aspects of mental health. In fact, what was actually found was that despite their very different backgrounds and experiences, the service users involved in the study were closely similar in their perspectives either to the psychiatrists or to the social workers.

Just why the perspectives of the service users in the study should have turned out to be so similar to those of the psychiatrists and social workers was not explored. A group of carers (not shown here) showed a very different pattern: they were all completely different one from another. But the match of perspectives between service users and service providers found in the study gives a completely new significance to the importance of a broadly based multidisciplinary team, representing different perspectives, in providing care that is genuinely person centred. Multidisciplinary teamwork is of course important in providing a range of different skills to support the different needs of individual service users. What this study showed was that, in addition to different skills, the different perspectives on a mental health problem of different team members are important in matching care plans to the different perspectives of individual service users.

The study also shows the importance of getting 'best evidence' on values, as on any other questions in health care. The study employed very careful empirical methods, developed and validated by Colombo (1997). In the next section we look at the relationship between values-based and evidence-based practice. Before moving on, though, you may find it helpful to review what you have learned so far about the four areas of clinical skills supporting values-based practice, by reflecting on the following case example.

Case Scenario 5.4: Risk Assessment (continued): Communication, Ethical Codes and Values-Based Practice

Scenario for reflection

Look back at Case Scenario 5.3. You will recall that we thought about the values bearing on the decision that the mental health practitioner, John, had to make about how to conclude the interview with Neil.

As noted above in this section, values-based approaches depend on good communication: this means transparently getting different and sometimes conflicting perspectives on the table and explicitly acknowledging them respectfully and sensitively. Values-based practice starts with the individual

---

involved and how they see the situation, and aims for a balance in decision making.

How we do this in practice depends on the situation, but it is always important to be as clear as possible about the often very different value perspectives that are likely to be involved. We all tend to assume that we understand other people's values. But as Colombo's (1997) study showed (Figures 5.4 and 5.5), and as we saw in the work noted earlier with a Community Mental Health team (Figure 5.3), we may not be fully aware even of our own values!

In this case, therefore, before finally concluding the interview with Neil, the practitioner took time out to discuss with colleagues. The main issues of the discussion were as follows:

- The practitioner had to respond to the neighbours' concern professionally. The process of assessment and access to mental health services and resources required the presence of a mental health disorder. The neighbour was frustrated and confused that although Neil was obviously distressed and not himself, he did not meet the criteria to receive services.

- The practitioner valued highly the support and comfort that could be given by friends and family, and questioned whether his concern that Neil was unsupported in this respect was generated by his personal value or by his sense of professional responsibility.

- Neil valued independence, being self-reliant and maintaining personal privacy; however, mental health systems and services promote a message of seeking help and getting support. In relation to the risk of self-harm, this can raise a particular tension between autonomy and choice and the responsibility to care and act in the best interests of the service user.

- The practitioner's colleagues were eager that Neil's estranged wife should be contacted in respect to her and her children. This was because they perceived a potential risk that she and the children could either be at direct risk of harm from Neil or indirect risk of harm if Neil harmed himself. This raised the difficult decision of whether to keep confidentiality, or because of the level of risk to break confidentiality.

Reflective questions

1. What are your thoughts on the key points raised by the practitioners? In what ways do they raise awareness of different values? How could this help in coming to a balanced decision about how to proceed?

2. How would you work with this diversity of values? How would you resolve the conflicts? Do the ways of reasoning about values noted above help here?

3. What ethical issues are raised? What ethical codes might help you to decide what to do? Make a list of any ethical codes or relevant law you are aware of, and how they could be applied in practice using values-based skills.

▶ Values-based practice and evidence-based practice

Values-based practice and evidence-based practice are very closely related. Both are processes for working with complexity – complexity of values, and complexity of evidence. And they come together in clinical decision making. Values-based practice aims to connect generalised best evidence, as derived from evidence-based practice and interpreted by experienced practitioners, with the unique values – the preferences, concerns, wishes and desires – of individual service users and their families.

Three particular aspects of the relationship between evidence and values are summarised in pointers 7, 8 and 9 of the '10 Pointers' shown in Figure 5.2. As these indicate, *all* decisions are based on values as well as evidence (pointer 7), but we only tend to notice values when they cause difficulties (pointer 8). Ethics focuses particularly on explicit conflicts of values, but as we have seen, values-based practice is concerned with raising awareness of values more widely. Pointer 9, about science and values, is also important. Ethics is sometimes seen as being in opposition to science (for example in research ethics committees). Values-based practice shows that as science increases the range of choices open to service users, so an ever-wider diversity of values comes into play. Hence advances in science and technology increase the need for values-based, as well as evidence-based, practice in health care.

The need to combine values with evidence in clinical decision making is well recognised within evidence-based practice. Evidence-based practice is usually thought to be all about best research evidence. But as Table 5.3 shows, one of the founders of evidence-based practice, David Sackett, actually defines evidence-based practice in terms of three elements, as 'the integration of best research evidence with clinical expertise and *patient values*' (Sackett *et al.*, 2000, p. 1, emphasis added). And as Sackett goes on to say, consistently with pointer 10 of values-based practice, it is only by bringing together these three elements that a genuine alliance between service users and service providers can be achieved.

In evidence-based practice, however, it has generally been assumed that the key difficulties for clinical decision making arise from the research evidence rather than from patients' values. Thus Sackett *et al.* focus in their book exclusively on the first of their three elements, best evidence, the implicit assumption being

Table 5.3   Definition of evidence-based medicine (EBM)

Evidence-based medicine (EBM) is the integration of best research evidence with
clinical expertise and patient values.

- By *best research evidence* we mean clinically relevant research, often from the basic
  sciences of medicine, but especially from patient-centred clinical research into the
  accuracy and precision of diagnostic tests (including the clinical examination), the
  power of prognostic markers, and the efficacy and safety of therapeutic,
  rehabilitative, and preventive regimens. New evidence from clinical research both
  invalidates previously accepted diagnostic tests and treatments and replaces them
  with new ones that are more powerful, more accurate, more efficacious, and safer.

- By *clinical expertise* we mean the ability to use our clinical skills and past experience
  to rapidly identify each patient's unique health state and diagnosis, the individual
  risks and benefits of potential interventions, and the patient's personal values and
  expectations.

- By *patient values* we mean the unique preferences, concerns and expectations each
  patient brings to a clinical encounter and which must be integrated into clinical
  decisions if they are to serve the patient.

When these three elements are integrated, clinicians and patients form a diagnostic
and therapeutic alliance which optimises clinical outcomes and quality of life.

Source: Sackett *et al.*, 2000, p. 1.

that service users' treatment preferences are likely to be more or less transparent.
That this is very far from being the case is shown by the work from values-
based practice illustrated in this chapter, as well as by a growing number of
service user narratives and of surveys and other research, indicating the extent
to which professionals misread their service users' values (Rogers, Pilgrim &
Lacey, 1993). There is evidence, furthermore, that even with training in broadly
service user-centred approaches, the values that service users themselves actually
bring to the clinical encounter are not sufficiently explored (Haynes, Devereaux
& Guyatt, 2002). This is why values-based practice is directly complementary to
evidence-based practice in supporting service user-centred care.

▶ Resources for values-based practice

The skills-based approach of values-based practice has been the basis for a
number of policy, service development and training initiatives, primarily in the
UK but increasingly with international partners. In the UK, the National Institute
for Mental Health in England developed a National Framework for Values (see
Table 5.4), that is explicitly based on the principles of values-based practice
(NIMHE, 2004).

The National Framework has in turn supported a number of policy and service
development initiatives in such areas as recovery practice, black and minority
ethnic services, audit, commissioning, and the development of mental health

Table 5.4   The NIMHE National Framework for Values-Based Practice

The work of the National Institute for Mental Health in England (NIMHE) on values in mental health care is guided by three principles of values-based practice:

1. *Recognition*: NIMHE recognises the role of values alongside evidence in all areas of mental health policy and practice.

2. *Raising Awareness*: NIMHE is committed to raising awareness of the values involved in different contexts, the role/s they play and their impact on practice in mental health.

3. **Respect**: NIMHE respects diversity of values and will support ways of working with such diversity that makes the principle of service-user centrality a unifying focus for practice. This means that the values of each individual service user/client and their communities must be the starting point and key determinant for all actions by professionals.

Respect for diversity of values encompasses a number of specific policies and principles concerned with equality of citizenship. In particular, it is anti-discriminatory because discrimination in all its forms is intolerant of diversity. Thus respect for diversity of values has the consequence that it is unacceptable (and unlawful in some instances) to discriminate on grounds such as gender, sexual orientation, class, age, abilities, religion, race, culture or language.

Respect for diversity within mental health is also:

- *User centred*: it puts respect for the values of individual users at the centre of policy and practice.

- *Recovery oriented*: it recognises that building on the personal strengths and resiliencies of individual users, and on their cultural and racial characteristics, there are many diverse routes to recovery.

- *Multidisciplinary*: it requires that respect be reciprocal, at a personal level (between service users, their family members, friends, communities and providers), between different provider disciplines (such as nursing, psychology, psychiatry, medicine, social work), and between different organisations (including health, social care, local authority housing, voluntary organisations, community groups, faith communities and other social support services).

- *Dynamic*: it is open and responsive to change.

- *Reflective*: it combines self monitoring and self management with positive self regard.

- *Balanced*: it emphasises positive as well as negative values.

- *Relational*: it puts positive working relationships supported by good communication skills at the heart of practice.

NIMHE will encourage educational and research initiatives aimed at developing the capabilities (the awareness, attitudes, knowledge and skills) needed to deliver mental health services that will give effect to the principles of values-based practice.

law in relation to involuntary treatment and capacity (Fulford, Stanghellini & Broome, 2004).

Building on the National Framework, the workbook *Whose Values?* (Woodbridge and Fulford, 2004) is part and parcel of, alongside evidence-based practice, the Ten Essential Shared Capabilities, a national training programme in the generic skills for mental health and social care (Department of Health, 2004), which in turn has supported a number of other key policies, in particular as these involve multidisciplinary and user-centred care.

Internationally, these developments have been picked up in a number of countries, including Sweden, France, Belgium, Spain, Brazil and South Africa, and through the World Psychiatric Association (Fulford, Stanghellini & Broome, 2004). There has also been important work on values and the way mental health problems are assessed both in the UK and in the USA (Sadler, 2005).

It is important to add that values-based practice is only one of a variety of new ways of working with complex and conflicting values that are increasingly being applied in health and social care. In addition to ethics and law, decision theory (Hunink *et al.*, 2001) and health economic theory (Brown, Brown & Sharma, 2005) provide powerful approaches in this respect. Values-based practice, however, differs from these other approaches, including ethics and law, in focusing on the diversity of individual values and the need to reflect this diversity in day-to-day decision making.

▶ Conclusions: values, evidence and service user-centred care

This chapter has given a brief introduction to values-based practice as a new skills-based approach to working with complex and conflicting values in health and social care. It is an approach that is complementary not only to ethics but also to evidence-based practice in supporting multidisciplinary teamwork and service user-centred care.

Key points from the chapter are summarised in Table 5.5.

Values-based practice is one of a number of practical developments in mental health arising from a dramatic revival of cross-disciplinary work with philosophy during the 1990s (Fulford *et al.*, 2003; Fulford, Stanghellini & Broome, 2004). Historically, these developments parallel similar developments in psychiatry in the early years of the 20th Century. Then, as now, there were unprecedented advances in the neurosciences. Then, as now, there was a strong, if more restricted, philosophy of psychiatry, in the foundational work on psychopathology of the German psychiatrist and philosopher Karl Jaspers. Then, as now, the drivers for these developments were the same: namely, that as the American psychiatrist and neuroscientist Nancy Andreasen has pointed out, advances in the neurosciences, far from reducing the importance of philosophy in psychiatry, actually elevate a whole series of philosophical and conceptual problems to the top of the practical agenda of day-to-day clinical care (Andreasen, 2001).

There are deep theoretical challenges here that continue to occupy philosophers. Andreasen had in mind such hotly debated metaphysical issues as

Table 5.5   Key points from the chapter

1. Values are wider than ethics and include all the many ways in which we express positive and negative evaluations, i.e. preferences, needs, wishes as well as ethical values.

2. Values-based practice is a new skills-based approach to working with complex and conflicting values in medicine, health and social care.

3. Ethical principles provide a framework of shared values – such as 'best interests' and 'autonomy of patient choice' – that guide the *outcomes* of clinical decision making supported by codes of practice and regulatory bodies.

4. Values-based practice is complementary to ethics in focusing on the *process* of clinical decision making: ethics focuses on 'right outcomes' (reflecting shared values); values-based practice focuses on 'good process' (reflecting complex/conflicting values).

5. At the heart of the 'good process' on which values-based practice depends are four key areas of clinical skills: awareness of values and of diversity of values; reasoning about values; knowledge of values; and communication skills, including skills in such areas as negotiation and conflict resolution.

6. Awareness of values and ethical reasoning illustrate how the skills-based process of values-based practice supports service user-centred care by raising awareness of the differences of values and value perspectives between service users and service providers; and showing how these differences can be both explored and balanced using a range of methods of ethical reasoning.

7. Knowledge of values and communication illustrate how the skills-based process of values-based practice supports multidisciplinary teamwork by improving understanding of differences of values between different team members – thus improving communication and shared decision making; and improving understanding of the particular and often very different values of individual service users and carers – thus improving the extent to which care and treatment are appropriately matched to the particular needs, preferences and wishes of each individual service user and their family.

8. In focusing on process rather than outcomes, values-based practice (concerned with complex and conflicting values) is fully complementary to evidence-based practice (concerned with complex and conflicting evidence) in clinical decision making.

9. In clinical work, values-based practice is supported by a wide range of training materials and is the basis of a number of both national and international developments in mental health, aimed at building a strong diagnostic and therapeutic alliance between professionals and service users in medicine, mental health and social care.

10. The skills-based approach of values-based practice is one of a number of disciplinary resources for working with complex and conflicting values in health and social care; in addition to ethics, other important disciplines include health economics and decision theory.

the nature of personal identity. Jaspers (1913) struggled with the still unresolved problem of reconciling empathic understanding of individual experiences with generalised causal-scientific explanations. Values-based practice itself builds on a 200-year and still actively developing line of philosophical enquiry into the logical relationship between description and evaluation (Fulford, 1989; Putnam, 2002).

The importance of such philosophical debates for mental health is not that they should come to final conclusions. To the contrary, some of the worst abuses in mental health have arisen from premature and dogmatic foreclosures on complex problems (Fulford *et al.*, 2003). Rather, the importance of philosophical debates for mental health is their practical spin-offs. On the model of values-based practice, such practical spin-offs extend our resources for working as effectively with what Jaspers characterised as the meaningful as with the causal aspects of psychopathology (Jaspers, 1913). It is in this way, therefore, by deepening the skills base for clinical decision making, that philosophy can contribute to the further development of mental health as a discipline that, perhaps uniquely within medicine, is not only science based but also and essentially service user centred.

▶ **References**

Andreasen, N.C. (2001) *Brave New Brain: Conquering Mental Illness in the Era of the Genome*. Oxford: Oxford University Press.

Beauchamp, T. L. & Childress, J. F. (1989; 4th edn 1994) *Principles of Biomedical Ethics*. Oxford: Oxford University Press.

Brown, M. M., Brown, G. C. & Sharma, S. (2005) *Evidence-Based to Value-Based Medicine*. Chicago: American Medical Association Press.

College of Occupational Therapists (2005) *College of Occupational Therapists Code of Ethics and Professional Conduct*. London: College of Occupational Therapists, www.cot.org.uk.

Colombo, A. (1997) *Understanding Mentally Disordered Offenders: A Multi-Agency Perspective*. Aldershot: Ashgate.

Department of Health (2004) *The Ten Essential Shared Capabilities: A Framework for the Whole of the Mental Health Workforce* (40339). London: Department of Health/NIMHE, NHSU, The Sainsbury Centre for Mental Health.

Faulkner, A. & Layzell, S. (2000) *Strategies for Living*. London: The Mental Health Foundation.

Fulford, K. W. M. (1989) *Moral Theory and Medical Practice*. Cambridge: Cambridge University Press.

Fulford, K. W. M. (2002) Values in psychiatric diagnosis: Executive summary of a report to the Chair of the ICD-12/DSM-VI Coordination Task Force (Dateline 2010). *Psychopathology*, **35**: 132–8.

Fulford, K. W. M. (2004) Ten principles of values-based medicine. In J. Radden (ed.) *The Philosophy of Psychiatry: A Companion* (Ch 14, pp. 205–34). New York: Oxford University Press.

Fulford, K. W. M., Morris, K. J., Sadler, J. Z. & Stanghellini, G. (2003) Past improbable, future possible: The renaissance in philosophy and psychiatry. In K. W. W. Fulford, K. J. Morris, J. Z. Sadler & G. Stanghellini (eds.) *Nature and Narrative: An Introduction to the New Philosophy of Psychiatry* (Ch. 1, pp. 1–41). Oxford: Oxford University Press.

Fulford, K.W.M., Stanghellini, G. & Broome, M. (2004) What can philosophy do for psychiatry? Special Article for *World Psychiatry*, **Oct**: 130–35.

Fulford, K. W. M., Thornton, T. & Graham, G. (2006) *The Oxford Textbook of Philosophy and Psychiatry*. Oxford: Oxford University Press.

Hart, H. L. A. (1968) *Punishment and Responsibility: Essays in the Philosophy of Law*. Oxford: Oxford University Press.

Haynes, R. B., Devereaux, P. J. & Guyatt, G. H. (2002) Physicians' and patients' choices in evidence based practice. *British Medical Journal* (clinical research edn), **324**(7350): 1350.

Hope, T., Fulford, K. W. M. & Yates, A. (1996). *The Oxford Practice Skills Course: Ethics, Law and Communication Skills in Health Care Education*. Oxford: Oxford University Press.

Hunink, M., Glasziou, P., Siegel, J., Weeks, J., Pliskin, J., Elstein, A. & Weinstein, M. (2001) *Decision Making in Health and Medicine: Integrating Evidence and Values*. Cambridge: Cambridge University Press.

Jaspers, K. (1913) Causal and meaningful connexions between life history and psychosis. In S. R. Hirsch & M. Shepherd (eds) (1974) *Themes and Variations in European Psychiatry* (Ch. 5, pp. 80–93). Bristol: John Wright.

Jonsen, A.R. & Toulmin, S. (1988) *The Abuse of Casuistry: A History of Moral Reasoning*. San Francisco, CA: University of California Press.

Lord Woolf (2002) Lecture to the British Academy, 15 Oct., quoted in *Hansard* 28 Oct., col. 607.

NIMHE (2004) *The National Framework of Values for Mental Health*. Available at www.nimhe.org.uk/ValuesBasedPractice. Also available in Department of Health (2004) and in Woodbridge and Fulford (2004).

Putnam, H. (2002) *The Collapse of the Fact/Value Dichotomy and Other Essays*. Cambridge, MA/London: Harvard University Press.

Rogers, A., Pilgrim, D. & Lacey, R. (1993) *Experiencing Psychiatry: Users' Views of Services*, London: Macmillan Press.

Sackett, D. L. Straus, S. E., Scott Richardson, W., Rosenberg, W. & Haynes, R. B. (2000) *Evidence-Based Medicine: How to Practice and Teach EBM* (2nd edn). Edinburgh/London: Churchill Livingstone.

Sadler, J. Z. (2005) *Values and Psychiatric Diagnosis*. Oxford: Oxford University Press.

Woodbridge, K. & Fulford, K. W. M. (2004) *Whose Values? A Workbook for Values-Based Practice in Mental Health Care*. London: Sainsbury Centre for Mental Health.

▶ Guide to further reading

This guide gives a selection of publications and Web-based resources for further study on values-based practice.

Training resources

- Woodbridge, K. & Fulford, K. W. M. (2004) *Whose Values? A Workbook for Values-Based Practice in Mental Health Care*. London: Sainsbury Centre for Mental Health.

  This training manual, which was developed in a partnership between the Sainsbury Centre for Mental Health and the Department of Philosophy and the Medical School at Warwick University, introduces the principles of values-based practice and includes detailed training materials.

- Woodbridge, K. & Fulford, K. W. M. (2005) Values-based practice. Module 4 in T. Basset & L. Lindley (eds) *The Ten Essential Shared Capabilities Learning Pack for Mental Health Practice*. London: National Health Service University (NHSU) and National Institute for Mental Health in England (NIMHE).
  This module on values-based practice gives a brief introduction with worked examples. The Ten Essential Shared Capabilities are all built on the twin resources of evidence-based and values-based practice.

- Fulford, K. W. M., Williamson, T. & Woodbridge, K. (2002) Values-added practice (a values-awareness workshop). *Mental Health Today*, **Oct**: 25–7.
  This paper describes the first of the series of training workshops that Kim Woodbridge, Toby Williamson and Bill Fulford developed and from which *Whose Values?* was subsequently developed.

- Woodbridge, K. & Fulford, K. W. M. (2003) Good practice? Values-based practice in mental health. *Mental Health Practice*, **7**(2): 30–34.
  This paper covers similar material to Fulford, Williamson & Woodbridge (2002) but in the form of an interactive workshop suitable for self-study.

- Fulford, K. W. M., Thornton, T. & Graham, G. (2006). *The Oxford Textbook of Philosophy and Psychiatry*. Oxford: Oxford University Press.
  Although this is a large textbook, the materials are all organised around readings and other self-training exercises, including self-test questions, key learning points and detailed guides to further reading. Part IV, on Values, Ethics and Mental Health, gives detailed introductions to ethics and ethical reasoning, medical law and values-based practice.

- Fulford, K. W. M. (2002) Many voices: Human values in health care ethics. In K. W. M. Fulford, D. Dickenson & T. H. Murray (eds) *Healthcare Ethics and Human Values: An Introductory Text with Readings and Case Studies*. Malden, MA/Oxford: Blackwell.
  This is an edited collection of classic papers of newly commissioned articles, literature and patient narrative, illustrating the diversity of human values in all areas of health care. The introductory chapter, 'Many voices', spells out some of the key differences between values-based practice and traditional ethics.

Theory of values-based practice

- Fulford, K. W. M. (1989, 2nd edn forthcoming) *Moral Theory and Medical Practice*. Cambridge: Cambridge University Press.
  This book sets out the theory underpinning values-based practice, drawing on ideas and methods from Oxford analytic philosophy.

- Fulford, K. W. M. (2004) Ten principles of values-based medicine. In J. Radden (ed.) *The Philosophy of Psychiatry: A Companion*. New York: Oxford University Press.

This chapter sets out the principles of values-based practice as they apply to mental health. It includes a detailed case history – of 'The artist who couldn't see colours' – running through the chapter in a series of episodes illustrating how the ten principles work out in practice.

- Colombo, A., Bendelow, G., Fulford, K. W. M. & Williams, S. (2003) Evaluating the influence of implicit models of mental disorder on processes of shared decision making within community-based multidisciplinary teams. *Social Science and Medicine*, **56**: 1557–70.
  This paper gives full details of the work described in the chapter. An account of the work was also published as Colombo, A., Bendelow, G., Fulford, K. W. M. & Williams, S. (2003) Model behaviour. *Openmind*, **125**: 10–12.

- Williams, R. & Fulford, K. W. M. (2007) Evidence-based and values-based policy, management and practice in child and adolescent mental health services. *Clinical Child Psychology and Psychiatry*, **12**: 223–42.
  This paper illustrates how values-based approaches can be applied to policy and service development using the example of CAMHS (child and adolescent mental health services).

Challenging inequality

David Pilgrim
University of Central Lancashire

The fourth essential shared capability is Challenging Inequality and the Department of Health (2004) describes this capability as:

> Addressing the causes and consequences of stigma, discrimination, social inequality and exclusion on service users, carers and mental health services. Creating, developing or maintaining valued social roles for people in the communities they come from.

This chapter takes a broad look at mental health and inequality and the role that 'services' have in influencing that relationship. I use the term 'influencing' here to suggest that 'services' are Janus or double-faced. I will argue that they can play a role in challenging inequality, but that they are also inherently involved in maintaining it. To be clear, this is not a reductionist argument. 'Services' are neither the whole solution nor the whole problem about mental health and inequality. However, they are one among several factors that play a part in affecting the mental health status of individuals in society.

Below I will set out arguments laid out in more depth in *Mental Health and Inequality* (Rogers & Pilgrim, 2003) and *A Sociology of Mental Health and Illness* (Rogers & Pilgrim, 2005). To condense relevant work from those texts here, I will focus on three main questions:

1. Do socio-economic inequalities affect mental health status?

2. Do the diagnosis and treatment of mental health problems influence the risk of socio-economic inequalities?

3. Which bodies of knowledge address these two questions?

Learning About Mental Health Practice. Edited by Theo Stickley and Thurstine Basset
© 2008 John Wiley & Sons, Ltd

▶ **Do socio-economic inequalities affect mental health status?**

Economic deprivation

Disadvantages typically attending poverty, such as poor education, low pay or unemployment, poor neighbourhoods and poor living conditions, aggravate both physical and mental health (Fryers, Melzer & Jenkins, 2001; Rogers & Pilgrim, 2003). Class position predicts both morbidity in its broadest sense and longevity in its specific sense. Not only do the poor consistently die younger, this pattern of early death is amplified in poor people who also have a psychiatric diagnosis (Knapp, 2001).

The social context of unemployment is crucial. Labour market effects are reliant on the presence or absence of state-provided income maintenance and on the circumstances in which a person becomes unemployed. In most developed countries, unemployed people obtain welfare payments. These ensure that poverty is relative and not absolute: resources are available to sustain food and shelter. But in many developing countries, this safety net is absent. For example, Patel (2001) notes that in India during the 1990s, bonded low-paid farmers lost everything when the monsoon destroyed their crops. They were thrown into absolute poverty and suicide levels dramatically increased. In the other direction, some forms of unemployment may actually be linked to improvements in psychological well-being (for example when getting a good retirement package, inheriting wealth or winning the lottery). Thus, the absence of paid work is not inherently bad for mental health; context is important to consider.

Poor employment not unemployment has the largest detrimental impact on mental health

When state-provided income maintenance is assured, the worst mental health is found not in unemployed people but in those on low pay and with poor task control or on short-term contracts. This is sometimes called 'inadequate employment' or 'underemployment' (Dooley, Prause & Ham-Rowbottom, 2000). The best mental health accrues from high wages, good task control and permanent employment. Thus unemployment may affect morale, but work, especially poor work, brings with it peculiar stressors, as well as status and earnings. Low-paid work leads to poverty in the domestic arena and, during work time, brings with it tedious and unfulfilling tasks.

Unemployment and low pay have indirect effects on mental health

Both ensure poverty and with them come both the environmental effects discussed later in relation to neighbourhood and the psychological effects of low status. In the case of becoming unemployed these effects can be compounded by multiple losses (Fryer, 1995). Identity for many is bound up with work roles (loss of identity). Daily meanings are bound up with the routines of work for many (loss of daily structure). For some, being unemployed is a source of shame (loss of face). And for those whose income levels drop significantly, there is the direct impact of the loss of money.

Macro-economic effects are important

Economic cycles create advantages and disadvantages for individuals (Kasl, Rodrigues & Lasch, 1998). For example, one generation of young people might encounter a period of growth and can access the labour market readily. The next generation may be less fortunate. Those in insecure employment will be buffered from its effects during times of full employment, but in more economically depressed times they will be very vulnerable (Pearlin & Scaff, 1996).

More than money: the impact of cultural and social capital

Cultural and social capital predicts mental health status

Apart from financial capital (income maintenance and savings) there is also an extensive discussion now of social capital and cultural capital. Financial capital can be framed in *structural* terms as social class, defined by a combination of earnings and type of employment. By contrast, cultural and social capital are better described in *functional or instrumental* terms: the ways in which people operate consciously or unconsciously to maintain or improve their social position, well-being and quality of life. Social class lends itself to objective indices such as earnings. However, cultural and social capital require descriptions that capture subjective and inter-subjective phenomena.

With a poor family of origin (a risk factor in mental health problems) comes a sense of particular cultural space to do with locality, schooling and family expectations about social status and prospects. Personal identity and 'knowing one's place' are set early in childhood. Bourdieu (1983) describes this development of a sense of one's place in life as a person's 'cultural capital'. This is bound up with the later connectivity people develop with others as adults: their 'social capital'.

Cultural capital does not neatly prescribe the quality and amount of later social capital, but it does predict it. This is why intra-generational and inter-generational social mobility is possible but not probable for most of us. Cultural position combines with economic position to predict mental health status. By implication, those of us from better-off families who are also likely to have greater cultural capital are less prone to this trajectory of mental ill-health.

The bridge between cultural and social capital in the latter regard ('who you know not what you know') was noted by Granovetter (1973). He described how social networks of better-off people involve multiple 'weak ties'. By contrast, poorer people have far less of these and tend to rely on the 'strong ties' of kith and kin relationships. This leads to the class contrast of multiple weak ties (the typical middle-class pattern of social networks) being stronger in its impact on well-being than a few strong ties (the typical pattern of poorer people).

Bourdieu (1983) also elaborated the same points about networks of influence inhabited by richer people, which exclude poorer people. For Bourdieu we all inhabit different 'fields' (the economy, education, the family, the scientific world etc.). Individuals tend to operate predominantly in one field although they can move between them, but some of us have more opportunities than others in this regard. To be locked into one field denotes 'entrapment', a concept that has been used as times to explain the emergence of both psychosis (Laing & Esterson, 1964) and depression (Brown, Harris & Hepworth, 1995).

Inter-generational and intra-generational effects of social class

In Britain, there have been two major and relevant longitudinal studies: the 1958 National Child Development Study (NCDS) and the 1970 British Birth Cohort Study (BCS). Sacker, School & Bartley (1999) summarise the implications for mental health and class position as follows:

- Both psychological problems and lower parental social class in adolescence increase the risk of mental health problems in adulthood (NCDS and BCS).

- The social position achieved in early adulthood is affected by both the father's class position and psychological problems in adolescence (NCDS and BCS).

- About 50% of the relationship between social class and mental health status is accounted for by these pathways from parental social class position and adolescent mental health problems by the age of 23 (NCDS) and 26 (BCS). By the time the age of 33 is reached these two factors account for nearly 100% of the relationship (NCDS).

- Mental health problems persist more from adolescence to adulthood in males than females (NCDS and BCS).

- Women show more inter-generational social mobility than men, but intra-generational social mobility is the same for men and women (NCDS and BCS).

Thus early mental health problems predict later social class position and vice versa. The greater persistence of problems in men from adolescence to adulthood is largely accounted for by behavioural or conduct disorders (substance misuse and chaotic and violent acting out). Successful suicidal action is also greater in young males. Whether these differences are accounted for by testosterone or masculine identity (or both), other predictors from families of origin include low parental social class, urban living, domestic violence and physical chastisement (Regier et al., 1988).

Ecological effects

It has been known since the 1930s that psychiatric diagnosis is geographically distributed (Faris & Dunham, 1939). These early Chicago studies demonstrated that not only were poorer people more likely to have a psychiatric diagnosis, the latter appeared more frequently in poorer areas. However, it also highlighted the 'ecological fallacy'. That is, not all people in poorer areas are poor and not all are prone to mental health problems. Thus ecological effects are evident, but where a person lives is not the only determinant of their mental health status.

Place affects mental health status

Urban life generally is more psychonoxious than rural life (Paykel *et al.*, 2000), notwithstanding our knowledge of pockets of rural poverty. This is due to more social disorganisation, environmental stressors (crime, vandalism, noise, litter and motor traffic). In areas of concentrated poverty, which are socially disorganised, the impact at the individual level is profound and negative. Not surprisingly, in these neighbourhoods there are raised levels of depression, anxiety and substance misuse (Aneschensel & Succoff, 1996).

Apart from the direct exposure to the external 'ambient hazards' of stress in these local contexts, they are less likely to have regular supportive social networks, particularly if there is a high turnover of residence (Sampson, 1988). Some particularly deteriorated localities contain higher rates of presentation of depressive symptomatology (Ross, 2000) *in all social groups*, including those with higher rates of forms of capital. Similarly, aggregate neighbourhood income predicts levels of diagnosis of schizophrenia and substance misuse (Goldsmith, Holzer & Manderscheld, 1998).

Some localities provide more 'opportunity structures' than others. These refer to the cultural and environmental possibilities for stress-free or health-giving public behaviour. For example, two neighbourhoods may be equivalent in terms of gross income, but one may have safer streets and more spacious green park areas for safe exercise than the other. Generally though, more affluent neighbourhoods provide more opportunity structures than poorer ones (Ellaway & Macintyre, 1998). This emphasises that social position can be defined as either an individual or a neighbourhood characteristic.

Race, ethnicity, gender and age

Mental health status is predicted by race and ethnicity

This point largely applies to post-colonial effects. For example, in the British context two ex-colonised people (whose historical origins were in Ireland or the West Indies) have higher rates of psychiatric diagnosis (Rogers & Pilgrim, 2005). The fact that the Irish are typically white suggests that ethnic minority status may be more important to consider than racial background. The epidemiological data on those from the Indian subcontinent is more ambiguous: not all studies show higher rates of diagnoses. In the post-colonial context a complicating factor is the type of migration involved, which could be forced or wanted by the migrant. These different conditions can make a difference between migration being experienced with hope or in a state of trauma and loss.

Mental health status is predicted by gender

Although much has been researched and written about gender and mental health, its relationship with detrimental outcomes of the latter remain ambiguous (Rogers & Pilgrim, 2005). More women than men are recorded as having mental health problems. However, this is mainly because of primary care presentations and because women live longer than men (so have a higher prevalence of both dementia and depression in old age). At the coercive end of services, men rather than women are over-represented. Moving from prevalence to type of mental health problems, women are more likely to be diagnosed with panic disorder and depression than men. In the case of the first diagnosis this may be because of the higher incidence of domestic violence with female victims (panic disorder is common after assault and other traumas). Men are more likely to be diagnosed with substance abuse and personality disorder (especially anti-social personality disorder). As a consequence, some argue that if all diagnoses are included then overall differences in the incidence of mental health problems disappear.

Another way that mental health is gendered is in relation to marital status. Men gain more than women by being married in this regard. Because of the ambiguity noted in this short section on gender, it is less salient when discussing inequality than is social class.

Age predicts mental health status

Across the life-span mental health problems are unevenly distributed. Young children and very elderly people are most at risk, creating a U-shaped distribution. This suggests that the notion of a middle-aged crisis is a myth. Indeed, some studies suggest that people in their 50s and 60s enjoy the best mental health (Rogers & Pilgrim, 2003). And yet the investment in service resources tends to be concentrated in the working years age group (services for older people and children and adolescents receive less investment). This financial pattern gives us a hint that mental health services are more about social regulation on behalf of socio-economic efficiency than an equitable response to need.

Developmental effects

Environmental factors begin to affect current and future mental health status from the womb onwards. For example, substances that cross the placenta can influence neurological development, which in turn can have a behavioural impact from birth. With regard to loss, abuse and neglect, all of these contextual factors impinge on the developing child. The aetiology of mental disorders remains controversial, but environmentalists have argued that consistent benign childrearing is at the centre of positive adult mental health. The least controversial claims relate to depression and anxiety states. Sexual abuse in childhood is highly correlated with contact with services. The most contestation surrounds developmental claims about infantile trauma and psychosis (Read *et al.*, 2003; Whitfield *et al.*, 2005).

▶ Do the diagnosis and treatment of mental health problems influence the risk of socio-economic inequalities?

Whatever the original causes of mental health problems, the negative social consequences of being in contact with specialist services and receiving a psychiatric diagnosis are considerable. The stigma and personal invalidation this brings are then joined by a good chance of exclusion from the labour market (Alexander & Link, 2003; Sayce, 2000).

The term 'mental health' is by and large a euphemism in its typical use by politicians (as in the phrase 'mental health policy'), managers (as in 'mental health services') and by practitioners (as in the phrase 'mental health professionals'; Pilgrim, 2005a). To be precise, only a tiny amount of government activity is funded genuinely to *promote* mental health. Most of what is called 'mental health policy' is about a socio-political response to mental disorder or 'mental health problems'.

A common observation is that 'health' services are really 'illness' services. And so it is with 'mental health services', except that a broader term like 'mental disorder services' more accurately tells us what they are about. Many patients in those services have diagnoses other than that of mental illness (for example of personality disorder or substance misuse).

When we turn to the notion of 'services', the general objection to the notion of 'health services' deserves more attention than usual: when mental disorder is involved, *who* exactly is being offered a service? The high rate of compulsion in these services, and the perennial threat of coercion to those who attend voluntarily (Szmukler & Appelbaum, 2001), render the notion of 'services' highly problematic. This point may seem pedantic, but if we are to be serious about 'mental health services' challenging inequality, then we need to appreciate what they are in business for. If they are often involved in serving third-party interests (of the courts, significant others or the voting public), how often are they truly a service to their patients? My point here is that they *are* services, but there is much ambiguity about who they are serving.

Thus, 'mental health services' have true service elements for their identified patients but they also serve third-party interests. They are part of the state apparatus of social control – some of this is done coercively and some by negotiation. The relevance of this to the topic of inequality is that the *routine success* of any 'mental health service' is marked by the exclusion of some people from society. Moreover, one consequence of that lawful social exclusion is the allocation of stigmatising roles (being a psychiatric patient) and stigmatising labels (the receipt of a psychiatric diagnosis).

Specialist mental health services can either be framed as a resource to be distributed equitably to those in need or as a part of the State apparatus to suppress residual deviance. As a consequence of these quite discrepant perspectives, services can either be viewed as a response to defined or expressed need or as a threat to well-being. If the first view is taken, then the arguments centre on the willingness of the State to provide adequate levels of funding for a 'fit-for-purpose' mental health workforce. In other words, patients who do not have access to these services are seen as suffering from a form of deprivation.

If the second view is taken, a totally different construction is evident. The challenge is not to access services but to avoid them or at least evade their iatrogenic impact. The latter term refers to all those aspects of service contact that have a *negative* impact on mental health. These include the life-diminishing and occasionally life-threatening effects of psychiatric drugs and the stigma of psychiatric diagnosis (Breggin, 1993; Pilgrim & Rogers, 2005). Even psychological therapies can create negative outcomes when incompetent or abusive therapists create 'deterioration effects' in their clients (Pilgrim & Guinan, 1999).

▶ Which bodies of knowledge address these first two questions?

In this section I will outline three different types of knowledge that inform debates about mental health and inequality. These are further informed by three distinct philosophical positions:

- *Medical naturalism* (sometimes called 'psychiatric positivism') starts from the premise that current medical terminology describing mental abnormality is valid and has global and trans-historical applicability. Diagnoses such as 'schizophrenia' or 'depression' are taken to be labels for naturally occurring phenomena embodied in their sufferers. Here the object (mental disorder) is assumed to precede the subject (those using the term). Mental disorder is assumed to exist 'out there' and to be independent of its observers or diagnosticians. In other words, its factual status is deemed to be non-problematic.

- *Radical constructivism* inverts the first position and assumes instead that subject precedes object. Here the emphasis is on how diagnoses are context-specific human products. They are deemed to be socially negotiated outcomes that reflect the cognitive preferences and vested interests of the negotiators (in this case in modern times the psychiatric profession being the most important, but not the only, group). In this view, mental disorder does not exist as an objective natural entity but is a by-product of psychiatric activity. This position is associated with Foucauldian reviews of psychiatric knowledge (e.g. Miller & Rose, 1988).

- *Critical realism* is a bridge between the two positions, in that external reality is deemed to precede the subject but is represented by shifting subjective or inter-subjective activity. The latter needs to be critically evaluated in order to identify interests operating (thus it supports the radical constructivist position to an extent). But critical realists concede the reality of some sort about mental abnormality (supporting to some extent the medical naturalists). Mental illness is not dismissed as being *merely* a by-product of professional activity, but it may be criticised for its poor conceptual validity (e.g. Pilgrim & Bentall, 1999). Recent critical psychiatrists move between radical constructivism and critical realism in their writings (e.g. Double, 1990; Thomas, 1997).

Thus the validity or legitimacy of knowledge claims about mental health is shaped by the pre-empirical assumptions held by researchers. Moreover, these assumptions are not only bound up with a view about reality but also about values. Is madness a defect or a heightened state of consciousness? Should mad be people be left alone or interfered with against their will?

How we answer these questions matters. If we frame madness as an illness that implies warranted state and professional paternalism, then we will find psychiatric epidemiology investigating the prevalence of 'schizophrenia' in order to plan appropriate levels of local mental health services. If we do not, then the latter would be irrelevant. For example, the radical edge of the users' movement has defended a counter-dependent position (Crossley, 2005). They want less not more statutory services and they argue that madness has value – it is not pathology to be discounted, interfered with or controlled. It is not the random noise produced by diseased brains (the assumption of biological psychiatry), but has meaning for the patient.

Any research agenda is shaped by a researcher's pre-empirical and non-empirical starting point. The latter determines which research questions they do or do not ask. Similarly, students reading and appraising literature will favour research that makes sense in terms of their pre-empirical and non-empirical assumptions. When they read literature that does not fit their assumptions, they will either discount it or be perplexed by it. These differing pre-empirical and non-empirical positions are very varied, but largely coalesce around the three epistemological positions I note above.

A central controversy in the field of mental health is the adequacy of psychiatric knowledge, with its emphasis on scientifically dubious diagnoses (Pilgrim, 2007a) and the dominance of medical naturalism. As Ingleby (1981) noted in his critique of the latter, while a bio-medical approach can be more or less adequate for the study of physical disease, it is inadequate for the study of mental disorder. The latter relies overwhelmingly on symptoms (what patients say and do) not signs (measurable bodily abnormalities). As such, it requires an interpretive rather than bio-medical approach of knowledge production.

Challenging inequality

The above discussion of the inter-relationship of services, knowledge and social variables suggests that if we are to challenge inequality then a complex set of actions is implied.

Political action is implicated

There is no technical fix for madness and misery. By the time mental health problems are established, professional interventions can make a marginal difference for some people some of the time. As I note above, it is important to distinguish the need for *mental health gain*, expressed by identified patients, from the *administrative success* of mental health services in controlling risky action. When there is success in the latter and not the former, then services compound or contribute to social exclusion.

This general point about the limited value of treatment applies to some extent to all health-care systems. However, what makes the iatrogenic impact of specialist mental health services more salient is that they exist in large part to provide actual or potential coercive social control of mental disorder. Accordingly, they provide one form of systematic lawful social exclusion.

Iatrogenesis and social control are recurring features of health-care interventions, but they are more striking in mental health services, which emerged in most developed countries from the 19th Century state asylum system. For example, when Talcott Parsons discussed the social control function of medicine in relation to the sick role (Parsons, 1975), his emphasis was on it being a negotiated position between the physician and patient. In mental health services there are indeed those who look for help and voluntarily enter the sick role – treatment is 'anxiously sought and gratefully received' (Rose, 1990). However, for many coercion is either evident or a background threat; this radically alters the nature of the social control involved.

As with most problems, prevention is better than cure. But what upstream political interventions are implied if we think about primary prevention or mental health promotion? The answer to this question resides in reversing the causal correlations identified earlier in the chapter about race, class and gender. It is only by reducing these inequalities that upstream solutions to mental health problems will be secured.

Local and national initiatives

The potential of the state and its employees to promote mental health and reduce inequalities exists despite the first point above about social control. An example of the varying balance of the two political imperatives has emerged recently in the UK about changes in mental health law (Pilgrim, 2007b). In England, the government had to weather the longstanding opposition of an umbrella group, the Mental Health Alliance, in its attempts to install new legislation to reinforce coercive powers. The London administration demonstrated a narrow preoccupation with the latter, including the refusal to include evidence of treatability as a condition of involuntary detention. By contrast, in Scotland the treatability criterion was honoured in its new legislation. Moreover, the Scottish Executive included a balancing policy of mental health promotion.

The point being made here is that there is a global convergence of mental health policy towards the use of legislation to single out mental disorder for particular scrutiny and control. However, nation-states can exercise discretion in what form that takes and whether the stick of control is mitigated by concessions to human rights (about treatability) and whether the carrot of investments in mental health promotion is also evident.

New social movements

If there is any doubt that mental health service are politically unusual in relation to the question of inequalities and social exclusion, we need only examine the growth of the mental health service users' movement (Crossley, 2005; Rogers & Pilgrim, 1991). A common complaint about health services in general is that there is a class gradient in access (with the sharp elbows of the richer groups in society gaining better access to care than poorer citizens). However, a reversal in that trend is evident when we examine mental health services. In the latter, the poor are over-represented, not under-represented.

Not only are the poor (and some ethnic groups) disproportionately detained and treated coercively in mental health services, thereby amplifying their social exclusion, the risk of iatrogenesis occurs more often under involuntary conditions. For example, while the risk of MRSA is present for any patient in a general hospital, they are not there against their will. In a psychiatric facility this is not the case.

A predictable political reaction to this state of affairs was that eventually psychiatric patients would respond collectively to their plight, with services and professionals becoming targets of their criticisms. The response of the state in turn has been to mollify and incorporate that opposition via 'user involvement' (Pilgrim, 2005b).

The prospect of progressive professionalism

Finally, I want to note the possibility of mental health workers challenging the status quo about mental health and inequalities. The first requirement in this regard is that professionals own up to their role. Mental health professionals *are* agents of social control. It is possible to remove the cloak of benign paternalism about their 'duty of care', their 'right to treat' and their 'response to mental health needs'. Indeed, simply to take the cloak away is a political act in itself. The second form of evidence about progressive professionalism would be a critical stance towards professional knowledge. The third aspect would be about testing the limits of user involvement and professionals showing evidence of their willingness to ally themselves with the users' movement. An honest reflection on the ambiguous role of specialist services and professional action is clearly required on these three fronts if practitioners are to make a persuasive case for their progressive stance towards inequality and mental health.

> **Activity 6.1**
>
> Think of a situation where you encountered inequality in your work as a
> mental health worker and answer these questions:
>
> ■ What form did the inequality take?
>
> ■ How were you able to challenge this inequality?
>
> **Activity 6.2**
>
> What contact do you have with your most local service user group?
>   If you have no contact, find out more about the group and consider how
> you can work in partnership with them to challenge inequality. Decide on
> some action.

▶ References

Alexander, L. A. & Link, B. G. (2003) The impact of contact on stigmatising attitudes
    toward people with mental illness. *Journal of Mental Health*, **12**(3): 271–90.
Aneschensel, C. S. & Succoff, S. (1996) The neighbourhood context of mental health.
    Journal of Health and Social Behaviour, **37**: 293–311.
Bourdieu, F. (1983) The forms of capital. In J. Richardson (ed.) *The Handbook of Theory
    and Research for the Sociology of Education*. New York: Greenwood.
Breggin, P. (1993) *Toxic Psychiatry*. London: Fontana.
Brown, G. W., Harris, T. O. & Hepworth, C. (1995) Loss, humiliation and entrapment
    among women developing depression: A patient and non-patient comparison. *Psycho-
    logical Medicine*, **25**: 7–21.
Crossley, N. (2005) *Contesting Psychiatry*. London: Routledge.
Department of Health (2004) *The Ten Essential Shared Capabilities: A Framework for the
    Whole of the Mental Health Workforce*. London, Department of Health/NHSU/Sainsbury
    Centre/NIMHE.
Dooley, D., Prause, J. & Ham-Rowbottom, K.A. (2000) Underemployment and depres-
    sion: Longitudinal relationships. *Journal of Health and Social Behaviour*. **41**: 421–36.
Double, D. (1990) What would Adolf Meyer have thought about the neo-Kraepelinian
    approach? *Psychiatric Bulletin*, **1**: 471–4.
Ellaway, A. & Macintyre, S. (1998) Does housing tenure predict health in the UK because
    it exposes people to different levels of housing related hazards in the home or its
    surroundings? *Health and Place*, **4**: 141–50.
Faris, R. E. & Dunham, H. W. (1939) *Mental Disorders in Urban Areas: An Ecological Study
    of Schizophrenia and Other Psychoses*. Chicago: Chicago University Press.
Fryer, D. (1995) Labour market disadvantage, deprivation and mental health. *The Psychol-
    ogist*, **8**(6): 265–72.
Fryers, T., Melzer, D. & Jenkins, R. (2001) *Mental Health Inequalities Report 1: A Systematic
    Literature Review*. Cambridge: Cambridge University, Department of Public Health and
    Primary Care.
Goldsmith, H. F., Holzer, C. E. & Manderscheld, R. W. (1998) Neighbourhood character-
    istics and mental illness. *Evaluation and Program Planning*, **21**: 211–25.

Granovetter, M. (1973) The strength of weak ties. *American Journal of Sociology*, **78**: 1360–80.

Ingleby, D. (1981) Understanding 'mental illness'. In D. Ingleby (ed.), *Critical Psychiatry: The Politics of Mental Health*. Harmondsworth: Penguin.

Kasl, S.V., Rodrigues, E. & Lasch, K. E. (1998) The impact of unemployment on health and well being. In B. P. Dohrenwend (ed.), *Adversity, Stress and Psychopathology*. Oxford: Oxford University Press.

Knapp, M. (2001) The costs of mental disorder. In G. Thornicroft & G. Szmuckler (eds), *Textbook of Community Psychiatry*. Oxford: Oxford University Press.

Laing, R. D. & Esterson, A. (1964) *Sanity, Madness and the Family*. Harmondsworth: Penguin.

Miller, P. & Rose, N. (1988) The Tavistock programme: The government of subjectivity and social life. *Sociology*, **22**(2): 171–92.

Parsons, T. (1975) The sick role and the role of the physician reconsidered. *Health and Society*, **53**: 3.

Patel, V. (2001) Poverty, inequality and mental health in developing countries. In D. Leon & G. Walt (eds), *Poverty, Inequality and Health*. Oxford: Oxford University Press.

Paykel, E. S., Abbott, R., Jenkins, R., Brugha, T. S. & Meltzer, H. (2000) Urban-rural mental health differences in Great Britain: Findings from the National Morbidity Survey. *Psychological Medicine*, **30**(2): 269–80.

Pearlin, L. I. & Scaff, M. M. (1996) Stress and the life course: A paradigmatic alliance. *The Gerontologist*, **36**: 239–47.

Pilgrim, D. (2005a) *Key Concepts in Mental Health*. London: Sage.

Pilgrim, D. (2005b) Protest and cooption: The voice of mental health service users. In A. Bell & P. Lindley (eds), *Beyond the Water Towers: The Unfinished Revolution in Mental Health Services 1985–2005*. London: Sainsbury Centre for Mental Health.

Pilgrim, D. (2007a) The survival of psychiatric diagnosis. *Social Science and Medicine*. In press.

Pilgrim, D. (2007b) New 'mental health' legislation for England and Wales: Some aspects of consensus and conflict. *Journal of Social Policy*, **36**(1): 1–17.

Pilgrim, D. & Bentall, R. P. (1999) The medicalisation of misery: A critical realist analysis of the concept of depression. *Journal of Mental Health*, **8**(3): 261–74.

Pilgrim, D. & Guinan, P. (1999) From mitigation to culpability: Rethinking the evidence on therapist sexual abuse. *European Journal of Psychotherapy, Counselling and Health*. **2**(2): 155–70.

Pilgrim, D. & Rogers, A. (2005) Psychiatrists as social engineers: A study of an anti-stigma campaign. *Social Science and Medicine*, **61**(12): 2546–56.

Read, J., Agar, K., Argyle, N. & Aderhold, V. (2003) Sexual and physical abuse during childhood and adulthood as predictors of hallucinations, delusions and thought disorder. *Psychology and Psychotherapy: Research, Theory and Practice*. **76**: 11–22.

Regier, D. A., Farmer, M. E., Rae, D. S. *et al.* (1988) Prevalence of mental disorders in the United States. *Archives of General Psychiatry*, **45**: 977–85.

Rogers, A. & Pilgrim, D. (1991) 'Pulling down churches' – Accounting for the British Mental Health Users' Movement. *Sociology of Health and Illness*, **13**(2): 129–48.

Rogers, A. & Pilgrim, D. (2003) *Mental Health and Inequality*. London: Palgrave.

Rogers, A. & Pilgrim, D. (2005) *A Sociology of Mental Health and Illness* (3rd edn). Maidenhead: Open University Press.

Rose, N. (1990) *Governing the Soul*. London: Routledge.

Ross, C. (2000) Neighbourhood disadvantage and adult depression. *Journal of Health and Social Behaviour*, **41**: 177–87.

Sacker, A., School, I. & Bartley, M. (1999) Childhood influences on socio-economic inequalities in adult mental health: Path analysis as an aid to understanding. *Health Variations*, **4**: 8–10.

Sampson, R. J. (1988) Local friendship ties and community attachment. *American Sociological Review*, **53**: 766–79.

Sayce, L. (2000) *From Psychiatric Patient to Citizen: Overcoming Discrimination and Exclusion*. Basingstoke: Macmillan.

Szmukler, G. & Appelbaum, P. (2001) Treatment pressures, coercion and compulsion. In G. Thornicroft & G. Szmukler (eds), *Textbook of Community Psychiatry*. Oxford: Oxford University Press.

Thomas, P. (1997) *The Dialectics of Schizophrenia*. London: Free Associations Books.

Whitfield, C., Dube, S., Felitti, V. & Anda, R. (2005) Adverse childhood experiences and hallucinations. *Child Abuse and Neglect*, **29**: 797–81.

CHAPTER SEVEN

Promoting recovery

Daniel B. Fisher

National Empowerment Center, Lawrence, Massachusetts

The fifth essential shared capability is Promoting Recovery and the Department of Health (2004) describes this capability as:

> Working in partnership to provide care and treatment that enables service users and carers to tackle mental health problems with hope and optimism and to work towards a valued life-style within and beyond the limits of any mental health problem.

Recovery has emerged in the mental health field around the world. It has assumed many meanings. The recovery movement has been generated from the cry and complaint of those of us who were labeled mentally ill and whose hopes for a full life were taken from us. We did not want mere remission of symptoms, in a life of reduced expectations. We did not want merely to function and be rehabilitated while remaining mentally ill. We have aspired to what everyone in society aspires to. We have wanted a full and meaningful life. So in the end, the recovery movement is based on the hope that is generated by the reality of people's lives.

'We are the evidence!' This was the repeated testimony of witnesses before the US President's New Freedom Commission on Mental Health (US Department of Health and Human Services, 2003). I, and thousands of mental health consumer/survivors, are the evidence that recovery from schizophrenia and other forms of mental illness is real. Our recovery stories are the spark to a vast recovery movement spreading around this planet. From person to person this torch of hope has lit the way to a new era in which, in the words of the Commission, there will be a 'future where everyone with mental illness will recover'. This chapter is a personal as well as a scientific description of the principles of how people recover from even the most severe forms of mental illness and how to use these principles of recovery to better assist people in their recovery.

Learning About Mental Health Practice.   Edited by Theo Stickley and Thurstine Basset
© 2008 John Wiley & Sons, Ltd

▶ **My personal recovery**

In the beginning most people want to know my story of recovery. So we will begin with a brief account of my recovery from schizophrenia. The world is still so convinced that people can never recover from schizophrenia that after I, and most of my peers, give testimony of our recovery, we are told, by professionals, that we must have been misdiagnosed. These professionals explain that we could never have given a coherent, well-delivered speech if we had ever had schizophrenia.

On the surface, my early life seemed normal. I succeeded in sports and academically. My behavior was good. In fact, I was probably a little too good. I was a little too eager to please teachers and other authorities. I was convinced that authorities possessed guidance and answers to my life. There was distress in my family as my father had Huntington's disease (a progressive degenerative disease of the nervous system), which we never discussed. We all knew that my siblings and I had a 50% chance of getting Huntington's, but still we did not discuss it. I suffered abuse at the hands of a teacher when I was 10. Again, not a word was spoken about it. Partly this silence on emotional issues was a product of my WASP (White Anglo-Saxon Protestant) upbringing. I was friendly, but had few close friends. In college, social pressures and love problems started to press in on me. In addition, I had chosen to pursue research into the chemical basis of schizophrenia. It was, I feel, partly as a result of the process and the culture of that work that I myself developed schizophrenia.

As a chemist, I was constantly trying to understand the mystery I was studying. I was, as is the field of psychiatry today, convinced that the secret of schizophrenia lay in our understanding the chemistry of the neurotransmitters such as dopamine and serotonin. The deeper I delved into these neurotransmitters, the more alienated I felt from my wife, my friends and myself. The inevitable consequence of such a mechanistic view of human feelings and thoughts was that we were all machines. Then one day, I became convinced that indeed everyone in the world, except myself, was a robot. I was so frightened by this belief that I retreated into my own world. I was unwilling to speak to anyone. I needed a safe place to overcome my fears. Then, as mostly now, there was only a psychiatric hospital. I was 25. They injected Thorazine into me and returned me to consensual reality and to my laboratory. This same sequence occurred again a year later. My second hospitalization lasted five months. During that time I realized I needed to make a major change in my life. Indeed, I said to myself I would return to everyday, shared reality only if I made a major change in my worldview, my relationships and my work. I wanted to go into psychiatry and find a new way to reach people going through the distress I experienced.

Though I was discharged with a diagnosis of schizophrenia, my psychiatrist, friends and family did not believe it was the end of my life. After my second hospitalization I decided to make major changes in nearly every realm of my life. Foremost, I decided to focus on building meaningful relationships with people and change from being a neurochemist to being a psychiatrist. I realized I needed to learn much more about myself and other people on a personal level.

During the next three years I worked diligently to become more in tune with my deepest self through every conceivable form of therapy and self-help. These included individual person-centered therapy, existential group therapy, radical therapy, psychodrama, peer support, and being a volunteer counselor in a free clinic. I also formed deep and lasting friendships, including in my marriage, and became a psychiatrist to help people and reform the system. I gained meaning in my life through my relationships, play and work.

My recovery, I believe, is complete, though I continue to work on my development and evolution as I feel every living creature needs to do. My third and last hospitalization occurred while I was in medical school, 32 years ago. I have been off meds and have been a practicing psychiatrist for the last 28 years. My recovery involved work on various levels of life.

On the intrapersonal level, I had a great deal of valuable psychotherapy. My therapist, a psychiatrist trained in the Sullivanian School, always believed in me. Shortly after being discharged from my second hospitalization, I told him I wanted to be a psychiatrist. Immediately, he said he would come to my graduation. Indeed, six years later, though I no longer saw him in therapy, he came to my graduation. I also learned to meditate. Even today I find that a valuable practice. I use a very simple form of insight meditation, in which I concentrate on my breathing. This practice allows me to regain control of my thoughts when they seem too crowded. I also exercise and watch what I eat. On an interpersonal level, I found group therapies and peer support that were helpful. In group therapy I learned to see myself through others. In peer support I learned how to take responsibility for parts of the running of a group. Providing help for others has been a significant part of my recovery. Dancing, canoeing, and other group activities were important. I have shared love with my wife and my two beautiful daughters who are now 22 and 24. On the community level, it has been very important to find a meaningful calling. I feel so fortunate that I love what I do. I am able to run an organization, the National Empowerment Center (NEC), that brings hope to people suffering mental illness around the world. I can directly see and feel the impact of my work in the eyes and hearts of people. I could never have dreamed of a better work.

▶ Research evidence of recovery

I am not an exception. There are many more people like me out in the world. The problem is that most professionals suffer what Dr. Courtenay Harding calls the 'clinician's delusion'. She said that most clinicians do not believe that people can recover from schizophrenia or other psychotic conditions, because they only see the consumers that remain in treatment and do not follow the ones that leave. Dr. Harding has published several compelling long-term studies showing that the moderate to complete recovery rate is about 65% even for people who had been hospitalized for several years (DeSisto et al., 1995; Harding, Zubin & Strauss, 1987). Since recovery for many people involves community integration such that others do not know your history, it is difficult to locate those of us who have recovered. So the only thing exceptional about me is that I disclose publicly. A famous case of the clinician's delusion involved Dr. Eugene Bleuler, the psychiatrist who coined the term schizophrenia in 1911. He generally believed that people did not recover. However, 63 years later his son, Dr. Manfred Bleuler, published his long-term studies of patients who were treated in the same hospital as his father. Manfred Bleuler found that a majority of people with schizophrenia recover (Bleuler, 1978). He pointed out that his father never saw patients after they left the hospital. Other long-term studies have up held these findings (Ciompi, 1984; Huber, Gross & Schottler, 1979).

Another important source of evidence that people recover from schizophrenia is found in cross-cultural studies. Far from being universally similar, schizophrenia rates vary greatly across cultures. In general, the rates are higher in industrialized countries. Jablensky *et al.* (1992) have shown significantly higher recovery rates in developing countries compared to industrialized countries.

▶ Recovery as a movement

During the last 15 years there has been a recovery revolution in the mental health field (Anthony, 1993; Davidson, 2003; Deegan, 1988; Fisher, 1994; Jacobson & Greeley, 2001; Onken *et al.*, 2002). This recovery movement has been recognized by the recommendations of the US President's New Freedom Commission for Mental Health for a transformation to a recovery-based, consumer-driven system (US Department of Health and Human Services, 2003). Change comes slowly, however. The deinstitutionalization movement of the 1960s and 1970s moved people with psychiatric disabilities from psychiatric hospitals to the community. That movement did not, however, change the forms of institutional thinking that had developed during more than a hundred years of institutional approaches to mental illness. This institutional perspective means that everyone continues to consider people with mental illness as forever ill and forever in need of professional services. The major mental illnesses are still considered incurable diseases, for which maintenance is the expected outcome.

Recently I was consulted by a mother and her 19-year-old son who traveled 3,000 miles to see me. He had done very well academically in high school, but suffered a psychotic breakdown in his first year of college. He was hospitalized, and diagnosed with schizophrenia. He and his mother were told by a psychiatrist to mourn his life, as he would never get better. They visited me because they wanted to hear a message of hope. Indeed, hope is a fundamental element of recovery. Increasing numbers of people with psychiatric disabilities, their families and advocates have refused to accept the prognosis of doom. These groups have spoken out, citing the evidence of the lives of thousands of people who have recovered.

To understand how people recover, the NEC (National Empowerment Center) in the USA has been conducting qualitative research for the last 10 years. From these interviews a consistent set of principles of recovery have emerged. These principles form the basis for a recovery-oriented approach to assisting persons in distress. NEC has called this Personal Assistance in Community Existence or PACE (Ahern & Fisher, 2001; Fisher & Ahern, 2001). The recovery principles are as follows:

1. People fully recover from even the most severe forms of mental illness.

2. Understanding mental illness as a label for severe distress that interrupts a person's major life roles helps in recovery.

3. People who believe in you play important roles in recovery.

4. The person in distress and those around them need to believe that the person will recover.

5. Trust is a cornerstone of recovery.

6. Mistrust leads to coercion and control.

7. Self-determination, dignity and respect are vital to recovery.

8. People in severe distress can connect emotionally and deeply yearn to do so.

9. Human connections are as important for people labeled with mental illness as for others.

10. Being engaged in emotionally safe relationships facilitates expression of feelings, which aids in recovery.

11. Understanding the meaning of severe emotional distress is helpful.

12. People need to express and pursue their own dreams to recover.

▶ Empowerment model of development and recovery

From these studies we have constructed a model that views recovery in a developmental context. We call this the Empowerment Model of development and recovery (see Figure 7.1).

Our description begins with the green circle on the right side of Figure 7.1, which we call the Spiral of Development.

The spiral of development

Our view of development is based partly on the work of Erik Erikson (Erikson, 1950). Erikson's description of the phasic crises in psychosocial development has great meaning in our model. Many people are diagnosed with mental illness during their late teens. According to Erikson, that is the period of identity formation. It is a necessary step towards being able to establish intimacy. If this step is not completed, the person relates superficially, experiences an identity diffusion and is more vulnerable to emotional distress. Kegan (1982) has viewed development of the person's self as proceeding in a spiral fashion.

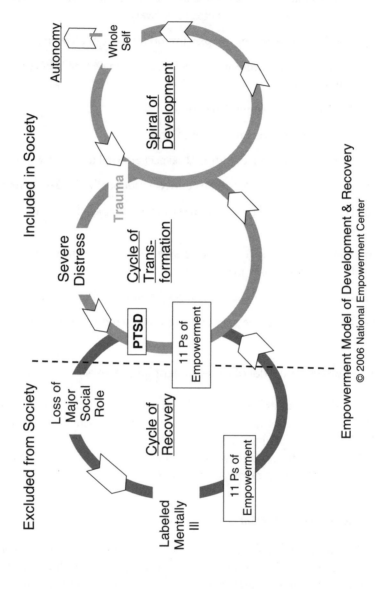

Included in Society

Excluded from Society

Autonomy

Whole Self

Spiral of Development

Trauma

Severe Distress

Cycle of Trans- formation

PTSD

11 Ps of Empowerment

Loss of Major Social Role

Cycle of Recovery

Labeled Mentally Ill

11 Ps of Empowerment

Empowerment Model of Development & Recovery
© 2006 National Empowerment Center

Figure 7.1 Empowerment Model of development and recovery.

The Empowerment Model is also influenced by the newer concepts of positive psychology (Seligman & Csikszentmihalyi, 2000) and self-determination (Ryan & Deci, 2000). These latter psychologists have emphasized that development depends on the active participation of the person as an actor, not a passive audience in their life. Recent research has shown that people are motivated to a greater degree by a wish for autonomy, competence and connection, which enable them to gain greater control over their life, than for externally supplied rewards and punishments (Ryan & Deci, 2000). Building relationships of trust and understanding are vital to gaining greater control over one's life. People need other people to gain the skills and resources they require to live an autonomous, self-regulated life. No man indeed is an island. In other words, community integration is an integral aspect of developing a whole self.

Throughout life, people work to develop as a whole person, through fully participating in the community by deepening emotional connections with others and ourselves. In the context of these relationships, each person truly comes to know their unique dreams and plan a life full of motivation and meaning. This increased self-knowledge deepens consciousness and extends one's autonomy. People work through stresses, losses and imperfect fit with their community, becoming architects of their own life and in so doing developing an empowered, hopeful self. Through this healthy spiral of development, people are able to find meaningful work and build a home of love through their network of mutually supportive family and friends.

Cycle of adaptation and accommodation

If, in the course of a person's development, there is a combination of trauma, loss, poor fit with one's environment, and/or insufficient supports, there is an interruption in the spiral of development. Individuals with traits or characteristics that are not accepted by their community are more likely to experience this interruption in their development. The cultural norms of a particular society determine which traits and people are rewarded and which are rejected. The degree of acceptance of a person's traits is frequently a function of the lack of tolerance by a society rather than a lack of the individual's capacities.

For instance, children with more visual, gestalt learning styles may fail in schools where they are expected to be aural, linear learners. In their frustration, they often experience severe emotional distress and unexpressed anger, and lose control over their behavior. They are then diagnosed as hyperactive and segregated from other children. They fail to form the relationships, learn the skills and gain the resources needed for their development. If they can share these feelings with significant, authentic people, the unexpressed emotions can be transformed into passion. Often, for people with psychiatric and physical impairments, peers who can share their experiential knowledge in a non-stigmatizing fashion can do this best through support. It also is vital to alleviate the source of their frustration by finding a more accommodating learning environment. The children can then resume their spiral of development through a belief in themselves, connecting with an accommodating social and learning environment, and thereby regain control of their lives. The environment needs to accommodate to the needs of the individual as much as the individual needs to adapt to the expectations of their community.

At various times in their lives, nearly everyone goes through some aspect of this cycle of adaptation and accommodation. The more often people and their environments go through this cycle, the less vulnerable they are to becoming disabled mentally or physically. A good example of a community accommodation is Gay Head, Massachusetts, where there were a large number of people with a hearing impairment. Rather than forcing those people with the hearing loss to adapt by speaking, the community learned sign language.

Cycle of recovery/independent living: labeled mentally ill and disabled

If people are unable to adapt and their environment is not sufficiently accommodating for them to fulfill their expected social role, 'symptoms' appear. These 'symptoms' are important messages from deep within that tell the person and those around them what the nature of the problem is between the person and their environment. All too often the person is blamed more than their environment and they need to tell themselves stories of their great-imagined accomplishments to overcome their rejection. There is then an interruption in a person's capacity to run their own life. Usually this results in hospitalization or some other form of psychiatric institutionalization in which the person's life is placed under the control of others. Often this process is involuntary, because few people give up that degree of control over their life voluntarily. The combination of an interruption in one's capacity to run one's own life, severe emotional distress and inability to fulfill one's expected social role results in the person being labeled as mentally ill. The form the mental illness takes depends on the stage of a person's development when the interruption occurred. People who exhibit an impairment in a major life function, who also are unable to reach a successful balance between their adaptation and the environment's accommodation, are labeled disabled. They are institutionalized. They also experience a loss of control over their life.

▶ Recovery/independent living

NEC reserves the term 'recovery' for resumption or establishment of participation in the community through an exercise of a social role other than mental patient. Recovery means (re)gaining a major social role, such as student, worker, parent and/or tenant, and control of one's life. Recovery involves reconnecting, being believed in, believing in oneself, and becoming empowered enough to resume one's cycle of and spiral of development. By this model, people can actually recover from mental illness, though they still continue to transform and heal. They may need to continue to need to take medication and require therapy, but they are the main decision makers in their life. After all, there are many people in our society who take medication and receive therapy but are not labeled mentally ill. The primary distinction seems to be whether the person has experienced a major interruption in their development and life, resulting in other people making their decisions for them.

NEC distinguishes between rehabilitation, remission and recovery. Remission is a medical term indicating that symptoms are reduced but one is still ill. Rehabilitation similarly means that a person regains their function but is still mentally ill.

Activity 9.1

Consider the Empowerment Model of development and recovery and apply it to somebody you know who has a diagnosis of mental illness. If it feels relevant, show the model to the person and discuss where they feel they are in relation to the model.

Our understanding of recovery has further deepened by translating the concept into other languages and cultures. In translating recovery into Spanish, the first word chosen was *recuperon*, which means 'recuperation'. Realizing how much broader recovery is in English, the translator then used the phrase *recobro de la vida*, which means 'recovery of a life'. In Korean, the best interpretation was 'recovery of one's humanity'. In that sense the most devastating aspect of mental illness is that one experiences a loss of one's humanity during the course of a breakdown and labeling.

In this context, it is understandable why the principles of the recovery movement focus on the most human aspects of our lives. We want more than anything to be regarded and addressed as full human beings, not just labels. So we see buttons that say, 'Label jars not people.' We want person-first language. We want be seen in the richness of our individual culture and history, not placed in a category. We want to be seen in all the dimensions of our being, on the levels of mind, body and spirit, not merely as a chemical equation. We want to lead a rich and fulfilling life in which we are the architect of our life based on our unique dreams and aspirations.

Recovery from mental illness is characterized by consumers living a full life in the community based on their making choices of the services and supports that enable them to control their life. These principles are the same as those on which the independent living movement for people with other disabilities is based. What do people with psychiatric disabilities mean by recovery? At this point our best description, based on interviews with people who have recovered, is:

■ Recovery means I am a full participant in the community and run my own life.

- Recovery means I no longer think of myself or am seen as being 'mentally ill', and instead think of myself as a worker, parent, student, neighbor, friend, artist, tenant, lover, citizen.

- Recovery means I rely mostly on personal and social support from outside the mental health system.

- Recovery means that I adapt to the stresses in life, use them as growth opportunities, and live life on life's terms. (National Empowerment Center, 2007)

What are people recovering from?

Though biology may play a role in varying vulnerabilities, we can learn a great deal by studying the psychosocial factors known to bring on psychosis-like states in animals. Nearly every species of animal has been shown to go into a state of immobility when confronted with an overpowering predator. The prey goes through a sequence of attempts to escape, such as squawking, aggressing, and then feigning injury. If these fail, the prey goes into an immobility response in which they appear dead (Ratner, 1975). If the animal is handled or tamed prior to the exposure to a predator, they are less likely to display an immobility response (Ratner & Thompson, 1960). It appears that this response to danger has an evolutionary advantage, because predators are less likely to attack an animal that already seems to be dead. This phenomenon of giving up is similar to Seligman's description of learned helplessness. He found that dogs exposed to unavoidable shocks eventually give up and end up lying down, allowing any number of shocks to take place without their protesting (Seligman, 1975). This animal reaction is similar to catatonic psychosis, in which the consumer holds the same position and becomes mute.

Empowerment as a central feature of recovery

Empowerment is a critical aspect of recovery, because it addresses the most central feature of mental illness, namely the loss of control over one's life through a loss of a voice in the world around one (Chamberlin, 1997; Fisher, 1994). In gaining a voice, people overcome the withdrawal and immobility cited in terror responses and learned helplessness above. NEC has developed a workshop called 'Finding Our Voice' to assist people in experiencing a greater degree of empowerment in their lives and being stronger advocates for others who are recovering. This emphasis on empowerment points out that recovery mainly relies on what the person is able to do for themselves, while treatment and rehabilitation are what professionals do to/for the person.

'Finding Our Voice' is based on the 11 Ps of Empowerment (Fisher & Chamberlin, 2007; see Figure 7.2):

- Personal Connections

- Positive Attitude

- Principles
- Passion
- Purpose
- Practical Plan
- Persistence
- Presence
- Presenting Publicly
- Persuasion
- Partnership

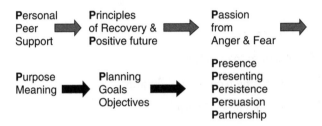

Figure 7.2   The 11 Ps of empowerment as the basis of recovery.

When people have experienced trauma, their voice is often stifled. This plays a role in the interruption of their development. When people can find their voice they can resume their development. NEC calls finding one's voice empowerment. A sequence often observed as people become empowered is summarized in Figure 7.2. This work can be done individually or in a group.

The first step involves connecting on a personal level. Peers have a unique advantage in forming these connections. There is an immediate sharing of experiences that forms a solidarity of suffering. Peers who have recovered bring an added element of hope by their life example. Sharing the principles of recovery can give a new framework for working through one's own issues. With deepening trust, a person feels safe enough to share the strong emotions that have interfered with development. Anger is often the most prominent repressed feeling. The anger is often the result of trauma and the ensuing interruption of one's development. When the anger can be safely expressed and accepted among peers (being in a group with one's peers is especially valuable for this step), then the person can experience passion. This transformation of anger into passion has been one of the most important steps in the finding of one's voice. Then a person can experience their passion and through it find their purpose and meaning in life. The person is then able to jointly re-author their life story through dialogue between their own perspectives and those of others. That way people get beyond thinking that they are either completely self-described or completely defined by others. Purpose then allows a person to dream and make plans again, for without purpose there is no reason to make plans. The next 4 Ps deal with how to communicate one's plan to those one works with. The final P, partnership, is the way people can move from their individual solution to a collaborative working relationship.

▶ Applying the principles of recovery to clinical care

Though recovery is primarily what the person does in gaining greater control in their life, providers can facilitate that process. In reviewing the steps involved in assisting people after traumas, disasters and mental illness (the 11 Ps discussed above), four phases of helping emerge. These are represented by the initials **CHEP**:

- **C** = Connecting
- **H** = restoration of Hope
- **E** = Expressing feelings and dreams
- **P** = Planning one's future

C: how to connect, especially when the person is in their own world

This essential first step in assisting people is the most challenging and the most rewarding. When a person has deeply retreated from the world around them, they have also retreated from themselves. This means that they have often lost, temporarily, the capacity to reconnect with themselves and thereby with the people around them. This also means that they need a person who can reach them in this state of withdrawal. Many of the following 12 key points come naturally to people who have been deeply in their own world. Others need to learn them.

1. Always believe in the person inside. This is an essential first principle of recovery-based care. It may appear that there is no one there when a person is not sharing in our consensual reality. During my early career as a psychiatrist, a gifted teacher would conduct an interview with a consumer who was in their own reality. At the end he would say, 'You see there is no one home.' When I tried to start a conversation with a consumer, another teacher said, 'You can't talk to a disease.' I was too afraid of being discovered in those days, so I did not tell them that I knew that was not true. I wish I had told them that no matter how unusual a person's appearance, behavior, or thoughts, there is always a person at home. When someone is in severe distress and is mute or talking to an unseen person, they are still there, inside, at home. In fact, at that time they are more present than someone not in distress.

The most frequently cited factor among people who have recovered was that 'someone believed in me'. They mean by this that, during the time that I had trouble believing in myself, there was someone whose belief in me sustained me. In daily conversation, people relate on a superficial level, relying primarily on spoken words for meaning. When a person is in severe distress, they yearn for a much deeper level of relating. This deep level of relating often takes place mostly at the emotional level. Therefore, the non-verbal elements of communication are the most crucial. People who have significantly recovered from mental illness frequently say they were greatly helped by someone who believed in them. One woman stated that there was a doctor who 'believed in me. She never gave up. She was the only one who didn't give up as far as [my] being in the hospital.' Another woman stated that for her it was a caring therapist. She said, 'He was the first person I encountered out of the ordeal that actually had some sort of feeling. He was sympathetic at least and was understanding. He was really helping me out and motivating. Motivating me to keep on fighting, don't give up... Don't let them get their way, just keep on fighting.'

Equally compelling is the centering and spiritual renewal coming for the person who does the believing in another. Whether it is for our children, lover, pet or person in need of help, there is deep meaning for the person who can step outside their world to support another's. A client I had seen through many hospitalizations recently had a long period free of such episodes. She clearly had a new light in her eyes. When I asked what had changed, she said now that she was working as a provider she had a sense of meaning and purpose in her life. Helping others gave her sufficient meaning that she felt her life was worth living.

These observations recall the research of Carl Rogers into the nature of the helping relationship. He stated, 'the safety of being liked and prized as a person seems a highly important element in a helping relationship' (Rogers, 1961). Martin Buber also describes the importance of having someone believe in you. He calls this characteristic 'confirming the other ... confirming means accepting the whole potentiality of the other. I can recognize in him the person he has been created to become.' Rogers echoes Buber's concept of confirming the other, 'if I accept the other person as something fixed, already diagnosed and classified ... then I am doing my part to confirm this limited hypothesis. If I accept him as a process of becoming, then I am doing what I can to confirm or make real his potential.'

2. Relate as if the person inside wants you to understand them. This approach of connecting to a person in another reality has been described by Gendlin (Gendlin, 1967). He states that it is the therapist's responsibility to move the therapy forward when a person is in severe distress. The therapist does this through the use of reflection of unformed, preconscious, but emotionally felt experience. Gendlin does this by using the sensible person hypothesis,

by which he means that when speaking to a consumer he always responds as if responding to a rational person. He emphasizes how the apparent irrelevant ramblings of a person in severe distress provide an important means of connecting. He states, 'The therapist's bit by bit solid grasp and response is [sic] like a pier in the patient's sea of autism and self loss. As each bit is tied to another person, who grasps it, the vast lost swampy weirdness goes out of things.' Prouty has given four concrete suggestions for reaching a person in another reality (Prouty, 1976). These all involve a form of reflection, which fits with the restoration of connection with another person as a way to understand oneself:

- Situational reflection: telling the consumer what they are doing and what the situation is.

- Body reflection: telling the consumer what they are doing with their body and/or mirroring their body movements with your body.

- Facial reflection: since feelings are directly related to facial expression, suggesting to the consumer what feelings they seem to be having based on the therapist's observation of their facial expression. (I can still recall very clearly the importance of a nurse telling me she heard sadness as I was singing a song.)

- Verbal reflection: repeating any word or sentence that the person says that makes sense of the seemingly chaotic verbalizations, even if this means repeating a single word.

Dr. Bert Karon (1992) gives a very good example of this way of connecting. It is about a man who was hospitalized for an acute psychosis. He perpetually bowed. When Dr. Karon asked why the man was bowing, he said he was not bowing. Dr. Karon demonstrated a bow and said, 'But you do this and this is bowing.'

> The man repeated, 'No I don't bow.'
> Therapist, 'Then what is it?'
> The man, 'It's balancing.'
> Therapist, 'What are you balancing?'
> 'Emotions.'
> 'What emotions?'
> 'Fear and loneliness.'

When he was lonely he wanted to get close so he leaned forward. But when leaning brought him too close to people, he got scared and pulled away by straightening up. Forming this connection was very important and the man completely recovered in eight weeks (Karon, 1992). It is vital for people to realize that they always have a healthy core.

3. Realize that the person in distress is acutely aware of every emotional nuance you are experiencing, so be honest and authentic. Carl Rogers called this feature of the helping relationship congruence (Rogers, 1961).

4. Your way of being with the person is most important; being here now is most appreciated.

5. Listen with all your heart first and foremost. In doing so you will help the person in distress to listen to their heart. One consumer, an engineer, shared that he heard voices when his heart stopped talking to him. When he was with friends his heart started talking again and he stopped hearing the voices.

6. Be humble, curious, respectful, leaving your theories at the door.

7. Be there deeply with the other person, sharing your full, centered self (regular meditation is good preparation for this). The alternative healing group called Windhorse uses an approach called basic attending, which is close to this way of being (Podvoll, 1991)

8. Minimize any distractions, especially of a mechanical nature.

9. Try to understand the person's meaning, realizing that distress appears crazy due to a lack of understanding by you and them of what the person in distress is trying to tell you and themselves about why they are upset. Carl Jung felt that understanding was so important that he said, 'When a person with schizophrenia is understood by another person they are no longer schizophrenic' (Karon & VanDenBos, 1981).

10. Always look for ways to increase the person's control through collaboration. Autonomy has been shown to be a stronger motivator than external rewards and punishment. Therefore, any way that we can assist a person in (re)gaining control over their life will increase their motivation to be part of their life.

11. Always build trust at the most basic level. Almost always, severe emotional distress involves a loss of trust in the important people in a person's life.

12. Find something to like about the person, especially when they find it hard to like themselves. Carl Rogers called this 'positive regard' and found it to be a central feature in the relationships formed by successful therapists (Rogers, 1961).

H: without hope recovery cannot even begin

There is always hope of recovery and it is vital to communicate that from the start in all mannerisms. Peers who have been through their own recovery are able to communicate hope by their very life example. By telling their story of recovery a peer can combat two of the central blocks to recovery: feeling they are the only one and feeling they have no future. Yet any practitioner can learn enough about recovery to be able to communicate this hope.

The importance of professionals feeling the hopefulness inside was highlighted recently during a trip to Japan. A professor of nursing had traveled a great distance to hear my talk. She said she had come to hear my story of recovery. She said that in the past she had only read that no one recovered from schizophrenia.

She wanted to meet me and hear my story in person so she could feel the hope in her heart. She felt that then she could carry that hope back to her students deeply enough that they would be able to give hope to the people they were helping. Preliminary research carried out by NEC has shown that exposing providers to evidence that people recover from mental illness increased their hopefulness in 65% of subjects (Zahniser, Ahern & Fisher, 2005).

Another example of the importance of hope, in the form of a song, occurred during my second hospitalization. A group of consumers would gather each afternoon and listen to Simon and Garfunkel's very hopeful song 'Bridge Over Troubled Water'. The image of someone being able to lie down and form a bridge over the troubled waters of one's life was very inspiring to us all.

E: expression of feelings and dreams

Once a person feels connected in a trusting fashion and feels they have a hopeful future, they can express the thoughts and feelings that have been unexpressed. These are often socially unaccepted emotions such as anger, fear or sadness. This feature of learning to express feelings and then transforming them into passion is elaborated above under the 11 P's of Empowerment.

P: planning

Having expressed the inexpressible, people can begin to make plans. Jumping too quickly to planning without some opportunity to express frustration or sadness can lead to no plans at all, however.

A good example of this CHEP approach occurred recently at a consumer-run conference in Portland, Oregon, US. A 20 year-old female consumer was attending while she was on pass from a state hospital. She became agitated and could not tell her peer advocate why she was so upset. The peer advocate kept saying to her she should be so happy that in one week she would be discharged from the hospital. But the advocate became worried that the young woman might need to return to the hospital right away. The peer advocate thought the young woman might need an extra dose of her tranquilizer. I and another peer supporter *connected* with the young woman, through striking up a conversation by focusing on her interest in soccer. She then expressed her despair that she would never get better. She was sure that her life was over. She felt hopeless. When she heard that both I and the other peer had also been mentally ill but had recovered to lead productive lives, she started to relax. She started to feel *hopeful* and that she could have a future. She continued to pace, however, and when we asked her if she was looking forward to leaving the hospital, she confided that she did not look forward to it. The advocate questioned her and she was able to tell the advocate too that she did not want to leave the hospital. She said she was treated more like an adult in the hospital than at home. Once she *expressed* this concern, she relaxed and stopped pacing. She was then able to make a *plan* to go swimming. The next day she reported that she slept well, felt relaxed and wanted to stay for the rest of the conference.

> **Activity 7.2**
>
> Think about the discussion of CHEP above and plan how you might use this approach with someone you are working with.

▶ Consumer-run alternatives to hospitalization

The Rose House (serving Orange and Ulster Counties, New York) is a good example of a recovery-based, peer-run alternative to hospitalization, as described on its Web site:

> This peer-operated house is designed to assist fellow peers in diverting from psychiatric distress, which may lead to a hospitalization. The program is located in a three-bedroom home set up and furnished for comfort. The house is equipped with a variety of traditional self-help and proactive tools to maintain wellness. Trained peer companions are the key ingredients in helping others learn self-help tools. Peer companions are compassionate, understanding and empowering.
>
> The Rose House offers a stay of up to five days to take control of your recovery and develop new skills to maintain your wellness. Peer companions staff the house 24 hours a day to address the needs of guests as they arise. Participation in the program is completely voluntary and free of charge. You are free to come and go as you please. We also will maintain contact and support for you, at your request, after you finish your stay.
>
> In-home support is also offered. Peer companions will meet with you at your home or in a comfortable place in the community. During these visits, the goal of a peer companion is to help you explore strategies for finding and maintaining wellness and to offer support through this process. In-home visits are one of the steps in developing a relationship with potential guests of the Rose House. (PEOPLe, 2007)

The director of Rose House, Steve Micchio, eloquently states the purpose of their work:

> The peer companions will always respect your right to make your own choices and work to enhance your sense of independence and empowerment. We meet you where you are. Peer companions have all experienced what it is like to be on the verge of a crisis, if not surrounded by it. We understand the need for support during these difficult times; that is why we offer hope, strength and knowledge of recovery to those individuals who need a more supportive environment. Transformation for me is simply changing the belief system in mental health and changing it to a system that believes everyone can recover or heal to a level that improves each person's quality of life. It is taking the 'can do' approach and putting action towards it in service delivery.

I am so inspired right now because I see so many people embracing transformation. While there still exists many barriers and obstacles, we are least at the table talking about how to overcome these barriers and we are becoming a mental health community of partners and collaborators. I believe that we all want the same thing in the end, but we just don't yet know how to get there. But get there, we must!

Another excellent example of a consumer-run respite program is Stepping Stones in rural New Hampshire. Stepping Stones consists of a 'warmline', overnight respite and a daytime recovery center. What is particularly unique about Stepping Stones is the excellent training in which all staff and regular members are continuously engaged. They practice trauma-informed peer support (Mead, 2001), which addresses trauma as well as the distress that is apparent in one's immediate experience. This means that after residents have passed through their crisis, they additionally have ongoing opportunities in the Stepping Stone community to understand the role that trauma has played in their distress. This allows for a deeper recovery than ordinary crisis services (personal communication, Lenora Kimball).

▶ Eight reasons for using a recovery approach in clinical practice

Clinicians often say that they either already are practicing a recovery approach or that it will increase their risk. The following is a list of reasons I cite when clinicians wonder why they should adopt a recovery approach:

1. *Recovery is central to system transformation.* The New Freedom Commission on Mental Health's Vision is: 'We envision a future when everyone labeled with mental illness will recover'; and a guiding principle is: 'care must focus on recovery and resilience not just managing symptoms' (US Department of Health and Human Services, 2003).

2. *A recovery approach reduces risk.* The factors most important to recovery – that is, trust, respect, hope, understanding and collaboration – are also the most important factors in building a positive relationship, decreasing the risk of negative behavior, improving communication, warning of trouble early, and reducing the risk of being sued. Lawsuits are more frequently the result of bad feelings than of bad outcome.

3. *Recovery builds an alliance instead of requiring compliance.* Building a positive, recovery-oriented relationship with a consumer improves the alliance with the consumer, improves motivation, and decreases the need for coercion and other compliance measures.

4. *Recovery improves motivation.* An emphasis on the recovery principle of self-determination and shared decision making improves motivation by the consumer because people are more likely to follow their own goals based on their dreams, and because autonomy is a primary motivator.

5. *Recovery improves team building.* Cultivating a recovery culture throughout an organization facilitates team building with consumers, families and staff, because respect and shared decision making mean that all team members feel valued and that they are meaningfully contributing, which improves communication and morale.

6. *Recovery decreases burnout.* A sense of hope and working together decreases staff burnout, keeps all staff members motivated and involved in their work; a recovery culture means that staff are encouraged to build a full life so they can bring a fuller personality and life to work.

7. *Recovery improves cultural competence and community integration.* Working in a recovery culture means that a person's culture, social network and story are seen as critical factors in their illness and their recovery; a recovery approach is always oriented towards sustaining, improving and building community connections with family, housing, vocational rehab and other natural supports.

8. *Recovery facilitates work with people with substance abuse.* The recovery culture is based on many of the same principles as substance abuse services and supports: these include the value of people taking responsibility, peer support, healing through fellowship and recovery through helping others.

▶ Conclusion

Above all else, remember that you need to be a bridge connecting the fearful and the isolated people who are in distress to the people around them and to themselves. There is no recovery program, because each person you help is an individual. There are recovery principles you will need to adapt to each person. You are the recovery program for each person. Who you are and what you learn about yourself are the most important assets you can have as a helper/therapist. Always realize that the more you learn, the more you can share. The more you can be, the more you can be there deeply with the person you are assisting.

▶ References

Ahern, L. & Fisher, D. (2001) *PACE (Personal Assistance in Community Existence)*. Lawrence, MA: National Empowerment Center, www.power2u.org.

Anthony, W. A. (1993) Recovery from mental illness: The guiding vision of the mental health service system in the 1990s. *The Psychosocial Rehabilitation Journal*, 16(4): 11–24.

Bleuler, M. (1978) *The Schizophrenic Disorders*. New Haven, CN: Yale University Press.

Chamberlin, J. (1997) A working definition of empowerment. *Psychiatric Rehabilitation Journal*, 20(4): 43–6.

Ciompi, L. (1984) Is there really a schizophrenia? The long-term course of psychotic phenomena. *British Journal of Psychiatry*, 145: 636–40.

Davidson, L. (2003) *Living Outside Mental Illness: Qualitative Studies of Recovery in Schizophrenia*. New York: New York University Press.

Deegan, P. (1988) Recovery: The lived experience of rehabilitation. *Psychiatric Rehabilitation Journal*, 11: 11–19.

Department of Health (2004) *The Ten Essential Shared Capabilities: A Framework for the Whole of the Mental Health Workforce.* London: Department of Health/NHSU/Sainsbury Centre/NIMHE.

DeSisto, M., Harding, C., McCormick, R., Ashikaga, T. & Brooks, G. (1995) The Maine and Vermont three-decade studies of serious mental illness. I Matched comparison of cross-sectional outcome II Longitudinal course comparisons. *British Journal of Psychiatry.* **167**: 331–42.

Erikson, E. (1950). *Childhood and Society.* New York: W.W. Norton.

Fisher, D. B. (1994) Health care reform based on an empowerment model of recovery by people with psychiatric disabilities. *Hospital and Community Psychiatry,* **45**: 913–15.

Fisher, D. & Ahern, L. (2001) Recovery at your own PACE. *Journal of Psychosocial Nursing.* **39**: 22–32.

Fisher, D. & Chamberlin, J. (2007). *Finding Our Voice: A Workshop based on the 11 P's of Empowerment.* Lawrence, MA: National Empowerment Center.

Gendlin, E. T. (1967). Therapeutic procedures in dealing with schizophrenics. In C. R. Rogers, E. T. Gendlin, D. J. Kiesler & C. B. Taux (eds), *The Therapeutic Relationships and its Impact.* Madison, WI: University of Wisconsin Press.

Harding, C., Zubin, J. & Strauss, J. (1987) Chronicity in schizophrenia: Fact, partial fact or artifact? *Hospital Community Psychiatry,* **38**: 477–86.

Huber, G., Gross, G. & Schottler, R. (1979) Schizophrenie: Verlaufs und soczial psychiatrische Lanqzeitundersuchungen an den 1945 bis 1959 in Bonn Hospitalisierten schizophrenen Kranken. *Monographien aus dem Gesarntgebiete der Psychiatrie, Bd. 21.* Berlin: Springen-Verlag.

Jablensky, A., Sartorius, N., Ernberg, G., Anker, M., Korten, A., Cooper, J. E., Day, R. & Bertelsen, A. (1992). Schizophrenia: Mainifestations, incidence and course in different cultures. *Psychological Medicine, Supp* **20**: 1–97.

Jacobson, N. & Greenley, D. (2001). What is recovery? A conceptual model and explication. *Psychiatric Services,* **52**: 482–5.

Karon, B. (1992) The fear of understanding schizophrenia. *Psychoanalytic Psychology,* **9**: 191–212.

Karon, B. & VanDenBos, G. R. (1981) *Psychotherapy of Schizophrenia.* New York: J. Aronson.

Kegan, R. (1982) *The Evolving Self: Problem and Process in Human Development.* Cambridge, MA: Harvard University Press.

Mead, S. (2001) Peer support: An alternative approach. www.mentalhealthpeers.com/booksarticles.

NEC (National Empowerment Center) (2007) *Voices of Transformation.* Lawrence, MA: NEC.

Onken, S., Dumont, J., Ridgeway, P., Ralph, R. & Dormon, D. (2002) *Mental Health Recovery: What Helps and What Hinders.* Alexandria, VA: National Research Project for the Development of Recovery Facilitating System Performance Indicators, NASMHPD.

PEOPLe (2007) Rose House, www.charityadvantage.com/people/RoseHouse.asp.

Podvoll, E. (1991). *The Seduction of Madness: Revolutionary Insights into the World of Psychosis and a Compassionate Approach to Recovery at Home.* New York: Perennial Press.

Prouty, G. F. (1976). Psychotherapy: A method of treating pre-expressive retarded psychotic patient. *Psychotherapy: Theory, Research, and Practice,* **13**: 290–94.

Ratner, S. C. (1975). Animal's defenses: Fighting in predator prey relations. In L. Pliner, P. Krames & T. Alloway (eds), *Nonverbal Communication of Aggression.* New York: Plenum Press.

Ratner, S. C. & Thompson, W. R. (1960). Immobility reactions of domestic fowls as a function of age and prior experience. *Animal Behavior,* **8**: 186–91.

Rogers, C. (1961). *On Becoming a Person.* Boston, MA: Houghton-Mifflin.

Ryan, R. M. & Deci, E. L. (2000). Self-determination theory and the facilitation of intrinsic motivation, social development, and well being. *American Psychologist,* **55**: 68–78.

Seligman, M. E. P. (1975). *Helplessness: On Depression, Development, and Death.* San Francisco: W. H. Freeman.

Seligman, M. & Csikszentmihalyi, M. (2000). Positive psychology: An introduction. *American Psychologist,* 55(1): 5–14.

US Department of Health and Human Services (2003) *The President's New Freedom Commission on Mental Health. Substance Abuse and Mental Health Services (SAMHSA).* Available at www.mentalhealthcommission.samhsa.gov.

Zahniser, J., Ahern, L. & Fisher, D. (2005) How the PACE program builds a recovery transformed system: Results from a national survey. *Psychiatric Rehabilitation Journal,* 29: 142–5.

CHAPTER EIGHT

Identifying people's needs and strengths

Lesley Warner

Registered mental nurse

The sixth essential shared capability is Identifying People's Needs and Strengths. The Department of Health (2004) describes this capability as:

> Working in partnership to gather information to agree health and social care needs in the context of the preferred lifestyle and aspirations of service users and their families, carers and friends.

Everyone who seeks help from mental health services, whether in community or residential settings, should have their needs and strengths assessed as the first stage in planning the care, treatment and intervention to be provided by the mental health team. While many workers, from different professional backgrounds, will contribute to the assessment, the role of the key worker/care coordinator is crucial in co-ordinating the assessment process and ensuring that a care plan is drawn up to meet the needs of the service user.

▶ The policy context: the care programme approach

The Care Programme Approach (CPA) is a system for planning, delivering and reviewing all care provided to mental health service users. Instructions for its implementation were published in 1990, when it was designed to be the framework for the care for people with mental health needs in England. It came into effect in April 1991, running in tandem with the local authority Care Management system, originally applying just to current inpatients at the point of discharge and new referrals to specialist mental health services. The CPA was later extended to include everyone in contact with specialist mental

Learning About Mental Health Practice. Edited by Theo Stickley and Thurstine Basset
© 2008 John Wiley & Sons, Ltd

health services. The key elements were the systematic assessment of individuals' health and social care needs, the formulation of a care plan to address those needs, the appointment of a key worker to monitor the delivery of care, and the regular review and, when necessary, amendment of the care plan in line with the service user's changing needs. The importance of close working between health and social services was stressed, as was the need to involve service users and their carers. The Mental Health Act Code of Practice emphasises that the CPA applies to everyone receiving specialist mental health care, including detained and informal hospital inpatients.

The CPA was revised and integrated with Care Management in 1999 to form a single care co-ordination approach for adults of working age with mental health needs, to be used as the format for assessment, care planning and review of care by health and social care staff in all settings, including inpatient/residential. Two tiers of CPA were established nationally, standard and enhanced, and key workers were replaced by care co-ordinators. Standard CPA is described as being for those people whose needs can be met by one agency or professional or who need only low-key support from more than one agency or professional, who are more able to self-manage their mental health problem, who pose little danger to self or others, and who are more likely to maintain contact with services. People on the enhanced CPA level are likely to have multiple care needs that require inter-agency co-ordination, to require more frequent and intensive interventions, to be at risk of harming themselves or others, and to be more likely to disengage with services. The CPA was introduced in Scotland in 1992, and in Wales in 2004.

The Care Programme Approach Association (CPAA) was established to support the implementation, operation and development of the CPA. Its members include professional and support staff working in mental health services, commissioners and other interested groups. They publish national standards, guidance for CPA care co-ordinators and information on auditing the use of the CPA, which can prove valuable to practitioners.

The CPA provides the framework for planning, delivering, monitoring and reviewing the care of people with mental health problems. It has been imperfectly implemented, and has a number of persistent critics for whom it will always be a flawed tool. However, many practitioners believe that its advantages outweigh its disadvantages, and that if there was no CPA we would be forced to invent something very like it. Under review by the Department of Health in 2006–7 and likely to emerge with some modifications, some form of the CPA is likely to continue to form the basis of care well into the 21st Century.

Activity 8.1

Find out more about how the CPA operates in your area/locality. How well is it working? Check out the last review into CPA in your area/locality.

▶ Why assess needs?

Most people in contact with mental health services will have been seen by a psychiatrist and been given a diagnosis. So is it not reasonable to treat everyone with the same diagnosis, for example of depression, in the same way?

There are some basics that should be included in all care packages, for example practising active listening, acting with empathy and safeguarding individuals' physical health and safety. However, beyond this, the care plan should be tailored to meet an individual's specific needs. So, unless there is a proper assessment, the appropriate care for that person cannot be provided. The National Service Framework for Mental Health (Department of Health, 1999) makes clear that all service users' health and social needs must be fully assessed.

Additionally, over time the repeated, documented assessment of needs, care interventions delivered, goals achieved and treatment outcomes becomes an important record of what is helpful for that individual service user in particular situations, and should remain part of their records to inform clinical teams working with them in the future.

▶ What type of needs should be assessed?

Comprehensive assessment of an individual's needs is an essential first step towards drawing up a CPA care plan, and should be undertaken in partnership with the service user, whose own assessment of their needs and strengths is crucial.

Many factors contributing to mental well-being need to be considered. These include:

- *Mental health.* This includes assessing the individual's mood, such as depression, anxiety, preoccupation, distress or elation; their thoughts, such as intrusive thoughts that seem to come from outside themselves, or compulsive thoughts that urge them to repeat actions; their behaviour and how they relate to other service users of staff. Other elements to be assessed are hallucinations, in which individuals generally hear voices talking to them, sometimes criticising or exhorting them to act in ways they would not normally choose, and delusions, in which the person holds a firm belief, not amenable to argument or persuasion, that seems at odds with reality as perceived by others. Their emotional state, how they are actually feeling, is also important.

- *Risk assessment.* This includes assessment of self-harm and suicide, violence towards other people, self-neglect, vulnerability to exploitation by other people, and the service user's social and housing context. Mental health services may have developed their own documentation for risk assessment, or will be using standardised risk-assessment tools.

- *Signs of relapse and crisis plan.* Service users are best placed to tell the worker what may trigger a relapse in their mental ill health, and what early warning signs of relapse may be observed by other people. They are also in the best position to explain what they find helps them most when this happens, to defuse the situation as much as possible, and what they would like the worker to do if this situation arises. Documentation of the signs and symptoms of relapse, with the agreed action to be taken, can help the worker respond appropriately when necessary.

- *Relationships with family and friends.* Whether the service user lives by themselves, with a partner, children, parents or friends will affect how their care plan is drawn up, and the mental health worker will need to be sensitive to how they want to involve the people they are closest to. Partners and parents may take on a caring role with the individual, as may adult children – and even younger children in some instances – and ideally their views and needs should also be determined, and the part they can plan in the care plan made explicit through discussion and negotiation. Some families find it hard to deal with a member who has mental health problems, and may benefit from information, education and even mediation sessions to improve the position of the service user within their family network.

- *Needs of carers and family members.* Carers and family members may express a wide range of emotions in response to the mental health difficulties of the person they are caring for. They may feel bewildered, uncertain or angry, deny anything is wrong, or insist on being involved to an intrusive extent. Carers' needs should be assessed, and steps taken to provide them with the information, support and practical help they may need.

- *Housing.* Having somewhere to live is a fundamental human need, so an individual's housing situation will inevitably affect their mental and physical health and well-being. They may be worried about losing their accommodation during a period of hospital admission, and will need help to ensure that their housing benefit, rent or mortgage payments are continued, or that negotiations take place to defer these until they are discharged. They may also be living in unsuitable housing and need help to find somewhere better, or they may be homeless with a pressing need to find somewhere to live. An individual's home circumstances may also include pets, and this should be noted so that arrangements can be made to care for them if necessary.

- *Activities of daily living.* These consist of the basic things that most people take for granted as part of getting on with their lives, but that some people with mental health problems may struggle with at times. They include the ability to take care of oneself in terms of keeping clean and getting dressed, budgeting and paying the bills, and the activities of shopping, cooking and cleaning.

- *Work and/or education.* Most people get satisfaction from taking part in regular work, on a paid or voluntary basis, or having some other regular daily activity such as an education or training programme. Feeling valued in an occupation enhances many people's feelings of self-worth, and status accrues to earning money. Education and training can be a means to the end of finding a job, or can be a satisfying end in themselves.

- *Financial, including benefits.* Like housing, having enough money for one's needs is a basic human necessity, and people who have no money or are constantly struggling to make ends meet will be unlikely to be able to focus on other, less important issues. It is crucial to assess an individual's source of income, commitments and outgoings, and to establish if there are state benefits to which they are entitled.

- *Leisure activities.* Some people will enjoy taking part in sporting activities, as a participant or spectator, while others may take part in artistic pursuits or enjoy socialising with others.

- *Spiritual.* Some people with mental health problems will have definite religious beliefs and will take part in the life of their local church, mosque, synagogue, gurdhwara or other place of worship. Others may describe themselves as religious but not take part in any collective form of worship, preferring to read holy books and pray in privacy. Others may not have any specific religious beliefs but still think of themselves as spiritual beings, having some notion of a force greater than that of humankind, maybe linked in with the force of the natural world. Spirituality means many different things to different people, and an individual's own assessment of how much of a part this plays in their life should be respected, and attempts made to meet the needs identified.

- *Cultural, including ethnicity.* A growing number of people in the UK have their family origins outside of these islands and remain connected to other ways of living and other family models, for example in relation to marriage and other relationships, and to parenting. Experience of racism may also be an important factor in relation to the effect this has on their mental health.

- *Physical health.* People with mental health problems experience higher levels of morbidity and mortality than other population groups. Risk factors including those associated with having a low income, medication side effects including weight gain, and the incidence of smoking lead to higher rates of diabetes, heart disease and stroke, and some cancers. Service users report that general practitioners tend mainly to see the mental ill health of their patients, and are less likely to investigate symptoms that might have a physical cause (Freidli & Dardis, 2002; Seymour, 2003). Both the National Institute for Clinical Excellence (NICE, 2002) and the National Service Framework for Mental Health (Department of Health, 1999) have highlighted the importance of assessing the physical health of people with serious mental ill health, so assessment of general health, including lifestyle and risk factors, and medication side effects is important.

- *Physical and sensory disability.* Linked with physical health, an assessment of any disability or impairment should be included, and steps taken to provide services or appliances to compensate for things like unsteadiness when walking, and poor eyesight or hearing.

- *Communication.* Effective communication between service user and mental health worker is the bedrock of all interactions, and without this any therapeutic intervention can only produce a limited result. First, with those whose English is not good it is important to use language that is easily understood, and not to resort to psychological jargon or acronyms. For those who speak poor or no English, in the absence of a mental health worker who can speak the individual's language, arrangements must be made for professional interpretation and translation services to assist them in making their needs and strengths known, and in discussion about the production of a care plan aimed at addressing them.

- *Advocacy.* Some service users may feel hesitant or unable to express their needs, and will need help to articulate them in order to obtain the services of their choice. Independent advocates should be available to help in this way.

- *Dual diagnosis.* Some people will have, in addition to a mental health problem, issues of substance misuse, relating either to alcohol, non-prescription drugs or other substances such as solvents. It is unfortunately the case that some mental health services are unwilling to work with this group, feeling that specialist drug and alcohol services would best meet their needs, while at the same time the drug and alcohol services protest that they feel unable to cope with service users' mental health problems. This leaves people who have a dual diagnosis firmly between two stools. In order to decide which service must take responsibility for such a vulnerable and needy service user, a proper assessment of the substances being used is essential, coupled with the previously described mental state assessment.

- *Gender.* It is sadly true that many female service users feel themselves to be unsafe when using mixed-sex services, especially inpatient and residential settings. More shockingly, some have been subject to assaults and serious sexual attacks in these settings. The need for single-sex facilities has therefore been recognised, and women should be asked if they would prefer this. An unfortunate result of this policy has been that many men are now also admitted to single-sex wards, which many of them find alienating and would not opt for if they had the choice.

- *Sexuality.* Mental health workers should be respectful of service users' sexual orientation, and be aware of the stigma and prejudice experienced by many lesbian, bisexual and gay (LBG) service users.

- *Dietary requirements.* Some dietary needs are inextricably linked with religious observance, for example the need for observant Jews to eat only Kosher food, and, similarly, for Muslims to have food that is Halal (permitted). Some vegetarians do not eat meat because of religious convictions, while others regard this a moral choice. There are also cultural reasons for choosing food with which a person is familiar, especially at a time of crisis when they are experiencing mental ill health and may be feeling dislocated from their cultural origins.

- *Unmet needs.* Finally, it is important to record if there are any needs that the service user and mental health worker have identified for which it is not possible to include an intervention in the care plan. For the individual, these should be reviewed regularly to see if the means to meet them have become available, and at the organisational level they should be aggregated and reported to feed into the service commissioning and planning cycle.

Activity 8.2

Consider the needs of a service user with whom you are working. Have their needs been assessed in a comprehensive way? Are there areas from the list above that may have been neglected?

▶ How can needs be assessed?

Assessments can be formal or informal, and it may take several days to cover all the elements. While there may be specific time limits to do with drawing up or reviewing care plans, in essence assessment should be a continuous process in which the mental health worker is constantly seeking to understand how the service user is feeling, what they are experiencing, and in what ways the worker can assist them through this process. The key skills needed are active listening and observation. The worker should listen to the service user, to their carer and to the other members of the team involved in their care. The worker should observe how the service user looks in terms of mood, their behaviour and interaction with others. Signs and symptoms of mental distress should be noted and used when drawing up the care plan. Crucially, the worker should try to discuss all aspects of their mental state with the service user, recognising that there will be periods when they are unable or unwilling to do this and the worker will need to come back to this at another time.

▶ Standardised assessment tools

A number of standardised assessment tools have been developed for use with mental health service users in clinical settings, some of which can also be used for evaluation and research purposes.

Developed at the Institute of Psychiatry at King's College London, the Camberwell Assessment of Need (CAN) consists of a series of questionnaires covering 22 aspects of the lives of people with mental health problems. The perceptions of carers and mental health workers can also be assessed, and the completed CAN may be used in drawing up a care plan. The CAN-C provides an in-depth assessment of needs, while a shorter version, the CANSAS, can be used to provide a summary of a service user's current problems and the care being provided.

The Institute of Psychiatry at King's College London also developed the CUES-U (Carer and User Expectation of Services) questionnaire, designed to elicit service users' views of the mental health and community support services they are receiving, along with ratings of practical issues including housing and financial matters, daytime activities and social life. It can be used as part of the care planning process, as part of evaluation and audit cycles, and can feed in to service planning and commissioning (Lelliott et al, 2001).

The FACE (Clifford, 2005) risk assessment profile is a tool to help mental health workers assess and manage all types of risk. If risk assessment is not documented as part of the routine CPA care planning process, the FACE profile proforma can be used to record an assessment of the service users' current risk status, risk factors and warning signs, the individual's and their carer's view of risk, and a plan for risk management and the action to be taken in the event of a crisis.

▶ The strengths model

If asked to describe ourselves to someone who does not know us, most of us will talk positively about the things we like doing or are good at. We might say 'I'm a poet', or 'I work as a teacher but my real passion is ballroom dancing', or 'I'm the father of two sons who like to watch sport on TV.' It is unlikely that we would start off by saying 'I find it hard to manage my financial affairs', or 'I'm a hopeless mum'. It is evident that our strengths are more important to us than our weaknesses, and our strengths enable us to cope with the stresses and strains of everyday life (Rapp, 1993 and 1998).

When someone is experiencing mental distress, this principle should also hold true. It is their strengths that will help them cope with their problems, so it is important that the worker understands what they are so they can incorporate them into the plan of care. Similarly, it is important for the individual not to lose sight of who they are as a person, what they are like when they are well. Acknowledging an individual's strengths in this way empowers the service user, giving them more control over the way their care and treatment are planned and delivered, as well as the goals that are to be achieved, and creates a more equal and less dependent relationship with the mental health worker.

Using this approach, which clearly forms a significant part of the Essential Shared Capabilities, moves workers away from a preoccupation and concentration on problems and deficits, which can have a demoralising effect on service users.

▶ The recovery model

The recovery model presents a way at looking at mental ill health that is very different to the traditional medical model of illness, treatment and cure. It assumes that everyone has the potential to change and develop, and includes the elements of hope and empowerment for the service user. Individuals' use of self-help skills and strategies to complement interventions by mental health workers enables them to achieve levels of wellness, stability and recovery (Allott, 2004).

▶ The tidal model

Developed by mental health nurses in Newcastle (Barker & Buchanan-Barker, 2004), this model of inpatient care depends on collaboration between the worker and the service user, empowers the individual by putting their experience at the heart of the care plan, and uses the individual's needs and strengths as the basis to resolve problems and promote their mental health. A holistic assessment, which is recorded in the service user's own words, is used to develop an overall care plan. Daily care planning focuses on how the person is progressing towards their goals, and a security plan records strategies for coping with identified risk factors.

▶ The care plan

The CPA care plan, drawn up after the individual's needs have been assessed and in conjunction with the individual, not only guides the worker by setting out what care they should be delivering, it can also be a therapeutic tool in its own right. It can be used to engage the service user in planning the care and treatment given, in setting the goals they are working towards and assessing to what extent they have reached them. Acknowledging that most mental health care is provided by staff working in teams, it can also ensure a continuity of approach and set out any specific interventions to be provided by staff from different professional groups. Care plans are important as a professional record of assessments carried out and care delivered, and may also have legal significance in some instances. Service users should always be involved in drawing up their care plan, and should also sign it to indicate this involvement. Signing a care plan may not always indicate that the service user is in agreement with all elements of it, and any comments or objections they have should be recorded, as should the reason for them not signing it if that is the case.

The care plan should set out, as specifically as possible, all the interventions and activities in relation to a service user's ongoing care and treatment. It is important to specify who is going to do what and by when. CPA care plans are subject to ongoing review.

▶ Involving service users

Involving service users in care planning and the whole CPA process is explicit in the guidance for its implementation, and some research has been done, much of it conducted by service users themselves, to find out how well service users have been involved in the process and what they think about the CPA. These studies

(Beeforth, Conlan & Graley, 1994; Rose, 2003) suggest that while service users are not universally involved in the CPA relating to their needs, when they *are* involved in the process they are happier with the services they receive.

There are examples of NHS trusts making good progress in this area. For example, South West London and St George's Mental Health NHS Trust has improved service users' involvement in their own care planning. Service users particularly welcomed the decision that all correspondence between professionals (e.g. mental health staff and GPs) must be copied to the person it referred to. The Trust also utilised the CUES-U to enable individuals to describe and record their wishes about the services they were getting. In addition, training was provided for staff, jointly led by service user and professional trainers, which covered not just the use of the CUES-U but also broader issues of service user involvement.

As part of its Partners in Care project, the Royal College of Psychiatrists produced a number of guides aimed at helping service users, carers and psychiatrists to work in partnership, available as free leaflets and downloadable from the Web site. The checklist for service users (Timms, 2004a) lists questions an individual may want to ask their psychiatrist about their diagnosis, treatment and care, including what to do in an emergency and how to make a complaint.

Activity 8.3

Look at a care plan for a service user with whom you are working. Does the plan state clearly what interventions and activities are to take place? Does it also specify who is going to do what and by when? How was the service user involved in drawing up the plan?

▶ Advance statements and advance directives

Service users can have a say in how they wish to be treated during future episodes of mental health care by formally recording them in the form of advance statements and advance directives. Drawing up advance statements or directives can be a useful tool to aid discussion and negotiation between service users, carers and staff, which can strengthen the therapeutic alliance and improve care planning.

Advance statements set out service users' wishes, which should be taken into account by those who are involved in providing care or treatment in the future. They enable the person to say in advance how they would like to be treated in a certain set of circumstances, for example in a situation when they were unable to communicate their wishes in other ways. Although they are not legally binding, mental health workers should respect advance statements as far as possible, and explain to the service user if some elements cannot be complied with. Advance statements can include service users' preferences about medication, financial matters and arrangements for taking care of their children, home and pets if they are admitted to hospital.

Advance directives enable service users to choose both to opt in and to opt out of various forms of treatment, such as a particular type of medication or other treatment, for example ECT. An advance directive in which an individual chooses to 'opt in' to a specific treatment is known as a Ulysses contract. Although not covered specifically by English legislation, advance directives are likely to be legally binding under common law. The position in Scotland is different, where recent mental health legislation provides for advance statements to come into effect when an individual is to be detained or receive compulsory treatment; this must be taken into consideration by those responsible for their care, but may be overruled by staff in certain circumstances.

A number of voluntary organisations (e.g. Age Concern, Alzheimer's Society, Mental Health Foundation, Mind, Rethink) have produced clear fact sheets for service users about advance statements and directives, which are available in paper form and free to download from the Internet, and several NHS Trusts have developed their own documentation to help staff and service users.

Activity 8.4

Find out what your organisation's policy is on advance directives and advance statements. Do any of the service users you are working with have advance directives or advance statements? Consider the needs of one service user: what issues would they like to have incorporated into an advance directive or advance statement?

▶ **Involving carers**

Mental health workers are sometimes unsure how to involve the carers of the service users they are seeing, and may be concerned to what extent they should be discussing issues that could be considered confidential. The key message here is that service users should always be involved in the decision to include their carers, but this may be done ahead of time and not necessarily at the time of admission to hospital or other crisis points. Explaining that it is beneficial for their carers to be included in the assessment of their needs and strengths and in drawing up their care plan, so as to gain the fullest picture of what their problems are and what may best help them, will in many cases secure the service user's agreement, and this can be recorded so that at some future date when they may be less receptive to discussions, the worker can ensure that the carer is not excluded. The use of advance statements is useful in this situation.

The Royal College of Psychiatrists has produced information on confidentiality and sharing information, and has published a series of checklists, including ones aimed at psychiatrists and at carers, which explore these issues and suggest questions that carers may ask psychiatrists and other mental health workers about the service user they are concerned for, aiming to involve them as much as possible.

▶ Conclusion

Involvement and working in partnership are key factors in the process of identifying people's needs and strengths in a comprehensive and holistic way. Central to this process is the service user, whose preferred lifestyle and aspirations form the starting point for any assessment of needs and strengths. Their family, carers and friends should also be involved wherever relevant and feasible.

▶ References, bibliography and resources for further study

Advance statements and advance directives

Age Concern (2003) *Advance Statements, Advance Directives and Living Wills.* Information sheet, Ref IS/5. London: Age Concern, www.ageconcern.org.uk.

Alzheimer's Society (2002) *Future Medical Treatment: Advance Statements and Advance Directives or Living Wills.* Information sheet. London: Alzheimer's Society, www.alzheimers.org.uk.

Beever, A. (2002) Advance statements in mental health. *Updates Research and Policy Briefings from the Mental Health Foundation,* 4(4). September. London: Mental Health Foundation, www.mentalhealth.org.uk.

Derbyshire Mental Health Services NHS Trust (2004) *Guidelines for People Making an Advance Directive.* Derby: Derbyshire Mental Health Services NHS Trust.

Hopkinson, P. (2003) *Advance Directives Policy.* Derby: Derbyshire Mental Health Services NHS Trust.

Mind (2005) *Legal Briefing: Advance Directives.* London: Mind, www.mind.org.uk.

Rethink (2002) *Advance Directives, Statements and Agreements and Crisis Cards. Policy Statement 51.* London: Rethink, www.rethink.org.uk.

Warner, L., Mariathasan, J., Lawton-Smith, S. & Samele, C. (2006) *Choice Literature Review: A Review of the Literature and Consultation on Choice and Decision-making for Users and Carers of Mental Health and Social Care Services.* London: Sainsbury Centre for Mental Health and The King's Fund, www.scmh.org.uk or www.kingsfund.org.uk.

Assessment

Askey, R. (2004) Case management: A critical review. *Mental Health Practice,* 7(8): 12–16.

Barker, P. (2004) *Assessment in Psychiatric and Mental Health Nursing. In Search of the Whole Person* (2nd edn). Cheltenham: Nelson Thornes.

Barker, P. & Buchanan-Barker, P. (2004) *The Tidal Model: A Guide for Mental Health Professionals.* London: Brunner-Routledge. See also www.tidal-model.co.uk for further resources.

Barker, P. & Whitehill, I. (1997) The craft of care: Towards collaborative caring in psychiatric nursing. In S. Tilley (ed.), *The Mental Health Nurse: Views of Practice and Education.* Oxford: Blackwell Science.

Clifford, P. (2005) FACE: An integrated assessment and outcome system for health and social care. *National Association of Primary Care Review*, **2**: 80–81.

Department of Health (1999) *National Service Framework for Mental Health*. London: Department of Health.

Freidli, L. & Dardis, C. (2002) Not all in the mind: Mental health user perspectives on physical health. *Journal of Mental Health Promotion*, **1**(1): 36–46.

Jones, A. (2004) Matter over mind: Physical wellbeing for people with severe mental illness. *Mental Health Practice*, **7**(10): 36–8.

Lelliott, P., Beevor, A., Hogman, G., Hyslop, J., Lathlean, J. & Ward, M. (2001) Carers' and Users' Expectations of Services – User version (CUES-U): A new instrument to measure the experience of users of mental health services. *British Journal of Psychiatry*, **179**: 67–72.

National Institute for Clinical Excellence (2002) *Schizophrenia. Core Interventions in the Treatment and Management of Schizophrenia in Primary and Secondary Care. Clinical Guidance 1*. London: National Institute for Clinical Excellence.

Phelan, M., Slade, M., Thornicroft, G. *et al.* (1995) The Camberwell Assessment of Need: The validity and reliability of an instrument to assess the needs of people with severe mental illness. *British Journal of Psychiatry*, **167**: 589–95.

Seymour, L. (2003) *Not All in the Mind: The Physical Health of Mental Health Service Users*. London: mentality. Available from www.scmh.org.uk.

Stevenson, C. & Fletcher, E. (2002) The Tidal Model: The questions answered. *Mental Health Practice*, **5**(8): 29–37.

Stickley, T. & Felton, A. (2006) Promoting recovery through therapeutic risk taking. *Mental Health Practice*, **9**(8): 26–30.

Care planning and the care programme approach

Care Programme Approach Association (2003a) *The CPA Handbook*. Chesterfield: Care Programme Approach Association. See www.cpaa.co.uk for further resources.

Care Programme Approach Association (2003b) *National Standards and CPA Association Audit Tool for the Monitoring of the Care Programme Approach*. Chesterfield: Care Programme Approach Association.

Department of Health (1990a) *Caring for People. The Care Programme Approach for People with a Mental Illness Referred to Specialist Mental Health Services*. Joint Health/Social Services Circular C(90)23/LASSL(90)11. London: Department of Health.

Department of Health (1990b) *The NHS and Community Care Act*. London: HM Stationery Office.

Department of Health and Welsh Office (1993) *Mental Health Act 1983. Code of Practice*. London: HM Stationery Office.

Department of Health (2006) *Reviewing the Care Programme Approach 2006. A Consultation Document*. London: Care Services Improvement Partnership, Department of Health.

NHS Executive and Social Services Inspectorate (1999) *Effective Care Co-ordination in Mental Health Services. Modernising the Care Programme Approach. A Policy Booklet*. Londo: NHSE/SSI.

Scottish Office Home and Health Department (1992) *Community Care Guidance on Care Programmes for People with a Mental Illness Including Dementia*. SOHHD DGM 1992/9 and SWI 1992/1. Edinburgh: Scottish Office Home and Health Department.

Timms, P. (ed.) (2004a) *Partners in Care. A Checklist for People with Mental Health Problems*. London: Royal College of Psychiatrists, www.partnersincare.co.uk.

Tunmore, R. & Thomas, B. (2000) Nursing care plans in acute mental health nursing. *Mental Health Practice*, **4**(3): 32–7.

Warner, L. (2005) *The Review of the Literature on the Care Programme Approach*. London: Sainsbury Centre for Mental Health, www.scmh.org.uk.

Welsh Assembly Government (2002) *A National Service Framework for Wales – Adult Mental Health Services.* Cardiff: Welsh Assembly Government.

Essential shared capabilities

Department of Health (2004) *The Ten Essential Shared Capabilities: A Framework for the Whole of the Mental Health Workforce.* London: Department of Health/NHSU/Sainsbury Centre/NIMHE.

Involving carers

Allison, S., Fadden, G., Hart, D., Launer, M. & Siddle, J. (2004) *Carers and Confidentiality in Mental Health. Issues Involved in Information Sharing.* London: Royal College of Psychiatrists. Available from www.partnersincare.co.uk.

Timms, P. (ed.) (2004a) *Partners in Care. A Checklist for Carers of People with Mental Health Problems.* London: Royal College of Psychiatrists. Available from www.partnersincare.co.uk.

Timms, P. (ed.) (2004b) *Partners in Care. A Checklist for Psychiatrists.* London: Royal College of Psychiatrists. Available from www.partnersincare.co.uk.

Involving service users

Beeforth, M., Conlan, E. & Graley, R. (1994) *Have We Got Views for You: User Evaluation of Case Management.* London: Sainsbury Centre for Mental Health.

Langan, J. & Lindow, V. (2004) *Living with Risk: Mental Health Service User Involvement in Risk Assessment and Management.* York: Joseph Rowntree Foundation/The Policy Press.

Lawson, M., Strickland, C. & Wolfson, P. (1999) User involvement in care planning. The Care Programme Approach (CPA) from the users' perspective. *Psychiatric Bulletin,* **23**: 539–41.

McDermott, G. (1998) The care programme approach: A patient perspective. *Nursing Times Research,* **3**(1): 47–63.

Perkins, R. & Goddard, K. (2004) Reality out of the rhetoric: Increasing user involvement in a Mental Health Trust. *Mental Health Review,* **9**(1): 21–4.

Repper, J. & Perkins, R. (2003) *Social Inclusion and Recovery: A Model for Mental Health Practice.* London: Bailliere Tindall.

Rose, D. (2003) Partnership, co-ordination of care and the place of user involvement. *Journal of Mental Health,* **12**(1): 59–70.

Webb, Y., Clifford, P., Fowler, V., Morgan, C. & Hanson, M. (2000) Comparing patients' experience of mental health service in England: A five-Trust survey. *International Journal of Health Care Quality Assurance,* **13**(6): 273–81.

Recovery model

Allott, P. (2004) What is mental health, illness and recovery? In Ryan, T. and Pritchard, J. (eds) *Good Practice in Adult Mental Health.* London: Jessica Kingsley.

Boston Center for Psychiatric Rehabilitation, USA. Further resources available at www.bu.edu/cpr/.

Copeland M. (undated) *Mental Health Recovery Including Wellness Recovery Action Planning.* Available from www.mentalhealthrecovery.com/art_wrap.html.

Frese, F., Stanley, J., Kress, K. & Vogel-Scibilia, S. (2001) Integrating evidence-based practices and the recovery model. *Psychiatric Services*, **52**(11): 1462–8.

Gillam, T. (2006) Positive approaches to schizophrenia. *Mental Health Practice*, **10**(4): 30–33.

Hamilton County Community Mental Health Board. Resources on the recovery model available at www.mhrecovery.com.

May, R. (2002) Making sense of psychotic experience and working towards recovery. In J. F. M. Gleeson & P. D. McGorry (eds) *Psychological Interventions in Early Psychosis: A Treatment Handbook*. Chichester: John Wiley & Sons Ltd.

National Institute of Mental Health in England. Resources on the recovery model available at www.nimhe.csip.org.uk/virtual-ward/empowerment-and-recovery/ self-direction /recovery.html?keywords=recovery.

Strengths model

Rapp, C. (1993) *Theory, Principles and Methods of Strengths Model of Case Management*. In M. Harris & H. C. Bergman (eds), *Case Management for Mentally Ill Patients: Theory and Practice*. Newark, NJ: Harwood Academic Publishers.

Rapp, C. (1998) *The Strengths Model: Case Management with People Suffering from Severe and Persistent Mental Illness*. New York: Oxford University Press.

CHAPTER NINE

Providing service user centred care

Laura Lea
Service user and coordinator of a service user group, teacher and trainer in mental health care

The seventh essential shared capability is Providing Service User Centred Care. The Department of Health (2004) describes this capability as:

> Negotiating achievable and meaningful goals; primarily from the perspective of service users and their families. Influencing and seeking the means to achieve these goals and clarifying the responsibilities of the people who will provide any help that is needed, including systematically evaluating outcomes and achievements

This chapter explores the context and delivery of service user centred care. It examines the rights of the service user and the values and attitudes that underpin service user centred care, with particular reference to the Human Rights Act 1998. Advocacy and communication are both highlighted as key ingredients and necessary requirements for goal setting within the context of the Care Programme Approach (CPA). A recovery approach and the Wellness Recovery Action Plan (WRAP) are outlined. Goal setting is explored in some depth. This chapter is written from the viewpoint of the service user and carer and reflects the concerns and experiences of service users and carers.

Figure 9.1 illustrates the range of factors that might affect any one person's mental well-being.

The causes and remedies of a person's mental distress are not just a matter of how the individual service user and mental health worker respond to a set of personal circumstances. Some problems lie outside the personal domain and are societal rather than personal. Research on the experiences of people from ethnic minorities in the UK supports the view that individuals within some groups are more likely to develop mental distress, and some of this distress may be

Learning About Mental Health Practice. Edited by Theo Stickley and Thurstine Basset
© 2008 John Wiley & Sons, Ltd

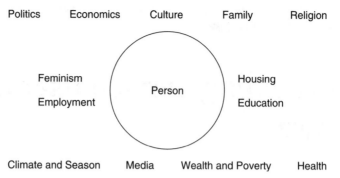

Politics   Economics   Culture   Family   Religion

Feminism   Housing

Person

Employment   Education

Climate and Season   Media   Wealth and Poverty   Health

Figure 9.1   Factors that affect well-being.

exacerbated or caused by the way mental health services respond to those groups. For example:

> Women born in India and East Africa have a 40 per cent higher suicide rate than those born in England and Wales. The suicide rate amongst young Asian women is twice the national average. Wives who cannot have children or produce only daughters seem to be at greatest risk. (Hatloy, 2004)

> Young black men [have been found] to be six times more likely than their white contemporaries to be sectioned under the Mental Health Act for compulsory treatment [even] though international studies showed they were not genetically more susceptible to serious mental illness. (Carvel, 2005)

Emphasising the individual aspects of mental distress is a failing of mental health service provision. In the past, mental distress has variously been identified as a matter of genetics, 'strength or weakness of character' and psychological make-up. However, culture, society and politics have a direct impact on the experience of mental ill health and the provision of care. These wider sociological issues play in to the specifics of everyday experience and care provision. Addressing mental distress only on an individual basis inhibits and denies the creativity required to provide real service user centred care.

Activity 9.1

Broadly speaking, what does service user centred care mean to you? Record some notes on this topic.

Here are some examples of what a service user might want from service user centred care:

- To be greeted warmly and with respect when ringing up.

- To be offered adequate information about the support services when discharged from hospital.

- Not to be told by the crisis team that 'the worker isn't here, try phoning the other number' (the one you just tried!).

- Not to have to knock on a reinforced glass window to attract attention when entering the building.

- To be able to get a decent hair cut while an inpatient.

- To be allowed to take communion while an inpatient.

Managing care so that these, and other ordinary needs are met is the foundation of service user centred care. These 'everyday' needs, when neglected, leave people feeling hurt and devalued. Generally the service user does not have the power to ensure that these types of need are met. Neither may it be a requirement of the individual worker's job description to ensure their provision. Yet each one of the examples given relates to achieving service user centred care and the basic right to be treated with dignity. Without an adequate response to these needs, any care offered by a worker, no matter how skilled they are in working with someone on an individual basis, will be inadequate.

▶ Human rights, values and attitudes

Some mental health workers and service users believe that the experience of mental distress may represent the only option left to the person living with that particular set of circumstances. Certainly it can be argued that the experience of distress is about a person having no other available resources to meet the demands of life at that time.

It is the experience of service users and the observation of workers that some people with distress are neglected because they are unable to voice their needs or, at the other extreme, regarded as a 'nuisance' and as 'difficult' (when workers might think or say 'oh no, not him/her again'). This neglects the reality that most service users and their families or carers are doing the best they can with what they've got. Take the following comments from a service user:

> I knew I had a problem but I didn't understand it and I didn't want to admit the extent of it. I turned down the first drug they offered – Lorazepam – because I knew it was addictive and I didn't want to get addicted. I didn't get offered the medication I thought I should have [chlomipramine, an antidepressant] but they agreed to offer me support and I suppose they were monitoring me too. It was only when I started to refer to myself as 'she' and really couldn't tell dreaming from waking that the nurse (whom I trusted) decided that enough was enough. I then got given some

heavy-duty drugs. In the end, it took three changes of drugs to get me on to the right antidepressant – Chlomipramine. I still can't express adequately how terrible it was.

Service Provision

In offering service user centred care, current policies require workers to continue to offer respect, dignity and hope even when faced with stuckness, repetitive behaviour and seemingly entrenched hopelessness. It is the task of the worker to develop a clear view of what service user centred care means, and indeed also to look after themselves as they work towards this gold standard.

The Human Rights Act (1998) enshrines in law the rights and freedoms guaranteed to European Union citizens by incorporating the articles of the European Convention of Human Rights. Articles that directly bear on the provision of mental health care and offering service user centred care are:

- Article 3: Prohibition of Torture. No one should be subjected to torture or inhuman or degrading treatment or punishment.

- Article 5: The Right to Liberty and Security. A person has the right to liberty and security of person.

- Article 8: The Right to Respect for Private and Family Life. A person has a right to a private life, family life, home and correspondence.

- Article 9: Freedom of Thought, Conscience and Religion. A person has the right to manifest their religion or belief in worship, teaching, practice and observance.

Workers are required to uphold the rights in each of these articles and to be centred on ensuring that they are met for both inpatient and community-based users of mental health services and their families. The complexities of maintaining human rights when both service users and staff may find themselves in sometimes extreme situations, particularly in acute mental health units, may focus the workers and service users away from these rights and towards mental health legislation that allows the compulsory detention and treatment of citizens who have not committed a criminal act. In these circumstances, the values enshrined in the Human Rights Act allow any worker or service user a standard against which care can be measured. The Human Rights Act (1998) provides the foundation on which mental health legislation should be enacted in practice. Human rights legislation applies to both formal/detained and informal/voluntary patients staying in hospital.

Both the *Acute Solutions* report on in patient care (Sainsbury Centre for Mental Health, 2006) and the *With Safety in Mind* report from the NHS National Patient Safety Agency (2006) report significant ongoing difficulties with inpatient care.

For example, the NHS National Patient Safety Agency (2006) report reveals 865 incidents of severe harm or death to patients and 122 incidents involving sexual safety, 19 of which included allegations of rape. In some cases this involved criminal behaviour by staff.

Health and social care practitioners who look back over their years as workers will probably, with hindsight, be able to identify a time when they witnessed poor or abusive practice. They may not have challenged it because they were too young, too inexperienced, didn't have enough knowledge, didn't notice it fully, were scared or felt it wasn't their business. They may not have been able to grasp the full implications of the situation. In many ways a worker's experience when they witness poor practice but do not intervene mirrors some of the experiences of the service user: events are not fully understood, there is no intervention and matters pursue their own course.

Providing service user centred care requires that mental health practitioners are awake to any oppressive and discriminatory practices found in their work settings, and to the experience that service users and carers have while using the mental health service. In situations where a person needs care and is fearful that this may be withdrawn if they don't cooperate, or if they raise a concern, a culture of silence may be reinforced.

Activity 9.2

Consider the following questions:

- To what extent do you feel that the care in inpatient units meet the expectations of the Human Rights Act?

- What will you do if you see practice that you believe is not service user centred and that violates someone's human rights?

- How will you look after the service user or carer?

- How will you look after yourself?

Advocacy

Advocacy addresses the questions: How will we speak for ourselves? And who will speak for us? Advocacy enables the powerless to speak when they have little or no power to speak confidently for themselves. The status, knowledge and employment rights that come with being a mental health professional ensure that power rests firmly in such professionals' hands. They are the 'gatekeepers' of the service. Any given event that takes place in a mental health setting belongs to their working world. The process of giving health and social care is managed by the practitioner. In contrast, the service user and carer's experience is very different. As receivers of care, they have little control or influence. Furthermore, it is the service user and carer's life that has been overwhelmed by mental distress.

Advocacy is founded on the belief that when someone is unable to speak for themselves they should be supported to express their needs, wants, concerns and goals. To provide advocacy ensures that the interests of justice, fair representation, citizenship and service user centred care are met.

The Advocacy Standards project at Mind produced these key recommendations (Mind, 2007):

- Advocacy is an essential process which supports individuals to negotiate the often daunting mental health system, have their voice heard, and be empowered when using mental health services. It must be commissioned and promoted as such and should never be viewed as secondary to care and treatment services.

- An appropriate advocate should be made available to anyone who is being sectioned under the Mental Health Act 1983.

The project offers points to best practice by highlighting gaps in advocacy services, including the need for substantial and on-going funding.

Activity 9.3

Consider and answer these questions:

- What do you feel you need to do to counteract the imbalance of power between yourself and service users and their families?

- What do you know about advocacy services that are available in your locality/area of work?

▶ Enabling service user centred care

Providing service user centred care means enabling a person to achieve their goals. The worker must have this as a significant priority. This requires the practitioner to ask questions and listen accurately while valuing the expertise of the service user and carer.

This seventh Essential Shared Capability gives some detail about how goals should be set. It requires the worker to be 'helping the service user to set goals that are realistic, achievable and meaningful' (Department of Health, 2004).

Health and social care workers need a wide enough perspective, either within themselves or by using the benefits of multidisciplinary or multi-agency resources, to see that success in achieving the immediate goals of the service user does not lie only in the worker's ability to facilitate goal setting, but also in their ability to be a radical advocate for change both within the organisation providing the care and within the community. In determining their next action the worker needs to be awake to the factors that may be influencing their thinking. By being explicit with the service user and carer about how the worker's knowledge, experience and opinions affect the situation, service users and carers are more able to separate their own ideas about goals from those of the worker and the health and social care system. This facilitates a more balanced negotiation of goals. In doing this, power is offered back to the service user and carer and a negotiation can take place.

As a person enters the mental health system, there is often no alternative but to accentuate the welfare (being looked after) and control aspects of mental health care. As the person is offered the opportunity to express their own needs and wants and ultimately set small and achievable goals, recovery and self-determination emerge.

While a worker may be communicating with a service user for many reasons other than to facilitate service user centred care, the key to enabling recovery is helping the person concerned to begin to understand that there are possibilities for a better, useful and hopeful life. This evolves as the service user and worker develop a shared understanding of what might bring pleasure and a sense of self-worth, success and achievement for the person concerned. When communication is service user centred, it leads to the process of rebuilding both internally and externally (in the person's environment). Communication that leans more heavily towards satisfying the service's need to make sure it is managing its resources and ensuring that it isn't making the headlines on the front page of a tabloid newspaper leaves service users feeling at best lost, and at worst badly cared for.

In order to achieve service user centred care and set goals that are realistic, achievable, meaningful and measurable, the worker will need to:

- Work alongside the service user to help them to describe their goals as precisely as possible in a way that is meaningful to them.

- Help the service user to identify and use their strengths to achieve their goals and aspirations.

- Identify the strengths and resources within the service user's wider network which have a role to play in supporting goal achievement.

- Ensure that any goal setting is driven by the needs of the service user.

- Ensure that any goals are achievable and measurable.

- Understand the difference between broader long term, short term and more specific goals.
  (All above quotes from Department of Health, 2004)

▶ Communication

One service user said: 'When I got ill, I couldn't say anything about anything, I just kept saying I'm confused, I'm confused.'

Many service users find it is their experience that they are unable to express important things about their lives to mental health workers. Some of the most important things in a person's life, such as their spirituality, may be held close to the service user who feels that this is too precious or inappropriate to be talked about, or that their dearly held beliefs may be labelled as part of an illness. Particularly in the area of spirituality, service users may feel that they will be judged harshly if they discuss their beliefs, and yet some 50% of service users say that their spiritual beliefs are significant to them (Mental Health Foundation, 1997).

This author would argue that the historical primacy of the medical model has led to practice where problems are looked for and then assessed (in order to find a pharmacological solution), rather than looking for solutions that are centred in the service user's daily experience of life (including, for example, in their spirituality or religious belief). The whole process of risk management and assessing and providing appropriate medication is built on being alert to problems and symptoms. It is not about finding where someone may already have a capacity or strength for building success.

Activity 9.4

Consider a service user with whom you are working and answer these questions:

- What sorts of questions are you asking about the person?

- How are you asking them?

- Are you aware of what you don't know about the service user's and their family's experience?

▶ The care programme approach (CPA)

For many service users, the experience of mental distress is all consuming. That is the power of mental illness. As their mental distress becomes both over-attended to in the sense of time, thought and feeling and at the same time under-attended to in the sense of finding management techniques and better narratives with which to view the problem, service users slip into an identity that does not always promote recovery. In the meantime, workers carry on doing their job, churning through the next intake of inpatients or referrals. By failing to address the service user's wider goals and by failing to offer strategies that enable the service user to notice small achievements, service users' lives and goals begin to coalesce around an identity of social exclusion, involving unemployment, poverty, family breakdown and dependence on services. Figures from the Social Exclusion Unit's report *Mental Health and Social Exclusion* (2004) reveal that adults with mental health problems are one of the most excluded groups in society:

- Only 24% of adults with long-term mental health problems are in work.

- Those with jobs have double the risk of losing their job.

- People with mental health problems are three times more likely to be in debt.

- People with severe mental health problems are three times more likely to be divorced than those without.

The Care Programme Approach (CPA) was introduced in 1991 and is designed to provide a framework for the delivery of effective mental health care within the statutory services. It covers the development of procedures; it is a process; and it incorporates a set of values that are aimed at promoting independence, involvement, risk taking and professional accountability for the duty of care. CPA recognises: 'All mental health service users have a range of needs which no one treatment, service or agency can meet' (Department of Health, 1999). Providing service user centred care can only take place if the needs and strengths of the service user have been adequately identified (as covered in previous chapters of this book).

Policy and guidance in relation to the CPA states that the service user should be given full information about the CPA process and be in possession of a copy of the agreed care plan, which should (Department of Health, 1999):

- Identify the interventions and anticipated outcomes.

- Record all the actions necessary to achieve the agreed goals.

It is unfortunate that despite this very clear requirement, the author's experience is that many service users are still not given a written copy of the care plan, do not understand its significance and are unable to use this process as a resource to promote their own recovery.

It is possible that, because CPA is so closely linked with service process and procedure and mental health workers need to ensure that they fulfil their legal and organisational responsibilities, it fails to be understood as a tool with which to help service users take responsibility for their own health and well-being. Generally, care plans are generated by the service and held by the service in a file. This, of itself, carries a strong statement about who owns the problem.

▶ The recovery approach, wellness recovery action plan (WRAP)

The recovery approach has its roots in the experiences of service users taking control of their health and life. Plans that arise from this approach have a greater likelihood of being service user centred. (Any goals belong to the service user, not the worker or the service.)

RECOVERY DEVON (2007) describe a recovery approach as one that:

■ Facilitates the recovery of a meaningful and satisfying life as defined by the person themselves.

■ Looks at the needs and strengths of the individual first, empowers people to manage their own health by giving appropriate levels of support, encourages independence or interdependence with less reliance on services and offers flexible, respectful and creative support.

■ Sees people beyond their problems and appreciates their abilities, possibilities, interests and dreams.

■ Helps people to recover the social roles and relationships that give their life value and meaning.

'The Wellness Recovery Action Plan (WRAP) is a self-management and recovery system developed by a group of people who had mental health difficulties' (Copelandcentre.com, no date). Originally developed by Mary Ellen Copeland in the USA, its use within the UK is now more widespread as both service users and service providers seek ways of developing a recovery process.

WRAP offers service users (and their supporters) a systematic approach to recovery, which is not always available within the CPA process. The service user is the central focus of the experience of completing the plan for managing and working towards recovery. The service user also has responsibility for monitoring their own health and developing strategies for dealing with escalating ill health.

WRAP is designed to:

■ Decrease and prevent intrusive or troubling feelings and behaviours.

■ Increase personal empowerment.

■ Improve quality of life.

■ Assist people in achieving their own life goals and dreams.

The person who experiences symptoms is the one who develops their personal WRAP. It enables them to:

■ Recognise their own early warning signs/symptoms.

■ Identify specific skills and tools to cope with these symptoms.

■ Create a crisis plan that lists their supporters.

■ Incorporate tools for staying well into their daily routine.

(Copelandcentre.com, no date)

When the service user sets goals and begins to achieve these, recovery is taking place. The Wellness Recovery Action Plan enables the service user to be the centre point of the process of finding a way towards better health, while also addressing the concerns of the service, such as having a:

- daily maintenance plan
- crisis plan
- post-crisis plan

In the hands of the service user, goal setting offers the person who wants to feel well a possibility of regaining a whole life, with tools to deal with the stresses of illness and living. Furthermore, this type of goal setting ensures that the solutions to 'feeling well' are likely to be the right ones.

Activity 9.5

Find out more about WRAP – is it being used in your locality/area of work? If possible, speak with a service user who has experience of using WRAP.

▶ **Setting goals**

In the frustration of trying to support a service user to set goals in a difficult situation, the worker can be tempted to impose goals. At its worst there is a real mismatch between the suggested goal and the service user's experience of life and likes and dislikes. This leads to a sense of increased isolation in service users, who feel they aren't being heard. Often they withdraw from the service, while the mental health worker may even believe that they have been involved in a successful piece of work. The real outcome may be that a significant mental health problem goes undiagnosed and unattended and leads to a lifetime of mental distress, with ramifications for the person, people around them and society.

For example, if a worker assesses a young mother as being isolated and suggests she needs to get some exercise by going swimming (which she probably knows already), but forgets to ask if she likes swimming and how she is going to get there and deal with three small children on her own, nothing has been achieved apart from increasing a belief in the service user that there isn't anyone who can help. The worker, with the best intentions, has attempted to impose a goal on the service user. Providing service user centred care requires the worker to elicit meaningful and small, achievable goals of significance and then to facilitate the outcomes.

But workers must be careful not to restrict service users' ambitions. Many service users describe limited opportunities for work. When they do achieve paid employment, it often does not reflect their abilities or potential.

The Social Exclusion Report (2004) states that only 24% of people with mental health issues in the UK are working, compared to 58% in the USA. One service user in the UK commented: 'My mental health worker told me not to worry about getting back to work. They had no idea how trapped I felt being at home.'

Some goals that service users set may seem unrealistic. But who is to determine what is realistic? It is easy to assume that because it appears that someone has made little progress in achieving their goals, this will always be the case. For example, it is possible for service users to begin work or return to paid employment after many years of ill health. Workers, family and friends might assume that because someone has been unemployed for five or ten years, this will always be the case. As another service user reported: 'None of my mental health workers understood how important it was for me to find a job. It took me eight years to find some sort of paid employment and ten years and three months to work enough hours to be eligible for working persons tax credit.'

Health or social care workers who don't recognise the issue of sustaining employment, or being involved in useful and confidence-building daytime activities, as a central goal for all service users are not addressing the issues of exclusion and isolation. If these are not addressed, the illness rather than the person is dictating lifestyle, and choice is removed from the service user concerned, with the consequence of further ill health.

Any goal needs to be specific and measurable. Often a goal is set with a service user for a piece of work. However, it might be very general. For example, a service user might say 'I want to stop worrying' or 'I just want it (the illness) to stop'. These statements reflect the goals and ambitions of the service users concerned. However, further analysis is needed to set a specific and measurable goal. A general statement such as 'stopping worrying' must be fully heard by the mental health worker. However, without more details, neither the worker nor the service user has a clear picture of what this involves or how they will know when things have changed.

If the goal is too general, then neither the service user nor the worker can see if any change has been achieved. To elicit more detailed information about a service user's goals, appropriate questions might be:

- What does this mean?

- How do you experience worry?

- When are the worst times for worry?

- What helps when you feel like that?

- How will you know you are worrying less?

- Tell me about times you worry less? What are you doing?

- What about the opposite way of seeing things – when do you feel fine?

- How can we build on that?

Activity 9.6

Try asking some of the questions above of a service user with whom you are working.

> Alternatively, have a discussion with a friend about life goals (such as giving up smoking or taking more exercise) and try to break these down to be as specific and measurable as possible.

'Brief solution focused' therapy (developed by Steve de Shazer) offers an additional perspective in enabling a service user or carer to set useful goals. This approach challenges the more traditional problem-focused methods of assistance, and provides for a strengths-based solution to creating change. In asking the key (miracle) question 'If you wake up tomorrow and everything is OK. What would be the first things you notice?' very specific goals are identified as a starting point (see www.brief-therapy.org/steve–miracle.htm).

> When there is a problem many professionals often spend a great deal of time thinking, talking and analyzing the problem. This can stop them thinking about what might help to get to solutions. Even the most chronic problems have periods or times when they do not occur or are less intense. By studying these times when problems are less severe or absent, it has been found that people do many positive things that they are not fully aware of. (www.brief-therapy.org)

Brief therapy examines not the problem, but the inbuilt human ability to keep on functioning in nearly all situations and to experience better moments even amid stress and illness.

Goal setting, and particularly noticing and celebrating the achievement of reaching a specific goal, acts as a building block in the process of recovery. In understanding a person's goals and aspirations, the mental health worker also achieves connection and offers the gift of fully hearing the person concerned. This makes it more likely that they will avoid delivering a service that is mismatched to the service user's and carer's needs and ambitions. Better outcomes are achieved for both the service user and the service.

A goal should be set within a given time frame. The time frame should allow for the goal to be reached with success. It helps people to have a time frame. As a service user noted: 'The nurse said he expected me to be better in a year. I didn't believe him but it gave me some sort of an idea and it meant someone thought it was possible.'

Service users often find that a mental health worker has a picture of how their illness might develop. This is often shared with the service user concerned. While it can give some comfort and hope, particularly if the information has been directly requested by the service user or carer concerned, this type of goal setting is not service user centred. It is about the expectations of the worker and the service for a reduction in symptoms, and probably a reduction in the involvement of the service.

It is best to avoid generalised goals such as 'being better' and to set specific goals such as 'going to the supermarket once a week' or 'being able to go into town for a cup of coffee when I feel like it'. These are measurable goals that can be set within a time frame and allow for a more ordinary life to emerge. In order to achieve these goals, more detailed analysis of any barriers that may prevent the service user reaching the targets would be necessary.

Goals need to be both short term and long term. Supporting someone to set small goals leads to the next small step and then the next – it is part of the process of beginning to believe in the possibility of well-being. Setting small goals enables the opportunity for success and the chance to reflect on achievement. Setting small goals also reduces the possibility of failure and allows for adjustment to a better next goal.

With all the constraints that exist in statutory mental health care, it might be argued that true service user centred care can only exist outside the statutory mental health services. Voluntary organisations like Rethink, Together and Mind have more flexibility than the statutory services. These organisations do not experience the demands of legislation and bureaucracy in the same way as the statutory mental health services. Within this sector, service users can come together to set and achieve goals that they as a group believe will benefit mental health service users and their carers.

Mind sets priorities that place the needs of the service user rather than the needs of the legislative and policy framework or the organisation above everything else, hence their priority in researching and providing an advocacy service to enable the service user to express their goals and desires.

Statutory mental health services are increasingly moving towards a recovery approach, which recognises the centrality of the experience of living life and seeks to move away from the outdated, yet tenacious, model of curing a set of symptoms, principally by prescribing medication. Commissioning teams and NHS Trusts are increasingly looking to ensure that the service user can be assisted in expressing an independent opinion. The Patient Advice and Liaison Services (PALS) provide this. By supporting PALS, recognition is given by policy makers of the legitimacy of the dialogue that needs to take place in order to air complicated issues, where many less than ideal factors produce an outcome with which the service user and carer are often unhappy. It enhances the probability that service user centred care will become a reality and redresses the imbalance of power between service user and service provider (see www.pals.nhs.uk).

Increasingly, citizens can gain access to information that previously only medical professionals held. Professional bodies now see it as part of their care to make extensive information available (see www.rcpsych.ac.uk). As part of the process of democratisation of medical, psychological and social knowledge, the Expert Patient Programme enables patients with a chronic health problem to approach their health issues with a basic understanding of how to set meaningful, achievable and measurable goals that promote better health (see www.expertpatients.nhs.uk).

> **Activity 9.7**
>
> Answer the following questions:
>
> - How can you ensure you make the most of the short time you have with the service user?
> - How do you keep centred on the service user's goals?

In the UK, many service users and carers now have access to more information about mental distress and the mental health services than ever before. Service users are finding ways of becoming more active in their approach to seeking recovery. However, it remains a fact that the terrifying, destabilising and disempowering effect of experiencing mental illness means that looking away from the medical approach to one that centres on recovery and self-management, independence and interdependence is still a little known concept for the majority of service users.

In the rush of working in stressed teams or wards where discharge is a significant goal for the worker, enabling service users and carers to understand the significance of setting their own goals, how to do this and how to obtain the support they need to achieve those goals is not always an essential priority. Nevertheless, providing service user centred care and enabling service users to set meaningful goals that they can achieve is the required standard of every mental health care worker.

If the mental health services have not yet fully adopted the concept of recovery and still tend towards a procedure-led model of CPA that fulfils the needs of the service and its goals without paying attention to its underlying values and principles, what criteria can be used to test out whether the movement of the service is towards service user centred care or towards service centred care?

Here are some suggestions:

- Service users need to be encouraged and supported to express their opinions. Service users and carers will often hold an opinion that is different to the worker and this will often be hidden from the worker.

- Workers need to be familiar with the different picture that they and the service user have of any given situation.

- Workers need to be confident in receiving feedback from service users and carers about the services that they and others offer, and treat this feedback in an open, respectful and responsive way.

- Workers need repeatedly to give information about options and opportunities, recognising the difficulties people have in absorbing information while under stress.

▶ **Conclusion**

All of us have dreams and ambitions and hopes. Goal setting is about stepping out towards finding these in our lives. Mental health workers need to understand this and ensure that goal setting by the service user is central to the care they provide. If they don't, then they do a disservice to all the people, the mothers, fathers, sons, daughters, employers, friends, and colleagues, with whom they work. By ignoring a person's goals, the possibility of further and ongoing mental ill health increases, leading to a life of exclusion and dependence. By focusing on the service user's goals, the possibility of providing service user centred care becomes a reality.

▶ **References**

Brief Solution Focused Therapy, see www.brief-therapy.org and www.brief-therapy.org/steve_miracle.htm.

Carvel, J. (2005) Move to end race bias in Mental Health Care, *The Guardian*, Jan 12, http://society.guardian.co.uk/mentalhealth/story/0,8150,1388368,00.html

Copeland centre.com, Wellness Recovery Action Plan, www.mentalhealthrecovery.com/vtrecovery.html.

Department of Health (1999) *Effective Care Co-ordination in Mental Health Services: Modernising The Care Programme Approach.* London: Department of Health.

Department of Health (2004) *The Ten Essential Shared Capabilities: A Framework for the Whole of the Mental Health Workforce.* London: Department of Health/NHSU/Sainsbury Centre/NIMHE.

The Expert Patient Programme, www.expertpatients.nhs.uk.

Hatloy, I. (2004) *Statistics 2: Suicide*, London: Mind, www.mind.org.uk/Information/Factsheets/Statistics/Statistics+2.htm.

Human Rights Act (1998) London: Stationery Office.

Mental Health Foundation (1997) *Knowing Our Own Minds.* London: Mental Health Foundation.

Mind (2007) *Advocacy Standards Project.* London: Mind, www.mind.org.uk/About+Mind/Networks/advocacy-standards-project/keyfindings.htm.

National Patient Safety Agency (2006) *With Safety in Mind: Mental Health Services and Patient Safety*, Patient Safety Observatory Report. London: National Patient Safety Agency, www.npsa.nhs.uk/site/media/documents/1846_FINAL.PSO2_MENTALHEALTH.pdf

Patient Advice and Liaison Services (PALS), www.pals.nhs.uk.

RECOVERY DEVON (2007) *Partnership for Mental Health*, Newsletter. www.recovery.co.uk.

Sainsbury Centre for Mental Health (2006) *The Search for Acute Solutions.* London: Sainsbury Centre for Mental Health.

Social Exclusion Unit (2004) *Mental Health and Social Exclusion.* London: Social Exclusion Unit.

CHAPTER TEN

Making a difference

Norman Young
Cardiff and Vale NHS Trust

Madeline O'Carroll
City University, London

Lorraine Rayner
School of Nursing, University of Nottingham

The eighth essential shared capability is Making a Difference. The Department of Health (2004) describes this capability as:

> Facilitating access to and delivering the best quality, evidence-based, values-based health and social care interventions to meet the needs and aspirations of service users and their families and carers.

In this chapter we aim to describe the transition from a novice to specialist practitioner in psychosocial interventions by detailing the goals of working with people who experience psychosis, the tasks frequently associated in achieving these goals and the general skills required to complete the tasks. Through a case example, we will illustrate how novice mental health nurses can practice in an evidence-based manner consistent with more advanced practitioners.

▶ Psychosocial interventions

Psychosocial interventions (PSI) encapsulate a range of approaches that improve outcomes for people who experience psychosis. The approaches used are based on best evidence, usually through randomised clinical trials, and are described in clinical guidelines, for example in the NICE guidelines for schizophrenia and bipolar affective disorder (National Institute for Clinical Excellence, 2003;

Learning About Mental Health Practice.   Edited by Theo Stickley and Thurstine Basset
© 2008 John Wiley & Sons, Ltd

National Institute for Health and Clinical Excellence, 2006). The types of interventions can be grouped into two categories:

- service-level interventions such as assertive outreach, systematic assessment and vocational rehabilitation

- psychosocial interventions such as cognitive behaviour therapy, family interventions and cognitive remediation

Pharmacological interventions and the monitoring of physical health complement psychosocial interventions.

People who experience psychosis value psychosocial interventions as a means to improve their health and well-being. The Thorn initiative is a leading programme for PSI skills training. The focus of this training programme is to prepare qualified mental health practitioners to practise psychosocial interventions as a speciality. After a period of consolidation and ongoing supervision, the practitioner may then look to additional training and education in order to practise at an advanced level.

Mental health practitioners during training for registration are benefiting from education and training in psychosocial interventions. For example, psychosocial interventions are among a broad range of competencies that pre-registration mental health nurses must fulfil, and in so doing reach a level of awareness of psychosocial intervention approaches. On registration, mental health nurses would only be able to practise a discrete set of interventions under supervision. As the majority of mental health nurses work with people who experience psychosis, it is imperative that, once registered, nurses continue to develop their skills in psychosocial interventions.

▶ Objectives, tasks, knowledge and skills

Peter Bates and Julie Cullen, in Chapter 27, identify the aim of psychosocial interventions as 'reducing the person's distress and promoting positive coping strategies that support recovery'.

In achieving this aim, mental health practitioners need to move away from a cure-based approach to mental health care and adopt a view that places the service user's experience at the centre of their work. Practitioners become concerned about the influence of mental illness on the service user's values, attitudes, goals, skills and roles (Roberts & Wolfson, 2004). A deeper appreciation of what recovery means to the person allows mental health practitioners to foster a collaborative relationship, through which they can take the role of coach or adviser to the person as they try to attain a personal sense of recovery.

In order to work towards recovery, it is essential that all practitioners possess a baseline of common attitudes, knowledge and skills. Hence the Ten Essential Shared Capabilities form the foundations of practice. Novice, or newly qualified, practitioners will have an awareness of psychosocial intervention approaches. In moving to specialist and more advanced practice in psychosocial interventions, practitioners focus on specific clinical objectives when working with service users. These are to:

- establish a collaborative working relationship

- complete an initial assessment

- engage in collaborative goal setting

- collaboratively formulate a working explanation for the person's situation that informs clinical decisions about interventions

- provide interventions

- review progress

Influencing how efficiently and sufficiently each objective is met are the practitioner's level of skill, the resources available to them and the receptiveness of the service user to work with them. For example, a practitioner will spend more time engaging, assessing and developing goals based on the immediate needs and goals of the service user if the person does not consider themselves in need of help from mental health services.

In unravelling how each objective can be met, it can be helpful to take a mechanistic approach and break down how progress from one objective to another is achieved. This can be done by subdividing each objective into a series of tasks. Let's take assessment as an illustration. Assessment consists of identifying and listing needs/problems/strengths, completing a history, completing a mental state examination, and administering specific tests. Practitioners will need to draw on a body of knowledge and a distinct set of skills in order to complete the tasks. Two types of knowledge will be drawn on: explicit knowledge, which can be written down and easily shared, for example signs and symptoms of psychosis; and tacit knowledge, which is often held within action and transferred through illustration, for example knowing when to soften your voice to demonstrate warmth.

Familiarity with the objectives and tasks of providing psychosocial interventions, coupled with increasing knowledge, moves the novice practitioner towards advanced practice. Novice practitioners hold a smaller knowledge base from which to draw, and therefore find filtering out relevant from irrelevant information more time consuming, spending more time selecting which action and skills to deploy at any given time. With advancing practice, the practitioner does not rely explicitly on rules and guidelines, but instead demonstrates an intuitive appreciation of situations derived from applying the principles of practice to many situations and across a range of settings. Because of this, they are able to direct their attention to the relevant presenting problem and quickly select the necessary intervention (Del Mar, Doust & Glasziou, 2006).

Self-assessment, ongoing coaching, training and supervision can improve a practitioner's knowledge and skills. Table 10.1 illustrates a self-assessment form that can be used to help practitioners reflect on their confidence and competence

Table 10.1   Self-rating of confidence and competence in cognitive behavioural session skills

Section 1: Tasks	I always have to ask for help, advice, and support **or** consult the manual to complete this task competently				I never need to ask for help, advice, and support **or** consult the manual to complete this task competently
Completing a functional analysis of a client's problem	1	2	3	4	5
Producing problem and goal statements	1	2	3	4	5
Completing a case formulation	1	2	3	4	5
Socialising the client to CBT	1	2	3	4	5
Coaching the client to link thoughts, feelings and actions	1	2	3	4	5
Coaching the client to identify the assumptions they may make	1	2	3	4	5
Coaching the client to balance the evidence supporting and not supporting their hot thoughts	1	2	3	4	5
Coaching clients to develop alternative explanations for events or experiences	1	2	3	4	5

Table 10.1   (continued)

Section 2: Skills	I always find this difficult and have to work hard at it				This skill is inherent in my practice that I never have to work hard at it
Set a collaborative agenda	1	2	3	4	5
Keep sessions on track – opening, pacing and closing	1	2	3	4	5
Provide and request feedback from clients	1	2	3	4	5
Convey understanding by summarising and reflecting back feelings as well as ideas	1	2	3	4	5
Balance the styles of teaching, leading, coaching and listening	1	2	3	4	5
Demonstrate warmth and empathy	1	2	3	4	5
Accommodate the client's wishes and suggestions	1	2	3	4	5
Elicit the client's thoughts, feelings and actions	1	2	3	4	5
Link thoughts and feelings, and elicit the client's assumptions	1	2	3	4	5

(continued overleaf)

MAKING A DIFFERENCE

Table 10.1   (continued)

Use guided discovery to determine the meaning a client attaches to an event; examine assumptions; and consider alternative explanations for events	1	2	3	4	5
Negotiate in-session and out-of-session work with the client	1	2	3	4	5

in using a set of skills to achieve therapy objectives. Using the form can aid novice practitioners in appraising their skills and planning their personal development.

> **Activity 10.1**
>
> Either use the self-assessment tool (Table 10.1) or construct your own list of tasks and skills required for your area of practice, and use the form to formulate an action plan for your personal development. Where you have identified areas that need development, write a plan that details what you will read, with whom you will talk and what clinical experiences you need to organise. Then plan out and place in your diary when these will be done.

▶ The influence of attitudes and context

In trying to define the behaviours that make up a complex intervention such as a psychosocial intervention, there is a risk that this can lead to a loss of context and detachment from the process of developing a therapeutic relationship. The environment, the patient and the practitioner form the context in which the decisions about the use of psychosocial interventions are made. Advanced practitioners are mindful of context and the broader influences on the delivery of care. They are aware that the nature of care is different when delivered at home or in a hospital environment. Hence the practice of psychosocial interventions must be placed in the context in which the practitioner and client find themselves.

In any context practitioners will act according to their attitudes and beliefs. Developing increasing self-awareness of their attitudes towards service users enables the practitioner to act from a reflective and informed position. In the case study that follows, we will see that attending to the principles of practice rather than focusing purely on tasks gives the practitioner greater scope and flexibility in their approach.

For example, one recurring task in psychosocial intervention is psychoeducation, the process whereby both clients and their families learn about mental health problems. If the practitioner is purely task focused, then they will complete this task by telling the person about their condition. However, a practitioner who at the same time attends to the principles of practice will approach the task differently. They will be aware that people should be enabled to manage their own mental health problems. They will draw on the patient's own knowledge of their condition and coach them in ways of finding additional information.

It is useful to deconstruct practice by dividing and defining its component parts. In doing so, the practice of psychosocial interventions becomes open and accessible. This also aids in the teaching and coaching of practitioners who are new to these interventions. However, the objectives and tasks need to be bound together with the principles of practice. When this is done, the practitioner is more likely to use their skills reflectively and pragmatically.

▶ psychosocial intervention skills in practice

A case example will be used to demonstrate how three objectives of psychosocial interventions can be met. These are:

- completing an assessment

- developing a shared case formulation

- delivering an intervention

For each objective, the tasks, knowledge and skills consistent with a novice practitioner will be described, followed by a discussion on how the practitioner can move forward to advanced practice.

A case example: Martha and Mathew

Martha works on an adult acute inpatient ward and is a primary nurse for five inpatients. She qualified as a mental health nurse a year ago and her confidence in taking the lead in organising and delegating work through the shift has increased over that time. Martha has an interest in developing her nursing and psychosocial intervention skills. In order to do this, she has obtained supervision and mentorship from a nurse practitioner who has

---

undertaken psychosocial interventions training through the Thorn training programme.

Mathew, aged 21, is one of the patients within Martha's primary nursing group. He was admitted to the ward a week ago following arguments at home. When he was at home, Mathew's parents were concerned about his level of self-care, his unusual behaviour and his thoughts of harming himself. Over the last year he had lost contact with his friends and was spending long periods in his room. Since leaving college, Mathew has not been able to hold down a job for very long. Each time he leaves a casual job he says that it was because he did not get on with the people there or because they did not like him.

A month ago Mathew's parents became very worried when he kept drawing the curtains and saying: 'The social are watching me.' His parents wondered whether he had done anything, but found that they only got vague answers from Mathew. They decided to call their GP, who questioned Mathew and discovered that he had been making plans to kill himself. The GP asked the crisis and home treatment team to take him on their caseload, however they considered that Mathew's mental state and his risk of self-harm were sufficient to warrant closer supervision and he was admitted to the ward that Martha worked on.

On admission, the multidisciplinary team felt that the present signs and symptoms indicated a psychotic illness. The psychiatrist decided on a working diagnosis of schizophrenia and prescribed Olanzapine 15 mg daily. Mathew was able and willing to talk about what led him to consider killing himself. His family were in contact with him through phone calls and visits to the ward every other day.

▶ Assessment

All practitioners need to be able to communicate clearly and through their communication convey emotional attunement. Less experienced staff can find it helpful to consider their contact with patients and service users as being guided by fixed rules, whereas the expert practitioner can draw on the underlying principles of 'the rules' in a much more flexible way. The first goal for any practitioner is to engage with the service user and their family. This is particularly important during a first episode of psychosis, as engagement will influence the contact that Mathew and his family have with services, and this could affect his prognosis.

Martha in practice

A sense of context is a useful place to start. In relation to Mathew, this means being curious about what happened in the period before he came into hospital, as well as knowing how long he has been an inpatient. In the context of his own life, his age is also a significant factor. Immediately this makes him quite different from someone in their middle or later years. The novice practitioner should draw on their knowledge of human development in order to have a sense of what some of the key issues are for people at this particular life stage. For example, personal identity and independence are of central importance to adolescents and young adults, and the experience of psychosis and hospitalisation can threaten both factors.

Some younger people will find it difficult to form a relationship with a nurse who is seen as an authority figure, and this difficulty may be compounded by the experience of active symptoms. One of the most important aspects of engagement is to demonstrate an empathic understanding of what it is like to be in hospital and to have strange or unfamiliar experiences that may be frightening and incomprehensible.

Engagement begins with the attitude one has towards the other person, for example whether 'assessing Mathew' becomes a task to be completed or an opportunity to get to know him. Using non-clinical language is one approach that may aid engagement, for example by using Mathew's own words to describe the experiences he is having rather than calling them hallucinations or delusions (May, 2004). The literature on early psychosis and the Ten Essential Shared Capabilities (Department of Health, 2004) recognise the importance of staff maintaining a hopeful and optimistic outlook.

It may be helpful for Martha to think about how having a psychosis might have affected Mathew. Recent conceptualisations of psychosis recognise that the impact of both psychosis and hospitalisation can be traumatic, and can result in anxiety that may also have a significant impact on coping responses (Henry, 2004).

It is not uncommon for assessment to be a prescribed activity, for example by the use of standardised documentation that the nurse has to complete within a specified time frame, particularly within inpatient settings. This type of assessment usually focuses on current mental state, identifying the presence of risk factors, personal and family history, as well as identifying strengths and needs.

A psychosocial assessment would also explore a number of additional areas. For the novice, it may be helpful to consider that much of what constitutes a psychosocial assessment is really finding out about the person's perspective and understanding of a number of key areas, such as:

- explanations for what has happened

- the impact of what has happened on personal identity

This involves finding out what Mathew thinks has happened to him. This includes exploring if he thinks he is ill or whether he has a different explanation for what has happened. Mathew may be quite puzzled about what has happened, for example he may know that 'the social' are after him but not have any idea why. By contrast, he may find the idea that he has a diagnosis of schizophrenia or psychosis quite devastating. This information is important to elicit, as it will influence subsequent interventions.

Interviewing skills are a significant part of this process and again, an awareness of context as well as the ability to manage emotions will be important (O'Carroll & Park, 2007). The interview should be used as an opportunity for exploration, and Martha may have to take care that it does not become an interrogation by her asking too many questions. The Socratic questioning method is a useful tool for getting the respondent to explore the process of what has happened (see Box 10.1).

Box 10.1 Socratic questioning.

What is it?

Socratic questioning or guided discovery is a technique used to help people explore a train of thought or belief that they hold. Typically the nature of the questioning guides the person being questioned to examine the logic underpinning their beliefs.

Why is it helpful?

The technique is useful because it avoids explaining people's experiences to them or assuming the reason behind their thinking. Through questioning the person participates fully in the search for explanations and is therefore more likely to believe in the conclusions that are reached.

How is it done?

Questions need to be understandable and address a particular goal. Secondly, questions tend to move from general questions that open up the subject area to specific questions that compare lines of thinking and help draw conclusions based on logic.

Returning to Martha and Mathew, Martha can begin to establish Mathew's knowledge about and possible commitment to starting relapse prevention work. An open question 'Mathew, in regard to your mental health, what benefits might there be for you in learning more about relapse prevention?' is preferable to saying 'Mathew, we think that you should do relapse prevention in order to avoid coming into hospital again'.

By asking Mathew the question, we anticipate that he will draw the conclusion that this is a good idea and that he uses the same logic 'in order to avoid coming into hospital'. If Mathew did not think it a good idea or could not see the point, the practitioner would draw on Mathew's response and develop specific questions that aim to elicit a conclusion that it is a good idea. Questions could be formulated to reach the conclusion through the following objectives:

■ Establish that Mathew experienced distress and impairment of his functioning prior to admission to hospital.

■ For Mathew to conclude that this distress is something to be avoided and is, at least in part, a result of mental illness.

■ For Mathew to conclude that distress and disruption in his functioning can be avoided through relapse prevention work.

Activity 10.2

Assuming that Mathew has no specific objections to doing relapse prevention work, but does not see any reason for it, devise a series of Socratic questions that will lead Mathew through to a conclusion that it is a good idea. As an aid, try looking up Socratic questioning on the Web site http://changingminds.org.

Moving towards advanced practice

Engagement

More experienced practitioners know that engagement is often the most important aspect of their work and are able to pay it the attention it requires. By contrast, the novice can sometimes become anxious that they are not 'doing' something else such as assessment, and in doing so pay less attention to the person. Martha will focus on what matters to Mathew and get to know about his interests and what he wants to do with his life. She will be aware that she is building a solid foundation for what follows.

Assessment

At this level, Martha will be able to conduct more complex assessments, including a cognitive behavioural analysis. This will help to identify the sequence of behaviours, for example whether Mathew smokes cannabis and then starts having paranoid thoughts ('the social are after me'). It might also help to provide information about why he was spending long periods in his room. This might have started as a coping strategy, but subsequently contributed to his isolation and paranoia.

Martha will be aware that the process of understanding what has happened to Mathew is as important as the information it produces. Martha will ask for the information in a calm, non-judgemental way, and will seek emotional information if it is not given, for example 'How did you feel when you thought the social were after you?' She will know that it is important for her not to jump to conclusions and assume that he felt angry or upset, but to check it out with him.

It is recognised that having a psychotic episode and being hospitalised can be extremely traumatic for some people (Henry, 2004). If this is not addressed, it can also contribute to the development of secondary morbidity in the form of anxiety and depression. Martha will be aware that she may be seen as part of the problem, and this is another reason for paying attention to developing a therapeutic alliance. She will explore with Mathew the impact of psychosis and hospitalisation on his social networks, and find out why he has lost contact with his friends. Maintaining and developing social support will be essential to his future well-being.

The assessment process requires the practitioner to manage themselves, the interaction with the other person and the information. This can be quite a complex process, and the novice will commonly find it difficult to pay attention to all of the elements. The primary focus can become the information at the expense of the interaction. Martha will have experience of both identifying and managing her own emotions, and also be alert to Mathew's emotional state. She will have developed the ability to manage the information that is produced, for example by the use of summaries and paraphrasing.

Another technique she will use is feedback – offering it to Matthew and seeking it from him. The use of feedback is an essential component of developing a collaborative style of working. Initially, she will give feedback such as 'that was very clear, I understand what happened' in order to reinforce his responses. Later, she might report her observations on his behaviour: 'Did you notice you started to look away when you spoke about your friends?' Martha will also seek feedback on her contact with Mathew. There are various ways of doing this, such as asking a general open question: 'How did you find the session?' She could also ask more specific questions, such as 'What did you like most about the session?' or 'Was there anything I said that you didn't understand or thought wasn't very helpful?'

▶ Developing a shared formulation

Case formulation is a method applied to enable both the client and the practitioner to make sense of what has led to the current circumstances and to guide the steps to recovery. The basis of any case formulation is a theoretical framework chosen because it is associated with the person's presenting problem. Case formulation is a cyclical process that is informed by the assessment and intervention phases, and these in turn direct further assessment and interventions (Tarrier, 2006).

Martha in practice

Martha will have gained a great deal of information about the events leading up to Mathew's admission to hospital. She will be keen to draw this information together, but in a way that will enable Mathew to make sense of his experiences. Martha will use the vulnerability/stress model of psychosis (Nuechterlein *et al.*, 1994) to develop a shared formulation and identify and prioritise areas for action.

The model proposes that psychosis is derived from an interaction between our genetic inheritance and our environmental experiences. Martha understands that Mathew will have inherited a level of vulnerability to psychosis and clues to the extent of this vulnerability can be obtained from taking a family history. In itself, genetic vulnerability to psychosis is not enough to trigger a psychotic episode. For this to occur, a number of personal and environmental factors must be in place. In Mathew's case, Martha is now aware that he tends to cope with stress by smoking cannabis, and that, in one of his early casual jobs, he was bullied. The interaction of these genetic and environmental aspects in some individuals is enough to trigger the development of psychosis.

Personal and environmental factors can also protect the person from psychosis. Martha knows that Mathew will have a degree of resilience to mental illness formed from his sense of self-efficacy in managing stressful life events. Having occupational and self-management skills and taking exercise both contribute to increased resilience. In addition to personal protectors, there are environmental influences such as a supportive family environment, having close friends and being in work. The interaction of both vulnerable and protective elements has led to Mathew moving from an 'at risk' state for psychosis to actually experiencing psychosis. Martha knows about Mathew's personal and family history and can see the factors that have protected him from psychosis. She also recognises those factors that have left him vulnerable to psychosis. At the same time, Martha is aware of the day-to-day issues that compromise his mental health, and the strengths Mathew can draw on to promote recovery.

Martha has finished her initial assessment and decided to move forward with her one-to-one sessions. She wants to progress from general support and day-to-day problem solving to defining the factors that have led Mathew to his present situation through a shared formulation. As a novice practitioner, Martha will be aware of the merits of adhering to the principles of the recovery approach. She will construct a shared formulation using the skills that ensure collaboration and the development of Mathew's self-efficacy. She uses the techniques of collaborative agenda setting, directing and Socratic questioning in sessions (see Box 10.1). She has enlisted Mathew as a collaborator in the process by directing him to complete the 'stress and vulnerability mind map' illustrated in Figure 10.1. Martha uses Socratic questioning to ellicit information for the map in preference to telling Mathew what she thinks are the important factors. Martha and Mathew reflect on the mind map and consider how accurately it accounts for events, and then explore the question: 'What needs to put in place in order to reduce vulnerability and promote recovery?'

Martha can see from the mind map that there is an opportunity to develop short- and long-term goals. In the longer term, Mathew will benefit from taking steps to return to work and changing the nature of his relationships with his friends. In the shorter term, he can develop ways to improve his compliance with

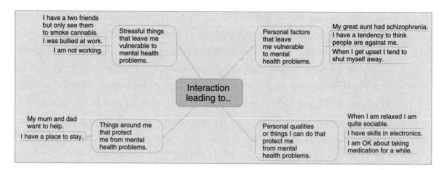

Figure 10.1 Shared formulation of stress and vulnerability mind map.

medication, help his family understand his condition and learn ways to question his suspicious thoughts.

Moving towards advanced practice

In moving towards more advanced practice in psychosocial interventions, Martha will need to increase her knowledge about models that explain how different mental health problems occur and how the problems are maintained. In working with Mathew, she will benefit from reading about advancements in the understanding of suspicious thoughts and paranoid ideas (Freeman *et al.*, 2002) and interventions for them (Freeman, Freeman & Garety, 2006) as well as family interventions (Pharoah *et al.*, 2006). Using this knowledge, Martha will be able to develop additional and specific formulations for each part of her existing mind map.

Let's take Mathew's suspicious thoughts as an example. With advancing practice, Martha's questions will be informed by the knowledge that when people are psychotic they tend to look for evidence to confirm their belief and ignore events that disprove it. People with psychosis are more likely to jump to conclusions and explain coincidences based on very little evidence. Martha can use the information that she gains to develop a cognitive model of Mathew's experiences (see Figure 10.2).

In future work, Martha can use the formulation to direct her interventions. The advanced practitioner will be keeping up to date not only with advances in treatments for psychosis, but also with how to search and appraise the literature. In thinking about therapeutic interventions for Mathew in the acute and early phase of psychosis, Martha may want to search the literature to find the evidence for the best intervention. She would formulate a search question based on defining the patient group, an intervention, the comparison and the outcome. In the care and treatment of Mathew, she would base a search on the question: 'What are the effects of psychosocial interventions for adults with psychosis compared to standard care in an inpatient setting?' Martha will need to appraise the papers she finds on the basis of costs, benefits and Mathew's preferences before coming to a decision and applying the intervention in practice.

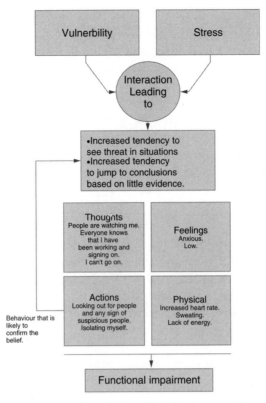

Figure 10.2 Cognitive formulation of Mathew's presenting problems.

Current evidence recommends the use of cognitive behaviour therapy for psychosis. However, in acute settings there is a lack of evidence of effectiveness. Nevertheless, Martha could set the foundations for this work by utilising the case formulation and direct her time to establishing the evidence that Mathew uses to confirm his belief that people are watching him. Once she has a clear picture of this, she can talk to Mathew about how he has come to reach the conclusions he has, and develop alternative explanations for the evidence he uses to support this belief. In order to do this work, Martha will have developed skills in cognitive behaviour therapy for psychosis and collected techniques and analogies, which she can use quickly and effortlessly in sessions (Blenkiron, 2005).

▶ Interventions: working with families

Working with families is a significant component of psychosocial interventions. Specific family interventions research has shown that working with families can have an impact on preventing relapse (Pharoah *et al.*, 2006). The NICE guidelines advocate that family interventions should be offered to all families who are living with or have close contact with a relative who has schizophrenia (National Institute for Clinical Excellence, 2003). Clearly there will be differences in the level of knowledge and skills between the novice and advanced practitioner when working with families. Also, when working with families confidence is particularly important. Fadden and Birchwood (2002) found that when staff lack confidence in the basics of talking to families, this lack of confidence is projected on to the family, with negative consequences. Pre-registration and basic professional training prepare practitioners to engage and work constructively with families, but do not prepare them to provide the more intensive, structured family interventions advocated by the NICE guidelines (National Institute for Clinical Excellence, 2003). Hence post-registration, post-qualifying psychosocial intervention programmes have a specific family work component that prepares practitioners to deliver this approach.

Martha in practice

Martha is aware of the major role that families play in the recovery from a first episode of psychosis and that without the support and collaboration of professionals, they may find it difficult to navigate the maze of emotions and challenges that come with psychosis. She sees that there are a number of objectives when working with families at this stage (Addington & Gleeson, 2003):

- Maximise the adaptive functioning of the family.
- Minimise the disruption to family life caused by the first episode.
- Minimise the risk of long-term grief, stress and burden experienced by the family.
- Aid the family to understand the impact of psychosis on the family system, individual family members and the interaction between the family and the course of the psychosis.

Martha is also aware that her role as primary nurse on an acute ward is limited in its capacity to achieve these objectives fully. She can start the tasks that will allow these objectives to be achieved, but it will be the role of the early intervention team to build on this initial engagement work and continue to work with the family on Mathew's discharge.

Martha is highly motivated to engage with the family and sees it as integral to her role as Mathew's primary nurse; however, she is aware of Mathew's right to confidentiality and the ethical and legal context in which she is working. She therefore discusses with him the need for his family to have information about his care and treatment. Mathew is happy for his family to have information and be involved. Raising the issue of confidentiality also leads to some discussion about the arguments that had occurred at home prior to his admission and about his relationship with his family. Furlong and Leggatt (1996) suggest that dealing with the question of confidentiality presents the opportunity for practitioners to build quality relationships with both service users and their families. They report that services and practitioners who have a positive attitude to families do not generally experience problems with confidentiality. Martha records Mathew's consent in his notes. It is important that the issue of confidentiality is brought up at an early stage and when the person is less acutely ill than may be the case later (Royal College of Psychiatrists, 2004).

The ward on which Martha works has a 'culture' of viewing families as partners in care, and therefore all staff welcome families and involve them as much as possible in the care and treatment of their relative. Small things can make a difference, so when Mathew is admitted, his parents who accompanied him are made tea and shown to a room designated for visitors. They are seen by the admitting doctor and by the nurse in charge, who gives them written information about the ward and visiting times.

Martha meets Mathew's parents at the first opportunity. As they visit regularly, this is easy to do. If this had not been the case, she could have phoned them and or written to them. Just as it is fundamental to view the service user first and foremost as a person, it is the same with family members. So though the family's experience is different from Mathew's, there will be similar processes at play, of bewilderment and a need to make sense of what has happened. Practitioners need to place themselves in the family's position and ask what they would like to happen if they were in the same situation.

One of the first tasks that Martha undertakes is to give an initial, clear explanation of psychosis to Mathew's parents. At this meeting, the parents are given written information to support the verbal information given by Martha. The leaflet provides some additional information sources available both locally and on the Internet. Martha follows this up at their next visit, by asking them how they found the leaflet. She answers their queries in a clear manner and addresses areas of misunderstanding that have arisen about Mathew's medication and how long he will need to take it for. At her meetings with Mathew's parents, she repeats the information about psychosis, but relates it to Mathew's experience. She is aware that psychoeducation cannot be as specific as with service users who have longer histories of psychosis (Addington *et al.*, 2005). Sometimes she meets the parents with Mathew, but she also sees them on their own, as this gives them an opportunity to talk about issues that they may not feel comfortable bringing up in front of Mathew. At these particular meetings Martha places emphasis on ensuring that they are managing their stress levels and taking care of themselves.

Families who are coming in contact with mental health services for the first time may find organisational structures puzzling and difficult to navigate. Therefore, the role of practitioners is to offer explanation and assist families through the system and its bureaucracy. Martha explains the purpose of the weekly reviews held on the ward, where Mathew's care and treatment are discussed and decisions made. She encourages the parents to attend and, when this is not possible, puts forward their views and concerns.

Martha's frequent, focused contact with Mathew's parents during his stay on the ward enables a good working relationship to be formed, one on which the early intervention team can build to begin to facilitate recovery.

Moving towards advanced practice

Martha can extend her knowledge and skills in various ways, from formal accredited modules on family work, attendance at relevant study days and conferences through to accessing resources on the Internet and appraising research papers on the topic. So she may, for example, consider a question such as 'What is the most effective way of providing family support to those who have relatives experiencing a first episode of psychosis?' and undertake a literature search. Clinical skills can continue to be developed on the ward. Confidence can be gained by working with a variety of families, with different kinds of needs.

If Martha worked in the community, for example in an early intervention team, some of the goals and tasks would not be any different from when she worked on the ward. She would still aim to develop a therapeutic alliance with Mathew's family, by giving frequent contact and high support. In addition, she would need to collect a detailed history of events leading up to Mathew's psychosis. This would complement the history obtained from him and would form the basis of relapse prevention work. Also, she would need to assess how the family is coping and their specific needs. In the initial weeks following Mathew's discharge, she would offer emotional and practical support. She would increase the family's knowledge of psychosis and specifically help them understand that the recovery process can take time and raise their awareness of the early warning signs of relapse.

Martha would also use the theory and research concerning expressed emotion to identify which families may need additional help. The term 'high expressed emotion' can be used to describe the responses of criticism and over-involvement displayed by some family members to their relative. Research has shown that service users living with relatives that display these characteristics are more likely to relapse (Brown, Birley & Wing, 1972; Brown & Rutter, 1966). Therefore Martha would use advanced clinical decision-making skills to recognise where families are finding it difficult to facilitate the recovery efforts of their relative and where they may engage in behaviour that may be detrimental to their own well-being. Families may also have particular patterns of communication that may have a negative impact on the service user. So in the example of Mathew, if there were continued arguments and tensions in the household or if he was not allowed to begin to develop an appropriate level of independence, Martha would use specific psychosocial intervention skills and offer specialised family work.

An advanced practitioner would be able to use different theories and assessments to consider the impact of psychosis on families. The skilled psychosocial intervention practitioner may use Leventhal *et al.*'s self-regulatory model (Leventhal *et al.*, 1997) to identify potential areas for intervention with first-episode families, preferring this assessment method for families new to mental health services over an assessment like the Relative Assessment Interview (Barrowclough & Tarrier, 1997), which may be more relevant to families with a longer experience of psychosis.

Martha as an advanced practitioner would recognise the importance of context and therefore be able to adapt the model of psychosocial intervention family work to take into account the context of the family. Therefore, though the model of psychosocial intervention family work emphasises the need for independence for family members, in some families from different cultures that place less emphasis on autonomy and more on the family as a single unit this may not be appropriate, and the model and the interventions may need to be adapted to take account of this cultural context.

An advanced practitioner will be aware that working intensively with families can be emotionally demanding and clinically challenging. Practitioners can feel overwhelmed with the issues that are presented during family work. It is vital that effective support systems, such as supervision, are available and accessed.

▶ Conclusion

With good use of supervision, an evaluative approach to one's practice and ongoing personal development, novice practitioners will develop towards more advanced practice. Advanced practice involves taking on the responsibilities of making decisions with greater associated risks and costs. In preparation for such a role, practitioners will benefit from understanding what it means to be an advanced practitioner and how experienced practitioners develop their knowledge and skills.

The case example illustrates that advanced practitioners successfully increase their knowledge and skills across the following areas of practice:

- *Assessment skills*: the extent to which the practitioner can use their knowledge base to elicit relevant information efficiently and sufficiently from the service user.

- *Knowledge base*: the extent and depth of knowledge that the practitioner has about psychosocial explanations of mental illness.

- *Specific psychosocial intervention skills*: the ability to agree objectives collaboratively, communicate these to the service user and enact specific therapeutic skills to achieve them.

- *Clinical decision making*: the ability to define problems, identify goals, search and appraise the literature, initiate shared decision making, and integrate the decision within the values of the practitioner and service user and within the context of practice.

- *Diagnosis and case formulation*: the ability to discriminate between signs and symptoms and to establish the probability of one condition over another. The ability to frame the service user's presentation within an explanatory model and come to a shared view on the causes, precipitants and maintaining factors for the problem.

- *Context*: an awareness of the how well the intervention fits and the ability to integrate it within the overall wider context for the work.

- *Self-regulation*: the ability to be mindful of the effect people have on the practitioner and the effect their interactions have on others.

- *Self-organisation*: the ability to organise, delegate and follow up work within the constraints of time and available resources.

While the advanced practitioner is mindful of the objectives and tasks associated with improving outcomes for people with psychosis, they carry out their work with an awareness of context and the principles underpinning the recovery model. The development of advanced practice is achieved through the continual challenging of one's existing practice and the search for new opportunities to learn and practise one's specialist skills.

▶ References

Addington, J., Collins, A., McCleery, A. & Addington, D. (2005) The role of family work in early psychosis. *Schizophrenia Research*, **79**: 77–83.

Addington, J. & Gleeson, J. (2003) Family intervention in early intervention. In P.D. McGorry & H.J. Jackson (eds), *The Recognition and Management of Early Psychosis*. Cambridge: Cambridge University Press.

Barrowclough, C. & Tarrier, N. (1997) *Families of Schizophrenia Patients: Cognitive Behavioural Interventions* (2nd edn). Cheltenham: Stanley Thornes.

Blenkiron, P. (2005) Stories and analogies in cognitive behaviour therapy: A clinical review. *Behavioural and Cognitive Psychotherapy*, **33**: 45–59.

Brown, G.W., Birley, J.L.T. & Wing, J.K. (1972) Influence of the family on the course of schizophrenic disorders: A replication. *British Journal of Psychiatry*, **121**: 241–58.

Brown, G.W. & Rutter, M. (1966) The measurement of family activities and relationships: A methodological study. *Human Relations*, **19**: 241–63.

Del Mar, C., Doust, J. & Glasziou, P. (2006) *Clinical Thinking: Evidence, Communication and Decision-Making*. Oxford: Blackwell Publishing.

Department of Health (2004) *The Ten Essential Shared Capabilities: A Framework for the Whole of the Mental Health Workforce*. London: Department of Health.

Fadden, G. & Birchwood, M. (2002) British models for expanding family psychoeducation in routine practice. In H. Lefley & D. Johnson (eds), *Family Interventions in Mental Illness: International Perspectives*. London: Praeger.

Freeman, D., Freeman, J. & Garety, P. (2006) *Overcoming Paranoid and Suspicious Thoughts*. London: Constable and Robinson.

Freeman, D., Garety, P.A., Kuipers, E., Fowler, D. & Bebbington, P.E. (2002) A cognitive model of persecutory delusions. *British Journal of Clinical Psychology*, **41**: 331–47.

Furlong, M. & Leggatt, M. (1996) Reconciling the patient's right to confidentiality and the family's need to know. *Australian and New Zealand Journal of Psychiatry*, **30**: 614–23.

Henry, I. (2004) Psychological intervention in recovery from early psychosis: Cognitively oriented psychotherapy. In J.F.M. Gleeson & P.D. McGorry (eds), *Psychological Interventions in Early Psychosis. A Treatment Handbook*. Chichester: John Wiley & Sons Ltd.

Leventhal, H., Benyamini, B., Brownlee, S. *et al.* (1997) Illness representations: Theoretical foundations. In K.J. Petrie & J.A. Weinman (eds), *Perceptions of health and illness*. Amsterdam: Harwood Academic, Amsterdam.

May, R. (2004) Making sense of psychotic experience and working towards recovery. In J.F.M. Gleeson & P.D. McGorry (eds), *Psychological Interventions in Early Psychosis. A Treatment Handbook*. Chichester: John Wiley & Sons Ltd.

National Institute for Clinical Excellence (2003) *Schizophrenia: Full National Clinical Guideline on Core Interventions in Primary and Secondary Care.* London: Gaskell/The British Psychological Society.

National Institute for Health and Clinical Excellence (2006) *Bipolar Disorder: The Management of Bipolar Disorder in Adults, Children and Adolescents, in Primary and Secondary Care.* London: National Institute for Health and Clinical Excellence.

Nuechterlein, K.H., Dawson, M.E., Ventura, J. *et al.* (1994) The vulnerability/stress model of schizophrenic relapse: A longitudinal study. *Acta Psychiatrica Scandinavia Supplement,* **382**: 58–64.

O'Carroll, M. & Park, A. (2007) *Essential Mental Health Nursing Skills.* Edinburgh: Elsevier.

Pharoah, F., Mari, J., Rathbone, J., & Wong W. (2006) Family interventions for schizophrenia. *Cochrane Database of Systematic Reviews,* **4**(CD000088).

Roberts, G. & Wolfson, P. (2004) The rediscovery of recovery: Open to all. *Advances in Psychiatric Treatments,* **10**: 37–48.

Royal College of Psychiatrists (2004) *Carers and Confidentiality in Mental Health.* Royal College of Psychiatrists and the Princess Royal Trust for Carers' Partners in Care campaign. London: RCP.

Tarrier, N. (2006) *Case Formulation in Cognitive Behaviour Therapy.* Oxford: Routledge.

◀ CHAPTER ELEVEN ▶

Positive risk taking: a framework for practice

Anne Felton and Gemma Stacey

School of Nursing, University of Nottingham

In the modern mental health system, the identification and management of risk are perceived as key roles for mental health workers. Historically, risk and dangerousness have been associated with mental illness, but now more than ever, staff working in mental health services are being asked to accurately predict and develop measures to control the behaviour of individuals experiencing mental health problems.

However, with the growing popularity of the recovery philosophy and new models of health-care delivery, there is a real opportunity to challenge the dominance of a risk agenda. We advocate movement from an agenda that is focused on restriction and control to one that is based on working collaboratively with service users to take positive risks that enable growth and change. This process is positive risk taking. Its importance is outlined in the ninth Essential Shared Capability, Promoting Safety and Positive Risk Taking. The Department of Health (2004) describes this capability as:

> Empowering the person to decide the level of risk they are prepared to take with their health and safety. This includes working with the tension between promoting safety and positive risk taking, including assessing and dealing with possible risks for service users, carers, family members, and the wider public.

▶ Risk

Risk, its assessment and control, has an ever-growing presence in modern society. The concept itself is associated with gambling theory and in its most literal sense refers to the probability of an occurrence and the significance of the resultant

Learning About Mental Health Practice. Edited by Theo Stickley and Thurstine Basset
© 2008 John Wiley & Sons, Ltd

loss or gain (Kettles, 2004). Within contemporary society, risk is perceived as a negative concept relating to a need to reduce danger. This is also reflected in mental health services. Risk is dominated by the need to assess and control negative outcomes, in particular violence towards others and suicide. In this respect, it is rarely seen in the context of gains that could result from taking risks. Morgan (2000) starts to challenge the narrow definition of risk that dominates clinical practice through introducing the language of potential and benefits into his definition of risk. The reframing of the concept to include opportunities, potential and gains is an essential foundation of positive risk taking.

Current policy frameworks place pressure on practitioners to view risk as something that has to be controlled by mental health services (Department of Health, 1999a, 1999b, 2001). This can be at odds with service users' recovery, as a focus is maintained on difficulties and problems of the past rather than goals and hopes for the future. Furthermore, evidence suggests that people with mental health problems are more likely to become victims of violence and harassment than the perpetrators (Office of Deputy Prime Minister, 2004; Read & Baker, 1996). This can be overlooked in the current climate, which heavily links violence with mental health problems.

▶ Positive risk taking

The concept of positive risk taking provides a framework to challenge this position. Positive risk taking refers to a collaborative process in which individuals make autonomous decisions about the options and resources available to them. This enables service users to make a choice to follow a certain course of action. Positive risk taking lies at the heart of being able to live a life that we choose. Taking risks is part of a normal human process that has enabled us to reach the places we have today. We all take risks in our choices about our relationships, careers and daily lives. However, for people with mental health problems there has been a long-held association between mental ill health and risk of harm, which has restricted the opportunities to take such risks. This association continues to be perpetuated by the media and can also be seen to be at the heart of current government proposals for new mental health legislation in the UK. Such a focus on harm may have contributed to a pressure to follow paternalistic practice rather than enhancing service users' autonomy, which is essential to growth and recovery.

Central to developing positive risk taking is a commitment to the belief that individuals can develop and change. Taking risks is a process that enables us to progress. In this context, if events don't have the outcome that we would have hoped for, this is as important as if we had achieved these goals. This process enables us to learn about our resources, our limitations and ourselves. We all learn from our mistakes. Positive risk taking creates opportunities to learn new skills and gain the confidence to follow choices.

It is essential to recognise that positive risk taking doesn't mean that the potential for negative outcomes is ignored or underplayed. In many respects, effective positive risk taking actually calls for more complex clinical skills and is supported by in-depth assessment of risk (in its truest sense, with an exploration of the potential for different courses of action) and open discussion about this with service users and their families. This clearly requires practitioners to be confident in these skills and is a challenge within a health culture dominated by a fear of violence. This chapter will use case studies and scenarios to explore some ways in which this potentially new approach to working can be achieved.

▶ The ethics of positive risk taking

Positive risk taking presents dilemmas for practitioners. When applying traditional approaches to managing risk, there is a tendency to focus on practices that are considered paternalistic at the expense of promoting client autonomy. This represents an approach to the consideration of ethical issues that is commonly known as 'principlism' (Beauchamp & Childress, 2001). Paternalism can be defined as 'the policy or practice on the part of people in positions of authority of restricting the freedom and responsibilities of those subordinate to or otherwise dependent on them' (Pearsall, 1998). Paternalistic practice raises ethical concerns because it can be seen to conflict with or override a person's right to autonomy, where autonomy is defined as 'the right or condition of self-government' (Pearsall, 1998). Respecting people's autonomy requires us to consult them and to obtain their agreement before we act on the person's behalf (Gillon, 1994). Paternalism is often justified in mental health care by invoking the concept of 'mental illness', which is used to suggest that a client has diminished capacity to govern themselves and therefore act in an autonomous manner (Beauchamp, 2000). When considered in this way, paternalistic practices are justified within mental health care if they ensure good (beneficent) outcomes or prevent harmful (non-maleficent) outcomes.

Childress (1982) argues that if a person is incompetent to make decisions and is also at risk, interventions against their will are not considered disrespectful. However, Beauchamp and McCullough (1984) warn that when this position is taken, it is easy for the mental health worker to focus on what the client needs as opposed to what they may prefer in an informed moment. Therefore, until a person's reasons are known, mental illness in itself does not exclude someone from making an autonomous decision. This argument will be considered in relation to practice-based scenarios throughout this chapter.

▶ Positive risk taking: a framework for practice

Positive risk taking embodies a certain philosophy of working with service users. In this respect it is an approach to be adopted in relation to working with someone to achieve their goals. This is clearly about more than just a way of responding to narrow clinically defined areas of risk. However, when exploring how positive risk taking is applied to practice, there are two areas that offer slightly different perspectives: working with risk and taking positive risks. It is important to consider how positive risk taking can be effectively promoted within each approach.

Working with risk

This relates to how risks are perceived negatively and dealt with. One example of this would be working with people who harm themselves. Self-harm is identified as an area of risk within clinical risk assessment tools, notably current care programme approach (CPA) frameworks in the UK. Traditionally, if service users harmed themselves it was perceived as a 'risk' behaviour, which may be a precursor to suicide. This has resulted in the focus on minimising the risk and therefore attempts to prevent people from hurting themselves. Service users have argued that this has led to an unhelpful and invasive approach in which their autonomy has been compromised by the searching of their belongings and themselves for implements. Preventing people from harming themselves can lead to a loss of control and enhance people's feelings of helplessness and hopelessness (Pembroke, 2006). This approach is enhanced by risk-assessment tools, which tend to reduce individuals to a statistic within a population, therefore overlooking their real-life experiences (Godin, 2004).

For a number of years service users have challenged the treatment of self-harm this way. This has contributed to debate within both the literature and practice about how to work with people who self-harm. Self-harm has begun to be recognised as an important way for some people to cope with emotional and psychological pain. The focus has shifted away from stopping the behaviour (and therefore reducing the incidence of risk) towards supporting individuals to take more control over this way of coping and helping manage the impact. For a young woman with whom one of the authors has worked, this involved us both writing a care plan that acknowledged self-harm as an important release of emotion and outlined how she was going to keep implements and wounds clean, as well as a commitment to a more long-term goal of employing alternative ways of dealing with the pain. This enables her resources at coping with her situation to be recognised and her to be encouraged to exercise her autonomy in making a choice, while being supported to deal with the consequences of this.

In this approach, the area identified as a risk is understood in the context of an individual's life rather than being reduced to a tick box on a form. This approach to working with areas traditionally perceived as being a risk is described as at the heart of community care, and yet can become invisible within the overriding political climate within the health service (Harrison, 1997).

Outlined in Scenario 11.1 is a case study exploring some of the issues that arise when working with service users who have been 'assessed' as being at risk in a certain area. It provides an illustration of how some of these concerns can be addressed within practice in a way that supports the service user's rights and autonomy.

Scenario 11.1

Brian is in his mid-30s. His belief in God is central to his life and he feels that this faith enabled him to gain the strength to leave hospital and get his life back on track after he was sectioned three years ago. Before Brian was sent to hospital, he started to hear the voice of a Methodist minister. This first started after losing his job and the breakdown of his marriage. He also believed that he was a child of God and as such, the public were plotting against him to have him crucified and sent to hell. While Brian was in hospital, he described hearing God's voice and seeing a vision, which asked him to celebrate his life's work by joining God. Brian felt this was a sign that meant the time had come to die and go to God. He decided he needed to fast and pray constantly. He stopped eating and drinking as an attempt to die.

While in hospital, a priest regularly visited Brian on the ward. They developed a relationship over a period of time, which allowed Brian to explore his beliefs and celebrate his closeness to God in other ways.

Brian is now living in a flat in the local village and is visited fortnightly by his community care co-ordinator. In the last visit from his care co-ordinator, Brian told her that God had spoken to him again and had visited him with another vision. He has recently had relationship problems with his new partner, which he has found difficult to cope with. Brian told his worker that he was planning to pray and fast for Easter the following week. The care coordinator expresses her concerns to the multidisciplinary team. There was some conflict among the team as to the appropriate course of action.

Reflective questions

What are your immediate thoughts about Brian's current situation?

List three possible options for how you might support Brian in this situation:

1.

2.

3.

How might the principles of autonomy and paternalism apply to Brian's situation?

Autonomy	Paternalism

How might this provide a rationale for your actions?

A positive risk-taking approach

Brian and his care coordinator explored the meaning behind his decision to fast. They identified that he did not want to die, but that fasting helped him to feel closer to God. They met to collaboratively write a support plan and agreed that Brian should have the right to exercise his autonomy and express his spirituality by going ahead with the fast. He felt that it was acceptable to drink tea and to be contacted by his care coordinator during the fasting period. The care coordinator also introduced Brian and his partner to a relationship counselling service.

Taking risks

Positive risk taking also involves taking positive action. Actively taking positive risks means supporting people to make choices about their own lives and act on these choices (Stickley & Felton, 2006). For instance, this might be for an individual in an inpatient environment to go on holiday, or for someone living in the community to return to employment. It could also include working with someone who has decided to come off their medication. Identifying the choices available, making a decision and following the course of action involves taking a positive risk for and with the service users. Recovery is not something that services can do to people, it rests within the individual. Working with people to take positive risks involves accepting that person as an expert in their own experiences, and supporting their decision means working alongside them in their recovery journey. This has the potential to make a significant impact on people's lives.

However, it is recognised that experiencing the distressing and sometimes disabling effects of mental health problems can make it difficult for service users to acknowledge the choices available (Perkins & Repper, 1999). This is compounded by the exclusion that is all too often a feature of using mental health services and paternalistic practice within health care which can contribute to feelings of helplessness. Practitioners have a key role in supporting service users to be aware of and make choices about the opportunities that are available. It is important to guard against the tendency to dismiss options identified by workers before exploring them with the service users involved (Repper & Perkins, 2003). This is also essential in order to mediate against the coercive aspects of mental health care, which Breeze (1998) identified as common within services. However, one of the main fears for practitioners is that these opportunities might not have the positive outcome that is hoped for (hence the risk!). There is concern that it may lead individuals with already damaged self-esteem to take further knocks. The fear is often expressed through concerns that we are setting people up to fail. This statement (while often made with genuine intentions) exemplifies the focus on paternalism rather than autonomy. Part of the process of taking positive risks is about facilitating individuals to take back more control over their lives. This can involve a shift in the balance of power in which individuals are supported to make their own decisions. We all need to be given the opportunity to make our own decisions: sometimes we fail, other times we succeed. Without these opportunities we will never progress in life.

This process will involve working collaboratively with service users to identify what resources and skills they have to support them to follow through the decision they have made. It will also involve an open discussion about the possibility of consequences that may not be the ones that are hoped for. For instance, in the example of someone coming off their medication, this may led to an increase in their distressing experiences or for the individual seeking a job that they don't keep it. The key to positive risk taking is the perception of this as a learning process rather than a preventable consequence that shouldn't be repeated. The most powerful way of learning is 'to do', thus enabling people to identify what worked and what didn't and what resources they may need in the future. This is important to facilitate effective change.

While the fear that service users are being set up to fail may be a genuine one, it is important to question whether this is underpinned by concerns that our ability and confidence as clinicians is judged by how well we control 'risk' (Perkins & Repper, 1999). To challenge this, there needs to be a shift in mental health culture that enables positive risk taking to be recognised as an essential process that enables people to develop and move beyond their mental health problems, which is surely the aim of the service.

Strengths

In many respects, the concept of positive risk taking is not new. It is underpinned by well-established approaches to mental health care. Rapp's (2006) approach to case management highlighted the potentially positive impact of working with clients' strengths and resources. The strengths model works on the premise that everyone with a diagnosis of mental illness has the capacity to grow and that staff have a responsibility to foster service users' self-determination and ability to follow their aspirations. If positive risk taking is about a collaborative process to enable service users to make decisions to follow a certain path, then strengths working is essential to identify what resources can be used to take that path. The focus of therapeutic interactions becomes people's successes, achievements and what skills enable them to reach those achievements.

For practitioners and service users this can be a difficult process. Traditionally services are focused on problems and difficulties, among which it can be hard to maintain hope. For clinicians, when faced with the complexity of people's lives it can be easy to become despondent. However, it is the fostering of this hope that has the capacity to help people have the self-belief for change. In order to deal with the impact of trauma, social exclusion and the distressing experience of mental health 'symptoms', individuals have strong resources. Working with someone to identify these resources can be essential when planning to take positive risks. This enables staff and service users to develop collaborative plans focused on goals and the resources that can be used to achieve these goals (Repper & Perkins, 2003).

Recovery

Recovery is defined and developed by people who have experienced mental distress and is not 'owned' by services. Anthony (1993) describes recovery as a process in which a person finds new meaning in life despite the presence of 'psychiatric symptoms' and consequences. Factors that were identified by service users as being important for their recovery included the ability to have hope and trusting in their own thoughts. Being supported to take positive risks can help to achieve this, as it allows the person to experiment and identify their own limitations and abilities. This will be on the person's own terms rather than professionally defined.

Deegan's (2001) exploration of the process of recovery acknowledges that taking risks and recovery are synonymous and that taking risks facilitates the acceptance stage of recovery. Recognising this is not to make the mistake of perceiving that recovery is achieved through certain prescribed elements. This is especially relevant as currently the knowledge and power associated with the concept of risk rest firmly with professionals, but Deegan (2001) simply highlights the centrality of positive risk taking to personal growth. Perkins (2003) describes hope as vital to the recovery process and suggests that hope in the form of mental health workers believing in the individual and their potential is especially powerful. Positive risk taking requires mental health workers to be committed to this hope and opportunity and to help unlock it in the people they are working with.

▶ **Promoting positive risk taking: from theory to practice**

There are a number of elements that support putting positive risk taking into practice.

Trusting relationships

The therapeutic alliance has been described as the essence of mental health care. Service users value qualities in staff that enable them to build such relationships (Forrest *et al.*, 2000). Much is written about the potential for the therapeutic relationship as a vehicle to support people to identify and deal with their difficulties (Peplau, 1988; Rogers, 1967; Watkins, 2001). The existence of trust and acceptance within a therapeutic relationship can foster hope. This enables service users to identify hopes and dreams that can spark the positive risk-taking process. For instance, in relation to Scenario 11.2, Paul felt safe and supported to share his dream of living on his own. The conditions within this relationship can facilitate service users to have the self-belief to follow these sorts of choices. In the culture of fear and risk minimisation that exists within society, coupled with the traumatic and stigmatising experiences of being a service user, the therapeutic relationship creates an important space to nurture such goals, which might feel out of reach.

The process of positive risk taking involves taking the chance that following these goals might not achieve what individuals would have hoped for. The therapeutic relationship can provide an important buffer within this process, essentially to help people identify learning and think about what happens next.

The trusting relationship: a vehicle for ethical decision making

This chapter has given examples of how autonomy and paternalism can be applied to practice-based scenarios (see Scenario 20.1). However, this approach to the consideration of ethical dilemmas in relation to positive risk taking in mental health care has been criticised for prioritising rational, universal and detached ethical reasoning (Roberts, 2004). As you have observed in this chapter, positive risk taking often represents a situation in which one principle will conflict with another. If an autonomous decision is respected, it could be argued that this will conflict with the principle of beneficence. Likewise, if a person's wishes are ignored on the basis of preventing harm and promoting good, this would be in conflict with the principle of autonomy (Breeze, 1998). It is this latter decision that would be considered to be a paternalistic action.

It is suggested that this sort of principlism fails to acknowledge the interpersonal relationships that exist between practitioners and clients. We argue that these relationships are central to our decision-making process. An alternative approach to principlism is known as the *ethics of care* and originated from the feminist writings of Carol Gilligan (1982). This approach stresses the importance of attending to particular contexts rather than general principles and is therefore useful when examining positive risk taking. Accordingly, each practice-based dilemma is said to call for a unique response that cannot be summed up by universal principles (Allmark, 1995). The ethics of care approach calls for 'engaged involvement' with clients and their goals rather than a detached consideration of theoretical concepts. This implies that rather than professionals focusing exclusively on the use of reason, a combination of both reason and emotion is said to be essential for appropriate ethical decision making. Therefore the consideration of how a client feels towards a scenario will introduce significant considerations into our ethical reasoning, which may have been ignored by principlism (Adshead, 2002).

This view is supported by *the virtue approach* to ethics, which takes into account a person's character within ethical decision making (McKie & Swinton, 2000). Therefore, rather than focusing on what a person *should do* in a given scenario, virtue ethics focuses on what a person *should be* in order to make ethically appropriate decisions. We have emphasised in this chapter the importance of collaborative working in relation to positive risk taking. Armstrong *et al.* (2000) recognise that working in this way will require the mental health worker to possess and demonstrate personal attributes such as compassion, patience and kindness. These qualities are identified as character traits and examples of moral virtues. They dispose the person to habitually act and feel in certain ways (Rachels, 1999), as they are an internal part of a person's identity (Armstrong, 2006).

The ethical principles identified and discussed in this chapter are examples of obligations, which are external to the person. They are socially constructed and imposed on the practitioner from the outside world, for example through professional bodies such as the Nursing and Midwifery Council in the UK (NMC, 2004). Such obligations need to be understood, interpreted and applied by people and therefore are inseparable from the person's character and the moral virtues they possess. By adopting a virtues approach, positive risk taking can be seen as an ethically complex scenario in which the moral character of those involved, the role of emotion and the significance of the relationship can be fully acknowledged. The mental health worker will be fully aware of the distressing nature of the ethical dilemma they face and the potentially damaging consequences that may arise. Furthermore, it is morally appropriate to feel emotions such as regret, anguish, guilt, hurt or loss (Hursthouse, 1999). This goes some way to explaining the anxiety expressed by mental health staff that they are setting people up for a fall when taking positive risks.

Principlism places a firm emphasis on solving the ethical dilemmas presented as a result of positive risk taking. Such a simplistic view can be problematic, as it assumes that all ethical dilemmas can be satisfactorily resolved by overlooking how the worker and client may feel during and after the scenario has occurred. Furthermore, virtue ethics acknowledges that conflicts between virtues will arise and it holds that exercising judgement is fundamental to morality and human flourishing.

In addition to this argument, Parker (2002) states that a mental health nurse cannot simply adopt virtues in order to cultivate a character that will ensure that appropriate decisions are made. Parker maintains that people are inextricably bound up with the communities of which they form a part. Therefore, rather than forming their own identity in isolation, *communitarianism* suggests that the mental health nurse's ethical decision making is also determined by the roles that they acquire as a member of a community (Roberts, 2004).

The application of each of the approaches to the ethical dilemmas presented within this chapter will involve the mental health worker engaging in self-reflection and in-depth discussion with the client. It will require them to exercise moral perception, which refers to their capacity to see the morally relevant features of a situation such as rights, motives and beliefs (Armstrong *et al.*, 2000). It will also necessitate moral sensitivity, which involves the ability to identify the client's needs in a collaborative manner. Finally, positive risk taking will involve the mental health worker exercising moral imagination that is closely linked with empathy. This refers to the worker's ability to place themselves in another's position. Moral imagination can be utilised by the mental health worker to promote reflection on what it might be like to be the client in this specific set of circumstances (Armstrong, 2006).

We recommend the consideration of dilemmas presented by positive risk taking in this manner because they can be described as context dependent, rational and inclusive. This description is complementary to the philosophy underpinning positive risk taking, which emphasises the importance of each of these aspects. It allows the mental health worker to acknowledge that making the decision to take a risk is an emotional process, and that our ethical decisions are not those with which we are certain: they are those with which we can live and prompt us to reflect critically on the scenario and our practice. Engaging in such a process will allow us to negotiate rather than eliminate ethical uncertainty (McCarthy, 2006). By its very nature it's impossible to predict risk. If we could predict it, then there would be no risk.

This can be seen in Scenario 11.2, through the work Leanne was doing with Paul to encourage him to identify what had enabled him to be happy living in his flat initially. The therapeutic relationship enables Leanne to hold some of distress that Paul experiences. This helped to act as a safety net from which Paul was able to bounce back after his admission to hospital.

Scenario 11.2

Paul has been living at Oak Tree Crescent (which is a rehabilitation unit providing ongoing support for people with mental health problems). Before he moved in to Oak Tree Crescent he had spent a long period on an acute ward, having become what he described as 'tortured' by his voices, which had resulted in him taking an overdose. Leading up to this deterioration in his mental health, Paul had moved in to a flat on his own and was being visited by outreach staff from Oak Tree Crescent. This was the first time Paul had lived on his own. He loved the flat and enjoyed visiting the pub across the road. However, after a few weeks he stopped visiting the pub and started refusing to let his keyworker visit him. His bad voices had increased, telling him that staff wanted him out of the flat and that no

---

one could be trusted, eventually leading to him taking all his prescribed medication and going to hospital.

Now that Paul is back at Oak Tree Crescent, he feels more in control of his voices and wants to move in to a flat of his own.

Paul's keyworker (Tom) does not think this is a good idea and is worried that if Paul moves into his own flat then his mental health would deteriorate and that the Oak Tree Crescent team would be 'setting him up to fail'. He is worried about Paul having all of his medication at the flat and wants him to consider moving to projects with 24-hour staff support. The multidisciplinary team had questioned Tom's actions after Paul took his last overdose.

However, the team's psychologist (Leanne) has a good relationship with Paul. Tom had referred him to see her to work with him on his voice-hearing experiences. During the individual work between Paul and Leanne, he has clearly said that he wants a flat of his own. He felt that during the first few weeks when he lived on his own before, he was really happy. Using a strengths approach, Leanne has worked with Paul to identify that in those first few weeks he was still visiting Oak Tree Crescent regularly and attending his voluntary work. They have also started to look at how Paul copes when his voices start to increase and what support he would like when this happens. Leanne is supporting Paul to work towards his goal. She has also offered to provide clinical supervision for Tom to enable him to explore reservations about Paul's move on. Paul has a Care Programme Approach review next month; this will provide a forum for Paul, Tom and Leanne to discuss the current situation.

1. In the above situation identify elements of:

    (a) Moral perception: this is seeing and providing meaning to the morally relevant features of a situation. This may include the outcomes of actions, moral rights, motives, beliefs, experiences.

    (b) Moral sensitivity: this involves identifying the client's needs and feelings in a collaborative manner to then inform actions.

    (c) Moral imagination: this involves reflecting on what it might be like to be the client in this specific set of circumstances.

2. Leanne and Tom both have ethically justifiable reasons for their concerns and actions. Identify what these might be.

Tom	Leanne

3. From the position of taking a positive risk, what actions might you follow?

Negotiated goals

Taking gradual steps towards a long-term goal can be an element of positive risk taking: working with service users to identify an aim and the short- and medium-term goals needed to achieve that aim. This may also assist in the management of negative risk, while still supporting the individual on their recovery journey. For instance, in the example of an individual in inpatient care who wants to go on holiday, this may mean that a fortnight abroad is their ultimate aim. The starting point for this service user could be supporting them to organise and plan a weekend away. For others, it may mean helping them to plan for contingencies during those two weeks, such as contact numbers for support. In Scenario 11.1, with the example of Brian and the prayer fasting, there was some negotiation between Brian and his key worker as to the length of the planned fast and the involvement of drinks. This enabled his key worker to meet her duty of care while respecting Brian's autonomy.

From a strengths perspective, this will involve enabling people to focus on their dreams and formulating this into a long-term goal. Once the long-term aims have been identified, the service user and their key worker will collaboratively define the steps needed to work towards this goal. This involves exploring the strengths and resources needed and the potential outcome of each step. Additionally, the potential barriers to achieving these goals should be examined and where possible addressed. This will enable the person to make informed decisions about their own level of risk (Department of Health, 2004).

▶ Effective risk assessment and care planning

Mental health workers have a responsibility to assess risks (for some professionals this is part of their duty). Godin (2004) suggests that trends within services have led to this assessment tending to be informed most heavily by paper documentation rather than contact with the service users involved. In this context, historical information is perceived as a key predictor of future risks, and for some service users this can contribute to them being held back by their past.

Positive risk taking is also underpinned by thorough assessment. This is essential whether the risk is in relation to taking positive action or working with a defined 'at risk' area (such as self-harm). Negative risks identified within assessments can act as barriers to taking positive risks, notably with reductionist risk-assessment tools, which provide limited accounts of the context in which people's experiences occur. Assessment of risk should build an understanding of the situation in which an event occurred and the stressors and protectors that existed for that person within that given situation. This enables mental health workers, service users, families and the multidisciplinary team to gain greater clarity about identifying situations when paternalistic action is truly justified.

Positive risk taking can involve a collaborative assessment of the pros and cons of different courses of action conducted within the trusting conditions of the therapeutic relationship. This enables service users to make informed choices about actions to take and provides a foundation for collaborative plans of care to develop, which reflect service users' priorities and not just professional ones. This process can be informed by a number of tools, which maximise choice and opportunities for service users throughout the path to following their goal. These can be even more central if the positive outcomes that are hoped for aren't initially reached or the service user experiences an increase in their distressing experiences. Advanced agreements provide a contract that can be agreed between service users and staff about who they want involved and what actions they would like to be taken if they become unwell. Working within an advanced agreement helps to ensure that an individual's wishes and autonomy can be respected at times when they may not be able to express this clearly themselves. While advanced agreements aren't legally binding documents, they would be an important addition to service-driven crisis plans within current CPA risk frameworks.

For some people who have used services for many years, it can be difficult for both that person and their key workers to recognise how well the person knows themselves, often as a result of services adopting the role of expert (Repper & Perkins, 2003). Working alongside service users to explore early warning signs and resources used to cope with their distressing experiences is important. This can be used to develop joint plans providing contingencies for courses of action taken, and contribute to fulfilling the requirements of working as a professional in contemporary mental health services.

▶ Multidisciplinary working

Contemporary mental health policy emphasises partnership and joint working as the best way to deliver effective services that meet clients' wishes and needs (Department of Health, 1999a, 2002). The majority of mental health services are structured to deliver support via a multidisciplinary team. One of the key elements of successful teamworking is sharing a common goal. Support from the multidisciplinary team for positive risk-taking practice is important. This is central to challenging defensive practice, which errs on the side of caution and prevents people from taking opportunities for growth and personal development. Working with risk and developing plans to enable service users to exercise their autonomy can be a stressful and challenging area. This is enhanced if individual professionals feel that they are solely responsible. Unresolved conflict within the multidisciplinary team could contribute to these feelings by developing a culture of blame in which fingers are pointed, particularly if the positive risk taken doesn't have the outcome that would have been hoped for.

Promoting positive risk taking within the multidisciplinary team is supported by open and honest communication in which the ethical dilemmas are recognised and explored by teams. In this respect, positive risk taking is a key agenda for existing multidisciplinary forums such as the care programme approach review, team meetings and reviews. This is supported by the Royal College of Psychiatrists, which suggests that therapeutic risk taking is a central approach in modern rehabilitation and recovery services (Royal College of Psychiatrists, 2004). Multidisciplinary support for a collaborative plan that outlines a positive risk such as going on holiday or reducing levels of intervention maximises the potential benefits. A consistent approach that emphasises an individual's strengths, resources and potential to follow their own goals could be undermined by team members remaining focused on barriers to this.

The positive risk-taking process will be underpinned by effective clinical supervision. In this context, the professional will be facilitated to explore the ethical conflicts that arise when attempting to promote positive risk taking. We have recognised within this chapter the emotional element of positive risk taking, and clinical supervision provides an important forum for this to be processed. This may encourage greater shared responsibility and contribute to a culture that promotes positive risk taking.

▶ Families and friends

Relationships are central to our lives and this is no different for people who use mental health services. Among many other things, they can be an important source of support for service users. However, the views of family and friends (commonly referred to as carers) are too often overlooked by services, notably when planning and delivering support to their loved ones. It is important to recognise this in relation to positive risk taking.

Families and service users have their own separate needs, which may result in competing agendas in relation to their lives and support needs. Most families and friends obviously don't want to see their loved ones going through pain or distress. This may also be compounded by poor relationships with services in the past, in which carers have been left to support the individual in crisis with limited input from services. There may be fears that this could happen again if they are supported to take any risk. There may be a tendency to naturally want to be cautious to protect the people they care about having to go through any potential pain or loss again. Without being involved in the process, there may also be frustration arising from being ill informed about the situation. Without effective communication, families could feel that they are unaware of the consequences and motivations behind supporting the person towards certain goals. Obviously, it is essential to respect confidentiality and the wishes of service users if working with families and friends. However, it is vital to acknowledge their perspective and where possible involve them in the positive risk-taking process through open communication and planning where appropriate. Equally, if this is not possible due to conflicting agendas or confidentiality issues, it is important to ensure that carers are aware of alternative sources of support and information.

▶ Conclusion

Positive risk taking presents mental health services with a challenge. It requires services to question the paternalistic and coercive approaches that are sometimes promoted through policy frameworks that emphasise public protection at the cost of an individual's opportunity to grow. This situation is also compounded by the media portrayal of violence and mental health, which fuels public support for policy of this nature. As a result, our understanding of risk is defined in terms of dangerousness and negativity.

The approach presented in this chapter opens the doors to an alternative perspective. Positive risk taking offers opportunity and hope, which need to be embraced. It is a collaborative process, which should enable people to realise their potential – a potential that is all too often buried beneath reductionist approaches to working with risk. This is outlined by the Ten Essential Shared Capabilities (Department of Health, 2004), which recognises the importance of the service user making an informed decision about their future through the level of risk they are willing to take. This chapter has demonstrated that positive risk taking should form an integral part of our approach to care: an approach that is synonymous with a recovery philosophy due to its focus on the service user's self-defined goals and wishes.

Positive risk taking cannot be separated from its ethical context. It will often place the mental health worker in a position in which ethical principles will conflict. However, if mental health services are to move towards a recovery approach, the consideration of ethics in terms of narrow, predefined categories will continue to act as a barrier. We argue that the ethics of each positive risk-taking situation need to be considered in the context of that individual and their therapeutic relationship with the mental health worker. This could break down such barriers to allow risk taking to occur. Taking positive risks will aim to shift the balance of power to enable people to take control of their future. After all, as the saying goes, if you don't risk anything you risk everything.

▶ References

Adshead, G. (2002) A different voice in psychiatric ethics. In K.W.M. Fulford, D.L. Dickenson & T.H. Murray (eds), *Healthcare Ethics and Human Values* (Chapter 6, pp. 56–62). Oxford: Blackwell.

Allmark, P. (1995) Can there be an ethics of care? *Journal of Medical Ethics*, 21: 19–24.

Anthony, W.A. (1993) Recovery from mental illness: The guiding vision of the mental health service in the 1990's. *Psychosocial Rehabilitation Journal*, 16: 11–23.

Armstrong, A.E. (2006) Towards a strong virtue ethics for nursing practice. *Nursing Philosophy*, 7: 110–24.

Armstrong, A.E., Parsons, S. & Barker, P.J. (2000) An inquiry into moral virtues, especially compassion, in psychiatric nursing: Findings from a Delphi study. *Journal of Psychiatric and Mental Health Nursing*, 7: 297–306.

Beauchamp, T.L. (2000) The philosophical basis of psychiatric ethics. In S. Bloch, P. Chodoff & S.A. Green (eds), *Psychiatric Ethics* (3rd edn, Chapter 3, pp. 24–48). New York: Oxford University Press.

Beauchamp, T.L. & Childress, J.F. (2001) *Principles of Biomedical Ethics* (5th edn). New York: Oxford University Press.

Beauchamp, T.L. & McCullough, L. (1984) *Medical Ethics*. Hemel Hempstead: Prentice Hall.

Breeze. J. (1998) Can paternalism be justified in mental health care? *Journal of Advanced Nursing*, 28(2): 260–65.

Childress, J.F. (1982) *Who Should decide? Paternalism in Health* Care Oxford: Oxford University Press.

Deegan, P. (2001) Recovery as a self-directed process of healing and transformation. *Occupational Therapy in Mental Health*, 17(3/4): 5–21.

Department of Health (1999a) *National Service Framework for Mental health: Modern Standards and Service Models*. London: Department of Health.

Department of Health (1999b) *Effective Care Co-ordination in Mental Health Services*. London: Department of Health.

Department of Health (2001) *The Mental Health Policy Implementation Guide*. London: Department of Health.

Department of Health (2002) *Community Mental Health Teams: Mental Health Policy Implementation Guide*. London: Department of Health.

Department of Health (2004) *The Ten Essential Shared Capabilities: A Framework for the Whole of the Mental Health Workforce*. London: Department of Health/NHSU/Sainsbury Centre/NIMHE.

Forrest, S., Risk, I., Masters, H. & Brown, N. (2000) Mental health service user involvement in nurse education: Exploring the issues. *Journal of Psychiatric and Mental Health Nursing*, 7(1): 51–7.

Gillon, R. (1994) Medical ethics: Four principles plus attention to scope. *British Medical Journal*, 309: 184–9.

Gilligan, C. (1982) *In a Different Voice: Psychological Theory and Women's Development*. Boston, MA: Harvard University Press.

Godin, P. (2004) 'You don't tick boxes on a form': A study of how community mental health nurses assess and manage risk. *Health, Risk and Society*, 6(4): 347–60.

Harrison, G. (1997) Risk assessment in a climate of litigation. *British Journal of Psychiatry*, 170(supp. 32): 37–9.

Hursthouse, R. (1999) *On Virtue Ethics*. Oxford: Oxford University Press.

Kettles, A.M. (2004) A concept analysis of forensic risk. *Journal of Psychiatric and Mental Health Nursing*, 11: 484–93.

McCarthy, J. (2006) A pluralist view of nursing ethics. *Nursing Philosophy*, 7: 157–64

McKie, A. & Swinton, J. (2000) Community, culture and character: The place of the virtues in psychiatric nursing practice. *Journal of Psychiatric and Mental Health Nursing Practice*, 7: 35–42.

Morgan, S. (2000) *Clinical Risk Management: A Clinical Tool and Practitioner Manual*. London: Sainsbury Centre for Mental Health.

Nursing and Midwifery Council (2004) *The NMC Code of Professional Conduct: Standards for Conduct, Performance and Ethics*. London: NMC.

Office of the Deputy Prime Minister (2004) *Mental Health and Social Exclusion, Social Exclusion Unit Report*. London: ODPM.

Parker, M. (2002) A deliberative approach to bioethics. In K.W.M. Fulford, D.L. Dickenson & T.H. Murray (eds), *Healthcare Ethics and Human Values* (Chapter 2, pp. 29–35). Oxford: Blackwell.

Pearsall, J. (ed.) (1998) *The New Oxford Dictionary of English*. New York: Oxford University Press.

Pembroke, L. (2006) Limiting the damage. *Mental Health Today*, **April**: 27–30.

Peplau, H. (1988) *Interpersonal Relations in Nursing*. London: Macmillan.

Perkins, R. (2003) Hope and opportunity. *Openmind*, **123**(Sep/Oct): 6.

Perkins, R. & Repper, J. (1999) *Working Alongside People with Long Term Mental Health Problems*. Cheltenham: Stanley Thornes.

Rachels, J. (1999) *The Elements of Moral Philosophy* (3rd edn). New York: McGraw-Hill.

Rapp, C. (2006) *The Strengths Model: Case Management with People with Psychiatric Disabilities*. Oxford: Oxford University Press.

Read, J. & Baker, S. (1996) *Not Just Sticks and Stones: A Survey of the Stigma, Taboos and Discrimination Experienced by People with Mental Health Problems*. London: Mind.

Repper, J. & Perkins, R. (2003) *Social Inclusion and Recovery: A Model for Mental Health Nursing Practice*. London: Bailliere Tindall.

Roberts, M. (2004) Psychiatric ethics: A critical introduction for mental health nurses. *Journal of Psychiatric and Mental Health Nursing*, **11**: 583–8.

Rogers, C. (1967) *On Becoming a Person*. London: Constable.

Royal College of Psychiatrists (2004) *Rehabilitation and Recovery Now, Council Report*. London: RCP.

Stickley, T. & Felton, A. (2006) Promoting recovery through therapeutic risk-taking. *Mental Health Practice*, **9**(8): 26–30.

Watkins, P. (2001) *Mental Health Nursing: The Art of Compassionate Care*. Oxford: Butterworth Heinemann.

CHAPTER TWELVE

Personal development and learning

Sharon Lee Cuthbert and Thurstine Basset

Independent training and development consultants

The tenth and final essential shared capability is Personal Development and Learning. The Department of Health (2004) describes this capability as:

> keeping up-to-date with changes in practice and participating in life-long learning, personal and professional development for one's self and colleagues through supervision, appraisal and reflective practice. This capability focuses on the need for the practitioner to take an active role in their own personal and professional development. In the same way that service users should be viewed as active partners in their care, not passive recipients, practitioners should be active participants in their own development.

The Department of Health (2004) also states that in order to meet this capability practitioners will need:

- Access to education and training based on the best available evidence.

- A personal/professional development plan that takes account of their hopes and aspirations and that is reviewed annually.

- To understand the responsibilities of the service in supporting them in meeting the goals set in the development plan.

- To understand their personal responsibility to achieve the goals set in their development plan.

- The ability to set personal/professional goals that are realistic and achievable.

- To recognise the importance of supervision and reflective practice and integrate both into everyday practice.

Learning About Mental Health Practice.   Edited by Theo Stickley and Thurstine Basset
© 2008 John Wiley & Sons, Ltd

■ To be proactive in seeking opportunities for personal supervision, personal development and learning.

This capability reinforces the notion that learning is life-long and that all mental health workers, from the least to the most experienced, are continuously learning. In this chapter we explore key factors that will enable you, as a mental health worker, to attend to your learning and development needs. The chapter is addressed directly to you as the reader and there are some activities you might want to complete as part of reading the chapter.

We will start with the importance of gathering information as part of developing a portfolio.

▶ Personal and professional profiles: developing a portfolio

Many mental health workers will have a curriculum vitae (CV), either stored in a paper format or on a computer. Usually it is an inventory of:

■ key facts such as your contact details

■ employment history

■ qualifications

■ education and training

■ membership of professional organisations

■ sources for references

A CV is generally updated when it is needed for a job or training application, and this usually just requires adding details of your most recent position or training you have attended. As most organisations in health and social care ask for applications on a standard form, CVs tend to be used simply as a memory prompt for key information. If you have not made an application for many years, your CV may be very out of date. In fact, it may not be contained in one document but in a variety of pieces of paper, perhaps stored with a collection of certificates from training that you have attended.

The CV is still essential in some commercial sectors, but rather than it being a list of facts, the trend is to use it as a marketing tool – selling you and your skills, knowledge and attitudes to the reader. For example, rather than beginning the CV with your contact details and employment history, specialists in CV design recommend starting with a mini profile or pen picture that describes your key abilities and achievements, showing how your skills and experience have developed over the years. This profile should be designed to hook the reader and draw them in, making them want to find out more about you. This shifts the focus of a CV on to your current competency rather than your work history and it should be based on evidence of achievements in particular roles. Instead of writing 'I worked for two years as a support worker in a mental health resource centre', you would describe what you achieved in that role, such as: 'I set up and facilitated a ten week self-management programme for people with depression.' This approach suggests to the reader that you are someone with ideas and organisational skills, whereas saying that you had a particular post gives no information about you as a person.

Activity 12.1

When did you last update your CV? Spend some time updating it now. Don't forget to include as much relevant evidence as possible and to focus on your achievements, skills and knowledge.

This new way of presenting yourself is sometimes known as *professional profiling*.

A professional profile is a focused selection of evidence that is prepared for a particular audience and purpose. This may be a job application, an application for a place on a learning programme, or as evidence of continuous professional development for registration with a professional body. The larger collection from which the information is taken is generally known as a *portfolio* and this draws together all the material that demonstrates your development over time.

There is no standard model for constructing a portfolio, but as a general guide it should contain three key types of information:

- *Factual information* includes that which would be included in a traditional CV, plus any records that you may need to refer to when completing a form. This may include information about mandatory and other training that you have attended, copies of certificates, memberships of professional organisations and registration numbers.

- *Professional development activity* refers to any activity that has taken place within a particular work role or a number of roles, and evidence of this will include notes from appraisals, supervision notes, personal development plans or work review meetings. The documents in this section will be copies of records from your current workplace and from previous employment. There may be some restrictions on what documents you can store in your portfolio, but it is considered best practice to ensure that employees are given copies of documents relating to their own supervision or appraisal.

- *Evidence of learning, development and achievement* is essential to a portfolio and it may come from a wide variety of formal or informal activities, including exercises carried out during training, learning diaries, reflective accounts of your work practice, notes from projects, practice-based assignments, presentations to colleagues, and feedback from others on your practice. It is important to note that this section is for evidence that shows you *actively* participating in your own development, not just certificates of attendance at training courses. A certificate simply shows that you were present and does not indicate what you learned and how you have put it into practice. Some learning activities produce evidence such as assignments based on your work practice that can be included in this section, but you may also have to capture and record learning experiences that would otherwise be lost. There is more on this later in this chapter.

Given that many people find keeping an up-to-date CV a bit of a chore, it may seem that to set up and manage your own portfolio would be a huge effort – especially if you need to draw on numerous sources of information held in different places. However, once you have designed a system that works for you, it should save time in future because everything is organised and in one place. Apart from job and training applications, the contents of a portfolio may also be useful for:

- providing evidence for accreditation of prior learning

- preparing for interviews

- demonstrating evidence of continuous professional development (CPD) to professional organisations

- providing evidence for competence-based qualifications

- writing assignments for a course of study

- preparing for an appraisal

It is worth noting at this point that national government policy is to move towards all health and social care workers being registered with a regulatory body. Currently the CPD requirements of such organisations ask applicants to prove that they have undertaken a specified number of hours of learning and development. This does not have to take the form of training courses but can be evidenced through a wide range of activities, and a portfolio is very helpful in preparing this information.

Some professional bodies and employers provide staff with a ready-made system, but it is important that the individual owns the portfolio because it should reflect the whole person rather someone in a particular job role. There are no absolute rules about the type of portfolio that you keep. A large ring-binder folder is portable and allows you easily to organise documents, but some people prefer to use a box file or to keep their portfolio in an electronic format. Whatever the format, your portfolio should be designed to be easy to use, because you need to update it regularly and it should grow and develop as you do. You could start by putting anything relevant in one box and organise it later.

As already suggested, a portfolio should contain copies of documents from professional development activity at work and it will be useful for activities such as your appraisal. The next section looks at how appraisal fits into the work-based cycle known as the performance management cycle and the place of this in your development and learning.

Activity 12.2

If you have not already got a portfolio, this is a good time to start one. Check out first if your employer has a ready-made portfolio that you can use.

▶ Professional development activity: the performance management cycle at work

Organisations have a responsibility to support and develop their staff and, in relation to some areas of practice such as health and safety, they also have a legal duty. Those organisations that seek accreditation for staff development activities or that are externally regulated and funded are expected to show an extensive commitment to their work force. In return, employees are expected to take personal responsibility for developing and maintaining standards and the quality of their practice. Employees also have some legal responsibilities such as ensuring that they know the content of policies and guidelines.

The systems that employers use to support and develop their staff vary according to the organisation's history, size, culture and context. For example, a small, voluntary counselling organisation may place a great emphasis on enabling its counsellors to become more skilled through regular one-to-one supervision with an experienced practitioner rather than through attending training courses. A large organisation may have a well-established short course programme with a clear progression from induction through foundation to advanced levels, with most training occurring away from the workplace. In such a situation, supervision may have more of a focus on tasks rather than practice development.

Whatever the actual system in operation, the theory is that professional development activities should be implemented through an overall process often known as the performance management cycle. This cycle has a parallel with the care planning cycle for working with service users, in that both have four key stages:

- assessment/appraisal
- goal planning
- implementation and monitoring
- evaluation and review

Each journey through the four stages should produce new information to be used at the beginning of the next cycle. Commonly, the cycle lasts a year, with meetings at fixed points during which records are completed. Organisations may use different names for the cycle and its components, but the essential principles should remain the same.

The purpose of the performance management cycle is to promote face-to-face discussion and two-way feedback about the work context and the performance of the individual within that context. It provides an opportunity for both parties to talk about and address any concerns and for the practitioner to have protected time to consider their development needs and career aspirations. One of several parallels between the performance management cycle and the care planning cycle is that as service users should be seen as active partners in their care and not passive recipients, practitioners should also be active participants in the performance management process.

The first stage of the process is a type of assessment that is generally known as appraisal. It is retrospective, looking back over a specified period of work. New workers may have appraisals at the end of a probationary period and perhaps yearly thereafter. An appraisal is an opportunity to ensure that a worker has a clear understanding of their job and how their work contributes to the wider aims and objectives of the organisation. It is a one-to-one meeting, usually with a manager or senior member of the team, which provides a space for a two-way discussion about how the appraisee is performing in their work role and their learning and development needs.

An appraisal usually takes place against some form of performance framework that identifies what is required of the worker in their particular role. This may be based on a set of competencies such as those contained in National Occupational Standards, which are phrased in terms of what a person should do within key elements of their role. For example, in relation to health and safety in the workplace a performance criteria may state: 'You report health and safety issues to the appropriate people.' Other performance frameworks are constructed around generic skills and qualities such as 'leadership' or 'communication'. Some organisations appraise their staff entirely against goals that were set in the previous performance period, and these may take the form of specific projects such as 'produce an information leaflet to promote the work of the centre'.

An often-quoted guideline about appraisals is that in the meeting there should be 'no surprises'. That is, although most organisations appraise via a formal meeting, feedback about performance should be continuous and the appraisal is then an opportunity to pull together what has already been discussed with a member of staff during the rest of the year. It is also important that an appraisal meeting is two-way, so that the appraisee can give feedback to the appraiser about what they have found helpful or unhelpful, or any obstacles they have encountered in carrying out their work and any ideas for improvements.

It is important for both parties to prepare for an appraisal to make best use of the time. In services where there is a very clear hierarchy, it is very common for staff to expect their manager to take the lead in an appraisal and bring any relevant documents. However, remember that an appraisal is *your* chance to have your say and to gain valuable development opportunities. If you are being appraised it is worthwhile reading beforehand or bringing the following to your meeting:

- Your job description.

- Your professional portfolio.

- Any previous objectives.

- Relevant information relating to your work such as organisational plans, changes to practice requirements.

- Any evidence about the quality of your work and feedback about your performance.

You could also think about and note down ideas about the following:

- Your strengths and areas in which you would like to improve.

- Your hopes and aspirations in relation to your career.

- Where you want to be in one year or in five years.

- Current obstacles and problems.

- Ideas and suggestions about improving your work practice or that of the team.

- Ideas for your short-term, medium-term, long-term work and development goals.

- Information on learning, training and development opportunities.

Many people feel quite anxious about appraisal meetings, as they carry with them notions of being assessed and judged. Sometimes appraisers feel uncomfortable about being in this position and it can lead to the meeting being treated as a 'paper exercise'. The success of the meeting will also depend on the skills of the appraiser, but both parties should try to stick to the following principles:

- Keep a ratio of 4:1 positives to negatives.

- Keep an open mind.

- Focus on exploring problems and ways forward rather than finding someone to blame.

In most systems the *goal-planning* stage usually follows on straight away from the appraisal, although ideally a break of a few weeks would be helpful, giving both parties time to think through what has been discussed. It is likely that during this second stage you should be agreeing goals for your work performance and for your personal development plan (PDP) based on your learning needs, and often these may go hand in hand. For example, if you have a work-related goal to develop a walking group for service users, you may have a personal development goal to attend training in developing exercise programmes in a mental health context or to research some information about best practice in this area.

Some personal development goals are not directly related to tasks and may be linked to regulatory requirements (for example mandatory training in health and safety) or your career aspirations, or other more general learning needs such as communication skills. Mental health services also have a responsibility to keep up to date with changes in practice and your goals should reflect this.

Any decisions about appropriate goals for your PDP will be influenced by what resources are available and therefore you will need to consider the following:

- What are my key learning needs – which of these must be met and which are my aspirations?

- What are the priorities for my service?

- What are considered priorities for my job role and grade?

- What is the current evidence about best practice in my area of work and how can this guide us in my PDP?

- What opportunities are there locally for learning and development?

- What is the balance between cost and benefit in relation to these opportunities?

- What different ways are available for meeting my learning needs – do I need to go on a course or could I learn more through shadowing someone with skills in this area?

Whatever method of learning you select, it is essential that goals are carefully thought through and well written. This is because badly recorded or 'woolly' goals such as in Example 12.1 can cause confusion and be misinterpreted or simply ignored. Writing goals is an essential skill, but with people often short of time goals are often quickly written at the end of the meeting with a view to getting the paperwork done.

The most important and yet often the most difficult aspect of completing objectives during an appraisal is ensuring that all objectives are *SMART*:

- *Specific*: exactly what do you have to do?

- *Measurable*: how will you know when it is achieved?

- *Achievable*: is it realistic and can you actually achieve this target?

- *Resourced*: what or who will you need to help you achieve your target?

- *Timed*: how long will it take or when will it be completed?

Example 12.1

The following is an example of a woolly work performance objective for Richard:

■ 'Richard to find out about setting up an art group.'

Problems with this objective are: What does 'find out about' mean? Because it's unclear what it means, it will be hard to agree on what the evidence will be that he has done it. Richard may think it enough that it is in his head, but his manager may want to see a full plan with back-up information. Likewise, how will it be possible to measure whether he has done it? When will he do it by? Achievability is hard to assess when the rest is unclear. Lastly, Richard will need resources but these are not specified.

A SMART version of the same objective is:

■ 'Richard will be reviewing the activities programme with the team in the staff meeting on 6 March in order to identify an appropriate slot for a new art group. He will also work with the occupational therapist in planning a series of 12 sessions and writing a budget for materials that his manager will purchase. The group will run between June and September, with the intention of producing a display for World Mental Health Day on 10 October.'

Activity 12.3

Review your own current personal development goals. Do they meet the SMART criteria? If not, consider how they could be made SMARTer.

Goals should be SMART because the worker needs to know exactly what they should do and what support they can expect. For this reason, complex goals are sometimes broken down into smaller steps.

Performance goals and professional development plans should be *monitored* throughout the *implementation* period. Too often they are seen as records that have to be done once a year and then are filed and forgotten. In your organisation there may be a formal system for having mini-appraisals at quarterly or six-month intervals, but if not, they should be a running item on the agenda for your *supervision*. This is important, because not only do you need to ensure that you are implementing your goals, you need to take note of any obstacles that are preventing you from achieving your goals and either address these or note them down ready for discussion at your review.

Evaluation and *review* is the point at which the cycle joins up, as it is an opportunity to see whether goals were achieved and begin the process again.

▶ The role of supervision in your personal and professional development and learning

Supervision is the term used to describe the regular meetings that are held between a practitioner and their supervisor to discuss the supervisee's work. Supervision has been given increasing attention and significance over the last 20 years and is now seen as an essential activity for all mental health workers. There are several reasons for this, including:

- The growing emphasis on lifelong learning for all practitioners, whatever their level of experience or position.

- Recommendations arising from inquiries into poor or dangerous practice where monitoring and support systems were not in place.

- Our increased understanding of what methods do or do not help people develop their practice and the value of ongoing, one-to-one coaching and mentoring as opposed to sending people on short courses.

- Continuous professional development requirements and standards set by regulatory and professional bodies.

- Employer responsibilities under health and safety legislation to monitor the stress levels of employees and take reasonable steps to prevent or reduce stress levels in the workplace.

- The role of supervision in the performance management cycle and the importance of ensuring that goals and plans are kept alive rather than just revisited once a year at an appraisal.

- The influence of counselling and psychotherapeutic approaches in mental health work and the significance that is given to supervision of practice in these fields.

As with the performance management cycle, the varying influence of these factors and differences in organisational cultures and structures have resulted in a wide variation in the way that supervision is organised and carried out. For example, supervision may be carried out in a one-to-one meeting with a team manager, whose main focus is to make sure that the service is being delivered to the right standard. Alternatively, a worker may attend group supervision, facilitated by a psychotherapist, with a focus on the quality of relationships between workers and service users.

Inskipp and Proctor (1995) have described the three tasks of supervision and, although they are derived from the field of counselling, they have been very influential in the development of supervision theory and models in health and social care. The three tasks are:

- *Formative*: to enable the practitioner to develop competence and confidence in their role.

- *Restorative*: to support the practitioner in coping with the demands of their role, deal with stress and ensure their fitness to practice.

- *Normative*: to monitor standards and ensure quality in service delivery.

These three tasks have a central purpose, which is to ensure that the worker offers the best service to the service user. The practice of supervision in different mental health settings will address these tasks to varying degrees, but ideally should achieve a balance between the three. Sometimes this is achieved by providing both management and 'clinical' (practice-focused) supervision for staff.

Activity 12.4

Consider your own supervision. Is it formative, restorative and normative? If one of these areas feels neglected to you, arrange to discuss it with your manager.

The reality of supervision in many mental health settings is that it may be constrained by several factors, including:

- Competing demands on time and the need to prioritise other activities.

- The level of experience and competence in supervision of both the supervisor and supervisee.

- Conflicting expectations of supervision.

In order for supervision to be successful, it is important that supervisor and supervisee anticipate these issues and establish a working alliance. This is the willingness to respect and be open with each other, to work towards common goals and to share the responsibility of ensuring that their meetings are productive. To help achieve the working alliance, it is very important that the following are put in place at the first meeting:

- A signed contract that identifies the responsibilities of each party and the focus of supervision.

- A timetable of meetings.

- An agenda for each meeting agreed by both parties.

- How agreed action will be recorded and followed up.

■ An agreement about how and when the supervision arrangement will be reviewed to ensure that there is an opportunity to give feedback to each other and make any necessary changes.

Because the idea of supervision can make practitioners feel very anxious, the working alliance is essential. The term 'supervision' carries with it thoughts of being overlooked, directed and criticised by a senior person. It is unfortunate that some people will have had a bad experience of supervision that has confirmed these fears, but at its best, supervision can be empowering and energising. Sometimes reflecting on our work can be uncomfortable, as it requires us to look back and to learn from our mistakes or to identify areas of weakness in our practice, or even aspects of our personalities that prevent us working well in a team. If there is mutual respect, supervisor and supervisee should be able to take a 'helicopter view'; that is the ability to rise up and look down at the supervisee's practice together and engage in a joint journey of discovery and learning.

▶ Ways of learning

The most common formative activities in supervision are:

■ Discussing critical incidents and what can be learned from these experiences (reflecting on practice).

■ Receiving help in a particular task such as filling in a form (coaching).

■ Exploring difficult situations and identifying options (problem solving).

■ Receiving guidance from someone with particular knowledge or more experience (mentoring).

Activity 12.5

Read Example 12.2. Note down when Sonia and Nelson do any of the above four common formative activities in supervision.

Example 12.2

Sonia is having a supervision meeting with her manager, Nelson. They begin by agreeing any additions to their agenda that has the following standing items:

1. Key working responsibilities.

2. Team and organisational issues.

3. Health and safety updates.

---

4. Practical issues: annual leave, absence.

5. Progress on performance and learning objectives.

Sonia says that she would also like to discuss a problem that she is having with a colleague in the team, because it is making her feel very stressed. Nelson suggests that as they have an hour, they should spend half an hour on the standing items and half an hour on the team problem, as it is clearly affecting Sonia very badly.

Sonia described a recent team meeting during which she believed a colleague was undermining her. She said that this person made many jokes at her expense and encouraged people to laugh at her because she did not feel confident in speaking in front of a group. Sonia said this had been happening ever since she joined the team six months ago.

Nelson asked Sonia some questions to explore the factors that may be influencing the relationship between this person and Sonia. It emerged that some of the goading of Sonia was focused on cultural differences, in particular that Sonia was from a different cultural background to three members of the team.

Nelson asked Sonia if there had been occasions when she had had a positive relationship with this person and she agreed that when they worked together on their own they got on better. Nelson suggested that the problem may be happening as a result of the person seeking status in the team and they explored some of the reasons Sonia found it difficult to set a limit with the person in the meetings. They discussed some different strategies for responding to the person when the problem happened, and the different ways she could speak up in an assertive way without escalating the situation. Sonia practised some phrases that she could use and Nelson gave feedback on their potential impact.

Nelson also said that it was very helpful to have this discussion, as it drew his attention to some of the team dynamics that he was unaware of. He said that he would suggest revisiting the ground rules for team meetings at the next meeting.

Nelson had the supervision record form and made notes of action points as they discussed the items. At the end of the meeting he wrote a brief summary of the key points discussed for each item on the agenda, ensuring that he did not record confidential information.

Hopefully you will agree that Sonia and Nelson covered all four of the common formative activities in supervision. These activities are often spontaneous rather than planned, perhaps arising because of something that is on the supervisee's mind or an event that has happened just before the meeting. We assume that

Sonia learned something about the dynamics between her and her colleague and some useful techniques for confronting difficult behaviour. These unplanned and informal ways of learning have probably been undervalued in the past in comparison with the attention and resources given to formal training through courses and workshops. Consequently, when a person identifies that they have a learning need, they tend to look for a course to attend. In Example 12.2, Nelson could quickly have distanced himself from the problem that Sonia brought to the meeting by suggesting she went on an assertion course. Instead, he used his skills to help her develop and took responsibility for his role in the team dynamics.

Gradually, forward-thinking organisations are coming to realise that employees should have access to a range of ways of learning and not just formal group sessions, because:

- Different people learn best in different ways.

- Different teaching methods work better for different topics.

- Transfer of learning into the workplace is more effective through particular methods.

- The greater cost of a particular method is not necessarily associated with the best outcome.

Attending a course often has a great appeal because it has other benefits, for example the opportunity to meet new people and to spend time away from work. However, if you really want to learn effectively it is worth exploring other methods.

Below are 14 different ways of learning, with examples of how they may suit particular learning and development needs.

1. *Coaching* from a skilled colleague.

   - Improving writing skills.

   - Using assertion skills.

2. *Mentoring* from someone who has the qualities and skills to act as a 'guide' based on their experience.

   - Setting up and running a new employment scheme.

   - Taking on new and unfamiliar management responsibilities.

3. *Structured work or research project* to help develop specific skills and/or knowledge.

   - Learning how to write a policy.

   - Finding out about the needs of carers in your locality.

4. *On-the-job instruction* working alongside someone who knows the job well – sometimes known as 'sitting with Nellie'.

- Induction into a new role.

- Learning how to organise a care plan review.

5. *Guided reading* such as studying a manual, reading a recommended article or book or researching information on the Internet, with an opportunity to discuss what you have discovered with someone.

   - Learning new policies.

   - The positive and negative aspects of a new medication.

6. *Reflective diary*: writing about an experience and reflecting on what happened, what you did, what you learned from it and what you will do differently next time.

   - How to handle conflict with people.

   - How to promote the rights of people.

7. *E-learning*: using the Internet or a CD-Rom.

   - Principles and values for mental health work.

   - Developing emotional intelligence at work.

8. *Shadowing*: spending time following another person and learning about what they do.

   - Finding out about the advocacy service.

   - How to work with people who have a dual diagnosis.

9. *Observation or visits* to a service that does similar work or is an example of good practice.

   - Getting ideas for new activities.

   - How to work with someone who has a form of mental distress that you are unfamiliar with.

10. *Mini teaching sessions for colleagues* through making use of time in team meetings or setting up a specific session time, for example a journal club.

    - New developments in health and safety practice.

    - What is meant by 'recovery'.

11. *Action learning groups*: a group of people meeting regularly to share their experiences at work and support each other in testing out new ideas and approaches to problems.

    - Managing a team for the first time.

    - Managing change.

12. *Action research*: a very structured approach that involves identifying an area of work that needs improving, gathering information and researching new ideas

or current evidence about effective practice, making a plan, implementing it and evaluating it.

- Introducing a new therapeutic technique.
- Setting up a service user consultation forum.

13. *Short in-house or external course* designed to meet learning needs that staff may have in common.

- Moving and handling techniques.
- Mental health legislation.

14. *Open learning course*, making use of distance learning materials.

- Theory and models in mental health work.
- The history of the service user movement.

Activity 12.5

Consider the 14 ways of learning that have just been described.
Make a record of the following:

- How many of these 14 ways have you experienced?
- Are there any you found very useful?
- Are there any you found not so useful?
- What about those you have not experienced – are there any you would like to try out?

▶ **Selecting the right learning method: do we have particular learning styles?**

The concept of reflective practice has been actively promoted in recent years in health and social care and in simple terms this is perhaps a more formal version of learning by experience – something that is a natural part of growing and developing. Schon (1983) is one of the key theorists in the field of reflective practice. He suggested that often there are no definitely right or wrong answers to complex problems, only good and not so good ones, and that the context in which professionals use their knowledge and skills is an important factor in the decisions they make. He described two types of reflection:

- Reflection in action: the process of using experience to make decisions in a situation while it is happening.
- Reflection on action: the process of looking back and thinking about something that has happened.

We all do both of these, to varying degrees, but reflective practice is a way of making these unconscious processes more explicit and capturing the learning points through discussing them or writing them down.

Some practitioners find the concept of reflective practice quite difficult to grasp. People tend to have preferences about ways of learning and sometimes this is due to only feeling comfortable with methods they are familiar with, or because they feel under-confident about a particular approach – perhaps because they believe that they are not good at writing. Our preferences are also influenced by our personalities and our particular strengths. For example, reflective practice may be a natural and normal part of the way that someone approaches their work and perhaps they are used to keeping a personal diary about key events in their life. Others may be 'doers' and prefer to look forward and to get on with trying out new ideas rather than thinking them through in advance.

There has been a considerable amount of research into what is called individual 'learning styles' to explore whether an approach such as keeping a reflective diary is suitable and beneficial for everyone. For example, Honey and Mumford (1992) have suggested that there are four key learning styles and that most people tend to have one or two preferred styles:

- The *activist* learns best from activities where they can get involved in a task or project and tackle a new challenge.

- The *reflector* learns through thinking about and reviewing their experiences or those of others, considering all angles.

- The *theorist* likes models, systems and ideas and emphasises the conclusions drawn from an activity, working in a logical fashion.

- The *pragmatist* moves forward and learns well when there is a link between theory and real work, returning from courses with ideas that they want to try out.

Although some have criticised this idea of putting people into categories and questioned whether the concept of learning styles is valid (Coffield *et al.*, 2004), it may be worth thinking about whether you can recognise a leaning towards any of these in yourself, as it may help you select appropriate learning methods. For example:

- The activist may prefer project-based learning, trying out an idea.

- The reflector may prefer reading and discussion.

- The theorist may enjoy seminars and presentations by experts.

- The pragmatist may benefit from visits and networking to find out about approaches that other people have found successful.

Activity 12.6

Which style do you think suits you best? Perhaps you like a mixture of styles?

▶ **Evidencing your learning for your portfolio**

Some learning activity will naturally produce evidence for your portfolio because there is a product such as an assignment or the results of a project. These can be added to your portfolio as evidence of your development and learning. Other learning experiences can easily slip away and you may need to make an effort to capture the essence of what you have learned and record the key points. In fact, the act of writing can be the moment at which the exact nature of what you have learned crystallises in your mind. If you think for example of a recent training course that you have attended, you may have been aware at the end of the day that you learned something really interesting and useful, but you are not quite sure what it is. It is worthwhile taking ten minutes to make a note for your portfolio and this is a simple structure to use:

- Date and activity.
- An outline of the content or what happened.
- Key learning points for me.
- How I will follow it up.

Example 12.3

Date and activity

5 April: We had a talk at our team meeting by a new psychologist about his role and service.

An outline of the content or what happened:

- Why the new service has been set up.
- The two types of therapies it offers: CBT and CAT.
- The similarities and differences between the two therapies.
- Who each therapy may be suitable for.

Key learning points for me

- Understanding why a service user has been turned down for CBT and referred for CAT as this wasn't explained to us at the time.

- The opportunities for learning more about both methods at the university.

How I will follow it up

- Download some information about the university taster sessions.

- Raise the service as an item at the next team meeting for us to consider how to ensure service users know about what is available.

This structure can be used for a wide variety of learning experiences including training courses, meetings, significant events, or even if you have just had the chance to do something new at work.

▶ Access to education, training and development opportunities

It is important to have access to education, training and development opportunities. Much will depend on where you are employed. The NHS, being a large and relatively well-resourced organisation, has work-force and staff development and training departments. Individual professions will have their own mechanisms for pre- and post-qualifying training. It may be harder to access education and training if you work in the voluntary sector. Workers who are not affiliated to a specific profession may also find it harder to access training, as career and qualification structures may not be in place (Cuthbert & Basset 2007). Similarly, if you are a service user or carer, you may find it difficult to gain access to helpful and relevant learning opportunities.

The 'learning and development toolkit for the whole of the mental health workforce' (Department of Health, 2007) may make access easier, with its emphasis on multi-agency education and training partnerships, whereby it encourages all key stakeholders to:

> have a part to play in supporting the learning and development of staff. The expectation is that, once informed about the current and future agendas for mental health, they will, in respect of their role, make the appropriate links with their key partners across health and social care. The aim is to help shape a local learning and development strategy, moulding the wider national agenda to fit their local; circumstances. (Department of Health, 2007, p. 8)

Finally, it is important to remember that although your employer will have responsibilities to you, you also have a responsibility yourself to be proactive in seeking out and making best use of learning and development opportunities.

▶ **References**

Coffield, F., Moseley, D., Hall, E., Ecclestone, K. (2004) *Should we be using learning styles? What research has to say to practice.* London: Learning and Skills Research Centre.

Cuthbert, S. & Basset, T. (2007) The non professionally affiliated workforce in mental health – who are these generic mental health workers and where do they fit within a workforce strategy? *Journal of Mental Health Workforce Development,* in press.

Department of Health (2007) *Mental Health Policy Implementation Guide: A Learning and Development Toolkit for the Whole of the Mental Health Workforce across both Health and Social Care.* London: Department of Health.

Department of Health (2004) *The Ten Essential Shared Capabilities: A Framework for the Whole of the Mental Health Workforce.* London: Department of Health/NHSU/Sainsbury Centre/NIMHE.

Honey, P. & Mumford, A. (1992) *The Manual of Learning Styles.* Maidenhead: Peter Honey.

Inskipp, F. & Proctor, B. (1995) *The Art, Craft and Tasks of Counselling Supervision.* Twickenham: Cascade Publications.

Schon, D. (1983) *The Reflective Practitioner.* New York: Basic Books.

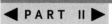

PART II

Issues for mental health practice

◀ CHAPTER THIRTEEN ▶

Social perspectives on mental distress

Jerry Tew

University of Birmingham

While it may seem obvious that there can be connections between mental distress and 'problems of living', we tend to lack conceptual models by which to map out these links more clearly. This chapter will explore how social factors may not only contribute to mental distress, but also play a key role in promoting resilience and recovery. For many people, making more coherent links between the 'inner' and 'outer' aspects of their experience can be crucial in making sense of their distress and laying the foundations for recovery.

The development of social perspectives involves building on a substantial body of work that has been undertaken over many years, but has tended to be marginalised as biomedical approaches have become more dominant in mental health practice (Double, 2005). However, since the introduction of the National Service Framework in England (Department of Health, 1999) and, more recently, the rolling out of the Essential Shared Capabilities for mental health workers (Department of Health, 2004), the pendulum has started to swing back towards a more holistic approach that embraces the social (Duggan, Cooper & Foster, 2002; Tew, 1999). This has met with an enthusiastic response from many service users and carers, who saw this as something that had tended to be missing from the psychiatric services they had been receiving.

▶ Social factors and vulnerability to mental distress

The stress–vulnerability model

The Stress–Vulnerability model (Zubin, Stuart & Condray, 1992) provides a useful starting point for conceptualising how social and biological factors may

Learning About Mental Health Practice. Edited by Theo Stickley and Thurstine Basset
© 2008 John Wiley & Sons, Ltd

come together to contribute to mental breakdown or subsequent relapse (see also Dohrenwend, 2000). It suggests that, faced with a currently stressful situation, some individuals may be more susceptible than others to become mentally distressed. While some of this vulnerability may come from genetic predisposition, a substantial part of the difference may result from social experiences (Brown & Harris, 1978; Tienari et al., 1994).

Rather than maintain an ideological opposition between biological and social approaches to vulnerability, recent research is demonstrating an interesting convergence. Developments in neurobiology are showing how early childhood experiences of trauma or deprivation can become reflected in the 'hard wiring' of neural pathways in the brain (Putnam & Trickett, 1997; Read et al., 2001; Shonkoff & Phillips, 2000). For example, if one's life experience has not provided the basis for learning how to trust others, one may not have developed all the neural connections by which to judge who is (or is not) trustworthy. In this way, social factors may become imprinted as neurological differences that may lead to difficulties and vulnerabilities in relation to navigating adult life. However, as there is evidence that the brain retains some continued malleability in response to environmental stimuli, then we have the possibility that, if a person goes on to have more positive social experiences (perhaps resulting from therapeutic interventions), this may result in more favourable neurological adaptations that would prove helpful in reducing their longer-term vulnerability.

Personal relationships and life events

Attachment theory suggests that difficulties in early relationships with primary caregivers can leave people with characteristic patterns in how they may approach relationships with others in later life. Research has shown how children may adapt when faced with situations of loss, no one being there for them in any real sense, or when key figures may be inconsistent and unpredictable (Ainsworth et al., 1978). They may tend to avoid closeness altogether, or have a sense of insecurity that may make it hard for them just to 'be themselves' in a relationship, and instead always feel that they have to please or manipulate the affections of the other. Such patterns may increase vulnerability to mental distress, as they may reduce the person's potential to access support and security in their personal relationships. Research has shown that the death of a parent in childhood correlates with increased likelihood both of depression (Brown & Harris, 1978) and schizophrenia (Bleuler, 1978). While concepts such as neglect or inconsistency are less straightforward to measure reliably, empirical support for the significance of attachment issues comes from recent inpatient surveys in which between one- and two-thirds of respondents reported experiencing physical or emotional neglect in childhood (Holowka et al., 2003; Lipshitz, 1999a).

There is strong evidence to suggest that the aftermath of experiences of trauma or abuse may contribute to subsequent vulnerability to mental distress (Myin-Germeys et al., 2003), particularly when there was the absence of a safe person to turn to for support at the time. Physically and psychologically invasive

236

acts such as sexual or emotional abuse would seem to be particularly frequent precursors of experiences of mental distress (Ensink, 1992; Staples & Dare, 1996; Williams & Watson, 1996). Other events, such as abandonment or witnessing domestic violence, may also be experienced as traumatic in this sense (Perry *et al.*, 1990). What may be seen as common to all these forms of trauma is that they render the person a powerless victim of circumstances or forces beyond their control, unable to negotiate their boundaries and relationships with others. It is this that may be seen to construct the social (as distinct to any physical) aspect of a traumatic experience, and may come to have a profound impact on a person's sense of self and how they negotiate relationships with others.

At a theoretical level, it has been shown how social trauma – and the subsequent emotional, behavioural and lifestyle adaptations that people may make – can render people vulnerable to a wide range of experiences of mental distress (Plumb, 2005). Particularly strong connections have been drawn between past experiences of childhood abuse and issues such as eating disorders, borderline personality disorder and substance misuse (Mullen *et al.*, 1993). Over recent years, there has been increasing awareness that such trauma may play a causal role in a much broader range of distress, including psychosis (Read *et al.*, 2004). Research with problematic voice-hearing experiences indicates that the majority of people could link their onset to some specifiable trauma (Romme *et al.*, 1994).

Social disadvantage and discrimination

There is strong evidence that adverse features of people's social environment may constitute vulnerability factors, including lack of education, unemployment and being brought up in a poor and socially disorganised neighbourhood, especially in inner urban areas (Fryer, 1995; Fryers, Meltzer & Jenkins, 2001; Harrison *et al.*, 2001; Rogers & Pilgrim, 2003). It has been suggested that it may be perceived injustice, in terms of *relative* disadvantage and exclusion from social opportunities, rather than *absolute* levels of deprivation, that may be more pernicious in its effects (see Dohrenwend, 1998). If a sense of injustice cannot be resolved, and where it may be compounded by experiences of powerlessness and isolation, anger and resentment may have to be internalised, leading to poor self-esteem, self-abusive behaviours, or an overwhelming sense of helplessness – which, in turn, may create vulnerability to mental distress (Elstad, 1998; Proctor, 2002).

There is wider evidence to suggest that subjection to any form of social discrimination may increase vulnerability to mental distress (Janssen *et al.*, 2003). Research has found that many ethnic groups are much more likely to be diagnosed with schizophrenia than are white British people (Fearon *et al.*, 2006). This is particularly the case for African Caribbean people, especially those born in Britain (Harrison *et al.*, 1984; McGovern & Cope, 1987a). They are also much more likely to be subjected to compulsory treatment (McGovern & Cope, 1987b). These differences cannot be explained by biological difference – as no such enhanced rates are to be found in countries of origin (Nazroo, 1997) – or by the impact of migration, as there is a higher incidence among British-born people. As Peter Ferns argues:

> We are therefore left with two possible hypotheses, each of which may be true to some extent. The experience of being Black in Britain may lead to a greater incidence of serious mental distress, and/or social attitudes and professional practice may lead to African-Caribbean people being selectively picked out and labelled as 'mentally ill' where this would not be the case if they were White British. (Ferns, 2005, p. 131; see also Fernando, 1999; Nazroo & King, 2002)

Both of these hypotheses implicate racism as the contributory factor that results in greater vulnerability, and this is supported by other evidence. Recent research shows that people from ethnic minorities are less likely to be admitted to psychiatric hospital if they live in a poor inner-city area with a high ethnic population than if they live in better-off, predominantly white areas (Boydell *et al.*, 2001). This unexpected finding would seem to be best explained on the basis of 'reduced exposure to direct prejudice' (Halpern & Nazroo, 2000, p. 34).

Gender-based oppression may also contribute to vulnerability to mental distress. Women can be disproportionately exposed to a range of vulnerability factors, from poverty to abuse (Williams, 2005). The overall incidence of mental distress (excluding substance misuse) among women has been significantly higher than for men, but this hides a more complex (and changing) picture in which women and men appear more or less prone to particular forms of mental distress (Prior, 1999). Women can tend to turn their anger and distress inwards, resulting in greater vulnerability to anxiety, depression and borderline personality disorder, whereas men can tend more often to push it outwards, leading to increased prevalence of substance misuse and anti-social behaviour. There has been little overall difference in rates for psychosis between men and women, although there have been significant differences in terms of age of onset (Read, 2004).

However, if we move beyond overall diagnostic categories and look at people's experiences of mental distress, then the oppressive force of sexism may be seen to be more strongly implicated. Both compliance with, and rejection of, normative gender roles may create particular vulnerabilities to mental distress (Chesler, 1972; Johnstone, 2000). In relation to people with a diagnosis of schizophrenia, studies indicate that:

> Men tend to be emotionally and socially closed down, have problems thinking clearly... and sometimes believe themselves to be extremely important. Meanwhile, women tend to have very strong feelings, to dislike themselves and to be frightened that others will hurt them. (Read, 2004, p. 179)

Over recent years, hospital admission rates (and particularly compulsory admission rates) for young men have been rising more rapidly than those for women, suggesting that social changes in terms of gender roles and expectations may be creating an increased vulnerability to mental distress among this group.

Lesbians and gay men may not only face the impact of sexist oppression, but also that of heterosexism and homophobia (Carr, 2005). Potentially this may lead to greater loneliness, isolation and internalisation of guilt and fear (Mcfarlane, 1998), less support from family than heterosexual counterparts (Jorm *et al.*, 2002) and experiences of victimisation resulting in lowered self-esteem (Otis & Skinner, 1996). The resulting increase in vulnerability is reflected in lesbians and gay men being 'greater users of mental health services' (King *et al.*, 2003, p. 557).

Family dynamics and communication issues

There is a long tradition, going back to the work of Bateson *et al.* (1956), Laing and Esterson (1964) and Lidz (1975), which has sought to identify particular patterns of family conflict or communication that may increase the likelihood of a child developing irrational or psychotic patterns of thinking in later life. Bateson describes the 'double bind', a recurring pattern in which a child receives simultaneous but contradictory messages to which they must respond and, due to their position of powerlessness, they neither have the option of seeking clarification nor of refusing to respond at all. As a result, whatever logical attempt they may make in order to comply will be doomed to failure: they are always going to get it wrong.

In a more systematic way, family communication patterns that are characterised by emotional over-involvement, intrusiveness or hostility (particularly where negative feelings are not owned by family members) have been shown to lead to more frequent experiences of relapse for people with psychosis (Kuipers, Leff & Lam, 1992). This type of interaction was termed, somewhat misleadingly, high expressed emotion. Subsequent work, particularly using behavioural family therapy approaches, has shown that honest and direct expressions of feelings (including 'difficult' emotions such as anger) have no adverse impact, whereas simmering or covert hostility (i.e. high *un*expressed emotion) can be very destructive to mental health. However, this body of work has tended not to countenance the possibility that, if such factors could increase vulnerability to relapse, then, by the same logic, they might also have a contributory role in making people vulnerable to breakdown in the first place (Johnstone, 1999). The latter view has been supported by a range of longitudinal studies, which have shown that family disturbance rather than genetics tends to be the main predictor of subsequent breakdown (Tienari *et al.*, 1994; see also Goldstein, 1985).

▶ Resilience

It is important not to take too deterministic a stance in relation to vulnerability factors. Only some of those who are faced with the range of issues described above may experience subsequent mental distress or breakdown. While this may be because they never encounter sufficient stressors in later life to 'tip them over the edge', it may also be because their vulnerabilities are protected by compensating areas of strength. A focus on strengths as well as deficits or vulnerabilities fits well with current approaches to recovery practice in mental health (Saleebey, 1996). It may therefore be helpful to conceptualise a second variable that relates to the impact of experiences of empowerment, recognition and support, which may become internalised as *resilience* (Rutter, 1990; Stevenson & Zimmerman, 2005).

Secure attachment experiences (not necessarily with primary caregivers) can imbue a positive sense of self-esteem and a basic confidence in one's ability to make and sustain personal relationships in later life – and deal with the 'ups and downs' that may go with this (Daniel, Sally & Robbie, 1999). Experiences of having someone supportive to go to in times of difficulty may provide the basis for developing help-seeking and problem-solving strategies, which can be utilised again in subsequent situations. Recognition of personal achievements and positive experiences of having influence in social situations can contribute to enhanced self-esteem. Experiences of solidarity with others can provide a power base, and a security of identity, from which to challenge and resist oppression (Ungar, 2001). Resilience may be understood as a repertoire of positive messages, strategies and interactional patterns that may be drawn from such experiences that enables the person to deal more effectively with challenging situations, so reducing the potential risk of mental distress or breakdown.

By looking at both vulnerability and resilience factors, we have a more dynamic model by which to see how one may outweigh the other, depending on people's past life experiences – see Table 13.1 and Figure 13.1 later in the chapter.

Table 13.1   Vulnerability and resilience factors

Vulnerability factors	Resilience factors
Neglect or inconsistency from primary care-givers leading to anxious or ambivalent attachment behaviour	Secure attachment experiences
Loss of, or rejection by, key others	Having someone safe to go to in times of difficulty
Sexual, physical or other abuse	Positive experiences of having influence within social situations
Exposure to patterns of hostile or intrusive communication	Achieving and having achievements recognised by others
Poverty, and social disadvantage	Positive sense of self-esteem
Poor educational attainment	Broad repertoire of social skills and problem-solving strategies
Discrimination and oppression on the basis of race, culture, gender, sexual orientation etc.	Experiences of solidarity with others suffering similar forms of discrimination or oppression

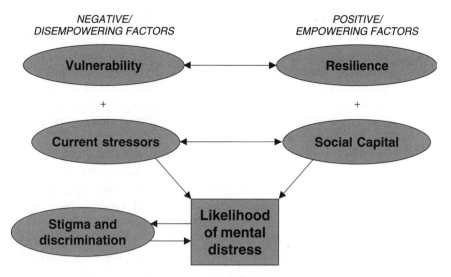

NEGATIVE/
DISEMPOWERING FACTORS

POSITIVE/
EMPOWERING FACTORS

Vulnerability

Resilience

+

+

Current stressors

Social Capital

Stigma and
discrimination

Likelihood
of mental
distress

Figure 13.1   Social factors and likelihood of mental distress.

▶ Social capital

Faced with a currently stressful situation, one's level of access to a range of social resources may be crucial in determining whether or not this may lead to adverse mental health consequences. There is evidence that factors such as being in employment, having the opportunities provided by a good level of educational attainment, and being part of supportive family or social networks can play a significant part in determining whether particular situations may or may not to provoke the onset of mental distress or breakdown. Such resources can be important in terms of offering choices and opportunities, and in providing options for social or practical forms of support. Theoretical understandings of social capital may be helpful in conceptualising the factors that shape both the quantity and the quality of people's social interactions (McKenzie & Harpham, 2006).

It is suggested that there are two aspects to social capital. First, there is the *cognitive* aspect: a person's situation within, and internalisation of, a set of subcultural attitudes and norms around belonging, reciprocity and entitlement to support. Secondly, there is the *structural* aspect of social capital: the existence in the here-and-now of actual networks of social connections and support systems that can be accessed. However, without being included within the cognitive aspects of social capital, a person may be unable to access (or even recognise) whatever support and resources may be available 'out there'.

What can be missing from some analyses of social capital is an acknowledgement of the degree to which social divisions and power relations within communities may determine one's position in relation to both cognitive and structural aspects of social capital. Overall indices of social cohesion, prosperity or community safety may cover over the varying experiences of women, ethnic minorities or others who may be subordinated within, or excluded from, the mainstream of community life. Sometimes, even when potential supports are available, the terms of accessing these may feel unacceptable, perhaps in terms of being patronised, having to be compliant or being treated as an inferior. The work of Bourdieu (1990) may be helpful in analysing inequalities in access to social capital, and exploring the defensive 'conservation strategies' whereby dominant section of society may actively seek to prevent those deemed marginal or deviant from 'joining the club' (Tew, 2005).

Although usually applied to communities, the concept of social capital may also be relevant at a smaller scale in terms of the functioning of close relationships with family and friends. In general terms, research shows that being in a partner relationship tends to reduce the likelihood of experiencing mental distress. However, the benefits for men can tend to be somewhat greater than those for women (Prior, 1999), suggesting that the shared understandings that may constitute cognitive capital may be skewed on gender lines, making it easier for men to access (or demand) support from women than the other way around.

▶ Current stress

There is already considerable research that suggests that many life events and transitions can be inherently stressful, as they tend to involve some dislocation of established ways of dealing with the world, of social identity, or of patterns of giving and receiving support (Dohrenwend et al., 1978). Transitions that involve losses, such as bereavement, separation or redundancy, can be particularly testing of people's resilience and social support systems. However, events with positive connotations, such as getting married or having a baby, may also be disruptive of former identities, social supports or coping strategies – and therefore act as stressors in relation to people's mental health.

Just as past experiences of trauma, abuse or oppression may contribute to vulnerability, similar experiences in the here-and-now may act as a trigger for mental or emotional breakdown. Where the current experience (e.g. sexual harassment) may resonate with past experiences (e.g. of sexual abuse), a relatively 'minor' occurrence may have an unexpectedly serious impact, acting as the 'straw that broke the camel's back'.

Longer-term scenarios may also act as stressors, such as facing, on a daily basis, incidents of racism, sexism or homophobia, while lacking sufficient support or power to challenge or resist this. Both over- and under-stimulation can be experienced as stressful, particularly when the person may feel powerless to regulate their level of involvement: either being burdened with more than they can deal with, or being excluded from spheres of activity that might be important to them.

Less visible, but equally stressful, may be having to negotiate between competing expectations from powerful others, for example having responsibility as a carer while balancing this with other responsibilities as a parent or an employee (see Milne & Williams, 2003). Conflicts or confusions around identity (perhaps on the basis of culture or sexual orientation), and the contradictory social pressures that may go along with this, can constitute pervasive and insidious forms of stress. Levels of stress may be compounded if a person feels powerless and stuck within a situation, unable either to challenge or to leave.

By including additional factors, in terms of resilience and social capital, we arrive at a more comprehensive model as to how social factors may influence the likelihood of a person experiencing mental distress (see Figure 13.1 later in the chapter). This opens up a broader vision of how social interventions may be targeted if the likelihood to breakdown or relapse is to be reduced – building on positives rather than just trying to minimise the effect of potentially negative factors.

Reflective exercise

Think of times when you have felt very stressed. List the events or circumstances that have caused the stress. When you have finished, see how many of these stressors are socially related.

▶ Living with mental distress: stigma, social exclusion and the social model of disability

Once someone's mental distress crosses a certain threshold and becomes socially visible, they become immersed in a new set of (not entirely welcome) social relationships and constructions. From a range of perspectives, different theorists from Schoff (1975) and Goldman (1991) to Foucault (1967) have sought to understand the process whereby people tend to lose their status as citizens and, generating apparently irrational levels of hostility from others, find that they are systematically excluded from participation in much of mainstream social activity (Tew, 1999). Theories of labelling, stigmatisation and discourse each grapple with the idea that the way that the threshold is defined, and the subsequent social reactions to those who are deemed to have crossed it, are much more social constructions that anything to do with the individual's presentation of mental distress. As Becker argues:

> Social groups create deviance by making rules whose infraction constitutes deviance, and by applying these rules to particular people and labelling them as outsiders... Deviance is not a quality of the act the person commits. (Becker, 1963, p. 9)

Within a social context in which 'mental illness' comes to mark a category of 'otherness', harmless but different behaviour, such as talking to one's voices or walking with an unusual gait, may evoke social responses of exclusion or outright hostility. Deviance theory can be particularly helpful in showing how quickly the imposition of a label (such as 'nutter', 'mentally ill', 'schizophrenic' etc.) can come to define the whole person within both lay and professional discourses, so that all their behaviour, beliefs and thoughts come to be seen as symptomatic of, and further evidence for, their label (Goffman, 1991). In turn, being labelled in this way may result in a denial of access to many forms of social capital (Breier *et al.*, 1991; Davidson *et al.*, 2001) and negative messages may quickly become internalised, undermining what may already have become a somewhat fragile sense of self-esteem (Corrigan, 1998). In this way, stigmatisation may be seen to be profoundly disempowering and oppressive.

Such perspectives link with the social model of disability. For many people, what is experienced as most disabling is not their impairment, but societal responses to it. These may be framed by a construction of 'normality' that puts down, patronises or excludes those who fall outside its definition.

Rejecting their construction as medical pathology or social tragedy, disabled people have sought to shift the terms of the discourse from blaming individuals for their failure to be 'normal' to challenging society for its failure to offer equality of citizenship and social participation to people who may appear different from pre-vailing constructions of 'normality' (Morris, 1993; Oliver, 1996). This has involved challenging much of conventional care practice and medical treatment, which had tended to be organised around individualised deficit models – a concern just with what people cannot do and how they are (implicitly) inferior to 'normal' people.

In many ways, this analysis may be seen to apply to people whose impairment is mental distress. For many people, living with mental distress may be difficult, but this may be nothing compared with dealing with the 'double whammy' of unhelpful or oppressive responses that they may receive from society at large, from friends and family, or from professional helpers (Laurance, 2003). However, there are also significant differences: whereas disabled people predominantly face being patronised or excluded, people with mental distress can face a more active hostility – a level of fear that can translate into their demonisation as a threat to 'normal' citizens and a risk to social order.

Mental distress would seem to be the location for some of the most invidious processes of social labelling that are faced by any identified social group within modern Western societies. This may be seen to be reflected both in media coverage (Philo *et al.*, 1994) and in the degree to which people with mental distress face discrimination in relation to housing, employment and participation in mainstream social and recreational activities. In seeking to understand this, it may be helpful to turn to a wider social and political analysis.

Within the implicit social contract of modern societies, citizenship may be seen to depend on a commitment to rationality and a capacity for self-regulation. While living the appearance of being free and self-directing, people must actually behave in a relatively predictable manner, sticking to commitments and taking respon-sibility for their actions. Social and economic opportunities come with being per-ceived as the 'right sort' of citizen. Historically, dominant social groups were able to define others (such as women and black and working-class people) as unstable and irrational – and hence a potential threat to the established social order. On this basis, they were excluded from full citizenship and 'kept in their place' (Pateman, 1988; Venn, 1997). Now, while such groups are (at least in theory) enfranchised, it is people with mental distress who are becoming increasingly constructed as an unruly group that must be contained at all costs for fear that they destabilise the social order. They have come to be 'deemed inimical to society or the state – indeed could be regarded as a menace to the proper workings of an orderly, efficient, progressive, rational society' (Porter, 1987, p. 15; see also Foucault, 1967).

Unlike other forms of impairment or disability, there is a further twist in the story for people with mental distress. However frustrating or demoralising societal responses to physical impairments may be, these do not have much potential to interact with the impairment and make it worse. For a person with mental distress, the 'double whammy' can become a 'triple whammy', with negative or oppressive societal reactions compounding other social stressors and impacting adversely on their mental distress – or at least impeding their possibilities for recovery and reclaiming social networks (Dinos *et al.*, 2004; Wright, Gronfein & Owens, 2000). In this way, there is a danger of a vicious circle with increasing distress triggering ever more hostile or exclusionary responses, and these responses, in turn, pushing the person into an even deeper mental health crisis (see Figure 13.1).

▶ **Power and powerlessness**

A common theme that runs through much of the discussion so far is that of power (Tew, 2005; see also Thompson, 2007). As we have seen, experiences of relative powerlessness, resulting from social disadvantage or systematic discrimination, may contribute both to acquired vulnerability and current stress. Stigma may be seen to depend on the operation of oppressive and collusive forms of power by mainstream social groups, expressed through patronising or hostile attitudes and behaviours directed towards those defined as 'different'.

At a more personal scale, inter-personal power relations can play a major part in defining whether particular events (or on-going situations) are simply perceived as difficult or frustrating, or whether they come to be experienced as traumatic or abusive – and hence likely to contribute to vulnerability or stress. One may find oneself effectively trapped within a situation in which one is subjected to oppression by more powerful others, or one is faced by a collusive 'wall of silence' or lack of concern if one seeks help. Alternatively, one may be part of relationships in which others can offer either protective power (perhaps providing a place of safety) or co-operative power (in the form of mutual understanding, support or collective action). It is one's positioning within such power relations that may determine the degree to which one has control or influence, what options are available, and whether one faces the event in isolation or has the support of others (see Tew, 2002, 2006).

As we have seen, resilience is typically developed through cumulative experiences of personal empowerment or co-operative power with others – and, in the here-and-now, it is one's linkage to various forms of social capital that may provide opportunities for accessing co-operative and protective power within community or family networks.

In Figure 13.1, disempowering factors are situated on the left and empowering factors on the right.

▶ Recovery and social inclusion

In its development of the term 'recovery', the service user movement has increasingly come to define it in social terms: as regaining active control over one's life and reclaiming a socially valued lifestyle rather than becoming 'symptom free' (Anthony, 1993; Deegan, 1988).

Historical analysis indicates that variations in overall rates of recovery can depend more on prevailing social circumstances than on availability of treatments and therapies. Recovery may often depend on opportunities for social inclusion (Repper & Perkins, 2003). Recovery rates have been shown to correlate with prevailing economic conditions, and hence the availability of work opportunities. Similarly, rates of recovery vary across cultures, with rates in the West being as little as half those in some developing countries where mental distress may be less stigmatised and irrationality seen as less of a threat to social order – and hence where people with mental distress may be expected to rejoin the work force and to slot back into valued social roles as soon as they are able to make a contribution, rather than face ongoing social exclusion (Warner, 1994).

This challenges the assumption that one has to get well first and then be assimilated back into 'normal' society. Instead, it suggests a more integrated approach that addresses the personal and the social at the same time. Progress depends on claiming the right to 'get a life', while working to resolve issues that contribute to vulnerability, building on strengths and coping strategies, and managing distress experiences with whatever supports or strategies work best (including medication or other forms of medical treatment). Many service users report that, as a result of taking on social roles of their choosing, their self-esteem is enhanced and, in turn, they feel more empowered to deal with their distress experiences (or these start to fade more into the background).

Progress towards social inclusion requires a 'twin-track' approach: support and coaching for the individual, coupled with networking and community development activity to enhance access to social capital. Research suggests that while educational approaches to tackling stigma may change reported attitudes among the wider community, they may have little impact on actual behaviour: it is only through direct contact with mental health service users that potentially exclusionary or discriminatory behaviour can start to be changed (Holmes *et al.*, 1999). This suggests that service users and service user groups may need to play a pivotal role in 'stigma-busting' strategies.

Conceptualising recovery in this way foregrounds the social as an important arena for change, and shifts the onus of responsibility away from the individual to a more equal partnership between individual and those around them. Building on the social model of disability, it is not for the person with mental distress to have to demonstrate that they are sufficiently 'normal' in order to be let out into the wider world, it is the wider world that has to become more tolerant, flexible and supportive – able to offer opportunities to the person on the basis of what they can do, rather than exclude them on the basis of what they cannot (yet) do. This suggests that interventions and supports to enable recovery should be as much community focused as they are individually focused (Figure 13.2). This may involve challenging the social attitudes, practices and assumptions that constitute barriers to people accessing whatever opportunities for education, work or social life they might wish to take up.

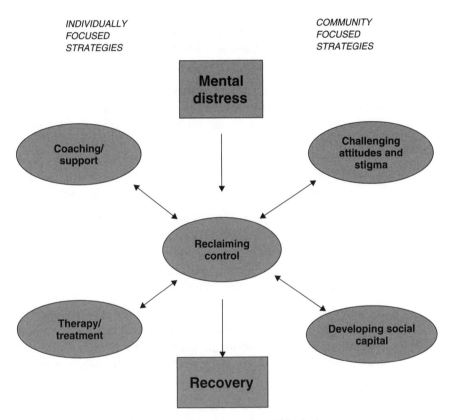

Figure 13.2   Recovery and social inclusion.

▶ Social perspectives informing practice

In this chapter I have outlined two models by which to conceptualise the role played by social factors, both in contributing to, and in protecting people from, mental distress (Figure 13.1), and the role of both individually and community focused strategies in enabling social inclusion and recovery (Figure 13.2). Together these suggest a variety of points at which socially informed interventions may make a major difference in terms of people's mental health. In particular, they suggest a focus on the following:

■ *Promotion of positive mental health*. Although identified within the National Service Framework, this has not yet received the priority it deserves. However, by using a social perspectives approach, it should be possible to target strategies to build resilience and social capital at a community level, with a particular focus on marginalised or excluded social groups.

■ *Preventive work with potentially vulnerable groups.* Many young people with high vulnerability to mental distress will already be known to education, social work and medical services, with children in the care system being a particular priority group. There may be great potential value in working with such people to enable them to deal better with the issues that may contribute to their vulnerability, build on their strengths and resilience, and develop their access to social capital as they move into adulthood. Particular approaches need to be developed and evaluated.

■ *Identifying vulnerability, stress, resilience and social capital in mental health assessments.* When people come into the mental health system, a comprehensive assessment needs to cover what social factors may have contributed to their vulnerability or constitute current stressors, what may be their areas of strength and resilience, and how well they are connected within family and community resources. This may differ from current approaches to assessment, where the focus may be more on diagnosis, risk and need for care services.

■ *Strategies to reduce vulnerability.* While adverse past experiences cannot be undone, they can be acknowledged, and people can be supported in resolving any 'unfinished business' that may arise from them. While for some, reducing their vulnerability may involve specialist counselling or therapy, others may find that peer support or other more informal strategies work better for them.

■ *Strategies to promote resilience.* Just as important as working to reduce vulnerability is a focus on enabling people to enhance their capabilities and self-esteem, for example through achieving (and have their achievements recognised), acting on their own initiative, developing problem-solving strategies and giving and receiving support.

■ *Promoting social inclusion and challenging discrimination.* Effective programmes to support social inclusion may need to include not just individual coaching and support, but also practical engagement with both community networks and providers of employment, housing, education and recreational activity. There would need to be a focus in developing not just structural but also cognitive aspects of social capital.

■ *Working with relationship and communication issues.* As well as working with wider social networks, there may also be a need to work on resolving relationship or communication issues within existing family or friendship networks, or helping to rebuild such networks if they no longer exist.

This list is by no means exhaustive and there may be many other ways in which socially informed strategies and interventions may contribute to providing more effective prevention and support for recovery in mental health. The emphasis on the social in this chapter should not be seen as a rejection of the potential value of more individually focused therapies or treatments, just as a call for a major rebalancing of effort so that 'inner' and 'outer' issues are dealt with in a properly integrated way.

▶ **References**

Ainsworth, M., Blehar, M., Waters, E. & Wall, S. (1978) *Patterns of Attachment*. Hillsdale, NJ: Lawrence Erlbaum.

Anthony, W.A. (1993) Recovery from mental illness: The guiding vision of the mental health service system in the 1990s. *Psychosocial Rehabilitation Journal*, **16**: 11–23.

Bateson, G., Jackson, D., Haley, J. & Weakland, J. (1956) Toward a theory of schizophrenia. *Behavioural Science*, **1**: 251–64.

Becker, H. (1963) *Outsiders: Studies in the Sociology of Deviance* (2nd edn). New York: Free Press.

Bleuler, M. (1978) *The Schizophrenic Disorders*. Hew Haven: Yale University Press.

Bourdieu, P. (1990) *In Other Words*. Cambridge: Polity.

Boydell, J.van Os, McKenzie, J., Allardyce, K., Goel, J., McCreadie, R. & Murray, R. (2001) Incidence of schizophrenia in ethnic minorities in London: Ecological study into interactions with environment. *British Medical Journal*, **323**: 1336.

Breier, P., Schreiber, J., Dyer, J. & Pickar, D. (1991) National Institute for Mental Health longitudinal study of chronic schizophrenia. *Archives of General Psychiatry*, **48**(7): 239–46.

Brown, G. & Harris, T. (1978) *The Social Origins of Depression*. London: Tavistock.

Carr, S. (2005) 'The sickness label infected everything we said' – Lesbian and gay perspectives on mental distress. In J. Tew (ed.), *Social Perspectives in Mental Health*. London: Jessica Kingsley.

Chesler, P. (1972) *Women and Madness*. New York: Avon.

Corrigan, P. (1998) The impact of stigma on severe mental illness. *Cognitive and Behavioral Practice*, **5**(2): 201–22.

Daniel, B., Sally, W. & Robbie, G. (1999) 'It's just common sense isn't it?' Exploring ways of putting resilience into action. *Adoption and Fostering*, **23**(3): 6–15.

Davidson, L., Haglund, K., Stayner, D., Rakfeldt, J., Chinman, M. & Tebes, J. (2001) 'It was just realising. . . that life isn't one big horror.' A qualitative study of supported socialisation. *Psychiatric Rehabilitation Journal*, **24**(3): 275–92.

Deegan, P.E. (1988) Recovery: The lived experience of rehabilitation. *Psychosocial Rehabilitation Journal*, **11**: 11–19.

Department of Health (1999) *National Service Framework for Mental Health*. London: Department of Health.

Department of Health (2004) *The 10 Essential Shared Capabilties: A Framework for the Whole of the Mental Health Workforce*. London: Department of Health.

Dinos, S., Stevens, S., Serfaty, M., Weich, S. & King M. (2004) Stigma: The feelings and experiences of 46 people with mental illness: Qualitative study. *British Journal of Psychiatry*, **184**: 176–81.

Dohrenwend, B.P. (ed.) (1998) *Adversity, Stress and Psychopathology*. Oxford: Oxford University Press.

Dohrenwend, B.P. (2000) The role of adversity and stress in psychopathology: Some evidence and its implication for theory and research. *Journal of Health and Social Behavior*, **41**(1): 1–19.

Dohrenwend, B.S., Askenasy, A., Krasnoff, L. & Dohrenwend, B.P. (1978) Exemplification of a method for scaling life events: The PERI Life Events Scale. *Journal of Health and Social Behavior* **19**(2): 205–29.

Double, D. (2005) Beyond biomedical models: A perspective from critical psychiatry. In J. Tew (ed.), *Social Perspectives in Mental Health*. London: Jessica Kingsley.

Duggan, M. with Cooper, A. & Foster, J. (2002) *Modernising the Social Model in Mental Health: A Discussion Paper*. Paper 1. London: Social Perspectives Network.

Elstad, J. (1998) The psycho-social perspective on social inequalities in health. *Sociology of Health and Illness*, **20**(5): 598–618.

Ensink, B. (1992) *Confusing Realities: A Study on Childhood Sexual Abuse and Psychiatric Symptoms*. Amsterdam: VU University Press.

Fearon, P., Kirkbride, J., Dazzan, P., Morgan, C., Morgan, K., Lloyd, T., Hutchinson, G., Tarrant, J., Fung, W., Holloway, J., Mallett, R., Harrison, G., Leff, J., Jones, P. & Murray, R. (2006) Incidence of schizophrenia and other psychoses in ethnic minority groups: Results from the MRC AESOP Study. *Psychological Medicine*, **26**: 1–10.

Fernando, S. (1999) Ethnicity and mental health. In M. Ulas & A. Connor (eds), *Mental Health and Social Work*. London: Jessica Kingsley.

Foucault, M. (1967) *Madness and Civilisation*. London: Tavistock.

Ferns, P. (2005) Finding a way forward: A Black perspective on social approaches to mental health. In J. Tew (ed.), *Social Perspectives in Mental Health*. London: Jessica Kingsley.

Fryer, D. (1995) Labour market disadvantage, deprivation and mental health. *The Psychologist*, **8**(6): 265–72.

Fryers, T., Meltzer, D. & Jenkins, R. (2001) *Mental Health Inequalities Report 1: A Systematic Literature Review*. Cambridge: Department of Public Health and Primary Care, University of Cambridge.

Goffman, E. (1991) *Asylums*. London: Penguin.

Goldstein, M. (1985) Family factors that antedate the onset of schizophrenia and related disorders. *Acta Psychiatrica Scandinavica*, **71**(suppl 319): 7–18.

Halpern, D. & Nazroo, J. (2000) The ethnic density effect. *International Journal of Social Psychiatry*, **46**: 34–6.

Harrison, G., Ineichen, B., Smith, J. & Morgan, H. (1984) Psychiatric hospital admissions in Bristol: Social and clinical aspects of compulsory admission. *British Journal of Psychiatry*, **145**: 605–11.

Harrison, G., Gunnell, D., Glazebrook, C., Page, K. & Kwiecinski R. (2001) Association between schizophrenia and social inequality at birth: Case – control study. *British Journal of Psychiatry*, **179**: 346–50.

Holmes, E., Corrigan, P., Wiliams, P., Canar, J. & Kubiak, M. (1999) Changing public attitudes about schizophrenia. *Schizophrenia Bulletin*, **25**(3): 447–56.

Holowka, D.W., King, S.I., Saheb, D., Pukall, M. & Brunet, A. (2003) Childhood abuse and dissociative symptoms in adult schizophrenia. *Schizophrenia Research*, **60**: 87–90.

Janssen, I., Hanssen, M., Bak, M., Bijl, R., De Graaf, R., Vollebergh, W., Mckenzie, K. & Van Os, J. (2003) Discrimination and delusional ideation. *British Journal of Psychiatry*, **182**: 71–6.

Johnstone, L. (1999) Do families cause schizophrenia? In C. Newnes, G. Holmes & C. Dunn (eds), *This Is Madness*. Ross on Wye: PCCS Books.

Johnstone, L. (2000) *Users and Abusers of Psychiatry* (2nd edn). London: Brunner-Routledge.

Jorm, A., Korten, A., Rodgers, B., Jacomber, P. and Christiansen, H. (2002) Sexual orientation and mental health: Tesults from a community survey of young and middle-aged adults. *British Journal of Psychiatry*, **180**: 423–7.

King, M., McKeown, E., Warner, J. *et al.* (2003) Mental health and quality of life of gay men and lesbians in England and Wales. *British Journal of Psychiatry*, **183**: 552–8.

Kuipers, L., Leff, J. & Lam, D. (1992) *Family Work for Schizophrenia*. London: Gaskell.

Laing, R. & Esterson, A. (1964) *Sanity, Madness and the Family*. Harmondsworth: Penguin.

Laurance, J. (2003) *Pure Madness: How Fear Drives the Mental Health System*. London: Routledge.

Lidz, T. (1975) *The Origin and Treatment of Schizophrenic Disorders*. London: Hutchinson.

Lipschitz, D. (1999) Perceived abuse and neglect as risk factors for suicidal behaviour in adolescent inpatients. *Journal of Nervous and Mental Disease*, **187**: 32–9.

McFarlane, L. (1998) *Diagnosis: Homophobic – The Experience of Lesbians, Gay Men and Bisexuals in Mental Health Services*. London: PACE.

McGovern, D. & Cope, R. (1987a) First psychiatric admission rates of first and second generation Afro-Caribbeans. *Social Psychiatry*, **122**: 139–40.

McGovern, D. & Cope, R. (1987b) The compulsory detention of males of different ethnic groups, with special reference to offender patients. *British Journal of Psychiatry*, **150**: 505–12.

McKenzie, K. & Harpham, T. (2006) Meanings and uses of social capital in the field of mental health. In K. McKenzie & T. Harpham (eds), *Social Capital and Mental Health*. London: Jessica Kingsley.

Milne, A. & Williams, J. (2003) *Women in Transition: A Literature Review on the Mental Health Risks Facing Women in Mid-Life*. London: Pennell Initiative for Women's Health.

Morris, J. (1993) *Independent Lives?* Basingstoke: Macmillan.

Mullen, P.E., Martin, J.L., Anderson, J.C. *et al.* (1993) Childhood sexual abuse and mental health in adult life. *British Journal of Psychiatry*, **163**: 721–32.

Myin-Germeys, I., Krabbendam, L., Delespaul, P. & Van Os, J. (2003) Do life events have their effect on psychosis by influencing the emotional reactivity to daily life stress? *Psychological Medicine*, **33**: 327–33.

Nazroo, J. (1997) *The Health of Britain's Ethnic Minorities: Findings from a National Survey*. London: Policy Studies Institute.

Nazroo, J. & King, M. (2002) Psychosis – symptoms and estimated rates. In K. Sproston & J. Nazroo (eds), *Ethnic Minority Psychiatric Illness Rates in the Community (Empiric)*. London: National Centre for Social Research, TSO.

Oliver, M. (1996) *Understanding Disability: From Theory to Practice*. Basingstoke: Macmillan.

Otis, M. & Skinner, W. (1996) The prevalence of victimisation and its effect on mental well-being among lesbian and gay people. *Journal of Homosexuality*, **30**(3): 93–121.

Pateman, C. (1988) *The Sexual Contract*. Cambridge: Polity.

Perry, J., Herman, J., Van der Kolk, B. & Hoke, L. (1990) Psychotherapy and psychological trauma in borderline personality disorder. *Psychiatric Annals*, **20**(1): 33–43.

Philo, G., Secker, J., Platt, S. *et al.* (1994) The impact of the mass media on public images of mental illness: Media content and audience belief. *Health Education Journal*, **53**: 271–81.

Plumb, S. (2005) The social/trauma model: Mapping the mental health consequences of childhood sexual abuse and similar experiences. In J. Tew (ed.), *Social Perspectives in Mental Health*. London: Jessica Kingsley.

Porter, R. (1987) *A Social History of Madness: Stories of the Insane*. London: Weidenfield and Nicholson.

Prior, P. (1999) *Gender and Mental Health*. Basingstoke: Macmillan.

Proctor, G. (2002) *The Dynamics of Power in Counselling and Psychotherapy*. Ross on Wye: PCCS Books.

Putnam, F. & Trickett, P. (1997) Psychobiological effects of sexual abuse. In R. Yehuda & A. McFarlane (eds). Psychobiology of PTSD. *Annals of the New York Academy of Sciences*, **821**: 150–59.

Read, J. (2004) Poverty, ethnicity and gender. In J. Read, L. Mosher & R. Bentnall (eds), *Models of Madness*. Hove: Brunner Routledge.

Read, J., Goodman, L., Morrison, A., Ross, C. & Aderhold, V. (2004) Childhood trauma, loss and stress. In J. Read, L. Mosher & R. Bentnall (eds), *Models of Madness*. Hove: Brunner Routledge.

Read, J., Perry, B.D., Moskowitz, A. & Connolly, J. (2001) The contribution of early traumatic events to schizophrenia in some patients: A traumagenic neurodevelopmental model. *Psychiatry*, **64**: 319–45.

Repper, J. & Perkins, J. (2003) *Social Inclusion and Recovery*. London: Bailliere Tindall.

Rogers, A. & Pilgrim, D. (2003) *Mental Health and Inequality*. Basingstoke: Palgrave Macmillan.

Romme, M., Pennings, M., Buiks, A. *et al.* (1994) Hearing voices in patients and non-patients. Paper presented at World Congress of Social Psychiatry, Hamburg.

Rutter, M. (1990) Psychosocial resilience and protective mechanisms. In J. Rolf, A. Masten, D. Cicchetti, K. Neuchterlein & S. Weintraub (eds), *Risk and Protective Factors in the Development of Psychopathology*. New York: Cambridge University Press.

Saleebey, D. (1996) The strengths perspective in social work practice. *Social Work*, **41**(3): 296–305.

Scheff, T. (1975) *Labelling Madness*. Engelwood Cliffs, NJ: Prentice Hall.

Shonkoff, J. & Phillips, D. (2000) *From Neurons to Neighbourhoods: The Science of Early Development*. Washington, DC: National Academy Press.

Staples, E. & Dare, C. (1996) The impact of childhood sexual abuse. In K. Abel, M. Buszewicz, S. Davison, S. Johnson & E. Staples (eds), *Planning Community Mental Health Services for Women*. London: Routledge.

Stevenson, F. & Zimmerman, M.A. (2005) Adolescent resilience: A framework for understanding healthy development in the face of risk. *Annual Review of Public Health*, **26**: 399–419.

Tew, J. (1999) Voices from the margins: Inserting the social in mental health discourse. *Social Work Education*, **18**: 4.

Tew, J. (2002) *Social Theory, Power and Practice*. Basingstoke: Palgrave/Macmillan.

Tew, J. (2005) Power relations, social order and mental distress. In J. Tew (ed.), *Social Perspectives in Mental Health*. London: Jessica Kingsley.

Tew, J. (2006) Understanding power and powerlessness: Towards a framework for emancipatory practice in social work. *Journal of Social Work*, **6**(1): 33–51.

Thompson, N. (2007) *Power and Empowerment*. Lyme Regis: Russell House.

Tienari, P., Wynne, L., Moring, J. *et al.* (1994) The Finnish adoptive study of schizophrenia: Implications for family research. *British Journal of Psychiatry*, **164**(suppl 23): 20–26.

Ungar, M. (2001) The social construction of resilience among problem youth in out-of-home placement: A study of health-enhancing deviance. *Child and Youth Care Forum*, **30**(3): 137–54.

Venn, C. (1997) Beyond enlightenment? After the subject of Foucault, who comes? *Theory, Culture and Society*, **14**(3): 1–26.

Warner, R. (1994) *Recovery from Schizophrenia: Psychiatry and Political Economy*. London: Routledge.

Williams, J. (2005) Women's mental health: Taking inequality into account. In J. Tew (ed.), *Social Perspectives in Mental Health*. London: Jessica Kingsley.

Williams, J. & Watson, G. (1996) Mental health services that empower women. In T. Heller, J. Reynold, R. Gomm, R. Muston & S. Pattison (eds), *Mental Health Matters*. London: Macmillan.

Wright, E., Gronfein, W. & Owens, T. (2000) Deinstitutionalisation, social rejection and the self-esteem of former mental patients. *Journal of Health and Social Behaviour*, **41**: 68–90.

Zubin, J., Stuart, R. & Condray, R. (1992) Vulnerability to relapse in schizophrenia. *British Journal of Psychiatry*, **161**: 13–18.

CHAPTER FOURTEEN

Socially inclusive practice

Peter Bates
National Development Team

Joanne Seddon
National Development Team

This chapter explores the nature of social inclusion and sets out some of its implications for people working in mental health services.[1] We aim to show how an understanding of social exclusion and inclusion is important for people working in mental health services, how all staff and all systems need to reflect this understanding, what can be done to promote opportunities for service users and how to avoid some of the common errors.

▶ What inclusion looks like

The terms 'social exclusion' and 'social inclusion' have many definitions that reflect their many attributes. Asking almost any group of people about their personal experiences of being excluded will reveal that, among other things:

- Exclusion hurts and the memory of it can last for years.
- It can be based on abuse of power, denial of rights and opportunities or simple lack of courtesy.
- It affects how people feel and think about themselves.
- It damages the person themselves, their family and the excluding community.

The term 'social exclusion' originated in France in the 1970s and blends concepts of poverty, unemployment and alienation (Levitas, 1998). The fluid nature of

---

[1] Some of the section headings that are used in this chapter also follow the structure of the material in a staff training pack (Bates, 2005a) and so readers wishing to find additional material and training exercises may use the two items as companion resources.

Learning About Mental Health Practice.   Edited by Theo Stickley and Thurstine Basset
© 2008 John Wiley & Sons, Ltd

the term and competing definitions reflect its rich and multi-stranded nature, which resists simplification into a simple or tidy concept. In this chapter, social inclusion is not merely another term for economic inclusion in the labour market (although unemployment is a powerful factor in exclusion), but is also about political, social and cultural participation. Inclusion is not merely the absence of exclusion, but is a positive force that converts tolerance into welcome, attendance into belonging and participation into contribution.

▶ What exclusion looks like

The evidence is that for many people who make extensive use of mental health services, exclusion is the norm. People using mental health services are less likely to be included among the economically active, and employment rates among people with serious mental illness are particularly low. They are less likely to have a decent income and home, be physically healthy or have access to health care. They are less likely to engage in continuing education or leisure activities, and they have smaller friendship networks than other citizens.

> I was working in a solicitor's as a trainee receptionist. I couldn't tell my boss I had to see a psychiatrist every week, so I told him I was on a training scheme one day a week. When I had to tell him I was being taken to hospital his reaction said it all. He sat back in his seat wanting to keep as far away from me as possible. As soon as mental illness is mentioned people literally back off from you. (Jo, mental health service user, in Dunn, 1999, p. 11)

Exercise 14.1
Examine local demographic data and first-person accounts to discover whether these findings are reflected in the particular experiences of people living in your area.

While collecting data on the prevalence of exclusion is of interest to public health specialists, it is enough for most staff to be aware of the possibility that people who use their services may need inclusion support. Commissioners, service users and staff involved in service design will be interested in three linked agendas, as follows.

Stop increasing exclusion of service users within services

> I can talk, but I may not be heard. I can make suggestions, but they may not be taken seriously. I can voice my thoughts, but they may be seen as delusions. I can recite my experiences, but they may be interpreted as fantasies. To be an ex-patient or even an ex-client is to be discounted. (Leete, quoted in Repper & Perkins, 2003, p. 14)

Some people describe mental distress as an experience of feeling out of control, and the professional mystique surrounding psychiatric services can transfer any residual control from the service user to staff. Difficulties in thinking or managing emotion can be reinforced by a loss of confidence in social situations to disempower the person further. Meanwhile, negative stereotypes suggest that the distressed individual has no worthwhile insights or information to share.

To combat these things, the voices of people using mental health services should be clearly heard in their own care-planning meetings and in the places where services are designed. There are currently three new threats that act alongside the forces of tradition that seek to reassert professional control. First, organisational turbulence resulting from frequent restructuring has combined with increasingly sophisticated clinical assessment and organisational development interventions, rendering the decisions that need to be made incomprehensible to some potential participants. Second, changes arising from the inclusion agenda have replaced some buildings-based services with individualised supports and so lost the convenience of consulting a gathered group that meets in an existing facility with a shared agenda. Third, after some years of expansion, recent financial constraints on mental health services have slowed and sometimes reversed the pace of development, and it is harder to involve people in the decisions about shrinkage and closure than it was to engage people in designing new opportunities.

Efforts to empower service users have been championed by the advocacy movement over the past three decades, and latterly the UK government has lent its support by adopting policies that promote choice, personal responsibility and community engagement. However, there is still much work to do, and one survey of 400 mental health projects that claimed to promote inclusive opportunities (Bates *et al.*, 2005) found a low level of service user involvement in decision making.

Service users also complain that mental health staff often hold low expectations. While these days it is unusual for people to be labelled 'unemployable', a service user may be offered skilled help from their care manager to claim long-term welfare benefits, while another staff member would have accompanied the same individual to the local jobs fair instead.

Services have traditionally been designed in a way that congregates users together and segregates them from wider societal roles and relationships. One way to classify the options for arranging support is to think of the three lights on the UK traffic light: red, amber and green. The 'inclusion traffic lights' then becomes a shorthand in which mental health buildings where almost all the people present are service users and staff are classed as 'red', groups of mental health service users in ordinary community buildings that are simultaneously used by the general public are classed as 'amber', and individualised support alongside the general public is classed as 'green'.

While there are many potential criticisms and abuses of this image (Bates, 2005b), it helps staff to recognise options for providing support. Thus the growth of social firms out of the sheltered workshop is often a change within 'red', since service users remain in a mental health building surrounded by other service users and staff, even if activities and relationships within the group are transformed. However, the move to supported employment is a move into 'green', while some further education programmes are a move into 'amber' if the college favours discrete 'mental health' classes. Indeed, some colleges have moved all their 'amber' classes into a separate building on the campus and recreated the 'red' setting, while others support individual students in a mainstream ('green') class.

The debate about how to commission an appropriate mix of red, amber and green support, how to ensure that each type is as good as it can be and how to ensure clear links between the different kinds of service will surely run for some time. Some staff view the colours as complementary 'stepping stones', while others fear that red services will increase institutionalisation, that proximity without relationship will increase discrimination in amber services, and that essential supports will be withdrawn in the name of creating green services. Table 14.1 summarises the main implications of each type of provision.

Exercise 14.2

1. Sort your programme of activity into red, amber and green. What do you learn?

2. Select an activity and review it against the relevant row of Table 14.1. How can you strengthen the positives and minimise the negatives that come with this format of service delivery?

Combat exclusion from the wider community

To tackle exclusion from roles and relationships in the wider community, there are a number of steps that can be taken by mental health services. Continuing positive action to influence media representation of mental health issues needs to be taken by people using services, staff and the general public. The UK has legislation that makes it unlawful to discriminate on grounds of disability or ill health, including mental ill health, and local mental health services that are active in combating exclusion will have a track record of efforts to uphold these rights.

As mental health service users have been shown to have poorer health and are often subject to diagnostic overshadowing, whereby physical health problems are wrongly attributed to the person's mental health difficulties, mental health services that are active in combating exclusion will be energetic advocates for high-quality primary care. Similar efforts will be taking place in relation to the allocation of housing, access to financial services and so on.

Table 14.1   Inclusion traffic lights – positives and negatives

	Positives	Negatives
Red	Sanctuary Shared experience builds friendship Free services Secure places can keep people safe Staff may develop specialist skills Cope with those who are very challenging or distressed by creating a controllable and planned therapeutic environment Economies of scale	Segregated and may be far from home Little variety of activities Minorities not well served Amplifies stigma, misuse of power, sick role People get stuck with low expectations of recovery and inclusion Money used on buildings, not support People lose their job, partner, home, friends, status
Amber	Provision can be near service user's home Non-stigmatised building More opportunities and potential for contact with other building users Can try out new places with the support of familiar people and a continuing sense of identity Increased access to new funding sources	Money used on room hire, not support Activities limited to those suitable for the group Teaches the public that service users 'need' to be batched into separate provision Increases the public perception of difference – proximity without relationships
Green	Retains lifelong roles Chance for new friendships Educates the community and can lever money in Increases personal responsibility and self-esteem More opportunities for support from the informal community It is what many service users want Gives people an opportunity to make a contribution	Support may mark out the person as different The public may be unskilled in supporting users Lonely in a hostile (fragmented, racist, discriminating) community Some may struggle with the opportunities and choices Expensive for users (travel costs, entrance fees) and more work for services

Removing or reducing exclusion has little to do with managing or minimising symptoms, but rather is based on accepting people as they are. The focus shifts to efforts that sustain citizenship roles and rights within the wider community.

Promote inclusion within the wider community

In 14 years as a service user, mental health professionals have never offered me help with working towards getting back to work. (Service user, quoted in Social Exclusion Unit, 2004, p. 54)

Lowering barriers within and outside mental health services is a necessary but insufficient step towards achieving inclusion. In addition, mental health services need to pay more attention to the positive aspects of inclusion, and that will involve work on recovery, friendship, belonging, self-confidence and assertiveness. Some of these elements are explored further below.

Inclusive assessment

An examination of how a local team understands and completes the assessment stage of care planning reveals many things about the team, including the focus of its work and how power is distributed between staff and service users and between professional staff groups. Table 14.2 shows how pressure of work, responding to crises and defensive practice can all narrow the focus of the team. Restoring a social inclusion focus (Bates, 2002) may demand action in all the areas outlined in the table.

Table 14.2   Widening the focus

Narrowed focus	A social inclusion focus adds the following dimensions	Review this by examining your work with one service user
The person's mental health state and identity as a user of mental health services	The person's positive social roles, such as householder, employee, parent, friend	Does the care plan include actions to support the person in these roles?
Responding to crisis and coping with today	The person's ambitions and goals for the future	Are therapeutic interventions designed to assist the person to identify and move towards their preferred lifestyle?
The person as a recipient of help	The person as a contributor to society	What opportunities does the person have to enrich the life of other people?
Community organisations that offer help	Community organisations that confer positive status and roles outside the mental health service	Do the people contacted by the care team represent *helping* or *community* organisations?
Growing strong teams within the mental health service	Building new alliances beyond the mental health service	(Thinking beyond this one service user now) How much staff time is ring-fenced for spending with people from non-mental health agencies?

Source: Bates, 2005a.

Exercise 14.3

What were your answers to the questions in the right-hand column of Table 14.2? Are there changes you or colleagues could make to become more socially inclusive in the work you do?

Promoting inclusive opportunities for services users carries the risk that mental health services will attempt to prescribe 'inclusion therapy', in which activity to promote inclusion is relegated from an issue about fairness and rights to a treatment, and inclusive outcomes are judged on whether they deliver improvements in symptoms. This risk can be avoided by ensuring that the service focuses on individual recovery journeys and person-centred approaches. One common strand in these approaches is the importance of paying attention to the individual's personal definition of wellness, quality of life and ambitions.

Several of the person-centred planning formats use the metaphor of 'dreams' to denote both preferences for a pleasant day-to-day quality of life and more substantial achievements, such as moving house or obtaining employment. While some people have clearly articulated and consistent ambitions, most human beings seem to us to dream in a rather more ambiguous and complicated way. Like nighttime dreams, our preferences are often muddled, confused and hard to interpret. Indeed, the metaphor of dreaming can be extended in this way, as shown in Table 14.3.

During our training sessions we have often asked staff to think of people they know who mirror these ways of dreaming in their ambitions and preferences. For example, some service users appear to have no ambitions at all. Perhaps they used to dream, but have been disappointed so often it seems less painful to give up. Perhaps they have cultivated the art of contentment, they express their preferences through their behaviour rather than through words, or they are describing ambitions that the worker fails to recognise. We have gathered advice from staff about how they can listen more carefully to each person's dream, reflect on their own attitude towards it, interpret what they hear and harness the positive motive power of the dream (Bates, 2006).

Table 14.3 Paying attention to dreams – ambitions and preferences

Serious and enduring dreams	Dreams that appear to be beyond reach	Dreams that are muddled and difficult to understand
Dreams that are clear, but change every time you ask	Dreams that unsettle the dreamer	Dreams that are private
People who seem not to have any dreams at all	Dreams that are all about basic human drives	Dreams of things that we must prevent happening

Exercise 14.4

1. Review a few completed assessments. Do you obtain a clear picture of the person's lifestyle preferences and ambitions?

2. Imagine deleting the person's name and other basic identifying data from 20 such assessments. Could your colleagues (assuming they knew the people) relabel them by using only the assessment information?

3. Consider the nine kinds of 'dreaming' shown in Table 14.3. For each kind, can you think of a service user who presents their preferences and ambitions in this way? How do you identify and harness the positive motive power of this dream?

▶ Working beyond the mental health service

> The great irony about service user action in the past 15 years is that while the position of service users within services has undoubtedly improved, the position of service users in society has deteriorated. As a result, it is at least arguable that the focus of user involvement needs adjustment. (Campbell, quoted in Bates, 2002, p. 73)

Promoting socially inclusive practice demands the kind of 'adjustment' that Peter Campbell refers to, not only for service users but for staff teams. The simplest and most direct situation in which mental health staff find themselves when promoting inclusive lifestyles is when they are out in ordinary community settings with one person who uses services. This is a more common experience for assistants compared with their professionally qualified colleagues, but it illustrates many of the challenges of socially inclusive practice. In our training sessions with staff teams we find that workers are very keen to share their experiences of the dilemmas and difficulties of this work, but have had few or no opportunities to clarify their thinking and practice. Table 14.4 offers some of their observations.

While the suggestions in Table 14.4 may seem little more than common sense, many staff will have experience of times when life seems to have moved far beyond the guidance available from their organisation's policies on lone working, information sharing and positive risk taking. Strengthening inclusive practice will require most mental health organisations to build up the quality standards and assurance mechanisms for how to respond in these situations.

Table 14.4   Providing subtle, one-to-one support in community settings

Ask the person

- What they want to do and how to identify and overcome the barriers to participation.
- How they want to be supported.
- How to negotiate disclosure and positive risk taking.
- About needs for additional support or flexibility.

Think about

- Who is the best person to provide support?
- Meeting someone you know.
- Managing your feelings about supporting this person.
- How will you deal with private matters in a public setting?
- What if the person is loud, visible or behaves inappropriately?
- Impact of weather, schooldays, time of day.

Plan

- Introductions and explanations.
- What the person can do without support.
- Transfer of support to other participants and discreet withdrawal by worker.
- Any adjustments that need to be made by the activity provider, so that the person is seen in the best light.

On the day

- How does the person feel today?
- Does that change your plans?
- Keep your words, tone and body language calm and positive.
- Be with the person and join in, but encourage them to make their own connections.

Avoid

- Being over-controlling.
- Showing off as the person who is in charge.
- Name badges and unsuitable clothes.
- Doing your own shopping and phone calls.
- Denying opportunities to people who don't behave prettily.

Exercise 14.5

Identify a situation from your own practice or that of a colleague where it was difficult to provide one-to-one support to a service user in a public setting. Bring this to a team meeting where colleagues can share in examining the issues and offering ideas about how best to respond.

While some of the situations that challenge support staff in community settings take place in community amenities (shops, cafés, pubs, parks, cinemas, museums, libraries and the like), mental health services need to locate other settings too. Longer-term groups where service users can interact with the general public on the basis of reciprocity form prime sites for the development of identity, roles and relationships. For this reason, mental health services need to develop a detailed knowledge of how people access these environments: employment, education, volunteering, arts, sports, faith and interest-based communities, as well as the informal web of connections that might be loosely titled 'neighbouring'.

But staff sometimes have a problem of perception. They may be thoroughly knowledgeable about the places in the community where help can be found, but have only minimal awareness of the ordinary community places where positive roles and relationships can be built. Instead of viewing the neighbourhood where they work as a rich oasis of opportunity, they can adopt a deficit mindset and conclude that their community is either a desert, devoid of life and connection, or in the midst of an ice age, where the only way to respond to such cold hostility is to hide away until discrimination is overcome and the atmosphere warms up. A socially inclusive approach does not require staff to become naïve and deny the reality of stigma and discrimination, but it does require them to move beyond a deficit model to a strengths model in their perception of the life of their local community.

Uncovering these places where community is built demands a heightened sensitivity from mental health staff and their allies. We have found that most staff already exercise some of this sensitivity, but it can be honed in much the same way that intuitive skills in listening can be extended. We have found that staff benefit from creating a checklist of issues to explore when visiting community settings and tailoring their checklist for each area of community life, so that the checklist for faith communities is quite different from the volunteering list (see Table 14.5).

In addition to clarifying how front-line workers behave in community settings and what is available locally, mental health services need to build strong links with gatekeepers in community settings. It is these mentoring links across agencies that provide the basis for changing the way communities work.

▶ Getting and keeping inclusion

Pursuing a journey of recovery includes finding out what helps well-being and improves quality of life, which almost always includes socially inclusive goals.

Table 14.5   Extracts from a community mapping checklist for faith communities

What activities are available?

- What happens when and how many people are involved in each activity?
- Where do the activities take place?
- What roles can newcomers adopt?
- What is the duration of activities and do you have to stay throughout?
- Is it noisy or quiet?
- Are refreshments provided?
- What do participants say about this community?
- Do friendships grow around the formal meetings?
- Do people listen? Smile?

What support arrangements are in place?

- Do people welcome and take care of each other?
- Are problems acknowledged and can you ask for extra support?
- Is there a hierarchy and how are decisions made?
- Public transport, access, toilet arrangements.
- Is the space warm and the furniture comfortable?
- Is this community already providing additional support to some members?

What do I have to do to participate?

- Are men and women treated differently?
- Are most participants male, young, in families, intellectuals?
- Do I need particular books, equipment or clothes?
- Am I expected to pay, pray, sing or otherwise join in?
- Do I have to share the group's beliefs to be accepted or join in with everything?
- Is the group trying to persuade people to support its views, recruit people or sell anything?
- What are the rules that members are expected to follow?

Administration

- Name and contact details of the person who completed this form and the contact at the community setting.
- Date of the visit.

Staff can be involved in helping the person to clarify their own ambitions and then find opportunities, get connected and sustain their participation. Some individuals will need a comprehensive inclusion plan, while others will need little more than encouragement or signposting from the mental health service to achieve their goal.

For those who need a comprehensive inclusion plan, we have published the *Social Inclusion Planner* (Bates & Dowson, 2006), a software-based catalogue of over 100 interventions grouped into seven primary categories that correspond to the stages of a full plan. Table 14.6 summarises the stages of the plan.

It is our impression that mental health staff routinely utilise only a few of the available strategies and so we have devised a training exercise that is designed to widen individual repertoires. We asked 500 staff to work in pairs and think about a person that one member of the pair knew, review brief descriptions of the 105 strategies from the *Social Inclusion Planner,* and then build a seven-step inclusion plan that might work for the individual concerned. Each member of the pair then compared the resulting plan with their own personal repertoire of strategies. This structured approach led to staff including two new strategies in an average seven-step plan. They were then encouraged to investigate the strategies further and, of course, start again and design a real inclusion plan *with* the person concerned, rather than *for* them.

Table 14.6   The seven stages of a social inclusion plan

1. *Getting to know the person.* Good assessment questions and approaches will help staff find out more about how the person thinks of their own recovery and what elements need to be in place to support that personal journey.

2. *Getting to know the community.* Find out about the informal community and its opportunities. Community development workers, voluntary-sector agencies and health-promotion specialists can help with this task.

3. *Building capacity in mental health services.* Help mental health services learn about mainstream community organisations, the mental health benefits of inclusion and which support strategies are effective.

4. *Building capacity in community organisations.* Staff need to build alliances, deliver training, dismantle barriers, and highlight the benefits to community organisations of including people who have mental health difficulties.

5. *Support for the whole of life.* Resolving other issues in the person's life (housing difficulties, health care, finances and so on) so that they do not interfere with the inclusion effort.

6. *Getting there and settling in.* Assistance with choosing the right setting, getting ready to go, travelling and induction.

7. *Sustaining participation.* Solve problems before they lead to the breakdown of the activity and transfer support to natural, informal processes so that the person can fully and independently participate wherever possible.

Source: Bates & Dowson, 2006.

Table 14.7   Most commonly chosen pieces of advice in how to support the growth of friendship

1. Is friendship considered an important goal? Be aware of all opportunities that could possibly extend networks. Support people to nurture friendship, to make and maintain connections.

2. Does the person have opportunities to give as well as receive in the setting?

3. Fix the person up with a mentor or buddy. Find the bubbly personalities.

4. Promote social skills and possibly offer training – but be clear what this is about. Learn when it is OK to touch, skills needed in meeting new people. Know the rules – recognise when it is OK to have a chat.

5. Raise expectations – everyone who wants to can have friends. Promote the value of friendship to family, carers and professionals. If necessary, work with the person to grow self-esteem and social confidence.

6. Do people with mental health issues use the same places, people and things in the setting as people without mental health problems?

The most elusive goal of many people's inclusion plan is to find new friendships beyond the mental health service. It seems that everyone has some homespun wisdom and insight on how friendship works, but few mental health staff have spent time formally studying the topic. Consequently, there is a tendency to adopt a number of unacknowledged assumptions – including that other people construct their friendships in a similar way to the one we choose, that those who construct their friendships in quite different ways lack 'real' friendships, and that friendships between people considered dissimilar are unlikely to succeed.

We asked 150 staff to think about how they could support the inclusive friendships of a service user whom they knew and then choose three pieces of advice that would be most helpful to them in their work from a list of 35. While some items that were rarely chosen may have been exactly right for the individual concerned, it is interesting to note the items that were most often chosen, as shown in Table 14.7.

Perhaps our 35 pieces of advice miss some key factors, people attending our training sessions are timid, or their subjects require conventional support, but we note that issues of personal presentation and sexual relationships are missing from this list. Sometimes there is a need to offer sensitive, respectful and honest comment on issues that might prevent the development of friendship, such as personal hygiene, appearance or personal habits. Secondly, raising the subject of friendship will sometimes generate discussion about sexual relationships. Staff may feel unsure about their role in this and unclear where their personal values and skills impinge on their duties as employees and the effect of mental illness on friendship and sexual behaviour.

> **Exercise 14.6**
> Find a colleague who is willing to let you take a 'friendship history'. How does their experience of friendship differ from your own? What would help to expand or deepen your friendships?

▶ Organisational and personal issues

If individual workers are to promote socially inclusive lifestyles, then they require both personal competencies and an organisation that supports their endeavours. Neither can be taken for granted, nor achieved simply by including the term 'social inclusion' in the organisation's mission statement. So we need to take a closer look at both organisational and personal factors.

Taking a closer look at the organisation

We have found that the following inclusion-friendly attributes are crucial:

- *Celebrating diversity* means acting to combat the multiple exclusion experienced by women, people from black and ethnic minority communities and those from other diverse communities who also have mental health problems.

- *Staff competencies* can be reviewed against the framework of inclusion capabilities (National Social Inclusion Programme, CSIP) that is built on the ten Essential Shared Capabilities for mental health practice (Hope, 2004). This informs the selection process for staff as well as their continuing development. A gap analysis may indicate a need for training, which should be non-hierarchical and include everyone from senior managers and commissioners to front-line staff, people who use services, carers and community members. Such events will provide an opportunity for everyone to invest time, work together, share ideas and experiences and develop a joint understanding and commitment to inclusive practice.

- *Performance indicators* need to capture evidence that people have more opportunities to take up and sustain participation in their communities. There are a variety of available measures (Bates & Hacking, 2007; Davis *et al.*, 2002; Huxley, 2007) and both service commissioners and front-line staff may need help to understand how using these measures can support the development agenda.

- *Creativity* can be crushed by the tactless introduction of performance management and protocols, yet effective social inclusion practice to match the unique gifts of individuals with their communities demands accountability and creativity in equal measure.

- *Policies* can provide a safe backdrop for staff to practise inclusively, but often need redrafting if they are to do so. Particular attention needs to be paid to the policies on risk, confidentiality and disclosure, as well as lone working.

- *Promotional opportunities* to provide information to the community about the work of the service should be harnessed to promote social inclusion and recovery. This includes introductory, referral and induction information available in GP surgeries, libraries, community centres and the media. People with direct experience should be supported to offer mental health and social inclusion training to the whole range of mainstream community agencies. People who have used services may need support to take up positions of influence with local government, advisory committees and consumer watchdogs. Employers, learning providers and community organisations that provide a respectful welcome should be praised without patronising them or implying that they have done any more than their moral duty.

Exercise 14.7

Carry out an audit of the community profile of your mental health service. Visit your local library and health centre to check for leaflets and posters and ask the staff for information. Call your communications department and local 'experts by experience' group to ask about their bookings diary for giving presentations to community organisations (don't count presentations to mental health audiences). Monitor your local newspaper's representation of mental health issues.

Taking a closer look at personal investment

Sometimes we forget the basics – that it is a privilege to work in people-related services, that it constantly stretches us to explore new ideas, that people need a warm smile and positive, hopeful humility as well as knowledge and technical expertise. We need to recognise our own potential to influence the lives of others and set this alongside integrity and a willingness to be managed. We sometimes serve as role models and so need to make our own journey of recovery within our own inclusive community. Sometimes this is as simple as staff remembering what they like about their job.

Staff working in inclusive services have overcome the uncertainty and divisiveness of competitive tendering by being good neighbours. Within teams, they overcome the isolation of lone working by genuinely learning from their colleagues and inventing really useful collaborations. They dare to visit services run by other agencies, find kindred spirits, host gatherings to share good practice and generously share food, stories and resources.

Finally, socially inclusive practice cannot be confined within the bounds of working hours or mental health services and it affects our conduct at the local supermarket, during conversation over a family dinner, as a passenger using public transport, or a member of a local faith or community group.

▶ **Conclusion**

Socially inclusive practice in mental health requires a sophisticated understanding of how exclusion and inclusion work, careful listening to people using services and their communities, organisational redesign and a personal journey. We travel together!

> **Exercise 14.8**
>
> ■ Can you say what 'inclusion' means to each person you support?
>
> ■ Do you have a detailed 'inclusion plan' as part of their care?
>
> ■ Where does 'inclusion' fit into your personal life and development plan?

▶ **References and links to further learning**

Bates, P. (ed.) (2002) *Working for Inclusion*. London: Sainsbury Centre for Mental Health.

Bates, P. (2005a) Developing socially inclusive practice. In T. Basset, P. Lindley & R. Barton (eds), *The Ten Essential Shared Capabilities: Learning Pack for Mental Health Practice* (Module 6). London: NHS University. Available at www.lincoln.ac.uk/ccawi/esc/default.htm.

Bates, P. (2005b) *Accidents at the Inclusion Traffic Lights*. Ipswich: National Development Team. Available at www.ndt.org.uk/ETS/ETILT.htm.

Bates, P. (2006) *Responding to Dreams in Person-Centred Planning: Stories and Tips*. Ipswich: National Development Team. Available at www.ndt.org.uk/docsN/ETDreams.pdf.

Bates, P. & Dowson, S. (2006) *The Social Inclusion Planner*. Ipswich: National Development Team. Available from www.ndt.org.uk/SIP.htm.

Bates, P. & Hacking, S. (2007) The Inclusion Web as a tool for person-centred planning and service evaluation. Unpublished paper, available from pbates@ndt.org.uk.

Bates, P., Morris, D., Churchill, S. *et al.* (2005) Learning from experience. *Mental Health Today*, May: 25–8.

Davis, F., Burns, J., Lindley, P. & Sutton, R. (2002) Assessing individual needs. In P. Bates (ed.), *Working for Inclusion*. London: Sainsbury Centre for Mental Health.

Dunn, S. (1999) *Creating Accepting Communities: Report of the Mind Inquiry into Social Exclusion*. London: Mind.

Hope, R. (2004) *The Ten Essential Shared Capabilities: A Framework for the Whole of the Mental Health Workforce*. London: Department of Health.

Huxley, P. (2007) SCOPE: A measure of social inclusion. Unpublished research instrument, available from Professor Peter Huxley, Centre for Social Carework Research, Department of Applied Social Sciences, University of Wales Swansea, Vivian Building, Singleton Park, Swansea SA2 8NN.

Levitas, R. (1998) *The Inclusive Society: Social Exclusion and New Labour*. Basingstoke: Macmillan.

National Social Inclusion Programme, CSIP (2007) *Capabilities for Inclusive Practice.* London: Department of Health.

Repper, J. & Perkins, R. (2003) *Social Inclusion and Recovery: A Model for Mental Health Practice.* London: Balliere Tindall.

Sayce, L. (2000) *From Psychiatric Patient to Citizen: Overcoming Discrimination and Social Exclusion.* Basingstoke: Macmillan.

Social Exclusion Unit (2004) *Mental Health and Social Exclusion.* London: Office of the Deputy Prime Minister.

◀ CHAPTER FIFTEEN ▶

Equality and rights: Overcoming social exclusion and discrimination

Liz Sayce

RADAR (Royal Association for Disability and Rehabilitation)

This chapter explores the experience of social exclusion and discrimination among people with mental health conditions[1] in the UK and offers suggestions for mental health practitioners on how to support social inclusion and challenge discrimination.

The learning outcomes are that readers should be able to:

- Understand recent policy developments that support equality and challenge discrimination on mental health grounds.

- Understand the evidence of discrimination and its impact on service users.

- Know the main evidence base for effective ways of combating discrimination.

- Reflect on their own role as mental health practitioners in supporting service users to challenge discrimination, and in supporting wider systems change to achieve greater equality.

▶ A brief history

In 1978, the mental health charity Mind sent a dossier of cases of employment discrimination experienced by people with mental health conditions to the

---

[1] There is no consensus on language to describe those of us who experience mental health difficulties and/or use mental health services and I respect self-definition. I have used the fairly neutral term 'people with mental health conditions' in preference to users of mental health services (since most communities do not define themselves by particular services they use) or people with mental health problems ('condition' leaves it open as to whether the experience is a problem or not).

Learning About Mental Health Practice. Edited by Theo Stickley and Thurstine Basset
© 2008 John Wiley & Sons, Ltd

(Labour) minister responsible for employment. He replied saying that he doubted there was sufficient discrimination of this kind to merit new law (Bynoe, Oliver & Barnes, 1991).

By 2004 the (Labour) government's stance had entirely changed:

> Adults with long-term mental health problems are one of the most excluded groups in society. Although many want to work, fewer than a quarter actually do – the lowest employment rate for any of the main groups of disabled people... Stigma and discrimination against people with mental health problems is pervasive throughout society... Fewer than four in ten employers say they would recruit someone with a mental health problem. Many people fear disclosing their condition, even to family and friends. (ODPM, 2004, pp. 3–4)

This landmark official recognition of pervasive discrimination was the result of concerted campaigning by mental health service users and survivors and allies. It would not have happened without their strenuous efforts.

This struggle did not begin in the 1970s. The Alleged Lunatics Friends' Society campaigned in 19th Century England against the way patients were 'first crushed and then discharged to live a milksop existence in society' as one of their members, John Percival, put it (cited in Sayce, 2000). But from the 1970s the civil rights movements of black people, women and gay people were providing new inspiration to disabled people and mental health 'patients' (the terminology still in vogue). Second-wave feminism was the precursor to second-wave campaigning against discrimination on mental health grounds.

In the 1980s the Thatcher government encouraged consumerism. The embryonic mental health user movement fitted the bill and organizations such as UK Advocacy Network, Mindlink and Survivors Speak Out secured modest funding.

During the 1990s, the people involved in combating discrimination on mental health grounds began to change: from radical activists, to mainstream leaders in professional bodies and government. Service users documented discrimination more and more fully, which prompted voluntary-sector and professional organizations to research and promote evidence. Government responded with legislation and policy to reduce discrimination. Selected milestones are in Box 15.1.

Box 15.1 Milestones on the way to ending discrimination.

> *1977* Judi Chamberlin, American mental health survivor leader, published *On Our Own*, the major survivor campaigning account; published in Britain in 1988 (Chamberlin, 1988)
>
> *1970s* British Mental Patients' Union and Campaign Against Psychiatric Oppression active in challenging the power of psychiatry

1986 Derbyshire national conference of users of mental health services, which stimulated a new wave of user activism leading to widespread 'user involvement' (a new concept in the 1980s) in mental health services

Early 1990s A few campaigners moved the focus from mental health services to wider civil rights in employment, fair media portrayals etc.

Early 1990s Small-scale bridge building with the wider disability rights movement

1994–5 Mind, Survivors Speak Out and others succeeded (against some opposition) in getting people with mental health problems and those with personality disorders included in protections from discrimination in the Disability Discrimination Act (DDA) 1995

December 1996 For the first time in British history it became illegal to refuse someone a job, or sack them, on grounds of current or past mental ill health (with the implementation of the DDA 1995)

1996 Publication of *Not Just Sticks and Stones*, highlighting discrimination in health services, employment, parenting decisions and public attitudes: 'they call me nutter', as one respondent put it (Read & Baker, 1996)

Late 1990s Campaigns launched to combat stigma/discrimination by Royal College of Psychiatrists (*Every Family in the Land*) and Mind (*Respect*)

Early 2000s DDA progressively introduced and strengthened in 1999, 2001, 2004, 2005, to cover goods and services, education, public functions and transport; to strengthen employment rights; and to place a duty on public-sector organisations proactively to promote disability equality and positive attitudes towards disabled people (including mental health service users). Special requirement that mental illness had to be 'clinically well recognised' for someone to seek rights under the DDA removed in 2005 following campaigning by mental health organizations

2000 Disability Rights Commission set up to enforce and promote the DDA. The first legal case it supported was Mr Kapadia *v* Lambeth Council. He won over £ 100,000 compensation after losing his job following depression

2000 Publication of *From Psychiatric Patient to Citizen*, a broad analysis of discrimination and how to combat it (Sayce, 2000)

2001 Professor Norman Sartorius of the World Psychiatric Association stated, 'There is no greater problem in the field of mental health internationally than stigma'

2002 Department of Health published guidance that overturned discriminatory recommendations on employing people with mental health problems in the NHS. From now on the positive contribution of people with personal experience was to be recognised and the 'two-year rule' no longer applied (this had stated that anyone who had received mental health treatment in the last two years could not enter or work in nursing; Department of Health, 2002)

2002 Royal College of Psychiatrists published *Employment Opportunities and Psychiatric Disability*, a comprehensive account of evidence, good practice and legislation to guide mental health practitioners to go beyond treatment – to support employment opportunities

2004 Government's Social Exclusion Unit published its report on mental health, which stated that discrimination on mental health grounds was endemic in society (ODPM, 2004)

2006 Professor Graham Thornicroft of the Institute of Psychiatry published *Shunned*, a comprehensive evidence base on discrimination and effective approaches to combating it. He found evidence that discrimination was both common and severe, and argued there was a need 'to demolish both direct and structural discrimination against people with mental illness' (Thornicroft, 2006)

2006–7 Evidence that 40% of people on Incapacity Benefit had a mental health problem as their primary impairment – rising to 60% if secondary impairments were included – made mental health and employment a national policy priority for the first time. Initiatives from Social Inclusion Action Plans to the Welfare Reform Act of 2007 and Pathways to Work placed a new focus on people with mental health conditions, rather than subsuming them into the generic category 'disabled people'

2007 DRC replaced by Equality and Human Rights Commission, tasked with working across six strands of equality (race, gender, disability, age, sexual orientation and religion/belief). DRC published two documents to influence the new Commission: *The Disability Agenda*, and *Coming Together – Mental Health Service Users, Equality and Human Rights*

▶ The twists and turns of change

While the last two decades have seen increased recognition of discrimination, and action to combat it, the process has not been linear. The 1990s was a decade of contradictions. On the one hand there was a major new impetus to bring the experience of discrimination to the surface and eradicate it; on the other, there was a 'moral panic' about the alleged dangerousness of people with mental health conditions, which intensified discrimination (Sayce, 1995, 2000). For a period, every homicide committed by someone with a psychiatric history was front-page news (not least because of a required public inquiry each time). Emblematic images of the same 'mad' killers were shown again and again each time any mental health story was in the news. Often the images chosen were of black men – like Christopher Clunis, who killed Jonathan Zito on an underground platform – fuelling a dangerous fusion of racism and discrimination on psychiatric grounds. Calls for increased control and coercion (supervision registers, compulsory treatment in the community) were strong, to keep the public safe. Government ministers, like Labour's Frank Dobson, stated that community care had 'failed'.

All this flew in the face of evidence. The proportion of homicides committed by people with mental disorders actually went down steadily over the period of de-institutionalisation – from about 35% in 1957 to 11.5% in 1995, according to Home Office figures (Taylor & Gunn, 1999). Evaluations of de-institutionalisation showed consistently that service users benefited overall from 'community care', on measures such as user satisfaction and social networks; although there was much further to go in terms of real opportunity and inclusion (Leff, Trieman & Gooch, 1996).

The 'moral panic' strand of the contradiction was much higher profile than the anti-discrimination strand. Probably as a result, repeated Department of Health surveys in the 1990s showed that the public's desire for social distance from people with 'mental illness' increased, and discriminatory attitudes worsened, as the homicidal images embedded themselves in the national psyche.

Successive governments passed policies designed both to reduce discrimination (see Box 15.1) and to increase control, in a form of double-think that left campaigners juggling competing priorities: to hold back the tide of coercive proposals (achieved with partial success through the Mental Health Alliance) and to strengthen the impact of disability rights policies specifically in relation to people with mental health conditions. At the same time, many user/survivor activists were active within mental health services, engaged in user involvement to improve their quality.

By 2000 one survivor leader, Peter Campbell (see also Chapter 16 of this book) noted that campaigning effort had not focused sufficiently on civil rights and opportunities:

> The great irony about service user action in the past 15 years is that while the position of service users within services has undoubtedly improved, the position of service users in society has deteriorated. As a result, it is at least arguable that the focus of user involvement needs adjustment. (Campbell, 2000)

Although some activists built bridges with the disability movement to capitalise on civil rights, this effort was diluted. There were also complexities in terms of which discriminations to challenge. In 1990 homosexuality was still formally classified in Britain as a mental disorder. At a seminar at Guy's Hospital in the early 1990s, practising psychiatrists could remember the use of aversion therapy in that hospital to 'cure' homosexuality. In 1992 at a joint Mind/Stonewall conference, Conservative minister John Bowis made a historic speech, ending the classification of homosexuality as a mental disorder, stating that never again should being gay be viewed as an illness, and wishing all present a happy Gay Pride. The speech was published in full in the *Independent* newspaper.

As the prevalence of abuse (physical and sexual) of women became better acknowledged, both as a precursor to mental health problems and within mental health services themselves, safety for women became a big campaign focus. Mind's Stress on Women Campaign prompted government to issue guidance in 1994 requiring single-sex wards (guidance that had still not been fully implemented by 2007, although some positive practice had developed). Evidence of extreme racial inequality in use of mental health services was mounting, particularly in relation to disproportionate use of coercive detention and treatment of African Caribbean men than other groups. Networks developed, conferences were held and policies gradually passed – though action, as compared to research, was slow.

Critical questions

- Can you think of other key milestones over the last 20 years that have made a difference to the position of people with experience of mental ill health in British society (or in the country where you live)?

- What have other communities done to reduce the discrimination they face? Does the mental health movement have things to learn from other social movements?

▶ The impact on services

With Government policies designed both to combat discrimination and to manage fears for public safety, policies imposed contradictory pressures on mental health services. At worst, services were expected entirely to contain risk – not to manage it, but to reduce it to zero. This can make clinical decision making overly risk averse, driven by fear rather than objective assessment and leading to restricted opportunity for individuals (Sayce, 1995). This conflicts with anti-discrimination policy: how can someone exercise their citizenship rights, get engaged in a full life of employment, relationships and leisure, if they are subject to compulsory detention or treatment, on a slight and unprovable chance that they may become violent in the future?

This applies most obviously in relation to risks to the public, but it is also highly relevant in relation to risks to self. What Corrigan calls the stigma of benevolence (Corrigan *et al.*, 2001) can entirely stifle people's opportunities, for instance by trying to protect mental health service users from the risk of potential failure, by discouraging them from pursuing their ambitions under the guise of being 'realistic'. Without risk, there can be no autonomy, no social participation and no achievement (see also Chapter 11 in this book).

Clinically, Repper and Perkins (2003) have noted that risk is essential for recovery – for resuming roles and attaining hope. No one can do anything without risk of failure, they argue. Every new relationship means risk of rejection, every job application means risk of not getting the job, every outing means risk of being run down by a bus. But without risk there is also no hope – confidence is eroded and opportunities limited. It is the job of mental health worker to support people in taking risks, not in systematically avoiding them (Repper & Perkins, 2003).

Arguably, the focus on risk in mental health services is part of a wider shift towards a risk-averse society, evident in increasing litigation and periodically absurd examples of removing health and safety risks (like no hanging baskets in case they fall on someone's head; see O'Neill, 2002; Sayce 2005).

Critical questions

- From your experience, can you think of examples of mental health services being too risk averse? If so, what could be done to change that?

- Can you think of examples of successfully supporting a mental health service user to take a risk? Or a situation where you would wish to?

- Whose risk is it if someone with mental health problems wants to try something that may fail – his or her risk, or the mental health service's risk?

- How would you want to balance supporting risk taking with the duty of care to service users?

▶ The experience of discrimination

People with mental health conditions have written and spoken eloquently about discrimination, how it feels and its impact. For example:

> Friends, family, people you meet everyday – people treat you differently. Like they are treading on eggshells...they think that if they say something wrong you're going to flare up or whatever. (cited in Repper *et al.*, 1997)

Sometimes rejection is more explicit.

> Friends avoided me and would not let their children play with my children any more. (cited in Read & Baker, 1996)

> When I went into psychiatric hospital the Minister didn't come and visit me. He always visits people when they are in hospital. But he didn't visit me. (cited in Sayce, 2000)

> My in-laws wouldn't have me in the house for 10 years after my mental illness. My wife and daughter visited them, but I was not permitted. (cited in Sayce, 2000)

The moment of hearing that you have a diagnosis like schizophrenia or personality disorder can seem like the end of life and hope. An ordinary life seems impossible. Dreams of a nice home, a decent job, family, friends are shattered by the images of 'the mentally ill' that are so often portrayed in the media and popular culture (see Dunn, 1999; Perkins & Sayce, 2006; Repper & Perkins 2003; Sayce, 2000).

On the one hand you are seen as incompetent, unable and unfit to participate fully in society, in need of others to look after you, make decisions for you. On the other, you are seen as unpredictable, dangerous, responsible for the 'rising tide of killings', one of the 'nuts' who should be 'caged for life' to protect others. Sometimes discrimination is overt. For instance:

> I applied for the post of Company Secretary with a leading construction company and was successful. A formal offer was made which, as expected, stated that it was subject to a satisfactory medical and references... The detail of the illness that the company received in the medical report was no more than one sentence, which referred to three, two-month hospital admissions due to schizo-affective breakdown. I received a curt letter from the Personnel Director stating that 'my standard of health did not measure up to the job, and therefore the offer was being withdrawn'. (Watkiss, 2001)

Mr Watkiss successfully challenged this discrimination under the Disability Discrimination Act 1995. Others have not been able to. Many people are afraid to be open about a psychiatric history at work for fear of discrimination. Secrecy brings strains and the fear of being found out.

Sometimes discrimination takes vicious forms. Read and Baker (1996) cite numerous examples of people who have been attacked in the street, had eggs thrown at them or dog faeces put through their letter box simply because they were known to have mental health problems. As one 71-year-old man recounted:

Various gangs in the district call me 'nutter' and spit on me. The gangs on the estate know I was a psychiatric patient and so I'm teased and harassed. (Read & Baker, 1996)

The Social Exclusion Unit report (ODPM, 2004) found that of all the problems experienced by people with mental health conditions, stigma came out top. Stigma was commonly worse than the mental health problem itself.

Some people with physical or other types of impairment have begun to recognise the extreme difficulties of the way discrimination on mental health grounds works. For instance, mountaineer Jamie Andrew was in hospital undergoing rehabilitation after losing all his lower limbs to frostbite. At the same time his friend Geoff was in hospital with manic depression. Andrew writes:

> What struck me as I learnt to get on with making the most of my life, was how similar our disabilities were and yet how differently we were treated. Both of our afflictions meant that we were incapable of looking after ourselves... Both of us would suffer our disabilities for the rest of our lives and were having to fight mentally to come to terms with that fact. And both of us, at that time, were doing our utmost to be able to leave the hospitals (Ward 6, both of us – a very significant fact according to Geoff) in which we were imprisoned. But whereas people were more than happy to come and visit me, all but Geoff's closest friends were reticent about going to see him, locked up in the 'loony bin', especially when he was down. I had support, encouragement from everyone I met, complete strangers were writing to me with words of admiration, and the newspapers were just about breaking down the hospital doors to get my story. Geoff had nothing, save for the few dedicated

staff in his forgotten corner of a forgotten hospital and the company of a handful of lonely and confused patients... People were happy to talk about me and how I was getting on, what I'd achieved recently. With Geoff it was different. Nobody could see his illness; no one could measure his progress. His disability was invisible and so was the battle he was fighting. Yet we were fighting the same battle. And in the end Geoff came out on top of his battle, every bit as much as I did mine. (Andrew, 2004)

Reflective question

Can you think of examples of discrimination from your own experience? It might be something you or someone close to you has experienced, or something you have witnessed. What do you think the person experiencing discrimination might find helpful to support them?

▶ Evidence as a basis for action

Evidence of discrimination has been categorised according to the content of stereotypes: for instance, the moral taint – madness being equated with rampaging lawlessness, criminality, immorality or amorality; and the worthlessness of service users' opinions – having incompetent judgements by definition and hence being disbelieved when reporting crimes or explaining symptoms to doctors (Sayce, 2000).

Discrimination has been described in terms of the behaviours of discrimination: social distance, leading to rejections when people try to enter a country or join a workplace or school; and in the extreme to complete segregation (Sayce, 2000). It has been summarised by social psychologists as a process: labelling difference, attaching negative connotations to the difference, separating 'them' from 'us' and finally excluding those who are 'different', with profound consequences for social exclusion (Link & Phelan, 2001). It has been categorised by field of discrimination: for instance in personal and family life, communities, employment, civil and social life, health and social care, media (Thornicroft, 2006). For evidence and theory on discrimination on mental health grounds and for evidence on effective ways to challenge it and promote equality, readers are referred to Link and Phelan (2001), Repper and Perkins (2003), Sayce (2000, 2003) and Thornicroft (2006). The evidence base is growing, as more attention has been accorded to discrimination as one of the most profound challenges facing mental health policy and practice. In some cases evidence is being used as a basis to bring focus to the need for change. Below are a couple of examples.

An equal chance of life itself?

In 2004–6 the Disability Rights Commission undertook a formal investigation into physical health inequalities experienced by people with mental health conditions and/or learning disabilities (DRC, 2006). Methods used included the most comprehensive study of primary care records and mental health issues in the world (8 million primary care records), coupled with area studies in four areas, extensive consultation with service users and providers, evidence reviews, and written and oral evidence taken by a high level Inquiry Panel, who made recommendations designed to work in the newly configured NHS. The investigation findings included the following.

People with schizophrenia, bi-polar disorder or depression have significantly higher rates of obesity, smoking, heart disease, hypertension, respiratory disease, diabetes, stroke and breast cancer than other citizens. The investigation also made an internationally completely new finding, that people with schizophrenia are almost twice as likely to have bowel cancer.

These people experience a triple jeopardy. Not only are they more likely than others to get these illnesses, they are also more likely to get them young – before the age of 55. And once they have them, they are less likely to survive for five years.

All these facts mean that they die younger than others. Social deprivation is one important factor, but the differences cannot be explained by social deprivation alone. As Hippisley and Cox (2006, cited in DRC, 2006) report, 'Five year survival rates show lower survival rates for patients with mental health problems for almost all key conditions.'

Despite these risk factors, these groups are actually less likely to get some of the expected evidence-based checks and treatments. Although people with schizophrenia are more likely to have coronary heart disease, and to die of it younger, than other citizens, they are less likely to be prescribed the main evidence-based treatment: statins, which lower cholesterol. As the authors of the investigation's clinical data analyses put it:

> CHD patients with schizophrenia have higher risks (as reflected in the higher prevalence of smoking), but are less likely to be screened for raised cholesterol and less likely to be in treatment so there is a need to raise awareness among general practitioners and consider ways in which this shortfall can be addressed. (Hippisley *et al.*, 2006a, cited in DRC, 2006)

Mental health service users experience 'diagnostic overshadowing'; that is, physical health problems being viewed as part of the mental health problems and not fully explored or treated.

The investigation also found that whereas mental health service users – and mental health practitioners – saw access difficulties as the responsibility of the service, primary care practitioners tended to see the problems as inherent to the individual (not attending because of a chaotic lifestyle).

> In almost all interviews with primary care staff, we heard about patients from these groups who don't follow advice as given, don't attend for appointments and can't cope with the implications of the advice they have been given. There did not seem to be any strategies in place to support these groups to follow any

advice or guidance they might have been given (Samele *et al.*, 2006, cited in DRC, 2006).

Where primary care did make 'reasonable adjustments', these were often at no or low cost: for instance, where someone had a difficulty waiting in a crowded waiting room, the arrangement was that they waited in their car until called by the receptionist on their mobile.

The investigation also identified low expectations: the attitude that people with mental health problems 'just do' die younger or 'just won't' participate in health services designed to improve physical health. And it found non-compliance with DDA duties to make reasonable adjustments to ensure equal access to the service, as well as a lack of policy impetus and leadership to create change right through the health system.

The investigation made recommendations designed to challenge low expectations, give service users more power through information on rights and give service providers and commissioners tools to support work to reduce these particular health inequalities. The recommendations range from the practical – enabling people to record their access needs on the patient record and then meeting them – to the strategic. For instance, assessing the physical health needs of people with mental health problems as part of local strategic needs assessments, commissioning new service models that meet the whole community's needs and tracking over time whether important health outcomes like early death from coronary heart disease are becoming more equal.

The Formal Investigation (FI) report was given formally to the Secretary of State for Work and Pensions and the Secretary of State for Health and Welsh Minister of Health in 2006. Progress in implementing the outcomes of the Formal Investigation is being assessed by a reconvened Inquiry Panel and thereafter it is hoped that health inspection bodies and the Equality and Human Rights Commission (EHRC) will track progress.

Medical organisations including the British Medical Association and Royal College of General Practitioners have responded to the investigation findings by issuing training materials to improve equality of outcomes, and in some cases making strong statements on the priority that should be accorded to reducing these particular inequalities. For example:

I was honoured to be part of the inquiry carried out by the Disability Rights Commission. . . it was an eye opener. Too often we have tended to rationalise the dreadful health outcomes of such groups, believing – with ignorance – that their early death or disability is part of their problem. Usually it is not. Take heart disease as a simple example. If we believe in screening, but leave a group of patients out of our services (either by using incomprehensible or frightening language, or by excluding them deliberately from our efforts) then we should not be surprised that their risk of developing coronary heart disease is much higher. That is not rocket science. And ignorance can be based on well-meaning but unacceptable levels of prejudice. I will never, ever forgive the GP who attended when my much loved sister in law, who happened to have Down's Syndrome, died suddenly of meningitis. His first words to her grieving mother? 'Well, I suppose it's for the best isn't it?' (Professor David Haslam, President, Royal College of GPs, in DRC and RCGP, 2007)

> ### Reflective question
>
> Do you think health service staff generally understand that making their services work equally well for people with mental health problems as for anyone else is a legal obligation, part of disability access? If not, why not? What can practitioners do to make sure that these duties are understood and that people know what they can do to ensure equal access?

An equal chance to contribute

People with mental health problems have the lowest employment rate (at 20%) of any group of disabled people (average 50%). If the British government is to reach its target of an 80% overall employment rate, it cannot do so without improving the employment rate of disabled people. The government target is for one million more disabled people to be in paid employment. Since 40% of those on Incapacity Benefit in 2007 had mental health difficulties as their prime impairment, rising to 60% if secondary impairments are included, improving their employment rates is critical to this mainstream government policy target.

There is extensive evidence of discrimination on the part of employers. For instance, only 37% of employers in 2001 stated that they would be prepared to employ someone with a history of mental illness, as compared to 62% who would take on physically disabled people, 78% long-term unemployed people and 88% lone parents (DWP, 2001).

Some discrimination is entrenched in law. If an MP is sectioned under the Mental Health Act, they are expected to stand down as an MP. The same applies to a company or charity director who develops mental incapacity. This means that whereas someone who (say) is admitted to hospital with a heart condition is welcomed back as a Member of Parliament or director once they are able to resume their duties, the person in hospital with (say) schizophrenia, who is temporarily incapacitated and/or sectioned, is required *by law* to stand down – even if they are quite capable of resuming their duties.

Many people with mental health problems are either not working, or are working at levels well below their capabilities. Good practice for employers includes making no assumptions, not asking questions about health and ill health until after a job offer, and making 'reasonable adjustments' (the mental health equivalent of the ramp): for instance, flexible working hours for someone who cannot travel in the rush hour, different shifts for someone who needs stability because of a medication regime, extra management support or time off for mental health appointments.

▶ Effective anti-discrimination approaches

It is possible to disrupt each stage of the process of discrimination as outlined by Link and Phelan (2001; Sayce, 2003). To discriminate, first, we link being 'different' to undesirable characteristics. To subvert discrimination we therefore link being different to positive characteristics and directly challenge the negative. For instance, a campaign in Norfolk by the mental health charity Rethink put up a statue of Winston Churchill wearing a straitjacket – and made clear in the campaign that he led a country through war while experiencing the 'black dog' of depression. When people objected that the statue degraded Churchill's memory, Rethink used this as an opportunity to raise further debate on attitudes: why, after all, is depression something that would damage a reputation? The campaign also used slogans like: 'Call me mad because I believe Norwich City will get promoted – not because I have schizophrenia'.

The campaign measurably improved public attitudes. Before the campaign, 24% of the public surveyed thought that people with mental illness should not be allowed to do important jobs. After the campaign, this dropped to 14%. Before the campaign, 33% thought that people with mental illness were often dangerous. After the campaign, this dropped to 21%. Before the campaign, 15% were prepared to say that they had experienced mental health problems; after the campaign, this had risen to 30% (Rethink, 2006).

Similarly, the 'Like Minds Like Mine' campaign in New Zealand used television and print advertising linked with local activities. It emphasised the contribution of people with mental health problems, ranging from famous rugby stars to people achieving ordinary successes, like working in a bakery. This mix is evidence based: using superstars grabs attention and gets discussion going, but celebrities are seen as exceptions; the point is not generalised. Ordinary role models build greater empathy and conviction. This campaign measurably improved public attitudes in New Zealand.

We also need to be careful not to reinforce existing negative stereotypes. The message 'mental illness is a brain disease/illness like any other' can reinforce the idea that people cannot make rational judgements, that they are incompetent (Read *et al.*, 2006). These messages should be avoided.

The second thing we do to discriminate is to separate 'them' from 'us'. To disrupt discrimination we therefore bring people together – to work, study or otherwise be together. The 'contact' theory (Hewstone, 2003) says that direct contact between people with mental health problems and other citizens changes attitudes – more than any amount of information (indeed, spending money on campaigns to tell the public what mental illness is, or how common mental health problems are is wasteful: it is likely to have no effect on attitudes). However, the contact needs to be on at least equal terms and needs to 'moderately disconfirm stereotypes': if the person is a superhero they will be seen as an exception; if they are completely disorganised or aggressive they will confirm stereotypes. Training programmes led by mental health service users with police officers, schoolchildren and other audiences have influenced attitudes; it has been important to select service users carefully and equip them with effective messages in addition to supporting them to share their own experiences (Thornicroft, 2006). The most effective way of all of achieving 'contact on equal terms' is through mental health service users working, studying and participating alongside others. Having someone who is open about having a mental health problem as a boss can massively affect attitudes. This is one compelling reason for shifting resources from sheltered to supported open employment (Department of Health, 2006).

The third thing we do to discriminate is treat 'them' unfavourably – heaping negative consequences of social exclusion on them. Therefore to subvert discrimination we stop the unfavourable treatment. One way of achieving this is by using legal rights. Since the DDA 1995 came into force, there have been many legal cases that have challenged discrimination faced by mental health service users: for instance, the cases of Ms Melanophy, Mr Watkiss, Ms Marshall, Mr Paul (see Sayce, 2003; Sayce & Boardman, 2007; DRC website at www.drc-gb.org). Some of these cases have resulted in compensation – and even more importantly, sent a message that refusing someone a job, or firing them, just because they have a mental health problem is illegal and unfair; and that employers have to make 'reasonable adjustments', like a gradual return to work, before concluding that someone is not able to do a particular job.

The evidence tells us that use of legal powers is likely to be important because, to cite Link and Phelan (2001), 'stigma is entirely dependent on social, political and economic power'. The power of the law is one effective way to challenge the power behind discrimination. However, recent work on equality and civil rights law suggests that individual cases alone are not sufficient. This is because an employer, service provider or college may lose a discrimination case – and perhaps pay compensation – but their practices may remain unchanged. Even if that one organisation changes, the case may well not prompt change right through the sector.

It is therefore important to use other methods to prompt system-wide change, drawing on the power of law but not relying only on individual cases. These include the following.

Active, positive promotion of good practice under the DDA

Imaginative communications rooted in market research (on what key audiences already think) can have a positive impact on attitudes. For instance, the Disability

Rights Commission (DRC) made a hard-hitting emotional drama film, *The Appointment*, that told a story of a hotel manager coming to terms with a new hidden impairment (diabetes), which forced him to rethink issues about disclosure and prejudice at work in relation to people with different hidden and overt conditions (including bi-polar disorder). This appealed to the small business audience effectively through reference to their humanity (the manager's experience at home and at work), their concern for business effectiveness and their need to comply with legislation.

One key to effectiveness is to ensure that the mental health experience is fully included in an 'equality and human rights' framework. For that reason the DRC, having found that most employers and service providers still understood 'disability equality' largely in terms of physical access (ramps, lifts and the like), adopted the practice of putting less expected examples first – for instance, listing the reasonable adjustment for someone with bi-polar disorder first in a list of adjustments that employers can make. As long as mental health issues are seen as separate and different from other equalities issues, people with mental health conditions will not benefit from general progress in Britain towards fairness and equality.

Formal investigations and other strategic legal interventions

Legal interventions can include enforceable action plans. The Health Formal Investigation described above is one example of a system-wide investigation designed to understand complex patterns of discrimination and recommend systemic solutions. If implemented, this could have far-reaching effects. Another DRC investigation into whether there is discrimination in the fitness standards required for someone to be a teacher, nurse or social worker is equally poised to have a system-wide impact: on the regulatory framework that can prevent people with mental health or other impairments from training or practising in their chosen profession.

The positive disability equality duty

In the UK, public-sector organisations have, since December 2006, been required positively to promote disability equality, rather than waiting until after the event of discrimination to offer redress. They have to collect evidence, involve disabled people, do impact assessments of policies and prepare action plans. For instance, in response to the Formal Investigation into health inequalities, it would be expected that health service commissioners would assess evidence of inequalities and local experience of disabled people, and commission services to close gaps of inequality, monitoring unequal life chances over time and acting to reduce them.

Putting disability in general – and mental health in particular – at the heart of mainstream policy and delivery

To give one example, mental health campaigners used to argue that with 80% of people with mental health conditions out of work, there were urgent problems of poverty for them and their families. The problem was that policy makers, unless concerned about people with mental health problems, took no notice. In the 2000s the argument was phrased differently: of all the British children living in poverty, one third has at least one disabled parent; and the families least likely to have moved out of poverty are those with a parent with a mental health problem. At this point mainstream policy makers took note.

In 2006 John Hutton, Secretary of State for Work and Pensions, stated, 'child poverty is a disability issue'. Similarly, the Treasury and No 10 Policy Unit focused on mental health and employment, in response to data that 40% of people on Incapacity Benefit (IB) have a mental health impairment. The winning argument is to start with the issue of concern to the policy makers – child poverty, or people on IB – and then show the high proportion of their problem accounted for by people with mental health conditions. Mental health and disability experts can then be poised to present solutions to the mainstream policy problem – reducing child poverty, or achieving an 80% national employment rate.

The DRC's Disability Agenda used this approach across a range of policy areas: skills (one third of people with no qualifications in Britain are disabled people), health inequalities, housing and more. The DRC's Mental Health Advisory Group followed up with a separate document, *Coming Together: Mental Health Service Users, Equality and Human Rights* (DRC 2007b), which made the mental health-specific case on the same policy priorities. Rather as the 'business case' explains to business why disability equality will help their economic, reputational and ethical position, 'putting disability at the heart of policy' shows policy makers how disability (or mental health) equality helps meet the main challenges for Britain, their policy targets and social justice imperatives.

In summary, the evidence suggests that systemic approaches to change work best. These approaches need to use tested messages, build contact between mental health service users and other citizens, and work to change whole sectors through systemic legal powers and putting mental health at the heart of policy.

Quiz

1. The DDA is rarely used by people with mental health problems to challenge discrimination. True or false?

2. It is harder to prove you are 'disabled' under the meaning of the Act if you have a mental health problem. True or false?

3. Under what conditions does contact between mental health service users and other citizens positively change attitudes?

4. In addition to individual legal cases, how else can legal powers be used to challenge discrimination and promote equality?

Answers

1. False. 23% of DDA employment cases have been brought by people with mental health problems.

2. Partly true. It used to be the case that people had to prove they had a 'clinically well recognised' mental illness – a requirement that did not apply to people with other types of disability. This requirement was removed in 2005. But it is still harder to demonstrate a disability, because the way disability is defined works in terms of day-to-day activities (walking, seeing etc.), which doesn't adequately reflect mental health impairments.

3. Contact on at least equal terms, where the stereotype is mildly disconfirmed.

4. Formal investigations. Enforceable action plans. Disability Equality Duty. Positive communications that reference the DDA.

▶ What can mental health staff do to support equality and combat discrimination?

Mental health staff have more contact with mental health service users than anyone else and are in a stronger position than anyone to let people know their rights and enable them to use them. For example:

> A man had worked in the construction industry for many years. He went off sick with depression and during this time was made redundant. He went to see a psychiatrist who advised him that he could have a strong DDA case and recommended that he seek legal advice. (DWP & DRC, 2004)

This simple piece of advice – that the man might have a strong DDA case – could make the difference between rights meaning everything or nothing. There is no need for mental health staff to know the legal detail, but advising people where to seek help could embolden them to challenge unfairness, not to give up.

Most challenges to discrimination through history have come from people seizing power – from women achieving the vote to gays and lesbians securing civil partnership. Anger is important. Armed with information and opportunities for peer support and contact, mental health service users may be able to achieve greater equality.

Equally, practitioners can familiarise themselves with the types of 'reasonable adjustment' that people with mental health problems have found helpful – from being able to travel outside the rush hour to avoid panic, to a gradual return to work – and provide this information to service users. This can make a huge difference to what people can then negotiate for, with their employer or college. RADAR's programme *Doing Work Differently* is written by disabled people, for disabled people, with examples of what people have found helpful in managing at work (RADAR, 2007). This type of material needs to be actively shared with service users, so they can benefit from what others have negotiated before them. For instance, what are the pros and cons of disclosing to your manager, in what situations, with what recourse if discrimination results? What adjustments at work have others negotiated, what might be considered 'reasonable'?

Practitioners can also provide expert opinion to employers, tribunals and others on who can work or take on a particular professional training. By knowing what others with mental health problems have achieved, and what can be achieved with adjustments, practitioners can guard against the all-too-common assumption that someone will not be able to hold down a responsible job, or enter a career, because it may be 'too stressful'. It may be that the practitioner has only seen the individual when very unwell, and doesn't realise their capabilities when well. Practitioners need to be aware that unemployment is generally much more damaging to mental health than employment, and that low expectations can sap confidence and opportunity. Practitioners have a key role in fostering hope.

Mental health staff can engage in system-wide change. Mental health services need explicitly to highlight equality and anti-discrimination as core values. This includes both equality on mental health grounds and equality on the other major grounds of sexual orientation, race, gender, religion/belief and age. An important start is to ensure that mental health organisations themselves exemplify good practice in employing people with personal experience of mental health problems – not only 'not discriminating', but valuing the contribution of personal experience and ensuring that managers are equipped to make adjustments and arrange support as needed. Staff should assess policies to ensure that they promote equality and do not impose barriers. For instance, do occupational health assessments help ensure that people get the reasonable adjustments they need? Or do they unnecessarily screen people out of the workplace on mental health grounds? Could the organisation adopt the practice of British Telecom, which states publicly that it will not discriminate against anyone on mental health grounds in recruitment, because it has abandoned pre-employment health screening as an unnecessary expense that tells the employer little about likely performance?

Mental health organisations can go further. They can embrace as their main purpose supporting mental health service users to participate in society, to exercise citizenship rights (Repper & Perkins, 2003). There is no point in treatment if it does not support people in living the lives they want. This lies at the heart of the Independent Living Bill, introduced by Lord Ashley in 2007, to transform services so that they support control and choice, on service users' own terms. This is a profound shift in service ideology – and in practice. It means adopting different end objectives, different measures of success, different clinical and management practices. It is the next major challenge for mental health services.

Finally, expertise in mental health and anti-discrimination is central to the whole British endeavour of equality and human rights; and central to successful policy making, from reducing child poverty to improving skills. Mental health threads right across equalities issues: racism, for example, affects mental health, and people from black and minority ethnic communities who have a psychiatric diagnosis experience particular challenges of discrimination. Mental health users/survivors and mental health practitioners, academics and campaigners understand these dynamics. There is a compelling need to share this knowledge with others working on equalities and human rights. Rather than playing catch-up with disability rights or other aspects of civil rights movements, it is time for the mental health world to take its rightful place: at the heart of equalities and human rights work, and at the heart of policy making on the central challenges facing Britain.

Reflective question

What would you like to see mental health practitioners do to:

1. Enable service users to assert their rights?

2. Ensure that the service itself promotes equality?

3. Make the service focused on social inclusion?

4. Contribute to wider equality and human rights work, and policy work?

▶ **References**

Andrew, J. (2004) *Life and Limb*. London: Portrait.

Bynoe, I., Oliver, M. & Barnes, C. (1991) *Equal Rights for Disabled People: The Case for a New Law*. London: Institute for Public Policy Research.

Campbell, P. (2000) The role of users of psychiatric services in service development – influence not power. *Psychiatric Bulletin*, 25: 87–8.

Chamberlin, J. (1988) *On Our Own*. London: Mind.

Corrigan, P.W., Edwards, A.B., Green, A., Diwan, S.L. & Penn, D.L. (2001) Prejudice, social distance and familiarity with mental illness. *Schizophrenia Bulletin*, 27(2): 219–25.

Department of Health (2002) *Mental Health and Employment in the NHS*. London: Department of Health.

Department of Health (2006) *Vocational Services for People with Severe Mental Health Problems: Commissioning Guidance*. London: Department of Health.

Department for Work and Pensions (2001) Recruiting benefit claimants: Qualitative research with employers in ONE pilot areas. *Research Series Paper No 150*, prepared by K. Bunt, J. Shury & D. Vivian. London: DWP.

Department for Work and Pensions & Disability Rights Commission (2004) *Monitoring the Disability Discrimination Act 1995, Phase 3*. London: DWP.

Disability Rights Commission (2006) *Equal Treatment: Closing the Gap. A Formal Investigation into Physical Health Inequalities Experienced by People with Learning Disabilities and/or*

Mental Health Problems. London: DRC. All research carried out for the investigation is available on the DRC Web site at www.drc-gb.org/health.

Disability Rights Commission (2007a) *The Disability Agenda*. London: DRC.

Disability Rights Commission (2007b) *Coming Together: Mental Health Service Users, Equality and Human Rights*. London: DRC.

Disability Rights Commission & Royal College of GPs (2007) *Learning Pack for Health Professionals. Equal Treatment: Closing the Gap*. London: DRC & RCGP.

Dunn, S. (1999) *Mind Readings*. London: Mind.

Hewstone, M. (2003) Intergroup contact: Panacea for prejudice? *The Psychologist*, 16(7): 352–5.

Leff, J., Trieman, N. & Gooch, C. (1996) Teams Assessment of Psychiatric Services (TAPS) Project 33: Prospective follow-up study of long-stay patients discharged from two psychiatric hospitals. *American Journal of Psychiatry*, 153(10): 1318–24.

Link, B.G. & Phelan, J.C. (2001) On the nature and consequences of stigma. *Annual Review of Sociology*, 27: 363–85.

Office of the Deputy Prime Minister (2004) *Mental Health and Social Exclusion. Social Exclusion Unit Report*. London: ODPM.

O'Neill, O. (2002) *A Question of Trust. The BBC Reith Lectures 2002*. Cambridge: Cambridge University Press.

Perkins, R.E. & Sayce, L. (2006) Social inclusion. In C. Gamble & G. Brennan (eds), *Working with Serious Mental Illness*. London: Elsevier.

RADAR (2007) *Doing Work Differently: Getting and Keeping a Job While Managing Impairment*. London: RADAR.

Read, J. & Baker, S. (1996) *Not Just Sticks and Stones: A Survey of the Stigma, Taboos and Discrimination Experienced by People with Mental Health Problems*. London: Mind.

Read, J., Haslam, N., Sayce, L. & Davies, E. (2006) Prejudice and schizophrenia: A review of the 'mental illness is an illness like any other' approach. *Acta Scandinavica*, 1–16.

Repper, J.M. & Perkins, R.E. (2003) *Social Inclusion, Recovery and Mental Health Practice*. London: Balliere Tindall.

Repper, J., Sayce, L., Strong, S., Willmot, J. & Haines, M. (1997) *Tall Stories from the Back Yard. A Survey of 'Nimby' Opposition to Community Mental Health Facilities, Experienced by Key Service Providers in England and Wales*. London: Mind.

Rethink (2006) Results of Norwich Anti-Stigma Campaign. *Presentation*. London: Rethink.

Royal College of Psychiatrists (2002) *Psychiatric Disability and Employment Opportunities*. London: Royal College of Psychiatrists.

Sayce, L. (1995) Response to violence: A framework for fair treatment. In J. Crighton (ed.), *Psychiatric Patient Violence*. London: Duckworth.

Sayce, L. (2000) *From Psychiatric Patient to Citizen: Overcoming Discrimination and Social Exclusion*. London: Macmillan.

Sayce, L. (2003) Beyond good intentions: Making anti-discrimination strategies work. *Disability and Society*, 18(5): 625–42.

Sayce, L. (2005) Risk, rights and anti-discrimination work in mental health: Avoiding the risks in considering risk. In R. Adams, L. Dominelli & M. Payne (eds), *Social Work Futures*. London: Palgrave Macmillan.

Sayce, L. & Boardman, A,P. (2008) Recent developments in the Disability Discrimination Act 1995, as amended in 2005. Implications for psychiatrists. *Advances in Psychiatric Treatment*, in press.

Taylor, P. & Gunn, J. (1999) Homicides by people with mental illness: Myth and reality. *British Journal of Psychiatry*, 174: 9–14.

Thornicroft, G. (2006) *Shunned: Discrimination Against People with Mental Illness*. Oxford: Oxford University Press.

Watkiss, A. (2001) Speech to National Mind Conference, Scarborough.

CHAPTER SIXTEEN

Service user involvement

Peter Campbell

Mental health system survivor and freelance trainer

Living with mental distress is, and is likely to remain, a difficult experience. Nevertheless, there are grounds for believing it is a better time to be a mental health service user in the UK (and numerous other countries) today than it was 25 years ago. A greater number of long-term service users in the UK now live in their own home rather than in large institutions. Although care and treatment rely heavily on medication, other options are slowly becoming more available. Service users' long-expressed desire for more talking and listening has finally received serious attention, currently focused mainly on the wider provision of cognitive behavioural therapy. While re-admission rates are high, there does seem to be a greater possibility, and certainly a greater recognition of the possibility, that living with mental distress and having a meaningful and contributing life need not be incompatible. The level of employment among long-term service users in the UK continues to be very low (less than 25%) and lower than for most groups of disabled people, but it is starting to rise. At the same time, opportunities to achieve some degree of equal citizenship have been assisted by the introduction and further development of legislation against discrimination on the grounds of disability. The journey in from the margin territories of distress, discrimination, poverty and disadvantage is undoubtedly long, but it is one that service users are increasingly able to begin.

One important aspect of these positive changes is the greater involvement of service users: in their own care and treatment, in the development of better mental health services and in social change more generally. We are living in an era of service user-centred services. Providing Service User Centred Care is one of the Ten Essential Shared Capabilities that establish the framework for current mental health practice in England (Basset, Lindley & Barton, 2005; and see Chapter 9, this volume). Service user involvement in the development and delivery of mental health services at a strategic level is a legal requirement under the Health and Social Care Act (2001). The public-sector duty to produce disability

Learning About Mental Health Practice. Edited by Theo Stickley and Thurstine Basset
© 2008 John Wiley & Sons, Ltd

equality schemes under the Disability Discrimination Act (2005) requires the involvement of service users (as disabled people). These are recent examples of a trend to promote service user involvement through legislation and guidance going back to the 1980s that includes the Disabled Persons (Services, Consultation and Representation) Act (1986), the NHS and Community Care Act (1990) and the Care Programme Approach (1991). At the very least, they reveal a significant and continuing desire to envision service users as active protagonists rather than mute recipients.

Inter-linked with this growing emphasis by government and service providers on involving service users at a range of levels has been increased enthusiasm by some service users about taking action to achieve positive change (Barnes & Bowl, 2001). One illustration of this is the development since the mid-1980s of service user networks within major mental health voluntary organisations (e.g. MIND, Rethink). Another is the emergence of service users as paid workers in and around mental health services (e.g. as advocates, freelance trainers, researchers, development workers, staff in service user-led services). Perhaps most notable has been the growth of independent service user-led action groups (Campbell, 2005). In 1985 there were less than a dozen in the UK. Today, although precise figures are difficult to obtain, there are probably more than 700 (Friedli, 2004b). The 1985 House of Commons Social Services Select Committee Report on Community Care complained about the difficulty 'of hearing the authentic voice of the ultimate consumers of community care'. In 2007, while there may be legitimate arguments about how 'authentic' the voice is and whether hearing has been translated into listening and action, the voice of service users is now present where once it was largely absent.

▶ Terminology

The term 'service user involvement', although widely used, has drawbacks. It is usually understood to relate to service users' relationship to various aspects of health and social care systems. Service users' relationship to society can also legitimately be seen in terms of involvement, but in recent years has been more commonly approached within a framework of 'social inclusion/exclusion'.

Even when restricted to health and social care systems, service user involvement can be applied to very different activities. A primary concern of most mental health professionals will be the involvement of individual service users in their care and treatment, but involvement also includes collective action. While many involvement issues are common to both areas, there are significant differences, not the least of which is that while service users can now only opt out of involvement in their own care and treatment with difficulty, collective action is something they have to opt into. At the level of collective action, it is quite possible to describe service users teaching mental health nurses about the Mental Health Act, or sitting on a committee to discuss the development of local services, or demonstrating outside the Royal College of Psychiatrists against the use of electro-convulsive therapy in terms of service user involvement. Whether doing so best helps us to understand the true nature of what is happening is more difficult to decide.

One danger in talking about service user involvement is that it is frequently taken to mean mental health professionals involving service users rather than service users involving themselves. In any working relationship questions of choice, goals and agenda setting are important. Whether we choose to use a framework of service user involvement or one of service user action in which involvement is an important element may depend partly on how much we are focusing on service users as individual recipients of care or as a collective force for change. Nevertheless, it is important to remember that service user involvement can range from activities that are spontaneously chosen and pursued, through ones that are taken up reluctantly because nothing better is on offer, to involvement that is actually imposed.

Exercise 16.1

Why should service users get involved?

Write down reasons service users should get involved in their own care and treatment. Make separate lists from these perspectives:

■ your own perspective as a mental health professional

■ the perspective of a service user

■ the perspective of government

■ the perspective of members of society not involved in mental health services

How similar are the lists?

Are any differences mainly due to different priorities or to reasons that appear on some lists but not others?

Do the differences really matter? If so, what can be done about them?

Are there reasons in your lists that are in direct opposition to each other – in particular on your own list as a professional and your service user list? Can anything be done about this?

Repeat this process with lists of reasons service users should get involved in developing mental health services and wider social change.

▶ The case for service user involvement

Thus making a case for the greater involvement of mental health service users is much less of a live issue today than 25 years ago. Most people now see involvement as 'a good thing'. There is a wealth of legislation, policy documents, guidance and training materials that make it clear that service user involvement is not just desirable but necessary. A similar emphasis on involvement has affected the lives of many other groups of health and social care users and disabled people. There is no doubt the direction in which the tide is flowing. More attention is currently given to how to make involvement effective than whether to encourage it or not.

Nevertheless, while the idea of involving service users more in their own care and treatment may never have been very controversial, believing they have anything significant to contribute to developing services or to mental health debates generally has been open to much greater challenge. The position service users currently hold in these areas has been brought about by a combination of factors, but it would be misreading recent history to conclude that they have always been warmly welcomed in. On the contrary, in the UK as elsewhere, access to the corridors of power has frequently been achieved only as a result of struggle by service user activists and their allies.

There are pragmatic reasons to support greater involvement. It can improve relationships between individuals and services. It can make care and treatment more effective. Collective action can lead to the development of better services and promote more sensitive public understandings of living with mental distress. But involvement is now also seen as a right. Article 4 of the WHO/UNICEF Declaration of Alma Ata 1978 states: 'people have the right and duty to participate individually and collectively in the planning and implementation of their health care' (WHO, 1978). Involvement is also clearly linked to consent to treatment, an issue that has a troubled history in relation to mental health services but has been given increasing emphasis since the Second World War (Fennell, 1996).

While the therapeutic benefits of an individual's involvement in treatment may be of particular interest to professionals, similar benefits from involvement in collective action should not be overlooked. Although service user activists are unlikely to prioritise these and there is evidence that action can contribute to as well as alleviate distress, the lives of numerous service users have changed for the better as a result of such involvement. Having an opportunity to work creatively with people with similar experiences and to put what has previously been seen as negative and unmentionable baggage to constructive use can significantly improve a service user's quality of life, regardless of whether they make a paid career out of it or use services less frequently as a result.

▶ Involvement in care and treatment

Consideration of involving service users in their own care and treatment must start by recognising that they may have no real choice over their contact with services. Some are 'sentenced' to treatment by the courts. Others are assessed and detained under Part One of the Mental Health Act. In 2005–6, the total number of detentions was 47 400. A snapshot survey of inpatients in England and Wales on 31 March 2005 found that 30% were detained patients. Non-white patients were 44% more likely to be detained. The fact that some service users prefer to call themselves 'service resisters', 'recipients' or 'psychiatric survivors' suggests that a degree of hostility about involvement may exist even among those who are not being compulsorily detained. A framework including the power to compel poses dilemmas for involvement, for example the insensitive use of actual powers (e.g. keeping people 'sectioned' when it is no longer strictly necessary) and the threatened use of powers (e.g. 'if you don't take your medication, we will section you'). The question of how far to go to involve service users is important and applies whether someone is actively resistant, reluctant or actively enthusiastic. That mental health professionals have access to compulsory powers and may be under pressure to use them can complicate matters.

Some of the enthusiasm for involvement is connected to a belief that it will increase the power to choose treatments, some to a belief that more involving treatments are more desirable. There has been a persistent demand from service users for more talking and listening and this has been recognised as a legitimate concern. Nevertheless, while the variety of supports available has increased and now includes more opportunities for talking and listening, drug treatment, not usually seen as an involving treatment, remains a mainstay (Appleby, 2007). In certain situations, notably the acute ward, talking and listening are in short supply, and measures like Protected Engagement Time are being hastily introduced to enable more interaction. It would be hard to argue that many acute wards are currently involving environments and we should be cautious about overestimating how involving care and treatment is generally. Research on a recent year-long initiative to improve acute ward care noted the following improvements in involvement: primary nurse meeting patient a minimum of twice a week – 38% to 60%; care and treatment discussed with nurse – 40% to 55%; asked if you wanted a carer/advocate involved in your care – 33% to 46% (Barry, Hughes & Lawton-Smith, 2006). This does show that worthwhile change can be achieved in a short period, but also that improvements are taking place within a low to medium rather than medium to high waveband of involvement.

Progress has been made, particularly in creating new mechanisms whereby service users can exert more influence on the choice and planning of their care and treatment. Whatever their misgivings about the nature of services or the choices available, service user-led organisations have seen these mechanisms as a vital area of concern, worked consistently in it since the 1980s, and pioneered some of the developments now seen to be essential to good service provision.

Written plans or statements have been an important element. They are often developed through service users working with professionals, but that need not always be the case. It is most unlikely that they will be produced without some involvement by the service user, although how meaningful that is may vary considerably.

The Care Programme Approach revolves around the creation of a written plan in collaboration with the service user and its subsequent monitoring and adjustment. It has been influential and stimulated interest in other types of plan like crisis plans. In the mid-1990s, service user-led organisations began to explore the use of advance directives/advance statements, whereby service users could indicate their treatment wishes at a time when they have decision-making capacity to influence responses when they are judged no longer to have it (Campbell, 2001). More recently, Wellness Recovery Action Plans (WRAP) have become an important element in the recovery approach.

While these new opportunities are usually welcomed, they have limitations. It may not always be clear what is on offer. A care plan suggests a degree of 'agreement to provide', but what redress is available if support does not materialise? It is not clear if an advance statement is effectively anything more than a wish list. What weight does it have and do service users realise that by writing they want a particular intervention they may put themselves under greater pressure if they change their mind without amending their statement? There is also a danger that written plans will be seen as essential for everyone or become an end in themselves. Writing about mental health wards as good workplaces, Henry Stewart said, 'The fact is that what people are prepared to do if they are self motivated and trusted to do it their way, is far beyond anything they can be managed to do' (Stewart, 2006). We should bear that in mind when developing involvement mechanisms for service users.

Box 16.1: Concerns about care planning (the Care Programme Approach)

Care planning has become the main mechanism for achieving cost-effective care and treatment. It should also mean that service users are more involved in decisions, and that care and treatment more closely reflect what they need and even what they want.

Major drawbacks include the lack of choice and the quality of services. Care planning does not directly address these issues. In terms of involvement, a number of concerns have been expressed since the Care Programme Approach was introduced in 1991, including:

- being seen by professionals as just a bureaucratic process (Continuous Paper Accumulation)
- variations in implementation
- service users not properly involved in the process:
  - do not know what CPA is
  - do not know who their care co-ordinator is
  - do not have a copy of their care plan
  - do not know when their plan is due for review

- the process values professional views more highly than service user views
- does it deliver the goods for service users?

Independent advocacy is an important element in effective involvement. While there may be different emphases on why it is necessary – incapacity of service users, shortcomings of professionals, proliferation of over-bureaucratic procedures – the need for advocacy is widely recognised. In the early 1980s there was little or no mental health advocacy and its provision was not a feature of mainstream debate in the UK. Now there is much wider provision and the introduction of a legal right to advocacy for detained patients has been secured across the UK.

A major factor in these developments has been the action of service users and service user-led organisations. They have been more enthusiastic about advocacy than have governments, service providers or voluntary organisations, and have led in campaigning for advocacy, setting up advocacy projects and developing principles and practice. The United Kingdom Advocacy Network (UKAN), a service user-led group founded in 1992, has played a vital pioneering role. The demand for advocacy comes very much from the grass roots and is reflected among all groups of health and social care users (Brandon, 1995).

The provision and practice of advocacy remain problematic. There are issues of availability and quality connected to inadequate funding and piecemeal development. Independent advocacy can make life more difficult for professionals. It can take up time and make their work more complicated. Advocacy often does not secure service users the outcomes they desire. Nevertheless, it usually increases their chances of influencing decisions and makes them more satisfied with the process whatever the results. It is clear both that many service users see advocacy as central to good services and that improving their involvement will require more and better advocacy provision.

Much of the rhetoric around service user involvement links it with greater choice and thus empowerment. One difficulty with this equation is the availability of choices (Main, 2006). How long do service users have to wait for talking treatments? Where do you go except the acute ward if you cannot be supported at home through a crisis? Is it possible to be a long-term service user and not on medication? Another problem is that involvement can focus on complying with a choice as much as making a choice. Indeed, medication compliance may be what the general public (and others) feel involvement should principally be achieving. We should not ignore the difficulty of service users making free choices under pressure of professional advice. We should not underestimate the degree of involvement work (e.g. compliance therapy, psycho-education) that is devoted to ensuring that service users comply with treatments that professionals have sanctioned and accept professionally approved frameworks of understanding. Greater involvement may have moved us to a point where partnership is a possibility, but there is no doubt where the power in the relationship still resides.

Exercise 16.2: How much do you know about service user action?

■ How many national or local service user-led organisations can you name (not including groups like Mind, Rethink, Together, which are not service user-led)?

■ How much do you know about their activities? Have you read any of their written materials?

■ How much input have service users had into your professional training?

■ Do you know if there is a service user-led group in your locality? Do you know anything about their activities? Have you ever met anyone from the group and talked about what they are doing?

■ Can you name any service user-led services in the UK?

■ How often have you read anything written by a service user about mental health services (apart from autobiographies)?

■ How often do you come into contact with service user activists about issues other than improving services?

▶ Service user action: an introduction

Service user action (the service user/survivor movement) in the UK has been a growing feature over the last 25 years, but has much earlier origins (Campbell, 1996). It is linked with and has contributed to action in other countries that dates back to the 1960s. In the 1980s it began to develop rapidly for a number of reasons, including the growth of health service consumerism, interest in individual rights, the example of other disadvantaged groups, contact with service user activists from other countries (e.g. USA and Netherlands) where action was better organised. Service user action has always contained a strong element of protest, although this may have weakened as more people became involved and service systems opened up to incorporate activists.

There are dangers in thinking that action is simply about developing better mental health services, although this remains an important goal. Action focuses on many aspects of a service user's life: levels of benefit, employment opportunities, discrimination. Meanings and identity are important as well as material circumstances, particularly as a mental illness diagnosis can be corrosive and unusual thoughts and perceptions devalued or dismissed altogether. What service users are struggling for is a more positive personal and social identity as much as anything else. Seeing action as basically a way for customers to obtain better services is a misunderstanding. Activists have spoken in terms of 'liberation of an oppressed group' and this should not be dismissed.

Service user action is diverse. People may be involved as individuals, within voluntary or other organisations, as members of a service user-led organisation or in a combination of these. Although most action is unpaid work, an increasing number will receive payment for some actions they take, while others will find full or part-time employment within the service user movement. Types of action are also wide-ranging, some with little or no connection to mental health services. Finally, although the movement in the UK is held together by common beliefs and goals, it contains divergent views and priorities and defies easy generalisations. While most share concern about compulsion and an over-reliance on medication, some are looking for radical changes in treatments, including banning the use of electro-convulsive therapy (ECT) or focus on the creation of alternatives to what they view as an unacceptable service system. Others see biomedical understandings as a major obstacle, or see discrimination and exclusion as the key issue. The use of creative arts as a means of self-exploration, self-expression and change is another area of increasing activity.

The *On Our Own Terms* survey that researched the service user/survivor movement in England (Wallcraft, Read & Sweeney, 2003) received 318 replies from service user groups in England and found:

- 75% groups in existence for less than 10 years

- 77% receive external funding

- 55% have a paid worker

- 72% groups meet at least once a month. Most commonly between 5 and 14 people attended each meeting

- Activities –

  - 79% self-help and support

  - 72% consultation work

  - 69% education and training

  - 41% creative activities

  - 38% campaigning

  - 36% advocacy

▶ **Service user action: types of action**

Many of the actions that services users and their organisations take will involve working with mental health professionals. One of the significant changes in the 1980s was that activists in the UK gave up their predominantly separatist stance.

Since then, action has usually taken place within a rhetoric of 'working together' or 'common concerns' or 'partnership'. Although this is connected with reality, it can obscure the fact that there are important differences between the reasons mental health professionals and service users come to work together in the first place, as well as between the goals they may be working towards. It is by no means clear that an assumption that we are all around the table for the same reasons and working on a shared agenda is the most effective starting point.

Consultation

Taking part in consultation around the planning, management and monitoring of mental health services is a key aspect of the work of most service user groups. The mechanisms used in such consultation may vary, from the use of questionnaires or interviews, through meetings organised by groups where their members can discuss issues with service providers, to the provision of service user representatives on committees and consultative groups. Often more than one of these mechanisms will come into play. In the eyes of government and service providers, consultations of this kind now seem to be the bread and butter of collective involvement, contributing an essential legitimacy to the process of developing services. It is more difficult to assess what service users feel. On the one hand, many groups have continued to devote time and energy to consultation. On the other, tokenistic involvement remains a frequent complaint.

Training and education

Training and educating mental health professionals has been an objective of service user activists in the UK since the mid-1980s. Survivors Speak Out, an early national networking group, had an unpaid training officer on its first executive committee in 1987. Since then service user input to training has increased steadily and it is now necessary for the training programmes of most mental health professions to include sessions by service users. Local action groups will often be involved in training in their area and may also contribute to the selection and induction of some staff. There is a small but growing number of service users working as freelance trainers, and service user contributions to conferences are widespread. Initially, service users' involvement in training might be restricted to 'telling their personal story', but critical analysis and examination of alternatives are now more common. Service users sometimes contribute to curriculum development or the production of training materials, but this is not yet general. While service user training is clearly valued, little research has been done to assess its impact on practice.

In the last 10 years, service users have begun contributing to mental health awareness and anti-discrimination education focused beyond those working in mental health services. A number of government initiatives have taken place in which service users have played an active role (e.g. the Shift campaign, 2004–9) Once again, it is possible that they are more likely to be transmitting or illustrating campaign messages than significantly influencing the nature and direction of the campaign. Mental Health Media's *Open Up Toolkit* project is an example of a project to give service users the skills required in this type of work and to support them as trainers.

Research

Service users have traditionally been the passive targets of research. In recent years, research on service users and other disabled people has become more participative. One aspect of this is that more research on service users' lives is actually being devised and carried through by service users themselves. User-focused monitoring is an early and influential example (Rose, 2001) and the Mental Health Foundation's Strategies for Living project was also important (Mental Health Foundation, 2000). There are now a number of research groups that focus on service user-led research. SURE (Service User Research Enterprise) has operated at the prestigious Institute of Psychiatry since 2001. Service user involvement in creating an evidence base is very significant in the overall process of shifting power away from professional experts and, not surprisingly, it remains controversial. Issues about the credibility and valuing of service user-led research are unresolved.

Understandings

There is a significant difference between service users providing evidence about what it is like to receive mental health services and providing new understandings of mental distress/illness. Although they are connected, the latter presents more profound challenges to the status quo and professional hegemony. It is by no means clear that the majority of service user activists in the UK currently see challenging traditional understandings as a priority, and opposition to an over-reliance on medication and rejection of the medical model are not the same thing. Nevertheless, certain service users and groups, for example the Hearing Voices Network and the National Self-Harm Network, are directly challenging professional assumptions and promoting insight and expertise based on personal experience (National Self-Harm Network, 2000; Romme & Escher, 1993).

Service provision

Service user-controlled services in the UK are not highly developed and less so than in some other countries. Nevertheless, a number exist and it is clear that some activists see providing their own services as an alternative to those run by professionals as an important way forward. Over the last 20 years, service user groups have played an important role in the establishment of local independent advocacy services. However, while these have sometimes been service user-controlled projects, it is increasingly likely that they will now be run by voluntary or other organisations in which service users will not have a decisive role. Groups have also pioneered alternative crisis provision and a number of these are service user-controlled (Mental Health Foundation/Sainsbury Centre for Mental Health, 2002). A few of the larger local groups are providing a range of drop-in or support groups and day services. Smaller groups may also be involved in self-help support.

It is important to recognise that many mental health professionals have direct experience of mental distress and may be current service users. The combined effect of government emphasis on service user involvement and action by service user groups has helped to create an atmosphere where this dual role can become more visible. It is now more likely that prominent mental health professionals will reveal their distress (Friedli, 2004a). Experience of mental distress and service use is no longer an automatic barrier to employment in mental health services and can sometimes even be an advantage. On the other hand, discrimination from colleagues against those who do 'come out' clearly continues.

Campaigning

The *On Our Own Terms* research (Wallcraft, Read & Sweeney, 2003) suggests that campaigning is not a key feature of service user action. This may be partly explained both by the way service user groups in the UK have become tied into the service system and the relative lack of public interest and sympathy over mental health issues. The dominance of large voluntary organisations over campaigning may also be significant. Nevertheless, service user activists have campaigned vigorously and persistently over the use of compulsion and proposals to extend it in a new Mental Health Act. This issue has brought service users together regularly over the last quarter of a century and reflects its central importance to service user organisations worldwide (European Network of Users and Survivors of Psychiatry, 2007). Other issues on which service user groups have combined across local areas include benefits, safety on acute wards and the use of ECT.

Creative arts

The involvement of service users and their organisations in creative arts has been increasing in recent years, both as a means of self-exploration and expression and as a tool for achieving change in services and society. For some activists it provides a more attractive alternative to committee work and the opportunity to address a complex range of issues. For many service users it is fun to do. Creative arts will often be an aspect of a service user group's activities. Some groups, for example Survivors Poetry (Survivors' Poetry, 1995), will be exclusively devoted to it. Promotion of a positive 'culture of madness' has been an enduring theme among service users worldwide. In the UK it has been actively pursued since the late 1990s by the group Mad Pride (Curtis *et al.*, 2000).

Self-help

Self-help is integral to individual and collective service user action. There is a shared core belief that people with direct experience can support each other effectively and often help more than professionals can. The value of running your own organisation is a common recognition. Although many of the groups included in the *On Our Own Terms* research were not primarily support groups, self-help and support remained the most common activity reported. Achieving a workable balance between support and action is a key challenge for service user-led organisations, which often have to meet their objectives while responding to the mental distress of some of their members. At the same time, promoting belief in the fundamental competence of people with a mental illness diagnosis and their ability to manage their own destinies is central to service user action. It has been influential in the increasing adoption in the UK of recovery approaches pioneered in the United States and New Zealand, and the development of self-management programmes run by Manic Depression Fellowship and Rethink.

Box 16.2: Working with service users to achieve change – practical issues

Although service users and mental health professionals in the UK have been working together to achieve change for at least a quarter of a century, it is clear that the process does not always work well. It is important that professionals (and service users) recognise and think about the challenges involved in coming together in non-clinical settings. For example, it is well worth thinking carefully about how formal meetings (e.g. committees) are likely to work and not to assume that they are unproblematic.

Research into effective and service-user friendly involvement suggests that the following are vital:

- Being clear what kind of involvement is on offer.

- Involving people from the start.

- Making the limits of involvement clear.

- Setting attainable goals.

- Making involvement accessible to all.

- Providing flexible involvement.

- Providing enough resources and support to enable people to stay involved.

▶ **Service user action: some key issues**

What has service user action achieved?

One of the best ways to assess the impact of action is to ask local service users and service user activists what has changed for the better in recent years and what part service user involvement has played in this. Readers are strongly urged to do this.

A common response to questions about the achievements of the service user/survivor movement in the UK is to mention the growing number of service user-led organisations in the last 25 years and the presence of service users as active agents in areas of the mental health system where previously they were entirely absent. This change has indeed been remarkable and significant, but in itself can no longer be seen as a sufficient indicator of success. The novelty of having service users in on the decision-making process should have worn off by now and the focus be switching to whether services are actually changing to meet their wishes. Changes in professional attitudes have also frequently been said to have resulted from the emergence of service users in a wider range of roles within services, and it is likely that many long-term service users would confirm this. Whether those changes really alter the key dynamics of the provider–recipient relationship is less certain and has not been sufficiently tested.

The difficulty of achieving change in mental health services is widely acknowledged. Despite the improvements in their status, service users remain stakeholders with quite limited influence. The majority of the changes that service user activists in the UK have been seeking in the last quarter of a century have been very slow in coming. The more radical demands have been largely ignored. Service users have been calling for more talking treatments since the 1980s, but it is only in the last two or three years that this reached the top of the agenda (Rogers, Pilgrim & Lacey, 1993). Service user groups were highlighting concerns about acute ward care in the late 1980s (Good Practices in Mental Health/Camden Consortium, 1988). Their concerns were largely ignored for 10 years. While the development of independent advocacy services can be seen as a success story, service user initiatives around alternative crisis houses have made limited progress. Campaigning on the Mental Health Act may have increased awareness of the impact of compulsion. It has not prevented the extension of compulsory powers. While it would be wrong to dismiss the role of service users in change or to deny that their opportunities to influence change are increasing, it might be difficult to identify many significant local or national changes where the demands of service users have been decisive.

Credibility and representation

The ability of service users to obtain the changes they want is limited by a range of factors. We should not assume that service users all desire the same things, or that government and service providers always want to involve them to influence change rather than sanction changes that have already been decided. The effectiveness of service user organisations themselves is crucial and is dictated by the resources and funding available. But a major underlying barrier to achievement is the continuing individual and collective lack of credibility of service users.

This is often expressed in official concern about representativeness: service user organisations do not reflect the full range of service users; service user activists are not 'typical' service users or are 'professional users'. While representation is a legitimate issue and it cannot be denied that certain groups have so far had a limited voice within the UK movement (e.g. black people and ethnic minorities, disabled people, young people, older people), it has often not been even-handedly addressed (Beresford & Campbell, 1990; Crepaz-Keay, 1996). Many activists observe how service providers choose their times to raise the issue and are content to cherry pick some representatives and then provide no support for them to consult their constituency. Coherent and open discussion of the relationship between the value of the evidence and analysis provided by service users and its representativeness is often missing. What are the criteria? Do they apply across the board and to all groups or only to service users? How important is it that a service user trainer should be representative? Is such a demand placed on educators with a professional background? Without a more honest approach to the real dilemmas involved, there is a danger that unresolved issues of representativeness remain a convenient pistol at the head of the service user contribution.

When professional experts and lay people come together in any field, there is likely to be a credibility gap favouring the professional. People with a mental illness diagnosis suffer a particularly severe credibility deficit. There is both no tradition of listening to them and a bias towards assuming that their diagnosis itself significantly prevents them from having anything worthwhile to say. The fact that they may become angry, distressed or personal when presenting evidence may not be challenged at the time, but will weigh against them in retrospect. We are a long way from creating a level playing field on which professionals and service users can come together. Madness and a lack of insight remain closely interlocked and, while criticism about the quality of services may be acceptable now, presenting new understandings of psychosis may remain a bridge too far.

Involvement and empowerment

The concept of empowerment has been frequently applied in the health and social care field. It remains both fashionable and controversial. Some mental health professionals have argued that they are themselves significantly powerless and not in a position to empower their clients (Gibson, 1991). Some service users are also sceptical. Two well-known activists have written 'No-one can give power to another person but they can stop taking their power away' (Read & Wallcraft, 1992) and there are certainly grounds for saying that professionals might be better focusing on the latter rather than the former. Although empowerment sounds most desirable and people talk about good involvement as empowering, there is a good deal of confusion about what it means.

One significant difficulty is that many people see service user empowerment largely in terms of increasing individuals' involvement in their own care and treatment. Having influence or control over mental health service provision or over the huge areas of life that have nothing to do with services are much less likely to be considered relevant. To a certain extent, both mental health professionals and service user activists focus on mental health services to the exclusion of the broader social and political canvas. The content of this chapter very much reflects this bias. Nevertheless, it is increasingly clear that service users' lives are not just about services, and that increased influence over care and treatment is quite inadequate unless it is accompanied by greater empowerment in the community. A sign of shifting emphasis is the way service users 25 years ago would complain that mental health services caused them more problems than they had originally, whereas now they will cite stigma and discrimination as their greatest problem in living with mental distress.

Whatever has happened within mental health services in recent years, it would be impossible to argue that mental health service users are not a powerless group. Although legislation and education programmes have been introduced in the UK to counter discrimination, government surveys show that some aspects of attitudes to mental illness have become less favourable (Department of Health, 2000). The majority of long-term service users remain, poor, unemployed, excluded and devalued. Their meaningful empowerment requires a broad programme of social and political change in which mental health professionals could play a more active role (Disability Rights Commission, 2007).

Exercise 16.3: Are we partners?

- Service user involvement and empowerment are frequently linked to the idea of partnership, but what does partnership really mean?

- What are the essential characteristics of partnership that make it different from other types of working with (on/for) people? Make a list of key points.

- Using your list, decide whether you think you are really working in partnership:

  o with your clients in their own care and treatment

  o with your colleagues

  o with service users in working for change

- What are the key barriers to working in partnership in these three areas? Is it possible to overcome them? If so, how?

- Do you think the idea of partnership is realistic in your working life?

▶ Conclusion

Despite the real obstacles outlined in this chapter, it is clear that service users are closer to the centre of their own care and treatment in the UK and that initiatives to increase that trend will continue. Personalisation of services is becoming fashionable, and it is likely that health and social services will increasingly look to give individuals budgetary control through direct payments and individual budgets (Coldham, 2007). The community mental patient thus becomes a customer with cash. Whether people with a mental illness diagnosis will at the same time become more respected as human beings or more equal as citizens is more problematic. Changing the mechanisms of service delivery and increasing individual involvement is unlikely to do the trick.

As far as most of society are concerned, 'the mentally ill' are still the problem, a burden on all of us, with little to contribute. For the best part of the last two centuries, mental health professions have done little to challenge that view and a good deal to encourage it. Now there is a greater recognition within mental health services that service users collectively might be at least part of the solution. Ultimately, better mental health services will only make sense if they lead to the better valuing, the liberation, of 'the mentally ill'. Individual customer involvement cannot achieve this. It demands collective action towards wider change.

▶ References

Appleby, L. (2007) *Breaking Down Barriers: The Clinical Case for Change*. London: Department of Health.

Barnes, M. & Bowl, R. (2001) *Taking Over the Asylum: Empowerment and Mental Health*. Basingstoke: Palgrave.

Barry, S., Hughes, G. & Lawton-Smith, S. (2006) Small is beautiful. *Mental Health Today*, June: 30–33.

Basset, T., Lindley, P. & Barton, R. (eds) (2005) *The Ten Essential Shared Capabilities: A Learning Pack for Mental Health Practice*. London: NHSU, NIMHE, Sainsbury Centre for Mental Health.

Beresford, P. & Campbell, J (1990) Disabled People, Service Users, User Involvement and Representation. *Disability and Society*, 9(3): 315–25.

Brandon, D. (1995) *Advocacy: Power to People with Disabilities*. Birmingham: Venture Press.

Campbell, P. (1996) The history of the user movement in the United Kingdom. In T. Heller, J. Reynolds, R. Gomm *et al.* (eds), *Mental Health Matters: A Reader*. Basingstoke: Macmillan/Open University.

Campbell, P. (2001) Crisis cards and advance directives. In T. Read (ed.), *Something Inside So Strong: Strategies for Surviving Mental Distress*. London: Mental Health Foundation.

Campbell, P. (2005) From little acorns – the mental health service user movement. In A. Bell & P. Lindley (eds), *Beyond the Water Towers: The Unfinished Revolution in Mental Health Services 1985–2005* (Chapter 6). London: Sainsbury Centre for Mental Health.

Coldham, T. (2007) Direct payments and individual budgets: Keys to independence. In C. Jackson & K. Hill (eds), *Mental Health Today: A Handbook*. Brighton: Pavilion.

Crepaz-Keay, D. (1996) Who do you represent? In J. Read & J. Reynolds (eds), *Speaking Our Minds: An Anthology*. Basingstoke: Macmillan/Open University.

Curtis, T., Dellar, R., Leslie, E. & Watson, B. (eds) (2000) *Mad Pride: A Celebration of Mad Culture*. London: Spare Change Books.

Department of Health (2000) *Attitudes to Mental Illness. Summary Report 2000*. London: Department of Health.

Disability Rights Commission (2007) *Coming Together: Mental Health, Equality and Human Rights*. London: Disability Rights Commission.

European Network of Users and Survivors of Psychiatry/World Network of Users and Survivors of Psychiatry (2007) *Declaration of Dresden Against Coerced Psychiatric Treatment*. Dresden: World Network of Users and Survivors of Psychiatry.

Fennell, P. (1996) *Treatment Without Consent*. London: Routledge.

Friedli, L. (2004a) Behind the scenes. *Mental Health Today*. October.

Friedli, L. (2004b) Power to the people. *Mental Health Today*, October.

Gibson, C. (1991) A concept analysis of empowerment. *Journal of Advanced Nursing*, 16: 354–61.

Good Practices in Mental Health/Camden Consortium (1998). *Treated Well: A Code of Practice for Psychiatric Hospitals*. London: Good Practices in Mental Health.

Main, L. (2006) What are we waiting for? Choice in the mental health system. In C. Jackson & K. Hill (eds), *Mental Health Today: A Handbook*. Brighton: Pavilion.

Mental Health Foundation (2000) *Strategies for Living: A Report of User-Led Research into People's Strategies for Living with Mental Distress*. London: Mental Health Foundation.

Mental Health Foundation/Sainsbury Centre for Mental Health (2002) *Being There in a Crisis: A Report of the Learning from Eight Mental Health Crisis Services*. London: Mental Health Foundation.

National Self-Harm Network (2000). *Cutting the Risk: Self-Harm, Self-Care and Risk Reduction*. London: NHSN.

Read, J. & Wallccraft, J. (1992). *Guidelines for Empowering Users of Mental Health Services*. London: COHSE/Mind Publications.

Rogers, A., Pilgrim, D. & Lacey, R. (1993) *Experiencing Psychiatry: Users' Views of Services*. Basingstoke: Macmillan.

Romme, M. & Escher, S. (1993) *Accepting Voices*. London: Mind Publications.

Rose, D. (2001) *Users' Voices: The Perspectives of Mental Health Service Users on Community and Hospital Care*. London: Sainsbury Centre for Mental Health.

Stewart, H. (2006) Making mental health wards great places to work in. In M. Janner (ed.), *Star Wards*. London: Bright.

Survivors' Poetry (1995) *Under The Asylum Tree*. London: Survivors Press.

Wallcraft, J., Read, J. & Sweeney A. (2003). *On Our Own Terms: Users and Survivors of Mental Health Services Working Together for Support and Change*. London: Sainsbury Centre for Mental Health.

World Health Organisation (1978) *Primary Health Care: Report of the International Conference on Primary Health Care, Alma Ata, USSR, 6–12 September 1978*. Geneva: World Health Organisation.

▶ **Further reading and resources**

Keeping in touch with the activities of your local service user-led group(s) is an excellent way to find out about service user perspectives. Large voluntary organisations in the UK that have service user networks within them include Mind, Rethink and Together. MDF The Bipolar Organisation and Depression Alliance are examples of service user-led networks addressing particular areas of concern.

Written material by service users is often not well covered in professional journals and teaching materials. Two regular magazines that often feature service users are *Openmind* and *Mental Health Today*.

Audiovisual materials focusing on service user experiences can be obtained from Mental Health Media.

If you are interested in the service user/survivor movement and the initiatives it has inspired, the following are useful resources:

Mind (2006) *Some Things You Should Know About User/Survivor Action: A Mind Resource Pack*. London: Mind Publications.

Read, J. (2001) *Something Inside So Strong*. London: Mental Health Foundation.

Wallcraft, J., Read, J. & Sweeney, A. (2003) *On Our Own Terms*. London: Sainsbury Centre for Mental Health.

◀ CHAPTER SEVENTEEN ▶

Connecting the parts to the whole: Achieving effective teamwork in complex systems

Steve Onyett

Care Services Improvement Partnership South West CSIP Network and the University of the West of England

▶ When is a team a team?

In the UK, the NHS National Staff Survey (Healthcare Commission, 2006) revealed that nine out of ten people thought that they worked in a team. However, this shrunk to only around four in ten when the survey explored whether the team in question fulfilled criteria for a clearly defined team. The definition of effective teamworking that was supplied included clear objectives, close working with other team members to achieve these objectives, regular meetings to discuss effectiveness and how it could be improved, and no more than 15 members. This finding suggests that there are a lot of people in the NHS who see themselves as working in teams and yet, depending on how you define 'team', might be better thought of as merely working in a multidisciplinary way. This echoes long-standing concerns that simply referring to a group of practitioners as a team avoids addressing the inevitable problems that arise in teamworking while co-ordinating complex community services (Ovretveit, 1986).

Teamworking can be an expensive and troublesome way to deliver services. It should therefore only be used where the complexity and range of need presented require team members with different backgrounds to combine their efforts to achieve successful outcomes. In health and social care this is usually true, but not always. So for example, work with people requiring more linear (assess – intervene – close case) approaches to more mild to moderate mental health problems would not necessarily require such co-ordinated work.

Learning About Mental Health Practice. Edited by Theo Stickley and Thurstine Basset
© 2008 John Wiley & Sons, Ltd

The ideal team from a user perspective is likely to be one that places them at the centre and coordinates a range of inputs to support them. This is very much in line with the recent policy agenda concerning 'personalised' care, the use of direct payments and individual budgets (Department of Health, 2006). It is the sources of these inputs, including carers, friends and members of the users' informal network, that effectively comprise the team. A 'team' as understood from a service perspective is the infrastructure that is required to make this a reality.

Reflection point on your team

You can do this alone or with colleagues.

Imagine you have put aside this book for today at this point. You do what you plan to do this evening and then you go to bed. While you are asleep, a miracle occurs. That miracle is that your team has become the very most effective and enjoyable-to-work-in team that you can imagine. However, you don't know this, because you have been asleep. When you go to work tomorrow, what are the first things that you notice?

When you have captured how things will be after the miracle, try to remember a time when you have seen little glimpses of that miracle (things that were even a little bit like it in some way).

Capture in detail what was happening at that time.

Consider how you might find ways of doing more of what was working then, even if it is in tiny ways.

▶ Features of effective teams

Perhaps the two most guiding considerations in designing teams are the clarity of the team's aims; and the best way to bring together the minimum number of people required to achieve these outcomes. More broadly, the conditions for effective teamworking include (Mickan & Rodger, 2005; Onyett, 2003; West & Markiewicz, 2004):

- A clear and motivating vision among the host organisations based on explicit human values.

- Clear, shared and motivating objectives, which are aligned with this vision and values.

- A need among members to work together to achieve team objectives.

- Diverse, differentiated and clear roles. Productive difference within the team can be maintained through a positive sense of identification with one's profession or discipline, where objectives are aligned at a professional, team, organisational and individual practitioner level. Professional distinctiveness can comfortably co-exist with team identification in contexts where the team's super-ordinate goals are salient and meaningful to those involved and where team members can see their particular contribution to these goals (Haslam & Platow, 2001).

- Cohesion and a positive sense of team identification, but not to the extent of creating impermeable boundaries around the team or demonising other local services.

- Mutual respect within the team and beyond.

- Effective communication, characterised by a depth of dialogue wherein people are able to suspend assumptions and judgements, while promoting active and attentive listening and individual and collective reflection.

- Ambition manifest in an expectation of excellence.

- The necessary authority, autonomy and resources to achieve these objectives.

- Time out for the team to review what it is trying to achieve, how it is going about it and what needs to change. This also requires that the team collects information in an ongoing way about what it is doing, who it is serving and how.

- Clear leadership both within and around the team to promote the features listed above.

Where the conditions for effective teamworking are in place, there is evidence that teamworking contributes to improved effectiveness of health-care organisations (e.g. Cohen & Bailey, 1997; West & Markiewicz, 2004). However, working in 'nominal teams' – those teams that are teams in name but have none of the features of effective team design described above – may be worse than not working in teams at all. Yan, West and Dawson (2006) found that working in well-structured, inter-professional teams was associated with better patient care (including lower patient mortality), more improved ways of providing patient care, work environments in which fewer errors occur, and less stress and more satisfaction among staff. However, those working in nominal teams were more likely to report higher levels of errors and stress, and lower levels of innovation and satisfaction, than those who are not in teams at all. The implications of this are quite profound in that the illusion of teamworking may be placing both users and staff at risk. The need for honest and transparent team design based on clarity of objectives can therefore not be emphasised enough.

Where teams have been designed to be effective, the following advantages have been claimed (Mickan, 2005; Mohrman, Cohen & Mohrman, 1995; Onyett, 2003; Opie, 1997):

- Improved quality of care for users (reduced time for users in hospital, better accessibility, enhanced user satisfaction, better acceptance of interventions and improved health outcomes) through the achievement of co-ordinated and collaborative inputs from different disciplines. This can be achieved through improved, better-informed and holistic care planning, the development of joint initiatives and thus more effective use of resources.

- Better use of information leading to improved decision making and better handling of risk.

- Increased learning and retention of learning.

- Saved time if activities, formally performed sequentially by individuals, can be performed concurrently by people working in teams.

- Increased innovation through the cross-fertilisation of ideas.

- More collegiality, friendship and emotional support from within the team, leading to increased staff satisfaction and professional stimulation.

Reflection point

As you think back, what examples can you remember of your own personal experience of really sparkling leadership? What did you notice about it that was effective?

Think about times when you have felt yourself to be a really effective leader or contributor to positive change.

What would others have noticed about you?

▶ Teamworking and leadership

The key determining aspect of team design is that form should follow function. All the literature on team effectiveness prioritises the overriding importance of clarity of team objectives as central to effectiveness. The problem is, as described above, that different stakeholders may have different views about what the team should be doing. It is therefore imperative that the context for teamworking is properly managed through effective leadership. Leadership is enacted strategically in the sense of being clear about what the whole local system of care should be achieving; operationally in terms of how this particular team contributes to that enterprise; and professionally in terms of how best to enable staff to make their optimal contribution to the work of the team. Crucially, these different types of leadership need to be aligned and working well together. As we shall see later, there are also issues concerning how teams work together at a local level. There is therefore an imperative for team leaders to make lateral connections with other local team leaders to ensure effective joint working, sharing of information, and smooth transitions for users and their supports when required.

Much is made of distinctions between leadership and management. While management narrowly defined is the determination of how things get done, the issue here is about engaging hearts and minds on the questions of why we do what we do. It therefore has a *creative* dimension that helps people make sense of their social worlds, and a *political* dimension concerned with valuing possible lines of action in different ways. It is this exercise of power within this political dimension that forms the bedrock of much of the ideological conflict within teams. Exploration of this aspect is beyond the scope of this chapter, but it is worth stressing that it is an issue that needs to be made very conscious and actively worked with to ensure successful team operation (see Onyett, 2003). The reflective space described later provides an opportunity for teams to do this.

Recent reviews of leadership behaviour emphasise that:

- Effective leadership is determined by the context and the task at hand.

- It is the quality of the relationship between leader and follower that matters most to performance-relevant attitudes and behaviour.

- It is the relationship with your immediate line manager that has most impact on how you feel about your work rather than the behaviours of people at the top of the organisation (Alimo-Metcalfe & Alban-Metcalfe, 2004).

- Leadership capacity is often dispersed within complex systems (e.g. Bolden, 2004; Millward & Bryan, 2005).

▶ Teamworking within the wider system

The World Health Organisation describes mental health as 'a state of well-being in which the individual realises his or her abilities, can cope with the normal stresses of life, can work productively and fruitfully, and is able to make a contribution to his or her community' (WHO, 2001). This definition helpfully embeds the experience of users within their local system and reminds us of the need to build on strengths and existing resources. This is a principle that needs to be enacted at all levels.

Stakeholder consultations by the Healthcare Commission and Commission for Social Care Inspection (2005) highlighted the need to promote a 'whole person' perspective that tackles social exclusion and overcomes discrimination. Stakeholders advocated better access to services, partnership working, and empowering service users and carers to get involved both in their own care and strategically in the delivery of mental health services. Teamworking means nothing if it does not support individual users and their supports to identify their care and treatment requirements and then, as far as possible, co-produce a care or treatment plan or assist the person in directing their own care and support in order to lead the life they choose to live.

Effective relationships are crucial to creating an environment in which users, their social networks and staff can work together to achieve the best outcomes given the prevailing conditions. Equally crucially, services must be able to offer evidence-based psychosocial interventions and access to other key resources, such as benefits advice (for example by working in partnership with an independent welfare rights agency or organising an outreach advisor service from Jobcentre Plus), and advice and support on employment and access to education, leisure activities and housing (see Sainsbury Centre for Mental Health, 2004a, 2004b).

▶ **The state of development of the major types of teams involved in mental health practice**

Leaders and managers of teams have not only to consider what makes a team effective, but also how their team complies with a range of organisational features for new team configurations required by government. Since 1999 there have been annual autumn reviews of the extent to which new team configurations comply with the Mental Health Policy Implementation Guides. Latterly, greater flexibility was permitted to allow providers to respond to local circumstances where the model proposed met the functions specified in the relevant guidance, for the right numbers of people, using an approach that had the support of local implementation teams (particularly users and carers) and was not simply proposed because it was cheaper (National Institute for Mental Health England, 2003).

In the UK, the Mental Health Policy Implementation Guide (Department of Health, 2001) describes the following kinds of teams.

Assertive outreach teams

The National Forum for Assertive Outreach (NFAO, 2005) described the key features of assertive outreach as follows:

- A discrete multidisciplinary team able to provide a full range of interventions.

- Most services provided directly by the team and not brokered out.

- Low staff-to-client ratios (1:10 to 1:15).

- Most interventions provided in community settings.

- Emphasis on engagement and maintaining contact with clients.

- Caseloads shared across clinicians. Staff know and work with the entire caseload, although a Care Programme Approach (CPA) care co-ordinator is allocated to and responsible for each client.

- Highly co-ordinated, intensive service with brief daily handover meetings and weekly clinical review meetings.

- Extended-hours, seven-day-a-week service with capacity to manage crises and have daily contact with clients where needed.

- Time-unlimited service with continuity of care.

A meta-analysis of assertive outreach trials concluded that well-designed teams achieve better engagement, reduced hospital admissions, increased independent living and increased user satisfaction (Marshall, cited in Department of Health & Care Services Improvement Partnership, 2005). In particular, the team approach where the team as a whole manages the caseload was seen as a key feature associated with better outcomes.

Data reported in a ten-year review of the National Service Framework for Mental Health (NSF) suggests that the target for assertive outreach was exceeded from 2003, peaked in 2005 and then slightly declined (Appleby, 2007). A survey of its members conducted by the National Forum for Assertive Outreach (NFAO, 2005) identified problems in achieving fidelity to the recommended model. In particular, dedicated medical input and access to inpatient beds were seen as lacking. The survey also identified continued problems of recruitment and retention and competition for funding among local teams, with teams seldom fully resourced to meet expectations. This mixed picture was also reflected in the 2005 annual autumn review on progress towards implementation of the NSF (Department of Health, 1999), in which only 77% of NSF local implementation teams considered their level of assertive outreach provision to be satisfactory.

A concern with the potentially coercive nature of assertive outreach has been evident since the NSF implicitly linked assertive outreach with risk management. However, despite early concerns (e.g. Spindel & Nugent, 1999), some users have found assertive outreach to be *less* coercive than provision by Community Mental Health Teams (CMHTs). This may be because it is also experienced as more informal and family oriented (see, for example, Killaspy *et al.*, 2006). Users appear to value the frequent contact with team members achieved through a team approach.

The need for effective engagement is the key imperative separating assertive outreach from more generic community teamworking. Priebe *et al.* (2005) explored the reasons for both disengagement and re-engagement among African-Caribbean and white British men, finding that disengagement was associated with three key themes: a desire to be an independent person; a lack of active participation and a poor therapeutic relationship; and a sense of loss of control due to medication and side effects. With respect to engagement, the key factors were social support and engagement without a focus on medication; time and commitment from the staff; and a therapeutic relationship based on a partnership model. A Department of Health and Care Services Improvement Partnership research seminar on assertive outreach suggested: 'Consideration should be given as to how the successful features of AO working should be extended to other parts of mental healthcare' (DH/CSIP, 2005, p. 6).

That said, there is no room for complacency about the potentially coercive nature of assertive outreach, particularly in anticipation of the likelihood of increased community coercion arising from the amendments to the Mental Health Act. This underlines the importance of effective advocacy, training and clear values as set out, for example, in the Ten Essential Shared Capabilities (see Chapter 1 of this volume).

Crisis resolution (or 'home treatment') teams

Having a community-based alternative to admission in place has been English government policy since publication of the NSF. The role of crisis resolution and home treatment teams (CRHTTs) was to ensure that individuals experiencing severe mental distress are served in the least restrictive environment and as close to home as possible. This requires a 24-hour service to users in their own homes, providing an alternative to hospital admissions where possible and thereby providing opportunities to resolve crises in the contexts in which they occur. To fulfil this role, teams usually need the capacity to provide immediate, multidisciplinary home treatment 24 hours a day, 7 days a week. They need to intervene in the pathway between community-based referrers and inpatient care, providing assessment and acting as gatekeeper to other parts of the local mental health service. The aim of CRHTTs is not to keep individuals out of hospital at all costs, but rather to make the most appropriate use of inpatient care.

CRHTTs have been shown to substantially reduce length of stay (Audini et al., 1994; Johnson et al., 2005) and rates of admission where teams provide out-of-hours cover (Glover, Arts & Babu, 2006; Johnson et al., 2005). There is also evidence for cost-effectiveness (Joy, Adams & Rice, 2001), high satisfaction with CRHTTs among users and families (Dean et al., 1993; Johnson et al., 2005; Joy, Adams & Rice, 2001) and better staff morale (Minghella, 1998).

The review of NSF progress again suggested that the target for CRHTTs implementation had been exceeded (Appleby, 2007). However, a survey of CRHTTs in England (Onyett et al., Psychiatric Bulletin) found that only 40% of teams in England saw themselves as fully set up, with lack of staffing reported as the key obstacle to effective operation; a finding corroborated by the survey data. Teams were composed largely of nurses and support workers rather than providing the full range of multidisciplinary skills advocated by the Mental Health Policy Implementation Guide (MHPIG). In particular, teams lacked and sought adequate senior medical cover.

The majority of CRHTTs were urban teams and these operated with greater fidelity to the MHPIG, and took on a larger proportion of referrals for ongoing work. Overall, fidelity to the MHPIG was variable and compromised by the finding that around a third of teams were not involved in gatekeeping and just over half offered a 24-hour, 7-day-a-week home-visiting service.

There was widespread concern reported about the lack of local support for CRHTTs, particularly from influential senior doctors, suggesting that existing provision may not yet be sustainable. Working collaboratively with other parts of the local service system was perceived as a significant challenge to proper implementation of an effective CRHTT function.

Despite trying to offer a targeted service, teams reported considerable pressure of referrals for assessments that are inappropriate and that do not subsequently lead to home treatment. Participants reported that this affected the team's capacity for home treatment and in turn the use of inpatient beds.

Although the implementation of CRHTTs was therefore evidently incomplete and patchy, it was equally true that where implementation was in place, and particularly where it operated on a 24/7 basis, benefits were being reported. The survey partly prompted a further round of Department of Health guidance on CRHTTs, highlighting the importance of the gatekeeping function, adequate staffing and a stronger and more recognised role of CRHTTs in local service systems (Department of Health & Care Services Improvement Partnership, 2007).

Early intervention teams

Early intervention teams specifically seek to serve people in the early stages of developing psychotic symptoms in order to reduce their longer-term dependency on services and promote better outcomes. There are 10 guiding principles to the operation of early intervention services (see www.iris-initiative.org.uk/ guidelines.htm):

1. A strategy for early detection and assessment of psychosis is an essential component of early intervention.

2. A key worker should be allocated as soon as possible following referral in order to develop engagement and rapport and to 'stay with' the client and family/friends through the first three years (the 'critical period'), preferably using an assertive outreach model.

3. An assessment plan and collaborative assessment of needs should be drawn up that are both comprehensive and collaborative and driven by the needs and preferences of the client and their relatives and friends.

4. The management of acute psychosis should include low-dose, preferably atypical antipsychotics and the structured implementation of cognitive therapy.

5. Family and friends should be actively involved in the engagement, assessment, treatment and recovery process.

6. A strategy for relapse prevention and treatment resistance should be implemented.

7. A strategy to facilitate clients' pathway to work and valued occupation should be developed during the critical period.

8. A key responsibility of the service is to ensure that basic needs of everyday living – housing, money, practical support – are met.

9. Assessment and treatment of comorbidity (i.e. co-occurring drug or alcohol misuse) should be undertaken in conjunction with that for psychosis.

10. A strategy to promote a positive image of people with psychosis needs to be developed locally.

Building on the pioneering work of Birchwood, Todd and Jackson (1998), randomised controlled trials have found that clients of early intervention teams report reduced re-admissions, improvement in symptoms and better quality of life (Craig *et al.*, 2004; Nordentoft *et al.*, 2002).

Early intervention is the area where there has been least progress in implementation, though again the NSF review describes the target as being exceeded (Appleby, 2007). According to the 2005 autumn review only 77% of local implementation teams were providing some level of service, and only 35% rated provision as being at a level that would meet local need (approximately the same figure as in the autumn review of two year previously). A survey in 2005 found 117 teams, of which 86 had funding and 63 were operational (Pinfold, Smith & Shiers, 2007). Only three teams met all ten features as listed above. Just over half the teams cited lack of funding as limiting development. The authors concluded that, despite a rapid growth in early intervention teams, there were marked regional variations in implementation and many were fragile. Around a third of the population in England was judged to have no local early intervention service.

Community mental health teams (CMHTs) or primary care liaison teams

The Mental Health Policy Implementation Guide states:

> CMHTs, in some places known as Primary Care Liaison Teams, will continue to be a mainstay of the system. CMHTs have an important, indeed integral, role to play in supporting service users and families in community settings. They should provide the core around which newer service elements are developed. The responsibilities of CMHTs may change over time with the advent of new services, however they will retain an important role. They, alongside primary care will provide the key source of referrals to the newer teams. They will also continue to care for the majority of people with mental illness in the community. (Department of Health, 2001, pp. 6–7)

CMHTs' operation is therefore contingent on the configuration of the other newer service models, though in practice, because of their longer- standing role locally, they often appear in practice to be difficult to redesign.

The Mental Health Policy Implementation Guidance update on CMHTs (Department of Health, 2002) focused on the functions that the team should achieve:

1. Giving advice on the management of mental health problems by other professionals, in particular advice to primary care and a triage function enabling appropriate referral.

2. Providing treatment and care for those with time-limited disorders who can benefit from specialist interventions.

3. Providing treatment and care for those with more complex and enduring needs.

People with 'time limited disorders [who can] be referred back to their GPs after a period of weeks or months' are described as the major client group of CMHTs and would be served through functions 1 and 2 above. However, another role of CMHTs is 'reduce stigma, ensure that care is delivered in the least restrictive and disruptive manner possible'. It is questionable whether involvement in a dedicated team process is the least stigmatising way to serve such individuals where they could be better served through individual practice-based counselling or therapy and the new national imperative to increase access to psychological therapies. In practice therefore, CMHTs are often evolving to prioritise the third function above and developing into 'rehabilitation and recovery teams'. Where there are complex issues such as difficulty establishing effective working relationships with users or multiple diagnoses, this function will also need to be successfully negotiated with local assertive outreach teams. In harmony with the attention being paid among some CMHTs to the recovery approach, many also appear to be specifically developing their role in promoting social inclusion for people with severe and long-term mental health problems (though at present data on this is scant).

▶ Creating more effective teams

The characteristics of effective teams have been described above. Achievement of these characteristics requires:

- Shared understanding and clarification of team members' roles and responsibilities, informed by clarity about the role of the team within the wider service system.

- Contact between teams and their managers within a local whole system of care to promote shared understanding of each other's respective roles and responsibilities and methods of working along care pathways.

- Direct and regular contact between those providing care, including family and other supports. This is promoted by named care co-ordinators, contacts or link workers and clear systems for referral.

- Understanding the vision, culture and methods of working of the organisations involved in collaborating.

- Good communication systems that build relationships and trust between users, carers and health-care workers.

- Access to practical local information about services and contacts.

- Individual commitment by all workers to a collaborative approach that is supported by their line managers.

- Organisational structures that support inter-agency collaboration (e.g. joint planning, commissioning and governance committees), and individuals with the shared vision, inter-personal skills and knowledge required to make collaboration effective.

- Change champions and groups to push forward inter-disciplinary/inter-agency initiatives.

- Opportunities for the team to reflect on its effectiveness, supported by good outcome-orientad evaluation data and the involvement of users, carers and others from outside the immediate team.

Generally, there appears to have been a paucity of good information to drive local development, not least in the area of how services are experienced by service users and their supports currently. The requirement for a strategic joint needs assessment conducted though Primary Care Trusts' public health staff and local authorities (Department of Health, 2007) should help where this high-level assessment connects with an assessment of how resources are currently being deployed, the effect of this deployment and the capacity available. Local leadership and improvement science need to come together to achieve wider application of improvement methods such as process mapping, which can then inform more systematic evaluation of demand and capacity in different parts of the local system. Process mapping is an effective means of incorporating users' view of the current situation and involving them from the outset in thinking about improvement (McLeod, 2005). Confue and Seward (2007) have developed a capacity planning framework that provides a dynamic planning tool for modelling demand and capacity within local service systems, based on an iterative process of analysing local data (e.g. on inpatient bed use), agreeing assumptions (e.g. on the functions of parts of the local service system), producing a model, and reviewing future activity against the model. A Capacity Management Framework for teams has also been developed by Training and Development for Health (see www.td4h.co.uk).

The National Institute for Mental Health England New Ways of Working initiative is working to modernise existing roles within the mental health system, and to introduce new roles of enormous potential benefit to community teamworking, such as support, time and recovery workers. It includes promoting a new role for psychiatrists that does not burden them with outdated notions of ultimate responsibility for the work of other disciplines. However, there remains an overriding imperative to systematically consider the deployment of human resources at local level to best meet the need of local communities. NIMHE has developed the Creating Capable Teams Approach (downloadable from www.newwaysofworking.org.uk), which will support teams in implementing new ways of working and new roles based on the skills and capabilities required to meet the needs of users and carers. However, as this approach acknowledges, this will only be effective if the functions and team context in which the roles are enacted are clear.

The newly launched Learning for Improvement Network for Leadership and Teamwork Development is pulling together resources for team development (see www.icn.csip.org.uk/leadership). These include the Integrated Team Monitoring and Assessment tool (ITMA; www.icn.csip.org.uk) and elements of the Effective Teamworking and Leadership in Mental Health (ETL) Programme (Onyett &

Borrill, 2003). ETL is an adaptable, action-learning-based programme for people who are dependent on each other to achieve positive outcomes for a defined group of users at local level. External evaluation (Rees & Shapiro, 2005) demonstrated the positive impact of the programme, particularly in the area of clarifying shared objectives and promoting effective participation. The opportunity to use learning sets to work on shared objectives with participants from other parts of the system was particularly valued by participants. This model of learning is in line with Goodwin's (2000) advocacy of the development of a 'local leadership mindset' rather than a focus on individual leadership skill development. He recommended a focus on locally based programmes that use action-learning principles, and concentrate on inter-organisational and shared leadership between organisations rather than leader–follower relationships within organisations.

▶ Taking a local whole systems approach

Even where specialist mental health services are well developed, it is important to improve co-ordination between them and other parts of the service such as inpatient services, CMHTs and primary care. If this is not done, care is often duplicated or poorly co-ordinated and delays occur when primary care workers seek help with patients in crisis (World Health Organisation, 2003). The survey of CRHTTs nationally highlighted problems in local whole systems working as a significant barrier to their achievement, and effective engagement of service users with a range of local services is a predictor of positive outcomes such as reduced admission (see for example Priebe *et al.*, 2004).

Teams require dedicated service improvement support and training that enables them to see beyond their own part of the service. We have described already the sorts of tools that can inform this by linking local capacity to demand. However, we also need strong leadership and management that help team members to identify not only with their immediate team but also with the work of the local mental health service as a whole. To complement the Learning for Improvement Network described above, a social networking site for people working to develop teams and team leadership has been established at www.leadershipdevelopment.ning.com. Managers need to come together from across teams within a locality to operationalise agreed priorities and functions across agencies. West (2004) advocated that all local teams include in their objectives that they will act in a spirit of co-operation with and altruism towards other local teams.

Improved integrated working at a local level requires clarity at commissioning level over the respective priorities of primary care trusts and local authorities, and how they come together. Informed by the shared framework offered by the health and social care white paper *Our Health, Our Care, Our Say* (Department of Health, 2006), these priorities need to be translated into shared eligibility criteria and joint working at local and practice level. There are concerns that the development of Foundation Trusts, with their greater financial autonomy, may undermine this collaborative approach. It will be crucial that the potential of the third sector to help achieve local equity of access, particularly for hard-to-reach groups, is fully realised (see also Priebe *et al.*, 2004 regarding the advantages of non-statutory assertive outreach services in this regard).

▶ The need for a reflective space for teams

The work of the Tavistock Clinic (Roberts, 2005) has long sought to equip leaders and managers with a sophisticated appreciation of the psychodynamics of organisational life through role consultancy, coaching or mentoring for managers, or the use of external consultants to achieve an independent and safe 'thinking space'. Its approach assumes that the emotional labour of work with people in pain and distress will inevitably create institutionalisation and defensive practice unless conscious measures are taken to create space for staff to consider the functioning of the organisation and the implications of the defence mechanisms evoked. These implications include a tendency towards 'de-humanising' users through avoiding emotional involvement, and dividing the care process into fragments so that each practitioner is responsible for only one function and no one person gets to know the whole person.

Organisations need systems that provide 'containment' (Bion, 1962) of staff anxieties. Like a 'good enough' mother, the organisation needs to be able to 'take in' the distress of painful experiences and work with it in a way that allows it be returned as understood and relieved. Without containment, 'there is the risk that staff talent is wasted, staff health both mental and physical is put at risk and the institution becomes "ossified", focusing on the accretion of further layers of defence mechanism rather than retaining the flexibility needed to survive in an ever-changing world' (Obholzer, 2005, p. 300).

Obholzer (2005) predicts other negative consequences for teamwork in the absence of attention directed towards addressing such defences. He observes that in times of stress, disciplines and individuals become defended islands. Instead of working in co-operation, they retreat into individual management structures, each managed by their own hierarchy somewhere else, while invoking the rhetoric of professional self-management and autonomy. Obholzer (2005) argues that team breakdown is inevitable at this point, because teams need each member to give up some personal and professional 'rights' to the greater cause of co-operative teamworking. Another consequence is that competence is projected 'upwards', sometimes leading to a 'why doesn't somebody do something' state of expectation, familiar from many a team meeting and awayday. This itself is seen as a flight from the position that progress could be achieved if people contributed what they can to the process of improvement. Where staff become accustomed to referring decisions up the chain of command, and assume no real responsibility, there is no sense of ownership of the task. The result is that no ideas are offered, depression and paralysis result, and all sense of agency is lost. These dynamics seem to operate not just within teams but also between them, with an increased risk of disrupted pathways and poorly co-ordinated care for users.

▶ Continuing to build from strengths

Some approaches (such as ITMA) are very powerful tools for highlighting the deficiencies of local teams. While this may be inherently useful, it is also important that such assessments take place in the context of development programmes that specifically offer support to teams to make effective use of the insights such tools offer, and recognise the strengths, assets and positive qualities that the team has to drawn on in taking small steps towards improvement. Strengths-based approaches are familiar to mental health practitioners through writing on case management (Onyett, 1998; Ryan & Morgan, 2004) and Steve de Shazer and Insoo Kim Berg's work on brief solutions-focused therapy. The growing disciplines of solutions-focused approaches to organisational change (Jackson & McKergow, 2002) and appreciative inquiry (Srivastva & Cooperrider, 1999) specifically seek out times when teams are at their most effective and capture what is happening that works well, with a view to then doing more of it.

Appreciative inquiry aims for cultural change by creating a self-reinforcing pattern of active discovery of the positive core of the organisation and the people within it. It operates from the premise that human systems move towards what they study. Therefore, consciously seeking out the ways in which people derive positive meaning from their work will in itself build relationships within systems and create more affirmative, positive and productive working environments. Appreciative inquiry is not coy about talking about the spirit of the organisation, and has much in common with the 'recovery approach' in mental health, in that it emphasises an on-going journey of healing and transformation where individuals reclaim a sense of meaning, hope and a positive sense of self (National Institute for Mental Health England, 2005). This is very different from the pervading 'culture of criticism' that has been highlighted in mental health services (Appleby, 2007).

▶ Key learning points

- Teams are not inherently useful by dint of being teams. They need to be designed with clear objectives in mind and the right structure, composition and process to promote the achievement of specific outcomes.

- These outcomes should be evaluated and teams need time to reflect on their effectiveness.

- Teams need to be understood as embedded within systems, both as a subsystem of a wider system and a system that subsumes and connects with other systems. The team needs to interact successfully with collateral parts of the local service system.

- The need for effective leadership within such systems is of considerable importance, both as dispersed expertise within the team, between teams, among higher managers who create the context for teamwork and among service users and carers as experts by experience.

- The different team types introduced by the NSF have demonstrated efficacy, but implementation is far from universally robust.

- Teamwork needs to continue to be addressed within local systems of care through the implementation of effective approaches to service improvement based on sound information on need, demand and capacity.

- The principle of building from strengths that is well founded in individual practice also has application at team and systems levels. This also works to counter the pervading culture of cynicism that risks dispiriting stakeholders and impairing their important contribution to continued improvement.

▶ **References**

Alimo-Metcalfe, B. & Alban-Metcalfe, J. (2004). Leadership in public sector organisations. In J. Storey (ed.), *Leadership in Organisations: Current Issues and Key Trends*. London: Routledge.

Appleby, L. (2007). *Mental Health Ten Years On: Progress on Mental Health Care Reform*. London: Department of Health. Available from www.dh.gov.uk.

Audini, B., Marks, M., Lawrence, R. *et al.* (1994). Home based versus outpatient/in-patient care for people with serious mental illness. *British Journal of Psychiatry*, **165**: 204–10.

Bion, W. (1962) Learning from experience. *International Journal of Psychoanalysis*, **43**: 306–10.

Birchwood, M., Todd, P. & Jackson, C. (1998) Early intervention in psychosis, the critical period hypothesis. *British Journal of Psychiatry*, **172**(Suppl. 33): 53–9.

Bolden, R. (2004). *What Is Leadership? Leadership South West Research Report*. Exeter: South West Development Agency, www.leadershipsouthwest.com.

Cohen, S.G. & Bailey, D.E. (1997) What makes teams work: Group effectiveness research from the shop floor to the executive suite. *Journal of Management*, **23**: 239–90.

Confue, P. & Seward, D. (2007) *Capacity Planning in Adult Psychiatric Wards*. London: Sainsbury Centre for Mental Health/Tribal/Research & Development in Mental Health. Download at www.tribalgroup.co.uk.

Craig, T.K.J., Garety, P., Power, P. *et al.* (2004) The Lambeth Early Onset (LEO) team: Randomised controlled trial of the effectiveness of specialised care for early psychosis. *British Medical Journal*, **329**: 1067–70.

Dean, C., Phillips, J., Gadd, E. *et al.* (1993). Comparison of a community based service with a hospital-based service for people with acute, severe psychiatric illness. *British Medical Journal*, **307**: 473–6.

Department of Health (1999) *National Service Framework for Mental Health: Modern Standards and Service Models*. London: Department of Health.

Department of Health (2001) *Mental Health Policy Implementation Guide*. London: Department of Health.

Department of Health (2002) *Community Mental Health Teams: Mental Health Policy Implementation Guide*. London: Department of Health.

Department of Health (2006) *Our Health, Our Care, Our Say: A New Direction for Community Services*. London: Department of Health.

Department of Health (2007) *Commissioning Framework for Health and Well-Being.* London: Department of Health.

Department of Health & Care Services Improvement Partnership (2005) *Assertive Outreach in Mental Health in England. Report from a Day Seminar on Research, Policy and Practice.* London: Department of Health.

Department of Health & Care Services Improvement Partnership (2007) *Guidance Statement on Fidelity and Best Practice for Crisis.* London: Department of Health.

Glover, G., Arts, G. & Babu, K.S. (2006) Crisis resolution/home treatment teams and psychiatric admission rates in England. *British Journal of Psychiatry.* **189**: 441–5.

Goodwin, N. (2000). The national leadership centre and the national plan. *British Journal of Health Care Management,* **6**(9): 399–401.

Haslam, S.A. & Platow, M.J. (2001) The link between leadership and followership: How affirming social identity translates vision into action. *Personality and Social Psychology Bulletin,* **27**(11): 1469–79.

Healthcare Commission (2006) *National Survey of NHS Staff.* London: Health Care Commission, www.healthcarecommission.org.uk.

Healthcare Commission & Commission for Social Care Inspection (2005) *Partnership Review of Community Mental Health and Social Care Services for Adults Aged between 18 and 65. Report on Consultation and Engagement Events.* London: Healthcare Commission.

Jackson, P.Z. & McKergow, M. (2002) *The Solutions Focus.* London: Nicholas Brealey Publishing.

Johnson, S., Nolan, F., Hoult, J. *et al.* (2005). Outcomes of crisis before and after introduction of a crisis resolution team. *British Journal of Psychiatry,* **187**: 68–75.

Joy, C.B, Adams, C.E. & Rice, K. (2001) Crisis intervention for those with severe mental illness (updated 2006). In *The Cochrane Library,* Issue 4, Oxford: Update Software.

Killaspy, H., Bebbington, P., Blizard, R. *et al.* (2006) The REACT study: Randomised evaluation of assertive community treatment in north London. *British Medical Journal,* **332**: 815–20.

McLeod, H. (2005) A review of the evidence on organisational development in healthcare. In E. Peck (ed.), *Organisational Development in Healthcare.* Oxford: Radcliffe.

Mickan, S.M. (2005) Evaluating the effectiveness of health care teams. *Australian Health Review,* **29**(2): 211–17.

Mickan, S. & Rodger, S. (2005) Effective health care teams: A model of six characteristics developed from shared perceptions. *Journal of Interprofessional Care,* **19**(4): 358–70.

Millward, L.J. & Bryan, K. (2005) Clinical leadership in health care: A position statement. *Leadership in Health Services.* **18**(2): xiii–xxv.

Minghella, E. (1998) Home-based emergency treatment. *Mental Health Practice,* **2**: 10–14.

Mohrman, S.A., Cohen, S.G. & Mohrman, A.M. (1995) *Designing Team-Based Organizations.* San Francisco, CA: Jossey-Bass.

National Forum for Assertive Outreach (2005) *Annual Report 2004–05.* London: NFAO, www.nfao.co.uk.

National Institute for Mental Health England (2003) *Counting Community Teams: Issues in Fidelity and Flexibility.* London: NIMHE.

National Institute for Mental Health England (2005) *NIMHE Guiding Statement on Recovery.* London: NIMHE.

Nordentoft, M., Jeppesen, P., Kassow, P. *et al.* (2002) OPUS project: A randomized controlled trial of integrated psychiatric treatment in first episode psychosis – clinical outcome improved. *Schizophrenia Research,* **53**: 51.

Obholzer, A. (2005) The impact of setting and agency. *Journal of Health Organization and Management,* **19**(4/5): 297–303.

Onyett, S.R. (1998) *Case Management in Mental Health.* Cheltenham: Stanley Thornes.

Onyett, S.R. (2003) *Teamworking in Mental Health.* London: Palgrave.

Onyett, S. (ed.) (2007) *Working Psychologically in Teams*. London: British Psychological Society/Care Services Improvement Partnership, WWW.bps.org.uk; WWW.newwaysworking.org.uk; WWW.mhchoices.csip.org.uk

Onyett, S.R. & Borrill, C. (2003) *Effective Teamworking and Leadership in Mental Health – Training Pack*. London: Leadership Centre.

Onyett, S., Linde, K., Glover, G. *et al.* (2007) *A National Survey of Crisis Resolution Teams in England.*

Opie, A. (1997) Thinking teams thinking clients: Issues of discourse and representation in the work of health care teams. *Sociology of Health and Illness*, **19**(3): 259–80.

Ovretveit, J. (1986) *Organisation of Multidisciplinary Community Teams*. BIOSS Working paper. Uxbridge: Brunel University.

Pinfold, V., Smith, J. & Shiers, D. (2007) Audit of early intervention in psychosis service development in England in 2005. *Psychiatric Bulletin*, **31**: 7–10.

Priebe, S., Fakhoury, W., Watts, J. *et al.* (2003) Assertive outreach teams in London: Models of operation. Pan-London Assertive Outreach Study, Part 3. *British Journal of Psychiatry*, **183**: 148–54.

Priebe, S., Watts, J., Chase, M. & Matanov, A. (2005). Processes of disengagement and engagement in assertive outreach patients: Qualitative study. *British Journal of Psychiatry*, **187**: 438–43.

Priebe, S., White, I., Watts, J. *et al.*, (2004) Characteristics of teams, staff and patients: Associations with outcomes of patients in assertive outreach. *British Journal of Psychiatry*, **185**: 306–11.

Rees, A. & Shapiro, D. (2005) *Effective Team Working and Leadership in Mental Health Programme. Evaluation Feedback Report to the NHS Leadership Centre*. Leeds: NHS Evaluation Group, University of Leeds.

Roberts, V. (2005) Psychodynamic approaches to organisational health and effectiveness. In E. Peck (ed.), *Organisational Development in Healthcare*. Oxford: Radcliffe.

Ryan, P. & Morgan, S. (2004) *Assertive Outreach: A Strengths Approach to Policy and Practice*. Edinburgh: Churchill Livingstone.

Sainsbury Centre for Mental Health (2004a) *The Supporting People Programme and Mental Health*. Briefing Paper 26. London: Sainsbury Centre for Mental Health.

Sainsbury Centre for Mental Health (2004b) *Benefits and Work for People with Mental Health Problems*. Briefing Paper 27. London: Sainsbury Centre for Mental Health.

Spindel, P. & Nugent, J.A. (1999) *The Trouble with PACT: Questioning the Increasing Use of Assertive Community Treatment Teams in Community Mental Health*. www.peoplewho.org/readingroom/spindel.nugent.htm, accessed 19/07/07.

Srivastva, S. & Cooperrider, D. (1999). *Appreciative Management and Leadership*. Euclid, OH: Lakeshore Communications.

West, M.A. (2004). Building a team based future. Presentation given at *Team Working Today* conference, Royal College of Nursing, 15 November.

West, M.A. & Markiewicz, L. (2004). *Building Team-Based Working*. Oxford: British Psychological Society/Blackwell.

World Health Organisation (2001) *Strengthening Mental Health Promotion*. Fact sheet no. 220. Geneva: WHO.

World Health Organisation (2003) *Mental Health in the WHO*. European Region Fact sheet EURO/03/03. Geneva: WHO.

Yan, X., West, M.A. & Dawson, J.F. (2006) *Good and Bad Teams: How Do They Affect Individual Well-Being?* Working paper. Birmingham: Aston Business School.

Problems associated with the use of the concept 'mental illness'

Anne Cooke

Salomons, Canterbury Christ Church University

> Depression is an illness with probable biological causes. (Eli Lilly, Prozac.com Web site, 2007)

> Schizophrenia is a devastating brain disorder. (Eli Lilly, Zyprexa.com Web site, 2007)

> The concept of schizophrenia is unscientific and has outlived any usefulness it may once have claimed. The label schizophrenia is extremely damaging to those to whom it is applied. (Campaign for the Abolition of the Schizophrenia Label, asylumonline.net, 2007)

Much writing about psychological distress, both in the specialist literature and in the general press, takes for granted the idea of 'mental illness'. There is often an assumption of underlying biological causation. As McCulloch *et al.* (2005) point out, however, this way of conceptualising certain types of behaviour and experience represents only one among a number of possible alternatives. The last two decades have seen a sustained and growing critique of the concept of 'mental illness' and associated terms. Some writers have concentrated on issues such as reliability and validity (e.g. Bentall, 1990) and others have pointed to political influence in the scientific process (e.g. Kutchins & Kirk, 1997). Others, however, have gone further to challenge the philosophical assumptions on which such classifications of human behaviour are based (e.g. Parker *et al.*, 1995; Raskin & Lewandowski, 2000). Many of these critiques derive from broadly social

Learning About Mental Health Practice.   Edited by Theo Stickley and Thurstine Basset
© 2008 John Wiley & Sons, Ltd

constructionist or critical realist approaches to knowledge. Such approaches assume that the ways in which we view phenomena are at least in part a product of cultural and historical norms, and are heavily influenced by the power and status of the decision makers (Foucault, 1965). This means that the validity ascribed to different accounts of the world cannot be judged in purely objective or value-neutral terms.

Accordingly, a number of writers (e.g. Beresford, 2002; McCulloch *et al.*, 2005; Tew, 2002) have stressed the importance of moving beyond considerations of reliability and validity to examine the *utility* of the concept: its effects on those who use it, on those to whom it is applied and in society more generally; that is, its 'social, ethical and political consequences' (Harper, 2001, p. 21). This will form the focus of this chapter.

A number of potential positive effects have been suggested, the most common being that the concept of mental illness removes blame from the person affected (e.g. World Psychiatric Association, 2001). Other arguments commonly put forward include the role of diagnosis in providing reassurance that the person in question is not the only one affected, and that professionals know what is wrong and can help. Some writers have pointed to positive practical consequences such as decreased pressure to fulfil certain social role expectations (Perkins & Repper, 1998), material benefits such as housing and benefit payments (Campbell, 2007) and access to care and treatment. These arguments have been well rehearsed and will not be repeated here. Instead, the current review will focus on the potential negative effects of the concept that a number of authors (e.g. Gergen & McNamee, 2000; McCulloch *et al.*, 2005) have suggested comprise a neglected area. Some have linked this neglect to the vested interests and power of the mental health industry and, in particular, of pharmaceutical companies (e.g. Boyle, 2007).

As schizophrenia is arguably the prototypical 'mental illness' (see e.g. Thomas, 1997) it will form the major focus of this review. However, many of the arguments apply equally to other diagnoses as well as to related concepts such as 'mental disorder' and 'mental health problems'.

The first section of the chapter will examine the social meaning of the concept, which, it is argued, is distinct from professional conceptions, but germane to any evaluation of its effects. The second will examine its practical consequences, and the third its psychological effects on those to whom it is applied. The fourth will examine effects on professionals and on services. Finally, a number of possible ways forward will be suggested.

▶ Method for reviewing the literature

An electronic database search was carried out using the keywords 'mental illness', 'psychiatric diagnosis' and 'Diagnostic and Statistical Manual'. Publications referred to by database-identified authors were also consulted, together with a number of authored and edited books. Given the relative paucity of empirical studies in this area and the nature of the subject, it was considered important also to include conceptual critiques. The growing archive of writings emerging from the mental health service user and 'survivor' movement, documented by Rose (2001), was also consulted. Rose (2001) suggests that such writings have traditionally been excluded from the mainstream literature for reasons pertinent to the subject of this review:

> There is a growing archive of material... by people with first hand experience of mental distress and psychiatric services... The way users and survivors describe their experience is quite different to – indeed, sometimes at odds with – the descriptions we find in both the psychiatric and social science literature... But power is at stake because dominant discourses and practices will always try to undermine us by pathologisation and exclusion. (Rose, 2001, p. 1)

In an attempt to redress this imbalance and to give due weight to 'distinctive user voices' (Rose, 2001), the current review will draw extensively on this archive in the form not only of citations but also of direct quotations. It is hoped that inclusion of this material will also protect against the 'clinician's illusion' (Mordock, 1997: the fact that clinicians only tend to see those people who are most distressed by their experiences, and whose distress continues), which arguably skews the information available to many reviewers.

▶ The social meaning of mental illness

Many writers stress the fundamental impact not only of the 'official' meaning of being designated mentally ill (i.e. that contained in the official diagnostic manuals) but also of its social meaning. The term 'mental illness' and associated terms are part of ordinary language and carry cultural meanings. For example, 'schizophrenia' is often understood as signifying a 'split personality', unpredictability and violence (Read & Harré, 2001; World Psychiatric Association, 2001).

Professionals sometimes criticise the 'wrong' use of mental illness concepts by non-specialists and attempt to educate the public about their 'true' meaning (see for example the Royal College of Psychiatrists' leaflet on schizophrenia: RCP, 2007).

However, there is evidence that such 'lay beliefs' not only differ from those of professionals but are also resistant to change. Barker, Lavender & Morant (2001) found that both service users' and relatives' beliefs about the nature of the problem differed significantly from professional conceptions. Furnham and Rees (1988) examined lay beliefs about schizophrenia and found associations concerning dangerousness, amorality, egocentricity and a vagrant nature. Rogers and Pilgrim (1997) found that lay people viewed the word 'mental' in negative terms. These negative connotations appear to be increasing rather than decreasing over time: a survey commissioned by the UK government found that perceptions of mentally ill people as violent increased between 2003 and 2007 (Department of Health, 2007).

A number of writers have suggested that such negative associations may be inherent to the idea of 'mental illness'. Susko (1994), for example, suggests that the concept of a 'diseased mind' not only evokes disability, but also implies potential unpredictability or violence. Similarly, Hill and Bale (1981, p. 290) suggest that it 'makes the "mentally ill" seem just as alien... as the witches seemed to fifteenth century Europeans'. May (personal communication) suggests that the social meaning of 'schizophrenia' is so negative and deeply ingrained that it is unlikely to be possible to 'reclaim' the term in the same way that other devalued groups have reclaimed terms, for example 'queer'. Empirical evidence in support of such an analysis is presented by Read and Harré (2001), who found that biological beliefs about 'mental illness' were associated with increased rather than decreased stigma. They conclude that traditional anti-stigma campaigns, which promote the message that 'mental illness is an illness like any other', may do more harm than good.

Raskin and Lewandowski (2000, p. 32) point out that professionals are themselves not exempt from the effects of stereotypes and 'cannot... fully detach themselves from their own internalised social constructions about the meanings of those labels'.

Activity 18.1

■ What are your beliefs about mental illness?

■ Where did you get those beliefs from?

■ What experiences have informed those beliefs?

Finally, a number of writers (e.g. Deegan, 1993; Hayward & Bright, 1997) note that that such internalised social constructions also have a significant impact on those who themselves receive mental illness diagnoses. This is discussed in more detail below.

▶ Practical consequences of the concept of mental illness for those so diagnosed

Chamberlin (2001, p. 7) highlights the discrimination and disadvantage faced by those designated 'mentally ill':

> Stigma will not be overcome by public relations campaigns... Discrimination against labelled people is real: (...) laws that provide for involuntary treatment, practices restricting employment opportunities and the like.

The various forms taken by this discrimination and disadvantage are examined in the following section, together with evidence that the concept of 'illness' is a significant contributing factor.

Avoidance

Martin, Pescoslido and Tuch (2000) conducted a large-scale study and found that respondents who labelled the behaviour described in a vignette as 'mental illness' also expressed a wish for greater social distance.

Harsh treatment

Mehta and Farina (1997) found that participants increased the intensity and duration of 'electric shocks' more quickly if they understood their experimental partner's problems in disease terms than if they believed that they were a result of childhood events. The authors suggest three possible reasons for this: that viewing distressed people as sick produces a patronising attitude in which they 'like children, must be treated firmly' (Mehta & Farina, 1997, p. 416); that a belief in biochemical aberrations renders those affected 'almost another species'; and that that the idea of (random) 'illness' makes people feel vulnerable.

Unemployment and financial disadvantage

Unemployment rates are extremely high in those diagnosed with mental illness (Sayce, 2000). There is evidence that this is often due to prejudice rather than impairment. Rothaus *et al.* (1963) found that 'patients' who presented to potential employers explaining their problems in terms of mental illness were evaluated less favourably than 'patients' explaining similar problems in terms of relationship difficulties. Link (1982) found that people with a 'mental illness' diagnosis were disadvantaged in terms of both income and work status relative to individuals with similar difficulties, but who had not received a diagnosis. Farina and Felner (1973) found that employers were less likely to offer positions to those with a mental illness diagnosis, even where other variables were controlled for. Some professions exclude applicants with certain psychiatric diagnoses: critics have suggested that such policies are based largely on prejudice (Perkins & Repper, 1998). Similarly, many insurance companies refuse life insurance to anyone with a 'mental illness' diagnosis (Dunn, 1999).

Denial of rights accorded to others

Freedland (1998, p. 4) points out:

> One group in the country has fewer rights than the rest of us . . . some can't even vote. They can be discriminated against at work and locked up even when they have committed no crime . . . now the Government is set to erode their liberty yet further. They are the mentally ill.

The British Psychological Society (2001) has pointed out that the existence of separate 'mental health' legislation targeted only at those deemed 'mentally ill' is inherently discriminatory: together with terrorists, those labelled mentally ill are the only group who can be detained without trial. It has suggested that a better way forward would to have laws dealing with capacity on the one hand (the ability to make relevant decisions) and dangerousness on the other. People with 'mental illness' diagnoses are also excluded from doing jury service and in some circumstances from driving (Dunn, 1999).

Activity 18.2

Think of a time when you were excluded from something for whatever reason. How did you feel?
Imagine what it would be like to have those kinds of feelings every day.

▶ Psychological effects of the concept of mental illness on those so diagnosed

A number of writers suggest that in addition to the 'real-world' effects, the concept of mental illness has important psychological effects on those so diagnosed.

Hopelessness and decreased confidence

An effect described by many is the hopelessness and lowered confidence that can often follow a diagnosis of mental illness (e.g. Sellar, 2000). Many of these authors conclude that that this is often a consequence of the label itself rather than the original problems.

A number of writers have suggested that this can lead to a vicious cycle of hopelessness and lack of confidence leading to withdrawal. Raskin and Lewandowski (2000, p. 17) quote a service user who avoided job interviews despite being employable, stating 'I can't hold down a job... I'm a schizophrenic'. There is evidence that outcome is worse for those who accept the label of 'mentally ill' than for those who reject that identity (Susko, 1994). May (2000a, p. 15) suggests that accepting the diagnosis of schizophrenia that he received would have led to a 'long-term career as a psychiatric patient'. Similarly, Campbell (1996, p. 57) writes:

> the idea of illness... is not a dynamic, liberating force... While we harbour thoughts of emotional distress as some kind of deadly plague, it is not unrealistic to expect that many so-called victims will lead limited, powerless and unfulfilling lives.

The social role of 'mental patient'

Several writers note that the concept of mental illness is closely associated with the social role of 'mental patient', which for many comes to dictate their primary identity: 'They are enjoined to become community mental patients, live an extremely restricted life and be socially excluded from mainstream society' (Rose, 2001, p. 2). Deegan (1993, p. 7), for example, describes her reaction to receiving the diagnosis:

> I was told I had a disease . . . I was beginning to undergo that radically dehumanising and devaluing transformation . . . from being Pat Deegan to being 'a schizophrenic'.

Some writers describe the 'perverse incentives' that can operate when the 'illness' role becomes someone's only source of power. Coleman (1999, pp. 160–61), for example, writes:

> In 1993 I gave up being a schizophrenic . . . not an easy thing to do, for it means taking back responsibility for yourself, it means that you can no longer blame your illness for your actions . . . Many of us think that our only power is this so called illness.

These concerns have been echoed in the professional literature. The best-known example is perhaps 'labelling theory' (Scheff, 1966), which recently appears to be attracting increased attention (e.g. Hannigan, 1999).

Decreased ownership and agency

A number of writers suggest that viewing one's experiences as symptoms of mental illness can lead to a reduced sense of ownership of the experiences and a decreased sense of agency in developing 'strategies for living' (Faulkner & Layzell, 2000).

Pilgrim (2000) suggests that while 'mental illness' terms may serve a function for professionals in marking what they consider their 'territory' and constructing them as experts, the mystique that they create is unhelpful and disempowering for others, including service users. A number of writers (e.g. Barham & Hayward, 1991) have suggested that this 'colonisation' by professionals risks militating against a sense of agency for those affected, and brings with it an implication that the only thing to be done is passively to comply with treatment, rather than mobilising one's own resources and coping abilities. Pembroke (1996, p. 34) describes such an experience:

> By giving up ownership of my experiences and the right to self-determination I was allowing my self-respect to be stolen from me. Ownership had gone to the blue file in the filing cabinet.

A number of empirical studies have reached similar conclusions. Birchwood *et al.* (1993), for example, found that people who accepted their diagnosis reported lower perceived control over illness. Fisher and Farina (1979) found that presenting a social learning explanation of their distress to clients led to more efforts to change than presenting a disease explanation.

Denial of the meaning of experiences and their possible relationship to the person's environment

A related point made by a number of authors is that to see experiences as merely indicative of 'illness' is to deny their subjective meaning, relationship to the person's history and environment, and possible function. May (2001), for example, describes his admission to hospital:

> Crucial in the next few months was that decision to . . . dismiss everything I was going through as a kind of a meaningless product of a carnivorous illness, a disease called schizophrenia, which I think is a very contentious idea. There's a lot of evidence to suggest that people's psychotic experiences . . . are actually responses to their environment [and] have an emotional meaning to them.

Of relevance here is the concept of 'insight', criticised by a number of writers as equating with agreeing with professionals, definitions of which often involve accepting that that one's experiences are meaningless symptoms of an illness (British Psychological Society Division of Clinical Psychology, 2000; Harper, 1999; Perkins & Repper, 1998). Some definitions of insight even include 'compliance' (e.g. David, 1990). The concept has also been widely challenged in the service user/survivor literature. Rose (2001), for example, suggests that dismissing service users' frames of reference as 'lacking insight' can be a means by which professionals exercise power. Campbell (1996, p. 57) writes that 'the concept of insight . . . lack of insight . . . is one of the most powerful and insidious forces eroding our position as competent, creative individuals'.

Other writers have suggested that psychiatric conceptions of insight are opposite to psychodynamic definitions, which often involve an acceptance that 'symptoms' have a meaning that needs to be explored and may be related to the person's history (Beck-Sander, 1998). With the exception of some psychoanalytic writers and of course the 'antipsychiatrists' (e.g. Laing, 1965; Szasz, 1961, 1979), however, until recently few writers in the professional literature had challenged disease explanations of 'psychotic' experiences. Nevertheless, in the psychological literature at least, a consensus now seems to be emerging that 'psychotic symptoms' can have meaning and function, for example playing a role in the emotional processing of traumatic experiences (e.g. Morrison, Frame & Larkin, 2003). In common with perhaps the majority of those writing from personal experience (e.g. Campbell, 2007; Coleman, 1999; May, 2000a, 2000b; Pembroke, 1996), many of these writers reject the concept of 'mental illness'.

Denial of the positive aspects of experience

A number of writers in the service user/survivor literature point out that there are positive as well as negative aspects to their experience, and many feel that these are denied by dismissing those experiences as 'illness'. Perkins (1999), for example, prefers the concept of disability to that of illness because of the implication that 'ill' people are unable to function. She writes:

> My manic depression is responsible for a great deal of the positive energy in my life. For a great deal of the time I am blessed with buckets of energy . . . My thoughts work like liquid crystal . . . I feel extremely engaged with, and part of, life. (Perkins, 1999, p. 137)

Similarly, O'Hagan (1993, p. 17) writes, 'How different my mood swings would have been if they were judged to be a talent rather than an illness'.

One of the stated aims of the organisation Mad Pride is to highlight and celebrate the positive aspects of 'madness', a term it is careful to distinguish from 'mental illness' (see www.ctono.freeserve.co.uk/mpname.htm). It has published an anthology of 'accounts of personal empowerment and liberation through madness' (Curtis *et al.*, 2000). An annual 'Bonkersfest' now takes place in South London. The Web site (www.bonkersfest.com) describes it as 'a free annual one day summer arts and music festival, illuminating creativity, madness, individuality and eccentricity' and claims to have 'identified normality as a mental health issue'.

May (personal communication) points out that pride and celebration can be selective:

> Mad Pride is about selectively valuing and celebrating the positive aspects of madness as perceived by the individual. For example . . . I am able to celebrate . . . creative aspects of my psychosis and see it as the initiation of a healing process.

Activity 18.3

Think of a time when you felt stereotyped or labelled.

- How did you feel?
- How did you cope?
- What did you do?

▶ Effects on professionals and services

In addition to the social and psychological effects on the individuals so labelled, the concept of mental illness appears to have far-reaching effects on services for psychological distress and on those who work in them.

A misleading impression of certainty

Coppock and Hopton (2000) suggest that one frequent consequence is the process of reification, whereby clinicians come to think in terms of real entities such as 'depression' or 'schizophrenia'. This can lead to circular reasoning in which the symptoms are seen as being caused by the 'disorder' (Pilgrim & Hewitt, 2001). There is evidence that clinicians often believe in the inevitability of a chronic, deteriorating course for 'schizophrenia' that, although not supported by evidence, can lead to hopelessness and therapeutic pessimism, which have adverse impacts on service users (Accoroni, 2000; Sellar, 2000). Barrett (1988) suggests that this belief also frames which symptoms are noted and reinforced, and how someone's history is interpreted, culminating in a characterisation of the person's life as 'an epic of failures' (Barrett, 1988, p. 93).

Promotion of 'them-and-us' thinking

Harper (2001) suggests that the idea of 'mental illness' set up the assumption that that those with mental health problems are 'Other'; that is, separate and different from 'Us' who are normal. This 'them-and-us thinking' is perhaps particularly evident in mental health services (Harper, 2001; May, 2000b). While it arguably fulfils a defensive function for staff (Hinshelwood, 1998; Menzies, 1959), many authors (e.g. Onyett, 1998) present evidence that its overall effect is to reduce job satisfaction and increase burnout, and that effects on service users are overwhelmingly negative. This view is echoed throughout the service user/survivor literature (e.g. Campbell, 2007; Coleman, 1999; Deegan, 1993).

A narrow conception of people's difficulties and of possibilities for change

White (1995) suggests that mental illness concepts offer 'thin descriptions': superficial ways of viewing phenomena, devoid of the richness of real life. A number of authors (e.g. Johnstone, 2000; Pilgrim, 2000) argue that the use of such concepts can lead workers to adopt an impoverished, reductionist view of their clients' difficulties, and can distort their focus of attention, for example directing attention away from aspects of people's problems that do not fit the label. Harper (2001) points out that this can lead workers to stop being curious about individual clients, seeing them as yet another example of 'anxiety' or 'schizophrenia', and assuming that we know in advance what they will find helpful. A number of writers in the service user/survivor literature (e.g. Campbell, 2007) describe the sense of alienation that can result.

Overemphasis on individual differences and individualised approaches to change

A number of writers have pointed out that to conceptualise a problem as 'mental illness' is to locate the problem within the individual rather than within their social context or even in the 'fit' between the two (e.g. May, 2007; Pilgrim, 2000). Some (e.g. Harper, n. d.) have characterised this as 'victim-blaming', and suggested that one effect of this has been the channelling of resources into services that attempt to change individuals at the expense of those that target social conditions. Approaches directed at the latter, such as community psychology projects (e.g. Holland, 1992) do exist, but in much smaller numbers than individual 'treatment'-based services.

Narrow conceptions of 'treatment' and 'treatment effectiveness'

A number of authors have argued that the idea of illness has led to an overemphasis on 'technical fix' approaches to distress such as medication or technique-based therapies, at the expense of broader, relationship-based approaches (Barker, Lavender & Morant, 2001; Deegan, 1993; Onyett, 2000; Pembroke, 1996).

Raskin and Lewandowski (2000) argue that the concept of mental illness advantages approaches that value symptom reduction over personal meaning. Similarly, Birchwood (personal communication) points out that treatment trials generally measure – and value – reductions in 'symptoms' (e.g. voices) rather than reductions in distress, increased life satisfaction or other variables considered relevant by the person concerned.

'Evidence-based practice' generally relies on studies and reviews that use diagnostic categories. Some of these (e.g. Roth & Fonagy, 1996) acknowledge that this is problematic, but usually claim that there are few alternatives. As services in the UK become more protocol driven, the power of diagnoses in determining the service someone receives is likely to increase.

Seligman and Peterson (2003) suggests that psychologists should resist this development:

> The search for empirically validated therapies has in its present form handcuffed us by focusing only on validating the specific techniques that repair damage and that map uniquely into DSM-4 categories . . . By embracing the disease model of psychotherapy, we have lost our birthright as psychologists.

Narrowing the focus of research

Pilgrim (2000) points out that current service provision is planned on the basis of 'psychiatric epidemiology'; that is, the numbers of diagnoses given rather than estimates of need, vulnerability or risk. More generally, most mental health research is based on an assumption of 'underlying illness' and categorises participants by diagnosis (Boyle, 1999). The vast majority is funded by drug companies (Coppock & Hopton, 2000). It is obviously in these companies' interests for a wide range of experiences and behaviours to be interpreted as symptoms of mental illnesses. Indeed, there is evidence that new diagnostic categories are enthusiastically promoted by drug companies because of the associated opportunity to renew patents on existing drugs (Johnstone, 2000). Moreover, even statutory and charitable agencies usually require the use of diagnostic groupings in research (Bohart, O'Hara & Leitner, 1998).

▶ Conclusion and possible ways forward

In conclusion, it appears that there are a number of problems associated with the concept of mental illness. This review has not attempted to compare these against the opposing arguments in order to arrive at a judgement. However, in order to inform future debate about this issue, it seems appropriate to end with a consideration of possible alternatives. A number have been put forward: space only permits a brief mention of some of these. They divide approximately into possible ways of *describing experiences* on the one hand and possible approaches to *offering help* on the other.

Alternative approaches to describing experiences and problems

Mary Boyle (1999, 2007) contrasts diagnosis with what she calls a 'descriptive' approach. Such an approach starts from the premise that we are not justified in ignoring any aspects of behaviour, experience or distress and that we must make as few inferences about them as possible. This means trying to account for what people do and what they say they experience, rather than for a hypothesised illness. Boyle also stresses the need to take into account the effects of the person's situation, and to acknowledge that people actively interpret their experiences.

A number of writers suggest drawing on people's own ways of describing and understanding their experiences (e.g. May, 2007; Read, 2001; Rose 2001), and stress the importance of working within the person's own frame of reference rather than imposing the worker's. Such an approach contrasts with the traditional 'expert' model where the role of the professional is seen as explaining to the client the 'true' nature of his or her experiences (Hulme, 1999). A number of popular self-help movements, notably the Hearing Voices Network (de Valda, 2001), are explicitly based on the principle that different explanations exist and are helpful for different people. This approach appears gradually to be gaining acceptance in the more mainstream literature. A report by the British Psychological Society Division of Clinical Psychology (2000), for example, states:

> Professionals and other mental health workers should not insist that all service users accept any one particular framework of understanding. This means, for example, that professionals should not insist that people agree with their view that experiences such as hearing voices and holding unusual beliefs are always symptoms of an 'underlying illness' such as schizophrenia. Some people will find this a useful way of thinking about their difficulties and others will not. (British Psychological Society Division of Clinical Psychology, 2000, p. 59)

Others (e.g. Perkins & Repper, 1998; Sayce, 2000) advocate a 'social disability' model that stresses the role of the social environment in determining the extent to which certain experiences (e.g. fluctuations in mood) prevent people from fulfilling desires and social roles (e.g. working). Such approaches incorporate certain aspects of more traditional approaches to 'psychiatric rehabilitation' (e.g. Wing, 1978).

Alternative approaches to offering help

A number of writers have suggested possible ways of offering help that do not draw on traditional notions of illness and treatment. Many of these arise directly from the approaches to describing experiences outlined above, and all stress the idea of collaboration.

Many stress the need for a 'holistic' or 'whole person' approach, which does not attempt to treat 'symptoms' in isolation from the rest of the person's life (e.g. British Psychological Society Division of Clinical Psychology, 2000; May, 2004). Others emphasise possibilities for self-help (e.g. Read, 2001), for recovery independent of 'treatment' (e.g. Deegan, 1993), or suggest focusing efforts on changing the environment rather than the person (e.g. Joseph, 2007; Perkins & Repper, 1998). A number of writers emphasise the importance of attending to people's own narratives about their experiences, and helping them to develop these (e.g. Barker, Lavender & Morant, 2001; May, 2007; Susko, 1994; White, 1987, 1995). Others suggest the need to study 'resilience' and the strategies that enable some people to cope with even quite severe difficulties or unusual experiences without ever coming to the attention of services (e.g. Harper, 2001; Romme & Escher, 1993). An increasing number of authors (e.g. Joseph, 2007; Social Perspectives Network, www.spn.org.uk) are drawing attention to the social origins of distress and calling for a 'public health' approach that focuses on changing social conditions (such as unemployment, poverty and poor housing) that are known to be associated with increased psychological distress.

With respect to more traditional psychology and psychotherapy services, there are calls to resist managed care initiatives and protocol-driven treatments (Holmes, Newnes & Dunn, 2001) and to eschew the 'expert' model of help in favour of 'collaborative conversation' (Hulme, 1999). Many authors stress the central importance of relationships rather than techniques, and draw attention to the potential damaging effects of compulsion in mental health services (e.g. Onyett, 2000).

An apt conclusion is perhaps provided by Wallcraft and Michaelson (2001, p. 185):

> It may be that the fundamental changes in law and service provision ... will only happen once popular notions of mental illness belonging to the discourse of psychopathology formulated in the 19th century have been transformed by the social action of the self advocacy movement and its allies.

▶ Acknowledgement

Many thanks to Dave Harper and Tony Lavender for helpful comments on an earlier version of this chapter.

▶ References

Accoroni, A. (2000) Professionals' beliefs about schizophrenic disorders. Unpublished doctoral dissertation. Salomons: Canterbury Christ Church University College.

Barham, P. & Hayward, R. (1991). From the Mental Patient to the Person. London: Routledge.

Barker, S., Lavender, A. & Morant, N. (2001) Client and family narratives on schizophrenia. *Journal of Mental Health*, **10**(2): 199–212.

Barrett, R.J. (1988) Clinical writing and the documentary construction of schizophrenia. *Culture, Medicine and Psychiatry*, **12**: 265–99.

Beck-Sander, A. (1998) A rejoinder to David's commentary on 'Is insight into psychosis meaningful?' *Journal of Mental Health*, **7**(6): 585–8.

Bentall, R.P. (1990) The syndromes and symptoms of psychosis, or why you can't play twenty questions with the concept of schizophrenia and hope to win. In R.P. Bentall (ed.), *Reconstructing Schizophrenia*. London: Routledge.

Beresford, P. (2002) Thinking about 'mental health': Towards a social model (editorial). *Journal of Mental Health*, **11**(6): 581–4.

Birchwood, M., Mason, R., MacMillan, F. & Healy, J. (1993) Depression, demoralisation and control over psychotic illness: A comparison of depressed and non-depressed patients with a chronic psychosis. *Psychological Medicine*, **23**: 387–95.

Bohart, A.C., O'Hara, M. & Leitner, L.M. (1998) Empirically violated treatments: Disenfranchisement of humanistic and other psychotherapies. *Psychotherapy Research*, **8**: 141–57.

Boyle, M.E. (1999) Diagnosis. In C. Newnes, G. Holmes & C. Dunn (eds), *This Is Madness: A Critical Look at Psychiatry and the Future of Mental Health Services*. Ross-on-Wye: PCCS Books.

Boyle, M.E. (2007) The problem with diagnosis. *The Psychologist*, **20**(5): 290–92.

British Psychological Society (2001) Reform of the Mental Health Act. Letter to the Secretary of State for Health, 4 June.

British Psychological Society Division of Clinical Psychology (2000) *Recent Advances in Understanding Mental Illness and Psychotic Experiences*. Leicester: British Psychological Society.

Campbell, P. (1996) Challenging loss of power. In J. Read & J. Reynolds (eds), *Speaking Our Minds*. Basingstoke: Macmillan.

Campbell, P. (2007) Hearing my voice. *The Psychologist*, **20**(5): 298–9.

Chamberlin, J. (2001) Equal eights, not public relations. Abstract for paper presented at World Psychiatric Association Conference *Together Against Stigma*, Leipzig, Germany, 2–4 September.

Coleman, R. (1999) Hearing voices and the politics of oppression. In C. Newnes, G. Holmes & C. Dunn (eds), *This Is Madness: A Critical Look at Psychiatry and the Future of Mental Health Services*. Ross-on-Wye: PCCS Books.

Coppock, V. & Hopton, J. (2000) *Critical Perspectives on Mental Health*. London: Routledge.

Curtis, T., Dellar, R., Leslie, E. & Watson, B. (eds) (2000) *Mad Pride: A Celebration of Mad Culture*. London: Spare Change Books.

David, A. (1990) Insight and psychosis. *British Journal of Psychiatry*, **156**: 798–808.

Deegan, P. (1993) Recovering our sense of value after being labelled. *Journal of Psychosocial Nursing*, **31**(4): 7–11.

Department of Health (2007) Attitudes towards mental illness. Government Press Release, 6 July.

De Valda, M. (2001) The Hearing Voices Network. In J. Read (ed.), *Something Inside So Strong: Strategies for Surviving Mental Distress*. London: Mental Health Foundation.

Dunn, S. (1999) *Creating Accepting Communities: Report of the Mind Inquiry into Social Inclusion and Mental Health Problems*. London: Mind.

Farina, A. & Felner, R.D. (1973) Employment interviewer reactions to former mental patients. *Journal of Abnormal Psychology*, **82**: 268–72.

Faulkner, A. & Layzell, S. (2000) *Strategies for Living: A Report of User-Led Research into People's Strategies for Living with Mental Distress*. London: Mental Health Foundation.

Fisher, J.D. & Farina, A. (1979) Consequences of beliefs about the nature of mental disorders. *Journal of Abnormal Psychology*, **88**: 320–27.

Foucault, M. (1965) *Madness and Civilisation: A History of Insanity in the Age of Reason.* New York: Pantheon Books.

Freedland, J. (1998) Out of the bin and glad to be mad. *The Guardian*, 21 January.

Furnham, A. & Rees, J. (1988) Lay theories of schizophrenia. *International Journal of Social Psychiatry*, **34**: 212–20.

Gergen, K.J. & McNamee, S. (2000) From disordering discourse to transformative monologue. In R.A. Neimeyer & J. Raskin (eds), *Constructions of Disorder: Meaning-Making Frameworks for Psychotherapy.* Washington, D.C.: American Psychological Association.

Hannigan, B. (1999) Mental health care in the community: An analysis of contemporary public attitudes towards, and public representations of, mental illness. *Journal of Mental Health*, **8**(5): 431–40.

Harper, D. (n. d.) Approaches to undergraduate psychology teaching: 'The psychology of delusions' and 'difference and discrimination in mental health', mhhe, www.mhhe. heacademy.ac.uk/casestudies/study7.asp#details.

Harper, D.J. (1999) Deconstructing paranoia: An analysis of the discourses associated with the concept of paranoid delusion. PhD thesis. Manchester: Manchester Metropolitan University, www.geocities.com/Athens/Sparta/5721/thesiso.htm.

Harper, D. (2001) Psychiatric and psychological concepts in understanding psychotic experience. *Clinical Psychology*, **7**: 21–7.

Hayward, P. & Bright, J.A. (1997) Stigma and mental illness: A review and critique. *Journal of Mental Health*, **6**: 345–54.

Hill, D.J. & Bale, R.M. (1981). Measuring beliefs about where psychological distress originates and who is responsible for its alleviation. In H. Lefcourt (Ed.), *Research with the Locus of Control Construct (Vol. 2).* New York: Academic Press.

Hinshelwood, R.D. (1998). Creatures of each other. In A. Foster & V. Zagier Roberts (eds), *Managing Mental Health in the Community: Chaos and Containment.* London: Routledge.

Holland, S. (1992) From social abuse to social action: A neighbourhood psychotherapy and social action project for women. *Changes: An International Journal of Psychology and Psychotherapy*, **10**: 146–53.

Holmes, G., Newnes, C. & Dunn, C. (2001) Continuing madness. In C. Newnes, G. Holmes, & C. Dunn (eds), *This Is Madness Too.* Ross-on-Wye: PCCS Books.

Hulme, P. (1999) Collaborative conversation. In C. Newnes, G. Holmes & C. Dunn (eds), *This Is Madness: A Critical Look at Psychiatry and the Future of Mental Health Services.* Ross-on-Wye: PCCS Books.

Johnstone, L. (2000) *Users and Abusers of Psychiatry: A Critical Look at Psychiatric Practice* (2nd edn). London: Routledge.

Joseph, S. (2007) Agents of social control? *The Psychologist*, **20**(7): 429–31.

Kutchins, H. & Kirk, S.A. (1997) *Making Us Crazy. DSM: The Psychiatric Bible and the Creation of Mental Disorders.* New York: Free Press.

Laing, R.D. (1965) *The Divided Self.* Harmondsworth: Pelican.

Link, B. (1982) Mental patient status, work and income: An examination of the effects of a psychiatric label. *American Sociological Review*, **47**: 202–15.

Martin, J., Pescoslido, B. & Tuch, S. (2000) Of fear and loathing: The role of 'disturbing behaviour', labels and causal attributions in shaping public attitudes toward people with mental illness. *Journal of Health and Social Behaviour*, **41**: 208–23.

May, R. (2000a) Recovery from early psychosis: A dual perspective. Paper presented at *Future Possible*, 2nd International Early Intervention for Psychosis conference, New York, 1 April.

May, R. (2000b) Routes to recovery from psychosis: The roots of a clinical psychologist. *Clinical Psychology Forum*, **146**(December): 6–10.

May, R. (2001) Taking a stand (radio interview). BBC Radio 4, 6 February.

May, R. (2004) Making sense of psychotic experiences and working towards recovery. In J. Gleeson & P. McGorry (eds), *Psychological Interventions in Early Psychosis*. Chichester: John Wiley & Sons Ltd.

May, R. (2007) Working outside the diagnostic frame. *The Psychologist*, **20**(5): 300–1.

McCulloch, A., Ryrie, I., Williamson, T. & St. John, T. (2005) Has the medical model a future? *The Mental Health Review*, **10**(1): 7–15.

Mehta, S. & Farina, A. (1997) Is being 'sick' really better? Effect of the disease view of mental disorder on stigma. *Journal of Social and Clinical Psychology*, **16**: 405–19.

Menzies, I. (1959) The functioning of social systems as a defence against anxiety. *Human Relations*, **13**: 95–121.

Mordock, J.B. (1997) The 'clinician's illusion': More evidence? *Clinical Child Psychology and Psychiatry*, **2**(4): 579–91.

Morrison, A.P., Frame, L. & Larkin, W. (2003) Relationships between trauma and psychosis: A review and integration. *British Journal of Clinical Psychology*, **42**(4): 331–53.

O'Hagan, M. (1993) *Stopovers on My Way Home from Mars: A Winston Churchill Fellowship Report on the Psychiatric Survivor Movement in the USA, Britain and the Netherlands*. London: Survivors Speak Out.

Onyett, S. (1998) An exploratory study of English community mental health teams. Unpublished D.Phil thesis. Liverpool: University of Liverpool.

Onyett, S. (2000) Understanding relationships in context as a core competence for psychiatric rehabilitation. *Psychiatric Rehabilitation Skills*, **4**(2): 282–99.

Parker, I., Georgaca E., Harper, D., McLaughlin, T. & Stowell-Smith, M. (1995) *Reconstructing Psychopathology*. London: Sage.

Pembroke, L. (1996) Chapter (unnamed). In L. Pembroke (ed.), *Self-harm: Perspectives from Personal Experience*. London: Survivors Speak Out.

Perkins, R. (1999) My three psychiatric careers. In P. Barker, P. Campbell & B. Davidson (eds), *From the Ashes of Experience: Reflections on Madness, Survival and Growth*. London: Whurr.

Perkins, R.E. & Repper, J. (1998) *Dilemmas in Community Mental Health Practice*. Abingdon: Radcliffe Medical Press.

Pilgrim, D. (2000) Psychiatric diagnosis: More questions than answers. *The Psychologist: Bulletin of the British Psychological Society*, **13**(6): 302–5

Pilgrim, D. & Hewitt, D. (2001) Mental Health Act Reform: Emerging challenges. *The Psychologist: Bulletin of the British Psychological Society*, **14**(10): 526–9.

Raskin, J.D. & Lewandowski, A.M. (2000). The construction of disorder as a human enterprise. In R.A. Neimeyer & J. Raskin (eds), *Constructions of Disorder: Meaning-Making Frameworks for Psychotherapy*. Washington, D.C.: American Psychological Association.

Read, J. (ed.) (2001) *Something Inside So Strong: Strategies for Surviving Mental Distress*. London: Mental Health Foundation.

Read, J. & Harré, N. (2001) The role of biological and genetic causal beliefs in the stigmatisation of 'mental patients'. *Journal of Mental Health*, **10**(2): 223–35.

Rogers, A. & Pilgrim, D. (1997) The contribution of lay knowledge to the understanding and promotion of mental health. *Journal of Mental Health*, **6**: 23–35.

Romme, M. & Escher, S. (1993) *Accepting Voices*. London: Macmillan.

Rose, D. (2001) Madness strikes back. Unpublished book proposal.

Roth, A. & Fonagy, P. (1996). *What Works for Whom? A Critical Review of Psychotherapy Research*. New York: Guilford Press.

Rothaus, P., Hanson, P.G., Cleveland, S.E. & Johnson, D.L. (1963) Describing psychiatric hospitalisation: A dilemma. *American Psychologist*, **18**: 85–9.

Royal College of Psychiatrists (2007) Scizophrenia. London: RCP, www.rcpsych.ac.uk/mentalhealthinformation/mentalhealthproblems/schizophrenia/schizophrenia.apx.

Sayce, L. (2000) *From Psychiatric Patient to Citizen: Overcoming Discrimination and Social Exclusion*. Basingstoke: Macmillan.

Scheff, T.J. (1966) *Being Mentally Ill: A Sociological Theory*. New York: Aldine.

Sellar, J. (2000) A study exploring the process of adjustment to the experiences of psychosis and a diagnosis of schizophrenia. Unpublished doctoral dissertation. Salomons: Canterbury Christ Church University College.

Seligman, M. & Peterson, P. (2003) Positive clinical psychology. In L.G. Aspinwall & U.M. Staudinger (eds), *A Psychology of Human Strengths: Perspectives on an Emerging Field*. Washington, D.C.: American Psychological Association.

Susko, M.A. (1994) Caseness and narrative: Contrasting approaches to people who are psychiatrically labelled. *Journal of Mind and Behaviour*, **15**(1&2): 87–112.

Szasz, T.S. (1961) *The Myth of Mental Illness*. New York, Hoeber-Harper.

Szasz, T.S. (1979) *Schizophrenia: The Sacred Symbol of Psychiatry*. Oxford: Oxford University Press.

Tew, J. (2002) Going social: Championing a holistic model of mental distress within professional education. *Social Work Education*, **21**(2): 143–55.

Thomas, P. (1997) *The Dialectics of Schizophrenia*. London: Free Association Books.

Wallcraft, J. & Michaelson, J. (2001) Developing a survivor discourse to replace the 'psychopathology' of breakdown and crisis. In C. Newnes, G. Holmes & C. Dunn (eds), *This Is Madness Too*. Ross-on-Wye: PCCS Books.

White, M. (1987) Family therapy and schizophrenia: Addressing the 'in the corner' lifestyle. *Dulwich Centre Newsletter*, Spring.

White, M. (1995) *Re-Authoring Lives: Interviews and Essays*. Adelaide: Dulwich Centre Publications.

Wing, J.K. (1978) *Reasoning About Madness*. Oxford: Oxford University Press.

World Psychiatric Association (2001) *Schizophrenia: Information for Educators*. Calgary, Canada: World Psychiatric Association.

Drugs, alcohol and mental health[1]

Tabitha Lewis
Middlesex University

Alison Cameron
Service user of mental health services

By the end of this chapter, the reader will have a greater knowledge of:

- The language and terminology used within the field of substance use.

- The role of attitudes, including their own, in the provision of care for those who use substances and who also have a mental health problem.

- The service users' experience.

- The substances that are commonly misused and their effects on mental health.

- The role of motivation in the care and treatment of those who use substances.

- How to assess for substance use.

- What treatment options may be available.

This will be achieved through reading the content and participation in the guided activities designed to enhance the reader's learning.

The Department of Health (2002, p. 4) states: 'Substance misuse is usual rather than exceptional amongst people with severe mental health problems.' In fact, substance *use* is usual rather than exceptional in the general population. Wherever you work, in whatever role, you will come across people who use substances.

[1] The term 'substance' is used throughout this chapter as a generic term referring to any substances, whether the substances be illicit, prescribed, over-the -ounter products or alcohol.

Learning About Mental Health Practice. Edited by Theo Stickley and Thurstine Basset
© 2008 John Wiley & Sons, Ltd

However, if we are to focus on mental health service users in particular, prevalence studies have repeatedly indicated that the co-occurrence of mental health problems and substance use is high. Within Community Mental Health Teams (CMHT) in the UK, the prevalence of service users with substance misuse and severe mental illness is 8–15% (Department of Health, 2002), whereas if you include substance misuse and any mental disorder the prevalence rises to between 30% and 50% (Menezes *et al.*, 1996; Regier *et al.*, 1990). In prison populations 79% of remand prisoners have been found to be drug dependent and have two or more mental disorders (Department of Health, 2002). One study of even more concern, which was conducted within three inner London psychiatric wards, found that not only were service users using substances, but that many were using on the wards and were even being introduced to substance use during their stay by other service users (Phillips & Johnson, 2003).

It is also known that people with mental health problems who use substances will have poorer outcomes. For example, they are more likely to experience worse symptoms and have more periods of hospitalisation, as well as to experience poorer social outcomes such as homelessness, poverty and involvement with the criminal justice system (Department of Health, 2002).

In addition, the presence of substance use with a mental health problem is known to present increased risks. For example, substance users are less likely to comply with treatment, and the presence of alcohol in particular is associated with an increased risk of suicide. The five-year report of the National Confidential Inquiry into Suicide and Homicide by People with Mental Illness (Appleby *et al.*, 2006) found that of the 1659 cases reviewed of homicide and suicide committed by people with mental illness, 27% of suicides and 36% of homicides were mentally ill people who also had a significant drug or alcohol problem.

In spite of these concerning facts, this group of people have typically received a very poor service, with service users being passed from one service to another with neither mental health services nor substance misuse services taking responsibility. The National Service Framework Mental Health (NSFMH) five-year review stated (Department of Health, 2004, p. 1):

> a key area for further action are... services for people with... mental illness and substance misuse – the most challenging clinical problem that we face.

But what has this got to do with you? The following case study illustrates some of the problems people often face in attempting to access help for mental health and substance use problems.

Case study of a service user's experience of services

Jayne was first diagnosed with post traumatic stress disorder (PTSD) and work-related depression by her GP in 1998 after her involvement in an

---

accident at work in which her colleagues were killed. She reported drinking heavily and having feelings of deep depression and suicidal intent, which had intensified following the accident. She was signed off work for a period of one year. In addition, she was seen by a trauma specialist who confirmed the diagnosis, and she was referred for cognitive behavioural therapy.

At this time I was already drinking on a 24-hour basis. I had been a workaholic and the realisation that I was not likely to be able to return to that job was a reality that was too hard for me to bear. I felt at the time that given the circumstances I had no choice but to drink. I was retired on ill health grounds from my job and this led to a further intensification of my drinking.

Given that I had the diagnosis of PTSD, I felt somehow justified in my drinking. It seemed to me to be some sort of official endorsement that I had been through something so traumatic that I had no choice but to drink. The approach at that time by my therapists and doctor was that if I could come to terms with what had happened to me at work, which governed what was going on for me mentally, the drinking would resolve itself. I turned up dutifully for therapy, often with supplies of vodka in my bag. Being intelligent, I quickly grasped what symptoms I should be displaying and what responses the therapist wanted me to give. I would sense when the therapist was getting too close to something I felt too painful to cope with and steer her deftly down some other garden path.

By this time I was drinking more than a bottle of vodka a day and I was not prepared to acknowledge this as even part of the problem. At this time I could not envisage living without alcohol as a buffer to the mental pain.

The psychiatrist prescribed me Antabuse and I moved back into my parents' house – having lost my home through spiralling debts. The combination of the Antabuse and the policing by my parents created an illusion of sobriety. However, just not drinking without taking any real steps towards changing the associated behaviour, I now know, was not in fact recovery at all.

Of course, as soon as I got myself to the stage where I found myself a new job and left town, free from the watchful eye of my parents, almost immediately, I relapsed on alcohol and went into a sharp decline. I did not even turn up for the new job and moved into a hostel. I had money from the compensation I had received from my previous employer, was adrift from all sources of support services, and so commenced round-the-clock drinking and destructive behaviour leading to several stays in hospital. I would be detoxed and despatched out again to start all over again.

I moved again. I knew something was wrong and felt that doing a 'geographical' would change things. The problems went with me however. In London, I drifted under the radar from support services, staying in bed and breakfasts to which I was sent by my Borough's Homeless Person's Unit.

The drinking was now at catastrophic levels. I didn't eat, didn't take care of myself, allowed myself to be used sexually by anyone with access to alcohol and whenever I tried to stop I had convulsions and delirium tremens. I had periods of total blackout. The worse one of those was the period of over a month in which I recall nothing of my whereabouts or actions. I was found in a strange part of London in a delirious state, put in an ambulance and taken to hospital. I was found to have slash wounds on my inner thighs and across my stomach which were infected with MRSA. I still to this day have no recollection as to how I came to be in that state. This episode finally led to me coming to the attention of the mental health services. I was transferred to a Mental Health Unit in my local NHS hospital.

I remained on the ward for over seven months and continued drinking while there. During that time, my drinking was addressed only as 'bad behaviour' and then only when it disturbed the order on the ward. I was a voluntary patient and therefore free to come and go as I pleased. In my case it meant going off for 'liquid lunches' and bringing alcohol back with me to the ward which I would share with the 'official alcoholics'' who had been diagnosed as such unlike me, with my PTSD label. I still clung to the belief that I did not have an alcohol problem.

Jayne was finally discharged into the community under the Care Programme Approach (CPA) system. She was given a social worker and accommodated in a 'therapeutic community' for people with 'severe and enduring mental health problems'. However, her drinking remained unaddressed. She was evicted from the therapeutic community for persistent destructive drink-related behaviour. Once more, she was sent into the world of bed and breakfasts populated with drug and alcohol users and those with severe untreated mental illness. In that environment, Jayne continued her pattern of drinking, which escalated on the occasion she was sent to a bed and breakfast in a remote part of North London in which she became totally isolated from any form of support. She failed to turn up to any appointments with her care manager, feeling unable to contemplate the journey to her home borough. She was hospitalised on several occasions and again was simply detoxed and discharged back out to continue.

Then one day I regained consciousness, to find myself once again in a hospital ward. On this occasion however, the doctor did not just make reference to my mental health problems and tell me that 'after all I had been through no wonder I drank' but spoke instead about my drinking. He said I had about 18 months to live if I continued in the way I had been. He gave me a leaflet about the primary care drop-in run by the Substance Misuse Services of the NHS. He also told me that in his opinion I would be likely to find Alcoholics Anonymous (AA) helpful. I went back to the Bed and Breakfast and resolved to go to the drop-in. I also phoned the AA helpline which I found in the phone book. They wrote to me immediately and I found that there was a meeting just round the corner. At the drop-in I was assessed and advised that I would be sent to a hospital for a proper detox. While awaiting a place there I was advised to attend AA. I went to my first meeting and there I found a group of people who did not seem to fit the label 'alcoholic' that I had in my mind. They were healthy, happy looking, prosperous seeming people all of whom introduced themselves as 'alcoholic' with no apparent shame. I had been so isolated. I only had contact with other drinkers and staff of Off Licences. Suddenly I was in a room full of people with whom on some level I could identify. I spoke at that meeting and also said I was an alcoholic. I felt an immediate sense of release and a sense of being somehow lighter. I believe that is when I finally came out of denial.

Jayne was admitted to hospital for a two-week detox, which incorporated a programme of group therapy and 12-step meetings. It was acknowledged there that it would be counterproductive to send her back to the drug- and alcohol-using environments in which she had been living and so she remained in hospital until a place was secured for her in a 12-week rehabilitation programme. She was allocated at that time a worker from the newly established Dual Diagnosis Service of her borough's Social Services Department, who obtained the necessary funding for the rehabilitation centre placement.

On completing treatment, she was housed by the Social Services Department in a project for adults with severe and enduring mental health problems and referred to a specialist Dual Diagnosis day programme. She was able to achieve longer and longer periods of abstinence, with periodic relapses when her mental health problems, notably acute anxiety, increased. She did, however, continue to attend regular AA meetings and develop a firmer support network. With the increased stability that abstinence brought about and a greater level of motivation to recover, Jayne began to engage more meaningfully with therapists.

With alcohol no longer clouding the issue to the same extent, the Dual Diagnosis worker and the therapist from a Dual Diagnosis programme looked again at her original diagnosis. It was felt that a more accurate description of what was going on for the patient was borderline personality disorder (BPD). Jane agreed with this assessment, having already met and clearly identified with other people in treatment who had BPD. She was able to complete an intensive period of cognitive analytical therapy and develop a far greater understanding of her complex condition. She now lives independently, maintains abstinence and is actively involved in using her experiences to help others with complex needs.

I believe very strongly that I was self-medicating my mental health problems with alcohol. I believe the substance itself is irrelevant. I believe that by treating solely my psychiatric diagnosis in isolation, I was in a way given licence to stay stuck in the spiral of destruction. I got myself into alcohol treatment. I was not referred there by any of the various professionals with whom I had consulted over the years. I took myself to AA. There were in fact AA meetings in the very hospital in which I was treated for seven months and they were not even mentioned.

I regret that it took such a long time for me to find the help that I needed. Given how vulnerable I was and the destructive situations in which I found myself, it is miraculous that I survived. I have chosen to involve myself at various levels in improving services for people with complex needs. My aim is to ensure that people like me don't find sources of support simply by chance. We should not be passed back and forth between substance misuse and mental health services with the result that we pass unnoticed through the middle.

To try to give me an accurate diagnosis when I was so evidently drinking to a massive degree was a rather futile exercise and in fact for me counter-productive as it enabled me to remain in a state of denial. By focusing on the label given me by one doctor years before, I was denied for a long time the help I needed to tackle my alcohol use. This help I eventually obtained through my own efforts. Some in my position are not lucky enough to have the moment of clarity which enabled me finally to realise what help I needed.

I have started meetings of Dual Recovery Anonymous in the UK run on the lines of AA but with a greater understanding of mental health problems. I note that things are improving and that there is a greater understanding of our complex needs in the health care system. I am pleased to note that in my area patients are no longer exited into oblivion once they have been discharged from the acute care ward. It was far too easy for me to slip under the radar with little integration between the Social Services, Housing and Mental Health services. Those with a Dual Diagnosis are far more likely than most to experience serious problems such as homelessness. If we are simply patched up by the medics, and dispatched back to the often unsafe environments from which we came, it is not surprising that we relapse.

I am immensely grateful to the Dual Diagnosis workers who finally found, me after five years stuck in the revolving door of the Mental Health Unit. Their help has been invaluable. However, I know I would not have reached the stage I am at now were it not for the contact with people in AA and Dual Recovery Anonymous who have been where I have and come out the other side. They taught me that people with a dual diagnosis can and do recover.

Not surprisingly, recent policies have been addressing the care of those with a co-occurrence of substance use and mental health problems (also some-times referred to as dual diagnosis, dual disorders or complex needs). The key document in the UK is the Dual Diagnosis Good Practice Guide (Department of Health, 2002). It introduced the notion of 'mainstreaming', which means that mental health services must take the responsibility for providing care, with substance-misuse services providing support and consultation. The importance of mainstreaming for individuals with severe mental illness and substance use, with clear care pathways and joint working agreements, have also been echoed in the *Dual Diagnosis Toolkit* (Hawkings & Gilburt, 2004) and the National Confidential Inquiry into Suicide and Homicide by People with a Mental Illness (Appleby *et al.*, 2006).

▶ **Language/Terminology/Attitudes**

You may have noticed that so far a variety of terms have been used to describe the level and severity of substance use. For example:

■ substance use

■ substance misuse

■ dependence

What other terms can you think of that describe the level and severity of someone's substance use?

You may have come up with terms such as:

■ experimental use

■ recreational use

■ psychological dependence

■ physical dependence

What do you think they all mean?

Below are the definitions/explanations for some of the words you may be familiar with. For other terms that are not listed, do an Internet search to find out what they mean. Be mindful that some terms are actual diagnostic labels, while others are merely value judgements.

Substance use

The term 'substance use' is used to describe the taking of substances, by whatever means, without implying any moral judgement about whether the behaviour is right or wrong. It seems to be normal in many cultures to use substances of some form or other in order to alter feelings, whether through alcohol, drugs, smoking or even tea and coffee (Gossop, 1993).

Experimental use

Typically, this describes the initial use of any drug, but extends to encompass the use of the drug on the first few occasions. Experimental use is driven primarily by availability of the drug first and foremost, then curiosity to experience an anticipated effect. Peer-group influence can be an important factor.

Recreational use

This describes a continuation from experimental use where the user seeks stimulation, relaxation or an altered state of consciousness as an added-value aspect of their lifestyle. The individual has learned to appreciate the pleasurable effects of the drug and minimise undesired effects. Generally, use of the drug causes minimal problems for the drug user or those around them.

Substance misuse

Unlike the term 'substance use', which offers no judgement about right and wrong, the term 'substance misuse' does make such a judgement and implies that the use is wrong. However, the point at which 'substance use' is defined as 'misuse' is largely subjective and is influenced by social, cultural, religious, legal and personal variables. The term 'substance misuse' would usually include substance dependence.

Note that the term 'substance abuse' is often used interchangeably with substance misuse. However, substance misuse is usually the preferred term in the UK as the term 'abuse' implies an even greater moral judgement.

Substance dependence

Dependence is often understood in terms of psychological and physical dependence.

- *Psychological dependence*: This can be thought of as a compulsion or craving to continue to take a drug because of the need for stimulation or because it relieves anxiety or depression. Psychological dependence can occur with almost any drug and is the most important factor to understand and address in helping somebody with a drug-related problem.

- *Physical dependence*: A state of bodily adaptation to the presence of a particular drug, manifesting in physical disturbances or withdrawal symptoms following cessation of use, with varying degrees of severity. The phenomenon is underpinned by changes to the body's chemistry, resulting in the person needing to continue to take doses of the drug to maintain normal functioning and avoid the onset of withdrawal symptoms. Physical dependence only occurs with alcohol, opiates and sedative hypnotics (like benzodiazepines).

Substance use and misuse attract stereotypes and labels. What follows is a series of questions. Take some time to think about them.

- What words do you know of that describe a substance user?

- What characteristics do you associate with substance user?

- Where did you get these attitudes from?

- How might your own attitudes affect how effectively you can work with a substance user?

Whatever answers you have come up, with they have no doubt included many with negative implications. Some of the words you have thought of to describe substance users may have been junkie, addict, dosser or alkie. The characteristics may have included dirty, untrustworthy and irresponsible.

So where did you get these attitudes from? You may be going by the personal experience of yourself, family or friends, or you may have been influenced by the media.

And how might these attitudes affect how you work with someone who is using substances? Negatively, no doubt. Thus it is important that before you can work with substance users, you address your own attitudes and beliefs.

Service users will also hold these attitudes about themselves. It is our job as mental health professionals to not reinforce them.

Substances

The next step to working effectively with substance users is to have an understanding of what the substances are that they are using.

What substances have you heard of (you don't need to know what they are)?

There are many, but your list may have contained:

- heroin

- cocaine

- crack

- amphetamine

- cannabis

- khat

- magic mushrooms

- caffeine

- nicotine

- LSD

- ecstasy

- alcohol

- prescribed substances such as benzodiazepines

- over-the-counter preparations such as Sinutab

Activity 19.1: Names, appearance and forms

Select up to 10 of these substances, from either your list or the one in this chapter, and for each record in Table 19.1:

■ The name of the substance.

■ Any slang names that are used for the substance (this may vary from area to area and across different sub-populations).

■ What its appearance is like/what forms it comes in.

■ How much it costs and for what quantity (note that this will vary from area to area, like the slang names).

Use the resources at the end of this chapter to help you, together with any other resources you may know of, not forgetting that a substance user is one of your best resources. To assist you, Table 19.1 has been completed for cannabis.

Table 19.1   Names, appearance and forms of various substances

Substance name	Slang name	Appearance/forms	Costs/quantities
Cannabis	Dope, blow, puff, herb, ganga, weed	Resin – a dark brownish substance that looks like a stock cube Herbal – a dried grass-like substance	Usually bought in ounces or parts of ounces, e.g. 1/16th, 1/8th. 1/8th of resin is approximately
		Oil	£ 10, with the stronger skunk variety of the herbal form costing £ 20 for 1/8th ounce

Substance name	Slang name	Appearance/forms	Costs/quantities

Activity 19.2

What substances do you use? Make a list and think why you use the substances you do. You might like to think of legal substances including alcohol, tobacco, coffee etc.

Effects

Why, then, do people use substances? Have a think and make a note of your ideas. Here are some of the reasons we can think of:

- fun
- sociability

- relaxation

- acceptance

- confidence

- dependence

- promote/inhibit sleep

- promote/inhibit appetite

Whatever the reason, it is usually something to do with the intoxicating effects. In general, these can be grouped in terms of the effect they have on central nervous system (see Table 19.2):

- uppers

- downers

- all-rounders

Table 19.2   Uppers, downers and all-rounders

Classification	Effect on central nervous system	Symptoms
Uppers	Stimulate	Increased blood pressure Increased pulse rate Sweating Disinhibition Restlessness
Downers	Depress	Lowered blood pressure Lowered pulse rate Drowsy Slurred speech
All-rounders	Alter perception	Visual hallucinations Paranoia

Activity 19.3: Uppers, downers and all-rounders

Complete Table 19.3 by putting a plus sign in the column that corresponds to each substance's effects. If you feel confident with that activity, perhaps you could indicate the strength of the effect by using multiple plus signs. The first one has been completed as a means of explanation. There are a couple of blank spaces to add other substances you may know of. You may want to refer to the resources you used for the previous activity to assist you with this.

Table 19.3   Effects of various substances

Substance	Upper	Downer	All-rounder
Amphetamine	+++		
Heroin			
Cannabis			
Cocaine/crack			
Alcohol			
Nicotine			
Caffeine			
Benzodiazepines			
Khat			
Magic mushrooms			
LSD			

How did you do?

Uppers include:

- amphetamine
- cocaine/crack
- nicotine
- caffeine
- khat

Downers include:

- heroin
- benzodiazepines
- alcohol

All rounders include:

- cannabis
- magic mushrooms
- LSD

Intoxication is not the only effect of taking a substance. Most substances will have a withdrawal effect. In most cases, the substance will have the opposite in withdrawal to its effect in intoxication. For example, cocaine causes feelings of euphoria and confidence in intoxication, but causes feelings of depression, anxiety and tiredness in withdrawal.

As with any rule there are exceptions. In this case it is because substance effects will vary depending on:

- The subtance itself, the amount taken and whether it is taken alone or with other substances.
- The person, their tolerance to the substance, their expectations – i.e. a person's experience of a substance may depend on their past experiences of that substance.
- The situation, for example in a crowded night club or in a field at a festival.
- The method of administration, whether it was smoked, injected, swallowed, snorted (any method that bypasses the liver, avoiding first possible metabolism, will take effect more quickly, e.g. injecting, smoking and snorting).

In addition, substance effects are not always just about intoxication and withdrawal or the effect on the central nervous system. Other effects can be grouped into the following categories:

- other physical effects
- social effects
- psychological effects

Activity 19.4 focuses on alcohol, as this is the most commonly used substance by people with mental health problems. In addition, it is possibly the most harmful substance in terms of its physical, social and psychological effects.

Activity 19.4: The physical, social and psychological effects of alcohol

Complete Table 19.4 using the Internet resources listed at the end of this chapter.

Table 19.4   The physical, social and psychological effects of alcohol

	Physical	Social	Psychological
Positive effects			
Negative effects			

The positive and negative effects of alcohol would no doubt be influenced by the amount and frequency that someone drinks. In the UK, the Department of Health offers some guidance on this and advises that men should not regularly drink more than 3–4 units of alcohol per day, and women should not regularly drink more than 2–3 units of alcohol per day. After an episode of heavy drinking, it is advisable to refrain from drinking for 48 hours to allow your body to recover. A unit represents the amount of alcohol a healthy liver can metabolise in one hour.

A unit of alcohol is calculated as follows:

$$\frac{\text{Volume in mls} \times \% \text{ of alcohol}}{1000} \quad \text{e.g.} \quad \frac{750 \text{ ml bottle of spirits} \times 40\%}{1000} = 30 \text{ units}$$

Substance use can have lots of effects, some desirable, some less so. What may seem desirable to us may be different to someone else, so never make an assumption regarding why someone is taking substances. Always ask. This is no less important when someone has a mental health problem. All too often it is assumed that people with mental health problems use substances to self-medicate their mental health problems, whether that be to mediate the positive symptoms such as hallucinations, or negative symptoms such as depression, or against the side effects of their medication. While there is some evidence for this (Khantzian, 1985, 1997) and it may well be true for some people, it may not be the only reason someone is using drugs or alcohol.

Activity 19.5 illustrates some of these concepts.

Activity 19.5: The effects of substances on people with mental health problems

Complete Table 19.5. List the effects of each group of substances on each group of illnesses. Remember to consider:

■ the effects of intoxication as well as withdrawal

- the positive and the negative effects

- the physical, social and psychological effects

- the effects on positive and negative symptoms and the side effects of medication

Table 19.5   The effects of substances on people with mental health problems

Physical/Social/ Psychological	Intoxication/Withdrawal		
	Uppers	Downers	All rounders
Psychotic illness			
Depressive illness			
Anxiety-related illness			

Activity 19.6: True or false?

Answer true or false to the following statements. The answers can be found at the end of the chapter in Table 19.12.

1. It is possible to drink so much alcohol that you can overdose and die.

2. A pint of beer contains the same amount of alcohol as one measure of whisky.

3. Alcohol affects women more than men.

4. Drinking small amounts of alcohol damages your health.

5. Alcohol is a stimulant: it wakes you up and gives you energy.

6. Smoking heroin is safer than injecting it.

7. You can get hooked on heroin the first time you try it.

8. Heroin kills more people than any other drug in the UK.

9. Once you're hooked on heroin you can't get off.

10. Methadone is a green liquid.

11. Methadone is more addictive than heroin.

12. Methadone is safer than heroin.

13. A doctor needs a special licence to prescribe methadone.

14. Opioids substances such as heroin can cause respiratory depression.

15. Opioids are highly addictive.

16. Opioids are analgesics.

17. Benzodiazepines are highly addictive.

18. It is not an offence to be in possession of benzodiazepines.

19. Cocaine is a brown powder.

20. Cocaine can be smoked.

21. Cocaine does you no physical harm.

22. Cocaine has no medical uses.

23. Crack is a new drug.

24. A few tries of crack and you are addicted.

25. Crack is not used by rich people.

26. Crack can be made at home in a microwave.

27. Amphetamines cause salivation, frequency of urination and pin-sized pupils.

28. Amphetamines are usually injected.

29. Amphetamines give you energy.

30. The smokeable form of amphetamine is known as ICE.

31. Cannabis is not a very harmful drug.

32. You can overdose on cannabis.

33. Cannabis does not affect your driving as much as alcohol does.

34. Some forms of cannabis are a lot stronger than others.

▶ **Assessment**

The National Service Framework for Mental Health (NSFMH; Department of Health, 1999) states that all mental health assessments should assess for substance use. This does not mean that all mental health workers need to have the same level of knowledge and skills as their colleagues who work in substance misuse services. What it does mean is that mental health workers should have the knowledge and skills to detect whether someone has a substance use problem so that the appropriate support can be offered to the service user.

Many mental health workers find it difficult to do this, partly because they do not feel they have the knowledge, but also because they do not know how to approach the subject matter with a service user. One way to initiate this can be using objective assessment methods, e.g. urine testing. The results of the test can guide your assessment and communications. It is also important to assess service users' general health status, given that people with mental health problems are more likely to neglect their physical health and substance users are likely to have health problems associated with their use and lifestyle. In some cases these problems can be life threatening if left untreated, so if you do not feel able to make such an assessment, ensure you can arrange for someone who can to do so. It is best to not rely on general practitioners to do this, as substance users are renowned for poor attendance at primary care services. You may be the only professional with whom they have contact. Thus assessment should be used for all service users and not just those who are suspected as being substance users.

Objective assessment

Objective assessment methods include the following.

Urine testing

Urine testing checks for the presence of substances in the urine. Like all tests it has its limitations. Most mental health services use 'dip sticks' for specific substances. But who decides on which substances to test for? What does the test tell you? As you can see from Table 19.6, a positive result only tells you that

Table 19.6 Drug detection times for urine screening

Drug	Detection time
Cocaine	12-72 hours
Amphetamine	2-4 days
Heroin	2-4 days
Codeine	2-4 days
Cannabis (casual use)	2-7 days
Cannabis (chronic use)	30 days
Benzodiazepines (casual use)	1-2 days
Benzodiazepines (chronic use)	6 weeks
Ecstasy	2-4 days

someone may have used a drug in the last so many hours, days or weeks. It does not tell you how much of the substance has been taken or their frequency and pattern of use. And without doing a more specific laboratory test, it may not tell you which type of drug either, for example the opiate test may not distinguish between heroin and codeine.

In addition, some prescribed substances cause a positive result, for example selective serotonin reuptake inhibitor (SSRI) antidepressants such as fluoxetine can sometimes cause a positive result for amphetamine, as can some over-the-counter decongestants, and pregnancy can cause false negatives. So be cautious when interpreting urine testing. Consider first the utility of the result and what you will do when you get it. This is particularly important when you consider the impact that taking a urine sample for drug testing may have on any therapeutic relationship.

Blood testing

A liver function test may highlight compromised liver functioning, which may be due to alcohol use, hepatitis or other physical conditions. If heavy alcohol use is expected, then a full blood count will also show a raised mean corpuscle volume (MCV) if this is the case. If you suspect hepatitis A, B or C, antibody tests can be done to confirm this with appropriate pre- and post-test counselling (Department of Health, 2001).

Primary observations

Primary observations will include, for example, temperature, pulse, blood pressure and respiration. Has a young man got very high blood pressure? Does he feel cold? A stimulant user during intoxication would experience both of these. Perhaps these observations indicate that someone is in withdrawal. For example, in alcohol withdrawal someone may have a high temperature and high blood pressure.

Weight

Has someone gained or lost weight in a short period without any other explanation? Chronic alcohol users commonly loose weight rapidly due to poor diet and poor absorption.

Breathalyser

This can be a useful assessment tool as well as a good educational tool to use with service users. There are a number of different types on the market, so be sure you know how to use the one you have and know what the result means in terms of alcohol units. If you do have one, try it for yourself: you will find it is very hard to blow enough breath to take a reading, so be mindful of people with respiratory difficulties. Sometimes your nose can be just as good at detecting the smell of alcohol on someone's breath. It is not always necessary to know the amount.

Physical signs

Physical signs include injection sites, pallor, presence of abscesses, level of consciousness, pupil size, smell of breath, behaviour. If someone looks yellow they may be jaundiced, indicating that they may have a problem with their liver functioning. This may have been caused by liver damage related to excessive alcohol use or viral hepatitis. If someone has constricted pupils, that may be a result of opiate intoxication; however be sure to rule out other reasons for constricted pupils such as bright light.

Subjective assessment

The next stage is a subjective assessment, which refers to the interview part of an assessment. This is where you ask the questions. Be mindful that when you ask questions about substance use, the service user may be suspicious of you and your intentions. It is likely that they will have had negative experiences in the past when they have been forthcoming about their substance use. Be open and honest about why you are asking the questions and explain your role regarding confidentiality.

Before you embark on this stage you may want to be clear about the following:

- What are the limits of confidentiality?

- Who should you share information with? Carers/service providers?

- At what point should you inform police of criminal activity?

So what questions should you ask? Essentially all the questions you need to ask can be summarised as follows: what, where, how, who with, how much, how often, how long? These are outlined further in Table 19.7. Before you ask a question, think about why you want to know the answer and if there would be any consequences attached to any answers. Many people will answer questions about drugs using slang names for the drug or methods of using it (see Table 19.8). Do not pretend to understand if you do not: not only will you lose your credibility as a worker, but also you may make an incorrect assessment. Remember that the service user is the one with the knowledge, so ask them to explain.

Table 19.7   Assessment questions

- What do you (did you) use? (substance)

- Where do you use it? (risk)

- Who do you use it with? (peers)

- How do you use it? (administration)

- How often do you use? (start time/frequency/pattern)

- How much do you use? (amount/quantity and price)

Table 19.8   Slang used by substance users

Slang	Meaning
Gear	Heroin (but not always, could be drug of choice)
Clucking	Withdrawal
Fixing	Injecting
Cooking up	Preparing heroin for injection
Gouching	Feeling sleepy after taking heroin
Skin popping	Subcutaneous injection
Works	Injecting equipment
Chasing	Smoking on foil

Table 19.8 lists some of the slang used by substance users in the UK. It is by no means exhaustive and can vary from region to region. Can you think of any other words from your own experience? If so, add them to the table.

In addition to a general assessment, you may want to do a risk assessment. What risks do you think you should be considering when assessing a substance user?

Some of the risks may include:

- Overdose: any history of accidental or deliberate overdose, do they use alone, is there anyone else around if they overdosed accidentally?

- Risk of transmission of blood-borne viruses such a hepatitis A, B and C and HIV via risky drug using practice (e.g. sharing cocaine 'straws' or sharing injecting equipment) or sexual practice.

- Administration risks: are they injecting, if so where, do they share equipment, do they used a fixed tourniquet?

- Storage: where do they store their substances, are they out of reach of children and non-tolerant adults?

- Children: where are they when the user is intoxicated?

Screening and assessment tools exist to help structure an assessment, but in a chapter of this length it is not possible to mention them in detail. However, there is one tool that is quick and easy to use: a drug/alcohol diary (see Activity 19.7). It can either be given to a user to complete themselves day by day, or can be completed retrospectively in session with a worker.

Activity 19.7: Using a diary

Table 19.9 is a diary. Try completing it for your own substance use over the last week. If you do not use any substances, then complete the diary for your chocolate or coffee usage!

Table 19.9   Substance use diary

	Drug	Time	Amount	Where	With
Monday					
Tuesday					
Wednesday					
Thursday					
Friday					
Saturday					
Sunday					

When conducting an assessment, it is also important to assess for the interaction between the substance use and the mental health problem and not just assess them separately. It is usual that the problems will be greater than the sum of the parts. For example, there may be a relationship between someone's anxiety and their level of alcohol use. Another simple tool that can assist you in doing this is a 'timeline'. See Table 19.10 for an example. This allows you to take a history of someone's mental health and substance use simultaneously and allows for connections to be made. The aim is to identify the predisposing, precipitating and perpetuating factors. For example, someone may have a parent with a mental illness (predisposing factor), they lost one of their parents when they were in their teens (precipitating factor) and they then got involved in heavy cannabis use when they were in their twenties (perpetuating factor).

Table 19.10 Timeline (example)

Age	16	17	19	20	21	22
Mental health	Isolating myself Feeling different to others	Started to hear voices	First admission to hospital Diagnosed with schizophrenia	Started on medication Voices reduced	Started to forget to take medication especially at weekends	Voices were increasing in intensity – admitted to hospital for three months
Substance use	Started smoking cannabis	Smoking cannabis most days	Smoking approx 1/4 ounce a day	Stopped smoking cannabis in hospital and for next six months	Got into clubbing scene and started taking ecstasy	Started using cannabis again to cope with 'come downs'

▶ **Motivation**

One outcome of the assessment may be identifying that someone may have a substance misuse problem, or that their use is having a significant impact on their functioning that would require intervention, but it is quite likely that the person will be in disagreement with your opinion and you are frustrated at their apparent denial of their problem. Why is this and how do you engage them in treatment?

To explain this, look at Figure 19.1. This is a visual representation of the transtheoretical model of change, also known as the cycle of change or wheel of change. This model proposes that change is a process (not a product) and that anyone embarking on change will pass through a number of stages before achieving their change. Let's look at each stage in turn.

Precontemplation

Precontemplation is the stage when a person has not identified that they have a problem and are happy the way things are. This is the stage the person may be at when they disagree about having a problem and it is the most likely stage at which you will meet people. So what can you do?

The most unhelpful approach is arguing or trying to convince someone that they have a problem when they don't agree. You will only end up entrenching their belief if you try this approach. Think about how you would react if someone told you to lose weight or stop smoking if you didn't perceive it as a problem. You may deliberately do the opposite!

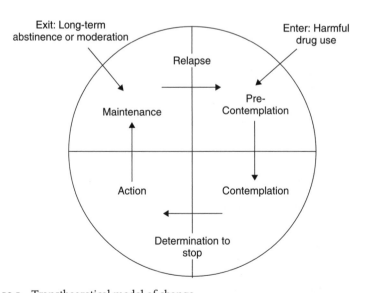

Figure 19.1 Transtheoretical model of change
Source: Adapted from Prochaska, J. O. & DiClemente, C. C. (1982) *Transtheoretical therapy: Toward a more integrative model of change*. Psychotherapy Theory, Research & Practice, *19*: 276–88.

What is more useful is just to try to engage the person. However, do not be fooled by attendance at appointments, for example, as evidence that someone is engaged. Many service users will attend appointments and so on, but only because they feel they have no choice due to pressure from others or perhaps they come to see you for other reasons. To engage someone give them what they want, whether that is help with benefits or a change in medication. Engagement is when someone is working collaboratively with you. Work with the problems that they present. In other words, do not mention the substance use until they do or you risk losing them.

One tool you can use to assess whether someone is ready to change, if it is not already evident, is the readiness to change exercise (Activity 19.8, adapted from Miller & Rollnick, 1991). It is likely that someone will score low in importance if they are precontemplative. Have a go using it on yourself for a behaviour you have been thinking about changing.

Activity 19.8: Readiness to change

Think of a behaviour you would like to change. Perhaps you would like to stop smoking, eat less chocolate etc. Now complete the following exercise to see how ready you are to make that change.

- First consider how *important* it is to change and give the importance a score between 1 and 10, where 1 is not important and 10 is very important.

- Now consider how *confident* you are about making the change, once again giving yourself a score from 1 to 10.

  If you have two 10s then you're ready to change. What is more likely is that there will be a discrepancy in your scores.

- Now consider what it would take for you to score a higher score for both importance and confidence. How would you know you were more confident or changing the behaviour held more importance?

  This is the key to what needs to be done.

Source: Adapted from Miller, R. & Rollnick, S. (1991) *Motivational Interviewing: Preparing People for Change*. New York: Guilford Press.

Contemplation

Contemplation is when a person is starting to think about a behaviour that they may want to change. It is identified by the ambivalence that someone may be expressing. For example: 'I really should stop smoking but I'm not sure I can do while I'm so stressed.' This is where you can start to highlight the problem behaviour by giving health promotion advice/literature and feedback from urine or blood results. In addition, you may want to complete a 'decision matrix' with the user (Activity 19.9, adapted from Miller & Rollnick, 1991), which explores the benefits and costs of their current behaviour and discrepancies between what the service user wants to achieve in life, where they are now and how their current behaviour affects that.

Have a go at completing a decision matrix using the same behaviour as you used in Activity 19.8. Remember that just because there are more things listed in one box does not mean they 'weigh' more than the items in the other box. Always start with looking at the benefits of not changing. This may well be the first time someone has ever asked the person this!

Activity 19.9: Decision matrix

Using the same behaviour you want to change from Activity 19.8, complete Table 19.11 by considering the benefits and costs of changing and the benefits and costs of not changing.

Table 19.11   Decision matrix

	Benefits	Costs
Not changing		
Changing		

Source: Adapted from Miller, R. & Rollnick, S. (1991) *Motivational Interviewing: Preparing People for Change*. New York: Guilford Press.

How does it feel to complete the exercise? Are you any clearer about changing? Is there a balance?

Preparation

Preparation is the stage where the service user, with your support, designs their plan of change. It is important that this plan is specific, measurable, achievable, realistic and timed (SMART). To assist with this you can use a change plan (see Activity 19.10 later in the chapter). An additional benefit of designing a change plan is that any lack of 'success' can be attributed to a fault in the plan rather than the person. However, it is not recommended that words such as success or failure should be used with the service user.

Action

Action is when the plan is put into action and the treatments in the next section are used.

Maintenance

Maintenance is just that, the maintenance of the new behaviour. This is not to be confused with 'success', as the person at this stage is still vulnerable to relapse.

Relapse

Relapse is included in the transtheoretical model of change as the model recognises that relapse may occur as part of any behaviour change. In fact, relapse is the most common outcome of any substance use intervention. It does not, however, mean that the person has to return to the beginning of the cycle. They may only need to return to the action stage or perhaps revisit the plan that they designed in the preparation stage. Relapse is discussed further in a later section.

Note that motivation is not something a person *has* but something a person *does*, despite the frequent incorrect attributions that are made that suggest that motivation is a fixed personality trait. Motivation will also fluctuate and vary from one behaviour to another.

▶ Treatment

Although expertise in providing substance use treatments have, until now, rested primarily with substance misuse services, there is a greater expectation that mental health services will either provide these treatments or work in collaboration with substance misuse services in their provision. Thus it is necessary to address them in this chapter. To start with, however, one must first appreciate the differences in treatment goals.

Treatment goals have long been a contentious issue between substance misuse services, mental health services and service users. In general, substance misuse services promote harm minimisation. That is, they do not expect service users necessarily to stop using substances, but to reduce the harm associated with their use. For example, heroin users are encouraged to stop injecting or at least use 'clean' injecting equipment and improve their injecting techniques. Mental health services, however, have typically promoted abstinence (complete cessation of use), based on the belief that *any* substance use has negative consequences for mental health. While this belief may be based on some truth, if this is not the belief of the service user then such a treatment goal will be unsuccessful (see the section on motivation and readiness to change).

Treatments fall into three broad categories: detoxification (coming off), rehabilitation (staying off) and substitute prescribing (of a pharmaceutical alternative in the same group of drugs, normally in a longer-acting form).

Detoxification

Detoxification (detox) is where an individual who is physically dependent on a substance is 'weaned' off it. This process may or may not involve the use of medication and usually does not require a hospital admission. Not all substances require detoxification. For example, cocaine users usually start treatment at the next phase because cocaine use does not result in physical dependency. However, opioid substances, such as heroin and methadone, and alcohol do require detox. Good practice is to follow detox with rehabilitation to reduce the likelihood of relapse.

Rehabilitation

Rehabilitation (rehab) is the phase after detox. It is a longer treatment time, anything from three months to a couple of years. During this time the individual addresses any psychological and/or social issues that may have been precipitating or maintaining their substance use and prepares for a life without substance use. Sometimes this can include taking adjunctive medications, such as acamprosate for alcohol misuse or naltrexone for opiate and alcohol dependence, to facilitate this (NICE, 2007b). The psychosocial elements of rehab can be provided as a residential or day service.

Substitute prescribing

Substitute prescribing or maintenance treatments involve either keeping an individual on their drug of choice or prescribing a safer alternative, which the person can be maintained on. The classic example of this is methadone maintenance treatment for dependent heroin users, where methadone (a longer-acting opioid) is prescribed in order to prevent withdrawal and stabilise their drug use. The other drug licensed for maintenance treatment in opioid dependence is buprenorphine, but methadone should be the first line of treatment (NICE, 2007a).

This approach is used either where an individual does not want to achieve abstinence or when repeated attempts at detox have been unsuccessful. It is the mainstay of community treatment for opiate dependence and has a well-tested evidence base, as it can engage individuals who are otherwise ambivalent about change and has been proved to reduce harm to the individual and to the community.

Relapse prevention

The concept of relapse prevention may be familiar to you with regard to developing a 'relapse drill' and 'relapse signature' with people with mental health problems. In the field of substance use, relapse prevention strategies also exist. Although very similar to relapse prevention strategies in mental health, there are a few terms or ideas that you may wish to add to your practice.

Relapse prevention in substance use views relapse as a learning process. It can be utilised with people reducing harmful use and/or those wishing to achieve abstinence. Fundamentally, it proposes that willpower is not enough; service users must have an awareness of the problem, and develop coping strategies to overcome it. First, there is the concept of high-risk situations. These situations can be anticipated and planned for. For example, a high-risk situation for someone trying to stop smoking may be going to the pub.

Then there are urges and cravings. These are the result of and an extension to high-risk situations. Although there is a distinction made between the two, it is not necessarily a helpful one, so for the purposes of this explanation they will be discussed as one and the same. This is when someone has a powerful desire to use whatever substance they are trying to control. This can be triggered by external factors such as specific environments or by internal factors such as thoughts and emotions.

Thirdly, there is a distinction made between lapses and relapses. Lapses are also known as 'slips'. That is, they are transient. Thus if the person from the previous example did smoke a cigarette one night while in the pub, it would not necessarily result in them returning to their previous level of smoking. Lapses are therefore part of the learning process and will assist in the development of a relapse prevention strategy. A relapse, however, is when someone returns to the previous level of behaviour; but note that a relapse is the most common outcome for individuals who undertake treatment for substance misuse.

Finally, there is the concept of lifestyle imbalance. Theory suggests that when someone is making a behaviour change, to protect against relapse they must address their lifestyle. For example, someone who drinks a lot of alcohol may have a partner who drinks heavily. It may therefore be necessary for that person to address that relationship if they are to maintain the desired behaviour change.

Thus, it is the role of the worker to assist the service user in identifying their high-risk situations, in developing the cognitive and behavioural skills required to overcome them and in addressing any lifestyle imbalance that may precipitate a relapse. The worker can also help the service user to learn from any lapse they have had and give them the encouragement to continue with their planned behaviour change.

Figure 19.2 has been adapted from the work of Marlatt and Gordon (1985). It gives an example of someone who has stopped smoking and then goes to a pub.

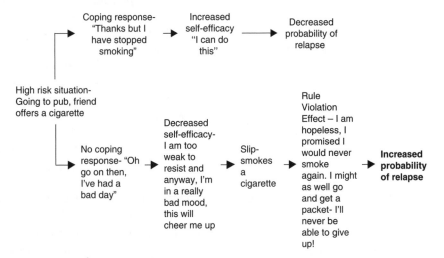

Figure 19.2 Relapse prevention
Source: Adapted from Marlatt, A. G. & Gordon, J. R. (1985) *Relapse Prevention*. New York: Guilford Press.

▶ **Where next?**

By now you may be feeling overwhelmed with all this new information and wondering where to start putting what you have learned into practice. In addition, while you may be feeling motivated to address your own practice, you may also be feeling powerless to change the workplace in which you work to facilitate improved services. But remember, Rome was not built in a day. Consider what you could do as an individual worker. If everyone does something then change will be facilitated. Keep in mind the case study you read at the beginning of the chapter.

To help you focus on where to go next you can complete Activity 19.10 (adapted from Miller & Rollnick, 1991). This is an exercise that is completed with service users embarking on change (as discussed previously under 'preparation'). Complete this activity for a change you can make to either your practice or workplace. An example is written in small text on the plan.

Activity 19.10: Change plan

The most important reasons I want to make this change	*I feel helpless when I have a service user who uses cannabis*	
The main goals for myself making this change	*To relieve feelings of helplessness and better help my service users*	
I plan to do these things in order to accomplish my goals	**Action** *Visit the local drug service*	**When** *In the next month*
Other people could help me with change in these ways	**Person** *My manager My partner*	**Ways** *Agreeing the time out Giving me space to read*
These are some of the possible obstacles to change, and how I could handle them	**Obstacle** *Reduced staffing so cannot get away*	**How to respond** *Rebook appointment straight away*

| I will know that my plan is working when I see these results | *My confidence to work with cannabis users has increased and I take a staff teaching session on the subject* |

Source: Adapted from Miller, R. & Rollnick, S. (1991) *Motivational Interviewing: Preparing People for Change.* New York: Guilford Press.

Table 19.12   Answers to Activity 19.6

1. TRUE: you can overdose by suppressing the activity of the region of the brain responsible for maintaining respirations and/or aspirate on vomit.

2. FALSE: a pint of 5% lager has 2.8 units where a 25 ml measure of whisky has 1 unit.

3. TRUE: in general, as women tend to be smaller and weigh less, but this is not always the case.

4. FALSE: The Department of Health advises that men should not regularly drink more than 3–4 units of alcohol per day, and women should not regularly drink more than 2–3 units of alcohol per day. After an episode of heavy drinking it is advisable to refrain from drinking for 48 hours to allow your body to recover.

5. FALSE: it is a depressant.

6. TRUE: in terms of avoiding injecting-related problems, but you could still overdose.

7. FALSE: it depends on the amount taken and how often.

8. FALSE: cigarettes kill the most with alcohol coming second.

9. FALSE: it is difficult but not impossible, as there are many treatments available.

10. TRUE: for the 1 mg/ml dilution, but there is also brown methadone, which is a 20 mg/ml dilution, and blue methadone, which is a 10 mg/ml dilution. It is also available in tablet and injectable forms.

11. FALSE: It just lasts longer in the body and therefore takes longer to be eliminated.

12. FALSE: methadone still poses the risk of overdose, a risk that is greater given its long half-life. It is however safer in terms of the route of administration, usually being oral.

13. FALSE: any doctor can prescribe methadone, but a special licence from the Home Office is required for a doctor to prescribe diamorphine (heroin) for the treatment of addiction.

14. TRUE.

15. TRUE.

Table 19.12   (*continued*)

16. TRUE.

17. TRUE: and they are very difficult to withdraw from.

18. FALSE: benzodiazepines are controlled under the Misuse of Substances Act as Class C substances, but the possession offence is waived so that it is not illegal to possess or use them without a prescription. It is an offence to sell or supply them to another person. The exception is temazepam, which is illegal to be in possession of without a prescription.

19. FALSE: cocaine is a white powder.

20. FALSE: cocaine is not combustible under heat, however it can be smoked in its freebase form known as crack.

21. FALSE: it can cause death due to heart attacks in healthy people.

22. FALSE: it is used as a local anaesthetic in ear, nose and throat operations.

23. FALSE: only the name is new, cocaine users have been making their own 'crack' for years.

24. FALSE: it gives a more intense 'high' than cocaine, primarily because it is smoked, and therefore its effects come on more rapidly, but it is no more addictive than cocaine.

25. FALSE: while it tends to be associated with those who are socially deprived, it is used across all sections of the population.

26. TRUE: crack is made from cocaine powder using chemicals and heat.

27. FALSE: the opposite is true.

28. FALSE: they can be, but they are usually snorted or swallowed.

29. TRUE: but it is 'borrowed' energy, as the user will feel tired, lethargic and depressed after the effects of the drug have worn off.

30. TRUE: ICE (also known as methamphetamine) is to amphetamines what crack is to cocaine.

31. TRUE: there is little evidence that it is harmful physically, but there is evidence that it does more harm to mental states. It will depend on how much someone is using and whether the cannabis user is vulnerable to developing or has a mental health problem.

32. FALSE: you may get dizzy and vomit but that's it.

33. FALSE: cannabis will affect co-ordination and judgement.

34. TRUE: 'skunk' has a higher THC (the active constituents of cannabis) content than resin and normal 'grass'.

▶ Conclusion

Substance misuse is endemic in our society and is unlikely to go away. Not surprisingly, as workers we meet substance users whatever our speciality, whether it be social work, nursing or mental health. Consequently, substance misuse services can no longer be the sole purveyors of substance misuse treatment and other mainstream services are going to have to provide treatment. This is not to say that substance misuse services cannot or should not be involved: they are there to support you. Perhaps you may wish to visit your local service and find out what they provide. Sometimes having a face to put to a name on the phone can help facilitate joint working.

But remember, as a worker you most probably will already have many of the skills required to meet the needs of substance users. This is not rocket science and can be a very rewarding area of work. So all the best with your work, and may you enjoy getting to know this service user group.

▶ References

Appleby, L., Shaw, J., Kapur, N. *et al.* (2006) *Avoidable Deaths: Five Year Report by the National Confidential Inquiry into Suicide and Homicide By People with Mental Illness.* Manchester: University of Manchester.

Department of Health (1999) *National Service Framework for Mental Health.* London: HMSO.

Department of Health (2001) *Hepatitis C: Guidance for Those Working with Drug Users.* London: HMSO, www.dh.gov.uk/en/Publicationsandstatistics/Publications/PublicationsPolicyAndGuidance/DH_4008723.

Department of Health (2002) *Mental Health Policy Implementation Guide: Adult Dual Diagnosis Good Practice Guidance.* London: HMSO, www.doh.gov.uk/mentalhealth/dualdiagnosis.htm.

Department of Health (2004) *The National Service Framework for Mental Health: Five Years On.* London: HMSO.

Gossop, M. (1993) *Living with Drugs* (3rd edn). London: Ashgate.

Hawkings, C. & Gilburt, H. (2004) *Dual Diagnosis Toolkit (Mental Health and Substance Misuse): A Practical Guide for Professionals and Practitioners.* London: Rethink, www.rethink.org/dualdiagnosis/toolkit.html.

Khantzian, E.J. (1985) The self-medication hypothesis of addictive disorders: Focus on heroin and cocaine dependence. *American Journal of Psychiatry,* **142**: 1259–64.

Khantzian, E.J. (1997) The self-medication hypothesis of substance use disorders: A reconsideration and recent applications. *Harvard Review of Psychiatry,* **4**: 231–44.

Marlatt, A.G. & Gordon, J.R. (1985) *Relapse Prevention.* New York: Guilford Press.

Menezes, P.R., Johnson, S., Thornicroft, G. *et al.* (1996) Drug and alcohol problems among individuals with severe mental illness in South London. *British Journal of Psychiatry,* **168**: 612–19.

Miller, R. & Rollnick, S. (1991) *Motivational Interviewing: Preparing People for Change.* New York: Guilford Press.

Miller, R. & Rollnick, S. (2002) *Motivational Interviewing: Preparing People for Change* (2nd edn). New York: Guildford Press.

NICE (2007a) *Methadone and Buprenorphine in the Treatment of Opiate Drug Misuse.* London: National Institute for Health and Clinical Excellence.

NICE (2007b) *Naltrexone for the Management of Opioid Dependence.* London: National Institute for Health and Clinical Excellence.

Phillips, P. & Johnson, S. (2003) Drug and alcohol misuse among in-patients with psychotic illnesses in three inner-London psychiatric units. *Psychiatric Bulletin,* **27**: 217–20.

Prochaska, J.O. & DiClemente, C.C. (1982) Transtheoretical therapy: Toward a more integrative model of change. *Psychotherapy Theory, Research & Practice,* **19**: 276–88.

Regier, D.A., Farmer, M.E., Rae, D.S. *et al.* (1990) Comorbidity of mental disorders with alcohol and other drug abuse. Results from the Epidemiological Catchment Area (ECA) study. *Journal of the American Medical Association,* **264**: 2511–18.

Royal College of Psychiatrists (1987) *Drug Scenes.* London: Gaskell.

▶ **Additional reading/resources**

Abdulrahim, D. (2001) *Substance Misuse and Mental Health Co-morbidity (Dual Diagnosis): Standards for Mental Health Services.* London: Health Advisory Service.

Banerjee, S., Clancy, C. & Crome. I. (eds) (2002) *Co-existing Problems of Mental Disorder & Substance Misuse (Dual Diagnosis): An Information Manual.* London: Royal College of Psychiatrists' Research Unit, www.rcpsych.ac.uk/cru/complete/ddip.htm.

Coyne, P. & Wright, S. (1997) *Substance Misuse: Guidance on Good Clinical Practice for Specialist Nurses.* London: Association of Nurses in Substance Abuse.

Department of Health (1999) *Drug Misuse and Dependence: Guidelines on Clinical Management.* London: HMSO.

Emmett, D. & Nice, G. (2005) *Understanding Street Drugs: A Handbook of Substance Misuse for Parents, Teachers and Other Professionals.* London: Jessica Kingsley.

Ghodse, H. (2002) *Drugs and Addictive Behaviour: A Guide to Treatment* (3rd edn). Cambridge: Cambridge University Press.

Rassool, G.H. (ed.) (2002) *Dual Diagnosis: Substance Misuse and Psychiatric Disorders.* Oxford: Blackwell Science.

Rassool, G.H. (ed.) (2006) *Dual Diagnosis Nursing.* Oxford: Blackwell Science.

Rollnick, S., Mason, P. & Butler, C. (1999) *Health Behaviour Change: A Guide for Practitioners.* Edinburgh: Churchill Livingstone.

Tyler, A. (1995) *Street Substances.* London: Hodder & Stoughton.

Wanigaratne, S., Wallace, W., Pullin, J., Keaney, F. & Farmer, R. (1990) *Relapse Prevention for Addictive Behaviours: A Manual for Therapists.* Oxford: Blackwell Scientific.

▶ **Resources for activities**

www.alcoholconcern.org.uk

www.ansa.uk.net

http://drinkwise.susu.org/

www.druginfo.adf.org.au/

www.drugscope.org.uk

www.knowyourlimits.gov.uk/index.html

www.rcpsych.ac.uk/mentalhealthinformation/mentalhealthproblems/alcohol anddrugs.aspx

www.release.org.uk

www.talktofrank.com/home_html.aspx

◀ CHAPTER TWENTY ▶

Gender inequality and the mental health of women and men

Jennie Williams
Director of Inequality Agenda Ltd.

Joe Miller
Devon Partnership NHS Trust

This chapter is about gender inequality, how it works in the western world in 21st Century and the implications for the mental health of women and men and service responses to their needs. Traditionally, mental health services have supported the social status quo by hiding the harm caused by inequalities and injustice. Our gender as both patients and workers has been rendered meaningless and irrelevant and the crucial links between mental health and our gendered lives dissolved. These days many staff know this is a problem, but work in contexts that do not offer the education, authorisation and support needed to support change. With dispiriting frequency we hear mental health workers say 'I don't want to take the lid off that can of worms' when explaining their reticence to listen to patients/clients talk about what has happened to them in their lives (Scott & Williams, 2004).

▶ About gender inequality

In the first instance it is important to acknowledge that gender inequality, at its most fundamental, is a system that advantages men at women's expense; an uncomfortable fact that is often ignored or sidelined in favour of talk about sex differences. The system of gender inequality gains stability from being opaque. It is hard to spot what is going on, particularly so if you are advantaged because

Learning About Mental Health Practice.   Edited by Theo Stickley and Thurstine Basset
© 2008 John Wiley & Sons, Ltd

you are less likely to have experiences that jolt a sense of injustice into awareness. Justifications and explanations for gender relations are woven into the fabric of society and our psychologies, which means that women as well as men can contribute to maintaining – as well as challenging - gender inequality (Peace, 2003).

Gender inequality not only confers privileges on men as a group but can further national interests. For example, gender inequality facilitates the delivery of large number of people (men) whose socialisation makes them well suited to military life (Busfield, 1982). Colonial history also provides clear illustrations of the ways in which political and economic interests have been shaped and served by the emphasis on competition, acquisition and domination that is the defining feature of masculinity. In contrast, gender inequality positions women as subordinate to men and orientates them to serve others in the home and wider society: work that is characteristically undervalued, unpaid or underpaid.

However, while gender inequality serves group and collective interests, this is at considerable cost to the mental health of individuals, which includes men as well as women. Understanding why this is the case, and knowing how to use this knowledge, is an essential competence for all people working in the field of mental health.

A gendered enterprise

Gender politics have shaped the emergence of theory and practice in the field of gender and mental health in striking ways. It is women – the group most poorly served by gender inequality – who have primarily given voice to the mental health implications of gender. In contrast, and with notable exceptions (e.g. Addis & Mahalik, 2003; Good, Thomson & Brathwaite, 2005; Miller & McClelland, 2006), men have largely been silent on the subject. When we ask mental health workers to explain this phenomenon, they consistently suggest it is because men are supposed to be strong and not have mental health problems, whereas women are known to be psychologically vulnerable. McCreary (2004), who is based in Canada, offers a very similar observation:

> Women banded together to work on problems with health delivery. Men don't want to do that. We have inculcated a culture in our society that men have to be tough, men have to be strong. Our society is very good at punishing gender deviation in men. Weakness is not considered to be masculine.

This public reticence to focus on men's gendered mental health needs parallels the private constraint that many men experience when it comes to talking about their experiences of distress. It also suggests that talking about men's mental health poses more of a challenge to the stability of gender relations – a phenomenon that is clearly detrimental to the interests of the many thousands of men with mental health needs.

An era of change

There are, however, signs of change. The mental health significance of gender, which has been recognised for many years by women (Busfield, 1982; Chesler, 1972; Gilman, 1899), is finally also being acknowledged by mental health policies (Department of Health, 2002, 2003, 2005). More recently there has been a tentative emergence around the world of government-led or government-supported initiatives taking men's health and mental health as their focus (Canadian Mental Health Association, 2004; Men's Health Forum, 2006; Mind, 2000). Recognition that gender inequality is a mental health issue is also increasingly evident in mainstream policy, which exhorts us to take gender, race, sexuality and other inequalities into account; though as yet these aspirational statements are not accompanied by directions about how they are to be achieved. The statement below is fairly typical in this respect:

> Like other health workers, mental health nurses also have legal obligations and duties regarding issues of equality, for example under the Race Relations (Amendment) Act (2000). In the future, public bodies will also need to ensure gender and disability equality in all aspects of policy, workforce issues and service provision. (Chief Nursing Officer, 2006)

Building competence

There is now a strong case for mental health workers to build an understanding of the mental health significance of the processes and practices that underpin gender inequality and help to keep us in our place. There are a number of routes that can be used; none are mutually exclusive. In an ideal world a major route would be training and preparation for working in mental health services. However, this describes the experiences of very few mental health workers (Cann *et al.*, 2001; Scott & Williams, 2004): the majority feel woefully ill prepared to help people whose distress is rooted in their gendered lives and experiences. Fortunately, there are other ways of building competence, which include actively seeking out relevant literature and work experience, and reflecting on our own lives and experiences. Here, we offer a map of the terrain as a resource for making this journey.

▶ Gender inequality and mental health

Gender inequality persists because the system is opaque and its scrutiny and opposition discouraged. The system is so deeply embedded in everyday life that it is very difficult for us as individuals and professionals to de-code the 'signs and symptoms' of associated psychological harm in ourselves, and in the clients and patients with whom we work. It is also difficult for us to identify ways in which the practices of mental health services are shaped by gender inequality, or to think through the implications for service development and delivery. Nonetheless,

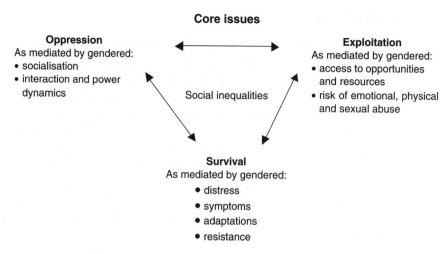

Core issues

Oppression
As mediated by gendered:
• socialisation
• interaction and power
  dynamics

Social inequalities

Exploitation
As mediated by gendered:
• access to opportunities
  and resources
• risk of emotional, physical
  and sexual abuse

Survival
As mediated by gendered:
• distress
• symptoms
• adaptations
• resistance

Figure 20.1   Mental health implications of inequalities.

there is now sufficient evidence to support the conclusion that gender inequality, in conjunction with the other inequalities that divide our society, is a major determinant of our lives and mental health.

The significant connections of which we need to take account in our work in mental health services are outlined in Figure 20.1.

Oppression is the generic term used to describe a range of processes and principles that help to keep people 'in their place' in systems of inequality. This includes psychological matters such as gender socialisation, and gendered interaction and power dynamics played out in private and public spheres of life. While the mental health risks are most commonly felt by those who are disadvantaged by these arrangements, they also carry mental health costs for those who are privileged (Rosenfield & Pottick, 2005).

Exploitation is manifest in the effects of gender on access to opportunities and resources, many of which are known to be generally beneficial to mental health. Exploitation is also causally linked to the gendered risk of emotional, physical and sexual abuse.

Our survival is also mediated by the effects of gender inequality, for example the psychological and material resources that are available, and the adaptations that are considered to be appropriate for people like us – whoever we may be.

Oppression

Gender socialisation

Social norms and attitudes as well as formal regulations define the desired qualities and accompanying behaviour for men and women, including those from different racial and ethnic backgrounds. They provide the raw material with which we construct our selves. Exercise 20.1 reminds us of the strength of social commitment to gender socialisation. This can also be detected by scanning the magazine racks in your local newsagent. Ask yourself what messages are being communicated about what it means to be a woman or man in 21st Century society. What are we being encourage to look like, be like, be interested in, responsible for and concerned about?

Exercise 20.1: Gender socialisation

In our society there are strong pressures to colour-code babies and young children.

Why do you think this happens? What does it tell us about gender inequality?

You'll find some answers at the end of the chapter.

We are living at a time of considerable change in gender expectations, which are evolving in the context of rapid social change affecting many areas of our lives. Exercise 20.2 suggests one way in which you can explore this for yourself.

Exercise 20.2: Changing expectations

Ask a same-sex older relative to tell you about what being 'female' or 'male' meant when they were your age. Did anything that was expected of them feel stressful or 'get them down'?

Then use yourself as a comparison to identify anything that seems to have stayed the same, or has changed.

Societal enthusiasm for gender division becomes internalised through our personal experiences of, and engagement with, these processes; and unsurprisingly, gender is a core component of identity. You can test this out for yourself in Exercise 20.3.

Exercise 20.3: Gender identity

One way to explore the centrality of gender to identity is to ask some friends to quickly write down six words that describe who they are.

You will find that most people include gender in their list; and that it is usually one of the first words elicited.

It is also important to appreciate the mental health significance of what is actually being differentiated along gender lines. For example, it has been recognised for many years (e.g. Baker-Miller, 1976) that people from subordinate social groups are socialised to develop psychological characteristics

Table 20.1   Desirable characteristics

Women	Emotional
	Understanding and concerned about the needs of others
	Unselfish and kind
	Good with children
	Reliable – mainstay of family life
	Hard working and able to multitask
	Deferential
	Feminine
	Slim, and to look good in all situations
	Appear to be less intelligent than men and to earn less
Men	Strong
	Self-confident
	Decisive
	Dominant
	In control of their lives
	In control of their emotions
	Providers
	Tough
	Confident at dealing with technical/practical tasks
	Keen on sport

that are useful and pleasing to the privileged, foster compliance rather than rebellion, and suggest that they are ill suited to acting autonomously or to exercising power. In contrast, those from dominant social groups are socialised to develop psychological characteristics that are consistent with the exercise of power. This phenomenon is evident when we look at the kinds of characteristics that are expected of women and men: there is an illustrative list in Table 20.1.

It is both difficult and risky to live outside of these expectations and each of us makes our own adaptations to them as we journey through our life. The work of researchers and clinicians, as well as what we can learn from reflecting on our own experiences, can help to pinpoint the embedded mental health risks.

Women and gender compliance

One of the main risks to women of being brought up to please men and to accommodate the wishes of others is of neglecting their own needs and losing the sense of their own entitlement. Jack (1991) calls this 'silencing the self'. Women are also placed in a double bind, because caring for others and being nurturing are socially undervalued activities. Should they feel angry about their lives and experiences, 'good women' are expected to stifle rather than express these feelings.

The psychological costs of this toxic combination of social expectations and injunctions are revealed in the accounts that some women offer of their lives (Hurst, 1999). A common theme in the lives of many women is that of 'getting on with it' and working very hard to 'hold it altogether', including minimising, normalising and coping with disappointment and distress in the service of being a 'good woman' (Scattolon & Stoppard, 1999). Given this, it is not surprising that depression is so common among women (WHO, 2000). 'Good women' are also sensitised to measuring self-worth through the success or failure of their relationships, and they can feel obligated to preserve those relationships even if it exacts a terrible personal cost (Rodman Aronson & Schaler Buckolz, 2001). Tolerance of family violence becomes more comprehensible when viewed from this perspective.

For some women, the dominant themes in their lived experience of inequalities are those of abandonment, betrayal, abuse, disappointment and frustration: experiences that assault the self and are a source of powerful emotions, including great sadness, anger and rage. Yet one of the injunctions that support the perpetuation of gender inequality is that women should not be angry. It is men in our society who are authorised to be angry and violent. The obvious implication for mental health services is that they should enable women to give voice to their experiences, and to find safe ways to expressing their anger and rage. Nevertheless, the dominant practices of mental health – especially the medicalisation of distress – function to manage and suppress emotion.

Gender and other social inequalities also have discernible effects on under-standings and definitions of mental health. So, even though femininity is demonstrably linked to clear mental health risks, studies find that women who have internalised the characteristics of femininity are generally considered to be normal and mentally healthy (Penfold & Walker, 1984, Chapter 4).

Finally, effective gender socialisation does offer women some potential advantages, most notably encouragement to become competent at relationships. Consequently, we know that women experiencing psychological difficulties are typically more ready than men to seek help and more able to address the causes of their distress in individual and group relationships (Bernardez, 1996).

Women: Gender non-compliance

Meeting gender expectations successfully for a day, yet alone for life, is not possible. However, it is what individuals do with the gap between gender expectations and the daily reality of their lives that holds mental health significance. When women shoulder responsibility for any shortfalls, gender inequality is protected at personal costs. Hence it is unsurprising that self-blame, guilt, depression and low self-esteem are common among women (WHO, 2000) and that body insecurity and hatred are of epidemic proportions. Even when women don't blame themselves, then others are often quite willing to do that for them. Derogatory and discouraging terms such as 'mad', 'bad', 'weak', 'sick' and 'crazy' are terms that are generally reserved for those women whose behaviour, sexual choices and lifestyles doesn't appear to be governed by expectations of femininity or might be 'read' as an indictment of injustice. This is particularly the case for women using psychiatric services, who are usually a poor match for the stereotype of a 'good' women or even a 'good' patient. Misogyny is widespread and painfully evident in the language used to describe women, their behaviour and needs (Williams, Scott & Bressington, 2004).

Men: Gender compliance

On the face of it, being born male seems to offer good prospects in terms of mental health, as it offers privileged access to a range of valuable and relevant resources. However, a closer examination reveals a more complex picture. One of the more telling consequences of being male is the injunction placed on emotionality, and the extent to which the internal world is under-valued. A key objective of male socialisation is to produce men that are 'strong and silent' and 'in control'. This offers psychological safety through an emphasis on the external world. However, since few men's actual lives are distress free, there is little scope to acknowledge and deal constructively with experiences of vulnerability or powerlessness, within the confines of traditional masculinity. This observation is illustrated by the consistent under-reporting of traumatic experiences.

To illustrate, numerous studies now demonstrate that boy children (as well as girl children) are victims of sexual abuse, physical violence and neglect. However, reviews of studies of sexual abuse in men consistently find that sexual abuse is under-reported and universal (e.g. Watkins & Bentovin, 1992). We can best understand this phenomenon as a defence against shock, embarrassment, fear, stigma, self-blame and, perhaps most significantly, on behalf of being male. Within the terms of masculinity, the consequences of abuse are exacerbated by a form of psychological emasculation, literally implying the loss of masculinity – that is, the loss of power – and the failure to be a man. An inability to acknowledge or express distress is now a recognised contributor to significant mental health outcomes such as suicide risk among younger and older men in particular, and also undiagnosed and diagnosed depression, post-traumatic stress disorder and substance abuse (Scottish Executive, 2005).

Compliance with traditional male norms also underpins male capacity to harm:

> Stated simply, the traditional ideology of masculinity is the central risk factor for men's health and the single, greatest obstacle to women's health. (Kimmel, 2004)

'Normative' male behaviour appears to include a high risk of violence within 'intimate' settings. Male socialisation encourages men to be dependent on women for psychological and other services, and to feel entitled to have their needs met. It is now well documented that a substantial minority – estimated at between 28% to 33% in White and Kowalski's study (1998) – of men manage this toxic mixture of dependence and entitlement through coercion, which finds expression in emotional, sexual and physical abuse. That this represents a significant risk factor for women's mental health is slowly being recognised within mental health services (Department of Health & Home Office, 2005) which until recently rarely considered emotional and physical abuse to be a central mental health issue.

Men: Gender non-compliance

Successful compliance with normative ideas about one's gender seems to be an important determinant of well-being. Men's feelings of personal satisfaction and psychological well-being seem closely tied to the extent to which they believe they are successfully discharging the male script; that is, the acquisition of conquest or entitlements, at work, at play and at home. White, middle-class heterosexual men may well gain some satisfaction from having fulfilled the male script, where economic power, ownership and authority are valued over all else (Dobash *et al.*, 1992). However, this is made less likely for men who deviate from the cultural and social norms. These will be men who need to reconcile the gap between the expectation of dominance and their experience of powerlessness, including men who become unemployed, who are more likely to feel frustrated and hopeless than their partners (Artazcoz *et al.*, 2004).

Men who do not comply with traditional male norms because, for example, they are gay, black, disabled, unemployed or have a mental health problem – are often subject to significant disadvantages and prejudices. As a lived reality, masculinity is a broad term that refers to a spectrum of overlapping 'masculinities', in which there can be dominant and dominated, mainstream and marginalised social groups. These different masculinities emerge, evolve or disappear over periods of social change, and are shaped by social class, age, disability, ethnicity and sexuality. In turn, these have an impact on the range of cultural messages that are available to men in developing their own identities. Certainly in Western societies, the 'male club' is hierarchically organised and men can be disadvantaged where they deviate from ascribed, heterosexual, white, middle-class norms. Thus a range of disqualifications may apply. Men from Asian or Afro-Caribbean cultures, for example, continue to have high admission rates to hospital under section, and are over-represented in secure units. They also have far higher rates of compulsory admission to psychiatric hospital than does the general population. They are more likely to be treated with drugs and electro-convulsive therapy, and are less likely to receive counselling or psychotherapy (Keating *et al.*, 2002).

Gendered interaction and power dynamics

One of the key competencies for the mental health workforce is to become sensitive and responsive to the power dynamics associated with gender, and other social inequalities. The dynamics are detectable in our own lives, in the lives of people using mental health services, and in the interactions that take place throughout mental health services. The evidence base for their existence and effects is scattered throughout the various inequality literatures, and we summarise these findings in Table 20.2. Building a vocabulary and understanding of the ways in which gender and other inequalities shape the relational world helps us to survive as workers and to become a resource for patients and clients.

Table 20.2   Power dynamics commonly associated with gender inequality

Practices and processes	Function	Risks for women	Risks for men
Attribution of inferiority and superiority 'I was classed as no good 'cause I was a single parent.'(quoted in ReSisters, 2002)	Supports the status quo in inequitable relationships	Damage to sense of self; limits control over one's body and labour, and access to resources	Anxiety, anger and frustration at not actually feeling powerful and invulnerable; risks to self and others of attempting to take more power and control; contact with criminal justice system
Blaming, derogating, ridiculing 'But that's what these men do... they make you feel so small that you agree that everything is your fault.' (quoted in Humphreys & Thiara, 2003)	Supports inequality by identifying a person or group as the problem, not inequality	Damage to identity and self-esteem; self-doubt; feelings of embarrassment, guilt, sadness and depression; and of being harmed not helped by mental health services	Erodes respect, including self-respect
Denial and indifference 'Doctors don't want to know about past domestic violence, just up the valium and I was walking around like a zombie.' (quoted in Barron, 2004) 'No action was taken and I was told "as I am good looking" I should expect it to happen.' (quoted in Baker, 2000)	Supports inequalities by denying, minimising and trivialising their consequences	Isolation, vulnerability, increased risk of further abuse; and of being harmed not helped by mental health services	Alienation and dehumanisation

Table 20.2   (continued)

Practices and processes	Function	Risks for women	Risks for men
Deference 'You know so much more than I do; so tell me, what should I do?' (quoted in Burstow, 1992)	Supports inequalities by giving power and authority to others	Internalisation of feelings of inferiority; loss of power and control and associated risk that this will be abused; acceptance of psychiatric authority	Overburdened by feelings of responsibility; personal development impeded by limited feedback from others; inflated sense of importance and entitlement; difficulty seeking help
Discrimination 'I went to see a psychiatric nurse who was assessing me. She was completely homophobic. . . she was so rude to me and so horrible to me. . . and I was very, very vulnerable and I thought I just can't face it.' (quoted in King & McKeown, 2003) 'Coming to this country (from Jamaica). . . working and working to bring up your family and every day being treated like that, people looking down at you.' (quoted in ReSisters, 2002)	Maintains and accentuates existing inequalities, may be unconscious or conscious	Blocks opportunities; limits access to valued resources; increases exposure to conditions that are damaging Denigrating views may be internalised, with implications for self-validation and social support Fear of seeking help from services	Can erode self-respect and personal integrity Fear of seeking help from services

(continued overleaf)

GENDER INEQUALITY AND MENTAL HEALTH

Table 20.2 *(continued)*

Practices and processes	Function	Risks for women	Risks for men
Exploitation and abuse 'The psychiatric problems have stemmed from the way I was treated as a child – physically abused by my mother, sexually abused when I was 10, raped when I was in care at 13, raped by other males in care when I was a bit older.' (quoted in ReSisters, 2002)	Validates and takes advantage of an inequality – this can also occur in the context of provider/user relationships in mental health services	Damage to sense of self; dissociation; alienation, chronic exhaustion	Alienation from meaningful intimacy, dissociation, damage to sense of male self, reluctance to express distress and seek help
Intimidation and coercion 'We have a catalogue of instances of intimidation, bullying, sexual harrassment, assault and rape of women by men patients.' (quoted in WISH, 2000)	Use of fear to preserve existing power relations	Erosion of self; feelings of fear and of being trapped and helpless	Objectifies self and others, prefers to see self as victim rather than perpetrator
Marginalisation 'Women's mental health issues appear to have a lower status and services rely heavily on professional having a personal interest.' (quoted in Williams, LeFrancois & Copperman, 2001)	Supports inequality by limiting power of disadvantaged groups	Not being heard or taken seriously	Limited access to relevant knowledge and understanding

Table 20.2   *(continued)*

Practices and processes	Function	Risks for women	Risks for men
Medicalisation and individuation 'Our needs are ignored, we are treated as illnesses.' (quoted in Williams, LeFrancois & Copperman, 2001)	Supports inequality by identifying a person or group as the problem, not inequality	Decreases chances of recovery Increases chances of experiencing further oppression and trauma	Curtails understanding, creativity and optimism
Normalisation 'Pathologising women who do not follow gender norms in lifestyle/behaviour.' (quoted in Williams, LeFrancois & Copperman, 2001)	Validates inequality and punishes deviance; normalises abuses of power	Constrains personal development and expression of anger – limits ways of coping	Constrains personal development and expression of vulnerability – limits ways of coping
Objectification (sexualisation, racialisation etc.) 'When I was in the 4th grade (at the crippled children's school), a man began to trap me in the hall and say sexual things as well as touch me inappropriately.' (quoted in Nosek *et al.*, 2001)	Power advantage embedded in inequalities is used to exploit the least powerful	Poor self-image; self-blame; risk of exposure to traumatic experience These experiences can be intensified within psychiatric services (Cohen, 1994; Keating *et al.*, 2002; Williams, Scott & Bressington, 2004)	False sense of entitlement; alienation from meaningful intimacy

(continued overleaf)

Table 20.2   (continued)

Practices and Processes	Function	Risks for Women	Risks for Men
Projection 'Klein's theories about projection, where an individual projects his/her own intolerable feelings into the other, are central to an understanding of the relationship between bully and target.' (Martin, 2004)	Power advantage embedded in inequalities used to get rid of unwanted feeling	Justification for male violence Resentful and demoralised staff can displace feelings onto patients	Detrimental to self-development and the possibility of genuinely caring about people
Resistance, challenge and change 'When people are pushed hard and when they're treated in a brutally unjust way, the reaction is sometimes the opposite of what you might expect. Sometimes the worm turns.' (Parris, cited in Pyke, 2004)	People from disadvantaged groups survive by being knowledgeable about the workings of the more powerful – in some conditions this leads to collective action	Can lead to personal empowerment	An opportunity for personal and moral development, i.e. to come to terms with the past and to take responsibility for our behaviour

An earlier version of this table appeared in Williams and Keating (2005) and is reproduced here by permission of the Sainsbury Centre for Mental Health.

▶ Exploitation

Access to opportunities and resources

So far, we have primarily focused attention on the mental health risks that men and women encounter as a result of gender socialisation as mediated by the impact on identity and associated psychological processes. It is also important to be alert to the systematic ways in which gender inequality patterns our lives and access to resources known to promote mental health, which include money, work, friendship, leisure, sleep and space. Data that can be used to explore these issues is readily available through government Web sites, social science research and advocacy organisations. This type of data is additionally valuable in alerting us to the ways in which gender effects are amplified by other inequalities such as those based on race, class, disability and sexuality; most people using statutory mental health services are surviving the cumulative effects of multiple forms of oppression and exploitation.

To illustrate, in Table 20.3 we summarise data that reminds us of the ways in which gender inequality and mental health can be mediated by poverty. Familiarity with this and other relevant research (e.g. Williams & Keating, 2005) is helpful in sensitising us to the issues that may be of importance to women and men, and which need to inform our thinking when talking to women and men about their lives, and when planning services to meet their needs.

The advantages of being born male are in the form of ownership rights, prestige, social status and employment. All these privileges have the potential to mediate mental health. For example, it is still the case that women, rather than men, shoulder the larger part of the burdens of domestic and child-care responsibilities regardless of their employment status. The income of married men tends to be greater than their female partners. Indeed, marriage as an institution owes its origins to the passing on of 'ownership' from father to husband. In many countries this is still very much the case. In the UK the process of gradual reform has led us to the point where it was only in the last decade that rape within marriage was recognised as a crime against the person. Male socialisation encourages men to believe that they are entitled to have their physical and psychological needs met by women, and to feel justified in their responses when thwarted. Hence, it is not surprising to find that home life

Table 20.3 Poverty is gendered

Poverty has a well known and well understood potential to undermine mental health, and a gender analysis reveals:

■ That women are more likely to be poor than men (Bradshaw 2003) because:

  – The jobs women do tend to be lower paid and of lower status.

  – Women are more likely to work part-time and to take time out of the labour market to bring up children.

  – They are more likely to be lone parents (25% of British families are headed by a lone parent and 90% of these are women) and to find it very difficult to work because of child-care responsibilities.

  – Women's disadvantages in the labour market also affect them in retirement: their entitlement to the basic pension is lower than men's at every age, and they are less likely to have an occupational pension.

■ Lone mothers and older single women are most likely to experience poverty (Equal Opportunities Commission, 2006).

■ Social attitudes towards young, single mothers on benefits are especially punitive (Bradshaw *et al.*, 2003).

commonly provides a better context for men's mental health than for women's (Cotton, 1999).

Exposure to emotional, physical and sexual abuse

The existence of structural inequalities creates opportunities for very serious abuses of power: abuses of power that also contribute to maintaining gender inequality by helping to keep women in their place. Gender inequality underpins commonly held beliefs among men that they should have their needs – including their sexual needs – met by women: that what they do or want takes precedence over the needs of women, and that their prerogatives should not be questioned. This sense of entitlement has been linked to rape, domestic violence, sexual abuse of children and sexual harassment. Physical and sexual violence and abuse, perpetrated overwhelmingly by men, are common and sometimes covertly sanctioned means of expressing and maintaining dominance in family and community settings. It is estimated that globally, one third of women have been beaten, coerced into sex or subjected to extreme emotional abuse (Heise, Ellsberg & Gottemoeller, 1999). The mental health implications of these forms of power abuse are becoming more widely acknowledged (e.g. Department of Health, 2002, 2003).

▶ Survival

The ways in which women and men survive the demands, deprivations and traumas of their lives are gendered. Evident differences in the prevalence and patterning of distress are unsurprising. As noted above, gender socialisation affects our responses and adaptations to such difficulties. Angry, demanding woman are deviant, as are tearful men who don't have control over their lives. Hence it is not surprising to find differences in pathways into, and out of, mental health services. Or indeed, to find women expressing their mental health needs in relationships and men keeping their misery hidden, or using aggression as the vehicle for expressing a range of emotions.

Women's training in relationships prepares them to provide services to others. It also enables them to give and receive help from each other with relative ease: group work with women is a well-trialled effective intervention. In contrast, gender socialisation makes it harder for men to be party to healing relationships, and group work does not have the same legitimacy. These gendered differences are also played out in inpatient services, where staff readily name the different demands of working on a male or female ward, but usually lack the training they need to make use of these observations (Scott & Williams, 2004).

Gender inequality is not only embedded in family life but in all social institutions, including mental health services. This can be detected in differential responses to the gendered needs and challenging behaviours of women and men using services. Misogyny is commonplace, as is collusion with denial of male distress. Hence a willingness to examine and question these unspoken ingredients of service culture is one of the hallmarks of an effective service.

▶ An opaque system

Gender inequality is a significant mental health hazard, which often causes harm in conjunction with other social inequalities such as those based on class, disability, age and race. Unpicking concepts such as oppression and exploitation helps us to appreciate their potential to compromise our mental health, and to build respect for the strategies individuals use to survive.

It is also evident that gender inequality persists because it is a feature of our social world and our personal lives that easily fades into the background and becomes part and parcel of normal life and working practices. To be effective mental health managers and workers, we must be willing to engage with these issues: to name gender inequality and be willing to discover and address its workings.

▶ Concluding thoughts

In this chapter we have sketched the main links that tie the current system of gender inequality to our mental health. These are the links we need to have in our minds when planning, managing and directly providing mental health services. While we find that many people working in the field agree with this statement, it rarely happens in practice. The central paradox is that addressing these issues reveals the working of inequalities and places us in conflict with the social status quo; resistance is encountered at every turn. Whether we like it or not, we are engaged in a political process. As yet, gender and other inequalities have not secured a central place in the training and preparation of the work force, and the dominance of medical and individualistic ideologies make it hard to define or defend other realities. Yet achieving this change is crucial. If staff don't have a well-grounded understanding of the workings and effects of gender and other inequalities, what can they hope to offer clients and patients?

▶ References

Addis, M. & Mahalik, J. (2003) Men, masculinity, and the contexts of help seeking. *American Psychologist*, **58**(1): 5–14.

Artazcoz, L., Benach, J., Borrell, C. & Cortès, I. (2004) Unemployment and mental health: Understanding the interactions among gender, family roles, and social class. *American Journal of Public Health*, **94**(1): 82–8.

Baker, S. (2000) *Environmentally Friendly? Patients' Views of Conditions on Psychiatric Wards*. London: Mind Publications.

Baker-Miller, J. (1976) *Towards a New Psychology of Women*. London: Sage.

Barron, J. (2004) *Struggle to Survive: Challenges for Delivering Services on Mental Health, Substance Misuse and Domestic Violence*. Bristol: Women's Aid Federation of England.

Bernardez, T. (1996) Women's therapy groups as the treatment of choice. In B. DeChant (ed.), *Women and Group Psychotherapy: Theory and Practice* (Chapter 9). London: Guilford Press.

Bradshaw, J., Finch, N., Kemp, P.A., Mayhew, E. & Williams, J. (2003). *Gender and Poverty in Britain*. London: Equal Opportunities Commission.

Burstow, B. (1992) Working with psychiatric survivors. In B. Burstow (ed.), *Radical Feminist Therapy: Working in the Context of Violence*. London: Sage.

Busfield, J. (1982) Gender and mental illness. *International Journal of Mental Health*, **11**: 46–66.

Canadian Mental Health Association (2004) *Men's Mental Health: A Silent Crisis*. www.canadian-health-network.ca/servlet/ContentServer?cid=1074435638245&pagename =CHN-RCS/CHNResource/CHNResourcePageTemplate&c=CHNResource, retrieved 11.03.07.

Cann, K., Withnell, S., Shakespeare, J., Doll, H. & Thomas, J. (2001) Domestic violence: A comparative survey of levels of detection, knowledge and attitudes in healthcare workers. *Public Health*, **115**: 89–95.

Chesler, C. (1972) *Women and Madness*. New York: Doubleday.

Chief Nursing Officer (2006) *From Values to Action: The Chief Nursing Officer's Review of Mental Health Nursing*. London: Department of Health.

Cohen, L. J. (1994). Psychiatric hospitalization as an experience of trauma. *Archives of Psychiatric Nursing*, **8(2)**, 78–81.

Cotton, S. (1999) Marital status and mental health revisited: Examining the importance of risk factors and resources. *Family Relations*, **48**(3): 225–33.

Department of Health (2002) *Women's Mental Health: Into the Mainstream – Strategic Development of Mental Health Care for Women*. London: Department of Health, www.doh.gov.uk/mentalhealth/women.htm.

Department of Health (2003) *Mainstreaming Gender and Women's Mental Health: Implementation Guidance*. London: Department of Health. Obtain free of charge from PO Box 777, London SE1 6XH, or download from www.doh.gov.uk/mentalhealth.

Department of Health (2005) *Supporting Women into the Mainstream: Commissioning Women-only Community Day Services*. London: Department of Health.

Department of Health/Home Office (2005) *Tackling the Health and Mental Health Effects of Domestic and Sexual Violence and Abuse*. London: Department of Health.

Dobash, R.P., Dobash, R.E., Wilson, M. & Daly, M. (1992) The myth of sexual symmetry in marital violence. *Social Problems*, **39**: 71–91.

Equal Opportunities Commission (2006) *Facts about Women and Men in Great Britain*. London: EOC.

Gilman, C.P. (1899) *The Yellow Wallpaper*. Boston, MA: Small and Maynard.

Good, G.E., Thomson, D.A. & Brathwaite, A.D. (2005) Men and therapy: Critical concepts, theoretical frameworks, and research recommendations. *Journal of Clinical Psychology*, **61**(6): 699–711.

Heise, L., Ellsberg, M. & Gottemoeller, M. (1999) *Ending Violence Against Women*, Population Reports, Series, L, 11. Baltimore, MD: John Hopkins University School of Public Health.

Humphreys, C. & Thiara, R. (2003) Mental health and domestic violence: 'I call it symptoms of abuse'. *British Journal of Social Work*, **33**(2): 209–26.

Hurst, S.A. (1999) Legacy of betrayal: A grounded theory of becoming demoralized from the perspective of women who have been depressed. *Canadian Psychology*, **40**(2): 179–91.

Jack D.C. (1991). *Silencing the Self: Women and Depression*. Cambridge, MA: Harvard University Press.

Keating, F., Robertson, D., Francis, F. & McCulloch, A. (2002) *Breaking the Circles of Fear. A Review of the Relationship between Mental Health Services and African and Caribbean Communities*. London: Sainsbury Centre for Mental Health.

Kimmel, M. (2004). We are our own worst enemy – and women's. In *Improving the Health of Men+Women*. London: EOC/King's Fund/Women's Health/Men's Health Forum/DH/European Men's Health.

King, M. & McKeown, E. (2003) *Mental Health and Social Wellbeing of Gay Men, Lesbians and Bisexuals in England and Wales*. London: Mind.

Martin, S. (2004) *A Psychological Understanding of Mutual Influence in Men's Abuse of Female Partners*. Canterbury: Tizard Centre, University of Kent.

McCreary, D. (2004) *Men's Mental Health: A Silent Crisis*. Toronto: Men's Health Network, www.canadian-health-network.ca/servlet/ContentServer?cid=1074435638245& pagename= CHN-RCS%2FCHNResource%2FCHNResourcePageTemplate&c=CHN Resource, retrieved 09.07.07.

Men's Health Forum (2006) *Mind Your Head*. London: Men's Health Forum.

Miller, J. & McClelland, L. (2006) Social inequalities formulation: Mad, bad and dangerous to know. In L. Johnstone & R. Dallos (eds), *Formulation in Psychology and Psychotherapy: Making Sense of People's Problems*. Hove: Routledge.

Mind (2000) *Men's Mental Health*. London: Mind Publications.

Nosek, M.A., Clubb, C.F., Hughes, R.B. & Howland, C.A. (2001) Vulnerabilities for abuse among women with disabilities. *Sexuality and Disability*, **19**(2): 177–89.

[1]Pyke, N. (2004). Alan Bennett comes out fighting as he recounts the night he was. *The Independent on Sunday*. Oct 31.

Peace, P. (2003) Balancing power: The discursive maintenance of gender inequality by wo/men at university. *Feminism and Psychology*, **13**(2): 159–80.

Penfold, P.S. & Walker, G.A. (1984) *Women and the Psychiatric Paradox*. Milton Keynes: Open University Press.

ReSisters (2002) *Women Speak Out*. Leeds: ReSisters.

Rodman Aronson, K.M. & Schaler Bucholz, E. (2001) The post-feminist era: Still striving for equality in relationships. *American Journal of Family Therapy*, **29**(2): 109–24.

Rosenfield, S. & Pottick, K.J. (2005) Power, gender and the self: Reflections on improving mental health for males and females. In S.A. Kirk (ed.), *Mental Disorders in the Social Environment*. New York: Columbia University Press.

Scattolon, Y. & Stoppard, J.M. (1999) 'Getting on with life': Women's experiences and ways of coping with depression. *Canadian Psychology*, **40**(2): 205–19.

Scott, S. & Williams, J. (2004) Closing the gap between evidence and practice: The role of training in transforming women's services. In N.J.T. Watson (ed.), *Working Therapeutically with Women in Secure Mental Health Settings*. London: Jessica Kingsley.

Scottish Executive (2005) *National Programme for Improving Mental Health and Well-Being: Addressing Mental Health Inequalities in Scotland: Equal Minds*. Edinburgh: Scottish Executive.

Watkins, B. & Bentovin, A. (1992) The sexual abuse of male children and adolescents: A review of current research. *Journal of Child Psychology and Psychiatry and Allied Disciplines*, **33**: 197–248.

White, J.W. & Kowalski, R.M. (1998) Male violence toward women: An integrated perspective.In R. Geen & E. Donnerstein (eds), *Human Aggression: Theories, Research, and Implications for Social Policy*. New York: Academic Press.

Williams, J. & Keating, F. (2005) Social inequalities and mental health: An integrative approach. In A. Bell (ed.), *Beyond the Water Towers: The Unfinished Revolution in Mental Health Services 1985–2005*. London: Sainsbury Centre for Mental Health.

Williams, J., LeFrancois, B. & Copperman, J. (2001) *Mental Health Services that Work for Women: Survey Findings*. Canterbury: Tizard Centre, University of Kent.

Williams, J., Scott, S. & Bressington, C. (2004) Dangerous journeys: Women's pathways through secure services. In N. Jeffcote & T. Watson (eds), *Working Therapeutically with Women in Secure Settings*. London: Jessica Kingsley.

---

[1] Parris is quoted in this report.

WISH (2000) *Minutes of Evidence Submitted to the Select Committee on Health.* London: House of Commons.

World Health Organisation (2000) *Women's Mental Health: An Evidence Based Review.* Geneva: World Health Organisation.

▶ **An answer to Exercise 20.1**

This is a very effective device for involving everyone in the gender socialisation of babies and guarantees their exposure to gender-typed expectations, attitudes and behaviour from the start. There is pressure to conform to this practice; it is obviously voluntary, but we can be made to feel churlish or irresponsible for not complying.

The trauma model of psychosis

Paul Hammersley
School of Nursing, Midwifery and Social Work, Manchester University

Peter Bullimore
Survivor activist

Magdalen Fiddler
Manchester University

John Read
University of Auckland, New Zealand

It would be incorrect to suggest that there is a single model of the relationship between traumatic life events and psychosis. A truer picture would be to suggest that there are a number of competing models of trauma and psychosis that interact with each other. However, these models all have one critical feature at their core: all attempt to address the overemphasis on biology in the traditional stress vulnerability model.

This chapter will outline the evidence base for trauma models, consider explanations for why this relationship exists and offer potential therapeutic solutions. Critical questions will be asked to reinforce the factors involved. The chapter will conclude with the real-life case history of Peter Bullimore from the UK Hearing Voices Network, who has made a full recovery from a trauma-induced psychosis.

▶ Stress vulnerability – A good idea is hijacked

The history of psychiatry shows a clear shift in thinking when biological psychiatry became pre-eminent. In the mid to late 1800s dramatic developments in

Learning About Mental Health Practice. Edited by Theo Stickley and Thurstine Basset
© 2008 John Wiley & Sons, Ltd

neurology led to the discovery that pellagra (a neurological disorder caused by severe vitamin deficiency and general paresis of the insane or syphilis of the brain) caused observable psychiatric symptoms. This convinced a number of prominent professionals that many – if not all – mental health problems had a medical basis, and that irrational or abnormal behaviour was caused by disease of the brain (Weitz, 1983). This led to a fruitless search for biological explanations of psychosis that has lasted over a century and continues today.

In the late 1970s and early 1980s a new model of psychosis was proposed that soon received widespread attention. The stress vulnerability model (Neuchterlein & Dawson, 1984; Zubin & Spring, 1977) suggested that psychosis arose from a combination of personal vulnerability factors and stressful life events or environmental factors. Biological psychiatry and the pharmaceutical industry responded to this new threat by effectively hijacking it (Read *et al.*, 2004). Individual vulnerability was deemed to be genetic and crucial life events were reduced to the marginal status of triggers. The originators of the stress vulnerability models never proposed that the vulnerability side of the equation was purely genetic and, quite correctly, subsequent research has shown that a number of environmental factors can make someone vulnerable to psychosis, including childhood abuse (Bentall, 2003; Read & Hammersley, 2005), smoking cannabis (Henquet *et al.*, 2005), poverty (Read *et al.*, 2004) and living in a city (van Os, Pedersen & Mortensen, 2004). Quite why biological psychiatry was so keen to distort the stress vulnerability model of psychosis is unclear. However, the fact that international sales of Olanzepine alone were worth $4.4 billion in 2004 may offer something of an explanation.

▶ Trauma and vulnerability to psychosis

The role of traumatic life events in psychosis has only emerged as a subject of serious study over the last five to ten years. Why has it taken us so long to face up to this obvious connection? The answer comes in four parts:

- The influence of psychoanalysis.
- Denial of the scale of the problem.
- Denial of the significance of the problem.
- Marginalisation of psychosis

The influence of psychoanalysis

Sigmund Freud who trained as a neurologist before developing psychodynamic theory almost made the connection between serious trauma in childhood and subsequent serious mental health problems in adulthood over 100 years ago. Almost, but not quite. His early writings were in keeping with many modern trauma theories. Molon (1996) points out that Freud, in his essay 'Inhibitions, symptoms and Anxiety', makes it clear that:

> Children who are repeatedly sexually abused with the accompaniment of violence or threats of violence if they resist or tell, are chronically in a position of helplessness in the face of overwhelming excitation. Emergency mental defences are brought into play. (Molon, 1996, p. 17)

Molon further describes how childhood sexual abuse according to Freud in his early work created an intense emotional time bomb, which would be triggered with the onset of puberty and lead to a severe psychological reaction in later life. However Freud, under intense pressure from his peers, soon changed his mind. Reports of childhood trauma were not viewed as expressions of genuine experience, but as projections and fantasies. Thus for much of the 20th Century in the then pre-eminent Freudian psychoanalytic theory, reports of childhood trauma were (with rare exceptions such as Sandor Ferenczi) thought to be about as significant as dreams.

Denial of the scale of the problem

Coupled with this denial of the truthfulness of reports of childhood trauma was a failure on behalf of the medical, legal and political professions to accept that such a problem existed and was worthy of any investigation. As recently as 1975 in the USA, *The Comprehensive Textbook of Psychiatry* estimated the prevalence of incest in America to be one per million of the population (Hammersley, Burston & Read, 2004). The actual prevalence of sexual abuse in the population is these days known to be closer to one in four females and one in six to eight boys (Sanderson, 2006). The staggering scale of the discrepancy between these two figures demonstrates clearly the level of complacency and denial that was commonplace in attitudes to childhood trauma until relatively recently.

Denial of the significance of the problem

The establishment was forced to take the issue of the prevalence of childhood trauma seriously, largely as a consequence of the emerging feminist movement who forced it onto the agenda (for a full historical review see Armstrong, 1996). The response was an acceptance that childhood trauma was more prevalent than had previously been thought, but a denial that it was a particularly significant problem in that the consequences were minimal. For example, it was common that if childhood trauma was revealed, it was often not mentioned in legal or medical reports.Mendel (1995) reported that in the USA when legislation was passed making the reporting of childhood trauma mandatory, reported cases of sexual abuse rose from 6000 in 1976 to 500 000 in 1992.

The marginalisation of psychosis

Finally by the 1990s the situation had changed markedly. Reports of childhood trauma were no longer regarded as fantasies: the true and shocking prevalence figures were accepted, as were the major long-term consequences of severe trauma in particular. Trauma was accepted as playing a key role in anxiety, depression, substance misuse, eating disorders, dissociative conditions and personality disorder, along with a myriad of physical health problems (Read *et al.*, 2005; Van der Kolk, 1994). However, for one group of service users, traumatic life events continued to be regarded as either imagined or irrelevant. The psychoses were still considered to be genetically determined, biologically driven chronic diseases of the brain, in the development of which traumatic life events played no part.

In the second part of this chapter we will review the evidence that challenged this belief.

Critical questions

1. Which model of psychosis replaced the purely medical model in the 1970s?

2. How did Freud's opinion change in his later work?

3. What was the prevalence estimate for incest in the 1975 *Comprehensive Textbook of Psychiatry*?

4. Which group of service users continued to be told that life events were irrelevant to their problems up until the last 5–10 years.

Traumatic life events and psychosis: the evidence

Two important points need to be made before discussing the relationship between childhood trauma and psychosis. First, much of the discussion so far has concerned childhood sexual abuse. However, sexual abuse is not the only traumatic event that may befall a child. Physical abuse, emotional abuse and neglect can have equally serious consequences (Romme, 2006). Secondly we are not claiming that the relationship between trauma and psychosis is 1:1. Many individuals are traumatised in childhood and do not develop psychosis; similarly, many individuals who display psychotic symptoms have not experienced childhood trauma. It is vital to make this point to avoid the situation that occurred in the 1960s where families of individuals with psychosis were often blamed for the problem. Nevertheless, the correlation is remarkably robust. Full reviews of the relationship between trauma and psychosis can be found elsewhere (Read *et al.*, 2005; Larkins & Morrison, 2006). For the purposes of this chapter we will briefly cover the smaller early studies and the five major later studies.

▶ Early studies

The early studies looked at very diverse populations (children, general population samples, adult psychiatric inpatients, homeless populations etc.). As is often the case in pioneering research, many of these studies were hampered by problems such as small sample size and poor study design due to financial restrictions, but their findings prompted further attention. Livingston (1987) found that in children admitted to a psychiatric unit, over 75% who had been abused were diagnosed as psychotic, as opposed to a diagnosis of psychosis for only 10% of the non-abused. Read and Argyle (1999) conducted a chart review of the notes of 100 psychiatric patients and found again that over 75% of individuals who reported a history of childhood abuse experienced one or more symptoms of schizophrenia. Reports of abuse are particularly strongly reported to be related to first-rank or 'Schneiderian' positive symptoms of psychosis. Ross and Joshi (1992) reported that in a large community sample, 45% of those who reported childhood abuse experienced three or more first-rank symptoms, compared with only 8% when no childhood abuse was reported. The first review of such studies was conducted by Goodman *et al.* (1997), who reviewed 13 studies that were deemed to be methodologically adequate. This review reported consistently higher levels of child abuse in women receiving treatment for psychotic illness.

An overview of the early studies of the relationship between childhood trauma and psychosis shows four findings that recur repeatedly:

1. There is a strong correlation between childhood abuse and psychotic symptoms in adulthood.

2. There is a particularly strong correlation between childhood sexual abuse and auditory hallucinations in adulthood.

3. There is a clear dose effect; that is, the more severe or the more frequent the trauma, the more likely it is that psychosis is reported.

4. Post-traumatic features and dissociation are common in psychotic trauma survivors.

▶ Later studies

Growing interest in this field led to the development of large-scale studies, with far better designs and data collection. Five in particular are worthy of mention.

Janssen et al. (2003)

This study analysed carefully derived data about childhood trauma in a non-psychotic Dutch population sample of 4085 people. It is important that the sample were non-psychotic, as this removes the problem of whether or not to believe retrospective reports of trauma in individuals who are psychotic. The researchers re-interviewed the sample three times over three years. They knew that in such a large group, a percentage of people would develop a psychosis over time. The results were startling. The individuals who had reported childhood trauma were far more likely to develop into psychosis. The dose effect was also present. Men who reported the most severe forms of abuse were 49 times more likely to cross over into psychosis.

Bebbington et al. (2004)

This was a large-scale population study of 8580 participants conducted by Paul Bebbington at the Institute of Psychiatry in London. This study used a standardised interview to collect data on psychotic symptoms and experience of lifetime trauma. The traumas were defined as re-victimisation experiences and were as follows: childhood sexual abuse, bullying, running away from home, time in local authority care, time in a children's institution, expulsion from school, homelessness, violence at work or serious injury or assault. The results again were clear. All but one of the victimisation experiences (running away from home) were correlated with subsequent psychosis; again, childhood sexual abuse had the strongest correlation. The researchers concluded that the relationship between childhood trauma and psychosis may be causal:

> In people with psychosis there is a marked excess of victimising experiences, many of which will have occurred in childhood, this is suggestive of a social contribution to the aetiology of psychosis. (Bebbington *et al.*, 2004, p. 22)

Whitfield et al. (2005), The ACE study

This was a very similar study to the Bebbington study, but was conducted on a larger scale, covering 17 377 participants from San Diego. In this study, prevalence of psychotic symptoms was analysed in relationship to adverse childhood experiences (ACEs). The adverse childhood experiences were very similar to Bebbington's victimisation experiences and consisted of emotional abuse, physical abuse, sexual abuse, battered mother, household drug or alcohol use, mental illness in household, parental separation or divorce, incarceration of a household member. The results again are consistent with previous findings: a strong relationship between trauma and subsequent psychosis, a clear dose effect (seven or more ACEs makes adult psychosis five times more likely), and in particular a very strong relationship between childhood adversity and hallucinations in adulthood. In fact, the authors concluded that the relationship between childhood trauma and hallucinations was so strong that 'Hallucinations may be a marker for prior childhood trauma that may underlie other common health problems'. In other words, hallucinations point to the presence of possible childhood trauma as opposed to schizophrenia.

Spauwen et al. (2006)

In this study, which was similar in some ways to the Janssen study, 2524 adolescents provided self-reports of psychological trauma and proneness to psychosis. They were then followed up and re-interviewed on average 24 months later. Once again there was a significant correlation between trauma and the emergence of psychotic symptoms. In this study the dose effect was particularly strong. The importance of both dissociation and post-traumatic stress disorder emerged in this study, as psychosis was strongly associated with trauma that caused intense fear, helplessness or horror. In this study the trauma exerting the strongest effect was natural catastrophe followed by physical threat. Sexual abuse had a lower effect than in the other studies. This may have been because the measurement of sexual trauma did not take timing, duration or severity into account.

Spataro et al. (2004)

Of all the five main studies this is probably the most interesting, in that at first glance it appears to contradict the findings of the other four studies. The Spataro study was designed to establish the absolute truth of the reports of childhood trauma in order to remove the possibility of unreliable retrospective self-reports. To achieve this, the researchers collected reports of childhood abuse from police and court records in Victoria, Australia, thus ensuring that all reports were genuine. These individuals were then followed up as adults to measure the presence of psychotic symptoms. They were then compared with a general population control group. The authors reported no significant relationship between childhood trauma and adult psychosis, a clear deviation from previous findings. However, the authors also reported that they were puzzled by the fact that they could also find no relationship between childhood trauma and subsequent adult drug and alcohol misuse, as there is a very commonly reported relationship between the two. This suggests that there is something unusual going on. There are indeed some problems with this study, including the presence of unrecorded trauma in the general population, and in particular the fact that the assessment of the presence of psychosis in men in this study was made when they were in their early 20s, which is simply too young.

These are, however, not the main problems. We have argued elsewhere (Read & Hammersley, 2005, 2006) that the main strength of this study is also its greatest weakness. The fact that the sample of participants was drawn from police and court records means that they will have been taken out of the abusive situation, and/or given assistance to recover. We argue that rather than show that there is no relationship between childhood trauma and psychosis, this study demonstrates that removing a child from a traumatic situation, and offering that child help, may prevent the onset of psychosis (and drug and alcohol misuse) in later life.

Critical questions

1. What are the three recurring findings from the early studies?

2. Name three or more diagnostic groups where psychotic symptoms appear in which childhood trauma has a correlation.

3. In the Janssen *et al.* (2003) study, which sub-group of individuals was 49 times more likely to experience psychosis following abuse?

4. What is Read and Hammersley's main objection to the Spataro *et al.* (2004) study?

▶ Explanatory models of how childhood trauma may lead to psychosis

As has been stated previously, no single model of the relationship between trauma and psychosis exists. The following are the main models that have been presented to date.

PTSD model (Jankowski, Meuser & Rosenberg, 2006)

This model, originally developed by Kim Meuser, is the closest to the current medical model understanding of schizophrenia and therefore is more acceptable to some. Meuser argues that schizophrenia is a real condition that has many outcomes from the benign to the chronic. The effect of severe trauma in someone diagnosed with schizophrenia, he argues, is to push a potentially mild clinical presentation into a much more severe arena with a far worse outcome. A clear analogy is made with substance misuse, which is known to worsen recovery rates in any medical or psychiatric diagnosis. Meuser suggests that the experience of severe trauma affects individuals diagnosed with schizophrenia in three ways: first, they are more likely to experience co-morbid post-traumatic stress disorder (Meuser, 1999); secondly, they are more likely to experience co-morbid substance misuse; finally, it is known that individuals who have experienced childhood trauma are more likely to experience further trauma in adulthood. Essentially, the model suggests that trauma makes a bad situation worse through a series of feedback loops that are very hard to escape. The strength of this model is the research evidence that exists to support it. The weakness, according to opponents, is that it continues to discuss schizophrenia as if it was a meaningful construct when it is not (Bentall, 2003; Read *et al.*, 2005), and ignores or minimises the evidence that trauma can cause as well as just worsen psychosis.

Dissociation models (Romme, 2006; Ross, 2005)

In the 1980s a highly influential model was proposed by British researcher Tim Crow (1980), who suggested that schizophrenia takes two forms. One, dominated by negative symptoms such as withdrawal and communication problems, he sought to explain in terms of abnormalities in brain structure. The second form was dominated by positive symptoms such as hallucinations and bizarre ideas, and was explained by chemical disregulation of the dopamine system.

Some influential trauma researchers accept Crow's observation of a clear distinction in presentation, but offer an entirely different explanation. Colin Ross, an American psychiatrist, has argued (Ross, 2005) that our understanding of schizophrenia and the relationship between trauma and schizophrenia is based on a fundamental misunderstanding.

There are some people (mainly men) who have a distinct clinical presentation. They may have been clumsy and non-communicative as children and may have often missed, or been late to arrive at, developmental milestones. These children are frequently noticed at an early age by teachers, who are very accurate in identification (Mendick et al., 1998). The clinical presentation in adulthood appears to be on a continuum with autism or Asperger's syndrome, with the most common reported problems being thought disorder, isolation, poor communication and difficulties with theory of mind (the ability to understand the mental states or even facial expressions of others).

An entirely different group also exists, mainly, but not exclusively, women. In this group childhood trauma is a crucial factor, and there is a dose effect. For this group of individuals the clinical presentation is completely different. Negative symptoms and thought disorder are almost entirely absent. Overwhelmingly, this large group reports auditory hallucinations, often of a critical nature, post-traumatic symptoms such as hyper-vigilance and re-experience phenomena. Self-harm and substance misuse are common. Ross argues that to diagnose both groups as 'schizophrenic' and to offer identical treatments is not just scientific nonsense but morally unacceptable. A potential solution may be the creation of an entirely new diagnosis, dissociative psychosis, which would recognise the importance of traumatic life events and offer psychotherapy rather than medication and case management.

Across the Atlantic, and for slightly different reasons, Professor Marius Romme from the Netherlands arrived at the same conclusion (Romme & Escher, 2000). After extensive work with 'voice hearers', Romme and his collaborator Sandra Escher (Romme & Escher, 1989) found that there is a clear, large and identifiable sub-group of individuals who experience psychotic symptoms for whom childhood and lifetime trauma is key to their experience. Romme and Escher suggest that coming to terms with the relationship between adverse life events is key to recovery for many people. In addition, most people who do recover do so outside of mainstream psychiatry, and through the assistance of friends or organisations such as the Hearing Voices Network. Romme has called for a new diagnostic criterion of traumatic psychosis, which is slightly different to Ross's dissociative psychosis, but based on very similar observations.

The catastrophic interaction model (Fowler et al., 2006)

A particularly sophisticated account of the relationship between traumatic life events and psychosis offered to date comes from David Fowler and colleagues. The catastrophic interaction model suggests that there are three routes by which severe trauma may lead to psychosis. The first route involves direct and indirect links between intrusive trauma memories that directly reflect previous trauma. The second involves information-processing biases that result from trauma, and cause traumatised individuals to over-estimate danger, under-estimate their own ability to cope and, most significantly, reach very firm conclusions about the nature of danger on the basis of little information (conclusion jumping). The third route involves hallucinations. It is suggested that negative opinions about oneself and habitual ruminations about relationships with previous abusive figures can give rise to distress about hallucinations rather than a more benign interpretation.

All of these processes can occur individually, however the model suggests that when they occur together (direct memories, information-processing biases and continual rumination about previous abuse experiences), a catastrophic reaction will take place that can end in a psychotic episode. The authors of this model ask for more clear research evidence, but the model holds much promise for direct psychotherapeutic interventions, in that intrusive memories, information biases and rumination and belief about the origin of hallucinations have all been demonstrated to be legitimate targets for treatment using cognitive behavioural techniques.

Critical questions

- With what does Meuser compare the effect of trauma on psychosis?

- Which researcher has called for a new diagnosis of 'dissociative psychosis'?

- What are the three component parts of 'catastrophic interaction hypothesis'?

▶ Trauma and psychosis: a cross-diagnostic phenomenon?

The majority of the content of this chapter so far has concentrated on the relationship between trauma and psychosis in what some would describe as the 'schizophrenia spectrum disorders'. However, these are not the only disorders in which psychotic experiences can occur. Hallucinations and delusional ideas can also occur in the major mood disorders, bipolar disorder and unipolar psychotic depression. This leads to a very interesting question: Are individuals who have experienced major trauma and have subsequently developed a major mood disorder also more likely to report psychotic experiences? If this is the case, it suggests that the relationship between traumatic life events and psychotic experiences is a genuine cross-diagnostic phenomenon, with the potential to affect individuals from different clinical groups.

The evidence to date is limited but extremely intriguing. In our study (Hammersley *et al.*, 2002), four trained cognitive behavioural therapists collected spontaneously disclosed information about lifetime trauma from almost 100 individuals diagnosed with bipolar affective disorder who were participants in a larger randomised control trial. At the same time, trained and supervised research assistants who were blind to the fact that we were collecting data on trauma, collected data on the presence of psychotic symptoms. We then asked the question: Are the participants who reported severe traumatic life events the ones who are also reporting psychotic experiences? The answer was an unequivocal yes, and was almost entirely explained by one factor. The participants who reported childhood sexual abuse were far more likely to experience auditory hallucinations. In fact, all participants who reported severe sexual abuse also reported hallucinations, predominantly critical or 'running commentary' hallucinations in the depressed phase of their mood cycle.

Some commentators found our findings hard to accept. It was suggested that that the hallucinating group must have had higher co-morbid substance misuse or borderline features. Neither was true. It was also suggested that our findings could have been purely random, and that, without a replication, could not be taken at face value. The replication came in the form of a small study conducted by Ruth Fox (Fox & Reid, in press). This study compared participants diagnosed with bipolar disorder who had been traumatised with non-traumatised bipolar participants and a non-psychiatric control group. The results were the same: the traumatised bipolar group reported more psychotic experiences, the relationship between childhood sexual abuse and hallucinations was by far the strongest correlation, and there was a dose effect. These studies need to be further replicated, on a larger scale and with better designs, but there is certainly enough to warrant further investigation.

The small number of studies that have looked at the relationship between trauma and psychotic experiences in major depression follow the same pattern. There is not enough room in this chapter to cover all the findings (for a review see Hammersley & Fox, 2006). The pattern is most clearly demonstrated by a study conducted by Zimmerman and colleagues in 1999. This study looked at 500 participants, some of whom were diagnosed with psychotic depression. Those diagnosed with psychotic depression were more likely to experience co-morbid post-traumatic stress disorder, the most commonly reported trauma was sexual abuse in childhood and the most commonly reported psychotic experience was auditory hallucinations.

Where does this research lead us? The trauma model requires more research. Nevertheless, the literature review conducted by Read and colleagues in 2005 prompted leading British psychologist Oliver James to state that the psychiatric establishment was about to experience an earthquake.

With caution, we can say this:

- There may be a genetic/biological influence on psychosis, but this appears to have been vastly over-estimated and is not specific to psychosis, but is rather a predisposition to be more sensitive to stress and trauma.

- There is certainly an environmental influence on psychosis (including environmental trauma), and this has certainly been under-estimated.

- The relationship between traumatic life events and psychosis does appear to be a causal one with a dose effect.

- The clearest correlation is between childhood sexual abuse and auditory hallucinations.

- Many, but not all, psychotic experiences are not symptoms of an illness as such, but are understandable responses to extreme experiences.

In June 2006 two of us (Read and Hammersley) had the great fortune to be invited to propose the motion 'This house believes that child abuse is a cause of schizophrenia' in a debate at the Institute of Psychiatry in London. After hearing the research evidence that we have summarised earlier, the motion was carried 114 to 52. Jacqui Dillon, the then national chair of the UK Hearing Voices Network, prepared the following press release for the debate:

> In our experience, gained through more than 15 years running a national network, listening to people who hear voices, many of them living with a diagnosis of schizophrenia, it is clear that there is a definite link between traumatic life events and psychosis. On a daily basis, we hear terrible stories of sexual, emotional and physical abuse, and the impact of racism, poverty and stigma on people's lives. We do not seek to reduce people to a set of symptoms that we wish to suppress and control with medication. We show respect for the reality of the trauma they have endured, and bear witness to the suffering they have experienced. We honour people's resilience and capacity to survive often against the odds. The reduction of people's distressing life experiences into a diagnosis of schizophrenia means that they are condemned to lives dulled by drugs and blighted by stigma, and offered no opportunity to make sense of their experiences. Their routes to recovery are hindered. Rather than pathologising individuals, we have a collective responsibility to people who have experienced abuse, to acknowledge the reality and impact of those experiences and support them to get the help they need. Abuse thrives in secrecy. We must expose the truth and not perpetuate injustice further, otherwise today's child abuse victims become tomorrow's psychiatric patients.

▶ Peter's study

Case studies in books like this tend to be anonymous mixtures of the life experiences of various individuals. This is different. Peter Bullimore, a veteran user's rights activist, former head of the Hearing Voices Network and director of Asylum Associates, has agreed to tell his own true story of recovery from trauma-induced psychosis.

My name is Peter Bullimore and I'm a voice hearer. I'm proud to call myself a voice hearer, they're my experiences and I own them. I rejected my diagnosis of paranoid schizophrenia over ten years ago and have made my recovery outside of the psychiatric system. These days I assist others to do the same. This is my story.

My psychosis has its origins in serious and prolonged childhood physical and sexual abuse. I was abused every Friday night by a female baby sitter from the age of 8 up until my middle teens. The abuse was sexual and violent, I was absolutely petrified and would deliberately harm myself on Friday evenings to try and prevent my parents going out. I never told anyone, my abuser said that no one would believe me and I was completely intimidated by her. I did begin to hear voices and go through what I now believe to be dissociative states at the time. These experiences diminished and stopped for a while in my late teens.

At the time of the birth of my first child I was self-employed in the manufacturing trade making iron fireplaces. The business was very successful turning over more than £1 million per year, but I was becoming increasingly stressed. I was working 14 or more hours per day seven days a week and struggling to cope with the new baby. This stress came to a head, the voices started up again, many voices, I could identify my abuser as the dominant voice. I was also experiencing visual hallucinations. On one occasion I saw Freddie Kruger from the *Nightmare on Elm Street* films in the back of my van. In addition my paranoia was worsening and I trusted no one. My fragile psychological state was noticed by a social worker who visited our house for another reason and I was admitted to the local psychiatric unit. So began a 20-year nightmare in the British psychiatric system. I'm not suggesting that everyone has had such a bad experience. I know there are many dedicated staff members out there of all professions, but my personal experience was not good.

I had been expecting that I would be given the chance to talk about my experiences, in fact it was over ten years before anyone asked me about my personal traumas. I was simply told that I had a brain disease, 'paranoid schizophrenia', and that I would never work again. I was prescribed strong anti-psychotic medication with such powerful side effects that I was often unable to move from my bed and saliva dribbled constantly from my mouth. I fell into a pattern of being compulsorily admitted to hospital, over-medicated, discharged, my medication would stop, re-admission and so on. My marriage collapsed and I became homeless, living on the streets for a time. I was also deeply depressed and shut myself away from all human contact. Some people called this behaviour 'negative schizophrenic symptoms'; for me it was more of an emotional shut-down, a bit like going on a life-support machine. I could just about function but I wasn't really there, I had no choice, it was shut down or die.

My recovery story, like those of so many, starts with a turning point. In my case it was the dedication of an occupational therapist who saw something in me, the possibility of recovery perhaps, and refused to give up on me. She helped me with my accommodation and invited me into her life. She was a constant source of support and encouragement. She tried to persuade me to go to a local Hearing Voices Network meeting, I went once, but I didn't go back immediately. I wasn't ready for it, but it must have struck a chord with me because I started to attend the meetings regularly some time later and ended up running them. Through the meetings and the shared experiences with other voice hearers, I began to see that there was a completely different explanation for my experiences than the explanation that mainstream psychiatry had given me, and one that I found much more acceptable. However, I knew that if the recovery was to be complete, I would have to deal with the issue of my abuse.

One of the main residual problems of my childhood abuse, apart from the flashbacks and the voices, were feelings of intense guilt and shame that had been planted in me by my abuser and continued to disturb me. I took a decision, I isolated myself for 48 hours and reviewed my experiences as though it was a court of law, examining evidence and establishing guilt. I found myself 'Not Guilty' and since that day I've never looked back. Through my involvement with the Hearing Voices Network I've had the opportunity to meet radical practitioners such as Alex Jenner, Marius Romme and Sandra Escher. I formed the UK Paranoia Network in 2006 and am a director of Asylum Associates, which campaigns for the rights of service users. I lecture and offer training all over the UK and Europe and am one of the co-founders of CASL – the Campaign for the Abolition of the Schizophrenia Label.

I often wonder what happened to the psychiatrist who told me I had an incurable illness, and that I'd never work again. She was far too quick to write me off. From the depths of my severe psychotic experiences I have made a full recovery, and so can anyone else. We all have potential.

More details about the CASL campaign can be obtained from CASL@asylumonline.

Armstrong, L. (1996) *Rocking the Cradle of Sexual Politics: What Happened When Women Said Incest.* London: The Women's Press.

Bebbington, P., Bhugra, D., Brugha, T., *et al.* (2004) Psychosis, victimization and childhood disadvantage: Evidence from the Second British National Survey on Psychiatric Morbidity. *British Journal of Psychiatry*, **185**: 220–26.

Bentall, R.P. (2003) *Madness Explained: Psychosis and Human Nature.* London: Penguin.

Crow, T.J. (1980) Molecular pathology of schizophrenia: More than one disease process? *British Medical Journal*, **280**: 66–8.

Fowler, D., Freeman, D., Steel, C. *et al.* (2006) The catastrophic interaction hypothesis: How do stress, trauma, emotion and information processing abnormalities lead to psychosis? In W. Larkins & A.P. Morrison (eds), *Trauma and Psychosis*. London: Routledge.

Fox, R.D. & Reid, G.S. (in press) Childhood trauma and symptom profiles in bipolar affective disorder.

Goodman, L.A., Rossenberg, S.G., Meuser, K. & Drake, R.E. (1997) Physical and sexual assault history in women with serious mental illness: Prevalence, correlates, treatment and future research directions. *Schizophrenia Bulletin*, **23**: 685–96.

Hammersley, P.A., Dias, A., Todd, G. *et al.* (2002) Childhood trauma and hallucinations in bipolar affective disorder: A preliminary investigation. *British Journal of Psychiatry*, **182**: 543–7.

Hammersley, P., Burston, P. & Read, J. (2004) Learning to listen: Childhood trauma and adult psychosis. *Mental Health Practice*, **7**: 18–21.

Hammersley, P. & Fox, R. (2006). Childhood Trauma and Psychosis in the Major Depressive Disorders. In W. Larkins & A.P. Morrison (eds), *Trauma and Psychosis: New Directions for Theory and Therapy*. Routledge Press.

Henquet, C., Murray, R., Linszen, D. & Van Os, J. (2005) The environment and schizophrenia: The role of cannabis use. *Schizophrenia Bulletin*, **33**(3): 608–13.

Jankowski, K., Meuser, K.T. & Rosenberg, S. (2006) Psychosis with comorbid PTSD. In W. Larkins & A.P. Morrison (eds), *Trauma and Psychosis*. London: Routledge.

Janssen, I., Krabbendam, L., Bak, M. *et al.* (2003) Childhood abuse as a risk factor for psychotic experiences. *Acta Psychiatrica Scandinavica*, **109**: 38–45.

Larkins, W. & Morrison A.P. (2006) *Trauma and Psychosis*. London: Routledge.

Livingston, R. (1987) Sexually and physically abused children. *Journal of the American Academy of Child and Adolescent Psychiatry*, **26**: 413–15.

Mendel, M.P. (1995) *The Male Survivor: The Impact of Sexual Abuse.* Thousand Oaks, CA: Sage.

Mendick, S.A., Cannon, T., Jacobsen, B. *et al.* (1998) School teacher ratings predictive of psychiatric outcome 25 years later. *British Journal of Psychiatry*, **172**(33): 7–13.

Meuser, K.T., Rosenberg, S., Stanley, D., Goodman, L.A. & Trumbetta, L. (2002). Trauma, PTSD and the course of serious mental illness: An interactive model. *Schizophrenia Research*. **53**: 123–143.

Molon, P. (1996) *Multiple Selves, Multiple Voices: Working with Trauma, Violation and Dissociation.* Chichester: John Wiley & Sons Ltd.

Neuchterlein, K.H. & Dawson, M.E. (1984) A heuristic vulnerability/stress model of schizophrenic episodes. *Schizophrenia Bulletin*, **10**(2): 300–12.

Read, J. & Argyle, N. (1999) Hallucinations, delusions and thought disorders among adult psychiatric patients with a history of child abuse. *Psychiatric Services*, **50**: 1467–72.

Read, J. & Hammersley, P. (2005) Child sexual abuse and schizophrenia. Correspondence. *British Journal of Psychiatry*, **184**: 76–7.

Read, J. & Hammersley, P. (2006) Can very bad childhoods drive us crazy: Science, ideology and taboo. In J.O. Johannessen, B.V. Martindale & J. Cullberg (eds), *Evolving Psychosis: Different Stages, Different Treatments*. New York: Routledge.

Read, J., Mosher, L.R. & Bentall, R.P. (2004) *Models of Madness*. Hove: Bruner Routledge.

Read, J., van Os, J., Morrison, A. *et al.* (2005) Childhood trauma, psychosis and schizophrenia: A literature review with theoretical and clinical implications. *Acta Psychiatrica Scandinavica*, **112**: 330–50.

Romme, M. & Escher, A. (2006). Trauma and Hearing voices in Understanding Trauma and Psychosis: New Horizons for Theory and Therapy. In W. Larkins & T. Morrison, Hove: Brunner-Routledge.

Romme, M. & Escher, S. (1989) Hearing voices. *Schizophrenia Bulletin*, **15**: 209–16.

Romme, M. & Escher, S. (2000) *Making Sense of Voices*. London: Mind.

Ross, C. (2005) Dissociation and psychosis: The need for integration of theory and practice. In J.O. Johanessen, B.V. Martindale & J. Cullberg (eds), *Evolving Psychosis*. New York: Routledge.

Ross, C. & Joshi, S. (1992) Schneiderian symptoms and childhood trauma in the general population. *Comprehensive Psychiatry*, **33**: 269–73.

Sanderson, C. (2006) *Counselling Survivors of Childhood Sexual Abuse*. London: Jessica Kingsley.

Spataro, J., Mullen, P., Burgess, P. *et al.* (2004) Impact of child sexual abuse on mental health: Prospective study in males and females. *British Journal of Psychiatry*, **184**: 416–21.

Spauwen, J., Krabbendam, L., Lieb, R., Wittchen, H.U. & Van Os, J. (2006) Impact of psychological trauma on the development of psychotic symptoms: Relationship with psychosis proneness. *British Journal of Psychiatry*, **188**: 527–33.

Van der Kolk, B. (1994) The body keeps the score: Memory and the evolving psychology of post-traumatic stress. *Harvard Review of Psychiatry*. **Jan–Feb**: 250–60.

Van Os, J., Pedersen, C. & Mortensen, P. (2004) Confirmation of synergy between urbanicity and family liability in the causation of psychosis. *American Journal of Psychiatry*, **161**: 2312–14.

Whitfield, C.L., Dube, S.R., Felitti, V.J. & Anda, R.F. (2005) Adverse childhood experiences and hallucinations. *Child Abuse and Neglect*, **29**: 797–810.

Weitz, D. (1983) Schizophrenia: Exploding the myth. *Phoenix Rising*, **3**(3).

Zimmerman, M. & Mattia, J. (1999). Psychotic subtyping of major depressive disorder and post-traumatic stress disorder. *Journal of Clinical Psychiatry*, **60**(5): 311–314.

Zubin, J. & Spring, B. (1977) Vulnerability: A new view of schizophrenia. *Journal of Abnormal Psychology*, **86**: 103–26.

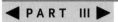

PART III

Approaches for mental health practice

◀ CHAPTER TWENTYTWO ▶

Carers' experiences of mental health services and views about assessments: Lessons from the Partnership in Carer Assessments Project (PICAP)

Julie Repper
University of Nottingham

Gordon Grant, Mike Nolan and Pam Enderby
University of Sheffield

A significant proportion of the UK population cares for someone with mental health problems. This is not surprising when one considers how many people have mental health problems: around one in six people of working age suffer from some form of mental illness; 10–15% of the population of 65 and over have a diagnosis of depression and around 600 000 have dementia. Indeed, it is estimated that around 1.5 million people are involved in caring for a relative or friend with a mental illness (Arksey, 2003). Even so, this group remain neglected and undervalued by services: research into the views of carers with mental health problems repeatedly shows that carers want more involvement with the services supporting their relative or friend, more information about the services and treatments available, and more recognition of their role (Hogman & Pearson, 1995).

Recent government policy has responded to carers' needs with a series of Acts providing carers with several rights, including the right to a separate assessment of their needs (see Table 22.1). Specifically in relation to carers of people with mental health problems, Standard 6 of the National Service Framework (NSF) for Mental Health, entitled 'Caring for Carers', states:

Learning About Mental Health Practice. Edited by Theo Stickley and Thurstine Basset
© 2008 John Wiley & Sons, Ltd

All individuals who provide regular and substantial care for a person on Care Programme Approach (CPA) should:

- have an assessment of their caring, physical and mental health needs, repeated at least on an annual basis;

- have their own written care plan, which is given to them and implemented in discussion with them.

Yet despite consistent research findings about the dissatisfaction of carers, and a concerted policy response, the experience of carers has changed little over the past decade. This scant progress is not confined to carers of people with mental health problems. The policy guide on implementing the Carers (Equal Opportunities) Act 2004 notes that 'progress in carrying out carer assessments is slow, and few separate assessments are carried out' (Social Care Institute for Excellence, 2005, Section 2, p. 2). Similarly, in a recent review of the implementation of the NSF for Mental Health over its first five years, Appleby (2004, p. 74) concluded that 'we have too little to report on improving the support we provide to carers'. Indeed, the data cited in the report were minimal, indicating a small increase in support services for carers and modest success in ensuring that carers of people on enhanced CPA had a care plan, but giving no information at all on the provision or uptake of carer assessments. (This compares with 'impressive' achievements in Standards 4, 5 and 7 and 'reasonably good' achievements in Standards 2 and 3; Appleby, 2004).

Table 22.1   Recent developments in carer policy in England

The Carers (Recognition and Services) Act (1996) gave carers who provided 'a substantial amount of care on a regular basis' the right to request an assessment of their ability to provide care and continue caring.

The National Strategy for Carers (1999) introduced the Carers Special Grant to develop flexible and innovative services to provide carers with a meaningful break from their caring responsibilities.

Standard 6 of the Mental Health National Service Framework (1999) aimed to ensure that health and social services assess the needs of carers who provide regular and substantial care for those with a severe mental illness and provide care to meet their needs. It states that all individuals who provide regular and substantive care for a person on the Care Programme Approach (CPA) should have an annual assessment and their own written care plan.

The Carers and Disabled Children Act (2000) empowers local authorities to provide services directly to carers who are providing regular and substantive care, and it gives carers the right to an assessment of their needs even when the person they care for has refused.

The Carers (Equal Opportunities) Act 2004 builds on existing support for carers, emphasising the need for all carers to know their entitlement to an assessment of their needs, and it places a duty on councils to consider carers' outside interests (work, study, leisure).

Clearly, the challenges of providing effective support for carers are not unique to those caring for a person with mental health problems, but it has long been recognised that difficulties relating to carers are exacerbated for mental health carers because of the fluctuating nature of problems, the potential for conflict between service users and carers' views, and the widespread fear and ignorance about mental health problems adding to the isolation and sense of guilt among carers (Hogman & Pearson, 1995).

▶ The Partnerships In Carer Assessment Project

This chapter draws on the findings of the first stage of the Partnerships In Carer Assessment Project (PICAP). This three-year study, funded by the Department of Health under its Service Delivery and Organisation (SDO) initiative, aimed to explore and evaluate how carers of people with mental health problems experience assessment processes, and to consider the type of help and support that they receive following an assessment of their needs. The project began with a series of consultation meetings in eight different regions of England. A total of 79 carers attended the meetings: a mix of relatives, male and female, and from various ethnic backgrounds, with a range of caring responsibilities (see Table 22.2). As a result of the discussions that occurred, a number of consistent themes emerged:

- carers' experiences of contact with mental health services
- what carers want from services overall
- carers' general views about assessment
- who should *get* an assessment
- who should *do* the assessment
- *when* assessment should be done
- *how* assessment should be conducted
- *what* assessment should cover
- dealing with conflicting views
- sensitivity to cultural and contextual issues
- *outcomes* of assessment

Overall, the consultations suggest that it is not possible to get a clear understanding of assessment without considering the carer's personal history and circumstances, particularly their previous contact with mental health services. These findings provide a useful guide for practitioners working with people with mental health problems. They illustrate the views and experiences of family

Table 22.2   Characteristics of carers participating in regional consultation meetings (total number 79)

Caring status	75 (94%) carers	Gender	24 (31%) male
	4 (6%) carer workers		55 (69%) female
Age	1 (1%) under 25 years	Ethnicity	61 (78%) white British
	23 (29%) 25–45 years		4 (5%) white Irish
	36 (45%) 46–65 years		1 (1%) black British
	19 (24%) over 65 years		2 (3%) Caribbean
			1 (1%) African
			6 (8%) Asian
			1 (1%) white American
			1 (1%) British Indian
Relationship to person cared for	33 (41%) mothers	Age of person cared for	10 (14%) under 25 years
	27 (34%) fathers		54 (77%) 26–45 years
	8 (10%) wives		9 (13%) 46–65 years
	1 (1%) husband		2 (4%) over 65 years
	1 (1%) niece		
	2 (3%) daughters		
	3 (4%) sisters		
	2 (4%) friends		
Number of years in caring role	2 (4%) under 5 years	Primary diagnosis of person cared for	48 (61%) schizophrenia
	35 (49%) 5–10 years		9 (13%) bipolar
	32 (48%) over 10 years		3 (4%) depression

Note: Where numbers do not add up to 79, this is due to missing data, or where one person cares for more than one person. Where percentages do not add up to 100, this is due to numbers being rounded up.

carers and offer an insight into their wishes and ideas for shaping services that recognise, value and include carers.

▶ Carers' experiences of mental health services

Although the consultation events were aimed primarily to inform good assessment practice, participants spoke primarily about their experiences of being a carer and their contact with mental health services (initials in the carer descriptions below relate to the region of the country). Many recalled early feelings of despair when they were unclear about what was happening, what they could do, who to turn to and how to find help and support:

> at first it felt as though I had a 500 piece jigsaw; all the pieces were there, some had straight edges and some had no picture and I had no idea how to put them together. I had no idea who to go to for what. (SE Carer)

Often the help and support they needed at this time was not forthcoming and carers felt as if they had been left to cope alone until a crisis point was reached:

> If ever I needed support it was in the early days...carers should be recognised as soon as possible and not left like me until things reach crisis point. (NE Carer)

As time went on, carers recognised that they were the main source of support and expertise for the person they cared for, but they often felt that services neither recognised this nor provided the back-up that they needed:

> Carers are there 24 hours a day and 7 days a week and yet we are having to re-justify who and what we are to professionals all the time; our expertise is not acknowledged. Recognition, communication and understanding of the limits of our involvement, are more important than 'assessment'. We need to be valued. (SW Carer)

Carers frequently spoke of the lack of information they received, about being kept 'outside the loop', yet 'expected to keep on caring whatever the circumstances':

> The 'confidentiality' smokescreen is used all the time to keep carers out of necessary dialogues. (WM Carer)

> Carers are not treated with common courtesy and respect, they are kept outside the loop. We are not informed of fundamental changes such as when a psychiatrist has changed, or when our daughter is being moved to a different home. We have to hear through third parties. (SW Carer)

Carers felt that they were treated unequally: professionals often wanted information about the service users' problems, but gave carers little or no information about treatment, plans or prognosis in return:

> They always want me to tell them when my son is well but they're not so keen to tell me about him. (NE Carer)

Carers were almost unanimously disappointed both with the attitude of service providers and the support provided by services. They used words like 'patronising', 'disbelieving', 'invalidating' and 'insulting'. More specifically, carers spoke of feeling that they were viewed negatively by services, and they were made to feel 'branded' as a 'problem child/parent', 'troublemaker', 'fusspot', 'always complaining', 'part of the problem rather than part of solution'. Several felt that the 'whole family is pathologised':

There is still a culture where they [the professionals] know best and are reluctant to admit that carers might also have a view that should be taken into account. We are important. We make an important contribution and they need to recognise that...a good indication of quality of care is just how much interest a service has in us. (WM Carer)

They [service providers] need to value my views, and believe my experiences. I am pro-active in calling them, so that they can do their job better, but they see me as troublesome. We have the same goal (they and I want the best for my mother) yet they do not consider my contribution to her well-being. (SE Carer)

Carers often felt that services, particularly primary care services, relied heavily on the support they provided for their relative, but paid little attention to their own needs. For example, one carer recounted how she went to her GP because she was feeling under severe pressure, only for his response to focus primarily on the needs of the service user, while also placing implicit pressure on her to continue in her role:

The GP told me 'you're the captain of the ship, we all rely on you...but don't tell your husband about your problems as he'll only dwell on them and that will make him worse. (NE Carer)

Poor recognition of carers' needs was not confined to primary care settings. Several recounted the difficulties and resistances they experienced when their relative had been admitted to acute care, often involuntarily:

I left that acute ward in floods of tears several times and the nurses used to watch me walk out. No-one once said to me 'look love, let's go and talk'. (NE Carer)

▶ What carers want from services

Several carers recounted positive experiences of services. Assertive outreach (AO) services were frequently praised for using a more carer-friendly approach, and several carers talked about the time and support provided by support workers. Interestingly, in neither of these scenarios was support the result of a formal assessment; rather. it was based on working 'with' the carer to optimise their ability to care, as opposed to seeing them as a difficulty to be assessed or worked round:

Assertive outreach workers provide very positive support for carers without calling on a specialist carer support service. The whole approach is based on engaging the person on the basis of their situation and their aspirations – starting where the person is at. There is a recognition of the social and psychological needs of individuals and that you can't divorce the person from their social context. You need to work with the carers in order to provide the most effective support – carers may not a need separate assessment in this situation. (SW Carer)

I'm happy with CPA. I didn't want full carer assessment. Our AO worker spends a lot of time listening to problems identified by us, the carers, and will respond quickly to emails that I send him. (London Carer)

We need pro-active support, regular phone contact, not just left to us to phone someone in an emergency. I have a support worker who has changed my life, listens, takes the initiative to phone me regularly to ask how I am, and doesn't wait for me to contact her. It has made everything easier. (NW Carer)

These accounts help us to formulate the sort of support that carers would find helpful: proactive, regular, responsive, working alongside, listening.

All carers had suggestions about how things could be improved, and identified the same qualities of a 'good' service. They emphasised the importance of their role, knowledge, views and expertise being understood and respected, and their limitations, fears and on-going grief acknowledged. They wanted information about services (who to turn to for what), as well as help to acquire skills to manage the challenges involved in caring for a person with mental health problems. They also wanted dependable support that fitted family and household routines and was delivered by a multidisciplinary team that communicated with carers, and with each other, so that carers did not always have to ask for help. In addition, they needed to 'offload' their emotions and feelings with someone who would acknowledge their role, their feelings, and help them with the difficulties that caring often caused (such as financial, employment, health and relationship problems). In addition, they wanted to feel that they could look forward to the future with hope and expectation:

Hope is an essential part of being able to care. It is hard to have hope after three relapses... you need help to grieve when your relative 'dies' – the loss of the person you thought they were. You have lost all the hopes and dreams that you had for them. (SW Carer)

We need help to understand and come to terms with what is happening to our relative. We need to know – from the start – what is happening, what to expect, and what we can do. (East Carer)

Carers' contact with services was often limited to times of 'crisis' and the response they received in such circumstances usually left a lasting impression. Unfortunately, it was frequently less than positive:

We need to be taken seriously. Too often you get the person to A&E – often with difficulty – and the psychiatrist says 'we can't do anything at the moment, take them home'. We have to cope and we know that they are going to get worse. The psychiatrist needs to believe us, and take our views and our knowledge of the person seriously. (London Carer)

It is difficult to represent our own needs at times. Carers are just ignored or blamed (even more so in the past), so it would be useful to have an advocacy service for carers, someone we could go to discuss our rights and who would go to meetings with us and help us to present our view. (East Carer)

Carers wanted greater flexibility, more thought given to future planning, and also attention to how caring affected their wider life, for example employment:

I think we need 'rainy day' agreements, not assessments, plans we can rely on about what will happen when things go wrong – contingency planning and preventative strategies. (SE Carer)

Employment should be a constant theme in work with carers: preventing loss of jobs and facilitating return to work. We have user employment workers, but there may be a case for carer employment workers to broker with employers and advocate on carers' behalf. (SW Carer Worker)

There was a general plea for a change in the culture of services so that people with mental health problems who had family help were seen to live within a community of support, with mental health workers being just one part:

Education is essential in order to change the whole culture and system of care so that it becomes family orientated rather than individually focused. (NW Carer)

There seems to be a need for a change in culture and values so that carers are seen as part of the solution, not part of the problem, and everyone is seen as part of a network of carers, not as an independent individual. (London Carer)

We need a change in culture so that carers are respected and involved throughout – a move away from blaming carers to seeing them as partners. (East Carer)

▶ General thoughts about assessment

In all of the discussion groups, one of the first issues that carers wanted to address was the term 'carer assessment'. Both the term 'carer' and 'assessment' were challenged. Many participants asked what was meant by the term 'carer', at what point a person was recognised as a carer, how and when they moved from being a 'person who cares' to a formal 'carer'. The term 'assessment' was also considered problematic, with carers feeling that it suggested an assessment of their mental health and/or competence to care, rather than of their own need for support. Assessments were also viewed more as a one-off 'measurement' rather than a long-term process of engagement and support. Many participants had not heard of 'carer assessments', and most had not been offered an assessment for themselves:

I didn't know I was a carer until I was told. I thought being a carer meant you had to take on extra responsibilities. (SW Carer)

There needs to be clarity of terms – assessment, reassessment, review all mean different things. We may need a formal separate carer assessment once a year, but this does not replace the ongoing flexible assessment of carers' needs as they change day by day in relation to the person they care for. (London Carer)

It must be clear that carer assessments are not about assessing our ability to care. We have been doing it for years regardless! Assessment should focus on our needs. (East Carer)

I refused a carer assessment... I always felt that they were judging *me*. (NE Carer)

Despite wanting recognition of their own needs, the main concern of most carers was the provision of adequate services for the people they care for. They repeatedly claimed that carer assessments would not be necessary if mental health services provided reliable, responsive and effective support for their relative. Indeed, several carers had chosen not to have an assessment when it was offered because they were unconvinced of its value and confused about its purpose:

There is confusion about the scope and purpose of assessments among carers, and who is responsible for doing them. Carer assessments don't mean a monkeys to me as long as my son is looked after. (SW Carer)

I don't want an assessment, I want people there to look after my son and for me to call on when I need it. (NW Carer)

Several carers who had been assessed considered many of the questions irrelevant, finding them designed primarily for carers of people with physical needs rather than mental health problems, or concerned with the needs of the service user rather than the carer:

Most conversations in carer assessments focus on the needs of the service user, to make things worse questions are often about physical care... you have to seriously wonder about their relevance. (NE Carer)

In my experience carer assessments are very restricting. They don't ask me about what I need. All of the things that I have said I would find helpful, I have been told are not available. I'd like two things: family intervention and mediation. I have been told that this won't be possible, they are not available, no resources, not prioritised. (London Carer)

The problem with the expectation of carers' assessment is that they are seen as a way of meeting the needs of a client. (NW Carer)

Assessments were generally seen as a 'tick-box', 'one-off' activity, required by local commissioners to meet 'targets', rather than being for the benefit of carers:

Carer assessments are part of the CHI [Commission for Health Improvement] review and LIT [Local Implementation Team] reviews so there is pressure to say they have been done; in danger of becoming 'tick box' activities, yet they will only make a difference to carers if they are a *'hearts and minds'* thing. (East Carer)

A carer assessment is not a one-off thing, it can't only be a piece of paper that you're left with, so people can say we've 'ticked that box'. (NE Carer)

Who should get an assessment?

Participants were concerned about the ways in which carers are defined for the purpose of assessment. They pointed out that many services only offer assessments to the carers of people on enhanced CPA (Care Programme Approach). This runs the risk of excluding many people, for example young carers; older carers; 'long-distance' carers; carers of people who refuse to use services; and carers who provide such good support that their relative manages without admission to mental health services.

There was agreement that *anyone* providing support for a person with mental health problems should be offered an assessment – whether they consider themselves to be a 'carer' or not. This places responsibility on primary care services to better understand the process of carer assessment and proactively to identify carers.

Carer Assessments need to take into account different needs over time, and the needs of carers before the service user agrees to use services; also that younger carers have different needs, knowledge base, experience and outlook. . . and people who refuse to use any services at all – their carers have an even greater burden. (NW Carer)

Older people care for each other, but at what stage do they become carers? They may be reluctant to see themselves as carers but often provide huge amounts of support from each other and a carer assessment may help to identify the help they need to continue caring. (SE Carer)

Who should do assessments?

The differing views about who should undertake assessments were largely influenced by personal experiences. Some participants had found that the care co-ordinator of the person they cared for was able to support them, as they had a good understanding of the service user. Others preferred a separate system of support for themselves, and considered that other carers were in the best position to assess their needs and understand their situation. Conversely, another view was that assessment should be carried out by a health or other professional with authority to act on the findings. There was concern that if carer assessment was separated from care delivery, it may well become a one-off event that does not lead to improved support:

The only people who can understand the situation of carers are other carers. Given training and authority, they could be best assessors. (NW Carer)

Ideally the person conducting the assessment should have some familiarity with the users' situation as well, in order to be able to see the carers' needs in an appropriate context. (NE Carer)

The skill of the assessor is very important, more important than whether the assessor has experience of caring themselves. (SE Carer)

The role of the assessor should be accorded value and status, and the person should have some authority to act upon the results of the assessment. (London Carer)

There was overall agreement that assessors must receive specific training in assessing carers' needs, managing conflicting views, legal rights and confidentiality issues, helping carers to manage difficult behaviour and to access local resources. It was considered that some of this training should be provided by carers themselves:

The assessor should be trained in assessment, clear about legal rights and confidentiality issues, have good knowledge of local resources for carers and authority to act upon results of the assessment. (NE Carer)

Professionals need education about information and confidentiality issues; there are ways of working openly with carers; staff often refuse to talk to carers when a client is ill. They can get over this by having crisis plans or advanced directives where a person makes plans for involvement of relatives when they are well because they are likely to become paranoid/angry with relatives when they are ill. (East Carer)

When should assessment be done?

As noted earlier, carers were clear that they needed support and information from the first days of trying to cope with caring for a person with mental health problems. However, this did not *necessarily* require a formal carer assessment. There was consensus that appropriate carer support should be provided as part of the routine care of the 'patient' from first contact with services. Carers consistently expressed the view that assessment should be a continuous, proactive and preventive process rather than an annual event or, worse, occurring only at a time of crisis.

Assessment needs to take place right at the start. We need to know what is best for me – how to handle my own emotions and needs, and what is best for my relative – so that I can help them to access appropriate support, and to help me to manage them. (WM Carer)

At times of crisis there is no time to do an assessment. We just need the support. Right from the very beginning we need support and care ourselves and for the person we are caring for. (East Carer)

How to do assessment: qualities of the process

There was much discussion about carers' experiences of being assessed and how they would like an assessment to be conducted. Carers advocated a flexible, loosely structured assessment in the form of a dialogue in which information was shared by both parties:

> I think there is a problem asking anyone what they need. Carers Assessments are not just about asking this question but about setting up a meaningful dialogue with a person they have built a good relationship with. You need to speak the same language, avoid jargon, explain what is available and what might be helpful to help me to define what will be best for me. (SE Carer)

On the basis of several discussions, a five-stage process could be identified: first, a loosely structured discussion where the assessor listened carefully; second, agreement over priority of needs; third, giving information about available services and resources; fourth, practical organisation of tailored support; and finally, regular review:

> What is important to us is being listened to first, followed by action and support. Being given information about what is available and what should be available as support. Often we don't know what exists. (SE Carer)

> The assessment should provide an opportunity to talk about their experience. (SW Carer)

The qualities of the assessor were considered to be paramount, in particular genuineness, sensitivity and a willingness to listen to *and believe* carers, while also valuing and respecting their expertise. Several people described how the assessment process in itself was tremendously supportive. This was largely because time had been dedicated to listening to these carers' views and experiences, as for most it was the first time this had happened. They recommended that sufficient time was allowed for a two-way discussion. This might need a number of meetings:

> A good carer assessment should meet the needs of my relative; offer me time to talk through things; recognise me as an expert; acknowledge the risks in my life as a carer; having a choice to take on this role; respite often needed, in its many forms. (SW Carer)

> Best carer assessments are not a one-off but continuous good practice in routine care, proactive, valuing, supportive. (NW Carer)

Carers wanted information about the assessment process in advance, with copies of the documentation to be used. However, they emphasised that the assessment should be flexible; for example, some carers preferred self-assessment, others formal interview, diary or informal conversation.

Overall, only five carers recounted positive experiences of being assessed, and even here they sometimes had to 'fight' for the attention they needed. However, they clearly identified the benefits of a supportive assessment:

> The carer assessment was the first time I could speak emotionally. Previously when speaking to the GP it was about my husband but the carer assessment was about me. I felt safe and there was time for me to be open and to be emotional. (SE Carer)

> My CA [carer's assessment] was really good. It wasn't about going through a form ticking boxes, it was listening and talking. The approach is as important as the content. (NW Carer)

> I requested a carer assessment for myself because I had physical problems and cared for three young children, but all the care was focused on my husband who has mental health problem... you may have to fight for an assessment. They are necessary because they are about our own needs and circumstances and identities – not part of the service users' care. In the end I got a good social worker who did an assessment and got the ball rolling. This made a difference because it looked at ways of helping me – I got a grant towards driving lessons to free me up. Also my daughter gets help for herself. (WM Carer)

Carers had different views about whether their assessment should be conducted with the person they care for or not. On balance, there was agreement that their needs overlapped but, for both the service user and carer, there were some issues that were best discussed separately. One (London) carer described, and illustrated this, as follows:

> What I want from carer assessment, I see this as some sort of continuum, a line on which the majority of my own needs and my son's needs overlap – and can be assessed together as part of routine care, but we each have discreet, personal needs that need to be assessed separately like this:

just the user	both user and carer	just the carer

[_____/_____/_____]

Others clearly highlighted the benefits of having an assessment without the service user present:

> I wouldn't have wanted my assessment to have been done with my mother because I couldn't speak openly. On my own I could say what I wanted to say without offending her. (SE Carer)

However, the interdependency of needs and care plans was also recognised and it was felt that ideally the carer assessment could be a route to creating a 'dialogue' between the carer and the user:

The needs of the carer and the relative are entangled, inextricable. Much of the relative's assessment will cover issues of importance to the carer, but there is a need for the carer to have their own assessment as an individual, not just in relation to the needs of the person they care for. (East Carer)

What should be assessed?

Carers specified a number of areas that they felt should be covered in assessments. These were not only about the difficulties they encountered in their caring role, but also their feelings about that role – their limitations and fears – and what would help, their engagement in community life, their general health, their views about services, and the skills they would like to help them cope:

> Issues that should be covered include basic needs – physical health and well being, emotional health, risks to physical and psychological health, impact of caring for life, impact on others' lives as a result of the carers' caring role... It would be helpful to ask carers how they feel about their role; whether they felt they have choice, control, are being manipulated. (SE Carer)

> Need to recognise our changing needs over time – recognising the implications of the onset and course of mental illnesses and the implications for how carers acquire knowledge and expertise. I felt there was no-one out there who can cope with him as well as I can – at least initially. I needed some certainty much earlier: a diagnosis, some idea of what might happen next, and when he would get better. (SW Carer)

> CA must take into account the needs of different members of the family – Mum, Dad, siblings all have different needs. A subset of carers will need a detailed assessment of their own need. They may need physical help to enable them to carry on caring. (NW Carer)

▶ Dealing with conflicting views

In all of the groups, carers discussed the difficulties that arose when their views differed from those of the person they care for and/or from service providers. This was most problematic when the carers recognised signs of deterioration that were not apparent to the person they cared for. This frequently resulted in conflict – both with the service user and with service providers who refused to increase treatment or admit that person. As carers pointed out, it was assumed that they would continue to care for the person even when they felt their views were not heeded, and when they felt that they and/or the service user were at risk in some way.

A central concern in this process was the exclusion of carers from decision making. Service providers claimed that they were unable to keep carers informed about progress and plans (even when these included discharge to live with the carers) because of the need to respect 'confidentiality':

> Workers always hide behind the need for 'confidentiality', they need to see us as part of the care team. (NW Carer)

Confidentiality is a veil of secrecy which workers hide behind. (NE Carer)

There is a tacit assumption by professionals that families are willing – or have a moral duty – to care under almost any circumstances. (SW Carer)

Carers felt strongly that they needed to be informed of, and ideally valued, in decisions that were made, for example about discharge:

At [the] very least, if the patient does not want [the] carer involved, the carer must be informed of any changes that effect their health and safety – they have a right to know. (SE Carer)

Frequently there are conflicting views between service user and carer when they have been admitted, often unpleasant process, paranoia, parents involved in sectioning etc., so [they] may have different views and [the] service user may not want carers present... but carers still need support. There are still situations when carers need to be present – i.e. when decisions are made that impact on the carer, particularly pre-discharge CPA meetings, carers' views about future living arrangement is essential. (London Carer)

There were suggestions about how conflict could be reduced. For example, the Royal College of Psychiatrists has issued guidelines for carers about confidentiality, and advance directives provide a plan of action formulated by service users in collaboration with carers and services. These plans specify what the service user would like to happen in a crisis or relapse, and who should be consulted and informed about decisions:

People who we care for want us to be involved. It's just when they get ill that they can become paranoid about us. You can get over this by having an advanced directive to plan what happens in a crisis and all agree to it. (NW Carer)

Planning ahead for potential difficulties can help although there are difficulties when plans are over-ruled... but there must always be agreement to breach contract for confidentiality in extreme circumstances. (SE Carer)

▶ Sensitivity to cultural and contextual issues

It was considered important that assessments should be sensitive to identities of carers and their role relationships, for example rural carers, those from black and minority ethnic groups, young carers, and carers with differing relationships to the user, such as spouses, siblings and parents. There were suggestions about how this could be achieved:

At [the] very least carers need a choice of worker, for example from the same culture or not, people from some cultures do not want a worker from [their] own culture as this potentially threatens privacy. (NW Carer)

For many Asian families, what needs to be understood is that services will not try to separate the family. I spent 2 hours with the CPN emphasising this on behalf of my parents. Families will not go near services if they fear being separated. (NW Carer)

Carers emphasised the need for staff training in cultural awareness, for example to ensure that the needs of people who are English speaking but from another culture are not overlooked:

Cultural differences are overlooked if we speak the same languages, so African-Caribbeans have different beliefs, different food etc., but this is often forgotten because they speak the same language. (WM Carer)

This is also the case with Irish people, different cultures overlooked because they have the same colour skin. There needs to be sensitivity to words and language. (WM Carer)

It was considered important that interpreters be booked in advance of assessments for carers who do not speak English, but it must also be recognised that people from other cultures may have additional difficulties understanding medical terminology and the UK health-care system:

When my husband became ill I had no idea how the medical system worked, how it differed from the Japanese system. I had to learn everything – who to tell, how to access services, what services existed. This was hard because my husband initially refused help and I was desperate but had no idea what to do. My husband's family saw supporting my husband as my role so I was very alone. (SE Carer)

Again, some positive suggestions for ways of meeting cultural needs were made, for example:

We have a team with members from different ethnic groups with people who speak different languages. We take a member of this team when we assess a person from an ethnic minority, not just as an interpreter, but also because of their cultural awareness. (SE Carer Worker)

▶ What should the outcome of the assessment be?

Carers were able to identify what they wanted to achieve through assessments. This included:

■ Bet ter support for the person with mental health problems:

Carer assessments should facilitate recovery of the client and identify where the carer fits into that and the support they require to do this.

■ Better understanding of carers' situations and expertise, leading to more respect and inclusion in the care team:

Agreements (rather than assessments) to agree roles, responsibilities, what will happen in given circumstances (a bit like a contract). (SE Carer)

- A clear plan to address carers' needs, with named responsible people and their contact details:

  Assessments should be 'followed up' in a flexible manner, with carers themselves having the name of a contact person who they could get hold of, if and when their circumstances changed. (NE Carer)

- More empowered carers, with better awareness of the type of help and support available and how to obtain it:

  The assessment process is an opportunity to give information, and to support carers and empower them to ask the right questions, identify the services that they need and the questions they might ask to ensure the best services for the person they care for. (NW Carer)

- More creative and innovative services, including wider use of direct payments to provide greater flexibility and choice:

  Any needs identified can be met through direct payments. It is important that people are aware of their rights for direct payments. Once a number of requests are put in for a service then commissioners become aware of the need for a new service/training etc. (SE Carer Worker)

- More attention to the options available if the carer feels that they are no longer able to continue in their role:

  The priority is to relieve the stress on carers by ensuring that their relative is adequately supported... then we need to plan what will happen when we are not here any more – this needs contingency planning. (WM Carer)

- A full account of any unmet needs in order to inform future service planning:

  It is essential therefore that assessments do establish what carers would want if it were available, rather than only offer them existing provision. We need to use assessments to shape services so that they meet our needs rather than us fitting into existing provision. (East Carer)

  If we use CA to identify unmet needs carers' assessment can become a driving force for change and improvement. (London Carer)

- Overall, carers felt that the assessment was a potentially important, but often missed, opportunity to provide emotional support, to give them information about mental health problems, treatment (including effects and side effects of medication), the type and range of support/help available, who to contact in a crisis, and ways in which they might manage the problems of living with the person with mental health problems, and strategies for managing their own distress, financial problems and employment issues:

We don't understand the language, the roles of different staff, shift patterns, who are staff and who are patients (no uniforms). We need an assessment to find out what we don't know and begin to answer our questions. (East Carer)

Information is absolutely essential from the very start – medication, side effects, treatment, symptoms, how to manage behaviour etc.; the whole family needs support as different views mean that family conflict arises. (London Carer)

▶ Conclusions

The main aim of the consultation exercise was to meet with carers at an early point in the PICAP study to ensure their views informed the study from the outset. It cannot be assumed that the views expressed by carers attending the discussion groups are necessarily representative of all carers; however, this is likely as carers raised very similar issues across eight differing meetings held throughout England, and the concerns they identified mirror very closely those arising from the review of the literature.

It is apparent that assessment is a complex matter, which cannot be understood fully without reference to the wider caring situation, particularly carers' prior experiences of mental health services. The consultation painted a poor picture of relationships between services and carers, but it also provided a list of suggestions to improve services and assessment practice for carers. Carers wanted services and staff that:

- Listened to them, valued their knowledge and expertise, and treated them as partners.

- Were proactive, dependable, consistent, responsive and family or community oriented.

- Respected their personal values and cultural beliefs.

- Took account of their established routines and ways of caring.

- Provided hope and positive ways of coping.

- Recognised other commitments such as employment and child care.

- Identified what to do and who to contact at times of crisis.

They also had a number of more specific views about assessments:

- The need for assessment to be a continuous process that recognised changing needs and circumstances, signalling the importance of regular reviews. One-off assessments were thought to have little value and typically yielded few results. Carers were especially critical when an assessment resulted in little or no action.

■ Good assessments should provide an opportunity for a full and frank exchange of ideas and expertise between assessors and carers. Partnership working was viewed as highly desirable, though it was acknowledged that potential conflicts of interest need to be accommodated.

■ Advance directives were advocated as a useful part of planning for the future, as they provided carers with a sense of security.

■ The need for assessments to be more sensitive to important issues of culture and ethnicity was highlighted.

As well as discussing the process of assessment, carers identified a number of desired outcomes, including:

■ Better support for the person with mental health problems.

■ Better understanding of carers' situations and expertise, leading to more respect and inclusion in the team and a clear plan to address their needs.

■ More empowered carers, with better awareness of the type of help and support available and how to obtain it.

■ More creative and innovative services, including wider use of direct payments to provide greater flexibility and choice.

■ More attention to the options available if the carer feels that they are no longer able to continue in their role.

■ A full account of any unmet needs in order to inform future service planning.

▶ References

Appleby, L. (2004) *The National Service Framework for Mental Health – Five Years On.* London: Department of Health.

Arksey, H. (2003) Scoping the field: Services for carers of people with mental health problems. *Health and Social Care in the Community,* **11**(4): 335–44.

Department of Health (1996) *The Carers (Recognition and Services) Act.* London: HMSO.

Department of Health (1999a) *The National Service Framework for Mental Health.* London: Department of Health.

Department of Health (1999b) *The National Strategy for Carers.* London: Department of Health.

Department of Health (2000a) *The Carers (Equal Opportunities) Act.* London: HMSO.

Department of Health (2000b) *The Carers and Disabled Children Act.* London: HMSO.

Hogman, G. & Pearson, G. (1995) *The Silent Partners: The Needs and Experiences of People Who Provide Informal Care to People with a Severe Mental Illness.* Kingston upon Thames: National Schizophrenia Fellowship.

Social Care Institute for Excellence (2005) *Practice Guide 5: Online Guide to Implementing the Carers (Equal Opportunities) Act.* London: SCIE, www.scie.org.uk/publications/practiceguides/carersguidance/index.asp (accessed 30 August 2007).

Therapeutic relationships

Theo Stickley
University of Nottingham

Dawn Freshwater
University of Leeds

The ability to know how to form, sustain and conclude therapeutic relationships is essential for all mental health practice. It is all too easy, however, to take for granted the nature of therapeutic relationships and come to rely too heavily on one's own personality and conversational habits. In this chapter, we present our understanding of the nature of therapeutic relationships, how they work and how they sometimes go wrong.

We have constructed a framework for education and practice that illustrates the nature of what we believe is fundamental to the development of an effective therapeutic relationship. It is fair to enquire where this framework came from and demand to know the research that underpins it. Both the authors of this chapter have worked for many years as nurses, counsellors, educators and supervisors. We have worked with literally hundreds of clients and practitioners, supervising their work with their clients. The framework originates from and represents some of what we have learnt doing this work. It is not comprehensive, but we think it is a 'good enough' explanation of the nature of therapeutic relationships and how to work with them. We consider the framework wholly relevant to all professions and workers in mental health care, and believe that what we present is necessary for underpinning mental health practice.

We acknowledge and appreciate the need for specialist workers – some who concentrate on social needs, those who concentrate on physical needs, some psychological and so on – but essential for every practice is the need primarily to create a human relationship that is therapeutic for the client. Before we proceed with the explanation of the framework, it might be expedient to begin with a working definition of what a therapeutic relationship actually is.

Learning About Mental Health Practice. Edited by Theo Stickley and Thurstine Basset
© 2008 John Wiley & Sons, Ltd

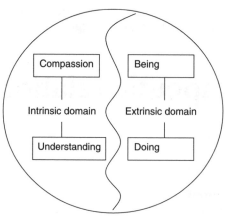

Figure 23.1   A framework for working in therapeutic relationships.

In the context of this book, we are using the term therapeutic relationship to mean any professional relationship that aims to foster and promote healing and growth in another person. Such a relationship is founded on several basic therapeutic tenets: these include respect, unconditional positive regard, trust, honesty and empathic understanding. In addition, a therapeutic relationship is one that requires workers to demonstrate a commitment to developing self-awareness through reflection and thoughtful sensitive self-enquiry.

Our framework for working in therapeutic relationships has two domains: the intrinsic (to do with our inner worlds, sometimes referred to as the intra-personal aspect) and the extrinsic (to do with what we do, often referred to as the inter-personal aspect). The framework does not attempt to explain the nature of what goes on in therapeutic relationships, for this largely depends on the people involved, the context and the content of the communication. However, we will identify common dangers and pitfalls associated with the development of helping relationships later in the chapter.

▶ The intrinsic domain of the therapeutic relationship

It is essential that people who work in mental health care have adequate levels of knowledge and understanding of the nature of mental health problems. However, not all of this knowledge and understanding can be learnt from textbooks such as this one. Students of mental health also require experiential knowledge. This way of knowing involves much more than intellectual or academic functioning. What happens during experiential learning is that a student engages with the subject on a personal and emotional level as well as intellectually. By reflecting on the impact of this learning, so the person has the opportunity to change and grow. From the outset, therefore, a therapeutic relationship involves the worker engaging with their own humanness. What we bring into our mental health work includes our past, our memories, our culture, our stereotypes, our prejudices, our beliefs and our emotions. For the benefit of this chapter, we divide this personal, intrinsic domain into two parts: understanding and compassion.

The first intrinsic component of the therapeutic relationship: understanding

Without an understanding of people and the cause and nature of mental health problems, we would argue that relationships might not necessarily be therapeutic. Fundamental to providing a therapeutic relationship, a worker requires understanding in a number of critical areas:

■ self

■ society

■ diversity

■ theories of being human

■ relationships

We now visit each of these areas in turn.

Understanding ourselves

Before we continue, we would like to raise a potentially tricky question: Should working in mental health care be therapeutic for the worker? In order to find a way into this subject matter, we ask that you take about an hour to complete the exercise in Box 23.1.

Box 23.1: Why you chose to work in mental health care

Step 1

Take a sheet of paper and in the centre draw a small circle. Then a few centimetres out form this circle draw a larger circle. Then finally draw another circle. Your page should look like this:

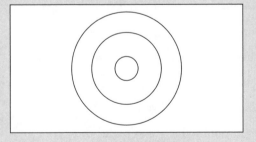

Step 2

Inside the smallest inner circle, write down the reason you came into mental health care. This might be an answer you have given to people who have made casual enquiries.

Step 3

Now inside the next circle, write down further reasons you came into mental health care. Take 10 minutes to do this. These may be the kinds of reasons you gave during your interview for training!

Step 4

Now take another 10 minutes to continue writing down your reasons for coming into mental health care in the outer circle. This time you need to think more personally, perhaps about your life experiences.

Step 5

Just when you thought you had exhausted your reasons for coming into mental health care, we now ask you to look even more deeply into yourself and continue writing in the space outside the circles. Continue on a separate sheet if you do not have enough room.

Step 6: Reflection

Hopefully by now your sheet of paper is full of writing. In this exercise we have deliberately encouraged you to begin with the superficial and gradually progress to thinking about yourself in a deeper way.

Reflective questions

- How self-aware do you think you are?
- How do you know how self-aware you are?
- How can you develop self-awareness?
- What will help you to develop self-awareness?
- What do you think blocks your development of self-awareness?
- What has surprised you doing this exercise?
- Who would you share this with?
- Who wouldn't you share this with?
- Why?
- And why not?

Now that you have finished the exercise in Box 23.1, let's go back to the question we asked: Should working in mental health care be therapeutic for the worker?

The exercise in Box 23.1 was designed to foster an experience of developing self-awareness. By thinking deeply about our reasons for first choosing a career in mental health practice, it may become evident for most people that we have chosen this path to get our own needs met (as well as wanting to help others). If we are getting our own needs met through our work – and this is perfectly natural – then working in mental health care is inevitably going to be therapeutic for the worker. The point we are emphasising is the need for self-awareness. We believe that problems in therapeutic relationships are inevitably caused by lack of self-understanding on the part of the worker. Self-awareness is therefore fundamental to our framework of therapeutic relationships.

On the one hand, it is normal to get some needs met through working in mental health. On the other hand, there are some personal needs that should not be met in our work. These include our need to be loved by others, our sexual needs, our need to express anger, and therefore a need to punish and/or control others. We return to these needs in the final section on common dangers and pitfalls.

The point here is that it is only through self-awareness that we can work out and understand our own motivations. Maybe through a process of self-enquiry some people find out that they have come into mental health care for the wrong reasons! This does not mean they should not pursue their chosen career; on the contrary, what is important is that they have leant something about themselves. Then they will be in a position to reflect on how these previously hidden motivations might affect the therapeutic relationships they later go on to perform.

On-going experiential learning regarding ourselves is essential for safe and effective mental health practice. There are several ways to achieve this. The first essential skill the mental health worker needs to develop is reflective practice. Reflecting on our practice is essentially a thinking process. It is all too easy to simply copy others or to do something because 'that's the way it's always done'. Being reflective means that we are able to question our actions according to our knowledge and professional ethics. There are various models for reflective practice with which we encourage the student to become familiar. Reflective practice, however, is not *only* a thinking process. Practitioners are also encouraged to consider their feelings and emotions. It is impossible to separate our personal feelings from our professional practices; we can, however, learn to discern the origin of our feelings. An incident in practice or a conversation with a client may evoke enormous personal feelings. Some of these are nothing really to do with the client or the incident, but the conversation or incident has re-stimulated unresolved feelings from the past. Once the reflective practitioner has acknowledged what is happening, they can then decide on a course of action to help resolve the uncomfortable situation.

Supervision is widely advocated as a way of reflecting on practice. Supervision should provide a safe place for the worker to talk freely about their work. Personal feelings should be allowed to be acknowledged and expressed when appropriate. During these opportunities for reflection on practice, the worker may consider engaging in personal counselling, especially if there are unresolved feelings that affect their work. People who work in mental health care have a responsibility to ensure that their own personal and emotional needs are met; otherwise, there is the potential for therapeutic relationships to be damaged.

Social awareness

We are all social beings: we grew up in families, have been to school and work, we join clubs, socialise and so on. All too often in mental health care, workers seem to forget the significance of society in people's lives. Mental health problems do not generally come from nowhere: there are often complex factors that cause them. The most obvious example is how mental health problems are highest in societies where economic inequality is greatest. This should not be confused with societies that are the poorest. Poor countries do not generally have more people with mental health problems. Furthermore, there are higher crime rates in less equal societies. So what happens in unequal societies (such as the UK and USA) is that the less well off tend to end up living in poorer areas. These areas become breeding places for crime and poor health. Sadly, people with ongoing mental health problems often become re-housed in such areas. These areas often become ghettos and also become stigmatised by the wider society. People who are born and grow up in such areas are understandably more prone to ill health (including mental health) because they are growing up in a sick society.

A further example of the social causes of mental health problems is racism. In spite of race laws that enshrine people's rights, institutional racism remains widespread. In the UK, for example, a black person is ten time more likely to be diagnosed with schizophrenia than a white person and ten times less likely to be offered talking therapies.

A social issue that features highly among people with mental health problems is childhood abuse and neglect. This is especially evident among people who have gone through the care system. We will not elaborate further on this subject, as Chapter 21 in this book is dedicated to research in this area.

We have given three examples of why it is necessary for mental health workers to have an understanding of how social issues affect people and how past experiences affect people's lives. The student of mental health will need to develop a sound understanding of this area in order to understand the needs of people with whom they work.

Diversity

Having already said that black people are more likely to be diagnosed with schizophrenia, it should be clearly stated that black people are over-represented in mental health services in predominantly white western countries. People who work in mental health services need to appreciate what it may feel like to be oppressed by society. Furthermore, people from all races and religions may come into mental health services. It may be impossible for the individual worker to learn about all races, religions and cultures, but every effort should be made to provide a culturally sensitive service. Again, Chapter 4 in this book addresses this subject in depth.

Diversity does not only relate to race and religion. People of a different age, gender or sexual orientation to us may pose difficulties in developing therapeutic relationships. Such difficulties need to be embraced by the mental health student/worker as opportunities to learn, grow and develop.

Theories of being human

It is not possible to describe all the major psychological theories in this chapter. However, it is our contention that it is essential for mental health workers to have a working knowledge of these theories. It is by understanding these theories that we can understand the origin of mental health problems. Such is our conviction that we would go even further and say that unless mental health workers have knowledge of psychological theories and are able to apply them in practice, they are not competent to practice. Having made such strong statements, we should explain ourselves. These theories are what underpin therapeutic relationships. Without these understandings, therapeutic relationships may by reduced to mere friendship or paternalism. In other words, if therapeutic relationships are not informed by theory, they are unlikely to be therapeutic. These psychological theories are the evidence base for therapeutic relationships. Therapeutic relationships form the cornerstone of mental health practice; without them, mental health practice is reduced to the role of a custodian, jailer or manager of care.

Psychodynamic theory

First developed by Freud as psychoanalytical theory, psychodynamic theory puts a great deal of emphasis on unconscious processes. Freud believed that each of us is born with a wild, libidinous id. It is through being parented that authoritative boundary setting challenges this id. The id is no longer allowed to be wild and have all its demands immediately met (notably the need for milk as an infant) and the super ego is formed. This super ego becomes the conscience and the internal parental voice. Through the dynamic working between the id and the super ego, the ego is formed. As children develop and become socialised, so the ego grows and the child develops a sense of identity. Any trauma or loss during this early period will cause a fragmentation or distortion to the ego. If these disturbances are not resolved, in adult life the person may exhibit neurosis or psychosis.

In order to protect our egos we develop ego defence mechanisms. If in some way we feel our ego is being threatened, we exhibit defensive behaviour. Box 23.2 lists some of the ego defences according to psychodynamic theory.

Box 23.2: Ego defence mechanisms

Defence mechanisms are not always destructive, only when they become maladaptive and interfere with ordinary life and relationships. Otherwise they are ways that people find of coping with threats to the ego. Here are some of the ego defence mechanisms identified by Freud.

Denial ('everything's OK')

An attempt to deny external reality by refusing to admit to oneself what is really happening. For example, in order to protect against the full impact of grief, a person may well experience periods of denial.

Projection ('pot calling the kettle black')

Attributing one's own (usually unacceptable) feelings or behaviour onto other people. For example, a client may accuse the nurse of being angry (when they are not), but the nurse in turn feels angry, having been wrongly accused. This interaction completes the client's unconscious drive not to have to acknowledge his own anger and successfully projects it onto the nurse.

Displacement ('kicking the cat')

Purposefully (but unconsciously) shifting feelings from one person to another in order to avoid conflict. For example, the client is angry with the doctor but hits a fellow patient. Another form of displacement is deliberate self-harm: instead of facing the inner pain, the body becomes the target for anger and frustration.

Reaction formation ('I am who I am not')

Trying to control what you feel by turning unacceptable feelings into their opposites. For example, obsessively tidy behaviour may be the activity of one who feels very 'messy' and disordered in their inner world.

Regression ('the big baby')

Changing one's behaviour to that of an earlier age to avoid conflicts and any challenge to the present state of development. For example, when it was time for the client to be discharged, he took to his bed in a foetal position and stayed there for two days.

A significant feature in psychodynamic theory is the importance placed on past events and past relationships. The past is always present, either consciously or unconsciously. It is therefore a normal part of human behaviour to project the patterns of past relationships onto present relationships. A simple example of this is how a university lecturer might remind you of a teacher at school; even though you know they are distinct humans, you may behave towards that lecturer the way you behaved towards your former teacher. Significantly, it is common for people to be attracted to others who are similar or opposite to their parents.

Behavioural and cognitive theories

Freudian ideas have fallen out of favour on and off, and more recently, policy makers, psychologists and psychiatrists have emphasised the role and value of cognitive and behavioural theories of understanding human interactions. These two theories are most often linked together and form a specific approach to creating and sustaining a therapeutic relationship. This approach is called cognitive behavioural therapy.

Watson, arguably the first behavioural psychologist, opposed Freud's rather introspective view of the person (i.e. the emphasis on the intrinsic domain), focusing instead on the formal study of observable behaviour. Skinner, another key theorist and practitioner of behaviourism, argued that all human behaviour is learnt and, so it follows, can be unlearnt.

The principle behind cognitive theory is that thinking (our rationality) informs our emotions, how and what we think about ourselves and about the world around us. Our thinking and emotions in turn have significant impacts on our behaviour. Hence, our behaviour can be seen as a complex interaction between our thinking and intellect and our emotions.

Humanistic theory

Humanistic theories of the person arose as a direct reaction to both Freud's seemingly deterministic approach and the rather objective, mechanistic perspectives presented within behaviourism. Humanism views the person as an individual, for whom no one theory could suffice or define. In other words, we are all unique individuals and as such have unique and different views not only of the world we live in, but of each experience that we encounter.

Rogers, an educationalist and counsellor, was a key figure in the evolution of humanism, developing the now famous client-centred approach to counselling, teaching and learning. Rogers was concerned with how a person made meaning of their experiences, believing that each one of us has the capacity and ability to identify, explore and solve our own problems. Thus, we are each the expert in our own life and are the only one qualified to comment on our own situation. Rogers' humanistic theory provides a very practical and useful schema for developing a therapeutic relationship that will or can facilitate the individual to explore, understand and develop themselves. In order for people to self-develop,

Rogers believed that the therapist (or teacher or parent) needs to provide the right conditions that will enable people to grow and change. These include genuineness, empathy, unconditional positive regard, honesty and transparency. If we can provide these conditions, the people with whom we are working will feel valued and good about themselves. These conditions will them to heal, grow and develop.

As the reader will appreciate, we have simply offered a sketch of each of the psychological theories. We would urge you to study each of these theories in more depth, and we provide references for further reading at the end of this chapter. We also wish to highlight that in our own experience as practitioners, all of the major human theories have proved useful and insightful. Rather than direct you to one specific theory, we would encourage a sensitive and informed blending of approaches when learning to understand the intricate and complex nature of human relationships. In Box 23.3 there is a worksheet to stimulate your studies.

Box 23.3: Two stories

Story 1

Amanda was an only child and her parents were both very academic. They put her under a lot of pressure to achieve three A grades at A-level so that she could take up a place at Oxford University to study politics and philosophy. Immediately prior to her exams, however, Amanda experienced a complete psychotic breakdown. She was found running through her local village in her nightclothes, believing she was the Virgin Mary and invisible to humans.

Story 2

Dan never knew his father and his mother gave him up for adoption when he was 18 months old. He refused to go to school because of being bullied. Aged 16, he made a serious attempt on his life.

Reflection

- For both stories, consider how various social and psychological theories may explain the onset of Amanda and Dan's mental health problems.

- How might your intellectual understanding influence the relationship you might form with them?

- When you think of working with Amanda and Dan, what personal challenges do you consider you might face?

The second intrinsic component of the therapeutic relationship: compassion

Intellectual understanding is essential for mental health practice. On its own, however, it is of little use. In order for intellectual understanding to be of use, it needs to be coupled with human compassion. Even though we use the word 'problems' in the expression 'mental health problems', people themselves are not problems to be solved by intellectual understanding alone. We are all complex creatures and intellectual understanding alone cannot fix our problems. As Maslow (1954) reminds us, the most fundamental human need after our physiological needs is the need for human love. Furthermore, this love needs to be unconditional (Rogers, 1961). On a human level, we can read the short descriptions of Amanda and Dan and conclude that here are two young people starved of unconditional love. We deliberately chose two people from contrasting social backgrounds to illustrate how mental health problems are so often to do with relationships. It is therefore understandable that the primary treatment for such 'problems' is relational too. As we have already stated, the forming of therapeutic relationships is foundational for mental health practice and should be the first point in every care plan.

Love and compassion

Providing love in a therapeutic relationship may be problematic for some workers. Some people may believe that love is reserved for family friends and intimate others. We would argue, however, that love for our 'fellow man' is fundamental in mental health care. It is acts of love, compassion and kindness informed by intellectual understanding that bring about change, growth and healing. Love is what Rogers (1961) calls unconditional positive regard. Love and the security that it brings feature in every major psychological theory, but for some reason receive little attention in mental health literature. It is our contention that the place of love in therapeutic relationships needs to be rightfully restored in mental health care.

Much of human caring has become technical, especially in nursing with machines and pumps used to deliver 'care'. Mental health has not escaped this drift towards efficiency, with an emphasis on quick-fix medication. The over-prescribing of antidepressant medication to combat human woe and restore happiness is alarming to any observer. Thankfully, there is a move towards greater provision of talking treatments, but these are often for limited periods and some people recommend that they are accessed on the Internet or through computer software. Standardised systems and care pathways, while not in themselves wrong, take the focus of care away from human relationships and emphasise the need to maintain the bureaucracy of the system.

Under-resourcing of mental health services further complicates the call for human compassion. If workers are required to fulfil their role with inadequate resources, it is understandable that morale becomes low and people find it difficult to produce emotional resources for helping others.

Respect

The word 'respect' invariably features in patient charters and hospital mission statements. In practice, however, it can be difficult to provide adequate respect in every given situation. Working in mental health care can be very personally demanding; workers are sometimes abused and not treated respectfully by both clients and colleagues. Sometimes maintaining respect feels over and above the call of duty. Nevertheless, respect for the individual, including respect for their age, gender, beliefs, culture and sexual orientation, is essential for providing a therapeutic relationship.

Carl Rogers was the first to articulate the non-judgemental attitude required for mental health work. To develop a truly non-judgemental way of working takes a good deal of self-awareness and a good deal of commitment. Given Rogers' core conditions for therapeutic relationships that we introduced earlier, there remains a conundrum for the worker: How can the worker maintain genuineness when they genuinely feel judgemental about the person with whom they are working? The worker needs to separate who the person is from what the person says or does. A compassionate approach requires the worker to lay aside their own judgements of the person's actions and words, and concentrate not on their own neediness but the needs of the client. Box 23.4 invites you to explore these issues in a practice-based situation.

Box 23.4

You are asked to assess a 45-year old man who has been detained under mental health law. He was arrested by police following the alleged rape and attempted murder of an 18-year-old student in a public park. The man is clearly mentally disturbed and has a diagnosis of schizophrenia.

Critical questions

- How do you feel towards this man?
- How might your feelings affect your assessment?
- What judgements do you think and feel?
- What do you think you should do with these judgements in order to work effectively with this man?

Empathy

Basic empathy may come more naturally to some people than to others. However, we would argue that empathic understanding can be learnt. Empathy requires both thinking and feeling processes. We could say that empathy requires multiple intelligence that is both cognitive and emotional. Empathy is achieved when the worker can imagine what it must be like and feel like to be that person; some have referred to this as 'putting ourselves in their shoes'.

One way of becoming empathic towards the client in Box 23.4 would be to imagine what he would have experienced throughout this episode. This is where empathic understanding becomes difficult; it is not easy to put ourselves in another's shoes, either literally or metaphorically. Next time you are in a group of people, experiment with wearing each other's shoes. The revulsion or challenge you might feel doing this is representative of the difficulty people have in putting themselves in another's shoes metaphorically. If we struggle with such a simple exercise, how much harder it is to put ourselves in another's shoes when we feel judgemental towards them. Developing empathic understanding is a complex and difficult business.

Some people say that empathy is easier to acquire and demonstrate if you have gone through the same experience. This may be true in some cases, but it may also be a disadvantage if the worker's feelings are negatively re-stimulated. Developing empathy for another's state of being is an art. As with any art form, empathy needs much commitment and practice.

Thus far in this chapter, we have identified the intrinsic components of the therapeutic relationship. Of course, these descriptions are not complete, but we believe we have laid the foundations for what is necessary for the mental health worker in terms of personal development. The intrinsic components of the therapeutic relationship are inseparable from values (discussed more fully in Chapter 5). The mental health worker's intellectual and emotional development needs to be on-going through further study, continuing reflections, therapy and supervision.

We now turn to the extrinsic components of the therapeutic relationship, in other words: How should the worker work? How should they be? What should they do?

▶ Extrinsic components of the therapeutic relationship

We have established the necessity for the mental health worker to have understanding and compassion for their clients. Once this is in place, then the worker needs to use their understanding and compassion for the therapeutic benefit of the client.

A word on evidence-based practice

In recent years, medical practice has called for all health care to be evidence based. Essentially what this means is that all treatments and therapies should be based on the best research evidence that proves their effectiveness. In medical science, this approach is highly recommended. If I were to be unfortunate enough to be diagnosed with cancer, I would want to know that I should be offered what had been proved to be the best available treatment in the hierarchy of evidence-based practice paradigm. The randomised control trial (RCT) is the pinnacle and I would certainly want to know that the treatment for my cancer had been subjected to RCTs and rigorously tried and tested (I certainly would not wish to be a guinea pig).

In our assertion that the therapeutic relationship is the most significant factor in mental health care, the reader may ask where the research evidence is to support this claim. Given the paradigm of EBP, this is a right and proper question. Where are the RCTs to support the therapeutic relationship? Of course, there are none. We say 'of course', because the whole idea of RCTs to test the effectiveness of a therapeutic relationship is unworkable, largely because it would be unethical to provide a non-therapeutic relationship to act as a control group.

The concept of human relations containing the potential to bring about healing and growth sits in a different paradigm to the one that measures effectiveness in RCTs. Having said this, the therapeutic relationship still needs to be evidence based, but what is required is a different sort of evidence to the kind of evidence that RCTs provide. This evidence is produced by case studies and the production of theories of human relations. If we carefully examine the original work of people who developed core theories of human relations (those we referred to earlier in this chapter), we see that the way these theories are created are through case studies. In the EBP paradigm, the single case study hardly features as significant evidence. In the paradigm of human relations, the single case study is paramount. This is why the counselling and psychotherapy literature is replete with case studies. It is through case studies that those who are professionals in human relating demonstrate the application of theory to practice.

So we now turn to applying the theory of therapeutic relationship to practice. What are the extrinsic components and how are they implemented?

Doing

Given the intrinsic qualities, values and knowledge the mental health worker should possess, what should the mental health worker do? In answering this question we propose the following subjects as essential for good therapeutic relationship:

- role

- boundaries

- responsibilities and rights

- communication

We deal with each of these four in turn.

Role

Throughout this chapter, we have referred to 'mental health workers' as if this were a generic role. We appreciate that readers of this book are from a multitude of professional backgrounds and each will fulfil their own special role. When we discuss role here we are speaking more generically, as we each maintain a professional role in the therapeutic relationship. The codes of practice that govern various professional practices will all support the creating/sustaining and ending of therapeutic relationships. Whatever our specific professional role, we all have a professional role to fulfil when we provide a therapeutic relationship.

The word 'role' originates in the theatre where an actor (one who on another occasion may be in the audience) assumes a costume and takes part in a play. This idea of a professional role in relation to the stage should not be taken literally, but metaphorically. The person who works as a professional assumes a social role. In therapeutic relationships, the professional has a specific role to fulfil. It is the role of one who provides a relationship that is therapeutic. If therapeutic benefit is not gained within the relationship, then the worker has not fulfilled their role. In reality, the professional role is multi-faceted and may include carer, quasi-friend, jailer, advocate, cleaner, adviser, housekeeper, protector, confidant and so on. While fulfilling each of these roles as appropriate, the worker needs to ensure that the intrinsic components of the therapeutic relationship are being put into external practice. In other words, whatever it is we are doing with our clients, we need to be able to offer compassionate care informed by our understanding.

Boundaries

Our professional role stipulates that professional boundaries exist, primarily for the protection of the client but also for the protection of the worker. Adherence to professional boundaries should keep everybody safe. When boundaries get blurred, people feel unsafe and mistakes occur. Sometimes boundary confusion does occur, for example being asked to work with somebody you attended school with, or inadvertently meeting a client in a public place in the company of mutual friends. All boundary blurring and transgression should be confessed and appropriate advice should be sought; hiding such issues will inevitably not be therapeutic for the client.

Responsibility

Mental health care is a very responsible role to fulfil. It is also a complex role with complex responsibilities. Mental health workers employed by statutory services are agents of the state with legal powers. At times, the worker is faced with ethical dilemmas, for example balancing the need to protect society while promoting the person's right to autonomy. It is argued in Chapter 11 that workers should always err on the side of promoting the person's freedom. It is argued that an over-emphasis on safety and risk prevention is un-therapeutic for the client. The worker is therefore often weighing up the responsibility of their role against the rights of the individual.

When we discussed blurring role boundaries, we used the word 'should'. By this we mean that the worker has an ethical responsibility to admit mistakes. When we discussed the intrinsic domain, we put much emphasis on the need for respect. Workers therefore have a responsibility to translate the respect in theory to respect in practice. Similarly, the worker has a responsibility to translate the understanding gained from applying theory to practice. Furthermore, the worker also has a responsibility to provide care according to their understanding of theory. Returning to Boxes 23.3 and 23.4 earlier in this chapter, now consider how your understandings of these examples might inform your approach in working therapeutically. How would each of the main theories inform your work?

Communication

All the compassion and understanding in the world will not help a person unless they are communicated. In developing a therapeutic relationship, ordinary human chitchat is essential. A therapeutic relationship does however need to develop from the superficial to the overtly therapeutic. We are not expecting the worker to make every interaction 'deep and meaningful'. However, we have a responsibility to communicate in a way that enshrines respect and an informed approach. Furthermore, individual and private time should be offered to the person for further development of the therapeutic relationship and for the opportunity to express themselves more fully. We would encourage all mental health workers to receive some form of counselling or psychotherapy training to enhance the skills needed for this type of work.

Being

We are all too familiar with the 'busyness' of professional practice. Students of mental health are not exempt from this busy, 'doing' culture. At times, it seems as though others are judging us not according to the quality of our work but on how busy we appear to others. In this day and age of surveillance, reporting and information technology, the art of human caring can be easily marginalised. This is intensified with threats of litigation that result in workers spending much time 'covering their backs'. This busyness and defensive practice can easily compromise the forming, sustaining and ending of therapeutic relationships.

Creating a therapeutic relationship requires time, and that time needs to be filled with so much more than information taking and giving. Primarily, the time required to build a therapeutic relationship should be taken up not with 'doing' but with 'being'. We are talking about the ability to lay aside both busyness and superficiality and be wholly present with the person in our care.

This presence is something that needs to be unconditionally offered. Box 23.5 gives examples of 'being' and offering presence in mental health practice.

Box 23.5

Rita

Rita did not believe in abortion, even though she was 42 years old and not in a relationship or in any fit state to parent a child. Having had mental health problems for many years, the thought of giving birth was too much for her to bear. Rita made a serious attempt on her life a month before her baby was due. The student nurse on the ward sat with Rita for an hour every day. Although Rita did not speak a word for four weeks, she later informed the student nurse how much it meant to her that he took the time every day to sit with her.

John

John was described as having personality difficulties, as he found difficulty maintaining any kind of conversation. As he worked with machinery all day, every day, his ability to communicate was seldom challenged. John was referred for counselling due to his inability to make any form of social contact. Every week during the hour-long counselling sessions, John hardly said a word. The counsellor did not feel a need to fill the silence and many of the 12 weekly counselling sessions were filled with silence. On the thirteenth week of counselling John began to cry. He had not expressed any emotions for many years and told the counsellor that the fact that she had remained 'present' for him for all of those silent hours had a major impact on him. He said that for the first time in his life he felt understood.

In these examples, the worker achieved a great deal in establishing a therapeutic relationship by actually 'doing' very little. In both examples, what the worker was doing was being with the client. During the many hours the workers spent with the clients, they were giving their full attention. Furthermore, they were not afraid to be still and calm and appear to be 'doing' nothing.

The ability to 'be with' a person in distress is not as easy as it may first appear. Being with a person in distress often raises two common responses: fear or the feeling of a need to rescue. Being aware of these responses and how to deal with them requires much self-awareness; neither fear nor the need to rescue is particular useful in mental health work. Self-awareness will help to turn these unhelpful feelings into helpful ones.

▶ **The good, the bad and the ugly**

The therapeutic relationship is the cornerstone of all mental health care; at least it should be. Human beings are not robots and when things go wrong emotionally or psychologically, human beings do not need fixing with machinery or chemicals. What people primarily need are positive helping relationships with significant others. If for whatever reason people enter mental health services, then the role of providing this therapeutic relationship falls on the mental health worker. The ability to form, sustain and appropriately end therapeutic relationships is not an optional approach for mental health work; it is fundamental to practice.

It might help to identify what it is that a therapeutic relationship provides. To do this, you might like to do the exercise in Box 23.6.

Box 23.6

Think of a time when you were distressed and somebody helped you. Now take a sheet of paper and list what exactly it was about that person that was helpful.

- What did they do?

- How did they treat you?

- What did they not do?

- What did they say?

- What did they not say?

- What did they provide?

This exercise might take a while. Usually people list about 30 factors.

While it may be necessary to contain people in distress (sometimes against their will), it should always be done therapeutically. In mental health training there is often talk about de-escalating violence, break-away techniques and managing aggression, but inadequate attention is usually given to the emotional and psychological aspects of people's distress. Of course workers need to be able to protect themselves, but if greater understanding and compassion were being offered in the first place, physical and chemical restraint would be required much less.

A good therapeutic relationship can provide people with the right conditions to grow, heal and change. This does not happen instantly and therapeutic relationships may be built up over a long period. When a person is first in contact with mental health services, being offered a therapeutic relationship is critical. Consider the contrasting practices in Box 23.7.

Box 23.7

Rudolph had become quite psychotic after the break-up of a three-year relationship. He was found in the street naked, making a pyramid from dustbin bags. The police were called and they escorted him to an acute admissions ward.

Hospital A

On arrival Rudolph was shown to his room by the police officers. One worker waited outside the room and another spent time with Rudolph. He was offered some medication to help him calm down. The worker spent several hours with Rudolph that day and most days the subsequent week listening to his (sometime garbled) story. Over the course of three weeks the worker gained a sense that he had really got to know Rudolph and had developed a trusting therapeutic relationship. After three weeks Rudolph was discharged and referred to counselling services.

Hospital B

On arrival Rudolph was shown to his room by the police officers. The worker told Rudolph that he must take a tablet to help him calm down and if he refused he would be forced to have an injection. At the mention of being forced, Rudolph raised his voice, objecting. The worker told Rudolph that he was not allowed to raise his voice and if he did so again he would be forcibly medicated. Feeling frightened and threatened, Rudolph attempted to run away. Within minutes he was restrained and forcibly medicated, and later detained under mental health law. For several weeks Rudolph was refused leave from the ward. He believed he was being kept as a political prisoner and remained on the ward for six months.

How true to life are these scenarios? Can human relationships have such causes and effects? Naturally, in the scenarios we have invented, the results are more than just the actions of individual workers; hospital culture and practices also need to be considered. Nevertheless, a positive human relationship between the person and a worker can make a difference to a person's life.

When things go wrong: dangers and pitfalls

Problems in therapeutic relationships often come to light when a worker feels out of their depth with a client. Sometimes, workers become over-involved or neglect or punish the person with whom they are working. Most of the time, workers are unaware that this is the case. When we begin to analyse what is wrong with specific relationships, it is often the case that a lack of self-awareness is evident. Such difficult situations can be avoided and overcome with increased self-awareness. As we already mentioned, some problems occur because of feelings of fear or the need to rescue the client. In all of these examples, workers become confused about the boundaries between themselves and their clients. In Box 23.8 you are invited to reflect on a difficult situation.

Box 23.8: a difficult situation

You enter a room full of people. The room is quiet, but you sense it is full of tension.

Reflective questions

■ How can you tell that there is tension in the room? (be specific)

■ What does this situation remind you of?

■ How might you have added to this tension?

■ What do you feel? (emotionally)

■ What do you feel? (physically)

■ How do you want automatically to react?

■ How might this reaction be different if you are in a professional role?

■ What does this situation remind you of?

■ If you decided you wanted to react differently in the future, what would you need to do to bring about a change?

In this exercise, we are deliberately encouraging you to think about yourself before you even begin to think about what might be going on in the room. All too often, mental health workers become involved in difficult situations without acknowledging what is going on for them first. Without this kind of self-awareness, there is the potential for the worker to react in this awkward situation in the same way they might have reacted to a similar situation in the family in which they grew up. If the worker grew up in a family with frequent tensions, these emotional memories may come flooding back and influence the way in which the worker responds in the here and now.

Often in mental health care, workers adopt a paternalistic role with their clients, and this is evident in the language employed. The worker may not realise that they are capable of punishing and controlling their clients, even with a tone of voice. Similarly, over-familiarity is a commonplace experience, especially when the worker feels the need to rescue the client, thus preventing the client from accessing and utilising their own resources. Workers may inadvertently foster relationships that become unhealthily dependent. Problems with such relationships often do not come to light until the worker leaves the service or the client makes a complaint against the worker. While we have advocated loving, compassionate relationships, we warn against the potential for falling in love. The self-awareness required when walking into the room described in Box 23.8 is the same self-awareness required to prevent the boundary breaking that would happen by falling in love with a client.

While it may be seen as abusive to have sexual relations with a client, it is equally abusive to be over-paternalistic or punishing. Both abusive scenarios stem from lack of self-awareness. The fear we referred to in distressing situations can cause us to behave in ways that are completely unfitting and un-therapeutic. Put crudely, a distressing situation may evoke within us a fight-or-flight response, neither of which are helpful. In such situations, we are required to examine our feelings and thoughts in the way we illustrated in Box 23.8. Naturally, this way of working takes time and practice. It is far easier to respond instinctively, naturally and without having to think and reflect. However, mental health practice requires us to be more skilled and informed than a layperson.

▶ Conclusion

Therapeutic relationships are essential to mental health practice. They are, however, often taken for granted and at times over-simplified. All human relationships are complex and often further complicated when people have experienced trauma and abuse. Whatever the origin of a person's mental health problem, the worker is required to have understanding of the nature of mental health problems and the theoretical underpinning for therapeutic approaches. Compassion is essential for this kind of work, although compassion on its own is not enough. For a therapeutic relationship to be effective, compassion and understanding need to be communicated to the person. Mistakes can easily be made in therapeutic relationships; these are largely due to lack of self-awareness on the part of the worker. Professional training for mental health practice should not be considered the end of the journey, but rather the beginning.

Finally, the opportunity to work with people experiencing mental health problems should be taken with sincerity and with joy. At times we are required to work with some of the most vulnerable people in society; at other times we are asked to provide the impossible with some of the most difficult. Mental health work requires immense patience and understanding for both constructing therapeutic relationships, but also having to work in systems that do not always appear to support the values required for the work. Ultimately, mental health workers need moral, ethical and human integrity to be the kind of workers we need to be. Our task is to provide the kind of relationship that we would want if we were in the client's shoes. Returning to the wisdom of the ancients, we would echo a fundamental tenet of most religions: 'Do unto others as you would wish to be done to.' If we can fulfil this principle, we have provided a 'good enough' therapeutic relationship.

▶ References

Maslow, A.H. (1954) *Motivation and Personality*. New York: Harper & Row.
Rogers, C. (1961) *On Becoming a Person: A Therapist's View of Psychotherapy*. London: Constable.

▶ Further reading

Therapeutic relationships have been identified in ancient cultures, notably in relation to shamanism and priesthood. You may like to read work about the role of the 'wounded healer' identified by Jung:

Jung, C.G. (1966) *The Spirit in Man, Art, and Literature*. London: Routledge & Kegan Paul.

Jung, C.G. (1989) *Memories, Dreams, Reflections*. Recorded and edited by Aniela Jaffé; translated from the German by Richard & Clara Winston. New York: Vintage Books.

These ideas have been applied to mental health practice by professors Phil Barker (nursing) and David Brandon (social work):

Barker, P. (1996) Working with mental distress. *Nursing Times*, **10 Jan**: 25–7.

Brandon, D. (1999) A necessary madness: The role of the wounded healer in contemporary mental health care. *Mental Health Care*, **21**(6): 198–200.

Brandon's classic text on social work practice is valuable reading:

Brandon, D. (1990) *Zen in the Art of Helping*. London: Penguin.

The seminal work of Carl Rogers brought person-centred therapy into the helping professions. His books have been hugely influential in education and all of the helping professions:

Rogers, C. (1951) *Client-Centred Therapy: Its Current Practice, Implications and Theory*. London: Constable.

Rogers, C. (1961) *On Becoming a Person: A Therapist's View of Psychotherapy*. London: Constable.

One of the earliest mental health nursing theorists was Hildegard Peplau. For her, the therapeutic relationship was central to mental health practice. Her seminal work is as relevant today as it ever was:

Peplau, H. (1988) *Interpersonal Relations in Nursing* (2nd edn). Basingtoke: Macmillan.

The following is a useful article for understanding the history of therapeutic relationships:

O'Brien, A.J. (2001) The therapeutic relationship: Historical development and contemporary significance. *Journal of Psychiatric and Mental Health Nursing*, **8**(2): 129–37.

For summaries of the psychological theories that underpin therapeutic relationships, it is worth beginning with psychology textbooks. For the application of those theories to practice, students will find it helpful to refer to the vast literature that has been developed in the field of counselling and psychotherapy. Although there are literally hundreds of different types of therapies and approaches, they will generally fall under the umbrella of the main approaches we have identified: psychodynamic, humanistic, cognitive and behavioural.

Some key texts for mainstream psychological and psychotherapy theories follow (this list is not exhaustive!):

Ellis, A. (1962) *Reason and Emotion in Psychotherapy*. Secaucus, NJ: Citadel Press.

Ellis, A. (1979) *A New Guide to Rational Living*. Hollywood, CA: Wilshire.

Jacobs, M. (2006) *The Presenting Past: The Core of Psychodynamic Counselling and Therapy* (3rd edn). Maidenhead: Open University Press.

Maslow, A.H. (1954) *Motivation and Personality*. New York: Harper & Row.

Skinner, B.F. (1993) *About Behaviorism*. London: Penguin.

Skinner, B.F. (2002) *Beyond Freedom and Dignity*. Cambridge: Hackett.

Psychological approaches to mental health

Rufus May

Bradford District Care Trust assertive outreach team

Anne Cooke

Salomons, Canterbury Christ Church University

Anthony Cotton

Bradford District Care Trust

This chapter begins with a personal account by one of the authors. The rest of the chapter considers various psychological approaches that may be used in mental health care.

A personal account of working with psychological approaches (Anthony Cotton)

My first experience of primary care services in mental health came in 1995. Following a series of traumatic life events – the deaths of several friends, the break-up of the band I was in, the physical illness and depression of my father – I had become extremely low in mood, spending most of my time in bed, unable to see the point of getting up to do anything, since I felt everything was ultimately useless. I began to contemplate methods of suicide on a daily basis. I rarely left the house in daylight, as I had feelings of paranoia about seeing other people. I thought everyone was talking negatively about me – friends, relatives, neighbours and strangers. To cope with these depressive and paranoid thoughts, I began to drink more heavily, mostly in the evening. During the early hours I would sometimes self-harm,

---

Learning About Mental Health Practice.   Edited by Theo Stickley and Thurstine Basset
© 2008 John Wiley & Sons, Ltd

stubbing cigarettes out on my arm. This seemed to temporarily relieve some of the mental distress I was feeling. The problem came to a head when my partner discovered the burn marks and said that if I carried on staying in bed all day I would end up dying there, to which I replied, 'Good'.

Hearing myself confirm to my partner that I wanted to die and realising I meant it came as a shock to me, even though I had thought about suicide innumerable times. My partner said that if I felt that way I should see a GP, and immediately arranged an appointment. Fortunately, my GP was sympathetic and understanding, prescribing Prozac straight away and offering me therapy within a few weeks. After about three or four weeks of Prozac, my mood improved, so that I was able to go out more. My interests in music and reading were rekindled, and I became much more sociable with friends. The drinking increased, however, largely because of this sociability.

The therapy offered was cognitive behavioural therapy (CBT), which I initially found too simplistic and often patronising. For example, at an early session I remember the therapist showing me two pictures of a vase of flowers, one in which the flowers were in full bloom, the other showing drooping, dead ones. This was supposed to illustrate the difference between positive and negative thinking. To me it seemed a crass, crude approach. I thought my depression a natural, logical reaction to the way the world was, rather than a form of individual 'faulty thinking' that could be quickly rectified. I had read books about the Holocaust and the Milgram experiment, which confirmed my pessimistic view of humanity. 'Happiness' seemed a superficial and stupid emotion in a post-Holocaust world. All my favourite artists and writers were depressives or had committed suicide. It seemed ridiculous that my therapist was trying to change these 'negative thoughts', which felt part of my being, seemingly as a 'quick fix' to project me back into a world that continued to avoid these unpalatable 'truths'. I also had difficulty when it came to doing the 'homework', particularly in writing down what I was thinking about immediately before I had depressive feelings, since the feelings often seemed to come before the thoughts. However, I did take on board some concepts of CBT, like 'catastrophising'.

I eventually established a good relationship with my therapist, who within a short period of time took a more eclectic approach, no doubt responding to my difficulties with pure CBT. It emerged that he was a practising Buddhist, and this soon became our main 'point of connection', as I had been interested in Zen Buddhism previously. Our sessions continued, often utilising Buddhist notions of 'mindfulness' and 'living in the present' as part of the therapeutic approach.

When the therapy ended after six months I felt better for a while, but relapsed a few months later. I was again referred by my GP and this time art therapy was suggested as an alternative to more CBT. My previous therapist had now retired and I felt that I needed a longer period of time to explore my feelings, and to work out where they came from, so the idea of two years of a more psychodynamic approach, again limited to one hourly session a week, made sense to me. I felt that CBT, offering one hour per week over six months, had not given me sufficient time to deal with my problems. Art therapy enabled me to discover the history of my depressive thoughts. I realised that I had felt unhappy for long periods of my childhood, particularly during my teenage years. These feelings were rooted in family deaths and my relationship with my parents and older brother. I painted dreams, nightmares and childhood scenes I remembered, as well as depictions of emotions I was experiencing in the present. There was no pressure to talk about these images, unless I wanted to. Some sessions would involve a lot of talking, but sometimes I just wanted to paint. In putting down on paper pictorial representations of my fears, I felt I was lessening their power over me. 'Dangerous' images were 'contained' within the frame of the paper.

After a while, I had a much clearer view of where these feelings originated, and this growing ability to identify and explain them to myself helped me to work through them. I became an archaeologist of my own past, my investigative curiosity overcoming former feelings of hopelessness. However, I did not feel as if all my problems had been 'solved' at the end of two years, only that in understanding them more fully I was able to cope with them more easily.

Within a couple years of completing art therapy I was studying full-time at college, and in 1999 I gained a place at university to undertake a degree in psychology. My father died shortly after I began my first year, but I coped with this in a better way than I had imagined I would. I have been prescribed other anti-depressant medication since therapy: Citalopram and Venlafaxine. The former was prescribed during my third year at university. I had stopped taking Prozac several weeks earlier, momentarily convinced that I would be fine without it. However, largely because of the pressure of work in the final year, I began to experience feelings of extreme anxiety. These emotions were new to me, and very frightening. I felt I was 'going mad', and thought I would end up in a mental health facility, being given ECT, as my father was. These new symptoms were very similar to my father's.

Fortunately, I had made a good friend at university, so I sent him a desperate text message. He immediately suggested I stay with him. He and his girlfriend supported me for several weeks, cooking me healthy meals, administering aromatherapy and reassuring me that I would be OK. Without their help I would probably have quit my degree and returned home. As it was, I deferred my final exams, but completed my degree successfully within a few months. The Citalopram I was prescribed during this period was counter-productive – it seemed to make me feel more anxious. I remember my dismay on finding anxiety listed as a possible 'side effect' of a drug I was told was designed to alleviate anxiety. Since then I have been prescribed Venlafaxine, which I have tried to come off several times. However, the resultant withdrawal effects, coupled with a fear of relapse, have meant that I have never managed to last without medication for longer than a few months.

Looking back on these experiences, several relevant points occur to me. First, being offered therapy on my first visit to my GP was a crucial factor in enabling me to cope with my depressive feelings. Medication alone would not have helped me to deal with the causes of my problems, but temporarily buried them by changing my outward behaviour. Secondly, making some kind of connection with the therapist was more important than the nature of the therapy itself. This was certainly true of my first encounter, where the therapist found something within my own experience, namely an interest in Buddhism, which could be successfully utilised in a therapeutic approach, rather than sticking to the prescribed CBT method. I discovered subsequently that he had also employed other psychological approaches in his attempts to find 'common ground' for dialogue.

Art therapy was different in its dynamic. While the therapeutic relationship was still a prominent factor in my progress, I felt that I was being given the space to establish a direct relationship with my unconscious self, which was emerging through my paintings. My therapist played an important role in creating a relaxed, safe environment in which I felt I could freely express these unconscious fears or desires, and she was always there to support and guide me through them. In contrast to the 'one-to-one' communication involved in the 'talking therapy' I had experienced previously, art therapy seemed to open up a three-way 'conversation' between my conscious self, the unconscious self represented in my artwork and my therapist. This new dynamic appeared to alleviate a lot of the potential tension involved in 'one-to-one' therapy. I felt a sense of relief from the pressure of constantly talking about my problems, and enjoyed the fact that I could sit and paint in silence, with the therapist inconspicuously present in the room, but always there if I needed to discuss anything. Another positive element of the therapy was being able to review my work over time, which gave me a strong feeling of purpose and progress. For instance, my early paintings were totally devoid of bright colours, the predominant black, grey and brown shades indicating not only my depressive mood, but also my distrust of happiness as an emotion. Looking back at my work after the first six months, I could see that I was coming to terms with this aversion as red, yellow, blue and orange splashes were gradually introduced, eventually displacing the dominant darker colours.

Unlike CBT, art therapy gave me the time and opportunity to explore my 'negative thoughts', rather than trying to change the thought processes that created them. For me, CBT was an introduction to the possibility of therapeutic change, which was later fulfilled by art therapy. Fortunately, as I ultimately related well to both therapists, I feel that I gained something from both encounters.

Finally, I would like to mention the significant role that others played in reassuring and supporting me through this period of my life. Without the concern and encouragement of my partner, my local GP, my friend at university and other friends at home in Bradford, I seriously doubt whether I would have been able to overcome these psychological problems. My thanks to them.

▶ Psychology as an alternative to medicine in mental health

A psychological approach to mental health is different to a medical approach to mental health. A medical approach describes the person's problem by allocating it to a diagnostic category. The assumption is that the primary cause of many problems is a biochemical abnormality. Psychiatric medicines are used to try to reduce the impact of the problem. Psychology can be defined as the study of behaviour and experience. A psychological approach to mental health aims to understand how people's past and present behaviour and experiences are linked, and how changing patterns of behaviour and thinking can alleviate levels of confusion and distress. It also aims to understand the psychological effects of social and environmental factors, including relationships and wider social and cultural influences. As an example of the difference between the two approaches, someone who as a child lost a parent in a road accident and becomes despairing and low in mood after a relationship break-up might be understood medically to be experiencing the symptoms of clinical depression. The same person might be understood psychologically to be in a grief state, which reflects not only the loss of a relationship partner but taps into suppressed emotional pain caused by unresolved childhood bereavement. A medical approach to treatment might involve the prescription of medication and if the problem remained and was severe, electro-convulsive treatment (ECT) might be tried. In contrast, psychological treatment would use emotional and psychological exercises try to understand, cope with and work through loss-related experiences and behaviours.

As we have seen in Anthony's example, the approaches can be combined and indeed many practitioners draw on both. However, this is not always the case and sometimes they can conflict. For example, there is much evidence that distressing psychological experiences such as hearing voices or experiencing feelings of low self-worth are likely to be related to past life experiences. In this way the signs of distress are clues to the underlying causes. Sometimes medication may suppress these clues and make tackling the roots of the distress more difficult.

Alternatively, it can be argued that used carefully, medical treatments can create enough emotional stability to enable the person to do some psychological work and to approach the world and their experiences more positively and less fearfully. The danger with this approach is that some drugs may be hard to come off, and used long term can sometimes have adverse health effects, for example tardive dyskinesia (a permanent Parkinsonian condition created by neuroleptic medication). The frustration in modern mental health services is that generally people do not get to make informed choices about which therapeutic route to take.

A psychological approach is currently the main alternative approach to understanding and treating health problems that is available in the medically dominated mental health system. Historically, as a result of its secondary status, proponents of a psychological approach have had to be careful not to be too challenging to the dominant medical paradigm, and it is often seen as complementary to a medical approach, rather than as an alternative. Psychological practitioners differ in the extent to which they ally themselves with medical concepts such as diagnoses and clinical language.

For example, many psychologists and other mental health professionals have sought to integrate psychological and biological approaches under the banner of 'biopsychosocial' approaches. However, Slade (2002, p. 8) suggests that 'this model leads to emotional disorders being understood primarily in biological terms (as disturbances in anatomy and physiology), with psychological and social aspects considered in so far as biological factors fail to account for the disorder'. Slade argues that psychological approaches are distinctively different from psychiatric approaches and have a superior evidence base. He argues that in this age of the consumer, service users should be able to choose between psychological and more medical models of treatment.

There are a number of different psychological approaches to therapy, each reflecting different practitioners' beliefs about the best way in which problems can be understood and addressed. These approaches are conceptual tools utilised by therapists and made available to their clients, rather than organised belief systems. They are not necessarily mutually exclusive: different combinations of approaches will be relevant to different clients. Often, therapeutic theories are saying similar things but expressing them in a different way, sometimes using different language. Service users considering therapy may find it difficult to decide which approach is most suitable for them, particularly if information about each approach is not readily available. There is currently a great need for good information to be made available to service users so that they can make a more informed decision about which therapy to undertake. We suggest that each practitioner or service, including those in the psychiatric field, should publish information about the nature of the approach(es) they offer. As Anthony's personal account suggests, knowledge of different approaches is likely to lead to a more flexible service that can adapt to the preferences of the person seeking help. The following list provides examples of some of these therapeutic approaches.

Behaviour therapy

Behaviour therapy focuses on modifying outward behaviour rather than exploring internal mental states. Therapists avoid 'endless introspection' about the meaning of symptoms. They concentrate on helping the person to act in a different way, for example by confronting feared situations in order to overcome anxiety, or by increasing activity levels if the person is experiencing low mood and has become 'stuck' in a vicious circle of inactivity and hopelessness. In this form of therapy the therapist's role is that of the 'technical expert', guiding the client through treatment.

Cognitive behavioural therapy (CBT)

CBT is probably the most common therapeutic intervention available to service users. CBT focuses on the client's thoughts and emotions, as well as their behaviour. The emphasis is on helping the client adopt coping strategies to alleviate psychological distress, and to recognise and change negative thought patterns that maintain unproductive behaviour. The meanings people ascribe to their experiences are considered to be crucial in determining their behaviour. Originally, CBT underlined the importance of 'faulty reasoning' in this process, but more recently there has been more concentration on the effects of mood states on thinking, rather than seeing 'wrong thinking' as necessarily causal. Clients are invited to take part in 'homework' between sessions, in which they can monitor their feelings and attempt to discover the psychological 'triggers' for problematic thoughts or behaviours. CBT has been widely used as a short-term treatment for depression. While CBT has emphasised the importance of a collaborative relationship, the therapist is seen as an expert guide who leads the person to a more rational view of themselves through techniques such as 'Socratic questioning'.

Psychodynamic therapy

The psychodynamic approach proposes that symptoms arise from the need to defend oneself from unconscious memories, feelings or impulses. Therapy is concerned with uncovering these unconscious thoughts, and bringing them into the client's conscious 'reality'. This requires not only a cognitive awareness of hidden feelings, but also a process of re-experiencing them. In this endeavour, the transference relationship between client and therapist, and the interpretation of unconscious thoughts, are of paramount importance. The therapist is seen as the 'expert' in the therapeutic exchange, as the client's own views may be 'defence mechanisms'. However, some therapists have adapted psychodynamic approaches to make them more transparent in sharing the therapist's views of the importance of addressing repressed emotional experiences and therefore more collaborative in style (e.g. Johnson, 2002).

Humanistic therapy

This approach overlaps with that of other psychological methodologies, such as existential models, client-centred models, gestalt therapy and personal construct therapy. The therapeutic assumptions are that people have an innate drive towards health and self-actualisation, and that the potential for positive mental health lies in a greater awareness and acceptance of inner feelings or impulses that may previously have been disregarded as a result of social conditioning. It is felt that positive change will occur naturally if the therapist provides the optimum conditions of warmth, empathy and unconditional positive regard. In this venture the therapist facilitates rather than initiates the possibility of change.

Community psychology

Community psychology proposes that psychological problems are mainly caused by the physical and social environment surrounding us. Proponents of this viewpoint cite evidence of the association between psychological problems and social deprivation; for example, the link between depression and unemployment. Therefore, more important than therapy is for psychologists to focus on social and community interventions and developments. This might include community-based group work that empowers people to come together to work collectively towards addressing social inequality issues (e.g. practical help in re-housing, education or employment training).

An example of a mental health community psychology project that has now developed into an independent community initiative is Evolving Minds (see www.evolving-minds.co.uk). This is a series of public meetings about different approaches to mental health. It has led to a Mad Arts festival, helping organise national protests against coercive psychiatric practice and a 'coming off medication' project.

Community psychology does not rule out individual work. For example, Smail (2005) outlines how 'consultation' can take place, consisting of three elements: the provision of comfort; helping the person to clarify the factors contributing to their difficulties; and encouraging them to make use of available powers and resources.

Social constructionist approaches

According to social constructionism, there is no one best way to view reality. There is therefore no way to take a truly objective stance on our social lives. Reality can only be known through language, which is made up of social constructs. Each way of describing reality amounts to a particular story that enables some ways of thinking and acting and restricts others. In this school of thought it therefore follows that psychological concepts, such as 'depression', are social constructs produced by particular societies or groups of people at particular times. Narrative therapy is an attempt to transfer these ideas into a therapeutic practice. Social constructionist approaches emphasise the social roots of knowledge about the world and oneself, particularly in family life, and attempts to assist the person in developing more enabling stories about events that have occurred in people's lives. The psychiatric service user/survivor movement draws extensively on these ideas.

Solution-focused therapy

This therapy eschews the often retrospective, 'problem-solving' approach of some other therapies in favour of an emphasis on the positive achievements of the client, and focuses on the best way of assisting the client to accomplish future goals. In this enterprise it reflects the ethos of the positive psychology movement, which aims to promote personal and collective psychological well-being, rather than concentrating exclusively on negative feelings of distress.

▶ The debate about 'evidence'

The recent climate within mental health services has placed a good deal of emphasis on the need for treatments and therapies to be 'evidence based', and various guidelines have been issued in the UK by the National Institute for Clinical Excellence (NICE) on what it considers to be the most 'evidence-based' treatments for different problems. However, there has also been a vigorous debate about what constitutes 'evidence' for a particular approach or treatment. NICE considers so called 'randomised controlled trials' to be the 'gold standard'. These are treatment trials where service users are randomly allocated to different forms of treatment and the results (generally measured by a combination of questionnaires filled in by the service users and judgements made by clinicians) are compared.

However, many professionals question the relevance of such trials within the mental health field. Critics point to a number of problems (see e.g. Marzillier, 2004; Slade & Priebe, 2001):

- Trials generally involve grouping service users according to 'diagnosis'. However, there is a debate about whether diagnoses are useful as a basis for treatment decisions, or indeed generally, in mental health. Critics point out that even where people have the same diagnostic label, they often have little in common. As shown in Anthony's example, treatment needs to be tailored to the individual's unique combination of needs and preferences; however, there are currently very few treatment trials conducted on this basis. Similarly, people often have a range of problems that do not fit neatly into one diagnostic category. Many psychologists feel that diagnoses are an inappropriately medicalised way of defining psychological experience, pointing out that people do not 'have' depression in the way that they might 'have' measles, for example. The experiences that might lead to such a diagnosis are ones that many people might have at points in their lives, and two people diagnosed with 'depression' might have very little in common, with very different reasons for their low mood.

■ Ironically, the better quality the research, the less use it is to clinicians. Good-quality research involves therapy carried out strictly according to a 'manual' for that therapy type, extensive assessment (e.g. the client fills out questionnaires every session), tape recording of sessions, and offered only to a highly selected group of service users whose experiences fit one diagnostic category and who have few problems in other areas. All of this makes it hard to say to what extent the results are relevant to 'real life', where things are necessarily very different. What does it mean, in these circumstances, to say for example that 'cognitive therapy is an effective treatment for depression'?

■ What counts as 'success' in a particular trial is usually decided in advance by the researchers. A common example might be a reduction of x points on a widely used questionnaire that claims to assess 'depression' or 'anxiety'. However, as shown in Anthony's example, different people are hoping for different things from therapy, and what counts as 'success' on a particular measure (or even a number of measures) may or may not accord with the person's own view as to how helpful the therapy was. Similarly, the aspects of the therapy that the person finds helpful may not be those that the therapist sees as particularly important.

■ Finally, critics point out that therapy is essentially a personal relationship. As Marzillier (2004), a respected psychologist and psychotherapist, writes:

How the therapist responds to clients is as much dependent on his or her skills and style as any technique. How can such complexity be reduced to a set of predetermined treatments or manualised procedures? When I am asked to recommend a therapist to someone, my first thought is about the personal qualities of the therapist. My next is about how experienced they are and whether they would suit the client and help them with their problems. (Marzillier, 2004, p. 394)

▶ Working with the individual in their social context

Mental health services are rooted in a tradition of coercive practice and biological ideology that continues to be an important factor in current provision. Pat Deegan (1993, 1994) has described how the coercive application of a narrow medical understanding of mental distress can have a 'spirit-breaking' effect on the person on the receiving end. There is evidence that for lay people at least, seeing someone's problems as caused by a 'mental illness' can lead to fearful attitudes and less respectful communication (Read *et al.*, 2006: for more on this see chapter 18 in this volume). For example, in his research looking at stigma and public perceptions, Read found that compared to psychosocial understandings, biogenetic causal theories and diagnostic labelling are both associated with increased perceptions of dangerousness, unpredictability, fear and a desire for social distance. Some writers in the service user/survivor literature also suggest that they experience more empathic understanding from mental health professionals who tend to see problems in psychological or social rather than in purely biological terms. Biogenetic explanations may also be more disempowering, as they arguably encourage the person to see themselves as a passive victim of an active and chronic disease process.

The evidence supporting the 'brain disease'/chemical imbalance explanation of mental health problems is gradually weakening. For example, recently the Royal College of Psychiatry has adapted its Web site so that depression is no longer explained as being caused by a biochemical imbalance. Despite this, biomedical attitudes remain dominant in mental health practice. Research over the last 20 years into how people cope with voice hearing has suggested that they find a broad range of frameworks useful in understanding their voice-hearing experience (e.g. Romme & Escher, 2000). For example, while some people find biological understandings helpful, others find psychodynamic (emotional), cognitive, spiritual and paranormal frameworks helpful. Some people blend different understandings together or hold seemingly contradictory models in parallel.

Recent research into the experience of hearing voices tells us that it is important for people to have choice in how they make sense of their experience, and that the traditional approach in mental health of seeking to impose explanation and promote 'insight' may be both harmful and counter-productive. It would seem that psychological practice should be as person centred as possible in allowing clients to choose and work within different cultural understandings.

We also need to be aware of the limitations of Western psychology, which has developed in a eurocentric cultural context. For example, Western psychology tends to assume autonomous thinking and a strong sense of self to be a universally desired state of being. In contrast, Eastern approaches to mental health tend to see self-cherishing as often leading to greed and loneliness. They suggest that while self-respect is important, developing a combination of detachment from self-serving thinking and a strong sense of connectedness and compassion towards others will promote positive mental health. Western psychological approaches to mental health can be criticised for their individualistic emphasis and their neglect of socio-economic factors and the importance of faith and spirituality. David Smail (2005) and others have observed how psychological therapy tends to minimise the impact of economic and political forces on individual well-being. Smail argues that psychological distress is mainly influenced by social processes such as poverty, exploitation, sexism and discrimination. If psychological approaches do not acknowledge these wider social realities, they risk seeing the individual and their 'faulty thinking' as wholly responsible and to blame for their problems. Secondly, an emphasis on individual psychological therapy may distract from the broader socio-political processes required to prevent the distress happening in the first place.

A community psychology approach seeks to address this by focusing on community interventions using education and empowerment to enable social groups and communities to create supportive resources and mobilise against unhelpful, oppressive socio-political processes. Supporting self-help networks is an example of putting this philosophy into practice (examples being the Hearing Voices Network, the Self-Harm Network, the Scottish Recovery Network and First Person Plural). The growth of self-help information and networks on the Internet is another exciting development.

In mental health services, psychological approaches need to develop so that they are accessible to a broad range of cultural and class backgrounds. This may mean psychological therapy diversifying, moving away from purely one-to-one consultations to a range of services including group work, self-help groups, community meetings, Internet consultations, and increasing the use of self-help literature and software. If psychology is genuinely to seek to promote choice in services, it will also mean working in partnership with faith groups, spiritual healers and other holistic therapists, as well as other mental health professionals.

The history of psychology is characterised by a valuing of rational and scientific understanding, so, with some exceptions (e.g. Jungian psychology), it has tended to avoid considering spiritual beliefs and practices in its research and practice. However, in (mental health) recovery research and accounts, spirituality is a common source of resilience, confidence and meaning in people's recovery journeys (e.g. Faulkner & Layzell, 2000; Thornhill, Clare & May, 2004).

▶ Using psychology creatively in mental health

In this final section we consider some creative ways in which psychology can be used to help people with mental health problems.

Recovery approaches

Service users/survivors and their allies have been keen to point out that mental health services are often too controlling and pessimistic in their approach to mental health problems. Treatment tends to be about 'symptom management' rather than helping people rebuild their lives and achieve their potential. Many survivors have been keen to pursue the concept of 'recovery', seeing it as a process that incorporates psychological healing, self-determination and the regaining of control. For example, Ron Coleman's book *Recovery: An Alien Concept* charts his journey from institutionalised psychiatric patient, diagnosed with schizophrenia, to international publisher and trainer: 'Recovery means learning to cope with our difficulties, gaining control over our lives, achieving our goals, developing our skills and fulfilling our dreams' (Coleman, 1999, p. 103). While believing that everyone can recover from mental health problems, Ron, influenced by the Mad Pride movement, also reclaims his psychotic experiences and has a tattoo that reads 'psychotic and proud'. Psychology is well placed to ally itself with such optimism in that it is not tied to notions of chronic disease and fatalistic ideas of biological determinism (see May, 2004).

The recovery process appears to follow three distinct stages, which are not completely linear and may at times run alongside each other. First comes a *safety* stage. During a period of intense distress and confusion, the person needs to learn ways to feel safe, which gives them a sense of autonomy. This could include psychological coping strategies and behavioural techniques, relaxation techniques, supportive relationships and holistic therapies. Learning an accepting (rather than avoidant) approach towards one's psychological experiences also seems to be extremely helpful. The second stage is *making sense of one's experiences*. This involves understanding how experiences link to thoughts, feelings and behaviour in the present and the past (including wider social and cultural forces). The third stage is *social reconnection*, where people find new ways to connect with others through social roles and activities. This may include improving one's housing, pursuing vocational activities and building family and friendship networks.

Psychological approaches can clearly play a vital role in supporting the recovery process, however in order to do so effectively they may need to be adapted from their traditional roots, in order for them to be as enabling as possible.

Making psychology less 'expert led'

Over the last 20 years, there has been a growing self-help movement that challenges traditional conceptions about 'them and us' in mental health services – in other words, who has the expertise and what form it takes. Psychology needs to respond to this movement. For example, in Hearing Voices conferences, academic studies of the voice-hearing experience and personal accounts of learning to live with voices are seen as of equal value and the presentations and workshops reflect this. Academic expertise and the expertise of experience are given the same status.

In its attempts to appear objective and scientific, psychology has traditionally tended to present itself as a dispassionate discourse that excludes the personal experience of the psychologist. This stance is likely to perpetuate 'them and us' boundaries. Therefore, psychologists who are able to reflect on personal experience of distress, which we all experience, and conduct research and other initiatives in a genuinely collaborative way will be offering service users a genuinely alternative way forward to deal with their problems and improve their lives.

Language

Earlier in this chapter we highlighted the problems with embracing medical terminology, which can encourage passivity and helplessness. Psychologists have also created their own professional jargon that can be experienced as exclusive and disempowering. An alternative approach is to help the person describe their own experiences in their own terms. This may mean using more experiential language such as talking about feelings of despair, loneliness, panic, dread or hearing voices, or describing coping strategies such as pacing self-harm, disassociation, distraction, avoidance and withdrawal. This language tends to put experiences into some meaningful relation to social contexts. Using a broader range of language prevents exclusivity. Describing someone's problems becomes a genuinely collaborative process. In this way, 'assessing' and 'formulating' an understanding of the person's problems become a subjective process of negotiation rather than attempting to describe experience using objective terms.

Conceptual work

As we have seen, even within psychological thinking there are a myriad of different ways of understanding behaviour and experience. This reflects the broader situation that mental health thinking and practice is a contested area. Disagreements in mental health thinking can seem extreme. For example, while some people believe that mental illness does not exist (e.g. Szasz, 2002), others believe that we are all mentally ill. Despite their apparent contradiction, it can be argued that both ideas may be useful at different times for different people. Social constructionism teaches us that each way of understanding opens up some possibilities for thinking and action and closes down others. As we have argued, a broad range of ideas will be useful to the recovery process. Research suggests that many people may hold seemingly opposing frameworks simultaneously.

In mental health systems many people get stuck with quite limiting accounts of their abilities and potential for change. Introducing new and different ways of seeing their situation can be potentially liberating. For example, the Buddhist idea that all of us are influenced by delusions and none of us sees the true nature of reality, can be a really useful concept to overcome the exclusive nature of being classified as 'mentally ill'. If everyone is mentally ill, the problem of recovery shifts from adapting to a 'well' society to finding a way to navigate unhealthy social systems and behaviours. In one self-help group, one of us facilitating the group looked at the problem of 'How do we survive in a sick society?' Such systemic understandings relieve the individual of a sense of unworthiness and avoid perpetuating the assumption that the social world is rational, fair and benign and the problem resides solely in the individual.

Working within different frameworks of understanding

As was observed earlier, research has found that people use a broad range of frameworks to make sense of their experiences of emotional distress (e.g. cognitive, emotional, spiritual, paranormal and biological understandings). Traditionally, mental health services have attempted to adapt people's irrational thinking to more 'normal' attitudes. People who refuse to do this and to adopt a medical view of their problems have been construed as 'lacking insight', and coercive measures have often been attempted to shift their standpoint. Psychologists also have traditionally excluded people from their services who are judged not to be 'psychologically minded'; or they have attempted to change the person's beliefs.

Psychological approaches used in self-help movements offer a different way forward. Hearing Voices, unusual belief and recovery self-help groups are often based an acceptance that there is no one best way to understand the world.

In other words, they respect different frames of reference or worldviews. For example, in the Bradford Hearing Voices group many people believe in spiritual possession, others believe that voice hearing is an emotionally driven experience, while others believe that it is the result of neurological problems (some people have adopted a number of these explanations, using them when it feels most suitable). One man believed that he was possessed and came to the Hearing Voices group because it respected his view. Initially the group supported him to gain access to a spiritual healer, which he found validating and beneficial. After two years he began to use psychological counselling in addition to the self-help group. He started to explore the idea that some of his feelings of being evil were related to feelings of self-blame and guilt related to difficult relationships he had had in the past with family members; at the same time he maintained his belief in the supernatural. Where people choose to, they are supported to test out the evidence for their beliefs, but this is with the total consent of the individual.

Psychology and changing social attitudes towards mental health

Mental health services remain largely biomedical in their philosophy and practice. This is despite the fact that in survey after survey, service users consistently ask for greater access to psychological approaches and holistic therapies. In the past, mental health systems have changed the most when social structures and public opinion have demanded social change. Psychologists have therefore sought to help educate the public about mental health from psychological perspectives. This has included getting involved in journalism, public meetings and campaigning work. The British Psychological Society Report (2000) on understanding psychotic experiences is an example of trying to make available in an accessible way psychological knowledge that challenges biomedical frameworks. It combined research findings with personal accounts of psychiatric treatment and psychotic experiences. Publication of the report led to a greater confidence among psychologists to speak up about diverse ways of understanding mental health problems and the recovery process.

Reflections on this chapter

- What has helped you when you have been distressed?
- How might this kind of help be similar or different to the approaches described in this chapter?

▶ References

British Psychological Society Report (2000) *Recent Advances in Understanding Mental Illness and Psychotic Experience*. Leicester: British Psychological Society. Available at www.understandingpsychosis.com.

Coleman, R. (1999) *Recovery: An Alien Concept*. Gloucester: Handsell Press.

Deegan, P. (1993) Recovering our sense of value after being labelled. *Journal of Psychosocial Nursing*. **31**: 7–11.

Deegan, P. (1994) Recovery: The lived experience of rehabilitation. In W.A. Anthony & L. Spaniol (eds), *Readings in Psychiatric Rehabilitation* (pp. 149–62). Boston, MA: Boston University Center for Psychiatric Rehabilitation.

Faulkner, A. & Layzell, S. (2000) *Strategies for Living Report*. London: Mental Health Foundation.

Johnson, B. (2002) *Emotional Health*. Sandown: James Naylor Foundation.

Marzillier, J. (2004) The myth of evidence-based psychotherapy. *The Psychologist*, **17**(7): 392–5.

May, R. (2004) *Making Sense of Psychotic Experiences and Working Towards Recovery*. Chichester: John Wiley & Sons Ltd.

Read, J., Haslam, N., Sayce, L. & Davies, E. (2006) Prejudice and schizophrenia: A review of the 'mental illness is an illness like any other' approach. *Acta Psychologica Scandinavica*, **114**: 303–18.

Romme, M. & Escher, S. (2000) *Making Sense of Voices: A Guide For Mental Health Professionals Working With Voice-Hearers*. London: Mind Publications.

Slade, M. (2002) Biopsychosocial psychiatry and clinical psychology. *Clinical Psychology*, **9**: 8–12.

Slade, M. & Priebe, S. (2001) Are randomised controlled trials the only gold that glitters? *British Journal of Psychiatry*, **179**: 286–7.

Smail, D. (2005) *Power, Interest and Psychology: Elements of a Social Materialist Kind of Distress*. Ross-on-Wye: PCCS Books.

Szasz, T. (2002) The myth of mental illness: Past and future. Lecture, 23 November. Rochester, MI: Oakland University.

Thornhill, H., Clare L. & May, R. (2004) Escape, enlightenment and endurance: Narratives of recovery from psychosis. *Anthropology and Medicine*, special issue, **11**(2): 181–99.

Turner, T. (2006) in a debate, 'This house believes that Psychiatric drugs do more harm than good'. Proposer Dr Peter Breggin, seconded by Dr Joanna Moncrieff. Opposer Dr Mark Salter, seconded by Dr Trevor Turner. Debate sponsored by the James Nayler Foundation, available on its Web site, www.jnf.org.uk.

Employment: What you should know and what you should do

Bob Grove

Sainsbury Centre for Mental Health

► Work, health and well-being

The association between work and improved mental health has been known for a long time. The physician Galen in the 5th Century described work as 'Nature's best physician'. The Quaker reformer William Tuke at the beginning of the 19th Century made work one of the central features of a radically new way of caring for people who were mentally ill. At The Retreat in York (which still exists as an independent mental hospital), Tuke introduced a regime in which people lived in good conditions in the country and worked for each other, as well as doing healthy activities such as farming. He had noticed that when people are happily occupied, their symptoms of mental ill health are less marked. The theory was that work would 'distract the mind from painful and injurious associations'.

Similar findings came from the seminal studies of mental hospital regimes in the 1960s by Wing and Brown (1970), thus giving evidential support for the development of industrial rehabilitation by psychiatrists such as Douglas Bennett at London's Maudsley Hospital. In Bennett's work there was a focus on reintegration into the labour market on leaving hospital. Unfortunately, this was later to be institutionalised into industrial therapy when it became less easy to find jobs due to economic downturn. This incorporation into the world of therapy served to reduce expectations about the possibility of people with severe mental health problems obtaining competitive employment. Indeed, those who

Learning About Mental Health Practice.   Edited by Theo Stickley and Thurstine Basset
© 2008 John Wiley & Sons, Ltd

ran industrial therapy units often developed a self-serving view that work on the outside might be damaging and that their workers should be protected from the harsh realities of the workaday world. The evidence of the effects of competitive employment on health and other non-vocational outcomes does not bear this out (Bond *et al.*, 2001a).

More recently there has been a review of the worldwide evidence on the association between health, work and well-being by Waddell and Burton (2006). Their conclusions are that across the whole population work is beneficial to heath and that unemployment is very damaging indeed. They produce evidence to show that unemployment is more dangerous than the most dangerous jobs in Britain today (e.g. working on oil rigs) and more damaging to health than smoking 200 cigarettes a day. Waddell and Burton acknowledge that sometimes work can be damaging to health, so they qualify their findings by saying that 'good work' is best for health and well-being, but this does not alter the main finding that on the whole people are overwhelming better off in all respects if they are in work.

Do people with mental health problems want to Work?

The short answer to this is yes. There is consistent evidence across many studies that people using mental health services – even if they have been unemployed for a long time – see employment as an important aspiration and a key element of the journey to recovery. In *New Thinking about Mental Health and Employment* (Grove, Secker & Seebohm, 2005), Patience Seebohm and Jenny Secker review some of this evidence and also describe a study they undertook in Sheffield in which 149 service users who mostly spent their days in day centres or other unpaid activities were asked about their employment aspirations. Only 5% of the group had paid work of any kind, but over 90% wanted to work as soon as possible or saw employment as a important aspiration for the future (Secker, Grove & Seebohm, 2001).

Findings such as these can come as a surprise to mental health professionals, who often tend to assume that people with more severe problems don't want to work and/or should be protected from work. This creates a culture of very low expectations – people believe their doctors when they are told they 'shouldn't overdo it' or that 'they will never work again'! This can, of course, then become a self-fulfilling prophecy. We will say more about the dangers of therapeutic pessimism later.

How do you tell if someone is likely to be able to work?

According to the Labour Force Survey, less than a quarter of people with mental health problems in Britain are in employment. Even the best employment-support programmes at present get only 50–75% of people with severe mental health problems into employment (Roberts & Pratt, 2007). This is a huge step forward, but still leaves a substantial number of people who are unable or unwilling to work. Researchers have put a great deal of energy into looking at indicators that might predict employability (Grove & Membrey, 2005). Their findings are not necessarily what one would expect. Diagnosis, severity of illness when in crisis, even social skills when out of work are all poor predictors of employability. Hospitalisation does have an association with unemployment, but the direction of causality is unclear (i.e. are people more likely to be unemployed because they have been in hospital or does unemployment lead to more frequent hospitalisation?). Having a previous history of employment clearly helps, but even this is outweighed, according to more recent studies, by a basket of characteristics (known to US researchers as 'self-efficacy') that include motivation, feelings of confidence and competence, and determination to succeed. The good news is that these are not stable personality traits, they change as people's circumstances and fortunes change. They can be improved by cognitive behavioural therapy (Cather, 2005) and other psycho-educational therapies (McGurk, Mueser & Pascaris, 2005) and most of all by getting a job!

So it is in fact very hard to predict who will be employable until the person has actually tried out a job. The best guide to both employability and readiness is what the people themselves say. Contrary to what many health professionals think, service users' preferences about the sorts of jobs they would like to do are both stable and realistic. Even when they appear not to be realistic, there is often a hint as to the sort of a job that would meet the person's abilities and aspirations. One person told his employment support worker (ESW) that he wanted to be a pilot. The ESW explained that being a pilot required long training and high levels of technical knowledge, but not wanting to be too discouraging, he arranged a visit to an airport open day so that the man could see for himself what flying planes was really like. While on the visit, they got talking to the baggage handlers and the job of driving the electric carts and the various other technologies was much admired. The outcome was that the person was taken on as a trainee baggage handler and loved it – especially being so near to planes, which was where he really wanted to be. Having a job he loved transformed that person's life, and although a great deal of on-going support was needed both for the employee and the employer, the determination to succeed on all sides won through. Had the ESW moved too quickly to douse the dream with 'reality', the eventual solution would never have been considered. When asked how people were selected for employment support in the programmes he helped set up, the famous American researcher Professor Bob Drake said, 'Whoever holds their hand up'!

How realistic is it to encourage someone to get paid employment?

Research and experience in the UK tell us that it is now possible to think of more than 30% of people in touch with specialist mental health services routinely being in paid work. This compares with present UK employment rates for adults of working age with schizophrenia of about 5%. The evidence for this comes from services such as that in the South West London and St George's Mental Health Trust (www.swlstg-tr.nhs.uk/work/user_employment_programme.asp) and in major studies such as EQOLISE (www.eqolise.sgul.ac.uk/team.htm).

The most important factor in improving employment rates is not finding the most employable service users, but rather offering the right kind of help. It is important, therefore, that service providers know what works. In my early days as a service provider, I worked on the re-provision of industrial therapy from mental hospitals that were closing. I could see that hospital workshops, however work-like and commercial, did not help many people into employment on the outside. They made very little effort to do so, in fact, because they needed the best workers to keep going. The one or two people who were employed usually got jobs in spite of the service and often in the face of considerable, self-interested discouragement. Naively, I thought that if only these workshops were out on industrial estates mixing with real businesses and their workers, the culture would change and more people would get jobs. How wrong can you be? The rates of employment from my community-based workshops were the same as from the hospital workshops – virtually nil.

There is only one model of service provision that has a strong evidence base for getting people with severe mental health problems into paid employment and that is called individual placement and support (IPS). Note the order of the words – not train and then place in work, but rather place in work and then support. IPS has been compared to train and place, sheltered work and 'clubhouse' models and has been shown to be more effective in placing people in work and in the duration of employment (Crowther *et al.*, 2001). There is some evidence that when clubhouses use a combination of their own model of 'transitional employment placements'[1] and IPS they start to become more effective. There is also some very recent evidence that short courses of CBT or cognitive educational preparation when combined with IPS increase its effectiveness (McGurk, Mueser & Pascaris, 2005).

However, the basic principles of IPS (to which we will return in a later section) represent the best technology we have for helping people with severe mental health problems to get into work and stay employed. Following the report and recommendations of the Social Exclusion Unit (2004), IPS now also has government approval. The government's most recent action plan (Cabinet Office Social Exclusion Task Force, 2006) and commissioning guidance for vocational services (Care Services Improvement Partnership, 2006) include the intention for every community mental health team to have a specialist employment worker and advice on commissioning services that adopt the core principles of IPS.

▶ The journey to unemployment and disability

Starting points and key decisions

Up to this point this chapter has been written as though it were based on two implicit assumptions. The first is that the topic of mental health and employment

---

[1] Transitional employment placements or TEPs are time-limited placements in paid jobs with local employers that are 'owned' by the clubhouse. If the worker becomes unwell, another clubhouse member of member of staff can take their place until they are ready to go back to work.

is mainly about people who have a severe mental illness; that is, psychosis, bipolar disorder. The second is that people with mental health problems are unemployed and have been so for some time, maybe all their lives. This is undoubtedly how most mental health professionals see the issue – understandably, because most people they see are in this position. However, although some people acquire a psychotic illness before they finish their education, let alone get work or have a career, this is a very uncommon starting point. Consider the figures: 1–2% of the population have some form of psychotic illness,[2] while one in four of us will have significant common mental health issues (depression, anxiety etc.) at some point during the course of our life. Doctors sometimes call common mental health problems 'mild' or 'moderate', but this can be misleading. It is true that people labelled as such mostly get better quite quickly, either without help or with some form of treatment obtained through the GP. However for some people – perhaps 700,000[3] across the UK – these 'mild or moderate' conditions can stubbornly refuse to go away, leaving the individual on the road to long-term unemployment and significant disability. How does this happen and can we do anything about it?

We have done some research with people in this situation (Thomas, Secker & Grove, 2003). The following story is based on things that a number of people told us about how they came to lose their jobs and what the consequences were for their lives.

Jane's Story

Jane Smith was in her thirties with two small children. She had always worked even when the children were young, because she and her husband needed the money. Jane enjoyed her work in the office of a medium-sized firm making electronic components and was good at it. However, after her second pregnancy she was very depressed for quite a while, eventually making it back to work part-time. Coming back to work was hard – colleagues were superficially sympathetic, but actually resented the extra workload created by Jane's extended maternity leave. There were a few jokey references to 'ladies of leisure', which Jane hated though she smiled and tried to work extra hard to get back into her colleagues' good books. Her manager was also less than helpful. He was very preoccupied with performance targets and also competing with another person on his own level for promotion to a senior post, so he unthinkingly gave Jane work that required tight deadlines at points when she could not arrange additional childcare.

---

[2] I am here using medical terminology that some people think is unhelpful. For an alternative view read Madness Explained by Richard Bentall (2003) – but beware, it is mind-blowing stuff.

[3] There are just under 1 million adults of working age with mental health problems on Incapacity Benefits. About two-thirds of these do not have severe mental health problems, nor are they in contact with specialist (secondary) mental health services.

Meanwhile, her marriage was under stress. Her husband was also in line for promotion and although he appreciated Jane's determination to work and to contribute to family income, he also wanted the house to be clean, meals to be on the table and the children not needing his undivided attention when he returned from work. He had started having drinks and heart to hearts after work with a female colleague who understood him.

Jane became very withdrawn at work, bursting into tears for no obvious reason and saying a perfunctory 'I'm OK' when colleagues tentatively enquired if there was anything wrong. Resentment started to creep in when Jane had not finished work and other colleagues had to do it instead.

Eventually Jane snapped and saying what sounded like 'I can't take any more' walked out of the office, leaving colleagues not sure whether they should feel sorry for her, guilty for having pushed her to this point or angry with her for putting them in this position.

The next day her manager received a doctor's certificate for four weeks, saying simply that Jane was unfit for work due to 'stress'. During the four weeks no one from work contacted Jane. Her colleagues thought about it, but decided not to say anything in case it made her worse. Jane thought that they were angry with her or else did not care whether she came back or not. She took the pills the doctor gave her, which took the edge off her depression eventually, but did not improve things much at home. Her husband was alternately over-protective, blaming her work and the GP for her continuing depression, or offering her advice on how he coped with low moods by pulling himself together and playing squash. He also passed on the thoughts of his unmarried female colleague on how to manage work/life balance.

Jane went back to her GP after four weeks and when he had established that, though the pills were helping a bit, she didn't feel much better, he signed her off for another month.

At work the matter had been passed on to the Human Resources Department (two people working to the Finance Director). Feeling under pressure from Jane's manager, who was also passing on the rising discontent among colleagues, the HR manager sent a letter to Jane under her boss's signature asking for a meeting and saying that they wanted a doctor's report. The tone of the letter was formal and used all the right words, but Jane couldn't help seeing it as a veiled threat, which was confirmed in her mind when she showed it to her husband, who immediately got angry and said she would be better off not working for a firm who treated ill people like that.

Jane agreed to her employer asking for a doctor's report. When it came, it simply said that Jane was suffering from depression, which was being treated, and that the GP thought she would recover within two to three months. HR took legal advice, which was that Jane might be eligible for protection under the Disability Discrimination Act because of her post-natal depression, but that her position was marginal and they should follow a formal procedure to establish the likelihood of her returning to work. When Jane received the letter asking her to attend a meeting with her manager, the HR manager and the Finance Director, her husband went into protective overdrive and said she was not going to face a lynch mob like that and she ought to resign. Jane could not face both her husband's rage and the pressure of what felt like a court hearing with her in the dock and sent in her resignation. Her former colleagues did not send a leaving card.

Questions to address

There are no easy or right answers to complex situations like this. However, a perfectly competent person who wanted to work was now unemployed, very depressed and feeling both angry and useless. She was clearly at risk of not working for a very long time, with consequences for her marriage, her feelings about herself as a mother, and worries about her families' financial future. Her deteriorating relationship with her husband was undoubtedly a complicating factor, but both the GP and her employer have a duty of care – at the very least to not make things worse and arguably, in the case of her employer, an interest in retaining a person who for most of the time has been a valued employee.

- What do you think has happened here and why has it been so difficult to stop this drift into unemployment?

- Were there any points in this journey to unemployment at which the people at work or the GP could have acted differently to slow down or stop the development of strained relationships, anger and mistrust?

- The longer a person is off work, the harder it is to get back.[4] What help or advice should she have been given and by whom?

- If the employer had decided that Jane was eligible for protection under the Disability Discrimination Act, what difference might this have made?

- What are the barriers to Jane getting back to work? How could these be overcome?

Some possibilities to consider

- Jane's firm could have had a mental health or stress policy in place setting out what employees can expect if someone becomes unwell or is starting not to

---

[4] By the time a person has been off work for six months there is only a 50% chance they will ever work again; 12 months and this is reduced to 25%. After two years, very few people indeed get back to work (Waddell & Burton, 2006).

cope. This at least 'normalises' the idea that work can sometimes be stressful and that employee well-being is something to which the firm is signed up. All employers should have disability policies and be aware of the provisions of the Disability Discrimination Act, 1995, which require employers to make 'reasonable adjustments' to enable a disabled person to do their job. Jane may well have had a case here, though a good employer would not worry about legal entitlement but rather see to it that someone in Jane's position would have a return-to-work plan and be supported to manage her workload and her childcare.

- Jane's colleagues and her manager not only felt somewhat resentful at having extra work, which is understandable, they also felt very uneasy about talking to Jane, not knowing how to deal with her distress and hesitant even to say how nice it was to have her back without also feeling they were putting her under pressure. There is training available, sometimes called Mental Health First Aid (see the Bibliography at the end of the chapter), which helps members of the public to identify and understand mental distress and, more importantly, to feel confident about talking to someone who is obviously in a bad way. If Jane's colleagues or her manager had this training, it may well have helped keep relationships going while Jane got back into a working routine. As it was, they went downhill very quickly, mainly because no one knew what to say. Some big companies will remind managers to stay in touch with people who are off sick with stress or depression and also tell them how often to phone and the kind of things it is helpful to say; BT is an example of a UK company that does this.

- The busy GP has very little time to reach a diagnosis and prescribe treatment, but it would undoubtedly have helped if Jane's GP had known how important it is not to delay return to work beyond a certain point. He could have said something like: 'I will sign you off now, but there will come a time – and it will be quite soon, maybe in three or four weeks – when we should discuss you going back to work. If we miss that point it will get harder and harder for you to go back.' He could have offered, with Jane's permission, to talk to her employer to reassure him that Jane would recover and to stress how important her job would be to Jane's future health. Maybe, as already happens in some places, there could have been an employment adviser linked to the practice who could have helped Jane to speak more openly to her employer. Even using the certificate as a way of communicating the GP could have been more helpful to the employer. In Jane's case, combining the prescribed medication with a course of CBT would also probably have helped her to develop strategies for managing the conflicting demands of her life with greater confidence and to challenge her own negative thinking.

- Once the matter had been passed further up the chain of command at work, the relationships get more difficult to resolve. The HR people probably didn't know Jane well and felt great responsibility to minimise the aggravation caused to her line manager and colleagues. The people who knew Jane, on the other hand, may well have felt relieved that a person whom they regarded as having specialist knowledge was now handling the matter. The net effect, however, is to make the resumption of normal working relationships more difficult. An enlightened employer might have recognised the need for mediation here – a case manager who could work between Jane and the work situation, not on one side or the other, but treating Jane's successful return to work as a team responsibility.

Of course, it is not always possible to do the right thing, even if you know what the right thing is. Waiting lists for CBT are long; the employer may not be able to find or afford skilled case management. Even with everything available, the problems that are not work related may be intractable. However, even doing the simple things well can help maintain good, open relationships at work while other issues are dealt with, and this above all is what is needed.

▶ Employment and recovery

Beginning the recovery journey

We have already seen that for people with mental health problems who have never worked or who have been unemployed for a long time, the barriers to employment are high. Not only does the person themselves feel lacking in confidence and competence, but the world will have made a harsh judgement about that person, based on stereotypes that we see reflected in the press and the rest of the media every day. The stigma of mental illness is often felt by people who experience it as the worst and most daunting barrier to overcome. Do you dare admit that you have been mentally ill? Do you need to tell your employer? How do you explain the reasons for the gaps in your employment record?

Other barriers are also totally or mostly outside the control of the individual. Moving off benefits is risky and complicated (though less so than it used to be). Family, friends and even mental health professionals may talk hopelessly of the benefits 'trap'. However, as we have seen, many people want to work despite the difficulties, because it is one of the best ways to regain control over your life and get access to the things that make life worth living – the state that people who use mental health services are increasingly referring to as being 'in recovery'. We have also seen that with the right kind of help, many more people than at present can get into employment.

What happens to enable people to make a start on recovery is one of the great mysteries. Sometimes it is hearing from an inspirational 'expert by experience' who is on the journey themselves. Other times it may be a wise professional who seems to believe in the person and who can stand by them, giving encouragement and helping to deal with the panic that accompanies setbacks. One or two people I have known say they reached a point where they realised that if they didn't take a few risks, life would have passed them by altogether. Of course, the recovery journey is not all or mainly about employment, but for most adults of working age employment or work in a broader sense (volunteering etc.) will be there somewhere as part of a full life.

The right kind of help

Once a person has made the decision to try to get a job, it will be very important that everyone in their life supports and encourages them. If the person feels that others who are important to them, including their doctor, social worker and community psychiatric nurse, believe in them, then they will be much more likely to succeed. Conversely, if professionals are constantly expressing doubts, urging caution, pointing out the risks, then this can slow up or stop the process by sapping the will of the individual – who will anyway have plenty of doubts of their own.

The next most important thing, as we have said earlier, is that the right technology is used to support the process of getting and keeping a job. Individual placement and support (IPS) is what it says on the tin. It is *individual* because everyone is different and because when it comes to persuading an employer to take someone on it is the individual person, their skills and their commitment that you want to sell, not the disability. Next comes *placement*, because once someone has made up their mind to try for a job, the biggest psychological barrier to overcome is actually doing it – and after all, the best place to learn about work is the workplace. The longer someone hesitates on the brink – even if they are having lots of work experience or training in an employment scheme of some kind – the more difficult actually taking the plunge will appear.

Finally and most critically comes *support* while in work, which should be time unlimited and offered to both the employee and the employer. Once a person makes the transition into work they are at their most vulnerable. Small things can go wrong that if not dealt with can become major crises and can trigger a recurrence of the illness or just make the person feel they have to give up. For people with mental health problems this support has to be carefully thought through. The employee will not want it to be too obvious in the workplace, but on the other hand the person may need adjustments that they do not feel confident enough to ask for. There are no simple solutions here, but experience shows that most difficulties are not about mental health and that the starting point for resolution is a regular meeting or phone call outside working hours for the first few weeks at least. On the whole, people say that they prefer the support worker to ring them at first just for a chat. In that context, asking for help does not seem so much like failure. One service user I know likened his support worker's phone calls to 'an aspirin in the pocket'. He didn't always need to take it, but it was reassuring to know it was there. The other support need is for the employer. It is certainly best if someone in the workplace knows the circumstances of the new employee and is prepared to take responsibility for seeing that the person is working in conditions that optimise the chances of success. Here again, it is necessary to get the relationship and the degree of visibility of that relationship right – but that is what being a skilled support worker is about.

The important components of IPS are:

- Rapid job search and placement with the minimum time spent in preparation – short, time-limited cognitive educational courses may be useful alongside job search.

- Attention to personal preferences – getting people the kind of job they want.

- Independent, individual, reliable benefits advice.

- Initial support and adjustment when in work.

- Time-unlimited availability of support at times of transition or difficulty.

- Integration of employment support and clinical management.

This last component is one of the most difficult to achieve, but it is absolutely critical. There are a couple of important reasons for this. The last thing people who are daring to try for work need is to lose the services they have been depending on to manage their illness. Pressures on community mental health teams and other services are often so great that there is a temptation to discharge people who seem to have recovered. *It is not necessary to be symptom free to get a job, nor is getting a job a sign of being fully recovered.* It can be a step on the journey to recovery, but unless the clinical team is working for the same goals as the employment support, then the process will quickly go wrong. This is why researchers think that the employment specialist should be a part of the clinical team (Bond *et al.*, 2001b). Having the employment specialist as part of the clinical team also means that everyone on the team's caseload is the responsibility of the employment specialist. Where the clinical team is separate from the employment support, a covert selection process seems to occur where the only people who are referred through are those the clinicians think are ready for work. As we have said before, clinicians tend to have very low expectations of people they work with and are often not the best people to ask about work aspirations.

Individual placement and support in action – jane's story continued

I am going to illustrate the next part of the chapter with a story. I have chosen to continue with Jane Smith, because I want to make the point that people with common mental health problems can become quite disabled through a combination of bad luck, poor clinical management and long-term unemployment and that when they are, their employment support needs are indistinguishable from those of people whose original condition appeared at the time much more severe, for example a psychotic condition. Remember I said earlier that diagnosis is a poor indicator of employability. I will consider the situation for people whose illness means that they have never been employed at the end of the chapter.

We are now ten or so years on from the last time we met Jane. These have not been good years. Jane's marriage broke up and following suicide attempts, she had several voluntary admissions to hospital. In the divorce Jane lost custody of the children, who went to live with her former husband and his new partner. Fortunately, they lived reasonably near and Jane kept up as good a relationship with the children as she was able and she also bought a small flat from the proceeds of selling the family home. Otherwise, it has been a bleak time. Eventually Jane reached the top of the waiting list for CBT, which certainly seemed to help, and gradually she became confident enough to seek out peer support through joining a local Mind group. Not only was she able to talk with people who had been through some of the things she had, she was also able to offer to help out in various ways, manning stalls, helping organise events and looking after the money side.

Jane was on Incapacity Benefit and periodically had to attend an interview with a personal adviser. Usually these were ordeals that she hated, but on one occasion the person she met seemed interested in her and her story. The personal adviser also pointed out that if Jane ever wanted to think about work, there were starting to be a number of schemes locally that might be able to help. Jane knew this because a friend at Mind had recently mentioned that her community nurse had introduced her to an employment specialist who was part of the community mental health team. She also was starting to feel that her life was going nowhere and that her daughters – now in their early teens - were treating her as an invalid rather than as a mother whom they could turn to for support.

Jane started to make enquiries with her community nurse to see if she was entitled to see a specialist employment worker. When she found that she was, she made an appointment. The employment worker was in no doubt that if Jane really wanted to work then she could find her a job. She took a careful inventory of Jane's skills and listened closely when Jane told her about the kinds of work she might be interested in doing. Jane felt that she could get back into administrative work quite easily and that she would enjoy it as long as the pressures were not too great. The employment worker said she had noticed that a couple of local schools were looking for additional help to manage their administration and Jane was attracted to the idea of working in a socially useful job around children. The employment worker did point out that Jane might have to face awkward questions and criminal record checks in order to work in a school, even in an administrative capacity, but she assured Jane that she would support her through the process and that employers were not allowed to discriminate against people with mental health problems because of the Disability Discrimination Act. To Jane's surprise, the employment specialist said she

> should start applying for jobs as soon as she fully understood her position as regards benefits. They went though Jane's finances and found that for the first six months she would be able to earn up to £ 85 per week on top of her benefits under the permitted work rules as long as she didn't work more than 16 hours per week. She also learnt that if all went well and she eventually decided to come off benefits, then if things went wrong within two years she would be able to go back to benefits at the same rate as before.[5]
>
> After some help with her CV, Jane started making applications and also went on a short 'Back to Work' course run by her employment worker and a colleague. After a couple of distressing rejections, Jane got an interview at a local church school and was offered three mornings a week doing specific administrative tasks and working to the school secretary. Jane increased her hours and came off benefits within six months and in a couple of years felt confident enough to apply for and get a post as school secretary at another local school.

So, if not a happy ending, at least a step on the road to recovery. Too straightforward to be true? Well, most of Jane's story is based on someone I know well.

Questions to address

- What do you think were the main factors that led Jane to take the first steps to recovery?

- What do you think should be the role of the care co-ordinator/community nurse in relation to employment in cases like Jane's?

- What were the barriers Jane faced and how were they overcome?

- What are the main points about the IPS method that would apply to anyone with a mental health problem who is thinking about employment?

- What would you need to do to adapt the IPS method to help a person with schizophrenia who never got as far as completing their studies?

Some points to consider

- IPS is not a magic wand. What it sets out to do is to address and overcome the problems and barriers that a person is experiencing in their daily lives that are

---

[5] Although these figures were correct at the time of writing, both rules and benefit levels change. It is best to consult a specialist welfare rights worker for up-to-date information.

stopping them doing what they want to do or achieving whatever it is they want to achieve. Once a person has travelled some way down the path to long-term unemployment and disability, they experience difficulties that are not the direct product of their original illness but are the result of the impact of that illness on their relationships, their social standing and their feelings about themselves. What IPS does is to provide a framework in which the individual can find a way to solve these problems and overcome these barriers at their own pace and in their own time. It is not, as some people think, a way of getting people into work quickly whatever the consequences. Rapid job search and placement aim to ensure that once a person has made the decision that they want a job, they are not held up by the anxieties of others. Taking the plunge, even in a part-time or entry-level job, overcomes a massive psychological barrier. There will be time for career development and promotion once the self-confidence returns. I think it is a bit like swimming – once you can take your feet off the bottom and tread water or do doggy paddle, then you have the possibility of learning breaststroke, front crawl and even diving of the side (if you can find a pool where they still allow you to dive).

- In my view, the IPS principles hold true for a person who has never had a job because they became ill before they had finished their education. If they want to resume their education, then you simply adapt the IPS principles and apply them to education. Similarly, the person may want to try a bit of volunteering, in which case the same applies.

- In general, I think it is extremely helpful if someone in the employment support team (or indeed everyone) is an 'expert by experience'. Having contact with someone who has walked the walk is enormously reassuring, especially when dealing with stigma.

▶ Conclusion

As a mental health professional, the two most important and precious things you can offer – which you have a professional duty to offer – are hope and belief: hope of something better in the lives of the people you work with and belief in the possibility of achieving it. We need to banish the 'we need to be realistic, I'm afraid you'll never work again' school of psychiatry for ever.

▶ References

Bentall, R.P. (2003) *Madness Explained: Psychosis and Human Nature*. London: Penguin.

Bond, G.R., Resnick, S.G., Drake, R.E. *et al.* (2001a) Does competitive employment improve non-vocational outcomes for people with severe mental illness, *Journal of Consulting and Clinical Psychology*, **69**: 489–501.

Bond, G.R., Vogler, K.M., Resnick, S.G. *et al.* (2001b) Dimensions of supported employment: Factor structure of the IPS fidelity scale. *Journal of Mental Health*, **10**(4): 383–93.

Cabinet Office Social Exclusion Task Force (2006) *Reaching Out: An Action Plan on Social Exclusion*. London: Cabinet Office, www.cabinetoffice.gov.uk/social_exclusion_task_force/publications/reaching_out/reaching_out.asp.

Care Services Improvement Partnership (2006) *Vocational Services for People with Severe Mental Health Problems: Commissioning Guidance*. London: CSIP, www.socialinclusion.org.uk/publications/DOH_Vocational_web.pdf.

Cather, C. (2005) Functional cognitive-behavioural therapy: A brief individual treatment for functional impairments resulting from psychotic symptoms in schizophrenia. *Canadian Journal of Psychiatry*, 50(5): 258–63.

Crowther, R.E., Marshall, M., Bond, G.R. & Huxley P. (2001) Helping people with severe mental illness to obtain work: Systematic review. *British Medical Journal*, 322: 204–8.

Grove, B. & Membrey, H. (2005) Sheep and goats: New thinking on employability. In B. Grove, J. Secker & P. Seebohm (eds) (2005) *New Thinking about Mental Health and Employment*. Oxford: Radcliffe.

Grove, B., Secker, J. & Seebohm, P. (eds) (2005) *New Thinking about Mental Health and Employment*. Oxford: Radcliffe.

McGurk, S.R., Mueser, K.T. & Pascaris, A. (2005) Cognitive training and supported employment for persons with severe mental illness: One-year results from a randomized controlled trial. *Schizophrenia Bulletin*, 31: 898–909.

Roberts, M.M. & Pratt, C.W. (2007) Putative evidence of employment readiness. *Psychiatric Rehabilitation Journal*, 30(3): 175–81.

Secker, J., Grove, B. & Seebohm, P. (2001) Challenging barriers to employment, training and education for mental health service users: The service user's perspective. *Journal of Mental Health*, 10(4): 395–404.

Social Exclusion Unit (2004) *Mental Health and Social Exclusion*. London: Office of the Deputy Prime Minister.

Thomas, T., Secker, J. & Grove, B. (2003) Getting Back Before Christmas, Avon & Wiltshire Mental Health Partnership Trust Job Retention Pilot Evaluation London IAHSP. Unpublished but available from bob.grove@scmh.org.uk.

Waddell, G. & Burton A.K. (2006) *Is Work Good for Your Health and Well Being?* London: TSO.

Wing, J.K. & Brown, G.W. (1970) *Institutionalism and Schizophrenia*. London: Cambridge University Press.

▶ Suggestions for further reading

New Thinking about Mental Health and Employment (Grove, Secker & Seebohm, 2005) has chapters dealing with the sorts of scenarios and barriers people face when it comes to getting into employment. There are also accounts from service users of the various ways in which they made progress (or not!) in achieving their employment ambitions.

Leading by Example is a practical guide showing how NHS managers and others can lead by example in employing mental health service users in the NHS workforce, and at the same time improve working lives and job retention for all staff. It brings together contributions from managers, service users and front-line staff who carried out this pioneering work and includes personal stories that show how employing people with mental health problems can be done well in practice. www.scmh.org.uk/80256FBD004F3555/vWeb/flKHAL6RCE3W/$file/leading_by_example.pdf.

Mental Health First Aid is a mental health awareness training programme that enables people to recognise and feel more confident about responding to mental distress. It is now in use in Scotland (www.healthscotland.org.uk/smhfa/) and is gradually spreading across the UK. Various versions for use in the workplace are in development. For further information, e-mail the author of the chapter (bob.grove@scmh.org.uk).

Treating creatively: The challenge of treating the creative mind

Peter Amsel

Composer, writer and health-care activist

▶ Creativity and mental illness

There are two things that exist in opposition to each other and yet, at the same time, they manage to generate a strange resonance with each other; those two things are creativity and madness. There is not an art class that can cover the *Expressionists* without touching on the brilliant insanity of Vincent Van Gogh and the masterpieces he created out of his unique view of the world. Similarly, literature classes that have not mentioned the agonised writings of Lord Byron, Ernest Hemmingway or Sylvia Plath would be incomplete in their surveys of the greatest minds, and the lists of other writers, of artists and of other similarly afflicted 'creatives' could go on and on, seemingly *ad infinitum*, with more and more examples of individuals who blurred the line between genius and insanity. Yet should we really be surprised? Would it perhaps be more surprising if there were not as many incidences among the artistic community of individuals with a mental illness existing alongside their great creativity: incidences among people who allow their passions to guide them in their labours, following their hearts as much as their minds as they toil at their art?

As human beings, we have the ability to be many things at the same time: we can love someone with tremendous passion and hate another with as much zeal; we can be kind to friends and be fearful of strangers; and, perhaps most peculiar of all, we are capable of being driven to create things even when our minds betray us with a madness that can have deleterious effects on other aspects of life. We live these lives of curious dichotomies and contradictions

Learning About Mental Health Practice. Edited by Theo Stickley and Thurstine Basset
© 2008 John Wiley & Sons, Ltd

and yet we function – or are able to function within a narrowly defined role relating to creative endeavours – and, for some individuals, we even manage to thrive under conditions that would seem to be conspired against us as we try to live our lives with a single-minded pursuit: to be successful in our creativity. While one might not immediately think that creativity and mental illness have anything in common, a growing body of literature exists linking this seemingly divergent issue, including a chapter entitled 'Manic-depressive illness, creativity, and leadership' in *Manic-Depressive Illness*, the 1990 ground-breaking work on the topic by Goodwin and Jamison.

The only way in which I can clearly describe what it is like trying to live with bipolar affective disorder while maintaining a life as a composer, poet and writer is to call it a 'roller-coaster ride from hell', which is one of the reasons I have never become overly enamoured with real-life roller-coasters: they simply do not impress me. Is it possible that there could be anything positive – the proverbial 'silver lining' perhaps – about being stricken with a disorder that, at times, leaves me nearly paralysed with debilitating depressions that rapidly alternate with feeling as though my mind is being torn apart as it ascends through dysphoric episodes filled with angst or agitation (or combinations of the two), occasionally landing in a rare hypomanic episode that can be enjoyable, though usually short lived? Then there are the mixed states, where it becomes increasingly difficult to cope with the feelings that seem to bombard me from every angle; what could possibly be positive about this type of illness?

My perspective comes as one who has lived with this 'beast' for the better part of 22 years and, after being diagnosed with the illness in 2000, immersed myself in the study of this topic in an effort to gain a more complete insight into what was exerting control over my life in such a dramatic manner. What I have been able to learn about the management of this illness and its relationship to my creativity has allowed me to see that bipolar affective disorder is truly both a curse and a blessing in my life as a creative individual. As a composer, as a poet and as a writer – and for anything else that I turn my creative attentions to – the one thing that I can be assured of is that the affective 'disorder' allows me to experience things at a more profound level than would normally take place.

This idea of being able to experience things, particularly those things that would normally be outside the realm of opportunity for the average individual to experience, is extremely important as it lies at the crux of our relationship with the arts: we look to the arts, to music and literature, to the fantasy or diversions that these 'entertainments' provide us, as a means of tapping into something that is untouchable under ordinary circumstances. The arts provide a means of escaping from the rigours of the 'real' world, and yet the question remains: What are we seeing when we go to an art exhibition? What are we truly hearing at a concert? What do the words of the songs being sung *really* mean, is there a hidden message buried within the melodies that caress and engage our imaginations with their clever inventiveness, or is it just something that was tossed together to entertain?

While people may be reluctant to expose themselves to the new creations being presented today, it is important to point out that what is being offered up to us by today's artists is nothing new, in the sense that 'classical' is only a relative term unto itself. Nothing exists today in the arts that has not been condemned or criticised for being 'too new' when it was first created. What we call 'classical' today, music that was composed in the times of Haydn, Mozart and Beethoven, was once labelled the *avant-garde*. When Beethoven was composing his music for the genteel audiences of Vienna, he was branded by many critics as an *enfant terrible* of new music. If the music of Ludwig van Beethoven, the composer of the *Moonlight Sonata* amongst other perennial favourites, can be considered to be an iconoclastic, ultra-modernistic 'new music' composer, jarring the blue-haired conservatives of the day out of their complacency, then how much more violent would those reactions be if those audiences could be transported into the beginning of the 21st Century where there seems to be as many styles of music as there are composers? Taste is relative; we must not be afraid to explore the varied opportunities the arts provide to experience a wide variety of emotional shades and hues that are not necessarily native to our everyday lives.

Creativity is so fundamentally important to our lives that it manages to find a role within the religious faiths of our planet: by ascribing the power of creativity to a 'higher power', to God, we ascribe an element of mysticism to the creative act for the simple reason that it is, ultimately, related to the archetype of divine creation; we view the act of creating something as being inherently holy, as being a part of the process of being co-creators with the divine. This is seen in the language we use surrounding creativity: we speak of the 'conception' of an idea, relating an intellectual idea to life itself. We speak of the 'birth' of a dream, or 'birthing' pains associated with projects, again relating ideas and non-living things to life itself. There is nothing inherently wrong with this, but it quickly demonstrates how important the issue of creativity is to our species, regardless of how an individual may feel about spiritual issues. The desire to approach that archetype, to create something that they can share with others or enjoy for themselves, is something to which many people feel driven; this is what may be defined as the 'creative imperative' and it is the difference between someone who is able to have a hobby that involves a creative outlet and someone who must dedicate their life to being creative.

▶ The pathology of creativity

Creativity is not about suffering for art or seeking a muse, though some artists will speak of their creative process in those terms for lack of a better frame of reference. The ultimate pathology of creativity, regardless of whether or not there is an illness present, stems from an overpowering desire to do something that is constructive or creative. Being able to shape a lump of clay into something with your own two hands makes you feel eminently more accomplished than simply going to a store and buying an ashtray or vase that was mass produced in some anonymous factory. People who devote their lives to the arts often do so without regard to the financial considerations: they do not expect to get rich, nor do they have any delusions that they are only one day away from 'being discovered'. True creativity is about the work, not the promise of future compensation or fame.

While that may sound grandly altruistic and insanely idealistic, it is spoken out of absolute experience: I am a composer for the simple reason that I compose. I write classical music, not because I want to, but rather because *I am driven to do so*. When I do not compose for prolonged periods of time, even a few days without sketching a few notes, I will begin to get physically ill, as well as severely depressed. The choice of 'going into' music was, for me, not a matter of choice at all; there was only one thing for which I had any 'why' for living, and that was to be creative. One does not become a composer of classical music in order to become wealthy or, for that matter, to be overly qualified for many other positions in the real world. My choice was governed by the fact that I had to compose: it is what I was, and who I am as an individual. I am a composer and a writer, and I have bipolar affective disorder.

Society accepts things from artists based on its willingness to accept both change and the eccentricities of the personalities behind the creativity. Given the eccentricities of Vincent van Gogh – the creator of some of the most treasured works of art from his time, if not all time – it is difficult to imagine how he would have fared in our modern society with the mental health laws and treatments that are designed to help people that are so obviously suffering. Could *Starry Night* (Figure 26.1) exist in an atmosphere where symptoms are eradicated, regardless of what benefits they may seem to impart to the individual? It is a difficult question, and there is no doubt that Vincent would have desired some deliverance from the torments he experienced, ultimately leading to his death; but could he have truly separated himself from his demons? The question is one

Figure 26.1 *Starry Night* by Vincent van Gogh (1853–1890). Oil on canvas; painted in June 1889. Permanent Collection; Museum of Modern Art, New York.

that artists have faced throughout history, and it is likely one that will continue to be asked as we examine the pathology of creativity in the light of mental illness.

We are granted a particularly brilliant insight into the nature of mental illness through the words that Sir Winston Churchill delivered to the students at Harrow School during the dark days of the Second World War when he revisited them in October 1941. Churchill's words, regarding the fact that things are not always as they seem, are an apt description of a life that may be spinning out of control as the result of uncontrolled symptoms and the importance of perseverance:

> You cannot tell from appearances how things will go. Sometimes imagination makes things out far worse than they are; yet without imagination not much can be done. Those people who are imaginative see many more dangers than perhaps exist; certainly many more than will happen; but then they must also pray to be given that extra courage to carry this far-reaching imagination. But for everyone, surely, what we have gone through in this period – I am addressing myself to the School – surely from this period of ten months this is the lesson: never give in, never give in, never, never, never, never – in nothing, great or small, large or petty – never give in except to convictions of honour and good sense. *Sir Winston Churchill, 29 October 1941, Harrow School.*

Understanding the pathology of creativity, or the creative process, begins with understanding the truth of what was spoken at Harrow so many years ago. *Sometimes imagination makes things out to be far worse than they are; yet without imagination not much can be done.* If we look at the world through the eyes of artists, through those who attempt to memorialise things for all eternity, we are sometimes provided with a glimpse of something that is not very attractive, but it is the vocation of those in the creative milieu to turn the ugly and the detestable into something that the rest of the world can look at without revulsion and relate to on an emotional level. Creatives allow us to experience the darkest aspects of the human psyche, the darkest side of the human condition, without having to leave the comfortably appointed museums and concert halls in which these dark visions are revealed.

While many of us may not want to acknowledge the existence of our individual 'dark' sides, or feel the need (or desire) to be able to better relate to it, particularly in a time when it seems to be increasingly difficult to feel safe in a world that gives every sign that it is collectively going mad, the arts offers an opportunity to touch something that has been experienced from the perspective of another, allowing us to enter their mind, if only for an instant, seeing the world through their eyes. By taking that opportunity, by touching the forbidden fruit that has been served up for us, already masticated – the poisons removed – we are permitted the visceral thrill of coming close to that line that we would not ordinarily cross.

The role that art plays in society may be debated until the end of time, especially when it comes to the question of the value of art and how much money should be invested into it; making culture a commodity is one way to guarantee that it shall be undervalued, just as the principal of preventive health care has been ignored for generations and we have reactive health-care systems, running around responding to disease instead of working to prevent people from becoming sick in the first place. What cannot be argued is that one of the many functions that artists fulfil is the provision of social commentaries through their works, drawing upon their experiences and what they observe in the world around them in order to create art that is reflective of the times in which they live. Whether this is accepted or not, from the perspective of an artist what must be understood is that what we experience in our day-to-day lives has a tremendous effect on our work, as well as the emotional aspect of our lives. What cannot be expressed through our art quickly spills over into the other parts of life, which is usually where things begin to get out of control.

Living in the 21st Century not only gives us the luxury of historical hindsight, but of having a vast repository of human knowledge and experiences available to us to draw upon when we are interested in learning something or if we merely desire entertainment. The propagation of new ideas has not always been as easy as it has been during the past decade. Individuals who wanted to have their works seen by others now have the Internet and other networks available to them to help spread the word that there is something new out there waiting to be discovered. Yet even in this post-modern age rife with electronic communications and immeasurable networks of computers and modern publishing that connect people around the world with a few keystrokes that makes it vastly easier to share ideas, it is still necessary to create them in order to share them with others. New ideas, works of art, poems and anything with any artistic merit was, at some point, born of the mind of a creative individual. What is wrought of the mind, even today, is still a reflection of the experiences of the individual creating the work, which was why I needed to understand as much as I could about the condition that was exerting so much influence upon my life.

The ultimate truth regarding creativity is that it can never escape what is popularly known as the 'human condition' for the simple reason that it is so inexorably connected to the humanity from which it stems. There is an almost 'romantic' appeal to the idea surrounding that existentialist dilemma faced by many artists of the past and the present and their genuine suffering that made the figure of the artist in the 19th Century such an image of romance and lore, as immortalised in Giacomo Puccini's seminal opera La bohème. The images we have of an artist struggling for their art is a well-known euphemism and recurring theme, having evolved out of the idea of the artist perceived as some monk-like figure, cloistered in a cell devoid of natural light and all creature comforts. The image continues with the artist wrestling with some intense, unseen force; an 'energy' that deigns to consider the artist worthy of their attentions – some divine visitation or intervention – that ultimately contributes to the final work of art being created before their very eyes. The truth of the matter is rather less spectacular, though perhaps not entirely inaccurate.

Whether it be a poem that has been birthed from the depths of the artist's suffering, a piece of music, or the memorialising of an image on canvas or in stone, the deed has been done: another work has been created where once before there was nothing. A page that had hitherto been blank has now been filled with the notes that a musician can read, turning the mysterious symbols into music that will fill the grandest halls with the sounds that had only been heard by the inner ear of the composer. What had only existed in my own mind as a composition is now on paper, waiting to be played, waiting to be discovered by a new generation of performers and by those who love music. When I sat down to compose the music could flow from my pen as easily as the ink flowing from the nib onto the page, filling the lines and spaces with the notes that would ultimately be transformed into cascades of sound, a sculpture in sound. The darkness of the deepest depression robbed me of the ability to even hear music: what had been constantly streaming through my mind – even when I was not composing – was now silent, a silence that was crushingly oppressive.

The mechanics of creativity are something that have eluded me until recently, but have nevertheless been of great interest. It would seem that many of the people that I have encountered want to know 'how I compose', which had always seemed like a strange question, but it also demonstrated how much interest there was in the creative process from those individuals who were not actively involved with this type of creativity. This interest in the process is what helps everyone relate to many of the things that we all do, that we all have in common, only on a different scale; and it all stems from the natural desire that humans have to create things. From the first paintings found in caves, depicting hunters and their catches, there has been a drive to express our inner feelings and ideas through a medium other than the spoken word. Even the spoken word, for the sake of art, can be taken to extremes in the various forms of poetry, singing and other performance art.

When considering the issue of bipolar disorder and its effect on my own creativity, I was confronted with the question as to whether there truly was a relationship between the disorder and my creative process. I can now answer this question with a categorical yes: there is an intrinsic connection between what goes into my creative process and how this affective disorder asserts itself upon my life. While I would have expected that my peak periods of creativity would have corresponded to my 'elevated' periods, those times when my mood seemed to be 'flighty', the truth was a bit more sobering, and not at all what you might expect. . . it was certainly not what I expected when I finally realized the connection.

The peak time for creative endeavours for most of those living with bipolar disorder are those times of elevated mood, hypomania (Jamison, 1989). This is an easy relationship to see: increased energy levels will often coincide with heightened intellectual abilities, the lack of sleep that corresponds to the drive to work, forcing oneself to work for extended periods of time: it reads like a list from the symptoms list for hypomania from the DSM-IV. This corresponds with the elevated mood, or with the period immediately before a major manic episode, so that, in a limited sense, increased creativity may be seen in some subjects as a prodrome to the worsening of symptoms and an indicator that, perhaps, some steps may need to be taken to protect the individual. However, this is also the type of situation that creative people with an affective disorder might long for, knowing it might signal the beginnings of a creative period, and many may try to achieve this end through the use of caffeine, nicotine and various other means at their disposal. This 'heightened' state of creativity can truly be a transcendent time in that it allows the individual involved in the creative act to make temporal relationships between seemingly unrelated things, something that lies at the core of the creative process. This allows creativity to flow with a far greater ease than at other times. The likelihood of someone seeking help as they are ascending to what they believe will be a creative state is, frankly, quite slim.

For the most part, and in what I can only describe a grand display of cosmic humour, I have discovered that my most creative moments seem to be accompanied by a low-grade depression that cycles frequently into a mixed state that includes something that can best be described as 'dysphoric angst' rather than the euphoric hypomania I occasionally experience and long after. While this seems to fly in the face of everything that I thought I knew about the 'fire' of creativity, particularly that expressed by Kay Redfield Jamison in *Touched with Fire* (1993), the illness only proved to be more complex in the manner with which it is able to express itself through a variety of symptoms. In my life that meant that the ups *and* downs present opportunities for creativity; the main difference being the manner in which the creative energy may be directed at a particular time.

In an effort to gain a better understanding of the 'big picture' after receiving a diagnosis that was at once devastating and illuminating, my goal became studying this disease so I could become a partner in my own treatment. There was a sense of devastation for what I did not know, for my own preconceived distortions relating to mental illnesses and of illumination for finally having that sense of, 'well, of course I have bipolar disorder, it's obvious . . . isn't it?' In a very real sense I became a student again, going on-line as often as I could, reading journals, books and everything else I could get my hands on regarding medications, treatments, psychiatric practices and so many other things that my family doctor finally told me I should consider entering medical school.

Once my treatment had begun my greatest fear was what might happen to my creative abilities in the absence of what I had perceived to be what made me the creative individual that I had become. There were also side effects from the medications that could result in a loss of my creative abilities; it all seemed like a cruel double-edged sword. While I had initially lost my ability to compose during a deep depression and had only regained it after my family physician prescribed a course of antidepressants, acting under the assumption that I was suffering from severe depression, the side effects from the first anti-manic agents prescribed for my case resulted in another descent into darkness, accompanied by a subsequent loss of the ability to compose.

While depression may be a debilitating disorder that is not readily associated with creative behaviour (Verhaeghen, Joorman & Kahn, 2005), what I discovered was that the mood stabilisers that were initially tried to even out my rapid cycles left me in a generally more depressive state than anything else. This was the point of revelation: what I had been able to accomplish while mildly depressed, in those times when the worst symptoms were not present, I was unable to do when under the influence of the over-controlling medications. It did not take very long for me to abandon treatment altogether – until I found myself standing on the edge of a very high cliff, thinking that it might actually be an interesting idea to see what would happen if I jumped off.

▶ Striking the balance

Nothing can describe the absolute thrill that accompanies what can only be described as having your 'creative juices' flowing so fast it is virtually impossible to record each thought as it takes shape in your mind, flowering into new, wondrous ideas that continue to transform themselves seemingly of their own volition. These ideas burst forth with the fluidity of a babbling brook, sometimes diverted into a tangent, but often flowing in the direction you desire, finally transforming themselves into that which was only a dream moments before. Nothing can describe the level of satisfaction that can be felt as you see your ideas come alive right before your eyes, but there can also be a price to pay for such elation: it can be utterly exhausting, both physically and emotionally, leaving you drained and totally enervated. Where once there was silence, nothing more than a blank page filled with obscure lines and spaces, devoid of life and character, it now contains a part of my soul, born out of the torment of my mind: awaiting the moment when it will be fully brought to life by musicians who will make the final transformation, turning the notes on the page into living music for all to hear.

Writing poetry merely truncates the final part of the process in the sense that once a work is completed all that is necessary for the work to 'live' is for *anyone* to read the words. A poem may still be *performed*, perhaps even by the author, but this is far less necessary than in the case of music. On a personal level, the writing of words never seemed as fulfilling an activity to me as the composing of music, until the illness provided me with a greater appreciation for the ability to create things in a time when it was impossible to do that one thing that I had, until that moment, identified myself with for almost half my life. While I could not compose in the depths of that deep depression I found that the writing of poetry was something that never really abandoned me; it was possible to partake of the creative fruits *even* when deeply depressed. There was, however, a trick: I had to *remember* to actually do so, which is more difficult than it sounds, particularly when you are feeling extraordinarily depressed, as I was when I was not able to compose.

While someone may say they 'know how you feel', it is really impossible to truly *know* what it is like to be in another individual's situation. Imagine what Vincent van Gogh was experiencing when he created the works we see in museums. Is *Starry Night* the way he really saw things? It may not have been, but visual disturbances may account for many of the unique techniques that he developed to communicate his message.

The poem 'Dragon Slayer' is an excerpt from a larger work, *Laments of the Lost*, which I wrote in 2005. While it was my intention to present the work as a whole, this particular *Lament* is especially episodic, and seems to poignantly reflect some things that are otherwise not particularly easy to describe, such as what a descent into insanity might be like – from the inside. As you read the poem what it might be like to believe that there is something as impossible as a dragon, or something equally fantastic, and you are pursuing it in real life.

Fifth Lament: Dragon Slayer

One day you awoke with the need to hunt down and
destroy the fire-breathing dragon
　　　　although you had never seen a dragon
　　　　let alone one that breathed fire,
　　　　you were quite certain that this was
　　　　necessary – of vital importance –

It was the quest you had been waiting for –
　　　　– *for your entire life* –
to give you meaning – a reason to live *in the moment*
beyond the here and now.
　　　　This was your Holy Grail –
　　　　it did not matter what others said,
　　　　you would find that dragon – and kill it –
　　　　if it was the last thing you did

You had to – it was your destiny

Travelling from town to town,
a Crusader of the new millennium, wherever you arrived
the people would see you – and take pity. . .
giving you food and a place to sleep –
　　　　but visions of the dragon would
　　　　come to you at night – and you would
　　　　leave . . . beds, un-slept in, half-eaten meals
　　　　left behind

Much like Cervantes' *Don*, your eyes would see
what wasn't there – an encroaching madness
distorted reality – twisting the world into a shadowy theatre –
you – the only source of light called upon to
hold back the darkness –
　　　　a hopeless struggle –
　　　　the dragon – coming towards you
raging in anger – a blaring war cry, trying to
scare you – to dissuade you from facing it. . .
But you, resolute in your mission,

---

stand your ground –
> even as the bright light of its flame
> *(strange how it does not burn)*
> blinds you – you do not move from your spot. . .

Standing in the mouth of the mighty cave,
> arms raised in defiance –
ready to strike a blow against the dragon,
> the rushing wind that precedes it
> surprises you, as you fall to the ground
> the dragon leaps from its lair –
> rumbling over the ground at tremendous speed. . .
> rolling towards you –

. . . .

Strange how the driver never saw the
> crumpled heap on the road
> in front of him –
> or barely felt the bump as
> the Dragon Slayer made his
>> last
>> desperate
>> stand.

Lament V/XIII
Source: Laments of the Lost © 2007 by Peter Amsel.

Creative individuals need to feel the fire of emotions in a different way than the person who does not attempt to tap into them as a source of inspiration. Unfortunately, it is this intimacy with the fires that fuel the creative flow that also makes it easier for people travelling that fine line of control to fall away from the path that they are on, becoming hopelessly lost amid unfamiliar territories. I decided to go off of my medications for the simple reason that what I would experience without them was, in my mind, preferable to what I had when I was taking the medications. Having to live with such side effects as nystagmus, fine tremors in my hands, ringing in my ears, a constant drowsiness that made me feel as though I was recovering from a drunken binge, and a worsening of an already chronic headache was simply too much for me to handle. Without the 'mood stabilizers' I cycled very rapidly, but – for a while – I was able to compose again, to write and do almost everything that I had done before my diagnosis.

One of the things that I had learnt when I embarked on my quest to learn as much as I could about bipolar disorder was that, in general, it did not get better on its own. On the contrary, there was a wonderfully terrifying concept called the *kindling effect*. The essence of this being that the 'switching' between moods, such as depression and hypomania, if left unchecked in a system will continue to escalate (Goodwin & Jamison, 1990). As things in my own life continued to spin out of control, it was not difficult for me to recognise the signs, especially when my chiropractor, one of my dearest friends, told me quite frankly, 'Peter, get help.' I did.

My fears about finding a psychiatrist who would understand and be sensitive regarding my needs as a creative individual were assuaged at my very first appointment: with a point-blank bluntness that I have developed a great appreciation for, my psychiatrist asked me, 'What do you want to do?' I took this question at face value and explained what being creative meant to me and how if I could not compose and write, I may as well not remain among the living. Some doctors may have taken this as a threat to commit suicide, but that was not what I was saying at all and, fortunately for me, Dr Miura understood the intent of my words. He smiled and told me the story of a psychiatrist who had a composer as a patient. When the composer was suffering from a depression and went to the doctor he prescribed one thing: 'You must work,' he said. 'You know if I cure your depression you can't compose!'

Whether this story is apocryphal or not is difficult to tell for sure, though I suspected that the composer in question was Benjamin Britten, who suffered from depression throughout his life (Carpenter, 2003). The point of Dr Miura's story was to say that he believed there was a role in my life for this illness. While he wanted me to be able to gain control over the symptoms that created problems for me, the ultimate goal was not to treat the illness; the goal was – and remains to this day – to treat the individual, to treat *me* as the creative person *living* with the illness. The first thing that I am asked when arriving at an appointment is, 'How is your writing?' My creativity is, to be sure, a barometer of my overall mental health.

Wie viel ist aufzuleiden!

'How much suffering there is to go through!' is a quotation from the poet Rilke that I encountered in Viktor Frankl's *Man's Search for Meaning* (Frankl, 1959) that, in a phrase, perfectly summed up the situation I was in: this illness exists, that is a fact, and it is something that I have to experience, that is also a fact; but at the same time, I *must* be able to have my life as a composer and writer, otherwise I am not alive. Through Frankl I understood the meaning of having a 'why' for living, and mine was – and is – to be a composer, writer, poet and, in general, a creative person. Having gone through a failed treatment protocol that felt worse than the illness itself, I vowed to myself that not only was this illness not going to be allowed to stand in the way of me pursuing my dreams, but I also was not going to stand for having the same thing happen as a result of the treatment.

With my doctor enthusiastically on my side I found that he not only wanted me to be part of my treatment plan, he *expected* me to play an active role. We not only discussed new medications that were available, but something else that had been discovered about my case: my extreme sensitivity to low doses of most medications. We debated the merits of different medications and their possible benefits for the headaches that have plagued me for so long, and we spoke of my creative goals. What began as a long experiment – looking for the right drugs that would work for me, at the proper dose, allowing me to *get through* the suffering and get on with creating – ended over a year later with a combination cocktail of several medications at low doses, two of which are extremely low.

Through the new generation of anti-seizure and novel anti-psychotic medications, I was able to emerge from the darkest moments of my life after a period of over one year in which I had not been able to compose a single note of music. More than anything else, I felt like a blind man who had been given the gift of sight again for one main reason: things that had been impossible for me to see only months before were now as clear as day, revealed in all their glory, and nothing could stop me from doing whatever I wanted to do, so long as I remained faithful to the protocol. Since the doses were relatively low, particularly in the case of the novel anti-psychotic that is only taken 'as needed' at bedtime, it is very easy to feel the difference when a dose is missed.

Minimal dosing is an important issue to individuals who are creative for many reasons, not the least of which being that the eradication of all symptoms may, as it did in my situation, result in more harm than good. The idea that someone entering treatment may not fully understand the ramifications of what they are about to receive is a serious issue, particularly at a time when there are so many new advances being made in medicine and the treatment of mental illness. At the same time, it must be stressed that there are inherent dangers, including the possibility of death, when these illnesses go without treatment. The problem, however, lies in the fact that an individual who has experienced moments of heightened mood that have been productive is going to be reluctant to accept the idea that this 'feeling' shall forever be lost to them, as this may also mean that their identity as a creative individual may also be lost.

There must be an understanding of what effect the eradication of symptoms will have on an individual's ability to work, and that can only come through a partnership of treatment between the creative individual and their mental health providers, as it has in my situation. One difficulty that I see from the perspective of the consumer is that doctors are not trained to fail; medical schools are training grounds to cure, when possible, and for providing an alleviation of discomfort when a cure is not available. Allowing someone to suffer when it is possible to provide relief goes against what a doctor is trained to do; but at the same time, how many people would accept some discomfort if it meant they could enjoy their favourite activity?

When asked if he felt there was an ethical dilemma in allowing me to experience the symptoms that I have, some of which are not pleasant, in order to provide me with the opportunity to maintain my connection with my creative energies, Dr Miura replied, 'No.' His position is quite simple: even the low doses of the medications that I am taking are exerting sufficient control to make a difference in the management of my symptoms, which is enhanced by techniques that were learnt through psycho-education at the psychiatric rehabilitation programme associated with the hospital. The ethical dilemma,

Dr Miura asserts, would have arisen had he treated me so aggressively that my ability to work disappeared.

Using the medications at the lowest effective dose has meant that my symptoms have not been completely eliminated: while I still experience episodes of depression, they are not as deep, nor for as long, and I cycle through many other states, though the 'roller-coaster' may actually be going slower – on some days. The medications have cut the worst symptoms, the ones that I found I could not easily cope with and would trigger irrational thinking, anxiety and too many other things to contemplate. I can sleep. That may seem like a silly thing to write, but there have been months at a time where I have averaged between 15 and 18 hours of sleep in a *week*. These were not periods where I was experiencing a manic episode: they were periods without sleep. In the last eight months the average has been 28–35 hours per week, which is a tremendous improvement, though it is still only between four and five hours a night.

The most important thing that Dr Miura and I have come to terms with in my treatment is that this is a treatment of more than a person, we must look at what makes a person *want* to live. Without that desire, without the fire and passion, no pill will help.

▶ The road ahead

The most important thing this illness has shown me is that we have to adjust the paradigm of current medical treatment if we are going to be successful in preventing the mental health issues at hand turning into an all-out crisis: unless there is a dramatic shift in the manner in which the health-care system perceives the issues it is being faced with, there is no way it can survive the next generation of aging citizens. Right now we have a system of medical care that is best described as being 'reactive' in its mode of functioning. You can generally get tremendous care once you are sick or need the services of a surgeon, but why should we be waiting that long? What about the things that can be prevented *before* they necessitate expensive hospital stays and surgery?

While the economic cost of having people stay in hospital is astronomical, there seems to be precious little emphasis placed on preventive health care. Instead of waiting until people need to be admitted to hospital for expensive inpatient care they could be provided with outpatient counseling that addresses the issues that lead to people being hospitalised. This is exemplified in the field of mental health care through Psychiatric Rehabilitation and is a reality that works, and works well. The Psychiatric Rehabilitation Programme at the Royal Ottawa Hospital offered many groups to both in- and outpatients providing a tremendous amount of support for individuals who were motivated to take an active role in their recovery process. Goal setting, symptom self-management and Dr Miura's group all provided different tools that complemented the medications being offered.

The future is at once bright and uncertain. I am constant in my inconsistency, continuing on my path while trying to enjoy the ride as much as possible, but things may be getting more difficult in the future. The Royal Ottawa Hospital began phasing out its Psychiatric Rehabilitation Programme several years ago. It has now been announced that the hospital is becoming a Tertiary Care Centre, and that psychiatric rehabilitation is no longer a priority. This means that the burden of providing the services that the hospital will no longer be providing will be falling onto non-existent community resources and volunteers.

For so long as the music is performed the composer lives.

Exercise

In order to foster an understanding about what the turmoil of an affective disorder is like, in a small sense, imagine what happens when creative ability is funnelled through a mind that is also being influenced by the internal havoc created by mental illness. Remember, artists reflect their identities through their works, so as you listen to the music and try to hear the underlying emotional current that is present. I would highly recommend an examination of the *String Quartets* of Robert Schumann, perhaps the greatest example of chamber music from the Romantic period. The music of Gustav Mahler, particularly his *Kindertotenlieder* (*Songs on the Death of Children*), is also highly evocative of an emotional state that would be very difficult to consider without the buffer that the artistic setting has provided. As you listen to some of the music imagine how the composer must have felt while composing this music.

As an alternate exercise, find a copy of Jamison's *Touched with Fire* and choose one of the artists, composers or writers that she identifies in the Appendix as having a mental illness. Try to find a work by this artist that reflects their illness. Be mindful of the fact, as demonstrated in 'Dragon Slayer', that not everything is as it seems: merely because an artist has an illness does not necessarily mean that their work will reflect elements of that illness. That is the difference between reflecting an identity and an emotional state: the great works appeal to us because they have more than 'surface' emotions, they are able to touch a deeper emotional level to which we can relate, even if our lives and experiential backgrounds are completely different.

▶ **Acknowledgements**

The author would like to thank a list of individuals too long to be given here, but without whom this chapter could not exist. For their continual encouragement, emotional support and professional advice, I would be remiss without specifically naming Drs Diane Bamford, Ron Bell, Carlos Miura and George Surko, each of whom provided an invaluable abundance of assistance, well beyond the professional insights that were garnered from them throughout the creation of this chapter. I am especially indebted to Theo Stickley for providing the opportunity to contribute to this endeavour and to Mylene for providing the requisite space to work.

▶ **References**

American Psychiatric Association (2000) *Diagnostic and Statistical Manual of Mental Disorders: DSM-IV-TR*. Washington, D. C.: American Psychiatric Association.
Carpenter, H. (2003) *Benjamin Britten: A Biography*. Faber & Faber, Essex.
Frankl, V.E. (1959/1985) *Man's Search for Meaning*. New York: Washington Square Press.
Goodwin, F.K. & Jamison, K.R. (1990) *Manic-Depressive Illness*. New York: Oxford University Press.
Jamison, K.R. (1989) Mood disorders and patterns of creativity in British writers and artists. *Psychiatry*, 52: 125–34.
Jamison, K.R. (1993) *Touched with Fire*. New York: Free Press Paperbacks.
Verhaeghen, P., Joorman, J. & Khan, R. (2005) Why we sing the blues: The relation between self-reflective rumination, mood, and creativity. *Emotion*, 5: 226–32.

▶ **Suggested reading list**

Andreasen, N. (1987) Creativity and Mental Illness: Prevalence Rates in Writers and Their First-Degree Relatives. *American Journal of Psychiatry*. **144**: 1288–1292.

Frankl, V.E. (2000) *Man's Search for Ultimate Meaning*. CambridgeL Perseus.

Jamison, K.R., Gerner, R.H., Hammen, C., and Padesky, C., (1980) Clouds and Silver Linings: Positive Experiences Associated with Primary Affective Disorders. *American Journal of Psychiatry*. **137**: 198–202.

Jamison, K.R. (1995) *An Unquiet Mind*. New York: A. A. Knopf.

Jamison, K.R. (2004) *Exuberance: The Passion for Life*. New York: Vintage Books.

Joormann, J. (2004) Attentional bias in dysphoria: The role of inhibitory processes. *Cognition and Emotion*. **18**: 125–47.

Ludwig, A.M. (1994) Mental Illness and Creative Activity in Female Writers. *American Journal of Psychiatry*. **151**: 1650–1656.

Marangall, L. (2004) The importance of subsyndromal symptoms in bipolar disorder. *Journal of Clinical Psychiatry*, **65**(Sup. 10): 24–7.

Shapiro, P.J. & Weisberg, R.W. (1999) Creativity and bipolar diathesis: Common behavioural and cognitive components. *Cognition and Emotion*. **13**: 741–62.

◀ CHAPTER TWENTYSEVEN ▶

Social inclusion and psychosocial interventions: Clash, compromise or coherence?

Peter Bates

National Development Team

Julie Cullen

Care Services Improvement Partnership

Among the array of current influences on UK mental health services, we find both the continuing development of psychosocial interventions (PSI) and the adoption of social inclusion (SI). This chapter records a dialogue that we have begun about the relationship between PSI and SI. After an introduction to each approach, we consider the similarities and differences at the level of the individual, the family and the community, followed by a discussion of evidence, the goals of intervention and staff roles, skills and values.

Throughout, our search is for the ways in which each model can highlight and stimulate reflection on the other so that our practice can improve. We have eased this search by simplifying on two axes: we write as if the 'PSI practitioner' and the 'SI practitioner' were different people with highly elaborated and distinct perspectives; and we write as if each approach comprised a fixed body of beliefs and knowledge. In reality, of course, the two perspectives are interwoven, evolving and sometimes utilised by the same person. Questions for reflection appear in boxes.

Learning About Mental Health Practice.   Edited by Theo Stickley and Thurstine Basset
© 2008 John Wiley & Sons, Ltd

► **A history of social inclusion**

An international network of people working to reverse the exclusion of people with physical, sensory and learning disabilities began to form in the 1970s and 1980s (O'Brien & O'Brien, 1996). Children in special schools formed one focus of their attention, although the value base was increasingly applied to a diverse range of people excluded for a variety of reasons.

This value base was informed by a range of innovators, including Carl Rogers (1961), who championed person-centred counselling and believed that people were the best architects of their own lives; Wolf Wolfensberger (1972), who developed and expanded the concept of normalisation in learning disability services; and Paulo Freire (1972), who as an educator and later a politician, highlighted the ways in which both individuals and communities could claim their power.

In Europe, these influences combined with other factors to form a favourable context for the concept of social inclusion: the development of the concept of social exclusion as a richer and more dynamic replacement of the old notion of poverty; the social model of disability that focused on disabling environments, systems and attitudes; and the development of legislation to combat discrimination on the grounds of disability.

Evidence demonstrating the social exclusion of people with mental health issues was cogently presented by the MIND Inquiry (Dunn, 1999), which highlighted the human and financial cost of exclusion for individuals and communities. The UK government duly published its own report on social exclusion and mental health (Social Exclusion Unit, 2004), setting out a 27-point plan for action across a range of public and community organisations.

Question 27.1

What influence do contemporary politics and policies have on how you view people with mental health issues, their circumstances and the right way to help?

The social inclusion perspective has also been supported by the parallel development of a variety of other policy and organisational factors, including:

■ A stronger focus on public health, starting with the publication of *The Health of the Nation* (Department of Health, 1992) and reinforced through the *National Service Framework for Mental Health* (Department of Health, 1999). Mental health promotion, suicide prevention and services for people with mental health difficulties have increasingly been recognised as issues for the whole population.

- The duty to undertake population assessments and commission health services in response to the findings has highlighted the needs of the large numbers of people with mental health issues who are outside specialist services.

- The adoption of 'Common Mental Health Problems' as a category and the development of services targeting the needs of this group.

- The creation in 1997 of the Social Exclusion Unit, with its interest in cross-governmental themes, which led to the National Social Inclusion Programme for mental health. More broadly, the formation of the Care Services Improvement Partnership in 2004 was one of a number of attempts to challenge 'silo' thinking, and seek frameworks that have broad application.

- The growing concern about the large number of people receiving Incapacity Benefit as a result of mental health issues, which has led to considerable political interest in initiatives that get people back to work. This has the potential to increase alienation as people with mental health issues feel harried and the public becomes less tolerant of benefit claimants.

These factors and others, such as the Human Rights Act, disability equality policy and efforts to equip society to be more accepting of diversity, have created a supportive environment for the development of SI work in mental health. This supports the inclusion of people with mental health issues by working both with the person and mainstream community organisations.

▶ A history of psychosocial interventions

'Psychosocial intervention' is:

> a generic term that describes a broad range of activities undertaken by services and clinicians, in collaboration with families and carers, that aim to improve the social functioning of people with serious mental health problems. (Baguley & Baguley, 1999)

Psychosocial interventions are based on the stress vulnerability model articulated by Zubin and Spring (1977). This model links increased stress levels to greater likelihood of both onset and relapse in psychosis. Nuechterlein and Dawson (1987) developed the model by showing how three factors – the individual's coping mechanisms, family relationships and social influences – affected the course of a person's illness. Social influences such as unemployment, poverty, isolation and other marks of social exclusion clearly exacerbate stress and so link PSI and SI approaches.

Individual psychosocial interventions aim to reduce distress and help promote coping. The approaches used to do this have been developed from cognitive behaviour theory, which considers that emotional disorder occurs as a result of chronic or profound misattribution of meaning to events and situations (Beck *et al.*, 1979). Although CBT began as a treatment for non-psychotic mental health problems, more recent work has developed the approach to form a range of evidence-based CBT interventions for people with psychosis (Kuipers *et al.*, 1997). Cognitive behavioural therapies received a considerable, if controversial, boost in profile in 2005 when Richard Layard advised the Prime Minister's Strategy Unit that the UK needed 10 000 additional psychological therapists trained in CBT. PSI draws on the evidence base for CBT, but takes a broader approach that takes the therapist beyond the clinical interview and adds other interventions such as skills training, modelling and family work.

Question 27.2

How much study, writing, practice training and other formal learning have you undertaken to use the particular interventions that you employ?

Brooker and his colleagues (1994) established the first UK PSI training programme in the late 1980s, and evaluation of this course showed that nurses trained in PSI achieved similar favourable outcomes with individuals and carers as those found in earlier trials of family work undertaken by clinical psychologists.

Manchester University and the Institute of Psychiatry in London then developed the Thorn Nurse Initiative. This aimed to teach nurses evidence-based PSI skills including case management, individual interventions and family interventions. From 1994, the programme emphasised multidisciplinary work and welcomed other mental health professionals to train alongside nurses. In 1998 the course was re-branded as the Collaboration on Psychosocial Education, and in 2004 secured a further five-year contract to deliver both undergraduate and postgraduate training.

Throughout this time, course participants have established satellite courses in their Mental Health Trusts and many universities have begun teaching PSI courses, especially on nursing pre-registration programmes. It has been estimated that more than 5000 nurses have completed full PSI training, with many more being exposed to short skills-based courses (Department of Health, 2006).

Question 27.3

What evidence do you have that your interventions are effective?

The growth of PSI coincided with a number of other factors that contributed to its profile within mental health services:

- The whole NHS became increasingly interested in evidence, and so treatments with proven efficacy were regarded more highly than those that did not, although custom and practice in services have been slow to change. This was especially important in mental health services, where (compared to other branches of health care) conclusive evidence is elusive.

- A national survey of community mental health nurses in 1990 found that 80% of people diagnosed with schizophrenia in England had not been on the caseload of a mental health nurse working in the community, and that much of the nurse's time was spent with people who had mild or moderate problems (White, 1991). The mental health nursing review (Butterworth, 1994) recommended that the main focus of work for mental health nurses should be with people who had a serious mental illness.

- In the 1990s policy guidance and referral criteria for specialist mental health services changed to target severely mentally ill clients (Department of Health, 1998). This happened for a number of reasons, including the growing litigious culture, relentless media attention on the small number of mental illness-related homicides, improvements in drug treatments and other interventions and hospital closures, which all kept the needs of seriously mentally ill people in the spotlight.

- Latterly, the integration of local authority and NHS services and the way in which the Fair Access to Care Services guidance (Department of Health, 2001) has been adopted in many places has reinforced the focus on people with severe illness. The recent launch of services for people with common mental health problems may shift this balance a little, but it remains a very small part of the overall budget.

However, a number of studies have shown that programme graduates have experienced difficulties in implementing their PSI skills in routine service settings (Brooker, 2001; Fadden, 1998). Lipsky (1980, cited by Repper & Brooker, 2002) stated:

> worker training is less important than the nature of working conditions themselves. Without a supportive network of working peer relationships, training to improve service capacity of workers is likely to wash out under the pressure of work context.

Repper and Brooker (2002) identified a number of issues that organisations needed to consider to integrate PSI skills into routine practice, including assessment of training needs, incorporating mapping of capabilities specific to PSI; developing a framework for clinical audit; short-course training for staff, including service managers; and addressing PSI in workforce planning and the commissioning of training and education.

Thus, PSI focuses on people with serious mental illness, while SI pays attention to the whole population. The next stage of the paper explores the two approaches at the level of the individual, families and the community.

Question 27.4

What is the balance of your caseload between severe and common mental health problems? Why?

▶ **Working with individuals**

In common with best practice across mental health work, both PSI and SI approaches lay great store on building a therapeutic alliance in which the person is able to develop openness and a feeling of trust in the worker. Both seat their work on a strong hope for recovery, and focus on overcoming the obstacles that currently hinder the person from getting on with their life.

PSI

In PSI, the worker engages individuals and families in a process of assessment, problem identification and formulation, intervention and relapse prevention. After paying attention to the person's problems and difficulties in the present, an incremental path is identified through which distress and symptoms might be alleviated while problems are reduced and coping strategies developed.

Aspirations for the future are broken down into short-term goals, some of which suggest interventions to reduce distress and unhelpful ideas or enhance medication compliance. Indeed, symptom management and reduction would be generally seen to be a vital prerequisite for working towards the other goals, since it is assumed that these are the factors that have interrupted the smooth progress of the person's life, while relapse prevention would be key to helping them maintain a preferred lifestyle.

PSI is therefore focused on issues that are plainly connected to the core business of mental health services and assumes that there is a need to ameliorate these problems before the person is ready to engage in the wider community.

Assessment

PSI workers are trained to conduct a detailed and standardised assessment that leads to a problem formulation built around a person's distress. The approach to assessment is one of collaborative enquiry based on the underpinning theory for PSI. The expertise of the worker can help some individuals feel secure, however there is also a risk that if handled clumsily this can reinforce the message to the service user that the professional is in charge over the compliant patient. The use of standardised forms categorises the person's experience, while statistical analysis drawn from these assessments can exclude people from the process of making sense of their own story. Furthermore, such an assessment could potentially be used to assist in determining entitlement to services, and therefore help staff to prioritise and ration the delivery of mental health care. Standardised assessment provides an opportunity to gain a deeper understanding of an individual's problems – particularly when supplemented with semi-structured assessment tools – but this approach is dependent on practitioners having high-quality engagement and collaborative skills to avoid the pitfalls mentioned above.

Question 27.5

What can you do to minimise the disempowering effects of your information-tion gathering?

At times, attention has been focused away from the purpose of the intervention and PSI has been reduced in some areas to 'doing a KGV' symptom assessment, rather than the KGV being a way of finding out about a person's experiences and engaging them in a helping relationship (KGV is an abbreviation of the authors who developed this assessment: Krawiecka, Goldberg & Vaughan). Indeed, many services set targets for numbers of KGVs and Social Function Scales that should be completed (Birchwood *et al.*, 1990). This adds PSI to the long list of helpful innovations that have been designed for selective, creative application and then have in some hands become slaves to an institutionally standardised, mechanical process that is rigidly applied to everyone in that service. SI could go the same way.

SI

While PSI offers a structured process for identifying and resolving mental health problems, SI emphasises the person's universal human needs. The difference is one of emphasis, as both models pay attention to the need for social networks and life goals. SI assists the person to clarify a compelling vision of how things could be and then uses this as a magnet to draw the person forward into a desired future. It assumes that people have a right to participate in the community now, and that there is no need to wait until someone else has deemed them to be 'ready'. Inclusion thinkers (along with allies in the recovery movement) expect people sometimes to choose social goals over symptom management, preferring perhaps to retain the job and the attendant stress and hospital admissions, rather than 'stress-free' unemployment. Some people, of course, will insist on achieving both their social and their mental health goals. But SI workers are not really very interested or skilled in reducing mental health symptoms, preferring instead to accept people as they are, work on reducing discrimination and arrange effective support and fair access to valued community activities.

Question 27.6

How do you stop a ladder of easy steps becoming a barrier that prevents the person having what they want straight away?

Self-assessment

PSI workers seek to personalise their work by listening respectfully, negotiating goals and selecting interventions that make sense to the person. In contrast to this personalised approach, some SI workers begin with a person-centred approach that moves mental health services to the periphery of vision. SI sees the person as a citizen with lifelong ambitions and achievements, informal networks and a myriad of actual and potential social roles and relationships. In this context, most life choices are made without much reference to the mental health services that are seen to play only a small part in determining life course or satisfaction. SI workers are keenly aware of the unplanned damage to identity, relationships and social roles that tends to follow contact with the mental health service, and so they seek ways of helping people minimise this damage through the development of a more 'inclusion-friendly' service.

Question 27.7

How do you support people to make their own life plans?

Person-centred approaches (Ritchie *et al.*, 2003) include a variety of ways to support the person to plan their own life. These person-centred planning formats assert that individuals and their allies have the resources to identify and work towards their ambitions. They utilise narrative, graphics and the person's own language to validate their sense of the world. Wellness Recovery Action Planning (Copeland, 1997) is one format for self-assessment that has been promoted within the mental health user movement and includes many features that would be consistent with other person-centred planning approaches. However, the celebration of ordinariness and lay insight may mask lazy thinking, a lack of rigour and denial of the professional's expertise. Furthermore, true person-centred plans are likely to be of little direct help to services wishing to prioritise and ration the delivery of care (although knowing what the person wants in their life will assist greatly in the design of helpful interventions).

Enthusiasm about self-assessment is often accompanied by cynicism about the merits of professional assessment, which is seen as a disempowering process for the person who misses the things that are truly important to them. Indeed, some projects have gone as far as to set aside professional assessment entirely, an approach that changes the fundamental basis of work with the person and may take it away from therapy entirely – as well as challenging the commissioning, eligibility, review and discharge arrangements.

Mature inclusion projects recognise that self-assessment leads to the identification of some needs that will be self-managed, others that will be met by family and friends, yet more that might result in an application or imposition of help from mental health services, and, finally, some that will remain aspirational and unmet. In this environment, self-assessment stands apart as a separate process from the professional judgement about the allocation of scarce public resources. Such judgements will be more effective if taken in the light of the person's own self-assessment, but they are not governed by it.

Question 27.8

In your work, how do you balance efforts to support positive roles in the community and working on mental health problems?

In summary, the focus of a PSI assessment is to find out about distress and the consequences of it on the rest of the person's life, as well as how other roles and relationships can support mental well-being. In contrast, the focus of a SI assessment is to find out how the person is meeting their need for connecting, contributing and belonging to the wider society.

Formulation

Following a PSI assessment, the worker and the person collaboratively draw up a list of problems and strengths. A formulation is then developed that helps to understand how different problems can interact and lead to escalating distress and other unpleasant emotional states. Formulations draw on the underpinning theories of PSI and may use the stress vulnerability model, antecedents and consequences, or the impact of beliefs on feelings and behaviours. Developing formulations is a collaborative process that helps develop a shared understanding of problems and the best way forward.

Short- and long-term goals can be agreed that help increase a person's level of activity and social interactions. In general, PSI sees the person with psychosis as a powerful actor on the social and personal stage of their own life, rather than a casualty of an unjust society. Consequently, interventions are personal and psychological rather than consisting of social and political efforts to challenge oppression, poverty and exclusion experienced by many people with mental health issues.

> **Question 27.9**
>
> How do you organise your observations into explanations?

SI practitioners do not appear to have an explicit 'formulation' stage in their work, and so may be unaware of how they blend their unacknowledged, implicit models with evidence to come to a decision about what to do next. However, a glance at the worker's diary or the support plans they write may reveal the extent of their belief in the power of accepting communities.

Interventions

PSI interventions at the level of the individual are primarily aimed at reducing the person's distress and promoting positive coping strategies that support recovery. Individual approaches include using normalising rationales (Kingdom & Turkington, 1991) to reduce the fear generated as a consequence of psychotic symptoms by placing them on a continuum with normal experience. For example, sleep deprivation, traumatic events, sensory deprivation, hostage situations, solitary confinement and sexual abuse are all examples of stressors that have been shown to have triggered psychotic symptoms in people with no psychiatric history.

Other interventions include coping strategy enhancement (Tarrier *et al.*, 1990) that aims to maximise the person's current resources and ability to cope with symptoms. Cognitive, behavioural, physiological and sensory strategies are explored after exploring antecedents and consequences of a person's symptoms. Other interventions include focusing techniques (Haddock, Bentall & Slade, 1996) and belief modification (Kuipers *et al.*, 1997). Intervention would usually include a focus on medication management and relapse prevention by identifying early warning signs and relapse-prevention plans (Birchwood *et al.*, 1989).

The suite of established SI interventions is much less well developed. Supported employment specialists have utilised a variety of approaches (Grove, Secker & Seebohm, 2005) and some of these have been adapted for other areas of community participation. Bates and Dowson (2006) have attempted to create a classification of generic SI interventions, but to date there is little agreement about the effectiveness of most of these ways of working.

▶ Working with families

The PSI approach to family intervention is based on the concept of expressed emotion (EE). Research carried out by Brown (1959) found that individuals returning from institutional care to live with family members fared worse in terms of relapse and symptom severity than those moving to hostel or supported accommodation. Further investigation led to the concept of EE, and in particular three aspects that increase the risk of relapse: criticism, hostility and emotional over-involvement. Workers therefore intervene with the whole family using CBT approaches to improve coping strategies, communication skills, stress management and relapse prevention. This focus on the family's contribution can sometimes result in family members feeling blamed for their relative's illness.

Barrowclough and Tarrier (1992) used the following rationale to introduce stress-management approaches for families:

- Living with a person who has schizophrenia can be difficult, and it is usual for relatives to feel stressed or upset at least some of the time and sometimes cope with this by excluding the person.

- When the person is living with family members, they can provide a lot of day-to-day help and rehabilitation. Helping family members manage their own stress and cope with difficult situations will improve the quality of the support that they provide.

- People with schizophrenia (along with others who have serious and long-term conditions) are often unusually sensitive to stress in others, and so by feeling more in control, the relative may indirectly help the person. It is worth noting here that stress levels of co-participants in inclusive community settings may be lower than in mental health settings, making inclusive environments safer for people with a diagnosis of schizophrenia.

While EE work assists families in managing stress and so reduces the risk of harm to the person, inclusive approaches see the family as a major source of strength. Some person-centred plans encourage the person to bring together an informal support group. Members are selected by the person and will often include relatives, who report that this process offers a refreshing validation of the love, support and insight that they offer (Short, Sanderson & Cook, 2003). Group members work together to develop a shared vision of a far-off and ideal future for the person, especially focusing on the person's preferences and ambitions in relation to social inclusion – home, job, friends and so on. During this process, past conflicts are often revealed to have been about short-term coping strategies rather than long-term ambitions, and so the new, shared vision forms the basis for future collaboration. Other inclusive approaches aim to help group members handle conflict by highlighting the competing perspectives that they hold. Beyond this, SI frameworks have little to offer to people seeking to work with families in conflict.

Question 27.10

How do you engage family members?

There is potential for SI to work with communities in the same way that PSI is working with families. Indeed, community groups would do well to understand not just how to avoid hostility (the usual target of mental health awareness campaigns), but also how to avoid overly controlling and critical expressions of concern for the person, as the studies on expressed emotion have shown how harmful this can be.

> **Question 27.11**
>
> In your area, who helps mainstream community groups learn how to create a mentally healthy culture for their members?

▶ Working with communities

Graduates from the early PSI courses used the Social Function Scale, which measures people's social engagement, interpersonal behaviour, positive social activities, recreation, independence in living skills and employment or occupation (Birchwood *et al.*, 1990). The assessment of social functioning is also likely to include managing anxiety in social situations, appropriate posture, conversation skills, and managing emotion in social rather than anti-social ways.

As PSI courses have developed there has been a greater focus on the effects of exclusion and ways of promoting inclusion. Despite these changes, PSI remains resolutely focused on the individual, along with their family and personal community of relationships and roles. In contrast, SI includes community development interventions such as building links with community organisations, offering guidance and support to key individuals in those organisations, and lowering practical barriers that prevent anyone accessing these community opportunities. This gives SI practitioners a perspective on the *local community* as well as the client's *personal community*, incorporating regular contact with mainstream organisations and recognition of the wider roles and relationships that people enjoy beyond the mental health system.

This means that they may spend time cultivating contact with organisations that do not yet figure in the specific inclusion plans of anyone on their caseload, as they consider this to be a sound investment for the future. Other implications include the following:

■ In their work with local communities, using mental health promotion, organisational development and mediation interventions, SI practitioners have to adopt a different viewpoint on confidentiality and disclosure than their PSI colleagues and others working in mental health services. Their anticipatory contacts with organisations mean that they are unlikely to have the chance to play the role of the unmarked 'friend' in visiting community venues. Moreover, the formal, sanction-driven disclosure agreements that mental health services often have with other agencies such as schools or the police are less relevant in the bar or the bowls club, and so different approaches have to be developed.

- SI practitioners work with people who want support to access community roles and opportunities. Unless care is taken, this can neglect people who prefer to remain inside mental health services at present, as well as people who have complex and longstanding issues that mean that they do not 'ask' for inclusion support in a conventional manner.

- The approach to risk management is different. Indeed, one inclusion project we know works from the basis that people using services have been trained to be unduly risk averse by their previous exposure to the mental health system, and positively encourages them to take more calculated risks in their life from the outset.

Therefore SI practitioners implicitly criticise the PSI perspective for its conservatism, in that it assists people to adapt to their circumstances rather than demanding and working towards societal transformation.

▶ Timing and combining interventions

Thus, while PSI pays attention to symptom alleviation and problem reduction in the context of social roles and relationships, SI is more interested in obtaining and retaining valued social roles and relationships, while acknowledging the person's problems. There is a need for both approaches, with the workers basing their collaboration on an understanding of difference (this can also be achieved by a single worker integrating and utilising both perspectives). For example, the vision of an inclusive lifestyle can provide the motivating reason to work on personal issues, while the person's grasp on home, job and friendship networks can slip if mental health difficulties are not addressed. The person-centred approach adopted by inclusion workers focuses on the person's life ambitions and current priorities, while the personalised interventions of the PSI worker concentrate on the causes and cure of distress and efforts to ameliorate its negative impact on social roles and relationships.

Rather than SI work starting when PSI finishes, the two approaches should work hand in hand, with the changing needs of the individual dictating the respective proportions of activity taking place in each aspect of the person's life. For example, if the person is experiencing psychiatric distress, the PSI therapist and SI worker would share out the work, to assist the person to consider both how they might respond to their voice hearing and what would help them maintain supportive and productive relationships with their employer.

Where a person is experiencing acute symptoms that affect the form and content of their thinking, the mental health service has traditionally either neglected the person's community roles or dictated when they are safe and ready to return in an approach that might be summarised as 'get well, then get back'. PSI practitioners recognise that some people need a holiday from burdensome responsibilities for a time and offer clinical intervention that reduce symptoms and distress. SI workers are keenly aware that a 'holiday' from inclusive roles can quickly turn into permanent exclusion, and so they work on retention of long-term roles and relationships from day one.

▶ Evidence of effectiveness

A key feature of reflective practice is to utilise evidence of what is working in order to improve practice. PSI and SI have taken different approaches to the importance of research and the selection of methods, evidence and outcomes. The whole of PSI rests on its alliance with the medical approach to evidence – replicable, randomised controlled trials of standardised interventions against specific outcomes – and so many different elements of PSI have undergone clinical trials and shown that it can deliver on the external targets set for mental health service providers.

These targets may not embrace inclusion-related outcomes. We have little formal evidence to suggest that PSI approaches are effective in helping people get and keep a job, a home or friendships, as these have not traditionally been the outcomes that the research trials have focused on. The converse does appear to be true, though, as attending to inclusion goals can yield improvements in mental health, and there is a growing body of evidence that employment, education, volunteering, exercise, participation in faith groups and other inclusive activities all have a beneficial impact (Becker et al., 1998; Drake et al., 1999; Pevalin & Rose, 2003; Warner, 1994). Despite this, few SI practitioners are aware of the research base, and most of those who are rely on qualitative, narrative-based models. Some find that the complexity of the concept slows progress on defining and delivering robust evidence of their practice.

To date, social inclusion thinking in mental health has largely focused on the two areas of population-level problem identification and values-driven change. Population-based research has demonstrated that people with mental health issues are subject to exclusion, while inclusion advocates have argued that shifting values, promoting creative and person-centred responses and redesigning mental health services will reduce this damage. Unfortunately, neither measuring exclusion, offering values training, promoting creativity nor redesigning systems offers much in the way of a tight definition of what inclusion practitioners actually do nor how the success of these interventions might be measured.

The first exception to this general position is perhaps in the arena of employment. Since the 1970s, academics have been investigating the effectiveness of the individual placement and support (IPS) approach in contrast to sheltered workshops and work-preparation programmes. The results have shown that IPS is a more effective intervention that can lead to more people obtaining and retaining suitable, well-paid jobs (Grove, Secker & Seebohm, 2005). A similar body of evidence on job retention and supported education is emerging. However, there have been few attempts to adapt the interventions or analyse their effectiveness in other inclusive settings.

The second exception might be evaluation of person-centred planning as a specific inclusion-focused intervention. While the values and practices underpinning person-centred planning have a lengthy history, its formal evaluation did not begin until recently, and the evidence is encouraging but remains sparse. In particular, there is little research evidence of the effectiveness of person-centred planning in a mental health context.

Question 27.12

How might you utilise the evidence base for PSI and SI work?

Thirdly, inclusion practitioners have the opportunity of drawing on a wide range of research evidence about more specific elements of their practice (Bates & Dowson, 2006), some of which are shared with their PSI colleagues. For example, practitioners may use motivational interviewing interventions to support the person in resolving their ambivalence around engaging in an inclusive setting; adult guidance interventions to help them select appropriate community activities; mental health promotion interventions to combat the ignorance and discrimination found in the setting; organisational development interventions to help the community group develop new responses; and mediation or restorative justice interventions to resolve difficulties that emerge during participation.

Despite the existence of these signposts that point towards clear evidence-based interventions, little work has been done to date and most front-line inclusion practitioners continue to work intuitively.

▶ Impact on staff and services

In mental health services no less than anywhere else in society, values are often taken for granted rather than clearly elaborated. So we may assume that the values and attitudes that underpin SI and PSI approaches are already held by mental health staff. These are assumptions that need to be tested both through research and in local services: What are these values? Do staff hold them? Is their practice consistent with the values? Are the key values underpinning PSI vital to effective SI work and vice versa?

Question 27.13

What are the core values that underpin your practice? How might you deal with the value differences between members of your team?

Growing pressures on mental health services have combined with a broader array of demands and increasing bureaucracy to divert qualified staff away from careful face-to-face work with people needing either PSI or SI skills. An opposing trend has led to an increase in the number of staff appointed to Community Mental Health Teams to work with people who have serious mental illness – but these newcomers have often been unqualified support workers.

This has meant that qualified staff remain responsible for work at the individual and family level, while the support worker aims to increase the person's social functioning. This allocation of time to social functioning has the potential to promote inclusion, but it has also meant that this activity may be accorded low status in the organisation and may lack professional rigour. Where support workers do adopt a social inclusion perspective, they can find themselves at odds with their professional supervisor, who perhaps wanted to recruit, train and supervise a PSI assistant.

The recent development of new roles in mental health services has identified a number of potential front-line SI workers, including support, time and recovery workers; gateway workers (graduate-level support staff working in primary care); people working in modernised day services; and some occupational therapists. In addition, a number of mental health services have appointed staff at a senior level to work on inter-agency and social inclusion issues, but these staff are unlikely to have a role with named service users. This means that the majority (but by no means all) of SI workers are comparatively unqualified in mental health terms and some may have weak academic credentials.

One implication is that the SI worker may need advice and support from their PSI colleague in order to respond well to the service user's complex delusional thoughts or other signs of distress. The relationship becomes reciprocal, as the PSI worker draws on the expertise of the SI worker in developing and supporting community participation.

Table 27.1 contrasts PSI and SI skills.

▶ Conclusion

In 2004 the government conducted a survey of user views about mental health services (Social Exclusion Unit, 2004) and one of its key findings was to identify the destructive culture of diminished expectations. Overcoming this pessimism will require sustained ambition to reduce both mental distress and exclusion. This ambition must be supported by evidence-based practice in psychosocial interventions and other treatments, as well as by evidence-based social inclusion work that supports both individuals and communities. If mental health service users are to have proper access to both PSI and SI expertise, then the process of exchange and dialogue that we have begun in this chapter must continue.

Table 27.1   PSI and SI skills compared

PSI skills	SI skills
Engagement with the service user and families	Engagement with service user and community organisations
Assessment – getting to know the whole person so that intervention makes sense in their life; and utilising standardised assessment formats including the symptom severity scale (KGV), Social Function Scale, Camberwell assessment of need, LUNSERS (neuroleptic side effects rating scale) and service user identification of problems and needs	Self-assessment – several person-centred planning formats invite the person and their friends and family to develop a rich picture of the person's gifts, preferences and aspirations. These processes are facilitated, but belong to the person themselves
Formulation – identifying problems and needs to develop a shared explanation of the person's distress and the way it can be resolved or managed	Asset identification – recognising the person's gifts and strengths in relation to participation in the wider community
Short and long term goals – reduce distress and its impact on the life of the person	Goals – obtain and retain valued roles in the wider community
Guidance and matching of the person with relevant helping agencies	Guidance and matching of the person with inclusive community opportunities
Interventions that help people cope and reduce symptoms, normalising approaches, coping strategy enhancement, focusing techniques and belief modification	Interventions that reduce the chance of exclusion, by working with the individual (to reduce their experience of exclusion and support their inclusion) and working with community organisations (to help them build capacity and lower barriers for participants with mental health issues)
Medication management and relapse prevention reduces stress in day-to-day life, identifies and respond warning signs and takes action to increase support as needed	Management of personal supports and exclusion prevention to build robust informal and formal supports in community settings so that they are resilient in the face of difficulties
Family interventions to support family in responding positively in the face of mental illness	Family interventions to support inclusion
Outcome measures include the relatives' knowledge about schizophrenia, family stress levels and the person's symptoms and social functioning	Social inclusion means engaging in roles that are valued by the person and the wider community. This will often include having a paid job, being a neighbour, enjoying friendships and leisure activities

▶ **Acknowledgements**

The authors appreciate the helpful comments on earlier drafts of this paper made by Sarah Joy Boldison, Tim Bradshaw, Fabian Davis, Carol Harper and Craig Wilson. Responsibility for the content remains with the authors.

▶ **References**

Baguley, I. & Baguley, C. (1999) Psychosocial interventions. *Mental Health Care*, **21**(9): 314–17.

Barrowclough, C. & Tarrier, N. (1992) *Families of Schizophrenic Patients Cognitive Behavioural Interventions*. London, Chapman & Hall.

Bates, P. & Dowson, S. (2006) *Social Inclusion Planner*. Ipswich: National Development Team.

Beck, A.T., Rush, A.J., Shaw, B.F. & Emery, G. (1979) *Cognitive Therapy of Depression: A Treatment Manual*. New York: Guilford Press.

Becker, T., Leese, M., Clarkson, P. *et al.* (1998) Links between social networks and quality of life: An epidemiologically representative study of psychotic patients in South London. *Social Psychiatry and Psychiatric Epidemiology*, **33**(7): 299–304.

Birchwood, M., Smith, J., Cochrane, R., Wetton, S. & Copestake, S. (1990) Social Function Scale: The development and validation of a scale of social adjustment for use in family intervention programmes with schizophrenic patients. *British Journal of Psychiatry*, **157**: 853–9.

Birchwood, M., Smith, J., MacMillan, F. *et al.* (1989) Predicting relapse in schizophrenia: The development and implementation of an early signs monitoring system using patients and families as observers, a preliminary investigation. *Psychological Medicine*, **19**: 649–56.

Brooker, C. (2001) A decade of evidence-based training for work with people with serious mental health problems: Progress in the development of psychosocial interventions. *Journal of Mental Health*, **10**(1): 17–31.

Brooker, C., Falloon, I., Butterworth, A. *et al.* (1994) The outcome of training community psychiatric nurses to deliver psychosocial intervention: Report of a pilot study. *British Journal of Psychiatry*, **160**: 836–44.

Brown, G. (1959) Experiences of discharged chronic schizophrenic mental hospital patients in various types of living groups. *Millbank Memorial Fund Quarterly*, **37**: 105–31.

Butterworth T (1994) Working in partnership: A collaborative approach to care. The review of mental health nursing. *Journal of Psychiatric Mental Health Nursing*, **1**(1): 41–4.

Copeland, M.E. (1997) *WRAP: Wellness Recovery Action Plan™*. W. Dummerston, VT: Peach Press.

Department of Health (1992) *The Health of the Nation*. London: Department of Health.

Department of Health (1998) *Modernising Mental Health Services: Safe, Sound and Supportive*. London, Department of Health.

Department of Health (1999) *National Service Framework for Mental Health: Modern Standards and Service Models*. London: Department of Health.

Department of Health (2001) *Fair Access to Care Services Consultation Papers*. London: Department of Health.

Department of Health (2006) *Chief Nursing Officers Review of Mental Health Nursing, Report and Recommendations*. London: Department of Health.

Drake, R.E., Hugo, G.J., Bebort, R.R. *et al.* (1999) A randomised clinical trial of supported employment for inner-city patients with severe mental disorders. *Archives of General Psychiatry*, **56**(7): 627–33.

Dunn, S. (1999) *Creating Accepting Communities: Report of the Mind Inquiry into Social Exclusion*. London: Mind.

Fadden, G. (1998) Family intervention. In C. Brooker & J. Repper (eds), *Community Mental Health Services for People with Serious Mental Health Problems: Policy, Practice and Research*. London: Balliere-Tindall.

Freire, P. (1972) *Pedagogy of the Oppressed*. Harmondsworth: Penguin.

Grove, B., Secker, J. & Seebohm, P. (eds) (2005) *New Thinking about Mental Health and Employment*. Oxford: Radcliffe.

Haddock, G., Bentall, R.P. & Slade, P.D. (1996) Psychological treatment of auditory hallucinations: Focusing and distraction. In G. Haddock & P. Slade (eds), *Cognitive Behavioural Interventions with Psychotic Disorders*. London, Routledge.

Kingdom, D. & Turkington, D. (1991) The use of cognitive behavior therapy with a normalising rationale in schizophrenia. *Journal of Nervous and Mental Disease*, **179**: 207–11.

Krawiecka, M., Goldberg, D.P. & Vaughan, M. (1977) A standardised psychiatric assessment scale for rating chronic psychotic patients. *Acta Psychiatrica Scandinavia*, **55**: 299–308.

Kuipers, E., Garety, P.A., Fowler, D. *et al.* (1997) The London–East Anglia trial of cognitive behaviour therapy for psychosis 1: Effects of the treatment phase. *British Journal of Psychiatry*, **171**: 319–27.

Nuechterlein, K.H. & Dawson, M. (1987) A heuristic vulnerability-stress model of schizophrenic episodes. *Schizophrenia Bulletin*, **10**: 300–12.

O'Brien, J. & Lyle O'Brien, C. (1996) *Members of Each Other: Building Community in Company with People with Developmental Disabilities*. Toronto: Inclusion Press.

Pevalin, D.J. & Rose, D. (2003) *Social Capital for Health: Investigating the Links Between Social Capital and Health Using the British Household Panel Survey*. London: Health Development Agency.

Repper, D. & Brooker, C. (2002) *Avoiding the Washout: Developing Organisational Context to Increase the Uptake of Evidence-Based Practice for Psychosis*. Lincoln: Northern Centre for Mental Health.

Ritchie, P., Sanderson, H., Kilbane, J. & Routledge, M. (2003) *People, Plans and Practicalities: Achieving Change Through Person Centred Planning*. Edinburgh: SHS.

Rogers, C.R. (1961) *On Becoming a Person. A Therapist's View of Psychotherapy*. Boston, MA: Houghton Mifflin.

Short, A. & Sanderson, H. with Cook, M. (2003) *Families Leading Planning*. Manchester: Helen Sanderson Associates.

Social Exclusion Unit (2004) *Mental Health and Social Exclusion*. London: Office of the Deputy Prime Minister.

Tarrier, N., Harwood, S., Yussof, L. *et al.* (1990)   Coping Strategy Enhancement (CSE): A method of treating residual schizophrenia symptoms in schizophrenic patients: Outcome. *British Journal of Psychiatry*, **162**: 534–2.

Warner, R. (1994) *Recovery from Schizophrenia, Psychiatry and Political Ecconomy* (2nd edn). London: Routledge & Kegan Paul.

White, E. (1991) *The 3rd Quinquennial National Community Psychiatric Nurse Survey*. Manchester: Department of Nursing, University of Manchester.

Wolfensberger, W. (1972) *The Principle of Normalisation in Human Services*. Toronto: National Institute of Mental Retardation.

Zubin, J. & Spring, B. (1977) Vulnerability: A new view of schizophrenia. *Journal of Abnormal Psychology*, **86**: 103–26.

◀ CHAPTER TWENTYEIGHT ▶

Spirituality and mental health

Peter Gilbert

National Institute of Mental Health in England; Staffordshire University; NIMHE

▶ The winding road

Travelling in Ireland in my student days on a motorbike, I once asked a friendly looking man at a crossroads which was the best road to take to my destination. 'Ah', he said, smiling gently and with a look of understanding on his face, 'if I were you, I wouldn't start from here!' This is an experience, although not always so kindly delivered, that many service users and survivors have in mental health services, when they are told that their best course would not be to start with where they are, or where they feel they are.

The journey of life is beset with difficulties for all human beings, because of the human condition; as John Banville puts it in his Booker Prize-winning novel *The Sea*: 'Are not the majority of men (sic) disappointed with their lot, languishing in quiet desperation in their chains?' (Banville, 2005, p. 93). This is more especially so for those who experience profound mental distress, who find the crossroads of life even more disorientating than when we are well. As Lewis Wolpert, Professor of Biology as Applied to Medicine at University College London, has written:

> It was the worst experience of my life. More terrible even than watching my wife die of cancer. I am ashamed to admit that my depression felt worse than her death, but it is true. I was in a state that bears no resemblance to anything I had experienced before . . . I was seriously ill. I was totally self-involved, negative and thought about suicide most of the time. (Wolpert, 2006, p. vii)

This disconnection becomes even more especially true in areas of spirituality and religious or humanistic belief. People continually talk about the paradox that their motivating force, what inspires and keeps them going through the valley

Learning About Mental Health Practice.   Edited by Theo Stickley and Thurstine Basset
© 2008 John Wiley & Sons, Ltd

of shadows, is routinely at best ignored, or at worst derided, by mental health professionals.

Mary Ellen Coyte, in a moving presentation to the first comprehensive multi-faith Symposium on Mental Health in the UK, spoke of the importance of recognising the spiritual dimension, because this approach, inextricably linked with the recovery approach, is about:

> Allowing someone with mental distress to have, or take back, control. It is not the same as cure. It involves things which I would call spiritual support, such as hope; opportunity – allowing the quest for meaning and value; spirituality . . .; coping with loss and good relationships. It spells out that it is hard to sustain hope if everyone around you, family, friends, professionals, think you will never amount to anything much. (Coyte, in Gilbert & Kalaga, 2007)

Having spoken to users and survivors across the country and in my work with the NIMHE Spirituality and Mental Health Project, I have been struck by how often people have been denied the means of expressing what it is that keeps a flame of light burning within them. Often it seems that mental health services, ostensibly designed to aid them, only serve to snuff out the candle of hope (see Moss & Gilbert, 2007). For me, almost my signature tune is the poem by Sue Holt, with its story of waiting for weekend leave from hospital, and having to deny her most precious beliefs to avoid being detained:

> I was excited; today was the Lord's birthday,
>
> And I was going home for dinner.
>
> I masked my emotions.
>
> Otherwise they would keep me.
>
> I had to behave myself today,
>
> *No talking of God.* (Holt, 2003, my emphasis)

In 2000 I experienced an episode of acute hyperactivity/anxiety followed by depression. As an essentially active, optimistic extrovert, the 'malignant sadness' (to use Lewis Wolpert's vivid phrase; Wolpert, 2006) of depression, came as a real shock to me. I had undertaken some tough roles in the past – active service as an Army officer; social work including as an emergency out-of-hours worker and ASW (approved social worker); a manager sorting out various problems across the country, including Staffordshire after Pindown (a method of discipline used in children's homes) – but as an essentially trusting person I had, perhaps naïvely, been unprepared for the political chicanery experienced as a Director of Social Services.

My first port of call was my GP, and her response was the first milestone of the winding road of a journey I had not expected to take. Her first words to me were: 'This is shit!' This was immensely liberating, because not only was it an intensely human response, but *this* and her subsequent linking of my illness (I deliberately call it an illness) to the financial problems in both health and social services locally, and the downgrading of Kidderminster Hospital (which has now become a political *cause célèbre*), took away some of my overwhelming sense of personal responsibility for a crisis that was not objectively of my own making. Other aspects of what was probably a relatively short session were:

- A very sound medical diagnosis of my condition.

- The offer of antidepressants for when I was in the right frame of mind to take them. This was a risk on her part, but gave me an element of control when I felt that my circumstances were profoundly out of my hands.

- Recognised my spiritual resources, such as a personal faith and running with my running club (see Coyte, Gilbert & Nicholls, 2007, Chapter 11).

Exercise 28.1

Please take a moment to think back to your experience as a user of health and social care services, and whether the person you sought help from met your human as well as your 'clinical' needs?
  What did you find helpful and unhelpful?

The allegory of a journey is one that has powerful resonances for us, as mythology (see Armstrong, 2005) demonstrates. Various stories have come down to us, such as Homer's *Odyssey*, Chaucer's *Canterbury Tales* and Bunyan's *Pilgrim's Progress*; and on to modern authors, sometimes mistakenly referred to as story-tellers for children, such as Tolkien's *Lord of the Rings*, Pullman's *His Dark Materials* and Ursula LeGuin's *The Earthsea Quintet*. This is reinforced by the work of geneticists such as Professor Brian Sykes of Oxford University (see Sykes, 2001, 2006), who has demonstrated the land- and sea-faring undertaken by our ancestors as they searched for a place to be at home. Science, religion and human stories, real, fictional and mythological, consider our search for our beginnings and endings; for our roots; for our sense of self; and for a sense of health and well-being.

One of the ironies of 'I wouldn't start from here' is that, while we experience profound senses of difference and the need to differentiate, which is often profoundly individual or tribal, we are also, essentially, both unique and bound together. As scientists such as Brian Sykes demonstrate, we all come out of common roots; for all Europeans, for example, seven essential maternal lines of descent. If we are religious then we believe we are created equal in the image of God. As the Chief Rabbi Jonathan Sacks puts it, we see as the basis of our humanity the fact that we are all ultimately the same. We are vulnerable. We are embodied creatures. We feel hunger, thirst, fear, pain. We reason, hope, dream, aspire. These things are all true and important. But we are also different. Each landscape, language, culture, community, is unique. Our very dignity as persons is rooted in the fact that none of us – not even genetically identical twins – is exactly like any other. (Sacks, 2002, p. 47)

or the Dalai Lama:

I travel to many places around the world, and whenever I speak to people, I do so with the feeling that I am a member of their own family. Although we may have been meeting for the first time, I accept everyone as a friend. In truth, we already know one another profoundly, as human beings who share the same basic goals: we all seek happiness and do not want suffering. (The Dalai Lama, 2002, p. 1)

We may not always be starting in the right place, with the best craft to voyage in, with adequate equipment and a compass, but that is where we *are* and we want those working with us to set sail from the same jetty, towards the same port – or how else are we going to find each other on life's ocean?

▶ Belonging . . . ? Believing . . . ?

It is increasingly said that the UK is becoming more spiritual and less religious, as people feel uncomfortable both with pervasive global consumerism and with the perceived constraints of organised religion.

Belief, in something other than what we can see and touch in front of us, is one of the major issues both in the field of mental health and generally in the world today. In their research for the Office of the Deputy Prime Minister and the Department of Communities and Local Government, the Mercia Group of Researchers, based mainly at the University of Warwick (Beckford *et al.*, 2006), state:

Over the last 50 years, the discourse in Britain about 'racialised minorities' has mutated from 'colour' in the 1950's and 1960's . . . to 'race' in the 1960's, 70's and 80's . . . to 'ethnicity' in the 90's . . . and to 'religion' at the present time. This focus on religion has been driven both by major international events which have highlighted the political demands associated with religious movements, and by an increasing recognition by academics, policy-makers and service providers, of the importance of religion in defining identity, particularly among minority communities. (Beckford *et al.*, 2006, p. 11)

Despite the complexity of the human condition, some proponents of a particular world view – materialist, scientific or religious – often fail to recognise that complexity, so that in some countries people's aspiration for a better material life, or greater freedom of expression, is suppressed for ideological reasons. Materialists often treat human beings as mere consumers, while some scientists hold the view that wonders will sometime cease as we discover the answers to all our questions. In the November issue of *New Scientist*, a group of scientists predicted that, within the next 50 years, we will be able to regenerate lost organs and lost limbs; find the evidence of dark energy; prevent ageing; communicate with animals; understand the 'Big Bang'; and create a unified 'theory of everything' (Jha, 2007; Smith, 2006). Human beings, however, appear to be annoyingly paradoxical, in that we search endlessly for answers but also seem to yearn for a sense of mystery at the same time. The universe, including us, appears to grant us some answers, but also the mystery of further questions. Physicist and cosmologist Paul Davies starts his recent book, *The Goldilocks Enigma* (Davies, 2006), with the statement:

> For thousands of years, human beings have contemplated the world about them and ask the great questions of existence: Why are we here? How did the universe begin? How will it end? How is the world put together? Why is it the way it is? (Davies, 2006, p. 1)

He goes on to state that it is extraordinary that the universe actually works in the way it does – or, indeed, at all – and then looks at current theories, including 'the lure of complete unification' of theories (Davies, 2006, Chapter 5), and decides that we are still looking. He quotes the lovely story (sometimes attributed to Bertrand Russell) about an academic lecturer interrupted by a woman who insists that the Earth rests on the back of a giant elephant, which stands on the back of a giant turtle (Davies, 2006, p. 244). Of course, this image has been used to great effect by Terry Pratchett, whose Disc World is founded on such a concept; Pratchett, as an agnostic, always seems to bring both the complexities and the prevalence of belief into his novels (see e.g. Pratchett, 1993; Pratchett & Gaiman, 1991).

It is often rather thoughtlessly stated that religion is in decline in the West, and this may be true for some religious traditions. The picture, however, is much more complex than that. *The Guardian* newspaper, before Christmas 2006, ran the front-page headline: 'Religion does more harm than good – poll'. It went on to say:

> Most people have no personal faith; the poll shows, with only 33 percent of those questioned describing themselves as 'a religious person'. A clear majority, 63 percent, say that they are not religious – including more than half of those who describe themselves as Christian. (*The Guardian*, 23 December 2006, p. 1)

In fact, the description of the poll on pages 12 and 13 of the paper shows a more intricate story:

- 33% of people do describe themselves as religious and 57% of people say they will visit a place of worship at least once a year.

- 62% see Britain as 'a religious country of many faiths'.

- While 82% of all respondents think religion causes division between people, 57% think that religion is a force for good.

Some commentators talk of people 'believing but not belonging', others of 'belonging but not believing' (see Davie, 1994; Francis & Robbins, 2004). As Davie concludes in her global study, the decline of religious observance in Western Europe should not be seen as the dominant paradigm (Davie, 2002).

Whether religious faith provides a moral framework, as argued cogently in the writings of someone like Chief Rabbi Jonathan Sacks (see Sacks, 2002, 2005), or a source of division – and in the field of mental health, whether it is a nurturing and supportive framework, or a constricting straightjacket and a source of oppression – is still very much up for debate (and in fact, in mental health terms, the question was the subject of a national symposium at Staffordshire University on 1 November 2006; see Gilbert & Kalaga, 2007). What is not in doubt is the growth of religious faith as a very present symbol. Driving down the arterial roads into the main cities in Britain, one is struck by the prominence of mosques, Hindu temples and Sikh gurdwaras. Some Christian churches have been converted into secular meeting places, but *The Guardian* poll points to an increase in Roman Catholic affiliation through the movement of Poles into this country (see also Vulliamy, 2006) as well as a major growth in Pentecostal churches in cities, partly based on worship from African-Caribbean and African congregations, but with an appeal wider than that. Television reporter Rageh Omaar speaks of the essential dialogue of secular society with faith and vice versa (Omaar, 2006).

Case study 28.1

Kimi was brought up in a household with a strong fundamentalist faith (faith not specified). The feelings of oppression and guilt induced were a contributory factor to a bout of acute mental illness, which saw her admitted to an Acute Psychiatric Unit. Still with a belief in a divine presence, but scarred by her previous experience, Kimi has been exploring other possible faith avenues. She realises that this may be difficult for her and also create barriers with her family, to whom she is very attached despite the difficulties she experienced.

How might you help Kimi on her voyage of discovery?

Whether religion has a basis in a genuine creational divine being or is a natural phenomenon (see Davies, 2006; Dennett, 2006; McGrath, 2005), people's religious faith and their spirituality are increasingly seen as having a part to play in their life. Increasingly, religious belief is being enshrined in law, in documents such as the *DSM-1V TR*, which recognises 'religious and spiritual difficulties as distinct, and deserving treatment'; and, more locally, the new guidance from England and Wales' Chief Nursing Officer on Mental Health, *Values into Action*, which enshrines people's spiritual and religious needs as an aspect of life to be addressed by mental health nurses (Department of Health, 2006).

For many people now, 'spirituality' or 'meaning' are words and concepts used to express a desire for our innermost being to be attended to. As psychiatrist Dr Julie Liebrich put it at the 21st World Assembly for Mental Health in 2001:

> The definition of mental health has much in common with the definition of spirituality, as both experiences are concerned with the experience of self. One reaches into dimensions of space to discover self, as the other realises freedom through the acceptance of self. (quoted in Blanton, 2006)

Paul Heelas and Linda Woodhead, in their influential *The Spiritual Revolution: Why Religion is Giving Way to Spirituality* (Heelas & Woodhead, 2005), explore a contemporary search for spirituality against the backdrop of more traditional religion. Interestingly, they quote the Queen's Christmas message of 2000:

> Whether we believe in God, or not, I think most of us have a sense of the spiritual; that recognition of a deeper meaning and purpose in our lives, and I believe that this sense flourishes, despite the pressures of our world. (Heelas & Woodhead, 2005, p. 1)

Intriguingly, the Queen's broadcast in 2006 took a slightly different slant:

> But the pressures of modern life sometimes seem to be weakening the links which have traditionally kept us together as families and communities ... there is always the danger of a real divide opening up between young and old, based on unfamiliarity, ignorance or misunderstanding.

> It is worth bearing in mind that all of our faith communities encourage the bridging of that divide. The wisdom and experience of the great religions point to the need to nurture and guide the young, and to encourage respect for the elderly. (www.royal.gov.uk/output/page5733)

The 'Soul of Britain' survey of 2002, conducted by Opinion Research Business, gives a broader overall support for more localised research, such as that by Heelas and Woodhead. Gordon Heald, writing on the publication of the survey, outlines some of the complexities:

> Many have faith that science will help mankind, but they do not think that it is capable of explaining the mysteries of life. On the contrary, the movement is in the opposite direction; the survey demonstrates very clearly that there has been a significant rise in the number of people who classify themselves as being 'spiritual' (as opposed to being 'religious'), which is why belief in a soul has increased significantly over the last two decades – to such an extent, that it now exceeds belief in God. (Heald, 2000, pp. 4–5)

Writing from Australia, David Tacey says something similar:

> The ideals of secularism, however well-intended, are inadequate for life, since our lives are not rational and we are hugely implicated in the *reality of the sacred*, whether or not this is acknowledged. (Tacey, 2004, p. 12, my emphasis)

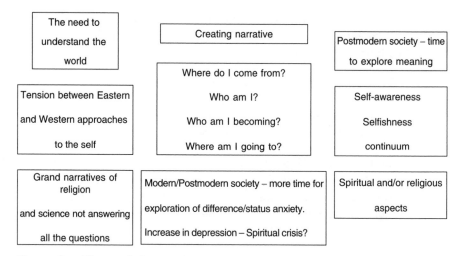

Figure 28.1 The search for meaning
Source: Gilbert, P, (2007) The role of spirituality in the journey of recovery, *The Pilgrim's Progress: The Pathway to Better Care in Geriatric Psychiatry*. Santiago de Compostela International Conference, 22 July.

Even in the ostensibly ultra-rational, hard-headed world of business, research and development institutes, such as the Roffey Park Institute in the UK, have found over the last 10 years an intense search for meaning in the workplace (see Holbeche & Springett, 2004). Interestingly, when the Financial Services Authority found that increasing regulation was having little or no effect on the integrity of business practice, it turned to the abbot of a Benedictine monastery, Christopher Jamison, and a management ethicist, Roger Steare, to bring in an ethical framework (see Soul Gym, 2003). Retreats of various sorts are increasingly used by individuals, community groups, public service groups and business organisations as a means of creating space and reorienting themselves (see also Jamison, 2006).

Many service users and survivors I talk with speak of their spirituality and/or faith as the essential element in regaining health and keeping well. It is fascinating that somebody like Professor Lewis Wolpert, in his honest and helpful *Malignant Sadness*, uses the language and concept of the soul:

> If we had a soul – and as a hard-line materialist I do not believe we do – a useful metaphor for depression could be *'soul loss'* due to extreme sadness. The body and mind emptied of the soul lose interest in almost everything except themselves. The idea of the wandering soul is widely accepted across numerous cultures and the adjective 'empty' is viewed across most cultures as negative. The metaphor captures the way in which we experience our own existence. Our 'soul' is our inner essence, something distinctly different from the hard material world in which we live. Lose it and we are depressed, cut off, alone. (Wolpert, 2006, p. 3, my emphasis)

Zoologist David Hay, in *Something There* (Hay, 2006), explores the nature of suffering and states:

> During 30 years of research in the field, I have come across the story again and again, in relation to unbearable suffering: the 'something there' that does not protect us from the pain, but is with us in the midst of it as we struggle through it. (Hay, 2006, p. 247)

As mental health professionals, if we cannot engage with this growing sense of unease, the search for meaning, the increase in certain religious groups, but also a decline in some traditional groupings and an exploration of individual spirituality, we will be fundamentally unable to deal with the profound questions that mental health raises for us, as mental ill-health rises up the league table of global disease and becomes the prime concern of knowledge economies (see Layard, 2005) in the developed and developing world.

Exercise 28.2

What aspects of your life hold most value for you?

▶ The genesis of the NIMHE project

It was this background of the increasing importance of faith as an international and national issue, and the less-defined, but still vital, ethos of spirituality as underpinning human life in the 21st century, that led to the setting up of the NIMHE Project in 2001. Most new schemes probably require a defining moment, and this one's was the discussion within the core group setting up NIMHE, under the leadership of Professor Antony Sheehan, around the effect that the traumatic and tragic events of 9/11 would have on everybody, but the Muslim population of Britain in particular. It is amazing how quickly '9/11' becomes a glib expression. But the shock of that event – the far-reaching nature of the assault on the iconic emblems of the modern Western state: the White House (political), the Twin Towers (global capitalism) and the Pentagon (the Western military machine) – was far-reaching. It, and subsequent events including the illegal (as defined by the United Nations) war in Iraq and the tube bombings in London on 7/7, made the world in general and our world in the UK in particular feel that bit less safe.

I was a practising social worker at a time of IRA bombings in London, and was acutely aware of many of my Irish clients feeling a sense of responsibility and also being under siege from these events. We know now that many Muslims, especially Muslim women, did not feel able to go outside their homes in the weeks after 9/11.

The aims of the Project, both in its NIMHE form and in partnership with the Mental Health Foundation between November 2003 and 2005, were to collate current thinking on the importance of spirituality and faith in mental health on an individual and group basis; to evaluate the role of faith communities in the field of mental health; and to develop and promote good practice in whole-person approaches.

Exercise 28.3

Are you finding service users and carers speaking about religious faith and secular spirituality as issues within mental health, mental illness and recovery?
What is your personal and professional response to this?

The Project has a number of elements to it designed to address these overall aims (covered in Cox, Campbell & Fulford, 2007, Chapter 10; and Gilbert & Nicholls, 2003), but now it will be important to try to define – and if that is not possible, at least to discuss – the concept of spirituality.

▶ Spirituality: weasel word or gateway?

Spirituality is a relatively modern word and concept. In fact, *spirituality* does not really appear in Jewish or Muslim writings and only features in certain strands of Christianity. Gordon Mursell (2001), the Bishop of Stafford, has written persuasively of Christian spirituality throughout the ages; and a Franciscan, Ronald Rolheiser (1998), has also set out a spirituality that looks at a relationship between self, the Other and our human companions.

The idea of human beings having a *spirit*, however, is very prevalent in most philosophical and religious traditions. Plato believed that there was something in each person that was not merely material, but was indestructible and essential to them. Linda Ross, who undertook one of the seminal works at the end of the 1990s on nurses' perceptions of spiritual care, quotes Plato as stating:

> As you ought not to attempt to cure the eyes without the head, or the head without the body, so neither ought you to attempt to cure the body without the soul . . . for the part can never be well unless the whole is well. (Ross, 1997, inside cover)

Aristotle is often portrayed as a materialist because of his fascination with the study of what was before him, but the philosopher saw beyond this and argued that a house is not a house because of the materials, but because of its structure and form. Likewise, he argued that the philosopher Socrates, while inevitably changing throughout life, was essentially still Socrates. Although many people debate the essential or non-essential nature of individuals, one of the most moving testaments to Aristotle's view I have read recently is Barbara Pointon's description of her relationship with her husband Malcolm (see Pointon in Coyte, Gilbert & Nicholls, 2007), where she perceives him, though stricken with early-onset dementia, as still essentially the person she has always loved. Aristotle would, I feel, be equally impatient of a religious theosophy that spoke only of the spirit and damned the material world as he would of a reductionist materialism that said 'what you see is what you get'.

In Abrahamic religions there are both congruencies and differences. Ray Anderson (2003) describes the Jewish concept of the person as comprising *basar* (flesh), *lev* (heart) and also components of soul, ego and spirit. While the soul is in some senses passive, being a part of the divine passed into human beings, *ru'ach* (spirit) is not just life but *vigorous or inspired life*.

Rabbi Jonathan Dove, in his presentation to the Multi-Faith Symposium at Staffordshire University, *Nurturing Heart and Spirit* (see Gilbert & Kalaga, 2007), depicted God as a craftsman blowing molten liquid glass, so that God:

> Formed the man (sic) of soil from the earth, and blew into his nostrils the soul of life; and man became a living soul. (Genesis 2:7)

The Qur'an (15:29) says of Allah that he 'breathed into him of My spirit (*ruh*)'. The Arabic word *ruh* has a similar connotation to *ru'ach*.

The Christian tradition speaks of God becoming a human being, so as to experience both the peaks and troughs of human existence, and of a spirit continuing to inspire and invigorate Christian communities: 'He is living in us, because He lets us share His spirit' (John 1, 4:13)

Hindus, through the spiritual teachings of the Vedas, say that every living entity is made up of a gross body (the flesh), a subtle body (mind, intelligence and ego) and a soul. The soul is the permanent self with its origin and ultimate destination in the spiritual world; and one of the three aspects of God is the *paramatma*, the aspect of God that resides in every living entity alongside the individual soul. This aspect of God is also present in every atom and molecule (see Kang in Gilbert & Kalaga, 2007).

From this we can see why a religious faith and a sense of a divine Other can be so important to people in the depths of despair. If there is a belief that we are created by a super-abundant being, and that being is linked with us in some way and either cares for us or, if not interventionist, will at some stage welcome us back into a spiritual host, then this may make life worthwhile. We know in our sufferings that the understanding and solidarity of another human being are of great importance. Divine empathy as shown through the manifestation of the divine, through some form of soul sense or through the interactions of other human beings, animals or the physical world may be all that sees us through the dark valley.

But for many people, the idea of some form of creator may appear either ridiculous and/or unhelpful. The often patriarchal nature of God as a concept can be profoundly alienating, and this was one of the issues explored at the *Nurturing Heart and Spirit* Symposium in 2006. In the Western world and, indeed, in fast-developing countries such as China and India, individualism is increasingly the dominant ethos. Even for deeply religious people, finding their own sense of spirit, of *ru'ach*, of invigorated and inspiriting life is essential, as is a form of spirituality that nurtures them. Certainly in the Christian faith, people may look to particular exemplars, such as Benedict of Nursia (e.g. see Jamison, 2006), Francis of Assisi and, in a more contemporary way, Thomas Merton. A number of Muslims would look to Sufi mysticism as a way of deepening their faith (see Greaves, 2005). Spirituality can be defined in a number of ways:

> A quality that goes beyond religious affiliation, that strives for inspiration, reverence, or meaning and purpose, even in those who do not believe in God. The spiritual dimension tries to be in harmony with the universe, strives for answers about the infinite, and comes especially into focus at times of emotional stress, physical (and mental) illness, loss, bereavement and death. (Murray & Zenter, 1989, quoted in Culliford & Johnson, 2003)

John Swinton and Stephen Pattison, coming from a health and theological perspective, described spirituality thus:

> Spirituality can be understood as that aspect of human existence which relates to structures of significance that give meaning and direction to a person's life and helps them deal with the vicissitudes of existence. It is associated with the human quest for meaning, purpose, self-transcending knowledge, meaningful relationships, love and a sense of the Holy. (Swinton & Pattison, 2001)

Religion encompasses most, if not all, of the aspects described above, usually in the context of belief in a transcendent being or beings, and with a meta-narrative that seeks to explain origins of the world and those living in it, and the questions that face human beings around life, suffering, death and re-awakening in this world or another.

Religion can provide a worldview that is acted out in narrative, doctrine, symbols, rites, rituals, sacraments and gatherings, as well as in the promotion of ties of mutual obligations (e.g. see Sacks, 2005). It creates a framework within which people seek to understand, interpret and make sense of themselves, their lives and daily experiences.

Exercise 28.4

- How might you define your spirituality?
- What makes your life an invigorated life?
- What gives you inspiration in life? In work?

My experience of mental illness and recovery has a number of links with the descriptions above. Like Lewis Wolpert, I found depression an extraordinary experience and unlike anything I had experienced before. I was fortunate to have certain resources open to me at a time when I could not have created any new resources to aid me (see also Gilbert, in Cox, Campbell & Fulford, 2007). One of these was running and, more than that, being a member of a running club (see Coyte, Gilbert & Nicholls, 2007, Chapter 10). Not only did the physical activity of running release endorphins, but the ability to remain in touch with nature while also being part of a social group, although not necessarily having to interact with people at a level that was not possible for me at that time, was a real life-saver. In some senses the membership of a formed social group had some of the elements of spirituality described above, giving a sense of harmony, affiliation and inspiration; but the social nature of a formed entity had some elements of a faith group, in its shared activities, routines, rituals and values.

In a similar vein, I returned to the Benedictine monastery with which I had had contact since my adolescence. I found the community extremely welcoming, and the Abbot at the time used to sit me down and let me talk things out and through. Belief in God was immensely difficult at that time. Trauma can increase faith or shake it, and I felt blocked off from any sense of a personal God – disconnected! What I did find helpful was sitting with monks in the choir and joining in the singing of the psalms. The rhythm and the sense of faith as family were major elements in my recovery. Friendships were vital, especially those with people who were either going through a similar experience, or had gone through one and who understood; and those where people were prepared to accept my strongly expressed feelings about the situation, both of sorrow and anger. Most people find strong emotion difficult to cope with, as it is very easy to think that any negative emotion is aimed at us. An ability to absorb and console and empathise with somebody who is expressing strong emotions is invaluable. Lastly, as I left one form of employment into the uncertainty of being an independent, it was the faith in me of those who said 'Come and work with us; we value you' that was a great restoration of faith.

Case study 28.2

David had worked as a mental health nurse in both acute residential settings and community for 12 years, before he experienced an episode of bipolar disorder following a period of stress at work due to increased demand and staff shortages.

Although in a mental health setting, and in a Trust that spoke of the importance of 'experts by experience' and sharing experiences, David had noticed that, in a recent survey within the Trust, very few people had felt able to indicate experience of mental ill-health, and the prevailing culture was, as one senior manager had put it, to 'grin and bear it'.

Trying to hide his symptoms, David became increasingly manic, creating problems for himself, his family, his colleagues and service users, and eventually arrived at his GP's surgery in such a state that he needed to access secondary care services, which caused him distress and a feeling of failure and being stigmatised.

Now back at work, David has found supportive colleagues and managers able to accept his experience and see it as valuable, and he has integrated this experience into his working life.

- Does this sound like an experience you recognise?

- How accepting is your organisation of the experience of mental ill-health among staff?

- How could David have been supported initially?

- Do you feel able to speak about your negative as well as positive experiences?

▶ An age of anxiety and anomie

In May 2006, a national newspaper carried the headline '1957, the year we felt much happier' (*Daily Mail*, 3 May 2006). This was based on a survey for the programme *The Happiness Formula*, a series broadcast on BBC2 in May and June. While in 1957 a similar poll by the Gallup organisation found that 52% of people were very happy and 42% fairly happy, the 2006 poll found a drop to 36% who were very happy and 56% fairly happy. This seems strange at a time when overall levels of personal income have risen, although a possible pointer to happiness, which will often be a relative concept, is the growing gap between what a *Guardian* commentator called 'the "haves and have yachts"' (Woollaston, 2007).

As human beings we appear to be programmed to seek happiness of various kinds. Psychologist Jonathan Haidt (2006) opines that the basic evolutionary urge towards a materialistic pursuit of pleasure often leads to no more than momentary satisfaction. As a number of commentators have pointed out:

> as the level of wealth has doubled or tripled in the last 50 years in many industrialized nations, the levels of happiness and satisfaction with life that people report have not changed, and depression has actually become more common. (Haidt, 2006, p. 89; and see Diener & Oishi, 2000; Hutchinson, Mellor & Olsen, 2002; Layard, 2005).

Many of the characteristics of modern life have seen human beings, who are basically social animals, becoming victims of what Daniel Goleman calls 'creeping disconnection' (Goleman, 2006). David Putnam describes the phenomenon whereby American workmates used to go ten pin bowling as a group many years ago and now go 'bowling alone' (Putnam, 2000).

These observations provide important contextual signposts that help to counteract the view that sees mental illness and mental distress as being the fault or weakness of the individual concerned. This pathologising tendency neglects the impact of wider forces and influences on individual health and well-being, and also fails to take into account the effect of the removal of previous fixed points in people's lives, such as shared values and mutual respect. When such flickering candles of hope are snuffed out, then the risks to mental, emotional and spiritual well-being are exacerbated (Moss & Gilbert, 2007).

Individuals, families, groups, communities and societies need some common values and culture to create the balanced tension of dynamism and harmony that people yearn for. UK Prime Minister Gordon Brown has started to talk increasingly about the concept of *Britishness*. Ironically, British society never felt, until recently, that it needed to define Britishness, but into an identity vacuum has stepped an increasingly contentious identity battle. Geoff Dench, Kate Gavron and Michael Young recently returned to the geographic East End of London, famously researched by Young with his then colleague Peter Willmott in the 1950s (Young & Willmott, 1957). The researchers found a very changed picture, where neither the inhabitants of the area in the 1950s nor those moving into the area since had been well served by the welfare bureaucracy within a changed social fabric of what the authors call 'the new individualism'. They conclude by stating that British social policy has created a 'greater emphasis on citizens' rights without working to create a national culture of responsibility, mutuality and solidarity' (Dench, Gavron & Young, 2006, p. 226). Jonathan Haidt makes similar claims for American society, where a measure of social cohesion has been lost.

The problem with secular societies is that secularism as such does not really provide a moral force; it simply provides a kind of ring, made up of legislative parameters that guard the outriders of morality without really affecting, influencing and shaping moral behavior. As Haidt puts it:

> My behavior was constrained only by the ethic of autonomy, which allowed me to do whatever I wanted, as long as I didn't hurt anyone else. (Haidt, 2006, p. 191)

We have tended to conflate secularism with humanism; whereas the latter provides a moral code, the former is only looking at the fence posts. This is often where organised religion, with all its faults, tends to come to the fore. One of the greatest exponents of the moral code of religion, Jonathan Sacks, speaks in his recent work, *To Heal a Fractured World: the Ethics of Responsibility* (Sacks, 2005), of the decline of social responsibility and the delegating of such responsibilities to governments, thereby 'substituting politics for ethics, law for moral obligation, and impersonal agencies for personal involvement' (Sacks, 2005, p. 7).

Sacks yearns for a renewed sense of community and solidarity. He defines community in vivid terms: 'A community is where they "know your name" and where they "miss you when you are not there". Community is society with a human face' (Sacks, 2005, p. 54). Dench, Gavron and Young have charted the destruction of London East End communities by planners, often for the best of motives. In his BBC Radio 4 programme *Knocking Down the Past*, Sarfraz Manzoor (BBC Radio 4, 27 November 2006) considered the destruction of communities in Scotland, who found that there was no space in and around their new flats for the community engagement that had been the lifeblood of the previous, albeit cramped, communities from whence they had come. As Haidt states, human beings are 'ultra social species' (Haidt, 2006), and if we deny this, we deny the essence of who we are, whether our beliefs are evolutionist or creationist.

In the world of work, Peter was struck by a meeting he had with a long-serving Director of Social Services, Ray Jones (later Chair of the British Association of Social Workers), in his works canteen. Ray stopped to speak to nearly everybody in the canteen. He did, in Sacks' words, 'know everybody's name'. Unfortunately, many leaders in public services, which are based on the concept of the vitality of human contact, seem to be faceless bureaucrats. As a Director of Social Services in Worcestershire, Peter visited one of his hospital social work teams and their nurse colleagues. One of the nurses remarked that it was good to see a senior manager visiting his staff, as she had not seen the chief executive of the Trust in the five years she had worked at the hospital, even though his office was immediately above her ward (see Gilbert, 2005).

It was the sociologist Emile Durkheim, writing his seminal work on suicide in the 1890s, who coined the term *anomie* (normlessness). Anomie is the state of a society where there is a lack of clarity and agreement around values, norms and rules. Haidt talks about anomie breeding 'feelings of rootlessness and anxiety', which 'leads to an increase in amoral and antisocial behavior' (Haidt, 2006, p. 176). He goes on to say that modern sociological research strongly supports Durkheim's conclusions that having strong social relationships strengthens both the individual and the community (Durkheim, 1897/1951). Haidt refers to modern sociological research indicating that a predicator of the health of an American neighborhood is the degree to which adults respond to the misdeeds of other people's children (Sampson, 1993). In the UK, recent research demonstrates that adults in Britain are the least likely in Europe to challenge young people misbehaving (Margo & Dixon, 2006). An ex-Army friend of Peter's was beaten up the other day for challenging youths who were vandalising a telephone box.

Thomas Friedman, in his new book *The World is Flat* (Friedman, 2006), argues that globalisation is fundamentally positive for both the developing world and the developed one. He sees huge opportunities opening out that will extend to every quarter of the globe and every section of society. Zygmunt Bauman, Emeritus Professor of Sociology at Leeds University, sees globalisation somewhat differently. Having recognised it as an inevitable process, Bauman points out a number of problem areas:

- Global elites have become like the 'absentee landlords' of an earlier time: people and money freed from social responsibility to those whose assets they own. Apparently democratically elected governments run, cap in hand, to media magnates who define national policy for them.

- A 'disconnection of power from obligations: duties towards employees, but also towards the younger and weaker, towards yet unborn generations and towards the self-reproduction of the living conditions of all; in short, freedom from the duty to contribute to daily life and the perpetuation of the community ... unanchored power' (Bauman, 1997, p. 9).

- Local groups and local places in a globalised world lose their 'meaning-generating and meaning-negotiating capacity and are increasingly dependent on sense-giving and interpreting actions which they do not control' (Bauman, 1997, p. 3).

In the work setting, Richard Sennett, who bridges the North American and European dimensions (MIT and LSE), also speaks of people being anchored or lacking anchors. He opines:

> Well-run companies provided a sense of pride; poorly-run companies provided at least an orientation: you came to know about yourself in relation to the frustrations or anger you experienced in an 'anchored' social reality outside yourself. (Sennett, 2006, p. 74)

As Haidt refers to Durkheim, Sennett looks to Max Weber and Michel Foucault. Foucault, in *The Archaeology of Knowledge* (1969/2002), outlines how an elite, through the powerful projection of ideas and ideologies, can dominate the more tied mass of the population and hold them in thrall. Sennett considers Weber's description of organisations and examines how we have moved from the solid to the 'liquid', into what some call postmodernity and Bauman calls 'liquid modernity' (Bauman, 2000). Sennett speaks for what is one of the most disillusioning experiences, hope betrayed, when he writes:

> The insurgents of my youth believed that by dismantling institutions they could produce communities: face-to-face relations of trust and solidarity, relations constantly negotiated and renewed, a communal realm in which people became sensitive to one another's needs. This certainly has not happened. The fragmenting of big institutions has left many people's lives in a fragmented state: the places they work more resembling train stations than villages, as family life is disorientated by the demands of work. Migration is the icon of the global age, moving on rather than settling in. Taking institutions apart has not produced more community. (Sennett, 2006, p. 2)

It is vital not to get too mawkish about the past and gloomy about the future. Fluidity is here to stay. Perhaps what we need is a conscious determination to throw the anchor down out of the boat into the tossing waves, so as to stabilise the vessel, even only for a measure of time. Holbeche and Springett, in their work surveying modern attitudes among managers in the workplace (Holbeche & Springett, 2004), speak of seeking to gain meaning in the workplace (see also Merchant & Gilbert, 2007). For some the community of meaning will be secular, such as a neighbourhood, socio-political or leisure group. Peter often uses the example of his running club in Worcester (see Gilbert, 2005); for others it will be a faith-based organisation. The catholic commentator Clifford Longley, speaking recently, stated: 'Religious identity is not primarily about ideas or views, but about identity – who you are. It is at the core of one's being, the soul.'

Perhaps one of the most moving and beautifully written journals of identity is that by a Polish Jewess emigrée to North America, Eva Hoffman (1998), in her *Lost in Translation* (the book, not the film; though the film gives a number of the same messages). Hoffman journeys with her family in adolescence from a Poland that they can no longer live in as Jews to an open welcome in North America. However, the family finds the welcome warm, but somehow vacuous. She misses the solidarity and community of a more communitarian country, despite its periodic oppressions. Polish friends ask why Americans go to psychiatrists all the time.

> Well . . . I say, it's hard to explain. It's a problem of identity. Many of my American friends feel that they don't have enough of it. They often feel worthless, or they don't know how they feel. Identity is the number one national problem here. There seems to be a shortage of it in the land, a dearth of selfhood amidst other plenty – maybe because there are so many individual egos trying to outdo each other and enlarge themselves. Everyone has to grab as much ego-substance as possible, and grab it away from everyone else; and they aren't sure it belongs to them in the first place . . . Or maybe it's because everyone is always on the move and undergoing enormous changes, so they lose track of who they've been and have to keep tabs on who they're becoming all the time.' (Hoffman, 1998, pp. 262–3)

Bauman, in his text on identity, challenges us that we are haunted by the 'specter of exclusion', and that the obvious temptation is to be attracted to a 'fundamentalist' message, secular, humanist or religious, and its promise of being born again into a home that is secure (Bauman, 2004, p. 97).

Exercise 28.5

- How would you describe the facets of your identity?
- Do you find the concept of 'travelling identity' helpful to you?

Case study 28.3

Shahana is a Muslim woman who trained as a pharmacist. She married Anton who, although not a strongly practising Roman Catholic, was seen as acceptable by Shahana's family, because he was a member of one of the three Abrahamic faiths (Judaism, Christianity and Islam). When Anton developed a bipolar condition, his behaviour in relationships with his wife and children and in his handling of money became unpredictable, and he started to undermine his wife's faith in front of the children.

Although receiving good support from the community team, Shahana finds her husband's behaviour difficult to cope with, and her own health is beginning to deteriorate as she becomes depressed. She is loyal to her husband, but also to her family of origin and her faith. Their daughter is following in her mother's footsteps, but their son has become very disillusioned with all belief systems.

How can the cultural and spiritual aspects of this family best be attended to?

▶ Knowing me, knowing you: implications for practice

With identity such a fluid concept, the words of the Abba song take on new meaning. It is hard enough to understand our own identity now, let alone other people's, as the whole issue of who we are and who we identify with becomes ever more mobile and complex.

Speaking about the work in mental health services in England to promote race equality and reduce discrimination, chair of the Mental Health Act Commission Professor Kamlesh Patel put the issue frankly:

> If you don't know who I am, how are you going to provide a package of care for me to deliver something? When you do not know how important my religion is to me, what language I speak, where I am coming from, how are you going to help me cope with my mental illness? And that is what I am trying to get over to people: the first step is about identity. It is absolutely fundamental to the package of care we offer an individual. (Mulholland, 2005, p. 5)

Of course, in one sense we can never know who another person is; the most honest of us probably recognises that we never completely know ourselves, and our engagement with others is partly to learn about ourselves through the eyes of others. But as Professor Patel makes clear, it is the dialogue and the engagement that are absolutely essential to create a service that actually does what it says it is going to do.

Exercise 28.6

Does your organisation consider people's:

■ religious beliefs?

■ spirituality?

How might you look to engage with an individual's spirituality?

To make spiritual care a reality, in whatever setting and whatever country or culture, we need certain conditions:

■ An overall policy direction and framework. Scotland brought out a visionary policy on spirituality in 2002 (NHS Scotland, 2002). England has had the NIMHE Project on Spirituality (see Gilbert & Nicholls, 2003) running since 2001, and Wales is currently consulting on a guidance document on spiritual care. Spirituality fits well with the growing accent on personalisation of care as set forth in a number of government policy documents; but policy does not always reach across the range of user experience, especially bridging hospital and community. NIMHE's Acute Services Collaborative is currently working with Staffordshire University to produce guidelines for staff.

■ Service users need to feel that they can express the fullness of their humanity, and for this to happen, staff have to experience a similar commitment from their organisation (see Aris & Gilbert, 2007). Many organisations truncate and curtail the creativity of staff, so that the person who is allowed to turn up to work is a pale shadow of who they really are.

Exercise 28.7

Does your organisation assist you to be a whole person, working with people to recognise their full humanity?
   If so, how does it do this?

■ Chaplaincy services are vital to promote the spiritual health of service users, carers and staff and to link with the wider community, especially as that community is increasingly likely to be multi-cultural and multi-faith. Staff training, however, should ensure that staff are comfortable with their own spiritual dimension, so that when a service user mentions spirituality and/or religion, the staff member they are talking to does not press the emergency button for the chaplain!

■ It is not always easy for communities and statutory services to trust each other, or even to have a mutual understanding of each other's role and value. Work is essential to build up confidence with a variety of communities, so that statutory services are seen as welcoming and approachable, and to foster understanding of an individual's spiritual and cultural needs.

If spirituality is about what makes us tick, what keeps us going, what helps us when life is at its toughest, then this must be an essential part of a value-driven and effective mental health service (see Aris & Gilbert, 2007). The drive for efficiency, although good in itself, must not be allowed to drive out humanity. The need for people to tick boxes and provide information must not get in the way of the human-to-human dialogue. As the poet T. S. Eliot put it: 'Where is the wisdom we have lost in knowledge? Where is the knowledge we have lost in information?'

Perhaps one of the greatest challenges for mental health services in the developed world is that recovery from severe mental illness sometimes seems to be a lot quicker and better in less economically developed countries. Is this because the essence of humanity and community is still much more evident and immanent? Services have to have a human face and, essentially, that human face is us.

▶ References and bibliography

Anderson, R.S. (2003) *Spiritual Care Giving as Secular Sacrament*. London: Jessica Kingsley.

Aris, S. & Gilbert, P. (2007) Organisational health: Engaging the heart of the organisation. In M.E. Cyte, P. Gilbert & V. Nicholls (eds), *Spirituality, Values and Mental Health: Jewels for the Journey*. London: Jessica Kingsley.

Armstrong, K. (2005) *A Short History of Myth*. London: Canongate.

Banville, J. (2005) *The Sea*. London: Picador.

Bauman, Z. (1997) *Postmodernity and Its Discontents*. Cambridge: Polity Press.

Bauman, Z. (2000) *Liquid Modernity*. Cambridge: Polity Press.

Bauman, Z. (2004) *Identity*. Cambridge: Polity Press.

Beckford, J., Gayle, R., Owen, D., Peach, C. & Weller, P. (2006) *Review of the Evidence Base on Faith Communities*. Warwich: University of Warwick/Office of the Deputy Prime Minister.

Blanton, K. (2006) Chaplaincy and holistic models of mental health. In *Social Perspectives Network, Reaching the Spirit*, SPN Study Day Paper 9. London: SPN.

Cox, J., Campbell, A. & Fulford, K.W.M. (2007) *Medicine of the Person: Faith, Science and Values in Healthcare Provision*. London: Jessica Kingsley.

Coyte, M.E., Gilbert, P. & Nicholls, V. (2007) *Spirituality, Values and Mental Health: Jewels for the Journey*. London: Jessica Kingsley.

Culliford, L. & Johnson, S. (2003) *Healing From Within: A Guide for Assessing the Religious and Spiritual Aspects of People's Lives*. Brighton: South Downs NHS Trust.

Dalai Lama (2002) *How to Practice the Way to a Meaningful Life*. London: Ryder Books.

Davie, G. (1994) *Religion in Britain Since 1945: Believing Without Belonging*. Oxford: Blackwell.

Davie, G. (2002) *Europe: The Exceptional Case*. London: Darton, Longman and Todd.

Davies, P. (2006) *The Goldilocks Enigma: Why is the Universe Just Right for Life?* London: Allen Lane.

Dench, G., Gavron, K. & Young, M. (2006) *The New East End: Kinship, Race and Conflict*. London: Profile Books.

Dennett, D.C. (2006) *Breaking the Spell: Religion as a Natural Phenomenon*. London: Allen Lane.

Department of Health (2003) *NHS Chaplaincy: Meeting the Religious and Spiritual Needs of Patients and Staff*. London: HMSO.

Department of Health (2006) *The Chief Nursing Officer's Review of Mental Health Nursing: Values into Action*. London: Department of Health.

Diener, E. & Oishi, S. (2000) Money and happiness: Income and subjective well-being across nations. In E. Diener & E.M. Suh (eds), *Culture and Subjective Wellbeing*. Cambridge, MA: MIT Press.

Durkheim, E. (1897/1951) *Suicide*. Trans. J. Spalding & G. Simpson. New York: Free Press.

Foucault, M. (1969/2002) *The Archaeology of Knowledge*. London: Routledge Classics.

Francis, L.J. & Robbins, M. (2004) Belonging without believing. *Implicit Religion*, 7(1): 37–54.

Friedman, T.L. (2006) *The World Is Flat: The Globalised World in the 21st Century*. London: Penguin.

Gilbert, P. (2005) *Leadership: Being Effective and Remaining Human*. Lyme Regis: Russell House.

Gilbert, P. (2007) The role of spirituality in the journey of recovery. *The Pilgrim's Progress: The Pathway to Better Care in Geriatric Psychiatry*, Santiago de Compostela International Conference, 22 July.

Gilbert, P. & Kalaga, H. (2007) *Nurturing Heart and Spirit: Papers from the Multi-Faith Symposium*. Stafford: Staffordshire University/Care Services Improvement Partnership.

Gilbert, P. & Nicholls, V. (2003) *Inspiring Hope: Recognising the Importance of Spirituality in a Whole Person Approach to Mental Health*. Leeds: National Institute for Mental Health in England.

Gilbert, P. & Watts, N. (2006) Don't mention God! *A Life in the Day*, 10(3): August.

Goleman, D. (2006) *Social Intelligence: The New Science of Human Relationships*. London: Hutchinson.

Greaves, R. (2005) *Aspects of Islam*. London: Darton, Longman and Todd.

Haidt, J. (2006) *The Happiness Hypothesis: Putting Ancient Wisdom to the Test of Modern Science*. London: William Heinemann.

Hay, D. (2006) *Something There: The Biology of the Human Spirit*. London: Darton, Longman and Todd.

Heald, G. (2000) The soul of Britain. *The Tablet*, 3 June.

Heelas, P. & Woodhead, L. (2005) *The Spiritual Revolution: Why Religion Is Giving Way to Spirituality*. Oxford: Blackwell.

Hoffman, E. (1998) *Lost in Translation*. London: Vintage.

Holbeche, L. & Springett, N. (2004) *In Search of Meaning in the Workplace*. Horsham: Roffey Park Institute.

Holt, S. (2003) Year 2000 on a Section 3. *Poems of Survival*. Brentwood: Chipmunka Publishing.

Hutchinson, F., Mellor, M. & Olsen, W. (2002) *The Politics of Money: Towards Sustainability and Economic Democracy*. London: Pluto Press.

Jamison, C. (2006) *Finding Sanctuary: Monastic Steps for Everyday Life*. London: Weidenfeld and Nicolson.

Jha, A. (2007) No religion and an end to war: How thinkers see the future. *The Guardian*, 1 January, p. 12.

Layard, R. (2005) *Happiness Lessons from a New Science*. London: Allen Lane.

Margo, J. & Dixon, M. (2006) Crisis of youth? Childhood, youth and the civic order. *Public Policy Research*, 13(1): 48–53.

McGrath, A. (2005) *Dawkins' God*. Oxford: Blackwell.

Merchant, R. & Gilbert, P. (2007) 'The modern workplace: surfing the wave or surviving the straightjacket?' *Crucible*, Jan/March 2007.

Moss, B. (2005) *Religion and Spirituality*, Lyme Regis: Russell House Publishing.

Moss, B. & Gilbert, P. (2007) Epilog: Flickering candles of hope: Spirituality, mental health and a search for meaning – some personal perspectives. *Illness, Crisis and Loss*, 15(2).

Mulholland, H. (2005) Counting on change. *Society Guardian*, 7 December.

Mursell, G. (ed.) (2001) *The Story of Christian Spirituality: Two Thousand Years, from East to West*. London: Lion Publishing.

NHS Scotland (2002) *Spiritual Care in the NHS Scotland*, Edinburgh: NHS Scotland.

Nicholls, V. & Gilbert, P. (2007) The sea, me and God. *Open Mind*, February/March.

Omaar, R. (2006) *Only Half of Me: Being a Muslim in Britain*. London: Viking.

Pratchett, T. (1993) *Small Gods*. London: Corgi.

Pratchett, T. & Gaiman, N. (1991) *Good Omens*. London: Corgi.

Putnam, R.D. (2000) *Bowling Alone: The Collapse and Revival of American Community*. New York: Simon & Schuster.

Rolheiser, R. (1998) *Seeking Spirituality: Guidelines for Christian Spirituality in the 21st Century*. London: Hodder & Stoughton.

Ross, L. (1997) *Nurses' Perceptions of Spiritual Care*. Aldershot: Avebury.

Sacks, J. (2002) *The Dignity of Difference: How to Avoid the Clash of Civilizations*. London: Continuum.

Sacks, J. (2005) *To Heal a Fractured World*. London: Continuum.

Sampson, R.J. (1993) Family management and child development: Insights from social disorganisation theory. Volume 6 of J. McCord (ed.), *Advances in Criminological Theory* (pp. 63–93). New Brunswick, NJ: Transaction Press.

Sennett, R. (2006) *The Culture of the New Capitalism*. Yale: Yale University.

Smith, L. (2006) Long life, aliens and a chat with fish – forecast for the year 2056. *The Times*, 16 November.

Soul Gym (Steare, R. & Jamison, C.) (2003) *Integrity in Practice: An Introduction for Financial Services*, at www.rogersteargroup.com/soulgym/ in response to Financial Services Authority (2002) *An Ethical Framework for Financial Services*, Discussion Paper 18. London: FSA.

Swinton, J. & Pattison, S. (2001) Come all ye faithful. *Health Service Journal*. 20 December.

Sykes, B. (2001) *The Seven Daughters of Eve*. London: Bantam Press.

Sykes, B. (2006) *Blood of the Isles: Exploring the Genetic Roots of Our Tribal History*. London: Bantam Press.

Tacey, D. (2004) *The Spirituality Revolution: The Emergence of Contemporary Spirituality*. Hove: Brunner-Routledge.

Vulliamy, E. (2006) The new Catholics: How our immigrant communities have revitalised the Church of Rome in Britain. *The Observer*, 17 December, pp. 4–6.

Wolpert, L. (2006) *Malignant Sadness: the Anatomy of Depression* (3rd edn). London: Faber & Faber.

Woollaston, S. (2007) City bonuses stretch gap between 'haves' and 'have yachts'. *The Guardian*, 6 January.

Young, M. & Willmott, P. (1957) *Family and Kinship in East London*. London: Routledge & Kegan Paul.

◀ CHAPTER TWENTYNINE ▶

Holistic approaches in mental health

Jan Wallcraft
Service user consultant, researcher and activist

▶ Healing minds

This chapter is based on *Healing Minds* (Wallcraft, 1998), a report on research, policy and practice concerning the use of complementary and alternative therapies in mental health, written as part of the service user-led Strategies for Living programme. In that report, I addressed holistic therapies that take into account the whole person and their physical, mental, emotional and spiritual being, within their life context. This is the approach that underlies many complementary and alternative therapies. The report covered a specific range of therapies for which some evidence exists of their mental health benefits, including ayurveda, traditional Chinese medicine, homeopathy, Western herbal medicine, nutritional medicine, spiritual healing, massage, aromatherapy, reflexology, hypnotherapy, exercise, yoga and relaxation.

In *Healing Minds* I set out to look at the policy context, types of evidence and underlying issues surrounding the introduction of holistic medicine and holistic therapies in mental health, as well as summarising the evidence base. I took this approach because the evidence base for holistic therapies is often seen as lacking, on the grounds that there are not many high-quality randomised controlled trials (RCTs) in existence that measure effectiveness and compare these therapies to conventional psychiatric medicine. I wanted to address the political issues about how to create a more level playing field in terms of the types of evidence regarded as valid in policy circles, given that many studies have shown that service users seek out and value holistic therapies.

This chapter is an update and development of the approach I took in *Healing Minds*, which means that I will be focusing on one aspect of holism in mental health; that is, the evidence base for complementary and alternative therapies in

Learning About Mental Health Practice. Edited by Theo Stickley and Thurstine Basset
© 2008 John Wiley & Sons, Ltd

Table 29.1 Complementary and alternative medicine (CAM)

The first group embraces what may be called the principal disciplines, two of which, osteopathy and chiropractic, are already regulated in their professional activity and education by Acts of Parliament. The others are acupuncture, herbal medicine and homeopathy. Our evidence has indicated that each of these therapies claim to have an individual diagnostic approach and that these therapies are seen as the 'Big 5' by most of the CAM world.

The second group contains therapies which are most often used to complement conventional medicine and do not purport to embrace diagnostic skills. It includes aromatherapy; the Alexander Technique; body work therapies, including massage; counselling; stress therapy; hypnotherapy; reflexology and probably shiatsu; meditation and healing.

The third group embraces those other disciplines. . . which purport to offer diagnostic information as well as treatment and which, in general, favour a philosophical approach and are indifferent to the scientific principles of conventional medicine, and through which various and disparate frameworks of disease causation and its management are proposed. These therapies can be split into two sub-groups. Group 3a includes long-established and traditional systems of healthcare such as Ayurvedic medicine and Traditional Chinese medicine. Group 3b covers other alternative disciplines which lack any credible evidence base such as crystal therapy, iridology, radionics, dowsing and kinesiology.

Source: House of Lords (2000) *Complementary and Alternative Medicine: Science and Technology – Sixth Report, Session 1999–2000*, 1 November.

mental health. As there is not space to look at all the therapies, I have singled out a particular example for which recent evidence is available, acupuncture for depression.

▶ What are complementary therapies?

Table 29.1 above sets out the list of complementary and alternative medicines examined by the House of Lords in the UK.

▶ Holism in mental health

The term holism (from the Greek *holos*, meaning 'whole') was coined by the naturalist Jan Smuts (1927) who defined it as 'the tendency in nature to form wholes that are greater than the sum of the parts through creative evolution'. The concept of holism is used in health in a variety of ways. For instance, recent government policy in the UK could be called 'holistic', in that it is concerned with 'joined-up' or seamless services, eroding the divides between health and social care and between professional disciplines. A more philosophic or spiritual understanding of holism relates to a view of mind, body and spirit as part of an indivisible whole.

According to Pert (1998), the origins of a divided or dualistic approach to health, splitting the realm of the psyche (mind or soul) from the somatic (physical body), resulted from a pragmatic deal that the philosopher and founder of modern medicine, Descartes, had to make with the Pope in the 17th Century in order to avoid condemnation from the church for his experimentation on human bodies. This division

> set the tone and direction for Western science over the next two centuries, dividing human experience into two distinct and separate spheres that could never overlap, creating the unbalanced situation that is mainstream science as we know it today. (Pert, 1997, p. 18)

Holism in health can mean taking more personal or social control over one's health and environment. Applied to health services, holistic medicine implies a partnership between professionals and patients. Symptoms are seen as clues to

Table 29.2   The principles of holistic medical practice

- Holistic physicians embrace a variety of safe, effective options in the diagnosis and treatment, including education for lifestyle changes and self-care, complementary alternatives, and conventional drugs and surgery

- Searching for the underlying causes of disease is preferable to treating symptoms alone.

- Holistic physicians expend as much effort in establishing what kind of patient has a disease as they do in establishing what kind of disease a patient has.

- Prevention is preferable to treatment and is usually more cost-effective. The most cost-effective approach evokes the patient's own innate healing capabilities.

- Illness is viewed as a manifestation of a dysfunction of the whole person, not as an isolated event.

- A major determinant of healing outcomes is the quality of the relationship established between physician and patient, in which patient autonomy is encouraged.

- The ideal physician – patient relationship considers the needs, desires, awareness and insight of the patient as well as those of the physician.

- Physicians significantly influence patients by their example.

- Illness, pain, and the dying process can be learning opportunities for patients and physicians.

- Holistic physicians encourage patients to evoke the healing power of love, hope, humor and enthusiasm, and to release the toxic consequences of hostility, shame, greed, depression, and prolonged fear, anger, and grief.

- Unconditional love is life's most powerful medicine. Physicians strive to adopt an attitude of unconditional love for patients, themselves, and other practitioners.

- Optimal health is much more than the absence of sickness. It is the conscious pursuit of the highest qualities of the physical, environmental, mental, emotional, spiritual, and social aspects of the human experience.

Source: Wallcraft,J., (1998) Healing Minds, Mental Health Foundation.

underlying problems and disharmonies, and treatments take into account the person's own natural healing processes and the wider aspects of the person's daily life and environment. The American Holistic Medical Association's set of principles for holistic medicine are included in Table 29.2.

Some writers have explored how holistic health debates can be related to mental health. For instance, McClanahan, Huff and Omar (2006) argue that the historic Cartesian mind – body dualism and the resulting conceptual separation of mind and body keeps mental health care too separate and too stigmatised for the holistic thinking that is now influencing US healthcare to spread to mental health.

Dr Chris Manning, Chief Executive of PriMHE (Primary Care Mental Health and Education) says:

> we're on a mission to dump Descartes. . . we think it is never going to be the case that we will get mental into the mainstream whilst people use mental as an alternative to physical. All the evidence is that we're wired for health. (Manning, 2003)

He argues that the artificial distinction between mind and body only serves to perpetuate the stigma attached to mental health and mental health problems:

> The factors that influence our mental health include not only our genetic make-up but also our upbringing, our life experience and our own skills, values and aptitudes. It is therefore important to take a holistic approach to assess and understand what treatment and support someone might require. We should also be looking at more upstream approaches to ensure promotion and prevention, making use of opportunities for volunteering, for exercise, for lifestyle enhancement etc. (Manning, 2003)

A House of Lords committee reporting on complementary and alternative medicine (CAM) recognised that there is a spectrum between reductionism and holism, and that complementary therapies should be seen as differing from conventional medicine in their underlying paradigms:

> The way that many CAM disciplines define health, illness and the healing process can depart significantly from the beliefs that underlie the practice of conventional medicine. It is essential to consider the different paradigms from which conventional medicine and CAM approach healthcare as these have implications for research and integration. (House of Lords, 2000)

The Prince's Foundation for Integrated Health argue that 'someone suffering mental distress is not a "patient" to be "treated", but a whole person to be supported in the complex and individual journey of their life' (Prince's Foundation, 2006). The Foundation has carried out a consultation exercise on complementary health care in mental health as the basis for developing a set of guidelines (due out in 2007) which could be influential in mental health policy and research. The Foundation's stated strategy is to help transform the

'National Illness Service' into a genuine National Health Service (NHS) through an integrated approach to health.

A conference, 'Black Women and Mental Health – Developing Holistic Interventions', held in May 2007, had key themes demonstrating an understanding of 'holistic' as related to personal experience, healing and recovery:

- Understanding the sources, process and impact of unresolved traumas and emotional distress experienced by black and Asian women.

- Reflecting on a range of black and Asian women's experiences of mental health services.

- Redefining and applying models of recovery and healing.

- Developing holistic, innovative and preventative emotional healing for black communities.

The theme of holistic mental health as preventive is addressed by Weare (2006) in relation to the mental and emotional health and well-being of children and young people. She argues that mental health work with children and young people has been focused on the identification, referral and treatment of their problems, but that child mental health work is now starting to take a more holistic and preventive approach.

Holism in mental health, therefore, has been seen as referring to approaches that treat the person as a whole, in the context of their wider environment, that aim to prevent problems by taking a wider approach to the context in which problems arise, that enable healing and recovery, and that are based on partnership approach in which people are enabled and supported in their own natural healing processes.

▶ The politics of holistic mental health

Service user perspectives

Healing Minds (Wallcraft, 1998) found a high level of demand from service users for greater access to complementary therapies, based on consultations carried out in the 1990s. The evidence showed that service users were dissatisfied with the limitations and problems of orthodox medicine, and sought holistic alternatives or complementary approaches that would have less adverse effects. The *On Our Own Terms* report (Wallcraft, 2003) showed that one of the main issues uniting service users was dissatisfaction with mental health services and seeking change and alternatives. Service user involvement with national government increased during the late 1990s and early 21st Century, and had some impact on the creation of the National Service Framework for Mental Health (Department of Health, 1999) and subsequent government initiatives to produce a more seamless and joined-up service, more focused on patient and carer-centred services.

However, change is slow to come about. A Mind survey on patient choice in primary care (Mind, 2002) revealed:

■ 98% of respondents visiting their GP for mental health problems were prescribed medication, despite the fact that less than one in five had specifically asked for it.

■ Over half (54%) of respondents felt that they had not been given enough choice.

■ Of those patients who have tried alternative treatments, over one in three had to take the initiative and ask for it (and often pay for it) themselves.

■ Almost 10% of all respondents had been unable to access alternative treatments because waiting lists were too long.

■ The top five alternatives to medication rated by respondents were counselling, group therapy, art/music/drama therapy, psychotherapy and aromatherapy.

Mind's recommendations add up to a more holistic approach in primary care:

1. Effective psychological therapies, including counselling, cognitive therapy and psychotherapy, should be available to those who want to try them.

2. Complementary therapies should be available as effective treatments for mental health problems and to help reduce negative side effects of medication.

3. People should be given sufficient information about medication to enable them to make informed choices before drugs are prescribed and throughout treatment.

4. Exercise on prescription schemes should be used for mental health.

5. Mental health problems do not exist in isolation and care and treatment should be individual and take account of a person's social, socio-economic and cultural background, lifestyle and preferences. (Mind, 2002)

The national consultation carried out by the Prince's Foundation (2006) involved nearly 300 people from the fields of mental health and complementary therapy, of whom 22% were service users or carers, 33% complementary therapists and 40% professionals in health and medicine. National events and a questionnaire were carried out. The therapies on which the participants sought guidelines were similar to those covered in *Healing Minds* (Wallcraft, 1998). They were:

■ diet and nutrition

■ exercise and movement (including yoga, chi gong/tai chi)

■ acupuncture

■ massage therapy (including shiatsu)

■ homeopathy

- reflexology

- herbal medicine

- aromatherapy

Similar to *Healing Minds*, the Prince's Foundation's (2006) consultation identified three alternative/traditional medical systems to be signposted:

- ayurveda

- traditional Chinese medicine

- anthroposophical medicine

Respondents also called for guidelines on self-management in mental health.

The consultation found that people thought the biggest barriers to integrated
mental health care were lack of funding, the resistance of conventional practitioners, education and evidence. Many wanted complementary approaches to
be taught in orthodox health professional training, and called for an evidence
base to be established and for appropriate evaluation and outcome measures,
including greater attention to patient choice, positive mental health and the
recovery approach.

Professional attitudes to complementary therapies

Healing Minds (Wallcraft, 1998) showed a shift in the attitudes of the British
Medical Association between 1986 and 1993, with a more co-operative attitude
emerging from GPs, and gradual acceptance that many patients are seeking
non-conventional treatments.

A survey of one in eight GP practices in 1995 (Thomas *et al.*, 2001) received
a high response, and found that 39.5% of GPs were providing access to some
forms of complementary therapies, and 24.6% had made NHS referrals for complementary therapies, with acupuncture and homeopathy the most commonly
available. The research shows that fundholding provided a mechanism for the
provision of complementary therapies, and the demise of fundholding was likely
to reduce this access unless Primary Care Trusts are prepared to support it.

Vickers (2000) found that complementary medicine is increasingly being practised in conventional medical settings. With regard to mental health, massage,
music therapy and relaxation are being used for mild anxiety and depression.
He considered this more open attitude to be related to the rise of evidence-based
medicine, so that those therapies where evidence is available are now more widely
accepted.

A leaflet on complementary medicine for GPs (Department of Health, 2000)
states that 58% of Primary Care Groups provide some access to complementary
and alternative medicine, including acupuncture, aromatherapy, homeopathy
and hypnotherapy.

A more open approach to complementary therapies in the NHS is supported by the House of Lords report (2000):

> we concluded that in view of the variable evidence bases which at present exist it might initially be unfair to restrict NHS provision only to those with firmly established efficacy. We recommend, however, that only those CAM therapies which are statutorily regulated or have robust mechanisms of voluntary self-regulation should be available through public funding.

The Department of Health leaflet for GPs (Department of Health, 2000) supports claims for the benefits of aromatherapy massage and hypnotherapy for anxiety, but does not support GPs referring patients to any complementary health services outside the NHS. GPs can, however, employ complementary therapists who are suitably qualified and delegate some patient care to them. The leaflet gives information on suitable qualifications and regulatory bodies.

Another survey of GPs and complementary therapists (Frenkel & Borkan, 2003) used a consultative method to develop an approach to greater integration of complementary therapies in primary care. The researchers concluded that given patients' demands and the numbers already utilising complementary and alternative therapies, despite the current lack of evidence, there is an increasing need to address how these therapies can be integrated into conventional medical systems. They suggest methods by which doctors can respond to patients' expectations and needs, but at the same time maintain accepted standards of medical and scientific principles of practice, through careful assessment of current knowledge, contraindications and dialogue with specific therapists.

A survey by *Which?* (Porritt, 2003) found that 80% of people with mental health problems are treated entirely by their GP, and most of these receive medication. Alternatives to drug treatment were often unavailable on the NHS. Porritt argued that alternative therapies with sufficient evidence of benefit should be available free.

It is clear that issues about the benefits and cost-effectiveness of complementary therapies are contentious and political. Canter, Thompson Coon & Ernst (2005), in a short review of complementary therapies and cost-effectiveness, conclude that in the majority of the small group of cost-effectiveness studies they reviewed, complementary therapies represent additional health-care costs. Although they show that the cost per QALY (quality adjusted life year, a measure of cost-effectiveness defined by Phillips & Thompson, 2003) was comparable to conventional treatment, they question the clinical relevance of these benefits.

Another study, more extensive and detailed, showed the limits of conventional cost – benefit analysis. Smallwood (2005) discussed the possibility that complementary therapies can meet 'effectiveness gaps'; that is, they may address health problems that are poorly dealt with by conventional medicine. Mental health is one area they cite. The report argues that there is a potential reduction in NHS financial and time pressures if complementary and alternative therapies are used to address such effectiveness gaps. This may be difficult to demonstrate, but Smallwood looked at studies that assess the frequency that GPs are presented with problems such as depression, anxiety, stress and a variety of physical problems such as chronic pain, which cause difficulties to doctors because they do not have effective treatments or cannot easily define the problem. Many of the GPs consulted in these studies believed that there were potential cost savings in some forms of complementary therapy such as relaxation, massage and hypnotherapy. Mental illness came ninth on a list of 16 conditions where cost savings could potentially be made if complementary therapies were integrated into primary care.

The complexities of measuring cost-effectiveness and finding suitable measures to apply to complementary therapies are underlined in an essay by Meenan (2001). He argues that the process of health care, as well as its outcome, can contribute to its value and benefit to patients, and that this applies particularly to complementary therapies. Therefore, accurate assessment of the health process as well as its outcomes should be made as part of cost-effectiveness analysis, and this is not part of the usual measurement system. Meenan argues that techniques such as qualitative analysis, which can give more information about the benefits of complementary medicine, should be explored.

▶ Government policy and its impact on holistic approaches

Government policy can play a major role in creating a level playing field in which holistic mental health treatments become available to service users. Some key aspects of policy are evidence-based medicine, outcomes measurement in mental health and the recovery approach.

Evidence-based medicine

Evidence-based medicine (EBM) and evidence-based health care are important government imperatives. Evidence-based medicine 'is the conscientious, explicit, and judicious use of current best evidence in making decisions about the care of individual patients' (Sackett *et al.*, 1996). Practice based on EBM, Sackett *et al.* say, integrates 'individual clinical expertise' with 'the best available external clinical evidence from systematic research'. According to Herts University (2007), EBM can be seen as

> a new paradigm, replacing the traditional medical paradigm which is based on authority. It is dependent on the use of randomised controlled trials (RCTs), as well as systematic reviews (of a series of trials) and meta-analysis, although it is not restricted to these. (Herts University, 2007)

Although EBM is not totally dependent on randomised controlled trials, clearly these are seen as the strongest form of evidence. The National Institute for Clinical Excellence guidelines manual (NICE, 2007, pp. 45–57) shows the hierarchy of evidence, with systematic reviews of RCTs at the top, and expert opinion or formal consensus on the lowest rung. Since it is rare that service users get to have any real influence on randomised controlled trials, the evidence base in mental health is still biased towards biomedical research funded by the pharmaceutical industry or the Medical Research Council, rather than evidence of service users' views and experiences, or the mainly small-scale research done by the voluntary sector or practitioners of complementary therapies.

Health Technology Assessment (HTA) commissions research for the NHS on the costs, effectiveness and impact of health technologies. A search on its Web site (HTA, 2007) shows that most of its mental health research is in the form of clinical trials or systematic reviews of clinical trials, and only two studies (interactive group art therapy as an adjunctive treatment for people with schizophrenia, and a pragmatic randomised controlled trial to evaluate exercise as a treatment for depression), both of which are currently under way, are looking at complementary or alternative therapies. However, at least a third of the trials are concerned with talking treatments or psychosocial interventions.

UK Mental Health Research Network (UK MHRN, 2007) is an organisation set up a few years ago by the Department of Health to provide the NHS infrastructure to support both non-commercial and commercial large-scale research in mental health, including clinical trials. Like the HTA's, UK MHRN's Web site shows a high proportion of trials looking at the benefits of talking treatments and psychosocial interventions, but other than this, the only trials that could be seen as looking at complementary therapies are the same two HTA trials mentioned above. It is encouraging to see that partnership with service users and patient choice is now a factor in more of the trials, both in terms of treatments offered and methodologies used (the list includes a pilot patient preference randomised controlled trial of admission to a Women's Crisis House compared with psychiatric hospital admissions, and an RCT on Joint Crisis Plans to Reduce Compulsory Admission for People with Psychosis). The clear finding, however, is that complementary and alternative therapies in mental health are still not being researched to any great extent.

Outcomes measurement and the recovery approach in mental health

Another important aspect of government policy that affects the likelihood of complementary and alternative approaches becoming more widely available is outcomes measurement. Traditionally, there was little attempt to measure the longer-term outcomes of mental health treatments, and patients with severe mental illnesses were not expected to recover. However, since the publication of the National Service Framework for Mental Health, it has become UK government policy that all mental health services should introduce routine outcomes measurement. Routine outcome measurement geared to service user priorities might provide incentives to develop holistic therapies that tend to have a preventive or recovery-oriented whole-person approach and lead to greater service user satisfaction with treatment.

Outcomes measurement has been described as a 'revolution in healthcare' (Relman, 1988) and as an 'outcomes movement [which] can be understood in social, political and economic terms' (Gilbody, House & Sheldon, 2003). The current interest in recovery in mental health, based on service user and family involvement in the US, UK, Australia and New Zealand (Turner-Crowson & Wallcraft, 2002), has brought increased pressure to bear on governments to bring in measures of outcomes in mental health, in order to assess which treatments and services best help patients and service users to recover a satisfactory quality of life. From the government's perspective, outcomes measurement is part of the drive towards improved quality and accountability of services, and will give managers a better understanding of the effectiveness of the services they deliver.

Gilbody, House and Sheldon (2003) carried out a study of outcomes measurement in psychiatric research, which showed it to be 'currently dominated by the measurement of psychiatric symptoms, with little reference to patient based measures'. They also found that UK psychiatrists rarely measure outcomes, and that there are 'substantial practical and attitudinal barriers to the use of outcomes instruments in NHS mental health services'.

However, there is some current work on developing outcome measures that reflect service users' concerns, for instance the HTA's Methodology Panel is commissioning a new service user-focused outcome measure in forensic mental health, and a measure named Psychlops, to be used in primary care, is being developed with service user involvement (Department of General Practice, 2007).

▶ Innovative projects

Another way in which complementary therapies become better known and more available to service users has been through innovative projects within the NHS, social services and the voluntary sector.

Healing Minds (Wallcraft, 1998) reported on a number of innovative projects such as the Creative Living Centre in Salford. The author's recent contact with this centre established that it is still operating, though it has struggled to retain funding and has had to reduce its opening times to three days a week plus Saturday evenings.

It is not uncommon for local Mind centres to offer complementary therapies. Some have run and evaluated pilot projects. Peterborough Mind (2007) set up a pilot project in 2000 with a group of therapists who work in the community mental health teams. The project offers service users with severe and enduring mental health problems a range of treatments including Indian head massage, aromatherapy, reflexology, Reiki and yoga.

Mind in Taunton and West Somerset hosts the Service Users Complementary Holistic Project (SUCH), which was developed by Maggi Rowan (Rowan, 2007) following receipt of a MIND Millennium award. SUCH was set up in 2003 to provide access to complementary and holistic treatments to those suffering mental distress, including service users, carers, volunteers or people working in the mental health system.

SUCH received Healthcare Trust funding in 2006–7 to carry out and evaluate a project (INSUCH) offering complementary therapies to inpatients in a local mental health acute unit to promote relaxation and well-being and to help reduce stress. A qualified therapist offered sessions of aromatherapy, reflexology, Indian head massage and hand massage for half a day per week over a period of 20 weeks. The external evaluator (Collings, 2007) used MYCAW, a well-being measurement scale developed by Paterson *et al.* (2003), and found significant improvements in patient well-being following treatment. Patients valued the direct effects of treatment (relaxing, stress reducing and calming) and the experience of being cared for, touched and listened to on a one-to-one basis. Staff at the inpatient unit appreciated the calming effects of treatment on their patients and wanted the project to continue and to expand.

Collings (2007) also did a cost – benefit analysis of INSUCH, which suggests that the availability of complementary therapy treatments reduced patients' demands on doctors' time, hospital admissions and community health team time. She argues:

> Investment in complementary therapies could be viewed as a preventative tool for community mental health teams to contribute to a reduction in admissions. (Collings, 2007)

Healthy Living Centres have provided an opportunity for some GPs to try to bring in holistic approaches. A leader in the field has been Bromley-by-Bow Healthy Living Centre. James (2002) wrote that mental health service users are frustrated by the lack of choice in treatment and many do not regard drugs as a panacea. He described the Healthy Living Centre in Bromley-by-Bow, which offers a holistic approach to health:

> Sure, the centre's doctors prescribe medication; perhaps no less than those at traditional surgeries. But patients can also be 'prescribed' gardening, exercise in a gym, homoeopathy, counselling, aromatherapy, acupuncture and employment training. Its professionals work on the premise that mental health problems are as much related to unemployment, bad housing, loneliness and poverty as they are with serotonin neurotransmitters...[GP Dr Sam Everington says] 'We are about looking at the whole person and their whole needs.' (James, 2002, p. 19)

Dr Everington cannot demonstrate statistically that a holistic approach in primary care works better than a traditional approach. But, as James reports, he claims that 'instinct tells you that no such proof is needed'.

▶ Evidence base for complementary and alternative therapies in mental health

Healing Minds (Wallcraft, 1998) examined a range of evidence for complementary therapies in mental health, including clinical trials, research reviews, outcome studies, project evaluations, case studies and accounts of personal experience.

Therapies or systems of medicine that claim to have treatments for mental health include ayurveda, traditional Chinese medicine, homeopathy, Western herbal medicine, nutritional medicine, healing, massage, aromatherapy, reflexology, hypnotherapy and the active therapies (exercise, relaxation and yoga). Evidence for each of these was gathered and summarised.

It was found that there had been a number of clinical trials of acupuncture, herbal medicine and nutritional therapies for schizophrenia and depression. There is strong evidence for some herbal remedies in depression, in particular St John's Wort. However, for the most part the clinical evidence came from small trials and often their methodology has been disputed as insufficiently robust. Most of these therapies and treatments did seem to be well accepted by patients and service users, and to have some positive impact on a wide range of mental health problems, with few adverse effects. Small-scale evaluations and qualitative surveys reveal that service users feel more valued and supported by complementary therapists who have time to listen to them, and appreciate therapies that relieve depression and anxiety, even if these effects are relatively short term. It was also found that therapies such as aromatherapy and reflexology combine well with talking treatments.

The *Healing Minds* report called for more co-operation between practitioners of complementary therapies and researchers to strengthen the evidence base for the effectiveness of these treatments, their cost-effectiveness, and how well they can be integrated with orthodox treatments.

There is no space here to update all the recent research on complementary therapies in mental health, although in fact a brief review has shown that there has been a paucity of new high-quality studies that could be cited. I have looked at one area that has been given recent attention, and that is acupuncture for depression. This example illustrates some of the political, scientific and philosophical debates that surround the apparently simple idea of creating an evidence base for complementary therapies.

A Cochrane review of acupuncture for depression (Smith & Hay, 2004) looked at seven trials comprising 517 subjects, five of which compared medication to acupuncture. The evidence was inconclusive, according to the authors, because the scientific design was poor and the number of people studied was small. However, they do explore some of the issues involved in transposing a treatment derived from a traditional Chinese medicine (TCM) into a Western medical context. Acupuncture, they explain, is based on the Chinese concepts of yin and yang and the five elements. Westernised medical acupuncture may exclude TCM principles and philosophy. Smith and Hay (2004) also note that there are different styles of acupuncture that may have different results. They argue that stronger randomised trial methodologies are needed for future trials, but also that there is a need to know more about the practitioners and their training, their rationale for using acupuncture in depression and the style of acupuncture used.

A small study (MacPherson *et al.*, 2004) sought to address design issues in clinical trials for acupuncture in depression. They did this by working with York and District Mind to involve service users in focus groups to look at the experience of depression and to discuss the plans for their research study. They also carried out an uncontrolled observational study of the acupuncture treatment of 10 patients with depression. These patients were under the care of their GPs, and were treated by professional acupuncturists in private practice, all of whom were members of the British Acupuncture Council. The research criteria were:

1. That the research is scientifically rigorous.
2. That it is respectful of the integrity of acupuncture as a system of medicine.
3. That it takes into account what patients experience and may value about acupuncture.

The acupuncture practitioners worked within a TCM framework, and practised as they would normally do, using additional treatments such as acupressure, massage, flower remedies and relaxation as they considered necessary. Standard depression rating scales were used. Two patients dropped out at the start, eight were treated and six responded to follow-up questionnaires. All had improved depression scores, though this was a modest improvement that could have come from a combination of factors.

The study did not conclusively demonstrate the value of acupuncture, but its purpose was primarily to look at study design issues. The focus group study of patients' experiences of depression showed diversity in how people experience depression, leading the authors to question whether it makes sense to see depression as one distinct condition. The acupuncturists, working within a TCM framework, diagnosed a range of different conditions among the patients, and the treated patients described benefits beyond symptom control, such as having learnt more about combating their depression, migraines stopping, feeling less fearful and more motivated. The authors additionally argued that while the literature shows stronger evidence for the benefits of acupuncture in mild to moderate depression, there may also be patients with severe depression who would benefit. They argue that it would be seen as unfair by service users to exclude this group from future trials for no clear reason. The therapeutic relationship emerged as an important factor, which they argue would be better demonstrated using in-depth qualitative interviews or observational methods. There were problems in reflecting the wider benefits of acupuncture using standard depression rating scales, and the authors suggest that other well-validated outcome measures might be found that assess these broader effects. Finally, they suggest that there should be a trial methodology that gives scope for practitioners to be flexible in their treatment repertoire in response to the variability of patients' conditions, as they would be in normal practice, rather than being constrained in their treatment approach by too much standardisation. They suggest that trial protocols need to have credibility with both the acupuncture community and the scientific establishment, and should be drawn up using clinical literature and expert opinion and tested with a representative sample of acupuncturists.

▶ Conclusions

There has been some progress in the development of holistic approaches in mental health in the nine years since *Healing Minds* was written. Debate still centres mainly around the scientific and philosophical differences between holistic approaches and conventional Western medicine based on the scientific method. Government pressure for evidence-based medicine has had the effect of creating greater debate on how to measure complementary and alternative medicines, though still there has been little investment in doing research on them, and much of the attempts to address this are still coming from the voluntary sector. The small-scale nature of innovation and research that can be funded in this way makes it hard for holistic therapies to make much headway in creating an evidence base.

Primary care is the location that offers the most promise for change, and there have been a number of studies aimed at finding out Gps' attitudes and educating and informing them more about complementary therapies. The developments in primary care will be a key area to watch in the future. New guidelines on complementary therapies in mental health will be emerging from the Prince's Foundation for Integrated Medicine, which may help to point the way forward.

Trial methods and outcome measures need to be developed that reflect patients' and service users' views and wishes much more than the standard methods and measures currently do.

Philosophical debates about holism and the mind/body split in medical thinking are still relevant as, despite moves in government policy to a whole-person approach, most research and practice are still governed by a reductionist scientific model based on the Cartesian world view.

▶ **References**

Canter, P.H., Thompson Coon, J. & Ernst, E. (2005) Cost effectiveness of complementary treatments in the United Kingdom: Systematic review. *British Medical Journal*, **331**: 880–81.

Collings, J. (2007) External Evaluation Report on INSUCH project. Unpublished report, available from Jane Collings, Ellbridge House, Broadhempston, TQ9 6BZ.

Department of General Practice (2007) *Psychlops*. London: Department of General Practice and Primary Care, King's College London, www.psychlops.org.uk/.

Department of Health (1999) *National Service Framework for Mental Health*. London: Department of Health.

Department of Health (2000) *Complementary Medicine: Information for Primary Care Clinicians*. London: Department of Health.

Frenkel, M.A. & Borkan, J.M. (2003) An approach for integrating complementary-alternative medicine into primary care. *Family Practice*, **20**(3): 324–32.

Gilbody, S.M., House, A.O. & Sheldon, T.A. *Outcomes Measurement in Psychiatry: A Critical Review of Outcomes Measurement in Psychiatric Research and Practice*. York: Centre for Reviews and Dissemination, University of York.

Herts University (2007) www.herts.ac.uk/lis/subjects/health/ebm.htm.

House of Lords (2000) *Complementary and Alternative Medicine: Science and Technology – Sixth Report, Session 1999–2000*, 1 November, London: Science and Technology Committee, www.parliament.the-stationery-office.co.uk/pa/ld199900/ldselect/ldsctech/123/12302.htm.

Health Technology Assessment (2007) *Evidence-Based Medicine*, www.hta.nhsweb.nhs.uk.

James, A. (2002) Prescribing choices: Bromley-by-Bow Healthy Living Centre has pioneered holistic health at primary care level. *Openmind*, **115**: 19.

Lane, A.M. & Lovejoy, D.J. (2001) The effects of exercise on mood changes: The moderating effect of depressed mood. *Journal of Sports Medicine and Physical Fitness*, **41**: 539–45.

Leason, K. (2003) There's another way. *Community Care*, June 5–11: 36–7.

Macpherson, H., Thorpe, L., Thomas, K. & Geddes, D. (2004) Acupuncture for depression: First steps toward a clinical evaluation. *Journal of Alternative and Complementary Medicine*, **10**(6): 1083–91.

Manning, C. (2003) Audio interview on the NHS National Electronic Library for Health, at www.nelmh.org/home_primary_care_manning_media.asp?c=16.

McClanahan, K., Huff, M.B. & Omar, H.A. (2006) Holistic health: Does it really include mental health? *TSW Holistic Health and Medicine*, **1**: 128–35.

Meenan, R. (2001) Developing appropriate measures of the benefits of complementary and alternative medicine. *Journal of Health Services Research and Policy*, **6**(1): 38–43.

Mind (2002) *My Choice Individual Services Survey*. London: Mind.

National Institute for Health and Clinical Excellence (2007) *The Guidelines Manual*. London: NICE.

Paterson, C., Thomas, K., Manasse, A. & Cooke, H. (2003) MYCaW: An individualised questionnaire for evaluating complementary therapies in cancer support care. *FACT (Focus on Alternative and Complementary Therapies)*, **8**: 527.

Pert, C. (1998) *Molecules of Emotion*. London: Simon & Schuster. Peterborough Mind (2007) www.cambsmentalhealthinfo.nhs.uk/services/pboro/complementary_therapies.html.

Phillips, C. & Thompson, G. (2003) *What is a QUALY? Evidence-Based Medicine What Is? Series* 1(6). Cambridge: Hayward Medical Communications, www.evidence-basedmedicine.co.uk/ebmfiles/WhatisaQALY.pdf.

Porritt, F. (2003) The hidden costs. *Health Which?* June: 10–13.

Prince's Foundation (2006) *National guidelines on complementary healthcare in mental health: Consultation and scoping report*. London: Prince's Foundation for Integrated Health.

Relman, A.S. (1988) Assessment and accountability: The third revolution in medical care. *New England Journal of Medicine*, **319**: 1220–22.

Rowan, M. (2007) SUCH project, www.suchproject.org.uk/index.htm.

Sackett, D.L., Rosenberg, W.M.C., Gray, J.A. & Haynes, R.B. (1996) Evidence based medicine: What it is and what it isn't. *British Medical Journal*, **312**(7023): 71–2.

Smallwood C. (2005) *The Role of Complementary and Alternative Medicine in the NHS*. London: FreshMinds, www.freshminds.co.uk/PDF/THE%20REPORT.pdf.

Smith, C.A. & Hay, P.P.J. (2004) Acupuncture for depression. *Cochrane Database of Systematic Reviews*, 3.

Smuts, J. (1927) *Holism and Evolution*. London: Macmillan.

Thomas, K.J., Nicholl, J.P. & Fall, M. (2001) Access to complementary medicine via general practice. *British Journal of General Practice*, **51**(462): 25–30.

Turner-Crowson, J. & Wallcraft, J. (2002) The recovery vision for mental health services and research: A British perspective. *Psychiatric Rehabilitation Journal*, **25**(3), www.bu.edu/cpr/repository/articles/turner-crowson2002.pdf.

UK Mental Health Research Network (2007) www.mhrn.info.

Vickers, A. (2000) Complementary medicine. *British Medical Journal*, **321**(7262): 683–6.

Wallcraft, J. (1998) *Healing Minds*. London: Mental Health Foundation.

Wallcraft, J. (2003) *On Our Own Terms*. London: Sainsbury Centre for Mental Health.

Weare, K. (2006) Taking a positive, holistic approach to the mental and emotional health and well-being of children and young people. In C. Newnes & N. Radcliffe (eds), *Making and Breaking Children's Lives* (pp. 115–22). Ross-on-Wye: PCCS Books, http://eprints.soton.ac.uk/24053/.

CHAPTER THIRTY

The capable practitioner of the future

Theo Stickley

University of Nottingham

Thurstine Basset

Independent training and development consultant

This book has focused on the Essential Shared Capabilities for the mental health workforce and has identified issues and approaches in mental health care. These issues and approaches can be said to come under the umbrella term of the 'psycho-social'. The book is not exhaustive: there are other issues and approaches that we have not considered.

Readers will have noticed the absence of anything very medical, in spite of mental health care being located in the health-care system. This has not always been the case, however, and may not always be the case in the future. Mental health care has only in recent centuries been the primary responsibility of medical practitioners. Previously, care for those who were considered 'abnormal', 'insane' or 'mad' was the responsibility of the wider community, for example families, friends, priests or, in some cultures, shamans.

It is our contention that mental health workers of the future will need to be far more community minded than medically minded. What is apparent today is that there is a growing consensus that a medical approach on its own is inadequate in providing answers for people with mental health problems. That is why there is a strong focus in this book on the social aspects of a person's life. An examination of the contents of the book reveals that it concerns itself not with people's 'illnesses' but with wider societal issues and the problems that people experience living in contemporary western culture.

Taking this broader view is important if mental health services are to avoid working in isolation from the mainstream of society. Some important elements of the capable practitioner of the future are rooted in this wider perspective.

Learning About Mental Health Practice.   Edited by Theo Stickley and Thurstine Basset
© 2008 John Wiley & Sons, Ltd

▶ Adopting a recovery-based approach

The concept of recovery has been referred to many times in this book, and its inclusion is vital for an understanding of the role of mental health workers of the future. The point about 'recovery' is that it is not about people becoming ill and getting better, but rather, it is about beliefs, values, principles and the potential for people to lead meaningful lives. It is also rooted in people's experiences and acknowledges the expertise of service users and their ability to manage their lives. The capable practitioner of the future needs to believe that people's problems are as much about society as they are about the people themselves. While there is research and theory that support genetic arguments for 'mental illness', the evidence for people's upbringing, environment and personal experiences as causing mental health problems is overwhelming. The prevalence of mental health problems in western society (up to one in four people in the UK) consigns to history any notion of generic groups called the 'mentally ill' and the 'mentally well' or 'us' and 'them'. The reality is that we are all susceptible to mental distress.

This is not an even distribution, however, as several contributors have observed. For where there is social and economic inequality, mental health problems will be more associated with the people who are less equal and more oppressed by the majority. That is why we have emphasised in this book the need to consider diversity, as well as wider social issues such as poverty, sexism and racism.

Recovery is also about working positively with people who are experiencing mental distress. There are many social 'voices' that add to distress; perhaps the most damning is the voice of the worker who condemns their client with 'you'll never be able to work again' or 'you'll never be able to have relationships and raise a family' (Perkins, 2001). These are the kinds of messages people have received in the past, and still sometimes receive today. A recovery approach encompasses optimism, believing always in people's potential for fulfilment. Workers need to value the person and encourage hope for the future (Basset & Repper, 2005). This is not an easy task when social pressures dictate other messages.

▶ Encouraging advocacy

Capable practitioners of the future will not only need to be aware of complex social issues, but also how to respond to the person in their care. The role of the advocate is as great today as it has ever been. Mental health workers can only take on this role if they are independent, and so this may often mean that workers will be confident and competent enough to refer service users and their families to independent advocacy services. It is also important to point out here that the service user movement is made up of large numbers of self-advocates who have learned to speak up for themselves and others.

There are laws in many modern countries to guard against racism or homo-phobia, but there are few laws that specifically protect the rights of people with complex mental health problems. Every country has mental health laws, but these invariably are designed to protect the public rather than ensure that people have equal rights as citizens. In fact, under most mental health laws people can lose their rights as citizens and can be treated worse than criminals. Furthermore, there are few laws that will protect people from blatant stigma and discrimination. While there are disability rights laws, these are not always easily applied to people with mental health problems. Western society has a long way to go in supporting people to become equal citizens.

▶ Forming good human relationships

Supporting virtually all world religions is the maxim: 'Do to others as you would have others do to you.' While we are not arguing for a religious approach to mental health work (although recognition of spirituality is essential), we emphasise the necessity for good human relationships. This maxim neatly summarises an appropriate philosophy to underpin mental health care. Although approaches in mental health care in the western world are much improved from years ago, we should not be complacent. Less than a hundred years ago, insulin shock treatment was the preferred therapy for schizophrenia. As abhorrent as it sounds today, it was the most advanced treatment available. Who knows if in a few decades' time the treatments widely offered today will be considered barbaric. The message of this book is loud and clear: mental health workers of the future need a deeper, clearer understanding of the nature of mental health problems. At the heart of responding to such problems is the need for good human relationships that respect the person, including their past and their hopes and aspirations for the future.

▶ Working in psycho-social ways and combating discrimination

Any care provision needs to be based on both social and psychological understanding of the person's life. People are not born into a vacuum. The person we are working with today was born into a family. We need to be asking what has happened in that person's life that has created the person we are working with today. Workers need to appreciate the social context of each person they work with. It is easier to avoid the delicate subject of possible abuse in childhood, but as Hammersley et al. (Chapter 21) have observed, much of what we see today as 'mental illness' may have its origins in childhood trauma. We therefore need a deep understanding of mental health problems and the compassion to offer therapeutic relationships and therapy where appropriate. As Sayce (Chapter 15) forcefully argues, it is not just the mental health problems that people experience that they have to contend with; it is also the blatant discrimination that exists that prevents recovery. The practitioner of the future will devote some of their time to the task of combating discrimination, and this is definitely something that can be done in partnership with service users.

▶ Practising in an evidence-based way

Nowadays there is a trend towards evidence-based practice (EBP). The message is loud and clear: all health-care interventions should be evidence based. The meaning of 'evidence based' in this context is that there has been scientific research that proves the efficacy of interventions to underpin practice. As the reader of this book will realise, the EBP agenda is seriously limited in mental health care. It is very difficult to provide 'scientific' evidence for the effectiveness of positive human relationships, or challenging stigma or therapeutic risk taking. Recovery is about worker/client relationships that inspire hope. How could hope be measured? Or compassion? This does not, however, mean that we should not be evidencing our good mental health practice; it simply means that we are barking up the wrong tree if we think good mental health practice will ever satisfy the 'holy grail' of medical science.

▶ Conclusion

At the heart of good mental health practice are certain qualities and activities: compassionate human relationships, deep understanding of psychological processes, effective therapies and social action. We encourage mental health students of today to grasp these intricacies and help mental health services of the future to become systems that enshrine values genuinely promoting recovery. Mental health care should be good enough for us all to recover if, at some point, we become recipients of the services. It is our fervent wish that society will change for the better. Indeed, it will always be judged by how it treats its more vulnerable citizens. Heyes (2007) believes that people with mental health problems provide a sort of 'early warning system' for society. He says:

> If dolphins start getting washed up on the beach, people start to think there might be something wrong with the environment, they don't blame the dolphins for their lifestyle.

This book aims to promote the rights of people who use mental health services. Mental health workers, whatever their profession or background, will be judged on the quality of their work. This book encourages the capable practitioner of the future to take a broad and holistic view of mental health and, when interacting with individuals on a personal level, to be constantly aware of the wider family, neighbourhood and society within which this person leads their life.

▶ References

Basset, T. & Repper, J. (2005) Travelling hopefully. *Mental Health Today*, **November**: 16–18.

Heyes, H. (2007) Interview by Clare Allan in *Society Guardian*, **August 15**: 5.

Perkins, R. (2001) The you'll nevers. *Openmind*, **107**: 6.

Index